Windows® 10
Anniversary Update
Bible

Windows® 10 Anniversary Update
BIBLE

Rob Tidrow

Jim Boyce

Jeffrey R. Shapiro

WILEY

Windows® 10 Anniversary Update Bible

Published by
John Wiley & Sons, Inc.
10475 Crosspoint Boulevard
Indianapolis, IN 46256
www.wiley.com

ISBN: 978-1-119-35633-2
ISBN: 978-1-119-35900-5 (ebk)
ISBN: 978-1-119-35903-6 (ebk)

Manufactured in the United States of America

10 9 8 7 6 5 4 3 2 1

For general information on our other products and services please contact our Customer Care Department within the United States at (877) 762-2974, outside the United States at (317) 572-3993 or fax (317) 572-4002.

Wiley publishes in a variety of print and electronic formats and by print-on-demand. Some material included with standard print versions of this book may not be included in e-books or in print-on-demand. If this book refers to media such as a CD or DVD that is not included in the version you purchased, you may download this material at http://booksupport.wiley.com. For more information about Wiley products, visit www.wiley.com.

Library of Congress Control Number: 2017932691

Rob Tidrow would like to dedicate this book to his wife (Tammy) and his two sons (Adam and Wesley).

About the Authors

Rob Tidrow has authored and co-authored more than 35 books on computers and technology. He specializes in operating systems, social media tools, live video technologies, Office suite applications, web technologies, and networking. Some of his books include *Windows 8.1 Bible*, *IBM Lotus Symphony for Dummies*, *Teach Yourself Visually Microsoft Windows Vista*, and *Teach Yourself Visually Wireless Networking* (Wiley). Rob has been a guest speaker at several industry events, including Indiana CTO Clinic, Blog Indiana, HECC Conference (Hoosier Educational Computer Coordinators), and the RCS eLearning Expo.

Today, Rob is chief operations officer for Richmond Comunity Schools in Richmond, IN (weRrichmond.com), where he leads several departments, including information technology, facilities/maintenance, food service, transportation, and security for more than 6,000 students and staff. He resides in Richmond, IN with his wife, Tammy, and two sons, Adam and Wesley. Follow him on Twitter (@robtidrow) and Facebook (http://www.facebook.com/robtidrow).

Jim Boyce has authored or co-authored more than 55 books on computers and technology, covering operating systems, applications, and programming topics. He has been a frequent contributor to Microsoft.com, TechRepublic (www.techrepublic.com), and other online publications. Jim has written for a number of print publications, including *Windows IT Pro*, *WINDOWS Magazine*, *InfoWorld*, and others, and was a contributing editor and columnist for *WINDOWS Magazine*.

Jim has been involved with IT in various capacities for nearly 40 years. He has been a CAD system administrator and trainer, college instructor, independent IT consultant, ISP owner, and practice director for managed services practices in a global environment. Today, Jim is a delivery management manager for Microsoft Services and a former Microsoft MVP.

Jeffrey R. Shapiro has worked in IT for more than 21 years. He has published more than 20 books on IT, network administration, and software development, and has written for numerous publications. Some of his books include *Windows Server Bible* (from version 2000 to 2008), *Building High Availability Windows Server Solutions*, and numerous books on Microsoft's server technologies, Visual Studio, and the .NET programing languages.

Jeffrey works for MISIQ (www.misiq.com), an organization that specializes in IT infrastructure and software architecture, systems, and development for large companies. MISIQ caters to cloud-based infrastructure, high-performance software for large web and line-of-business solutions, and Windows Server and Windows migration strategies.

About the Technical Editor

Vince Averello has been a professional geek for more than thirty years. During those often funny, sometimes frightening, but always interesting years, he's worked for more than ten organizations lending his expertise to a variety of projects. Every one of them has been a learning experience, so now he knows a little bit about a lot of things ranging from the Internet to garment trucking. Vince lives in lovely midtown Bayonne, New Jersey, with his loving wife, daughter, and two cats with delusions of grandeur.

Credits

Project Editor
Martin V. Minner

Technical Editor
Vince Averello

Production Editor
Barath Kumar Rajasekaran

Copy Editor
Martin V. Minner

Production Manager
Katie Wisor

Manager of Content Development & Assembly
Mary Beth Wakefield

Marketing Manager
Carrie Sherrill

Professional Technology & Strategy Director
Barry Pruett

Business Manager
Amy Knies

Executive Editor
Jody Lefevere

Project Coordinator, Cover
Brent Savage

Proofreader
Nancy Bell

Indexer
Johnna VanHoose Dinse

Cover Designer
Wiley

Cover Image
iStockphoto.com/Aleksandar

Acknowledgments

We want to recognize Carole McClendon for bringing us this opportunity. This project would not have stayed on track without Marty Minner pushing and pulling us. Finally, we offer our appreciation and thanks to Vince Averello for his technical review of the manuscript.

It was a great experience.

Contents at a Glance

Contents

Contents

Contents

Contents

Part X: Appendixes   711

Introduction

Welcome to *Windows 10 Anniversary Update Bible*. If you're familiar with Windows, you might know that the Windows operating system has existed for three decades. In that time, it has transformed in many ways as computer hardware has changed dramatically.

Windows 10 is the latest edition in the Windows family and builds on the usability and performance improvements in Windows 7 and Windows 8.x. One of the biggest differences, however, is the introduction of a cross-platform model that brings the same code base and user experience to a wide range of platforms including the PC, tablets, phones, Xbox, and even small devices like the Raspberry Pi!

Although we've tried to cover as many of the features and capabilities as Windows 10 offers, some naturally fall through the cracks because we have only so much space in this book. With a good understanding of the key features, however, you're well on your way to getting the most from your Windows PC.

Who This Book Is For

Not everyone wants to be a computer expert, and few have the time to become one. Most people just want to use a computer to get things done, or even just to have some fun. This should come as no surprise. After all, not everyone who drives a car wants to be a professional mechanic. Not everyone who uses a cellphone wants to be an electrical engineer. So, why should everyone who uses a computer want, or need, to be a computer expert? They shouldn't. Some people just need to be computer *users* — people who use the computer without being total nerds about it.

This book is for those computer users — the people who just want to use their computers to have some fun and get some things done. It may seem like an awfully big book for such an audience. The reason it's such a big book is because you can do *so many* things with Windows 10.

Most of us prefer to learn by discovery, by exploring and trying things out. It's much more fun that way and typically much more effective. However, a couple of problems are evident with that approach. For one, you can get yourself into a bind from time to time. For another, when you get to a place where you don't know what's going on, sometimes you need to fill in some gaps before you can continue learning by discovery.

A book can help with that by covering all the stuff everyone else assumes you already know. Especially if that book is divided up into sections and chapters that deal with one topic at a time, so you can focus on just the thing you need to know, when you need to know it. Which brings us to . . . .

How to Use This Book

A book that supports learning by discovery needs to have some elements of a tutorial and some elements of a reference book. You can say it has to be a reference book divided into multiple mini-tutorials, so you can learn what you need to know about one topic, whenever it becomes important to you. To that end, this book is divided into nine major parts, each of which covers a large topic.

Each part, in turn, is divided into multiple chapters, each chapter covering a smaller topic. Chapters are divided into sections and subsections, all designed to help you find the information you need, when you need it. The table of contents in the front of this book covers all the specifics. The index at the back of the book helps you find information based on a keyword or topic. The only thing missing is a high-level view of just the parts. So, that's what we provide here:

Part I: Getting Started: How you get started with Windows 10 depends on where you're coming from. This part covers all fronts. If you're an experienced Windows user, you probably want to know what's new. Chapter 1 covers that turf. Chapters 2 and 3 cover important "getting started" topics for everyone, and help you learn to navigate the Windows 10 environment. Chapter 4 touches on security and safety. Chapter 5 provides solutions to common problems with getting started.

Part II: Personalizing Windows 10: We all like to tweak things to suit our personal needs, taste, and style. That's what this part is all about. But it isn't just about changing the look and feel of your computer environment. It's about really making the computer a useful tool for whatever your work (or play) requires.

Part III: Windows 10 for the Enterprise: The share of Windows 10 installations in medium to large companies has increased over the past year. We will continue to see that share grow as organizations replace client computers on users' desktops and tablets. The chapters in this part cover setting up and configuring Windows 10 Hyper-V, using computers remotely, and managing Windows 10 Hyper-V in an enterprise.

Part IV: Managing Your Content: We all have to make some effort to get our stuff organized and keep it organized. Otherwise, we spend more time looking for files than actually *doing* things. This part covers the necessary housekeeping chores to help you focus on productivity — and fun.

Part V: Printing and Managing Printers: Sometimes, you just have to get something off the screen and onto paper. That's what printing is all about. This part covers printing and managing printers.

Part VI: Installing and Removing Programs: Hot topics here include adding and managing Windows 10 applications, installing and upgrading legacy programs, getting older programs to run, repairing and removing programs, setting default programs, managing programs and processes, and troubleshooting software problems. After all, what good is a computer without some programs to run on it?

Part VII: Hardware and Performance Tuning: *Hardware* is the computer buzzword for physical gadgets you can hold in your hand or that sit on your desk. As the years roll by, hardware keeps getting smaller, better, faster, cheaper, and, well, cooler. This part covers everything you need to know about adding and removing hardware, using wireless Bluetooth devices, performance-tuning your system, and troubleshooting hardware problems.

Part VIII: Networking and Sharing: This part focuses on networking features of Windows 10. Whether you have 2 PCs or 20, eventually you may want to link them all together into a single private network so they can share a single Internet account and printer, or perhaps several printers. You also learn about imaging Windows 10, using group policies, and how to protect against malicious software in this part.

Part IX: Managing Windows 10 in an Enterprise: For those responsible for managing and administering Windows 10 in a corporate or enterprise setting, this part devotes chapters to imaging and deploying Windows 10, how to use Windows 10 group policies, and ways to enhance Windows 10 security in an enterprise.

Part X: Appendixes: Rounding out the book are four appendixes, where you find information on how to install a clean copy of Windows 10 or upgrade an existing Windows 7 or Windows 8.x installation. We also provide details on Windows gestures and hotkeys.

That's a lot of topics and lots to think about. But there's no hurry. If you're new to Windows, or your experience is limited to basics like e-mail and the web, Chapters 2 and 3 are probably your best first stop. If you have more extensive Windows experience, you may want to hop over to Chapter 1 for a quick look at things that are new in Windows 10.

Part I

Getting Started

What's New in Windows 10

I f you have been using Windows 8 or Windows 8.1, you'll find Windows 10 both familiar and new. Windows 10 builds on the significant development done for Windows 8.x but adds improved usability. Windows 10 isn't just a tweak to Windows 8.1, however. Not only does Windows 10 offer a better user interface, but you'll find a long list of new and enhanced features.

If you are currently using Windows 7 or even Windows XP, you'll find Windows 10 to be a bit of a departure from your current experience in some ways. In other ways, Windows 10 isn't much different from Windows 7. For example, the Windows desktop still functions the way it does in Windows 7. With the changes introduced in Windows 8.1 and refined in Windows 10, you'll find that working in Windows 10 — whether on the Windows desktop or with the Start menu — is really not that different from your current experience. That means you can become productive with Windows 10 in a very short time.

In this chapter, we don't focus on the features you've encountered in previous versions of Windows — we explore the new and changed features in Windows 10. This chapter provides an overview of these features, and other chapters provide a deeper explanation. Although we can't cover every new feature in this chapter, we hope to give you a good overview of the key features and conceptual changes introduced in Windows 10.

Now, whip out that new Windows 10 tablet or PC, start reading, and start taking advantage of the great new features that Windows 10 has to offer.

New Platforms and Devices

One of the most significant additions to Windows 8 was its support for platforms other than the traditional PC. Windows 8 moved beyond the Intel and AMD x86 processor family to support System on a Chip (SoC) devices from both the x86 and ARM architectures. Windows 8.1 naturally also supported the ARM architecture, as does Windows 10.

ARM, which stands for Advanced RISC Machines, was developed by the company now known as ARM Holdings. Although you may not have heard of ARM processors, they are common in tablets, cell phones, MP3 players, gaming consoles, computer peripherals, and many other consumer electronics devices.

While the traditional PC portable form factor continues to shrink with ultra-light tablets and notebooks, SoC support for Windows 10 offers the capability to provide a Windows experience on small form-factor tablets, cell phones, and smaller handheld devices, in addition to the generally larger (and typically more powerful) traditional PC platforms. For ARM devices, the result is an opportunity for device manufacturers to provide a new selection of handheld devices running a Windows operating system (dubbed *Windows 10 IoT Core*) with support for applications like those in the Microsoft Office suite.

For users, it means a consistency of user experience across a broad range of devices. For example, your experience can be largely the same on your notebook, your tablet, and your cell phone. A single app can give you the same data and user experience across each device, with only small interface differences driven by screen size. Support for ARM also opens up some interesting possibilities for embedding Windows in consumer electronic devices. Someday soon your TV may be running Windows and giving you the same streaming experience as your PC. Devices such as these are loosely labeled as *Internet of Things (IoT)* devices.

Windows 10 Mobile and IoT Core

In addition to the more traditional PC editions for home, professional, and enterprise users, Windows 10 is available for a variety of IoT devices. Windows 10 supports a common

1

platform for universal apps and drivers across all of these types of devices, which further reinforces the capability to deploy apps across a very broad range of devices. But even with a common platform, the user experience on these three categories of devices is different depending in part on which edition of Windows 10 the device runs.

Windows 10 Mobile targets mobile devices and provides features such as a familiar and consistent user interface, instant on, and long battery life. Windows 10 Mobile supports universal apps, meaning an app developed for a desktop or tablet device can also run on a mobile device. Although Windows 10 Mobile does not support classic Win32/.NET apps, it provides lockdown capabilities to enable developers to create and deploy line-of-business (LOB) apps to mobile devices. For example, the app you use to submit and approve expense reports on your PC can also deploy and run on a special-purpose handheld device running Windows 10 Mobile as well as your Windows Phone, also running Windows 10 Mobile. Windows 10 Mobile is also available in an Enterprise edition that provides additional device management capability and security.

Windows 10 IoT Core is a small-footprint edition of Windows 10 with a subset of features that targets small devices and single-purpose devices, and has lower requirements for RAM, processer, and storage. Windows 10 IoT Core supports universal apps and drivers, the same development tools as for all Windows 10 devices, and the key features that Windows 10 provides on other platforms, such as security, update capability, manageability, and Windows apps.

> **NOTE**
> Apps designed for the new Windows 8.x and Windows 10 interface and available through the Microsoft Store were originally called *Metro apps*, then *Modern apps*, and now, simply *Windows apps*. Legacy apps written for previous editions of Windows are called *Windows desktop apps*. The term *Windows app* throughout this book refers to these modern Windows apps.

> **NOTE**
> Windows 10 IoT Core supports headed devices (those with a video display) as well as headless devices (those without a display).

However, Windows 10 IoT Core does not include any Microsoft branding or Windows UI, has no Windows shell or apps, and does not include the apps you would otherwise expect on a tablet or other multi-use device, such as Windows Explorer, the Mail app, or a browser. Windows 10 IoT Core is geared toward device-specific user experience scenarios. For example, a GPS manufacturer might design a GPS device that uses Windows 10 IoT Core as its operating system, or a wearable technology company might use Windows 10 IoT Core as the underlying OS for a new smart watch.

Xbox and Windows 10

Xbox has been the leading game console for several years, and although users have been able to control and integrate with their Xbox from a Windows 8.x PC, they could play Xbox games only on their Xbox consoles. Windows 10 changes that paradigm.

Windows 10 enables users to play Xbox games on their Windows 10 PCs and tablets. The games do not run natively on the PC, but instead stream from the Xbox to the other device using the Xbox app on the Windows 10 device. For example, if you're playing a game on your Xbox but need to move to another room, you pick up your tablet, connect to the Xbox, move to the other room, and continue playing.

If you have visions of playing Xbox games at work, that's still a dream (unless you have an Xbox at work). The only way Windows 10 streams is via Wi-Fi on a local network, and you can stream to only one device at a time. In addition, the game must be designed specifically to support streaming.

The Windows 10 Xbox app (Figure 1.1) enables you to stream compatible Xbox games to your Windows 10 device as well as to interact with your Xbox console and Xbox Live.

HoloLens

HoloLens is a new product from Microsoft that was conceptualized as part of the initial Microsoft Kinect project. HoloLens is essentially a wearable computer in the form of a headset that Microsoft touts as the "first fully untethered holographic computer" (see Figure 1.2). HoloLens is a perfect example of Windows 10 IoT in action. The device is fully self-contained and does not require an external computer to drive it.

HoloLens overlays holographic content on your real-world view for an augmented reality experience. The device has obvious potential in the gaming world, but even more so as a means for artists, engineers, educators, and many others to change the way we work, teach, and learn.

FIGURE 1.1

Use the Xbox app to stream games to your PC.

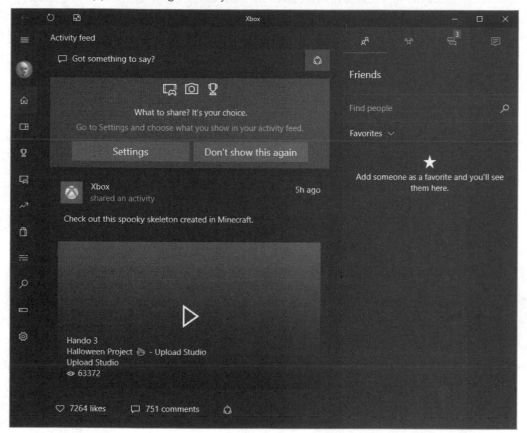

Surface Hub

Microsoft's Surface Hub is a large-screen, hybrid TV/computer/tablet device designed for in-person collaboration as well as video conferencing through Skype for Business. The Surface Hub is essentially a giant touchscreen TV with an integrated PC running

Windows 10 (see Figure 1.3). The Surface Hub includes built-in cameras, speakers, micro-phones, Wi-Fi, Bluetooth, and Near Field Communication (NFC). It uses OneNote to enable people to collaborate on a digital whiteboard, supporting both finger and pen input. Surface Hub also includes other Office apps as well as Skype for Business, and can run other Windows apps in a large-screen format. You can even connect apps from your personal device and drive them from Surface Hub.

FIGURE 1.2

Microsoft HoloLens is a wearable holographic PC running Windows 10.

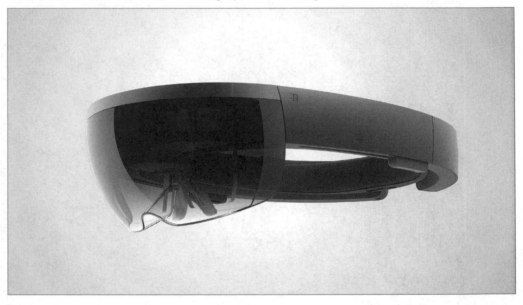

Microsoft Surface Hub is available in two sizes, 55" HD and 84" 4K. A variety of stands and wall mounts are available to enable you to either position Surface Hub in a fixed location or move it as needed.

FIGURE 1.3

Microsoft Surface Hub is a large-format, touchscreen PC running Windows 10.

The Windows 10 Interface

Windows 8 represented a fairly significant departure from the traditional Windows interface found in previous versions, in large part to support a new genre of touch-enabled devices. Windows 10 maintains much of the user interface found in Windows 8.x, reintroduces some familiar legacy experiences, and introduces some new features. This section covers the most significant changes in the Windows 10 interface.

The Start menu

One of the main complaints from users about Windows 8, after they got past the Start screen, was the removal of the Start menu. Many users were accustomed to getting to their programs and settings through the Start menu. As Figure 1.4 shows, Windows 10 brings back the Start menu, although it is in a somewhat modified form that marries the Start menu with the Start screen.

Clicking the Windows icon in the lower left corner of the display opens the Start menu. On the left side of the menu are icons for your most used apps, links to commonly used resources such as File Explorer and Documents, and your apps in alphabetical order.

FIGURE 1.4

The Start menu is back in Windows 10.

The right side of the Start menu should be fairly familiar to Windows 8.x users because it is similar in concept to the Start screen in Windows 8.x. Tiles on the Start screen give you access to apps, and, as on the Start screen, can display dynamic data within the tile (known as *live tiles*).

1

Items in the lower-left part of the Start menu provide quick access to your account, Power options (such as Sleep, Shutdown, and Restart), and Settings. You can resize the Start menu like other windows, simply by dragging the edge of the Start menu to make it larger or smaller. Figure 1.5 shows the Start menu resized to a much larger size.

FIGURE 1.5

You can expand the Start menu to fill much of the display.

The Windows 10 Start menu and the methods you can use to modify it are covered in other chapters.

Tablet Mode

Windows 10 Tablet Mode is intended to optimize the user's touch experience on tablet devices. Essentially, Tablet Mode switches the device to a full-screen Start menu and causes apps to open in full-screen mode. Apps that are already running in a window automatically switch to full-screen mode. Clicking the Restore button in Tablet Mode has no effect because no "windowed" app experience exists. However, you can drag apps to dock them.

You can turn Tablet Mode on or off through the Settings app. In addition, when you switch the device from a traditional desktop configuration to a tablet configuration, Windows 10 detects the change and asks if you want to enable Tablet Mode. For example, if you disconnect the keyboard from a Surface running Windows 10 or fold the keyboard to the back of the device to use it as a tablet, Windows 10 prompts to ask if you want to switch to Tablet Mode.

> **TIP**
> You can configure Tablet Mode behavior in the Settings app, configuring Windows 10 to always stay in the current mode without prompting you, prompt you to confirm a switch, or automatically switch modes without prompting.

The Taskbar

The familiar Taskbar is still a component of the Windows 10 interface; it behaves in much the same way as in previous versions of Windows. For example, if the Taskbar is unlocked, you can position it at any of the four edges of the display. Figure 1.6 shows the Taskbar docked at the left edge of the display.

You can pin apps to the Taskbar as you can in previous versions of Windows, including both Windows apps and legacy Windows desktop apps. The Taskbar retains the notification area, which shows icons and messages for running apps and services, with the date and time at the far right corner (when the Taskbar is docked at the bottom of the display). The Taskbar by default shows the Search box at the left next to the Start button. The Taskbar includes an icon for Task View, which is described in the following section.

> **TIP**
> The Taskbar remains when you switch to Tablet Mode, but changes slightly. For example, the Search box changes to a Search button and shortcut icons on the taskbar are hidden.

Task View

Experienced Windows users are familiar with the Alt+Tab feature in Windows, which enables you to switch between running applications. The Task View is a similar feature that is available from the Taskbar, both in desktop mode and Tablet Mode. Clicking or tapping the Task View icon in the Taskbar displays a filmstrip of the running apps (Figure 1.7).

You can then click or tap an app to make it active and bring it to the foreground. You can also close apps from the Task View by first highlighting an app and then clicking or tapping the close button in the upper right of the app's tile.

FIGURE 1.6

The Taskbar is docked at the left edge of the display.

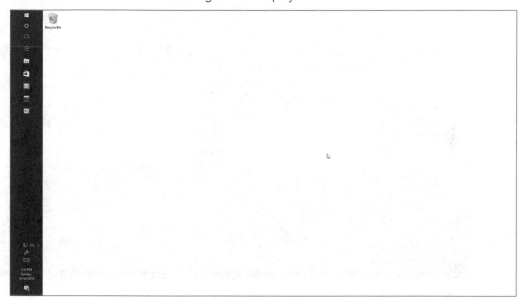

Multiple desktops

In Windows, the term *multiple desktops* refers to the capability to create more than one virtual desktop, each with one or more apps running on that virtual desktop, and switch between desktops. Windows has supported multiple virtual desktops for several years in multiple versions, although not as a mainstream feature. Windows 10 is the first version to offer multiple displays as a prominent feature of the interface.

If your device has multiple displays, you may be wondering why you would want to create multiple desktops; after all, you can simply move apps from one display to another and group them as needed. Multiple desktops let you group together apps onto a virtual desktop. Although they are most useful on single-display devices, multiple desktops can also be useful on multi-display devices.

FIGURE 1.7

Use the Task View to switch between running apps.

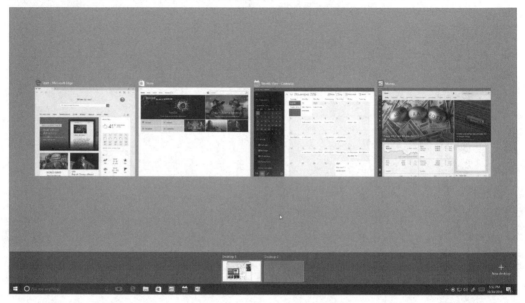

For example, you may be multitasking between work and personal activities. In this scenario, you can create a desktop for your work apps and another for your personal apps and switch between the two desktops as needed. Even on a multi-display device, you may find multiple desktops useful for helping you group specific apps together so you can focus on them as a set.

Creating a virtual desktop is easy. Just open the Task View from the Taskbar and click or tap New Desktop. Then open the apps that you want to use on that desktop. When you need to switch between desktops, either use the Task View or press Windows Key+Ctrl+Left Arrow or Windows Key+Ctrl+Right Arrow.

Action Center replaces Charms bar

One of the Windows 8.x interface elements that is gone from Windows 10 is the Charms bar. In Windows 8.x, the Charms bar expands out from the right side of the display to give you access to settings, device functions, search, and other features. Many of these items have been moved into other parts of the Windows 10 interface. For example, Search has been integrated into the Taskbar.

Even though the Charms bar is gone, something similar to it remains in Windows 10. In the Taskbar, next to the date and time, is a Notifications button that, when clicked or tapped, displays the fly-out interface element called the Action Center, shown in Figure 1.8.

FIGURE 1.8

The Action Center replaces some of the functions in the Charms bar.

The Action Center shows notifications, and through a selection of tiles at the bottom, gives you quick access to the Settings app, tablet mode, airplane mode, and other settings and features. When you need to change display brightness, for example, open the Action Center, tap the Display tile, and then use the brightness slider in the Settings app that subsequently opens.

Web Browsing

Internet Explorer (IE) has long been a love/hate app. Some users love it, but other users hate it (and often move to Firefox or Chrome because of IE's drawbacks). In addition, application compatibility for line-of-business apps and in-house apps has long been a consideration with IE for businesses that have sometimes struggled to keep their apps compatible with IE as the browser evolved.

Windows 10 ships with a new browser named Microsoft Edge (Figure 1.9). Some of the key goals of the Edge development team were to streamline the interface, integrate Cortana for faster search and better discoverability, optimize browsing across multiple platforms, provide a great experience on touch devices, and add features such as the capability to annotate web pages. Edge is a single browser designed to work across the entire Windows 10 device family.

FIGURE 1.9

The Edge web browser provides a streamlined browsing experience.

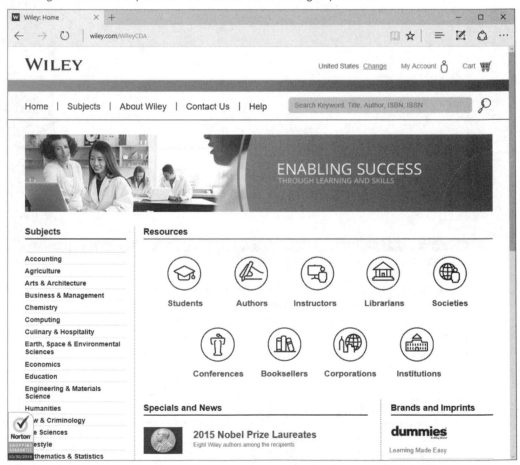

Edge moves from the markup used in IE to the same markup used in other modern browsers. Edge introduces a new proprietary rendering engine, dubbed EdgeHTML, that replaces the Trident rendering engine found in IE. In the initial beta releases of Edge, the new browser incorporated both the legacy Trident rendering engine and the new Edge rendering engine. During the development cycle, however, Microsoft decided to use only the Edge engine in Edge. In order to support legacy sites that require the Trident engine, Windows 10 ships with both the new Edge and legacy IE 11 browsers. Organizations can choose to designate the default browser through group policy, enabling them to ensure that IE 11 is the users' default browser if needed to support intranet sites or line-of-business apps that require IE compatibility.

In addition to a new rendering engine, Edge also integrates Cortana as a built-in search assistant, a new reading list that enables you to gather content to read and even export web pages to PDF, and as mentioned previously in this section, the new inking features that enable you to mark up and annotate web content and share those comments with others.

Cortana

Cortana, named for the fictional artificial intelligence character in the Halo game series, was introduced on the Windows Phone 8.1 platform. It is an intelligent personal assistant that can help you set reminders, perform searches, answer questions, recognize music, and launch apps using voice or text commands. If you speak a question, Cortana typically speaks the answer. If you type a question, Cortana answers with a text response.

Cortana (if you let her) can learn about you, your interests and habits, locations you often visit, and other information to simplify your work or personal life. For example, Cortana can search for and detect flight schedules in your e-mails and add the information to your calendar for you, or identify tracking information in e-mails to keep you up-to-date on whether your online orders are in transit or still sitting in the seller's warehouse.

Office Universal Apps

Windows 10 includes touch-optimized versions of the popular Office apps Word, Excel, PowerPoint, and OneNote. The apps are preinstalled on Windows phones and small tablets running Windows and are available as a download from the Windows Store for other devices. These apps enable you to view and edit Office documents and send and receive e-mail. Although the Office apps included with Windows 10 don't give you the same range of features as the full versions of the Office suite, they provide the most commonly used features for reading and editing documents and can minimize the number of times you need to switch from your phone or tablet to your PC to work with a document.

The Windows Store

Another change in Windows 10 is a complete revamp of the Windows Store. A key aspect of this change is that the Store is a single point of app delivery supporting phones, tablets, and PCs. In addition, IT organizations can deploy a customized version of the Windows Store that integrates in-house apps and public apps. A web-based management interface enables IT staff to assign apps, manage updates, and accomplish other Windows Store management tasks. So, when you need that line-of-business app installed on your new work PC running Windows 10, you can open the Windows Store and download it.

Another important change in the new Windows Store is the type of apps you can download. Previously, the Windows Store supported only Windows apps. The revamped store enables you to obtain Windows apps, traditional Windows desktop apps, and hosted web apps. The latter enable developers to convert components of their web sites into apps that they then make available through the Windows Store. These web apps are hosted on the vendor's infrastructure rather than being downloaded to the users' devices but have access to the notifications, camera, calendar, Cortana, and other features on the device.

Finally, the new Windows Store integrates content as well as apps. You can purchase and stream TV shows, movies, and music from the Windows Store to your Windows 10 devices.

Windows 10 Anniversary Edition Update

Windows 10 build 1607, known as Windows 10 Anniversary Edition, includes several updates and new features that were developed during the first year after Windows 10's initial release. This section explores many of these features and updates.

Start menu tweaks

One update in the Anniversary Edition is a collection of small changes to the Start menu. Previously, the Start menu displayed your most recently used apps and a selection of icons for common items including File Explorer, Settings, and Power. Clicking All Apps showed an alphabetized list of all installed apps. In the new Start menu (Figure 1.10), the Start menu by default shows your most-used apps and recommended apps, along with what was formerly the All Apps menu. Buttons at the left edge of the Start menu give you access to your account, Settings, and Power.

Action Center updates

Like the Start menu, the Action Center sees a bit of a change in the Anniversary Edition. You'll find Cortana now integrated into the Action Center, where it can offer alerts and notifications on things like stocks, sports scores, and more. The Action Center layout is also improved, grouping notifications so that a single, chatty app doesn't fill the Action Center and hide notifications from other apps.

FIGURE 1.10

The Start menu has been updated.

Notification badges

Universal Windows Platform apps can now display information on their taskbar icons. For example, a UWP mail app could display the number of new messages in your Inbox. Note that notification badges are not available for legacy Windows desktop apps, or for Windows apps that are not developed as UWP apps.

Taskbar calender

The taskbar calendar is improved in build 1607 to add meetings and events, as shown in Figure 1.11. You can view the items in the calendar, or click on an item to open it in a window, as shown in Figure 1.12.

FIGURE 1.11

The taskbar Calendar is much improved.

Pin apps to all virtual desktops

Virtual desktops in Windows 10 enable you to create multiple workspaces in Windows, each with its own set of apps. Previously, an app in Windows 10 appeared only on a single virtual desktop. With the Windows 10 Anniversary Update, you can pin an app to all virtual desktops, which is useful when you want to keep a particular app visible and easily accessible from every virtual desktop. To pin an app in this way, press Windows Key + Tab to open the Task View, then right-click the app and choose Show This Windows on All Desktops.

FIGURE 1.12

You can open calendar items from the taskbar.

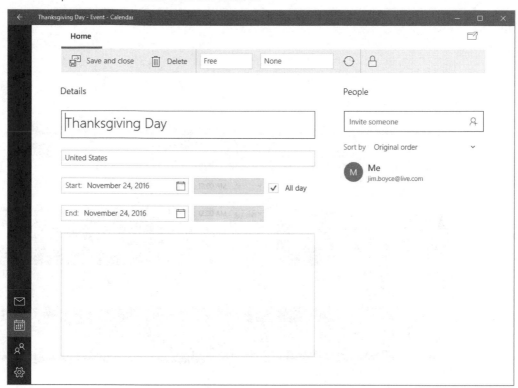

Edge improvements

Edge, the new web browser introduced with the initial release of Windows 10, gets some welcome improvements in the Anniversary Edition. For example, Edge now supports extensions. This capability enables developers to extend Edge with new features, such as ad blocking and enhanced experiences for certain sites like Amazon. To add extensions, click the ellipsis in the upper right corner of the Edge window and choose Extensions. Then, click Get Extensions from the Store. Figure 1.13 shows the Store with Edge extensions available as of this writing.

FIGURE 1.13

Use extensions to add new features to Edge.

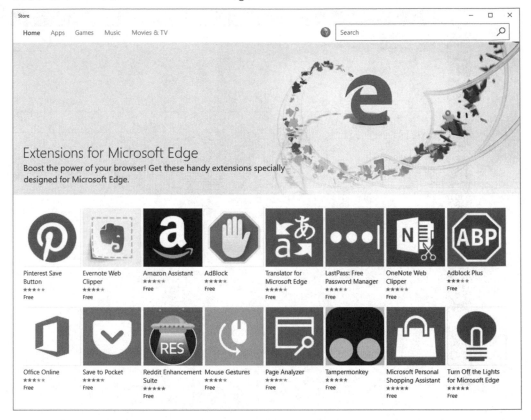

Xbox Play Anywhere

This new feature enables you to buy a game from the Store and play it on a Windows 10 PC as well as an Xbox One console, with settings, game saves, and other game data moving from device to device along with the game itself. Games must be specifically written to support Xbox Play Anywhere, but this new feature will be a welcome addition for gamers.

And more

Windows 10 Anniversary Update offers many more new features in addition to the ones covered in this chapter. For example, a Dark Theme is now available for users who want a darker color scheme. This feature is particularly helpful if you use your device in darker environments. An Activation Troubleshooter helps you work through Windows activation problems. Some additional features for Windows Ink improve the user experience when using a stylus. Cortana also has several enhancements and improvements, not only making it function better but also integrate within more apps.

You'll find additional enhancements and new features scattered throughout Windows 10. What's more, a host of new features have also been announced for the next Windows 10 update, named the Windows 10 Creators Update, due out in early 2017. With the new Windows 10 release model, you can be sure to see new features appear throughout the year.

1

Wrapping Up

Windows 10 is by far the most significant change in the Microsoft operating system ecosystem, potentially rivaling the shift from DOS to Windows in the early days of the PC.

This chapter scratched the surface of what's new in Windows 10. Some of the topics, such as HoloLens, Surface Hub, and Windows 10 IoT are not covered in detail in this book. Instead, we focus on helping you understand how to interact with and get the most from Windows 10 on your PCs and tablets. Where appropriate, we cover mobile devices and the key features that Windows 10 brings to these devices.

Your next step is to dive into Windows 10 and become familiar with the user interface. Chapter 2, "Navigating the Windows 10 Interface," helps you do just that. So, turn the page and dive in!

Navigating the Windows 10 Interface

IN THIS CHAPTER

Introducing the Windows 10 interface

Using the Start menu

Using the Action Center

Using the taskbar

Working with Windows 10 apps

Getting to the desktop

If you've been using previous versions of Windows for a while, you're no doubt familiar with the Windows desktop and how to work with Windows and Windows applications. If you've been using Windows 8.x, you'll find the transition to Windows 10 easy. If you've been using Windows 7 or earlier, however, you may find the Windows 10 interface very different. Gestures such as swipe, tap, tap and hold, slide, and so on may be foreign concepts. Fortunately, Windows 10 uses many of the same general gestures and actions you find on other touch-based devices. So, the Windows 10 interface should feel familiar to you.

If you don't have much experience with touch interfaces, this chapter gets you up to speed. You learn to navigate through the Windows 10 interface, use modern Windows apps, and even work with that familiar Windows desktop! Armed with some basic concepts, you'll be navigating the Windows 10 interface like a pro in no time.

If you've been using Windows 8.x for a while and are new to Windows 10, this chapter helps you understand the changes that Microsoft introduced in Windows 10. These changes make Windows 10 easier to use, particularly for those of us who missed the Start menu in Windows 8.

Introducing the Windows 10 Interface

The interface introduced in Windows 8 and fine-tuned in Windows 8.1 represented a shift toward touch-based interaction with the Windows operating system and applications, driven in large part by the growth of the tablet and handheld device markets. Although Windows 10 continues that touch-based focus, the Windows 10 interface is not only about touch; it's also about simplification and putting data and applications within easy reach. In addition, Microsoft has melded the positive aspects of the new interface with the Start menu familiar to users of Windows 7 and earlier versions.

If you have configured Windows Hello on your device and it has a Windows Hello–compatible camera, Windows 10 tries to recognize you and log you on automatically. If not, Windows 10 displays the Windows 10 logon screen (see Figure 2.1), which you use to log in to the device. Although Chapter 3 explains how to log in and out of Windows, we cover it briefly here. Windows displays a list of user accounts available on the device (see Figure 2.1) with the most recently used account shown in the middle of the display. To log in with the most recently used account, just tap or click in the Password box, type the password for the account, and press Enter or tap the arrow key beside the Password box. Or, if you have created a PIN on the device or have a virtual smart card installed, you can click the corresponding icon below the password box and type the PIN. To use a different account, tap (touch or click) on a user in the list at the left corner of the display, enter the password for that user account, and then press Enter or tap (or click) the arrow icon to the right of the password field.

If the device is locked but your account is logged on, Windows displays the same logon screen shown in Figure 2.1. As when logging on, just type your password and then press Enter or tap the arrow key.

After you log in, you see the Windows 10 desktop, shown in Figure 2.2. The desktop should be familiar to you, regardless of which version of Windows you have used previously, because the desktop is a key feature of all previous versions of Windows. However, the Windows 10 desktop is a little different from the others.

The first difference is the Start menu. To open the Start menu, click the Windows button at the left edge of the taskbar. As shown in Figure 2.2, the new Windows 10 Start menu is a melding of the Start menu found in Windows 7 and the Start screen found in Windows 8.x. On the left are frequently used apps, settings, and folders, and on the right are tiles for apps. You can start an app just by clicking or tapping on its tile or in the list at the left of the Start menu.

Before we dig deeper into the Windows 10 interface and its elements, let's look at the gestures and actions you can use within the interface.

FIGURE 2.1

The Windows 10 Logon screen.

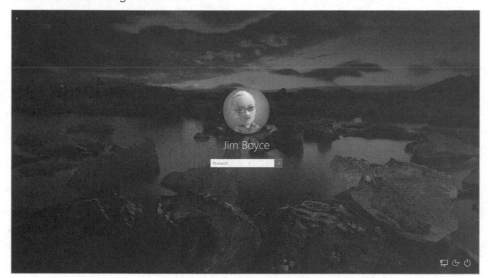

FIGURE 2.2

The Windows Start menu and desktop.

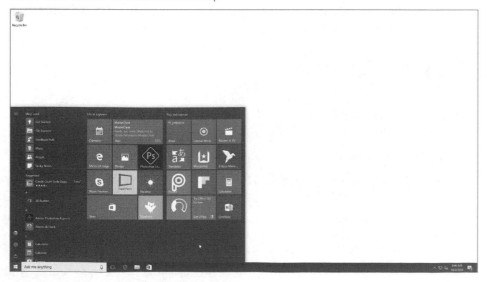

Working with Gestures and Mouse Actions

There are a handful of touch-based gestures you'll use with Windows 10, along with mouse-based alternatives for use on non-touch devices (or when you have a mouse connected to a touch device). The following list summarizes Windows 10 gestures, along with corresponding mouse actions:

- **Tap/Left-click:** Touch a finger to the object you want to select, and then remove your finger from the screen. With a mouse, left-click the object (point to it, click the left button, and then release the button).

- **Tap and hold/Click and hold:** Put a finger on the object you want to select, and hold your finger there. Tap and hold is typically followed by another gesture, such as sliding. For example, to relocate a tile on the Start screen, you tap and hold the tile, and after small buttons appear on the right corners of the tile, you can slide it to a new location. The equivalent mouse action for tap and hold is left-click and hold.

- **Swipe:** Slide your finger across the display, left, right, up, or down. For example, to view the tiles at the right side of the Start screen if they're off-screen, swipe from right to left.

- **Slide (drag)/Click and drag:** After you've selected an object, you can slide it on the display. Tap and hold to select the object, and then simply slide your finger across the screen to move the object. The mouse equivalent is to click and drag the object.

- **Swipe from the edge of the screen inward:** There are a handful of tasks you can accomplish by swiping from the edge of the display in toward the middle of the screen. For example, swiping from the left edge lets you switch between apps. Swipe from the right edge to display the Action Center. The mouse equivalent varies depending on the task. To view options for the app, right-click the app.

- **Pinch:** Place two fingers on the screen and move them apart or toward each other to zoom in or out, respectively.

Using the Start Menu

Now that you know some basic gestures and their corresponding mouse actions, you're ready to start navigating around the Windows 10 interface, starting with the Start menu, previously shown in Figure 2.2. Use any of these actions to open the Start screen:

- Press the Windows key on the keyboard.

- Use the mouse to place the cursor at the bottom-left corner of the screen, and then click the Start menu icon.

To move around the Start screen on a touch device, simply swipe the display up or down to view additional tiles. Then, tap a tile to open its associated app. You can also use the scroll wheel on the mouse to move through the Start menu.

You'll find that tiles on the Start menu can be *live,* meaning they can dynamically display information. For example, after you add an account to the Mail app, the app tile shows a preview of messages in your Inbox. The Weather tile is also live; it shows the current weather conditions (assuming your device is connected to the Internet). Other tiles show similar dynamic data. Figure 2.3 shows some examples of live tiles.

FIGURE 2.3

Live tiles on the Windows Start menu.

> **TIP**
> On a touch device, swipe from the left edge of the screen to display the Task view, which you can use to switch among running apps.

Using the Action Center

The Action Center (Figure 2.4), located at the right edge of the display in Windows 10, replaces the Charms bar found in Windows 8.x. To open the Action Center, click or tap the Notifications button on the taskbar just to the right of the time and date. Or, slide in from the right edge of the display.

Where the Charms bar gave you access to settings, devices, search, and a handful of other functions, the Action Center integrates many of those features with system notifications. For example, using the Action Center, you can quickly switch between tablet mode and regular mode, turn on or off airplane mode, and access display and other settings.

FIGURE 2.4

Access settings with the Action Center.

Using the Action Center is fairly intuitive. Some of the buttons on the Action Center pane function as toggle switches that turn functions on or off. Examples include tablet mode, airplane mode, and rotation lock. Other buttons open the Settings app to enable you to change settings. For example, if you click or tap VPN in the Action Center, The VPN page of the Settings app opens (see Figure 2.5).

In addition to buttons for settings and modes, the Action Center shows system notifications, if any are present.

FIGURE 2.5

The VPN page of the Settings app controls VPN connections and settings.

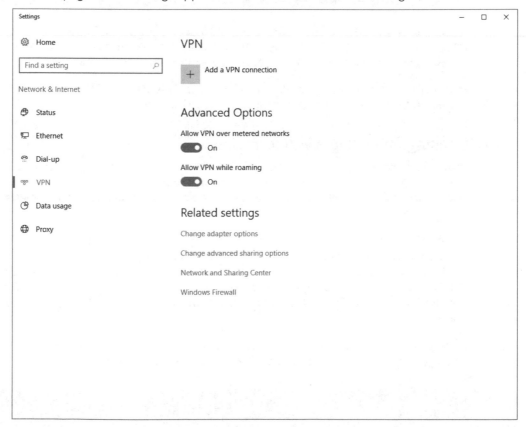

Working with Windows 10 Apps

If you're working on a traditional PC with Windows 10 installed, some (potentially many) of your apps will be "traditional" Windows apps. But, as more and more modern Windows apps are published, you'll no doubt have several favorites. On touch devices such as tablets and smaller handhelds, many of your apps will probably be modern Windows apps.

> **NOTE**
>
> The term *Windows app* refers to an app that is designed for Windows 8.x and later Windows versions. Formerly called *Metro apps* after the original name for the Windows 8 interface, Windows apps generally have a streamlined, minimalist appearance. Legacy Windows apps created for Windows 7 and earlier are called *Windows desktop apps*.

In general, working with a Windows app should be fairly intuitive. The gestures and actions you use to work with the Start menu and other Windows 10 screens are the same for apps. For example, to scroll up or down in the Maps app, just swipe up or down.

Rather than focus on specific modern Windows apps, this section of the chapter focuses on actions and methods you use in general to work with Windows apps.

Opening and using a Windows app

Opening a Windows app couldn't be any easier. Just open the Start menu, locate the app's tile, and tap or click the tile. If you're working on a non-touch device, and you have a mouse with a scroll wheel, you can use the wheel to scroll through the Start screen's tiles. Then, just click the tile for the app you want to open.

Unlike in Windows 8.x, which runs Windows apps only in full-screen mode, Windows 10 enables you to run apps in a window or full screen and change between full screen and windowed mode just as you can with a legacy desktop app. When Windows 10 is running in tablet mode, however, all apps run full screen. When running in a window, the apps display minimize, maximize, and close buttons just like a desktop app. Use these buttons to change the window state.

How you work in a Windows app depends entirely on the app, but relies on the standard touch gestures and mouse actions described earlier in this chapter.

> **NOTE**
>
> The term *Windows app* refers to apps written for Windows 8.x or later versions. In this chapter, the term *app* refers to these Windows apps.

Snapping apps on the screen

At first, it may seem that you can view and work with only one app at a time when running in tablet mode because all apps run full screen by default. But, you can actually snap two apps to the screen at once and easily switch between them. You can even view the desktop and any running apps there side-by-side with an app, or snap a legacy app beside a modern app.

To snap two apps to the screen, follow these steps:

1. Open the two apps.
2. Using the app's title bar, drag the app to the left or right side of the screen. Either action snaps the second app to the left or right of the screen. If the title bar isn't visible, slide down from the top of the display over the app to make the title bar visible.

Figure 2.6 shows two apps snapped side-by-side.

You can snap a modern Windows app beside a legacy app, enabling you to see and work with a traditional Windows app on the desktop while also using a modern Windows app. For example, Figure 2.7 shows the Windows 10 Store app snapped beside Notepad.

To snap the desktop and a modern Windows app, first switch out of tablet mode (if the device is not already in window mode). Then, open the app in a window. If you want to work with a desktop app, open it from the desktop or Start menu. With either app in the foreground, drag the title bar of the other app to the left or right side of the screen to dock the app. You can drag the edge of an app's window to resize it as needed.

FIGURE 2.6

Two Windows apps snapped side-by-side.

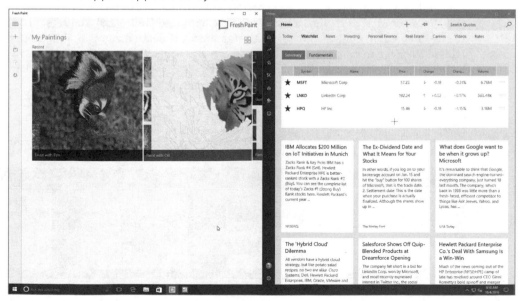

FIGURE 2.7

Notepad and a Windows 10 app snapped side-by-side.

Switching between apps

If you're an experienced Windows user, you'll be happy to learn that the methods you've used in the past to switch between apps are still available in Windows 10. For example, you can press Alt+Tab to view a list of running apps (see Figure 2.8) and select one to bring to the foreground. Continue pressing Alt+Tab until the desired app is highlighted; then release the keys to switch to that app. You can also press Windows+Tab or swipe in from the left edge to open the task view showing thumbnails of your running apps (see Figure 2.9). Click or tap on an app to bring it to the foreground.

FIGURE 2.8

Use Alt+Tab to switch between apps.

FIGURE 2.9

Use Windows+Tab to switch between apps.

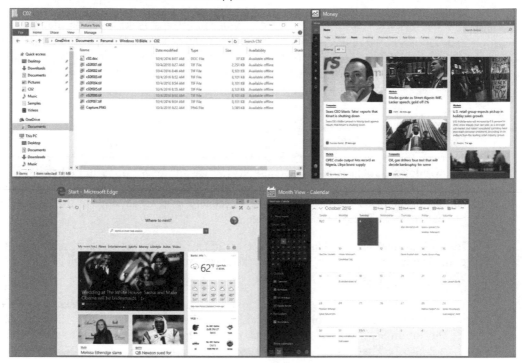

Closing a modern Windows app

Closing a modern Windows app is easy, although you may not have figured it out on your own if Windows 10 is running in tablet mode. Just grab the app at the top and drag it down to the bottom of the display.

This method isn't very intuitive, but it's the easiest way to close a app. When using a mouse, move the cursor to the top of the app until the title bar appears; then click and drag the app by its title bar to the bottom of the screen. When using a touch device, swipe down from the top to the bottom of the screen. The app should close.

Getting to the Desktop

Unless Windows 10 is running in tablet mode, the desktop has the same prominence as in Windows 7, which means that if you aren't running any apps in full screen mode, you see the desktop. If you can't see the desktop, you can simply minimize apps until it is visible.

Or, you can click the right edge of the taskbar (to the right of the Action Center button) to minimize all apps.

If Windows 10 is running in tablet mode, you can bring a desktop app to the foreground by tapping or clicking Task view in the taskbar and selecting the app. You can also use the Alt+Tab and Windows+Tab methods described previously in this chapter. If you truly need to view the desktop, for example to access a shortcut on the desktop, simply take the device out of tablet mode using the Action Center.

Using the Taskbar

The Windows taskbar remains a prominent fixture on the Windows 10 desktop and is visible even if you are running Windows 10 in tablet mode. The Windows taskbar deserves mention here, if for no other reason than that you probably want to pin apps to the taskbar so you can get to them quickly from the desktop.

Figure 2.10 shows the taskbar at the bottom of the desktop with a small selection of apps pinned to it. As in previous versions of Windows, you can open or switch to an app by tapping or clicking its icon on the taskbar.

You can pin legacy Windows apps and modern Windows apps to the taskbar, as well as app resources such as File Explorer. To pin an app to the taskbar, open the Start menu or search for the app in Search, right-click or tap and hold the app's tile, and in the app menu, tap or click Pin to Taskbar.

FIGURE 2.10

The taskbar remains an important fixture in the Windows 10 interface.

Wrapping Up

Windows 10 melds the best of the modern Windows interface with the familiar desktop interface. With the return of the Start menu, you can open apps in much the same way as in Windows 7 and earlier. If you've become enamored of the Start screen in Windows 8.x, the Windows 10 Start menu, whether running as a menu or full screen, provides essentially the same capabilities and look-and-feel as the Windows 8.x Start screen.

This melding of old and new is not limited to the Start menu. Windows 10 lets you run apps in either full screen or a window, just as you can with legacy apps. This capability makes it easier for people who haven't yet switched from Windows 7 or earlier to make the transition to the new Windows 10 interface.

Getting around the Windows Desktop

In today's busy world, few people have the time to sit down and learn to use a computer. Many books and online tutorials don't help much because they assume you already know all the basic concepts and terminology. That's a big assumption because the truth is that most people don't already know those things. Most people don't know a file from a folder from a megabyte from a golf ball. These aren't the kinds of things we learned about in school or from our day-to-day experiences.

This chapter is mostly about the things everyone else assumes you already know. It's for the people who just bought their first computer and discovered it has this thing called Windows 10 on it, or for the people who were getting by with an older computer but now have a new Windows 10 computer and want to know more about how to use it.

We often refer to the skills in this chapter as "everyday skills" because they're the kinds of things you'll likely do every time you sit down at the computer. In this chapter, we point out the name and purpose of many elements you'll see on your screen. Together, these bits of information provide basic knowledge about how you use a computer to get things done. It all starts with logging in.

Logging In

The first step to using a computer is to turn it on. Shortly after you first start your computer, the Windows 10 logon screen appears (see Figure 3.1). Windows displays the list of user accounts available on the device. You learn more about user accounts in Chapter 4, but for now, all you need to know is that if you see user account icons shortly after you first start your computer, you have to click one in order to use the computer. Click or tap the account you want to use.

FIGURE 3.1

The Windows logon screen.

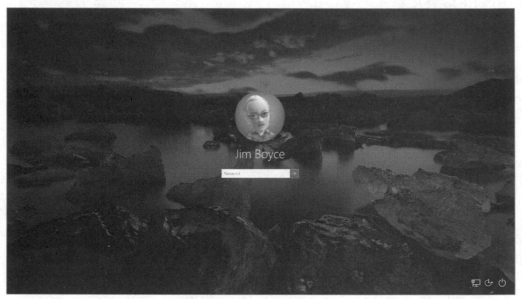

 You also can use a Windows 10 feature called Picture Passwords to log in to Windows. The Picture Passwords feature is covered in Chapter 4.

TIP

Buttons located at the bottom right corner of the logon screen provide access to actions other than logging on. The left button enables you to connect to a network before logging on. The middle button provides Ease of Access options for the visually impaired. The button at the right lets you turn off the computer rather than log in.

If the user account isn't password protected, the Windows desktop appears automatically. If the user account you clicked is password protected, a rectangular box appears instead. You have to type the correct password for the account to get to the Windows Start screen. The letters you type don't show in the box by default. Instead, you see a dot for each letter you type, as in Figure 3.2. This prevents others from learning your password by looking over your shoulder as you type it on the screen. To temporarily see the characters you enter, press and hold the eye icon on the right side of the password box. This toggles on the characters so you can see that what you typed is what you intended to type.

FIGURE 3.2

Typing a password.

After you type the password, press Enter or click the arrow to the right of the password box.

Pressing Windows+L on the keyboard locks the computer and displays the Lock screen, which is similar in look and function to the logon screen. The Lock screen displays the name of the currently logged on user, along with a password box. Enter the password to unlock the device.

After you've successfully logged in, the Windows desktop appears. Before we dive into the desktop, let's cover the Start menu.

Windows Start Menu

After you log on, you see the Windows 10 desktop. Clicking or tapping the Start menu button in the lower-left corner of the display (at the left of the taskbar) opens the Start menu, shown in Figure 3.3. The Start menu serves much the same function as the Start menu in previous versions of Windows, but it melds the look and feel of the Windows 8 Start screen with the familiar Start menu. Square or rectangular tiles give you quick access to apps, external resources such as OneDrive, folders, and settings.

FIGURE 3.3

The Windows Start menu.

At the left of the Start menu are a small number of buttons, one of which gives you access to your account settings. The button has either a stylized picture of a user, or your account picture. You can click or tap on the button to lock the device, sign out, or change account settings. Other buttons on the left portion of the Start menu give you access to File Explorer, Settings, and power options.

The right portion of the Start menu contains tiles for various apps, gathered into groups. To open an app from the Start menu, just click or tap its tile. The left side of the Start menu provides quick access to the most recent and frequently-used apps, and you can open those apps just by clicking or tapping on them. If you don't see the app you need, click or scroll through the alphabetical list of all of the apps on the device to find the one you want.

> **TIP**
> Click a letter heading in the apps list to open a matrix where you can select a specific letter.

Using the Windows Desktop

The *Windows desktop* is the electronic equivalent of a real desktop. It's the place where you keep stuff you're working on right now. Every program that's currently open is usually contained within some program window. When no programs are open, the desktop and all your desktop icons are plainly visible on the screen.

What's on the desktop

Users upgrading from previous Windows versions are familiar with the Windows desktop, the primary place for users to start their work in earlier versions of Windows. You work with programs on the Windows desktop in much the same way you work with paper on an office desktop. With Windows 8.x, the Start screen was intended to replace the desktop as the primary work environment. In Windows 10, however, the Windows desktop is still very much a part of Windows, and it's the environment in which you run legacy Windows applications and modern Windows apps — you no longer need to switch between the Start screen and the desktop to switch between legacy apps and Windows apps.

The desktop may get covered by program windows and other items, but the desktop is still under there no matter how much you clutter the screen. It's the same as a real desk in that sense. Although your real desktop may be completely covered by random junk, your desktop is still under there somewhere.

Below the desktop is the taskbar. The desktop is where everything that you open piles up. The taskbar's main role is to make it easy to switch from one open item to another. Everything you'll ever see on your screen has a name and a purpose. Virtually nothing on the screen is there purely for decoration (except the wallpaper). Figure 3.4 shows the main components of the Windows desktop and other items. Your desktop may not look exactly like the picture and may not show all the components. Don't worry about that. Right now, focus on learning the names of the most frequently used elements.

Here's a quick overview of what each component represents.

> **TIP**
>
> You learn to personalize your desktop in Chapter 9. But here's a quick hint: Virtually everything you'll ever see on your screen, including the desktop, is an object that has properties (characteristics of the object that you can specify, such as color). To customize any object, right-click that object and choose Properties.

- **Desktop:** The desktop itself is everything above the taskbar. Most programs you open appear in a window on the desktop.
- **Desktop icons:** Icons on the desktop provide quick access to frequently used programs, folders, and documents. You can add and remove desktop icons as you see fit.

- **Quick Link menu:** The Quick Link menu provides access to commonly used Windows programs and apps. To see it, right-click the Start button at the bottom-left side of the screen, or press Windows+X.

- **Taskbar:** A task is an open program. The taskbar makes switching among all your open programs easy. Right-clicking an empty place on the taskbar or on the clock in the taskbar provides easy access to options for customizing the taskbar and organizing open program windows.

FIGURE 3.4

The desktop, taskbar, and other items.

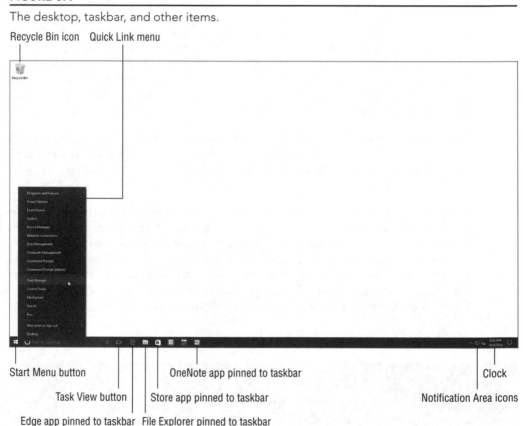

Recycle Bin icon   Quick Link menu

Start Menu button   OneNote app pinned to taskbar   Clock

Task View button   Store app pinned to taskbar   Notification Area icons

Edge app pinned to taskbar   File Explorer pinned to taskbar

- **Notification area:** This area displays icons for programs running in the background, which are often referred to as *processes* and *services*. Messages coming from those programs appear in speech balloons just above the notification area.

- **Clock:** The clock shows the current time and date.

That's the quick tour of items on and around the Windows 10 desktop. The sections that follow examine some of these items in detail.

About desktop icons

The desktop can have any number of icons on it. Most desktop icons are shortcuts to files and folders. They're shortcuts in the sense that they duplicate icons that are available elsewhere, such as on the Start menu. You can open the item associated with a desktop icon by double-clicking or double-tapping on it.

Rules always have exceptions. When it comes to desktop icons, the Recycle Bin is the exception. The Recycle Bin icon exists only on the desktop, and you won't find it anywhere else. The role of the Recycle Bin is that of a safety net. Whenever you delete a file or folder, the item is just moved to the Recycle Bin. You can restore an accidentally deleted item from the Recycle Bin back to its original location.

TIP

To learn more about the Recycle Bin and how to use it, see Chapter 19.

In addition to the Recycle Bin, you have other built-in desktop icons from which to choose. If you want to take a shot at adding icons, right-click the desktop and choose Personalize. In the resulting Personalization page of the Settings app, click Themes, then click Desktop Icon Settings.

NOTE

If you don't see Personalize when you right-click the desktop, that means you didn't right-click the desktop. You right-clicked something that's covering the desktop. You learn to close and hide things that are covering the desktop a little later in this chapter.

A *dialog box* named Desktop Icon Settings appears (see Figure 3.5). It's called a "dialog" box because you carry on a sort of dialog with it. It shows you options from which you can pick and choose. You make your choices and click OK. You'll see menu dialog boxes throughout this book.

To make an icon visible on your desktop, select (click to put a check mark in) the check box next to the icon's name. To prevent an icon from appearing on the desktop, click the check box to the left of its name to deselect it (remove the check mark). In the figure, we've opted to show just the Recycle Bin.

FIGURE 3.5

The Desktop Icon Settings dialog box.

You can choose a different picture for any icon you've opted to show on the desktop. Click the icon's picture in the middle of the dialog box. Then click the Change Icon button. Click the icon you want to show and then click OK. If you change your mind after the fact, click Restore Default.

Click OK after making your selections. The dialog box closes, and the icons you choose appear on the desktop. However, you might not see them if that part of the desktop is covered by something that's open. Don't worry about that. You learn about how to open, close, move, and size things on the desktop a little later in this chapter.

If nothing is covering the desktop, but you still don't see any desktop icons, they might just be switched off. We cover this topic in the next section.

Arranging desktop icons

As you discover in Chapter 9, you have many ways to customize the Windows 10 desktop. But if you only want to make some quick, minor changes to your desktop icons, right-click the desktop to view its shortcut menu. Items on the menu that have a little arrow to the right show submenus. For example, if you right-click the desktop and point to View on the menu, you see the View menu, as shown in Figure 3.6.

The last item on the View menu, Show Desktop Icons, needs to be selected (checked) for the icons to show at all. If no check mark appears next to that item, click the item. The menu closes, and the icons appear on the desktop. When you need to see the menu again, just right-click the desktop again.

FIGURE 3.6

Right-click the desktop.

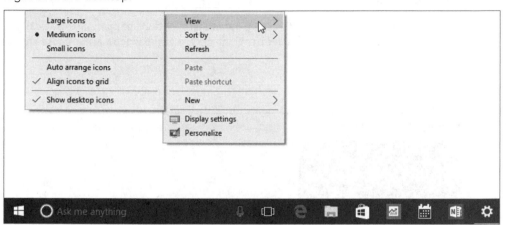

The top three items on the menu — Large Icons, Medium Icons, and Small Icons — control the size of the icons. Click any option to see its effect. If you don't like the result, right-click the desktop again, choose View, and choose a different size.

TIP

If your mouse has a wheel, another way to size icons is to hold down the Ctrl key as you spin the mouse wheel. This technique gives you an almost endless range of icon sizes. Use one of the three items in the View menu to get them back to one of the three default sizes.

The Sort By option on the desktop shortcut menu enables you to arrange desktop icons alphabetically by Name, Size, Item Type, or Date Modified. However, no matter how you choose to sort icons, the built-in icons are sorted separately from those you create.

 You learn more about personalizing your desktop in Chapter 9.

Using Jump Lists

Jump lists were a new feature of Windows 7 that enhance the usefulness of the icons and pin items on the taskbar. Windows 10 continues to use Jump Lists. Jump Lists add the most recently used objects from the application to a pop-up menu. Right-click the icon to view the Jump List (see Figure 3.7).

You don't need to do anything to set up Jump Lists — they happen automatically. Whenever you want to use a Jump List, right-click a taskbar icon and choose the item you want to open.

FIGURE 3.7

A Jump list for File Explorer.

Running Programs and Apps

You can start any program or app that's installed on your computer by finding the program's icon on the Start menu or by searching for it using Cortana, and then clicking that icon. There are other ways to start programs as well. For example, if an icon for the program is pinned to the taskbar, you can click that icon. If a shortcut icon to the program exists on the desktop, you can click (or double-click) that icon to start the program.

TIP

"Pinning" an app to the taskbar adds a shortcut icon for that object on the taskbar. You can open the associated app or object using that shortcut icon. You can also pin items to the Start menu and use those shortcuts in the same way as shortcuts on the taskbar.

 Cortana and search are covered in detail in Chapter 17.

Every time you start a program or app, that program opens in a program window. No rule exists that says you can have only one program open at a time. Some programs even enable you to open multiple copies of the same program. (Modern Windows apps, however, limit you to running only one copy of that app at a time.) You can have as many programs open simultaneously as you can cram into your available memory (RAM). Most programs allow you to run multiple copies. The more memory your system has, the more stuff you can have open without much slowdown in performance. Windows can also create a special *page file* on disk to mimic RAM, enabling you to actually use more memory than is physically present in the device.

NOTE

When it comes to using programs, or apps, the terms *start*, *run*, *launch*, and *open* all mean the same thing — to load a copy of the program into memory (RAM) so that it's visible on your screen. You can't use a program or app until it's running.

3

Most programs you open show their own names somewhere near the top of the program window. You see its name in the title bar at the top of the window, appearing either by itself or as part of a string of items. Figure 3.8 shows the Map app open on the desktop.

Most items that you open also appear on the taskbar. By default, Windows 10 shows only an icon on the taskbar for open items, with no label. However, you can configure the taskbar to show labels. The name in the taskbar button matches the name of the item.

When you have multiple program windows open, they stack up on the desktop the way multiple sheets of paper on your real desktop stack up. When you have multiple sheets of paper in a pile, you can't see what's on every page. You can see only what's on the top page because the other pages are covered by that page.

Program windows work the same way. When you have multiple program windows open, you can see only the one that's on the top of the stack. The program that's on the top of the stack is the *active window*.

> **NOTE**
> Some programs have an option called "Always on Top" that makes them display on top of the stack even when they aren't active. So, a program could be active but not necessarily on top of the stack. For the purposes of this chapter, however, assume that the active window is always the one on top of the stack.

FIGURE 3.8

Sample title bar and taskbar button.

Title bar

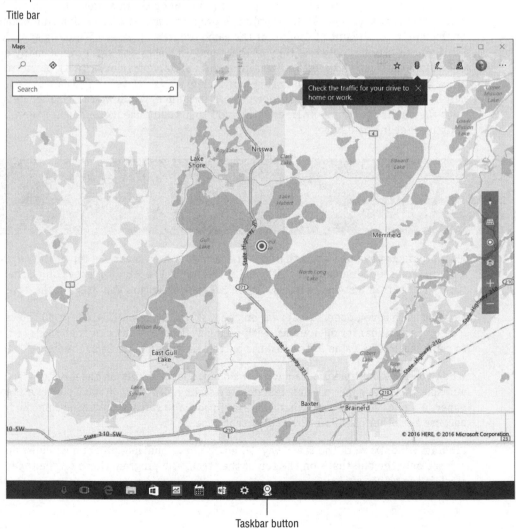

Taskbar button

The active window

When two or more program windows are open on the desktop, only one of them can be the active window. The active window has some unique characteristics:

- The active window is usually on the top of the stack. Any other open windows will be under the active window so that they don't cover any of its content. The exception is a window configured for Always on Top, as described in the preceding Note.

- The taskbar button for the active window is highlighted with a brighter foreground color.

- The title bar for the active window is a different color from the inactive ones.

- Anything you do at the keyboard applies to the active window only. You can't type in an inactive window.

Switching among open programs

When you have two or more programs open at the same time, you want to be able to switch among them easily. You have several ways to switch among open programs, as discussed in the sections that follow.

NOTE

The taskbar shows a miniature version of the window by default. Pointing to a taskbar button reveals a tooltip with the name of the window or program. You can set the size of the icons used by the taskbar through the properties for the taskbar. See Chapter 10 to learn how to set taskbar properties.

Switching with taskbar buttons

As mentioned, almost every open program has a button on the taskbar. When you have multiple open programs, you have multiple taskbar buttons. To make a particular program active, click its taskbar button. If you're not sure which button is which, point at each button. You see the name and a miniature copy of the program that the button represents, as in Figure 3.9.

TIP

If any part of the window you want to bring to the top of the stack is visible on the screen, you can click that visible part of the window to bring the window to the top of the stack.

Switching with the keyboard

If you prefer the keyboard to the mouse, you can use Alt+Tab to switch among open windows. Hold down the Alt key and then press the Tab key. You see a thumbnail image for

3

each open program window, as in the example shown in Figure 3.10. Keep Alt pressed down and keep pressing Tab until the name of the program you want to switch to appears above the icons. Then release the Alt key.

FIGURE 3.9

Pointing to a taskbar button.

FIGURE 3.10

Alt+Tab window.

You can also use Windows+Tab to switch between running apps. Pressing this key combination or clicking on the Task View button on the taskbar opens the task view, where you can click or tap the app you want to make active.

Arranging program windows

You can use options on the taskbar shortcut menu to arrange all currently open program windows. To get to that menu, right-click an empty area of the taskbar, or right-click the clock in the lower-right corner of the screen. Figure 3.11 shows the options on the menu.

The four options that apply to program windows on the desktop are similar to the options you get when you right-click a taskbar button that represents multiple instances of one program:

- **Cascade Windows:** Stacks all the open windows like sheets of paper, fanned out so that all their title bars are visible, as in Figure 3.12.

- **Show Windows Stacked:** Arranges the windows in rows across the screen, or as equal-sized tiles.

- **Show Windows Side by Side:** Arranges the windows side by side. As with the preceding option, if you have too many open windows to show that way, they're displayed in equal-sized tiles.

- **Show the Desktop:** Minimizes all open windows so that only their taskbar buttons are visible. You can see the entire desktop at that point. To bring any window back onto the screen, click its taskbar button. To bring them all back, right-click the clock or taskbar again and choose Show Open Windows.

The best way to understand these options is to try them out for yourself. Open two or more programs. Then try each of the options described to see the effect on your open program windows.

FIGURE 3.11

Taskbar shortcut menu.

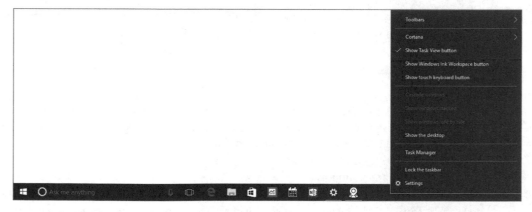

Sizing program windows

As a rule, program windows can be any size you want them to be, but this rule has a few exceptions. For example, the tiny Calculator program can't be sized at all. Some programs shrink down only so far. But in general, most open program windows can appear in three sizes:

- Maximized, in which the program fills the entire screen above the taskbar, covering the desktop.
- Minimized, in which only the program's taskbar button is visible, and the program window takes up no space on the desktop.
- Any size in between those two extremes.

FIGURE 3.12

Cascaded program windows.

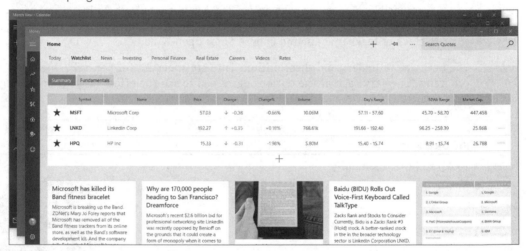

Often, you want to work with two or more program windows at a time. Knowing how to size program windows is a critical skill because working with multiple program windows is difficult if you can't see at least a part of each one.

Maximize a program window

A maximized program window enlarges to its greatest window size, which in many cases causes it to fill all the space above the taskbar. This makes it easy to see everything inside the program window. If a program window isn't already maximized, you can maximize it in several ways:

- Click the Maximize button in the program's title bar (see Figure 3.13).
- Grab the title bar and move the window to the top of the screen. Pause for a moment and then release the mouse button.

- Double-click the program's title bar.
- Click the upper-left corner of the window you want to maximize and choose Maximize. Optionally, right-click anywhere near the center top of the window and choose Maximize.

TIP

Few buttons on the screen show their name. But you can find out a button's name just by touching the button with the tip of the mouse pointer to display a tooltip.

Minimize a program window

If you want to get a program window off the screen temporarily without losing your place, minimize the program window. When you minimize the program window, the program remains running. However, it takes up no space on the screen, so it can't cover anything else on the screen. When minimized, only the window's taskbar button remains visible. You can minimize a window in several ways:

FIGURE 3.13

The Maximize button in a title bar.

- Click the Minimize button in the program's title bar (see Figure 3.14).

FIGURE 3.14

The Minimize button in a title bar.

- Click the program's taskbar button once or twice. (If the program isn't in the active window, the first click just makes it the active window. The second click then minimizes the active window.)
- Right-click the program's taskbar button or title bar and choose Minimize.

Size at will

Between the two extremes of maximized (consuming the entire desktop) and minimized (not even visible on the desktop), most program windows can be any size you want them to be. The first step to sizing a program window is to get it to an in-between size so that it's neither maximized nor minimized (called *restoring* the app). You can do that in one of two ways:

- If the program window is currently minimized, click its taskbar button to make it visible on the screen.
- If the program window is currently maximized, double-click its title bar or click its Restore Down button to shrink it down a little. Optionally, use the Cascade Windows option described earlier to get all open program windows down to an in-between size.

Minimize versus Close

Everything that's "in your computer," so to speak, is actually a file on your hard disk. The stuff on your hard disk is always there, whether the computer is on or off. When you open an item, two things happen. The most obvious is that the item becomes visible on the screen. What isn't so obvious is the fact that a copy of the program is also loaded in the computer's memory (RAM).

When you minimize an open window, the program is still in memory. You can tell that because the program's taskbar button is still on the taskbar. When you want to view that program window, click its taskbar button to make it visible on the screen again. It shows up looking exactly as it did before you minimized it.

When you close a program, its window and taskbar button both disappear and the program is removed from the RAM (making room for other things you might want to work with). The way to get back to the program is to restart it from its icon. However, this new program window is an entirely new running copy of the program, unrelated to any other copies that were running.

After the program window is visible but not consuming the entire screen, you can size it to your liking by dragging any edge or corner. You have to get the tip of the mouse pointer right on the border of the window you want to size so that the pointer turns into a two-headed arrow, as in Figure 3.15.

FIGURE 3.15

Use the two-headed arrow to resize a window.

When you see the two-headed arrow, hold down the left mouse button without moving the mouse. After the mouse button is down, drag in the direction you want to size the window. Release the mouse button when the window is the size you want.

You can also size a program window using the mouse and the keyboard. Again, the program window has to be at some in-between size to start with. Also, note that you always begin the process from the program window's taskbar button. Follow these steps:

1. Click the program window's control menu button (upper-left corner of the window) and choose Size. Note that the control menu is not available on all apps.
2. Press the navigation arrow keys ($\leftarrow$, $\rightarrow$, $\uparrow$, $\downarrow$) until the window (or the border around the window) is the size you want.
3. Press Enter.

Moving a program window

You can easily move a program window about the screen just by dragging its title bar. However, you can't start with a minimized window. You have to get the program window to an in-between size or maximized size before you begin. Then place the mouse pointer somewhere near the top center of the window you want to move, hold down the left mouse button, and drag the window around. Release the mouse button when the window is where you want it on the desktop. This works for both in-between sized and maximized windows.

Dialog boxes work the same way. You usually can't size or minimize a dialog box, and dialog boxes don't have taskbar buttons. But you can easily drag a dialog box around the screen by its title bar.

Moving and sizing from the keyboard

As you've seen, most of the techniques for moving and sizing program windows rely on the mouse. There are some keyboard alternatives, but they're not available in all program windows. To find out whether these work in the window you're using at the moment, press Alt+Spacebar and see whether a system menu drops down from the upper-left corner, as in Figure 3.16.

FIGURE 3.16

A system menu from a program window.

If you see the menu, you just have to press the underlined letter from the menu option you want to select. For example, press the letter *x* to Maximize or *n* to Minimize. If you press *m* to Move or *s* to Size, you can then use the arrow keys (←, →, ↑, ↓) to move or size the window. Then press Enter when the window is positioned or sized to your liking.

> **TIP**
>
> Sometimes, a window can be outside the viewable area of the desktop. This can happen if you extend your Windows desktop onto another monitor but that monitor isn't connected or turned on. If you can press Alt+Tab and determine that a program is running, but you can't see it on the desktop, press Alt+Tab and select the program (make it active). Then press Alt+Spacebar, press M, and use the arrow keys on the keyboard to move the window into a viewable area of the desktop.

Closing a Program

When you're finished using a program, you should close it. Every open program and document consumes some resources, mostly in the form of using memory (RAM). The computer also uses *virtual memory,* which is basically space on the hard disk configured to look like RAM to the computer.

RAM has no moving parts and, thus, can feed stuff to the processor (where all the work takes place) at amazing speeds. A standard hard disk has moving parts and is much, much slower. Newer solid state drives do not rely on moving parts, but you still have speed differences between RAM and solid state drives. As soon as Windows has to start using virtual memory, everything slows down. So, you don't want to have stuff you're not using to remain open and consuming resources.

You have many ways to close a program. Use whichever of the following techniques is most convenient for you, because they all produce the same result — the program is removed from memory, and both its program window and taskbar button are removed from the screen (until the next time you open the program):

- Click the Close (X) button in the program window's upper-right corner.
- Right-click the title bar across the top of the program window and choose Close.
- Choose File ⇨ Exit from the program's menu bar, if the program provides a File menu.
- Right-click the program's taskbar button and choose Close Window.
- If the program is in the active window, press Alt+F4.

> **TIP**
>
> You can close a Windows app by dragging the window down to the bottom of the screen. You can also move the mouse pointer to the top right of the app until the Close button appears, and then click the Close button.

If you were working on a document in the program and you've made changes to that document since you last saved it, the program should ask in a message box like the example in Figure 3.17 whether you want to save those changes.

FIGURE 3.17

Save changes to a document before closing the app.

Never take that dialog box lightly. If you click Don't Save/No, any changes you have made in the app will be lost. Your options are as follows:

- **Save/Yes:** The document is saved in its current state; both the document and the program close.
- **Don't Save/No:** Any and all changes you made to the document since you last saved it will be lost forever. Both the document and the program close.
- **Cancel:** The program and document both remain open and on the screen. You can then continue work on the document and save it from the program's menu bar (choose File ⇨ Save).

Using the Notification Area

Over on the right side of the taskbar is the notification area (also called the *system tray* or *tray*). Each icon in the notification area represents a program or service that's running in the background. For example, antivirus and antispyware programs often show icons in the notification area so that you know they're running.

To conserve space on the taskbar, Windows 10 gives you the option of hiding inactive icons. When inactive icons are hidden, you see a button with up and down arrows on it at the left side of the notification area. Click the button to see icons that are currently hidden.

As with any icon or button, you can point to an icon in the notification area to see the name of that icon. Right-clicking an icon usually provides a context menu of options for using the item. Clicking or double-clicking the icon usually opens a program window that's associated with the running background service.

> **NOTE**
>
> A *context menu* is a menu that offers commands that are in the context of the selected item. In other words, the commands apply specifically to the selected item, not to other items. To open a context menu, right-click an item (such as an icon).

For example, the Volume icon provides a simple service: It lets you control the volume of your speakers. To change the volume, you click the icon and then drag the slider (shown in Figure 3.18) left or right. Optionally, you can mute the speakers by clicking the button at the left of the slider. Click it again to remove the mute.

FIGURE 3.18

The volume control slider.

The icons in the notification area don't represent programs that you *can* run. They represent programs that *are* running. The icon simply serves as a notification that the program is running, although in most cases, the icon also provides options for closing the program or changing how it runs. Different computers have different notification area icons. The following are some common examples:

- **Network connections:** You might see an icon that lets you disconnect from the network, view and connect to wireless networks, and open the Network and Sharing Center.

- **Security programs:** Programs that protect your system from malware (such as viruses and spyware) often display icons in the notification area.

- **Power:** An icon indicates the charging status and battery capacity of your mobile device.

Windows 10 includes a selection of system icons that can appear in the notification area. These include Clock, Volume, Network, Power, Input Indicator, and Action Center. Other icons can also appear in the notification area. The following section explains how to turn these icons on or off.

Showing/hiding system and notification icons

You can choose for yourself which notification area icons you do or don't want to see at any time. You rarely need to see them all, so you can hide some if you prefer. To make choices about those icons, right-click the clock and choose Customize Notification Icons. On the resulting Taskbar page of the Settings app, scroll down and click Turn System Icons On or Off to open the settings page shown in Figure 3.19.

FIGURE 3.19

The Turn system icons on or off page.

The Taskbar page provides options for controlling the types of notifications that appear and when and where they appear. Click the link Select Which Icons Appear on the Taskbar to choose which icons you want displayed. Click the link Turn System Icons On or Off to show or hide specific system icons from the tray.

Chapter 10 discusses additional techniques for customizing the desktop, taskbar, and notification area.

Responding to notification messages

Icons in the notification area may occasionally display messages in a speech balloon. Many messages just provide some feedback and don't require any response from you. These messages generally fade away on their own after a few seconds. But you can also close the message by clicking the Close (X) button in its upper-right corner.

Using scroll bars

Scroll bars appear in program windows whenever the window contains more information than it can fit. You may not see any on your screen right now. But don't worry about that. The trick is to recognize them when you do see them, to know what they mean, and to know how to work with them. Figure 3.20 shows an example of a vertical scroll bar and a horizontal scroll bar.

When you see a scroll bar, it means that there's more to see than what's currently visible in the window. The size of the scroll box (the bit inside the scroll bar area that looks like a long button) relative to the size of the scroll bar tells you roughly how much more there is to see. For example, if the scroll box is about 10 percent the size of the bar, it means you're seeing only about 10 percent of all there is to see.

To see the rest, you use the scroll bar to scroll through the information. You have three ways to use scroll bars:

- Click a button at the end of the scroll bar to move a little bit in the direction of the arrow on the button.

- Click an empty space on the scroll bar to move the scroll box along the bar toward the place where you clicked. That moves you farther than clicking the buttons would move you.

- Drag the scroll box in the direction you want to scroll. To drag, place the mouse pointer on the button and hold down the left mouse button while moving the mouse in the direction you want to scroll.

If your mouse has a wheel, you can use that to scroll as well. If the window shows a vertical scroll bar, spinning the mouse wheel scrolls up and down. If the window shows only a horizontal scroll bar, spinning the mouse wheel scrolls left and right. Some mice have a horizontal scroll button (or wheel) that you can push left or right to scroll horizontally.

You can also use the keyboard to scroll up and down. But understand that the scroll bars work only in the active window (the window that's on the top of the stack). If necessary, first click the window or press Alt+Tab to bring it to the top of the stack. Then you can use the up and down arrow keys ($\uparrow$ and $\downarrow$) to scroll up and down slightly. Use the Page Up (PgUp) and Page Down (PgDn) keys to scroll up and down in larger increments. Press the Home key to scroll all the way to the top (or all the way to the left). Press the End key to scroll all the way to the end.

FIGURE 3.20

Examples of scroll bars.

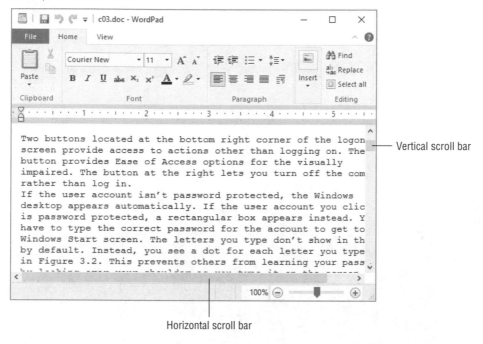

Vertical scroll bar

Horizontal scroll bar

Using Back and Forward buttons

Back and Forward buttons help you navigate through multiple pages of items. As with scroll bars, they appear only when useful, so don't expect to see them on your screen right now, or all the time. At times, they may be *disabled* (dimmed), as at the top of Figure 3.21. At other times they are *enabled* (not dimmed). Also, you won't find Back and Forward buttons in every program window.

A disabled button isn't broken. When an item is disabled, it's just not appropriate at the moment. For example, when you first open a window, both buttons may be disabled because you have no page to switch to yet. When you click a link that takes you to another page, the Back button is then enabled because now you *do* have a page to go back to (the page you just left). After you go back to the previous page, the Forward button is enabled because now you have a page to go forward to — the page you just left.

When a button is enabled, you just click it to go back or forward. When a button is disabled, clicking it has no effect.

FIGURE 3.21

Back and Forward buttons.

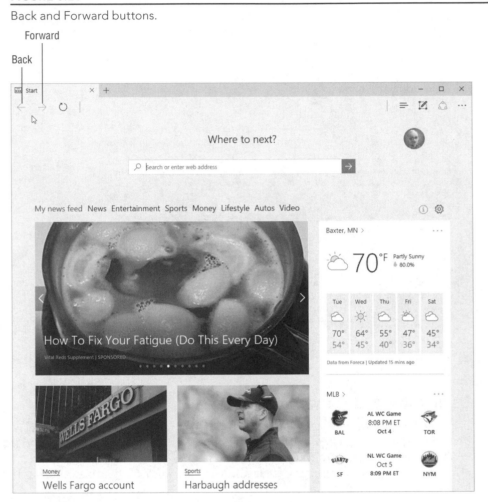

Using Multiple Virtual Desktops

You can think of the Windows 10 desktop as a workspace where you interact with your apps. If you work with a number of apps at one time, however, you may find that one desktop just isn't enough space to contain everything.

If you have more than one display connected to your device, the desktop extends across all of those displays, and you can move apps from one display to another as needed.

Whether you have only one display or just want more flexibility in how you organize your running apps, you can actually work with more than one desktop in Windows 10. Think of these virtual desktops as additional work surfaces, each containing its own set of open apps. For example, you may use one desktop for your work apps and create a second desktop for some personal apps.

To create a virtual desktop, click or tap the Task View icon on the taskbar. Then, click or tap the New desktop link in the bottom-right corner of the display. Windows 10 creates a new desktop, as shown in Figure 3.22. Then, simply drag apps from the task view to the desired desktop to move them to that desktop. If you want to add apps that are not yet open, close the task view and open the apps. Then, click the Task View icon and drag the now open apps to the desired desktop.

FIGURE 3.22

You can create multiple desktops in Windows 10.

TIP

You can quickly create a new virtual desktop by pressing Windows+Ctrl+D without opening the task view.

To switch to a different desktop, press Windows+Ctrl+← or Windows+Ctrl+→. These keystrokes cycle through the virtual desktops in order. You can also open the task view and click or tap a desktop to make it active. To remove a virtual desktop, open the task view, hover the mouse over the desktop's icon and click the Close button. Removing a desktop does not close any apps that are on it. Instead, the apps move to the next virtual desktop to the left.

CAUTION

Virtual desktops do not survive logging off or shutting down the device. You can't create and save virtual desktop configurations. Instead, you must create them each time you log on to the device.

Logging Off, Shutting Down

Here's a question many people ask: "Should I shut down my computer if I won't be using it for a while, or should I leave it on?" Everybody has an opinion about this. So here's ours: It doesn't matter. It's fine to leave your computer running. Many people shut down their computers only when they need to, such as when installing certain types of hardware. Aside from that, their computers are on, and online, 24 hours a day, 7 days a week. With today's green PCs, turning off the computer every day isn't as important as it once was. Perhaps more important, leaving the computer on means you can start working with it almost right away, instead of waiting for it to boot.

What about wear and tear? If your device is configured for power saving options, such as shutting down the hard disk after a certain period of inactivity, the device receives little to no wear when idle. With solid state storage devices becoming more common, hard disk wear and useful life are becoming non-issues. So, don't worry about wearing out your device by leaving it running all the time.

> **NOTE**
>
> Windows 10 provides a much quicker startup process than previous versions of Windows. In some cases, the boot-up time is only a few seconds, which is substantially quicker than Windows 7.

The Power button in Windows 10 is located on the Start menu. But you also can access the power commands from the Quick Link menu. Figure 3.23 shows the power commands in the Quick Link menu. Figure 3.24 shows the Power button in the Start menu.

> **CAUTION**
>
> Turning off a PC isn't quite the same as turning off a TV or radio. You shouldn't press the main power switch to shut down while you have files open and unsaved. Close all your documents and apps first. Then click the Power button and choose Shut Down. If your device is locked up and unresponsive, however, you may need to power down the device and turn it back on to get it to respond again.

Although shutdown is much faster in Windows 10 than previous versions, don't expect the computer to turn off immediately. Windows takes a few seconds to get everything closed up and ready to shut down. On most computers, you don't have to do anything else. The computer eventually shuts itself down completely.

FIGURE 3.23

The power commands available from the Quick Link menu.

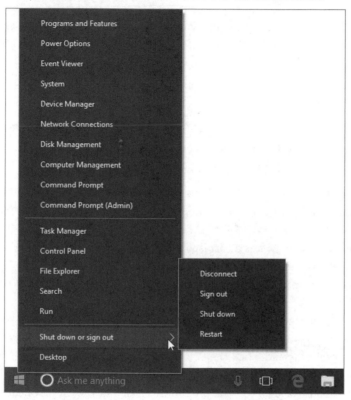

FIGURE 3.24

The Power button available from the Start menu.

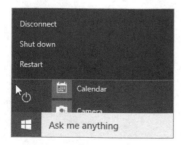

Wrapping Up

That wraps up the main terminology and basic skills. Much of what you've learned in this chapter is the kind of stuff most people assume you already know. You may have to read the chapter a few times and practice the skills before it all sinks in. Use the Windows Help for more information and for hands-on practice.

Here's a quick summary of the most important points covered in this chapter:

- The Windows desktop is the primary place you'll do your work.
- Unless you have a touchscreen device (such as a mobile phone or tablet), you'll use your mouse and keyboard to operate the computer.
- Most of your work will involve opening and using programs and apps.
- You can start any program that's installed on your computer from the Start menu.
- Each open program appears in its own program window on the desktop. Program windows stack up like sheets of paper.
- Each open program window has a corresponding taskbar button. The taskbar buttons help you switch from one open program window to another.
- You can move and size program windows to see exactly what you need to see, when you need to see it.
- You can create multiple virtual desktops to organize your running apps.
- When you finish using your computer and want to shut it down, don't reach for the main power switch. Instead, click the Start menu, choose Power, and then click Shut Down.

That's enough for now about the desktop and programs. These days, with just about everyone using a computer to access the Internet, security is a major issue. So, we begin to address that topic in Chapter 4 with a discussion of user accounts and how they relate to computer security.

Sharing and Securing with User Accounts

IN THIS CHAPTER

Why user accounts?

Creating and managing user accounts

Using user accounts

Recovering forgotten passwords

User account control secrets

Managing credentials and online IDs

E very person who uses your computer is called a *user,* and each user should have his or her own *user account* on the computer. Giving each person a user account is like giving each person his or her own separate PC, but much cheaper. Each user can personalize the desktop and other settings. Each person can have a separate collection of pictures, music, videos, and other files. Each user can also set up a separate e-mail account.

User accounts allow parents to create and enforce parental controls in Windows 10. This is a great tool for parents who can't always monitor when and how children use the computer. Parental controls allow you to control and monitor children's computer use 24 hours a day, 365 days a year, even when you aren't around to do it yourself.

User accounts also add a level of security to your computer. Many security breaches occur not because of a problem with the computer or Windows, but because the user is in an account that grants malware (bad software) *permission* to do its evil deeds. Of course, people don't realize that they're granting permission because the program doesn't ask for permission. It gets its permission automatically from the type of user account you're currently logged into.

Creating and managing user accounts is easy. But before getting into the specifics, this chapter looks at how you, as a user, experience user accounts.

Logging In and Out of User Accounts

When you start your computer, Windows 10 presents the Lock Screen. This screen shows a background picture and can run background apps such as a calendar app or mail app before you log in. To advance beyond the Lock Screen, click a mouse button, gesture down (press the down arrow on your keyboard), press the spacebar, or press Enter. If you're on a tablet, swipe up to get to the login from the lock screen. You're shown the login screen. This screen displays the last user logged in at that computer. If you have multiple user accounts on your computer, you can log in using the previous user account (if that's you) or select a different user.

To log in, enter the password for the chosen account and press Enter or click the arrow at the right end of the password text box. If you want to log in using a different login name, click the Sign-in options link under the default user name or choose from the list of users that appears at the bottom left side of the screen. You can also click on the user name list at the top of the Start menu, which presents a list of users who can log in to the computer. Select the user you want to log in with, and then enter that user's login credentials to start Windows 10.

For accounts that don't have an associated password, simply click the name for that user, and Windows loads to the Windows 10 Start screen.

Where am I now?

To see the name of the user account you're currently logged in to, look at the middle of the Windows 10 Start menu. In Figure 4.1, the user account name is Jeffrey Shapiro, but you'll see a username that has been set up on your computer. If Windows 10 came preinstalled on your computer, the username may be a generic name, such as Owner or User.

Switching accounts

You have a few ways to switch from the account you're currently logged in to to another account (assuming that you have more than one user account on your computer already).

The quickest way is to display the Start menus and then click your account name in the middle of the screen. Figure 4.2 shows an example of a list of users. You can use the following methods to change users:

- **Click Sign Out:** This option logs you out of Windows and sends you to the Windows startup screen. Press Enter, slide the screen up, or roll the mouse button down to display the sign on screen. Select a username by clicking the back arrow to display all users set up on this computer.
- **Click a username:** When you click your username at the Start menu, all user accounts for your computer appear. Click the name you want to switch to. Windows

suspends the current user and displays the login screen for the selected name. Enter the password for that username to continue.

FIGURE 4.1

Username on the new Windows 10 Start menus.

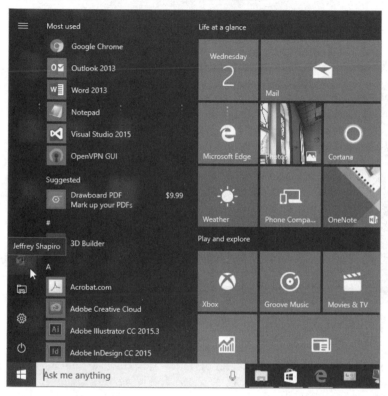

Why Switching Users Can Be Bad

When you switch users, all the programs and documents on your desktop remain open and in memory. This feature is useful if you need to leave your computer in a hurry and don't need to shut down all the stuff you're working on; however, it leaves less working memory for other users in their accounts.

If multiple users consistently switch users to leave their accounts, an enormous amount of memory remains constantly tied up. The likely result is that the computer runs much slower for everyone.

Ideally, every user should save all open files, exit all programs, and sign off from his or her account when finished using the computer.

FIGURE 4.2

Available users who can log in to the current computer.

You also can change users by using the Power options. Click the Start button, then click the Power icon. Three menu options appear, as shown in Figure 4.3. The options are described in the following list:

- **Sleep:** This option saves the system state to disk and powers down the computer, but the computer can be restored more quickly than shutting down and starting up.

- **Shut Down:** This option closes all open programs and shuts down the computer. Press the power button to restart the computer and show the login screen. The Power Options/System Settings applet allows you to decide what the power button does when you press it. You may need to change your computer's BIOS configuration as well.

- **Restart:** This option closes all programs, shuts down the computer, and then restarts the computer to the login screen.

- **Hibernate:** This option turns off the PC, but the apps stay open. When you turn the PC back on, you resume where you left off. By default this option is not checked. If you want to have this option shown in the list of power options, check mark it in the Power & Sleep settings in the Control Panel. To find the settings, press Alt-X, select Control Panel, and then select Hardware and Sound. Under Power option, select Change what the power options do. Select the Change settings that are currently unavailable and check the Hibernate button.

FIGURE 4.3

Windows Power options.

> **CAUTION**
>
> If your user account isn't password-protected, other people aren't really locked out of your account. Anyone can come along, click your user account name, and be at your desktop. In addition, once someone is at your desktop, she can use the Accounts screen to set up a password of her own. Unless she gives you that password, you can be locked out of your own account. In most cases, particularly when your computer is shared with another user or has the potential to be available to others, take precautions and set up a password for your account.

Sign-in Options

Windows 10 provides several sign-in options, available from the Accounts panel in Settings. To access the options, click the Accounts panel and then click the Sign-in options link.

The six options are the following:

- **Require sign-in:** This link lets you toggle on or off the requirement to sign in when you wake your computer from sleep.

- **Windows Hello:** This allows your computer to recognize either your face your fingerprint. You need to have additional hardware installed for this feature to work.

- **Password:** This link takes you to the page where you can create and manage your passwords (see the next section).

- **PIN:** Clicking this link prompts you for your password, after which you can enter and confirm a number with which to log on.
- **Picture password:** This link takes you to the page where you can create and manage a picture password (see "Picture Passwords" later in this chapter).
- **Lock Screen:** This option is under the Related settings section of the sign-in options screen. It lets you set the background picture, Screen timeout settings, and screen saver information.
- **Privacy:** This option shows your email address on the sign-in screen.

The Sign-in Options page is shown in Figure 4.4.

FIGURE 4.4

Windows sign-in options.

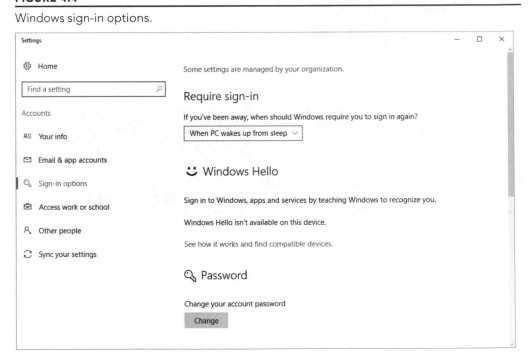

Creating Strong Passwords

In this section we talk about techniques for creating, managing, and password-protecting user accounts, but before we get into the details, we provide some basic information on passwords in general. These tips are useful not only for passwords for user accounts, but for all types of accounts you create, including online accounts.

A password that's easily guessed is a weak password. A strong password is one that isn't easily guessed and is immune to *password-guessing attacks*. The two most common forms of password-guessing attacks are the *dictionary attack* and the *brute-force attack*. Both types of attacks rely on programs that are designed to try to crack people's passwords and gain unauthorized entry to their user accounts.

A dictionary attack tries many thousands of passwords from a dictionary of English terms and commonly used passwords. A brute-force attack tries thousands of combinations of characters until it finds the right combination of characters needed to get into the account.

Both types of attacks are rare in a home PC environment. They'e also easily frustrated by common techniques such as forcing a person to wait several minutes before trying again after three failed password attempts. Nonetheless, the general guidelines used to protect top-secret data from password-guessing attacks can be applied to any password you create. A strong password is one that meets at least some of the following criteria:

- It is at least eight characters long.
- It does not contain your real name, user account name, pet name, significant date (such as birthday), or any name that's easily guessed by other family members or co-workers.
- It does not contain a word that can be found in a dictionary.
- It contains some combination of uppercase letters, lowercase letters, numeric digits, and symbols (such as !, &, ?, @, and #).

We realize that few people need Fort Knox–style security on their personal PCs. You don't want a password that's difficult to remember and a pain to type. But any steps you take to make the password less easy to guess are well worth the effort. Some websites offer *password checkers,* programs that analyze a password and tell you how strong it is. Or go to any search engine, such as www.google.com, and search for "password checker."

Remembering passwords

The most common problem with passwords is forgetting them. When you set up a password for a website, you can usually be reminded what the password is by clicking an "I forgot my password" link at the sign-in page. But no such link exists for passwords that protect your Windows user accounts. Therefore, be sure *not* to forget your Windows passwords!

Before you password-protect a user account, take the time to come up with a password that you (or the user) can remember. Make sure you use exactly the same uppercase and lowercase letters that you'll be typing. Windows passwords are always case sensitive, which means the difference between uppercase and lowercase letters matters.

4

For example, say you jot down your password as Tee4me!0 (with a zero as the last character). But later you type it in as tee4Me!o (with the last character being the letter *o*). Still later, you forget the password and dig out the sheet of paper. The tee4me!o you wrote down doesn't work, because the password is actually Tee4Me!0.

CAUTION

On a typewriter, the number 0 is basically the same as an uppercase letter *O* and the number 1 is basically the same as a lowercase letter *l*, but that is *not* true of computers. You must use the 1 and 0 keys near the top of the keyboard or on the numeric keypad to type 1 (one) and 0 (zero).

Devising a password hint

With Windows passwords, you can specify a password hint to help you remember a forgotten password. But still, using hints is tricky. Anyone who uses your computer can see the password hint. So, the hint shouldn't be so obvious that it tells a potential intruder what the password is. For example, create a hint that triggers your memory of the password but doesn't repeat the exact uppercase and lowercase letters you used.

Writing down your passwords isn't a good idea because other people may be able to access them. But if you need to keep track of multiple passwords, consider using a password-protected Excel spreadsheet to store all your passwords. Then, you need to remember only one — the password for the Excel file. Alternatively, password-keeper applications are available to achieve the same result.

TIP

If you decide to store your passwords in an Excel file, make a copy you can open on another computer in case your computer crashes or you forget the password to log on. Better still, get a secure password storage program you access from your computer or mobile device.

The bottom line on remembering passwords is simple: You have no margin for error. A password that's "sort of like" the one you specified is not good enough. It must be *exactly* the one you specified. You must treat passwords as though they are valuable diamonds. Keep them safe and keep them secure, but don't keep them so safe that even *you* can't find them!

If you choose to not have a password, you will not be able to use the other sign-in options.

That's enough general advice about passwords. Next, you need to find out about types of user accounts.

Picture Passwords

Picture passwords were introduced in Windows 8, and Windows 10 extends this new way to log in to your computer. Picture passwords are designed to be used with touchscreen PCs and tablets so you don't have to type in characters. Instead you choose a picture, draw a combination of three gestures on the picture that become your "password," and then save those combinations with that picture. You use those gestures to gain access to your computer, much like what happens when you type in a password on your keyboard.

Creating a picture password

You set up a picture password through the Accounts area in Settings. Click on the Sign-in options link and then click Add, shown in Figure 4.5, to display the Create a Picture Password dialog box. Type your user password and click OK to verify your password. Now you're now ready to select a picture and set up gestures to create the picture password.

Click Choose Picture and select a picture you want to use. Click Open to see the picture. Figure 4.6 shows an example of a picture that can be used for setting a picture password. If you are happy with your choice, click the option "Use this picture."

It's time to draw the gestures to create the combination you want to use for the password. You can draw any combination of these three gestures: taps, circles, and straight lines. Remember the following when you set up the gestures:

- Position of the gestures
- Size of the gestures
- Direction of the gestures
- Order in which you make the gestures

4

FIGURE 4.5

Creating a picture password.

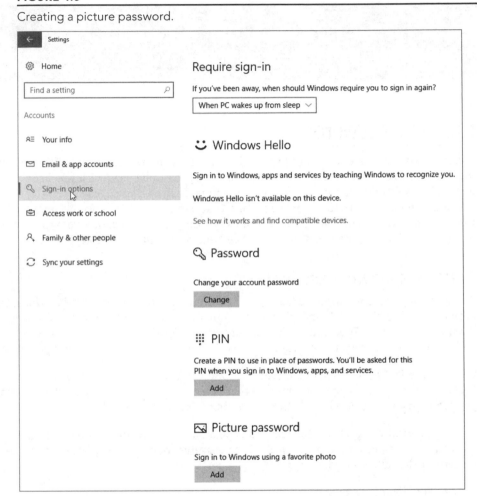

For example, on a picture of the flag of the United States, the following are suggested gestures:

- Draw a circle around three stars on the flag.
- Tap the lowest white stripe.
- Draw a straight line from the top-right corner of the blue border down to the bottom of the lower red stripe.

FIGURE 4.6

Use any picture, like the one shown here, for your picture password.

As you draw each gesture, Windows does two things. First, it shows each gesture using a white outline arrow for straight lines, a white circle outline for circles, and a white dot for taps. Second, it shows the sequence of each gesture as 1, 2, or 3.

If you make a mistake, click Start Over and restart the gestures.

After you complete the gestures once, you must confirm them before they're saved. Simply repeat your three gestures. If you forget one, click Start Over and redraw the gestures — and be sure to remember your gestures this time!

When you've successfully redrawn the gestures in their correct order, click the Finish button, shown in Figure 4.7. You're returned to the Users screen of PC Settings.

Testing your picture password

After you create a picture password, test it soon to commit the gestures to memory. To do this, return to the Windows Start menu and sign out. Sign back in to your account, this time using the gestures on the picture that displays. After you draw the correct gestures of your picture password, you're presented with the Windows desktop and Start menu.

FIGURE 4.7

Windows confirms that your picture password is complete.

Types of User Accounts

Windows 10 offers five basic types of user accounts: the built-in Administrator account, user accounts with administrative privileges, standard accounts, the Guest account, and Microsoft accounts, which can be used to access Microsoft resources and services such as Office 365 and the Family Safety features of Windows 10. They vary in how much privilege they grant to the person using the account.

 Family Safety and family accounts are discussed in Chapter 5.

With Windows 10, you also have the choice of setting up the user accounts as local or Microsoft accounts. You can read about these types of accounts in the following sections.

Microsoft accounts

With Microsoft accounts, you have the greatest flexibility for taking advantage of many of the newest Windows 10 features. To set up a Microsoft account, you must use a valid e-mail address. You can use an existing account, such as one you use at your office or a third-party account such as Gmail, Yahoo! Mail, or something similar. If you don't have one, you can set up an e-mail account during the Windows 10 user account setup.

A Microsoft account provides the following features:

- Allows you to log in to a computer on which you haven't previously set up a user account. (Conversely, with local accounts, you must set up a local account on each computer on which you want to log in.)

- Provides access to Microsoft services like Office 365, Windows Phone accounts, and OneDrive.

- Enables you to download apps from the Windows Store.

- Syncs settings across multiple computers. For example, if you work on two or more computers, logging in with the same Microsoft account on each one enables you to keep your favorites, history, sign-in info, and languages synced between the two computers.

- Enables you to access your saved files and photos from multiple computers if using OneDrive.

Creating a new e-mail address for a Microsoft user account

If you don't have an e-mail address, you can set one up as you create a new Microsoft user account. First, click the Accounts panel in Settings. The accounts options panel is displayed, as shown in Figure 4.8.

FIGURE 4.8

The Microsoft account page.

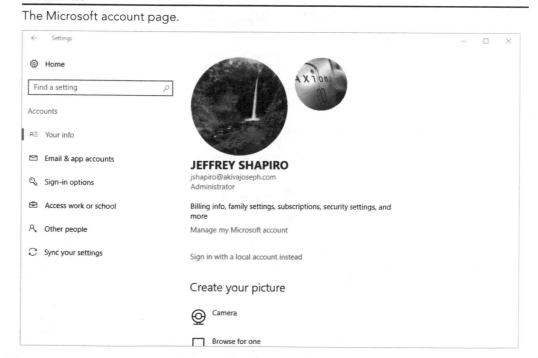

You have two ways to add a new Microsoft account. The first way is to click the link that reads Sign in with a Microsoft account. If you have another Microsoft account, enter the e-mail address and password for that account. If you don't have an account, you can click Add an account to create one.

The other way is to click Family & Other people and then click Sign in with a Microsoft account. This page is shown in Figure 4.9.

Now click the Add someone else (+) button to this PC link. The option to choose how this person will sign into Microsoft appears as shown in Figure 4.10.

Windows 10 enables you to set up a new outlook.com, hotmail.com, or live.com e-mail address, or an e-mail address for your own domain. Enter an e-mail address and wait for Windows to validate it as shown in Figure 4.11.

FIGURE 4.9

Other user accounts page.

FIGURE 4.10

Adding more users to the PC.

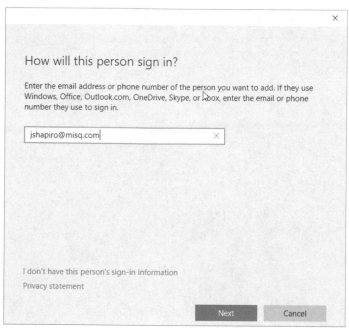

Now that you have validated the e-mail, you can begin to set up the user account.

You also can access your school or workplace network. To do so, simply click the Access work or school link on the left of the Accounts page and click the Connect button on the right. Enter the e-mail address associated with the account that was just validated and then click Continue. Windows 10 connects to your server or organization on the Internet or local network and begins to set up the user account on the computer automatically.

Local accounts

Local accounts are useful when you do not need to keep computers synced. When you use local accounts, you set up accounts for each user that will be using a computer as a stand-alone user. If you need to set up one account that can be used on multiple Windows 10 computers, you must set up Microsoft accounts or domain accounts.

Local accounts are also limiting in that you cannot use them to access the Windows Store to download apps, or services like SkyDrive. Remember that to access Windows Store apps, you must set up and use a Microsoft account.

FIGURE 4.11

Successful validation.

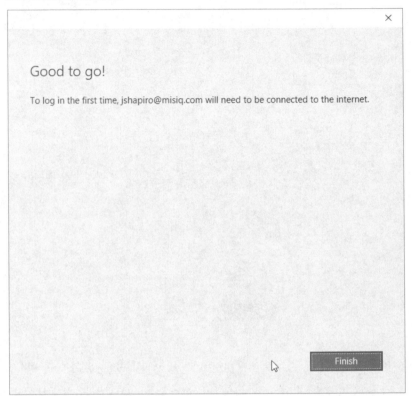

> **Good to go!**
>
> To log in the first time, jshapiro@misiq.com will need to be connected to the internet.
>
> Finish

The built-in administrator account

A single user account named Administrator is built into Windows 10. This is not the same as an administrative account you create yourself or see on the login screen. This account is hidden from normal view. It doesn't show up on the usual login screen.

The built-in Administrator account has unlimited computer privileges. So, while you're logged in to that account, you can do anything and everything you want with the computer. Any programs you run while you are in that account can also do anything they want. That makes the account risky from a security standpoint, and very unwise to use unless absolutely necessary.

In high-security settings, a new computer is usually configured by a certified network or security administrator who logs in to the Administrator account to set up the computer for other users. There, the administrator configures accounts on the *principle of least privilege*, where each account is given only as much privilege as necessary to perform a specific job.

When the administrator is finished, he or she typically renames the built-in Administrator account and password-protects it to keep everyone else out. The account is always hidden from view, except from other administrators who know how to find it. All this is standard operating procedure in secure computing environments, although hardly the norm in home computing.

In Windows 10, you really don't need to find, log in to, and use the built-in Administrator account unless you're an advanced user with a specific need, in which case you can get to it through Safe Mode. As a regular home user, you can do everything you need to do from a regular user account that has administrative privileges.

 Experienced users who need access to the built-in Administrator account can get to it through Safe Mode. We talk about that in Chapter 11. But if you aren't a professional, we suggest you stay away from that and use an administrative account, discussed in the next section.

Administrative user accounts

Most of the time when you hear reference to an Administrator account in Windows 10, that reference is to a regular user account that has administrative privileges. This is an account that has virtually all the power and privilege of the built-in Administrator account. But it also has lots of security built in to help thwart security threats that might otherwise abuse that account's privileges and do harm to your computer.

Ideally, you should create one user account with administrative privileges on your computer. If you intend to implement parental controls, you need to password-protect that account to keep children from disabling or changing parental controls.

Standard accounts

A standard user account is the kind of account everyone should use for day-to-day computer use. It has enough privilege to do day-to-day tasks such as run programs, work with documents, use e-mail, and browse the web. It doesn't have enough privilege to make changes to the system that would affect other people's user accounts. It doesn't have enough privilege to allow children to override parental controls. And most important, it doesn't have enough privilege to let malware such as viruses and worms make harmful changes to your system.

If you use a standard account all the time, and use a built-in administrative account only when absolutely necessary, you'll go a long way toward keeping your computer safe from Internet security threats.

4

Guest account

The optional Guest account exists to allow people who don't regularly use your computer to use it temporarily. Basically, it lets them check their e-mail, browse the web, and maybe play some games. It definitely doesn't let them make changes to your user account or anyone else's. Its limited privileges also help protect your system from any malicious software they might pick up while online.

Creating and Managing User Accounts

The best way to handle user accounts in a home setting is for one person to play the role of administrator, even if that person isn't a professional. In a home environment, that person most likely is a parent who needs to define parental controls. To begin, log in to a user account that already has administrative privileges. If you have only one user account, or you're taken straight to the desktop at startup, that account probably has administrative privileges.

As with most configuration tasks, you can create and manage user accounts through the Computer Management application, which you can access by right-clicking the Start button. Or you can create local accounts from the Accounts applet we just used to create a Microsoft account.

If you're in a standard account on a computer that already has a password-protected administrative account, you must enter the password for the Administrator account. Or, if the administrative account doesn't have a password, press Enter to leave the password box empty.

Changing user accounts

When you create a user account, you give it a name and choose a type. After you've created a user account, you can change the name and type to better suit your needs. Use the Setting, Accounts page shown in Figure 4.8 or the Accounts screen shown in Figure 4.10 to make changes to accounts.

> **CAUTION**
>
> If you aren't careful when you delete a user account, you can delete all the files in that account. Read the section "Deleting User Accounts" later in this chapter before you delete an account. If you make a mistake, you can delete photos or other documents that may be difficult or impossible to recover.

Changing a user account type

You can change an Administrator account to a standard account, or vice versa, from the main Accounts page. For example, if you've been using an administrative account for your day-to-day computing since buying your computer, you may want to change it to a standard account for the added security that a standard account provides. At least one user account must have administrative privileges, so you can make this change only if at least one other user account on the system has administrative privileges.

To change an account's type, click the account's icon or name on the Accounts page. Then click the Change an Account link at the bottom right of the accounts page. That page lets you change the account in a number of ways when you click Change, or simply remove the account.

Password-protecting an account

You have the option to set up local accounts without password protection (Microsoft accounts require passwords). If you share your computer with other people, chances are you want to keep some people out of the Administrator account. Likewise, you want to keep some users from having administrative privileges. Passwords are especially important with parental controls. If the administrative account isn't password-protected, the kids won't take long to figure out how to bypass your controls.

> **CAUTION**
>
> Don't forget the password you set on the administrator account if it's the only administrator account; otherwise, nobody has administrative privileges, and that causes a world of headaches. So, think up a good password and password hint, and make sure you enter the password correctly when you set it.

To password-protect a user account, go to the main page for the user account. For example, if you're on the Accounts page, click the user account that you want to password-protect and then click Sign-in Options. You're taken to the page that lets you change the password. If you've been using the account for a while without a password, heed the warnings. If it's a brand new account, you have nothing to worry about.

To password-protect the account, type your password in the New Password text box. Then press Tab or click the Confirm New Password text box and type the same password again. You don't see the characters you type — only a placeholder for each character.

> **TIP**
>
> When you type passwords, the characters are always hidden to prevent shoulder surfing. *Shoulder surfing* is a simple technique for discovering someone's password by watching over the person's shoulder as he or she types it.

4

Next, enter a password hint in the Type a Password Hint text box. The hint should be something that reminds you of the forgotten password, but not a dead giveaway to someone trying to break into the account. Click Create Password after you've filled in all the blanks.

If you see a message indicating that your passwords don't match, retype both passwords. Make sure you type the password exactly the same in both boxes. Then click the Create Password button. You're taken back to the main page for the user account when you've successfully entered the password in both boxes and provided a password hint.

You can repeat the process to password-protect as many accounts as you wish. If you're creating user accounts for people other than yourself, set a default password for the account and let the other users manage their own passwords. In our opinion, every account should have a password.

> **TIP**
>
> Why have a password on all local accounts? First, it's basic security. Second, if you have more than one child using a shared computer, creating a password for each child helps prevent a younger child from using an older child's account to bypass parental restrictions.

Changing the account picture

Every user account has an associated picture. The picture is like an icon, giving you a quick visual reference without having to read the name. The picture you choose can be any one of several built-in pictures, or it can be a picture of your own choosing.

If you decide to use your own picture, try to avoid using one that comes straight from a digital camera. The file size for such pictures is too large for a user account picture. Your best bet is to crop out a section from a photo and size it to about 100 × 100 pixels. The picture you choose can be of almost any format. By selecting all files, you can see the file types that are available.

> **TIP**
>
> If you don't know enough about pictures to meet the requirements, you can use built-in pictures. Then, after you've acquired some of the skills covered in Chapter 17, you can create a suitable user account picture and apply it to any user account.

To change the picture for a user account, click Accounts and then click Your Account. As shown in Figure 4.12, the panel shows the Account Picture, which is the current picture of the selected user (or the default image if you didn't select one). Click Browse and then select the area on your computer to locate a new picture. For example, click This PC, and then Pictures, to display your Pictures folder. You also can use an attached webcam to snap a picture or a five-second video to use as an account picture. To do this, you must have a webcam connected to your computer. On the same page, under Create a Picture, click Camera to start your camera (of course, this technique doesn't work if you don't have a camera or webcam working on your computer):

FIGURE 4.12

Account Settings page with user account picture options.

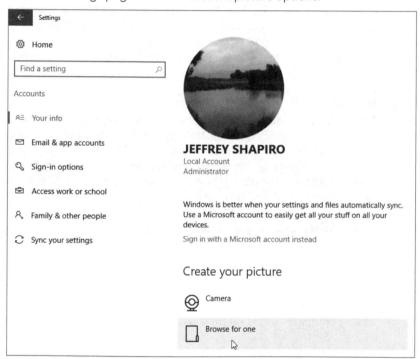

- To snap a still picture, click the screen. Use the cropping and resizing tools to select the portion of the picture to use. Click OK to save that picture as your new account picture.
- To take a five-second video, click Video Mode and click the screen to start the video. Click the screen again to stop the video and to review the video. Click Retake if you aren't satisfied with the video. Click OK when you want to keep the video and to set it as your account picture.

The picture or video you selected replaces the original picture.

Enabling or disabling the local Guest account

Every Windows 10 has a built-in Guest account. The Guest account is for anybody who needs to use your computer on a temporary basis. For example, on a home computer, you might use the Guest account for houseguests so that they can check their e-mail and browse the web. The Guest account has limited privileges, so you don't have to worry about guests messing things up while using your computer.

The Guest account is turned off by default. You can keep it that way until you need it. To activate the Guest account, go to the Computer Management application and drill down on Local Users and Groups under the System Tools tree and expand the list of users. Click the Guest Account icon. On the General tab, uncheck the Account is disabled option. Likewise, if you ever need to disable the Guest account, simply check the same option. To change or set a password, simply right-click on Guest and choose the first option, Set Password.

Navigating through user account pages

In Windows 10, user account management involves using two environments, including the Control Panel and the Accounts page on the Settings application. You can use the Control Panel to complete almost all user account tasks described earlier, even those that use the new Accounts page on the Settings application. When you get to a task, all you need to do is choose options and read text that's right on the screen. Windows provides links to advance to configuration screens. Some links are blue text (the standard web hypertext color), and others use new Windows 10 buttons to display new settings or options for a task. You use Back and Forward buttons to move from page to page.

Cracking into standard user accounts

If a local standard user forgets his or her password, you can use an account that has administrative privileges to reset the standard user's password. If you're an administrator and you want to see what a standard user is up to, you can use the same technique.

To change the password for a local standard user account, follow these steps:

1. Log in to a user account that has administrative privileges.
2. Go to the Manage Accounts page (press Windows Key+X and choose Control Panel, click User Accounts, and click Manage another account).
3. Click the password-protected account for which the user has forgotten the password.
4. Click the Change the password link.
5. Enter a new password, and then enter it again to confirm it.
6. Type a password hint.
7. Click Change Password to save the new password.

The local standard user account now has a new password. Share this password with the user so he or she can sign into Windows.

Deleting User Accounts

An administrator can easily delete user accounts. If nobody has ever used a user account, deleting the account is no big deal. But if someone has used the account, the decision to delete it is more complicated. When you delete a user account, you also delete all e-mail messages downloaded to the computer, Internet favorites, music, pictures, and videos. You can also delete that user's saved files if you aren't careful. Doing this by accident is a disaster because you have no way to undo the deletion.

> **CAUTION**
> Deleting a user account can have serious consequences. Don't do it unless you fully understand the ramifications.

If you want to save the user's e-mail messages and Internet favorites, export them to the user's Documents folder first. Read the Windows online Help for more information on exporting Microsoft Edge favorites. Also, refer to your e-mail program's help for information on saving e-mail messages to a local drive — for example, to your Documents folder.

Assume you understand the consequences and have no intention of deleting an account just for fun. Only administrators can delete user accounts. So if you're in a standard account, you at least need to know the administrative password to delete a user account. You also need to log in to any account except the one you intend to delete. Then follow these steps:

1. Display the Control Panel, click User Accounts, and click Manage Another Account.

2. Click the account you want to delete.

3. Click Delete the Account and read the resulting message. Then click one of the following buttons:

   - **Delete Files:** Click this button only if you intend to delete *everything* associated with the account, including all files that the user has created and saved.

   - **Keep Files:** Click this option to save the user's files. You will still lose the user's saved e-mail messages, Internet favorites, and user account.

4. Read the next page to make sure you understand the consequences of your choice. Then click Cancel if you change your mind, or click Delete account if you're sure you know what you're doing.

If you choose Delete account, the user's account no longer exists. If you choose Keep Files, the user's saved files (those from his account's profile) move to a folder on the desktop.

That folder has the same name as the user account you just deleted. Otherwise, nothing of the user's account, not even the saved files, remains. (If you choose Cancel in Step 4, the entire account remains intact and unchanged.)

If you create a new user account with the same name as the one you just deleted, the new account is still an entirely new account. It doesn't inherit any files or settings from the account you previously deleted.

NOTE

If the user's Documents folder contains no documents, Windows doesn't create a copy of the folder on your desktop when you delete the account (because you have nothing to save).

Using User Accounts

As mentioned at the beginning of this chapter, each user account is like its own separate PC. Every user has his or her private Documents, Pictures, Music, and Video folders for storing files. Each user account can have its own Windows apps, e-mail account, and Internet favorites. Each user can customize the desktop, Start screen, and other settings to that user's own liking.

When you start your computer, the Windows lock screen appears. Press Enter, swipe up (on a tablet or touch screen), press the spacebar, or roll the mouse wheel up to display the sign-in screen. You also see the sign-on screen when you sign out of your user account. If you click a user account that isn't password-protected, you're taken straight into the account. But if you click the picture for a password-protected account, a password prompt appears.

To get into the account, enter the appropriate password. If you enter the wrong password, a message appears letting you know that the user account name or password is incorrect. You can click OK to try again. You can't get into the user account until you've entered the correct password for that account.

The first time you or someone else logs in to a new user account, the process is just like starting Windows 10 on a brand new PC. The desktop has the default appearance. All the document folders in the account are empty. You have no e-mail accounts, no Internet favorites, and no Windows apps installed. To use e-mail, the user must set up the Windows account with an e-mail account, preferably an account used only by that person.

The user has access to all the programs installed on the computer (except for rare cases in which someone installed a program for personal use only). The user likely has Internet connectivity through the same network or Wi-Fi as all other user accounts.

If the user account is a standard account, some limitations control what the user can do. For example, Windows settings are not synced with other devices, such as a Windows Phone or tablet. In addition, the user can't make changes to the system that would affect other users. That's where Windows 10's User Account Control security comes into play.

Understanding User Account Control

User Account Control (UAC) is the general term for the way administrative and standard user accounts work in Windows 10. As you scroll through pages in the Control Panel, notice that many links have a shield icon next to them.

Items that have a shield icon require administrative approval. Items without a shield icon don't. For example, any user can change his or her Windows password, with or without administrative approval.

Options that have a shield icon next to them require administrative approval. But you don't have to be logged in to an administrative account to use those options. You only have to prove that you have administrative privileges. To prove you have administrative privileges on this computer, enter the password for the administrative user account and click Submit (or OK in some dialog boxes).

When someone who doesn't know the administrative account password encounters the User Account Control dialog box, he or she is stuck. Users who don't know the password can't go any further. This prevents the standard user from doing things that might affect the overall system and other people's user accounts. It also prevents children from overriding parental controls. (You learn how to set up parental controls in Chapter 6.)

Privilege escalation in administrative accounts

If you happen to be logged in to an administrative account when you click a shielded option, you don't need to enter an administrative password. After all, if you're in an administrative account, you must already know the password required to get into that account. You don't need to prove that you know that password again. But, by default, you still see a prompt telling you that the program you're about to run makes changes to the system. Click Continue to proceed.

Clicking something to get to the item you clicked may seem irritating, but the prompt works that way for a reason. The dialog box lets you know that the program you're about to run is going to make changes to the overall system. You expect to see that dialog box after you click a shielded option. With time and experience, you'll learn to expect it when you do other things that affect the system as a whole, such as when you install new programs.

Sometimes the prompt appears when you don't expect to see it. For example, when opening an e-mail attachment, you don't expect to see that message. After all, opening an e-mail attachment should show you the contents of the attachment, and not make a change to the system as a whole. Seeing the warning in that context lets you know that something fishy is going on, most likely something bad in the e-mail attachment. Click Cancel to *not* open the attachment, thereby protecting your system from whatever virus or other bad thing lies hidden within the e-mail attachment.

On a more technical note, UAC operates on a principle of least privilege. When you're in an administrative account, you run with the same privileges as a standard user. This arrangement protects your system from malware that would otherwise exploit your administrative account to make malicious changes to your system.

When you enter a password or click Continue in response to a UAC prompt, you temporarily elevate your privileges to allow that change to be made. After the change is complete, you return to your more secure standard user privileges. This procedure has been common in high-security settings for years, and it's considered a security best practice.

Turning UAC on and off

If possible, you should follow standard best practices and keep UAC active on your own computer. But if UAC proves to be impractical, you can turn it off.

Even though UAC is much improved from Windows Vista, Windows 7, and 8/8.1, UAC is not always a very popular Windows 10 feature. After all, nobody wants a feature that makes them do more work, even when the extra work is nothing more than an occasional extra mouse click. Furthermore, sometimes UAC is just impractical. For example, if you give your kids standard user accounts, they can't install their own programs. But if you give them administrative accounts, you can't institute parental controls.

 See Chapter 5 for setting up Child accounts.

Before you turn off UAC, we recommend that you first ensure that all the other security measures discussed in Part II of this book are installed and working on your PC. UAC is just one component of an overall security strategy. The more components you have on and working, the better.

> **NOTE**
>
> UAC in Windows 10 employs similar functionality to that used in Windows 8.1 and earlier versions to make it less obtrusive to the user. In contrast to how UAC functioned in Windows Vista, Windows 7, and Windows 8/8.1, in which UAC was an on-or-off feature, UAC in Windows 10 offers a range of settings to tailor the end-user experience.

Changing UAC settings is a simple process. From the Windows 10 Start menu, select Control Panel, and click User Accounts. Or from the desktop, press Windows+X and click Control Panel. Click User Accounts. Click User Accounts again, and then Click Change User Account Control settings. If prompted to do so, enter an administrative password to get to the dialog box shown in Figure 4.13.

FIGURE 4.13

User Account Control Settings dialog box.

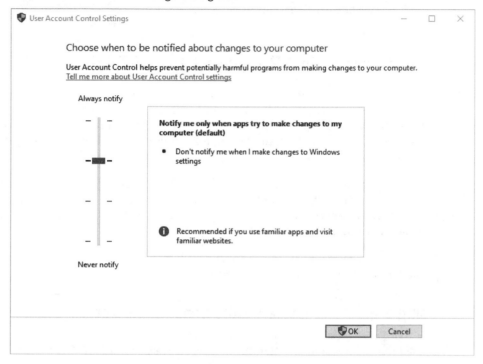

You can choose from the following options:

- **Always Notify:** Windows notifies you if programs try to install software or make changes to the computer, or if you make changes to Windows settings.

- **Notify Me Only When Apps Try to Make Changes to My Computer (Default):** Windows does not notify you when you make changes to your computer, but if programs attempt to make changes, Windows notifies you by dimming the desktop and displaying a warning.

- **Notify Me Only When Apps Try to Make Changes to My Computer (Do Not Dim My Desktop):** Windows does not notify you when you make changes to your computer, but it notifies you when programs attempt to make changes. However, Windows does not dim the desktop; instead, it displays a message.

- **Never Notify:** Windows does not notify you of changes (this option turns off UAC). The only safe time to use this option is when you need to install a program that doesn't work with UAC. Turn off UAC, install the program, and then turn on UAC again.

To turn UAC off, drag the slider down to Never Notify. Or, if it was already off and you want better security, drag the slider up to the desired level. Then click OK.

If you turned off UAC, when you click a shielded option you receive no prompting for credentials or status checking. The settings are basically the same as they were in Windows XP and other earlier versions of Windows.

Creating and Using Password Reset Disks

A password reset disk is an important part of any password-protected PC. It's the only method of password recovery that allows you to retain all data in an account in the event of a forgotten password. Advanced features such as EFS (Encrypting File System) encryption, personal certificates, and stored network passwords can be recovered only by using a password reset disk.

The trick is that you need to create the password reset disk *before* you forget the password. You can't create the disk after you've forgotten the password. Keep the disk in a safe place where you can find it when you need it, but where others can't find it to gain unauthorized access to the administrative account.

A USB flash drive or memory card works equally well. However, a memory card works only if your computer has slots for inserting a memory card.

Choosing a memory device for the password reset

A *USB flash drive* (also called a *jump drive*) is a small device that plugs into a USB port on your computer and looks and acts like a disk drive. A *memory card (SD Card)* is a storage device commonly used to save pictures in digital devices, such as cameras or smartphones. If your computer has slots for such cards, you can slide a card into the slot and treat the card just as you would a USB flash drive.

To see examples and prices, check out some online retailers. Then search the site for *flash drive, jump drive,* or *memory card reader* to view available products. If you're considering memory card readers, the kind that plug into a USB port are the easiest to install. Many retail department stores that sell computer or office supplies also carry flash drives.

To create the Password reset disk, perform the following steps:

1. Insert your Flash drive or SD card into the computer.
2. Press Windows+S to bring up the search bar. Type **User Accounts**.
3. Select User Accounts.
4. Click Create a password reset disk.
5. Click Next.

6. Select Next.

7. From the drop-down menu, select the device where you want the password reset disk to be created.

8. Type your password (this is the password that you use to log in to your computer from the login screen).

9. Click Next.

10. When the progress bar reachs 100 percent, click Next.

11. Click Finish.

Running Programs as Administrator

Most newer programs work with UAC's privilege escalation on the fly. But sometimes a program doesn't work, especially if it's an older program. You can run many programs with administrative privileges by right-clicking the program's startup icon and choosing Run as Administrator, as in the example shown in Figure 4.14.

If the option to run the program as an administrator is not available, one of the following is true:

- The program doesn't require administrative privileges to run.
- You're already logged in to an administrative account.
- The program is always blocked from running with elevated privileges.

FIGURE 4.14

Run a program as administrator.

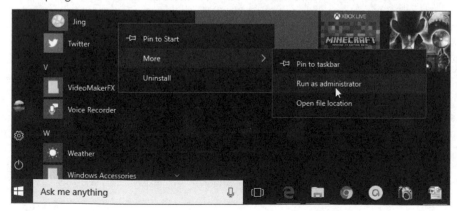

Add the Built-in Administrator Account to the Login Screen

The built-in Administrator account is intentionally hidden to discourage users who don't have sufficient knowledge to understand the risks involved in using such an account. Typically, the way to get to it is by starting the computer in Safe Mode. If you're an advanced user and you want to be able to get to that account from the sign-on screen, you simply have to enable the account. Here's how:

1. Log in to an account that has administrative privileges.
2. At the desktop, press Windows+X and click Computer Management.
3. In the left column of the Computer Management tool that opens, click Local Users and Groups.
4. In the center column, double-click the Users folder.
5. Right-click the Administrator account and choose Properties. You can also double-click the account to get the properties screen.
6. Clear the check mark beside Account Is Disabled and click OK.
7. Close the Computer Management window.

When you log out of your current account, you see the Administrator account on the sign-on screen. It also appears there each time you start the computer.

Advanced Security Tools

IT professionals and highly experienced users can also use the Local Users and Groups and Local Security Policy consoles for more advanced security configuration. Detailed instructions on using these security configuration tools are beyond the scope of this book and not something for the average user to mess with. However, if you want to access the Local Users and Groups tools, at the desktop press Windows+X and click Computer Management. Then click Local Users and Groups in the left column.

To get to Local Security Policy, type **local** in Search and click **Local** Security Policy. To find the new settings related to UAC, expand Local Policies in the left column and then click Security Options. The new UAC settings are at the bottom of the list in the content pane.

Using Credential Manager

Credential Manager (see Figure 4.15) enables you to manage your usernames and their associated passwords (collectively called *credentials*) for servers, websites, and programs.

These credentials are stored in an electronic virtual vault. When you access a server, site, or program that requests a password, Credential Manager can submit the credentials for you so that you don't have to type them yourself. If your password cache has dozens of sets of credentials in it, you'll be more than happy to have Credential Manager at work for you.

FIGURE 4.15

Store usernames and passwords in Credential Manager.

Type the address of the website or network location and your credentials

Make sure that the user name and password that you type can be used to access the location.

Internet or network address
(e.g. myserver, server.company.com): `misqdc01.azure.nry`

User name: `jshaprio`

Password: `••••••••••••`

OK   Cancel

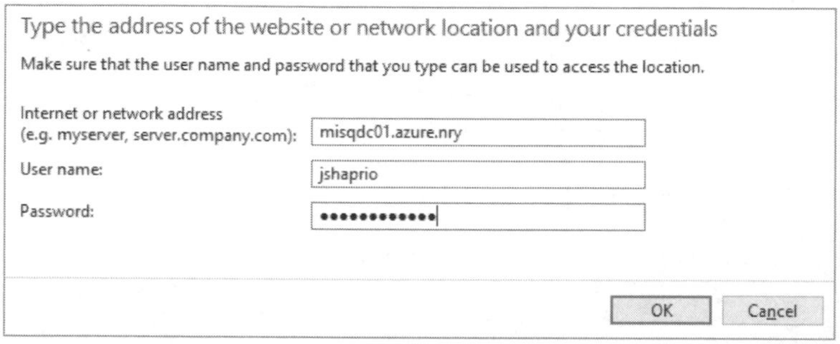

> **NOTE**
>
> Credential Manager can't interact with every website that requests credentials. For example, when you log in to your online banking site, the site probably displays a form in which you enter your credentials. Credential Manager can't store this type of form-based credential, but you can have Microsoft Edge remember the credentials for you.

Although you can add credentials to your vault directly, you don't need to do so in most cases. Instead, you can let Windows do it for you. To do so, navigate to a server or other computer on your network or to a web server that prompts you for credentials. Enter the username and password in the Windows Security dialog box, select Remember My Credentials, and click OK. Windows stores the credentials in Credential Manager.

You can add credentials directly to your vault if you want to. For example, if you have lots of credentials you use with multiple servers or sites, you may want to prepopulate your credential vault so that you don't have to wait to enter them until the next time you visit that resource.

To add credentials directly, open the User Accounts and click Credential Manager. Click the Windows Credentials icon and then click Add a Windows Credential. In the resulting form (as shown in Figure 4.16), enter the following:

- **Internet or Network Address:** Type the path to the resource. For example, enter \\ **fileserver\Docs** to specify the Docs share on a server on the network named *fileserver*. Or, enter **portal.mycompany.com** if your company intranet portal is located at `https://portal.mycompany.com`.

- **User Name:** Enter the username you want to use to log on to the specified service.
- **Password:** Enter the password associated with the username.

FIGURE 4.16

Manually add a Windows credential.

You can also add a certificate resource, which associates a network resource with a security certificate that is already installed in the Personal certificate store on your computer. In this case, verify that you've already installed the certificate, click Add a Certificate-Based Credential (see Figure 4.16), type the resource URL, and click Select Certificate to select the certificate.

The final type of credential you can add is a generic credential, which is used by applications that perform authentication themselves instead of relying on Windows to perform the authentication. As with a Windows credential, you specify the URL, username, and password for a generic credential.

Managing Profile Properties and Environment Variables

From the earliest days of DOS, the PC operating system we old computer geeks used before Windows came along, *environment variables* have been used to store information used by the operating system. For example, the `TMP` and `TEMP` variables tell Windows where to store temporary files. The `PATH` variable tells Windows where to look for programs if it can't find them in the current directory. A number of other system and user variables serve similar purposes.

In most cases, you don't need to change environment variables. But if you do — such as when adding a folder to the `PATH` variable — you can do so through your user account properties. Open the User Accounts object in the Control Panel and click Change My Environment Variables. In the Environment Variables dialog box, shown in Figure 4.17, click the user variable that you want to change, click Edit, modify as needed, and click OK. You can also click New and then add a new user environment variable.

4

Wrapping Up

When two or more people share a computer, user accounts enable each person to treat the computer as though it was his or her own. Users can personalize settings to their liking and keep their files separate from other users. Windows 10 Microsoft Accounts provide an account structure that enables multiple devices (Windows computer, Windows Phone, Windows tablets, and so on) to sync settings, apps, and other personalized items.

FIGURE 4.17

The Environment Variables dialog box.

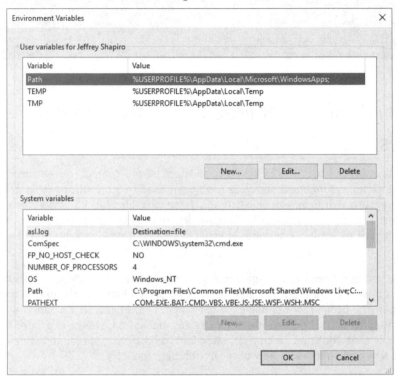

User accounts also work in conjunction with parental controls. A parent can set up a password-protected administrative account and then use that account to set up parental controls. You can create standard accounts for children and allow them to log in to their own accounts only.

 The parental controls in the Family Safety options are covered in Chapter 5.

User accounts also add security to your system by requiring all users to have limited privileges. The general term for security through user accounts is User Account Control (UAC). Some key points to keep in mind:

- At least one person should play the role of administrator for the computer. That person should create a password-protected user account with administrative privileges.
- The administrator should create a standard account for himself or herself and one for each person who shares the computer.

■ All users (including the administrator) should use their standard accounts for day-to-day computing.

■ All accounts should have strong passwords.

■ All the tools for creating and managing user accounts are accessible from User Accounts and Family Safety in the Control Panel.

4

Troubleshooting Startup Problems

IN THIS CHAPTER

The computer doesn't start

The computer takes too long to start

Resources for troubleshooting startup problems

When programs don't start

Several of the parts in this book end with a troubleshooting chapter like this one. The troubleshooting chapters are short and focused; they provide quick solutions to common problems.

The Computer Doesn't Start

If the computer does absolutely nothing when you turn it on, your first move is to check all cable connections. Make sure the power plug on every device that plugs into the wall is firmly plugged in. Also, make sure the mouse, keyboard, and all other devices are firmly plugged into their slots.

If you're troubleshooting a desktop computer, look for a 0/1 power switch on the back of the computer and make sure it's on (flipped to the 1 position).

If your computer is a laptop or tablet device, make sure the battery is connected correctly. Ensure that the AC adapter is plugged in.

Turn on the computer again and, as it is powering up, push the button on the CD or DVD drive. If a disk is in the drive, remove the disk.

If the computer sounds as though it's starting up but you don't see anything on the screen, make sure all plugs to the monitor are firmly seated. If you're working on a desktop computer, make sure the monitor's power cable is firmly attached to the monitor and wall socket. Confirm that the cable connecting the computer to the monitor is firmly attached at both ends of the cable. Make sure the monitor is turned on. Then restart the computer.

Non-system disk or disk error message

This type of message appears when the computer attempts to boot from a disk on which Windows is not installed, or if the disk is corrupted. Remove any removable media from the device, and disconnect any drive that's connected to the computer through a USB port. Press any key to continue startup. If that doesn't work, press Ctrl+Alt+Del or restart the computer with the main on/off switch.

Computer starts but mouse and keyboard don't work

If the computer starts but doesn't respond to the mouse and keyboard, turn off the computer. Unplug both the mouse and keyboard from the computer. For USB mice and keyboards, unplug each and re-connect them. Ensure each USB connection is tight and secure. If the plug is round and green, make sure you plug it into the PS/2 port for the mouse (usually colored green), but only when the PC is turned off. Make sure nothing is resting on the keyboard and holding down a key. Then firmly plug in the keyboard. If the plug is round and purple, plug it into the PS/2 port for the keyboard (only when the PC is turned off). Check *all* cable connections to the computer one more time. Then restart the computer.

Screen turns blue during startup and then stops

This is commonly referred to as the "blue screen of death." It doesn't mean your computer is permanently broken. A frequent cause of this problem is a device driver for a hardware device that doesn't work with Windows 10. If you recently connected or installed a new hardware device, disconnect or uninstall it. Then start the computer again.

If you still see the blue screen, you'll very likely have to boot to Safe Mode and disable the device through Device Manager. Typically, the average user does not attempt this procedure — leave it to a professional. But if you want to take a shot at fixing this problem yourself, follow the instructions in this section and see Chapter 37.

If the error persists, look for an error number on the blue screen of death page. It most likely starts with the characters 0x. Jot down that number on a sheet of paper. Then, if you can get online through another computer, go to Microsoft's site (http://www .microsoft.com) or your favorite online search engine (such as Google or Bing) and search for that number. You might find a page that offers an exact solution to your problem.

If you can get online through another computer, consider posting a question at the Windows Communities site (http://answers.microsoft.com/en-us/windows). Be sure to include the error number in your post. You may find someone who has already experienced and solved that very problem.

Computer Takes Too Long to Start

On most systems, Windows 10 is optimized to decrease boot time from many seconds or minutes to just a handful of seconds. For example, a laptop may take approximately 35 seconds to boot to Windows 7. Windows 8.x cut that to generally less than 10 seconds. With Windows 10, the boot time is only about 8 seconds. You may or may not see that much of a decrease in wait time, but you should pay attention if the boot time takes longer and longer each time you start your computer.

When the computer takes much longer to start than in the past, the problem usually is caused by too many programs trying to auto start. Consider uninstalling any programs you don't use, as discussed in Chapter 30. Configure the remaining programs so that they don't start automatically (see Chapter 11).

Many things that prevent a computer from starting have nothing to do with Windows 10. Diagnosing and repairing startup problems often take even seasoned pros many hours. But before you resort to the repair shop, here are some other things you can try.

Restore system files to an earlier time

The Windows 10 Advanced Startup options (described in the "Advanced Startup" section of this chapter) include a System Restore item that enables you to restore your system to a previous state if System Protection is turned on. Windows 10 creates restore points automatically, and you can create additional restore points using the Recovery item in the Control Panel. To recover your system to a previous state, boot using the Advanced Startup options as explained later in this chapter, and then choose System Restore from the Advanced Options screen. Follow the prompts to choose a restore point from which to restore.

Alternatively, if you can get the computer to start in Safe Mode, you can use System Restore to restore your PC. Boot to Safe Mode and then open the Control Panel. In the Restore item, click Open System Restore to choose a restore point and start the restore process.

Windows 10 Automatic Repair Mode

If Windows 10 automatically detects an issue with your startup, you see a light blue window (not the blue screen of death) that reads "Automatic Repair." This is the Windows 10 Automatic Repair Mode. The screen informs you that Windows could not start properly and that you can use a System Restore point to attempt to repair the issue.

5

Chapter 19 discusses the System Restore process and how you should consider keeping this feature activated for situations like the one you're experiencing.

System Restore turns the clock back to a previous setup when Windows was working correctly. During the System Restore process, you don't lose any personal data that you added to the system. Instead, programs and apps that were installed after the latest System Restore point and time are uninstalled from your computer. The assumption is that a program or app may have damaged your operating system installation. By removing the programs and apps, Windows may be able to start properly.

If you decide to choose to restore, the process cannot be undone. You have the option of canceling, but you must do it from this initial screen; don't try to cancel after you start the restore process. If you decide to cancel, click the Cancel button now.

To continue, click the Restore button and respond to the onscreen prompts.

Repair Windows 10 Install

If you have Windows 10 on a DVD, you can boot from that disk and do a repair installation. Put the disk in the DVD drive and start the computer. Watch the screen for the message "Press Any Key to Boot from CD or DVD" (or a similar message); then press Enter or the spacebar.

If the option to boot from the CD or DVD never appears, and the computer doesn't boot from the disk, you need to change your BIOS options to boot from the CD/DVD drive. How you do that varies from one computer to the next. Typically, you start the computer and then immediately start pressing the F1, F2, F12, or Del key repeatedly as the computer is starting. (Try each one in turn, rebooting each time if necessary, until you identify the right key.) This should take you to the BIOS Setup options where you can configure the computer to try booting from the CD or DVD before trying to boot from the hard drive. Close and save the new settings. The computer restarts, and this time you should be able to boot from the Windows DVD.

If you can boot from the DVD, the first screen you see very likely asks about your language and locale. Make any necessary changes and click Next. On the next page, click Repair Your Computer (not the Install Now option). Then follow the onscreen instructions to do a repair install of Windows 10.

Advanced startup

If you can boot into Windows 10, but you're having issues with the boot process, consider using Windows 10's Advanced Startup tool. This tool assumes you can boot into Windows and navigate to the PC Settings area.

To use this tool, perform the following steps:

1. Click or tap the Start menu and choose Settings.
2. Click Update and Security.
3. Click Recovery, and then click Restart Now in the Advanced Startup group, as shown in Figure 5.1.

FIGURE 5.1

Advanced startup option in the Update and Recovery settings.

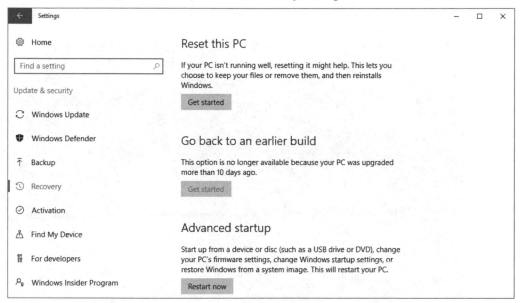

4. After Windows 10 restarts, it displays a screen similar to the one in Figure 5.2.
5. Click Troubleshoot.
5. Click one of these options (see Figure 5.3) and respond to the onscreen prompts:
   - **System Restore:** Use this option to restore your PC using a previously created restore point.
   - **System Image Recovery:** Recover Windows 10 using a recovery image file.
   - **Startup Repair:** Restart the device and perform a diagnostic repair.
   - **Command Prompt:** Open a command prompt to use console commands for troubleshooting and repair.

- **UEFI Firmware Settings:** Configure firmware settings.
- **Go Back To the Previous Build:** Use this option to revert to a previous build of Windows 10 (think of a build as a set of updates to the Windows 10 code, or as a Windows 10 mini-version identified by its build number). Microsoft releases new builds periodically, and using this option restores Windows to the previous build.
- **Startup Settings:** Configure Windows startup behavior (see the following section).

FIGURE 5.2

Troubleshoot startup problems.

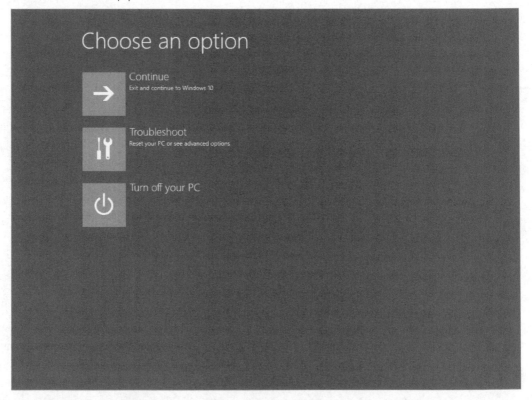

> **NOTE**
> Some of the options in this list can vary somewhat depending on the device.

FIGURE 5.3

Advanced options for troubleshooting startup problems.

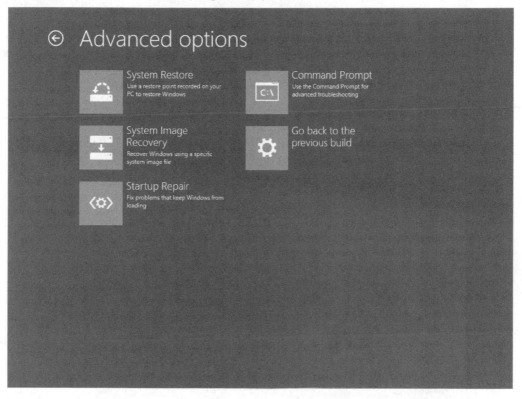

> **CAUTION**
>
> Do *not* use the Reset Your PC option until you've made a backup of your critical files. Use the Reset Your PC option only as a last resort — when all other troubleshooting tasks fail.

Start in Safe Mode

For many experienced Windows users who have dealt with faulty Windows startups, Safe Mode has become a close friend. Safe Mode offers a way to start Windows in a *barebones* setup. This means Windows starts with just enough system files, programs, and services to allow it to run so you can diagnose issues, remove programs, and perform other tasks that can be done only at the graphical user interface level.

5

To enter Safe Mode in Windows 10, access the Advanced Startup options as described in the previous section. Click Troubleshoot, click Advanced Options, and click Startup Settings. On the resulting page, click Restart.

Although Safe Mode looks like a normal instance of Windows, many programs and features do not work. It is simply a place where you can modify system settings, such as those for Device Manager, MSCONFIG, the Windows Registry, Control Panel applets, and the like. You cannot, for example, start some Windows apps or other programs.

After you finish repairing Windows, shut down Safe Mode and restart normally.

Another way to boot into Safe Mode is to set Windows to do so at reboot. To do this, press Windows+X and choose Run. Type **MSCONFIG** in the Open dialog box and click OK. The System Configuration dialog box appears (see Figure 5.4).

FIGURE 5.4

Windows 10 Safe Boot options in the System Configuration tool.

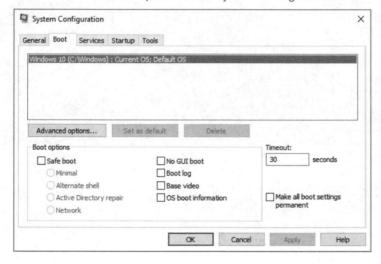

Select the Boot tab and click the Safe Boot option. Click Apply and then OK. You're prompted with a dialog box that has Restart or Exit without Restart buttons. Click Restart so that Windows reboots. When it restarts, you're in Safe Mode. Use Safe Mode to diagnose or repair Windows.

When you want to leave Safe Mode, you need to undo the Safe Boot option in the System Configuration tool. To do that, press Windows+X, choose Run, and enter **MSCONFIG**. On the Boot tab of the System Configuration dialog box, clear the Safe Boot option and click Apply; then OK. Click Restart to shut down and restart Windows into its normal view.

The instruction manual that came with your computer

Most computer manufacturers provide some means of helping you troubleshoot and repair startup problems. Be sure to look through your computer's documentation and find the manufacturer's recommendations. That's your best bet because all computers are unique in some ways. The manual that came with your computer provides information that's specific to your exact make and model of computer.

Resources in this book

We've thrown lots of technical terms and concepts at you in this chapter. But when you're solving startup problems, learning some new terms is unavoidable. Here are some additional resources in this book that may help you solve a startup problem:

- **Restoring from previous file versions:** If you've backed up your entire hard disk using File History, see Chapter 19 for information on restoring from that backup.
- **Restoring to an earlier time:** For information on restoring your computer to an earlier time, see "Using System Protection" in Chapter 19.
- **Removing programs:** If you think a faulty program may be preventing your computer from starting, you can uninstall the program using techniques described in Chapter 25 (assuming that you can get to Safe Mode so that you have access to that program).
- **Removing hardware:** When faulty hardware or drivers are preventing Windows 10 from starting, techniques described under "Removing Hardware" in Chapter 29 might help.
- **Troubleshooting hardware:** Startup problems are often hardware problems. See Chapter 32 for more information on troubleshooting hardware.

Resources in Windows Help

If you can start the computer in Safe Mode, you can get to Windows Help. The Help window should open automatically as soon as you enter Safe Mode. If it doesn't, click the Start button and choose Help and Support. Then search using the keywords "Safe Mode" for additional information on using Safe Mode to troubleshoot startup options.

Online resources

If you can start in Safe Mode with Networking, you can access online resources. Try searching Windows Communities (which you can get to from Windows Help) for words related to the startup problem, or post a question describing the problem in as much detail as possible.

In addition, you can search Microsoft's website for words that describe the problem you're having. Be sure to include the number 10 in your search. Otherwise, the search result very likely will include other irrelevant Microsoft products. Starting your search from http://

5

support.microsoft.com helps limit the search to Microsoft rather than including the entire web. If that doesn't help, try searching the entire web from www.bing.com, www.google.com, or your favorite search engine. If you aren't a technical person, don't expect the process to be easy. As we said, startup problems can be difficult to troubleshoot, even for the pros. If all else fails, you may have to take the system to a repair shop. Or call a mobile service that sends a computer geek to your home or office.

Programs Won't Start

If a favorite old program won't start, most likely it's incompatible with Windows 10. Try right-clicking the startup icon for the program and choosing Run as Administrator. If that doesn't help, try the program compatibility features, as discussed in more detail in Chapter 24.

> **NOTE**
> See Chapter 24 for more information on getting older programs to run with Windows 10.

Wrapping Up

This chapter discussed ways to troubleshoot your computer when you're experiencing problems. Some fixes are easy, and others may require you to reinstall Windows 10. If the steps and methods described in this chapter don't help, we've referred you to other chapters for tips on additional troubleshooting steps.

Part II

Personalizing Windows 10

IN THIS PART

Protecting Yourself with Windows Firewall

IN THIS CHAPTER

Understanding how firewalls protect your computer

Using Security Center

Using Windows Firewall

Configuring Windows Firewall

I f you use the Internet, a firewall is a must-have security tool. It isn't the only tool you need, but it's important. It protects your computer from hackers and worms. *Hackers* are people who attempt to access your computer through the Internet without your knowing it. *Worms* are programs, such as viruses, that are usually written to do intentional harm.

Windows 10 comes with its own built-in firewall. If you didn't know about it before going online, relax. The firewall is enabled by default. So, most likely, it's been protecting you since the very first moment you went online. (In addition, your Internet service provider protects you from most invasions.) In this chapter, you learn how the firewall works and how to configure it for maximum protection.

How Firewalls Work

To understand what a firewall is, you first need to understand what a network connection is. Even though you have only one skinny set of wires connecting your computer to the Internet (through a DSL phone line or cable outlet), that connection consists of 65,535 *ports*. Each port can simultaneously carry on its own conversation with the outside world. So, theoretically, you could have 65,535 things going on at a time. Of course, nobody ever has that much going on all at one time. Most people use a handful of ports at one time.

The ports are divided into two categories:

- **Transmission Control Protocol (TCP):** This generally is used to send text and pictures (web pages and e-mail), and includes some error checking to make sure all the information that's received by a computer matches what the sending computer sent.

- **User Datagram Protocol (UDP):** This works more like broadcast TV or radio, where the information is sent out with no error checking. UDP generally is used for real-time communications, such as voice conversations and radio broadcasts sent over the Internet.

Each port has two directions: incoming (or *ingress*) and outgoing (or *egress*). The directions indicate whether data traffic is coming *into* your computer from the outside — over the Internet — or going *out* from your computer *to* the Internet. Data traffic coming *into* your computer is what you have to watch out for. You can't close all ports to all incoming traffic, because if you do, you have no way to get the good information in. But you don't want to let everything in, either. You need a way to separate the wheat from the chaff, so to speak.

Anti-spyware and antivirus software are good tools for keeping out viruses and other bad things that are attached to files coming into your computer. But hackers can sneak worms and other bad things in through unprotected ports without involving a file in the process. That's where the firewall comes into play. A *stateful* firewall, such as the one that comes with Windows 10, keeps track of everything you request. When traffic from the Internet wants to come in through a port, the firewall checks to make sure the traffic is something you requested. If it isn't, the firewall assumes a hacker is trying to sneak something in and, therefore, prevents the traffic from entering your computer. Figure 6.1 illustrates how a stateful firewall works.

FIGURE 6.1

A stateful firewall.

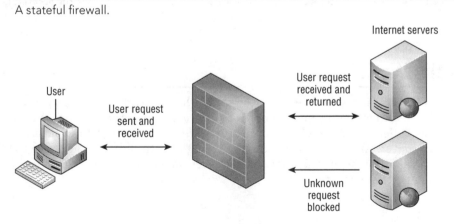

116

Firewall security means more than having a port open or closed. It's also about *filtering* — making sure that data coming into an open port is something you requested and not some rogue, uninvited traffic sent by a hacker. Many of the worms that infected computers in the 1990s did so by sneaking in undetected through unfiltered ports. To prevent such things, make sure you have a firewall up whenever you go online.

What a Firewall Doesn't Protect Against

A firewall alone is not sufficient protection against all Internet threats. A firewall is just one component in a larger defense system. Specifically:

- Windows Firewall *doesn't* protect you from spyware and viruses.
- Windows Firewall *doesn't* protect you from attacks based on exploits. Automatic updates (see Chapter 7) provide that protection.
- A firewall *doesn't* protect you from pop-up ads.
- A firewall *doesn't* protect you from phishing scams.
- Windows Firewall *doesn't* protect you from spam (junk e-mail).

So, a firewall isn't a complete solution. It's only one important component of a larger security strategy.

NOTE

The preceding list indicates that Windows Firewall doesn't provide certain types of protection, such as spam or virus blocking. Many hardware firewalls *do* provide this type of protection. This is sometimes referred to as *perimeter protection* because it protects your network from threats at the perimeter of your network. This type of firewall can cost from several hundred to several thousand dollars, so they aren't always the best bet for a home network. They can be extremely valuable, however, for business networks.

Security and Maintenance

Before you explore Windows Firewall, take a look at the Security and Maintenance Control Panel program. This program is a single point of notification for most of your PC's security. You can open Security and Maintenance in several ways. Use the method that is most convenient for you:

- In Cortana, type **maint** and click Security and Maintenance.
- On the desktop, press Windows+X, choose Control Panel, and then click System and Security and then Security and Maintenance.

Whichever method you use, the Security and Maintenance window opens. Figure 6.2 shows an example. We clicked the arrow button to the right of each heading so that you can see the descriptive text under each heading. You can click that button to show or hide the descriptive text.

FIGURE 6.2

Security and Maintenance Control Panel program.

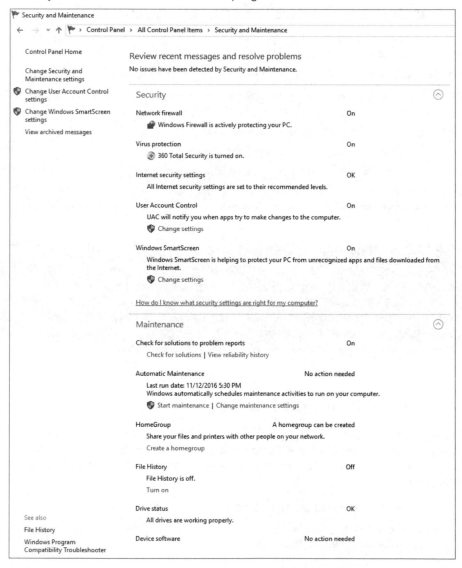

How you know Windows Firewall is on

By default, Windows Firewall is turned on and working at all times, so Security and Maintenance should show "On" beside the Firewall item. (You see only the Network Firewall item in Action Center if you click the arrow beside the Security heading.) If Security and Maintenance on your computer shows Off or Not Monitored, you may have a third-party firewall program running in place of Windows Firewall. Many such programs are available, such as McAfee, Symantec, and Check Point. If your firewall is turned off and you don't know why, find out the reason — perhaps from your computer manufacturer or a support person who worked on your computer. If you don't have any firewall up, definitely turn on Windows Firewall.

CAUTION

Don't run more than one firewall simultaneously. A second firewall doesn't offer any advantage and is likely to cause problems.

Turning Windows Firewall on or off

To turn Windows Firewall on or off, you must have administrative privileges. In the System and Security Control Panel window, click Windows Firewall. You should see the current firewall status in the right pane, and options for controlling the firewall in the left pane. Click Change Notification Settings or Turn Windows Firewall On or Off in the left pane to see the options shown in the foreground of Figure 6.3.

TIP

Use the Block All Incoming Connections check box to temporarily disable exceptions when connecting to public Wi-Fi networks. You can find more on that topic in the sections that follow.

If you have a third-party firewall that you feel is more secure than the Windows Firewall, you can choose the Turn off Windows Firewall option to turn off Windows Firewall. Just make sure you have a firewall up when you go online. Otherwise, you don't have anything to stop uninvited traffic on your network connection after the traffic gets past your Internet service provider.

TIP

If you have a firewall at home, such as a wireless access point (WAP) or a cable or DSL modem that provides firewall features, and those features are turned on, you can safely turn off Windows Firewall. However, leaving Windows Firewall turned on usually has no downside, even when an upstream firewall is in place. The exception is when you are trying to play multiplayer games or accomplish networking with other computers on the network and can't get the ports right in Windows Firewall to make it work. In these situations, turn off Windows Firewall on the computers.

FIGURE 6.3

Settings for Windows Firewall.

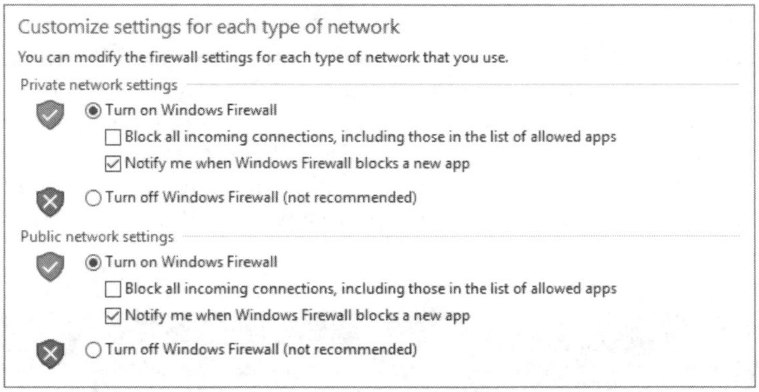

Customize settings for each type of network

You can modify the firewall settings for each type of network that you use.

Private network settings

- ⦿ Turn on Windows Firewall
  - ☐ Block all incoming connections, including those in the list of allowed apps
  - ☑ Notify me when Windows Firewall blocks a new app

- ◯ Turn off Windows Firewall (not recommended)

Public network settings

- ⦿ Turn on Windows Firewall
  - ☐ Block all incoming connections, including those in the list of allowed apps
  - ☑ Notify me when Windows Firewall blocks a new app

- ◯ Turn off Windows Firewall (not recommended)

Making Exceptions to Firewall Protection

When Windows Firewall is turned on and running, you don't have to do anything special to use it. It remains on constant vigil, automatically protecting your computer from hackers and worms trying to sneak in through unprotected ports. Ports for common Internet protocols, such as e-mail and web browsing, remain open and monitored so that you can easily use protocols safely.

Internet protocols that don't use standard e-mail and web ports may require that you create an *exception* to the default firewall rules for incoming traffic. Examples include instant messaging programs and some online games. When you try to use such a program, Windows Firewall displays a security alert.

The message doesn't mean the program is "bad." It means that to use the program, Firewall has to open a port. If you don't recognize the program name and publisher shown, click Cancel. If you want to use the program, decide for which networks the exception should be allowed. For example, if the traffic is coming from another computer on your local network, select the Private Networks option. For traffic coming from the Internet, select Public Networks (you can select either or both, as needed). Then click Allow Access. Allowing access for a program doesn't leave the associated port wide open; it only creates a new rule that allows that one program to use the port. You're still protected because the port is closed when you aren't using that program. The port is also closed to programs other than the one for which you unblocked the port. If you change your mind in the future, you can reblock the port, as described in the next section.

Manually configuring firewall exceptions

Normally, when you try to use a program (also referred to in Windows 10 Firewall as an *app*) that needs to work through the firewall, you get a security alert message. Occasionally, you may want to manually allow or block an app through the firewall. If you have administrative privileges, you can do that through the Allowed Apps page shown in Figure 6.4. To open that page, click Allow an App through Windows Firewall in System and Security (near the Windows Firewall item in the Control Panel).

Items on the list with a check mark beside them represent apps that work through the firewall. You also see any exceptions you created in response to a security alert.

You probably aren't familiar with most of the apps listed in the Allowed Apps and Features list, so you shouldn't guess which ones to select or deselect. Leave the selections as they are. If you later decide to use one of the listed features, you're prompted at that point to allow access for the app or program if necessary.

Adding an app exception

You can unblock ports for apps that aren't listed under Allowed Apps and Features. Do this only if specifically instructed to do so by an app manufacturer you know and trust.

FIGURE 6.4

Windows Firewall Allowed Apps and Features.

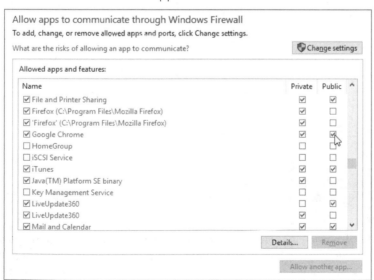

If the app for which you want to create an exception isn't listed under Allowed Apps and Features, you can do the following:

1. Click Change Settings and then click the Allow Another App button. When you do so, you see a list of installed apps that might require Internet access, as shown in Figure 6.5.

2. Click the app that you want to add to the list. Optionally, if the program isn't listed, but you know where it's installed, you can use the Browse button to get to the main executable for that program (typically the .exe file).

3. Clicking the Network Types button lets you define the addresses from which any unsolicited traffic is expected to originate. For example, if you're using an app that provides communications among programs within your local network only, you don't want to accept unsolicited traffic coming to that port from the Internet. You want to accept unsolicited traffic coming only from computers in your own network. When you click Network Types, you see the options shown in Figure 6.6. Your options are as follows:

FIGURE 6.5

Add an App dialog box.

- **Private:** Use this for home or workplace networks. If the program in question has nothing to do with the Internet and is for your home or business network only, choose this option to block Internet access, but allow apps within your own network to communicate with each other through the program.

- **Public:** Use this option for public networks, such as those in an airport or coffee shop. If you want the app to be able to connect to the Internet, choose this option.

■ **Domain Profile:** Windows can automatically recognize networks on which it can authenticate access to the domain controller for the domain to which the computer is attached in this category. No other networks can be placed in this category.

4. Click OK to save your settings.

FIGURE 6.6

The Choose Network Types dialog box.

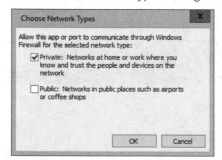

> **TIP**
> You can choose the scope for the program within the Allowed Programs and Features list by placing a check mark in the Private or Public columns for the program.

IP Addresses on Home/Office Networks

When you set up a network using the Network Setup Wizard described in Part IX of this book, each computer is automatically assigned a 192.168.0.x IP address (the x represents a number that is unique to each computer). For example, if the computers are sharing a single Internet connection, the first computer may receive the address 192.168.0.1, and the subsequent computers will have addresses in that same address space.

All computers on the network have the same subnet mask of 255.255.255.0. The subnet mask tells the computer that the first three numbers are part of the *network address* (the address of your network as a whole), and the last number refers to a specific *host* (computer) on that network. The 192.168... addresses are often referred to as *private addresses* because they can't be accessed directly from the Internet.

To see the IP address of a computer on your local network:

1. Go to that computer, display the desktop, press Windows+X, and choose Command Prompt.
2. At the command prompt, type **ipconfig /all** and press Enter. You see the computer's IP address and subnet mask listed along with other Internet protocol data.

Disabling, changing, and deleting exceptions

The check boxes in the Allowed Apps and Features list indicate whether the exception is enabled or disabled. When you clear a check box, the exception is disabled and traffic for that program is rejected. You can easily enable or disable a rule for a program as needed because the program name always remains in the list of exceptions.

To change the scope of an exception in the exceptions list, click the check box in the Private or Public column. To remove a program from the exceptions list and stop accepting unsolicited traffic through its port, click the program name and then click the Remove button.

TIP

You can't remove the default programs from the list — only those you've added.

Advanced Firewall Configuration

The rest of this chapter goes well beyond anything that concerns the average home computer user. It's for advanced users and network and security administrators who need to configure Windows Firewall to comply with an organization's security policy. All these options require administrative privileges. We don't go into great detail about what the options mean because we assume you're working to comply with an existing policy.

CAUTION

If you aren't a professional administrator, stay out of this area altogether. Don't guess and hack your way through these settings to see what happens. Doing so could leave you unable to connect to the Internet or exposed to attacks.

Open Windows Firewall with Advanced Security

To get to the advanced configuration options for Windows Firewall, open Windows Firewall from the System and Security item in the Control Panel. Then click the Advanced Settings link in the left pane. The firewall console, shown in Figure 6.7, opens.

You have three independently configurable profiles to work with:

- **Domain Profile** is active when the computer is logged in to a Windows domain, such as in a corporation or business setting.
- **Private Profile** applies to computers within a local, private network.
- **Public Profile** protects your computer from the public Internet.

FIGURE 6.7

The Windows Firewall with Advanced Security console.

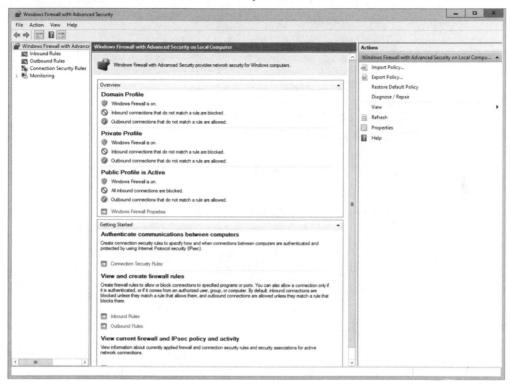

Changing firewall profile properties

Clicking the Windows Firewall Properties link near the bottom of the console takes you to the dialog box shown in Figure 6.8. You can use tabs at the top of the dialog box to configure the Domain, Private, and Public settings. The fourth option applies to IPsec (IP Security), commonly used with virtual private networks (VPNs), which are described later in this section. By default, Inbound Connections are set to Block and Outbound Connections are set to Allow. You can change either setting by clicking its button.

Firewall alerts, unicast responses, local administrator control

Each profile tab has a Customize button in its Settings section. Clicking that button provides an option to turn off firewall notifications for that profile. Administrators can also use options on that tab to allow or prevent unicast responses to multicast and broadcast traffic. You also have an option to merge local administrator rules with rules defined through group policy.

FIGURE 6.8

Windows Firewall advanced properties.

Security logging

Each profile tab offers a Logging section with a Customize button. Click the Customize button to set a name and location for the log file, to set a maximum size, and to choose whether you want to log dropped packets, successful connections, or both. You can use the log file to review firewall activity and to troubleshoot connection problems caused by the firewall configuration.

Customizing IPsec settings

The IPsec Settings tab in the firewall properties provides a way to configure IPsec (IP Security). Clicking the Customize button under IPsec Defaults reveals the options shown in Figure 6.9. The Default settings in each case cause settings to be inherited from a higher-level group policy object (GPO). To override the GPO, choose the options you want to apply to the current Windows Firewall instance. When you override the default, you can choose key exchange and data integrity algorithms. You can fine-tune Kerberos V5 authentication through those settings.

Clicking OK or Cancel in the Customize IPsec Defaults dialog box takes you back to the IPsec Settings tab. There you can use the IPsec Exemptions section to exempt ICMP from IPsec, which may help with connection problems caused by ICMP rules.

FIGURE 6.9

The Customize IPsec Defaults dialog box.

6

Why Outbound Connections Are Set to Allow

Contrary to some common marketing hype and urban myths, having outbound connections set to Allow by default does not make your computer more susceptible to security threats. Firewalls are about controlling traffic between trusted and untrusted networks. The Internet is considered "untrusted" because it's open to the public. You need to block inbound connections by default so that you can control exactly what comes in from the Internet.

Things that are already inside your computer (or local network) are generally considered "trusted." That's because, unlike on the Internet, you have control over what's inside your own PC or network. Your firewall and anti-malware programs also help to keep out bad stuff. Therefore, you shouldn't need to block outbound connections by default.

Some exceptions exist. In a secure setting in which highly sensitive data is confined to secure workstations in a subnet, blocking outgoing connections by default makes sense. That way, you limit outbound connections to specific hosts, programs, security groups, and so on. You can also enforce encryption on outbound connections.

> **NOTE**
>
> IPsec is a set of cryptographic protocols for securing communications across untrusted networks. It is commonly associated with tunneling and VPNs.

That covers the main firewall properties. You can configure plenty more outside the Properties dialog box, but most of these go far beyond anything the average home user needs to be concerned with. Advanced users needing more information can find plenty of information in Firewall's Help section.

Inbound and outbound rules

In the left column of the main Windows Firewall with Advanced Security window, shown back in Figure 6.7, you see Inbound Rules and Outbound Rules links. These provide very precise control over Windows Firewall rules for incoming and outgoing connections. Figure 6.10 shows a small part of the possibilities there. Scroll up or down to see more.

FIGURE 6.10

Advanced outbound exceptions control.

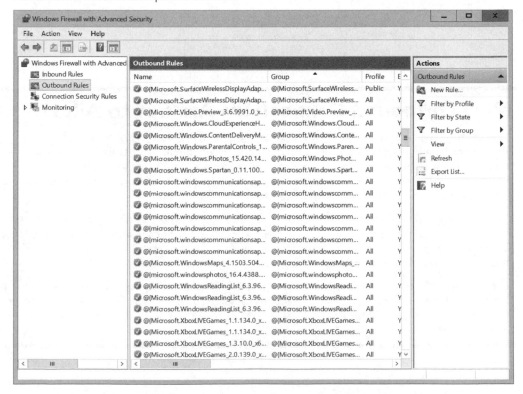

The settings in this window go beyond the scope of this book but should be a simple matter for most professional administrators. Options (and the Help link) in the Actions column on the right provide additional information to assist you. You can also change any exception in the center column by right-clicking and choosing Properties.

Wrapping Up

A firewall is an important component of a larger overall security strategy. Windows 10 comes with a built-in firewall that's turned on and working from the moment you start your computer. The firewall is automatically configured to prevent unsolicited Internet traffic from getting into your computer, thereby protecting you from worms and other hacking attempts. The Windows 10 firewall also provides advanced options for professional network and security administrators who need more control over its behavior. In summary:

- A firewall protects your computer from unsolicited network traffic, which is a major cause of worms and other hack attempts.

- A firewall does not protect your computer from viruses, pop-up ads, or junk e-mail.

- You don't need to configure the firewall to use standard Internet services such as the web and e-mail. Those work through the firewall automatically.

- When you start an Internet program that requires access to the Internet through a closed port, you're given a security alert with options to Unblock, or Keep Blocking, the port. Choose Unblock to use that program.

- Windows Firewall is one of the programs in the System and Security Control Panel section. To open System and Security, press Windows+X and choose Control Panel ⇨ System and Security.

- To get to Windows Firewall configuration options, in Cortana type **firewall** and click Windows Firewall.

- Exceptions in Windows Firewall are programs that are allowed to work through the firewall.

- Professional network and security administrators can configure Windows Firewall through the Windows Firewall with Advanced Security console in Administrative Tools.

Automatic Updates as Security

Internet security is a never-ending cat-and-mouse game between the security experts and the hackers who seem to have endless amounts of time to search for new ways to exploit the basic programmability of PCs. Every time the good guys find a way to patch some security hole that the bad guys have learned to exploit, the bad guys find two more holes to exploit.

Windows 10 is the most secure Windows version ever, by a long shot. But no computer is 100 percent secure because people can always find a way to turn something good into something bad. So, in addition to the security features discussed in Chapter 6, you need to keep your computer up to date with security patches as they become available.

Windows Update in Windows 10 builds on one of the most essential components in the OS engine: its self-healing and self-patching ability. An operating system can never be defect-free, and when a defect is discovered that must be "fixed" quickly, Windows Update kicks in. In Windows 10, Microsoft has installed the technology that may once and for all end the idea of an "upgrade." That's what Windows Update and this chapter are all about.

Understanding Automatic Updates

Many people are afraid of Windows Update—they're afraid that the updates will break something on their system that they can't fix. It's true that any change to your system can create a problem. But keeping up with updates is unlikely to cause any significant problems—certainly nowhere near as many problems as you expose yourself to by *not* keeping up with updates. In addition, Windows Update creates restore points before installing many updates (but not for all updates), so you have the added security of being able to restore the system to a point prior to the update.

Other people fear that Microsoft will somehow exploit them through automatic updates. That isn't the way updates work. Microsoft has tens of millions of customers and tens of billions of dollars.

It doesn't need to exploit anybody to be successful. Microsoft is also a publicly held company on the stock exchange, which means it's subject to constant scrutiny. When you're making up your mind about which companies to trust, large, publicly held companies are by far the most trustworthy, if for no other reason than that they can't afford to be untrustworthy.

A third common fear of automatic updates centers around the question "What's this going to cost me?" The answer to that is simple: Absolutely nothing. This brings us to the difference between *updates* and *upgrades*.

Some Hacking Lingo

The hacking world is replete with its own terminology. A *zero-day exploit* is one that exploits a problem in software before the software vulnerability is known by the software company. A *black hat* is a bad guy who has sufficient technical knowledge to find and publish exploits. A *script kiddie* is someone (sometimes simply an inexperienced programmer who doesn't have enough skills to create or discover his own exploits) who runs scripts and malware created by more experienced hackers. A *white hat* is one of the good guys — the security experts who find ways to thwart the efforts of black hats and script kiddies.

Updates versus upgrades

People often assume that the terms *update* and *upgrade* are synonymous. We certainly use the terms interchangeably in common parlance. But in the computer world, there is a big difference. Upgrades usually cost money and involve a fair amount of work. For example, upgrading from Windows 8.1 to Windows 10 costs you some money and takes some time. However, updating your existing version of Windows 10 to Windows 10 Anniversary Edition is actually a free upgrade (for at least a year after it's released) and your previous version simply morphs into Windows 10. You don't even need to hire someone to verify that the upgrade worked.

Why updates are important

Automatic updates are an important part of your overall security. Many forms of malware, especially viruses and worms, operate by exploiting previously unnoticed flaws in programs. The term *exploit,* when used as a noun in computer science, refers to any piece of software that can take advantage of some vulnerability in a program in order to gain unauthorized access to a computer.

Some hackers actually publish, on the Internet, exploits they discover, which is both a good thing and a bad thing. The bad thing is that other hackers can use the exploit to conjure up their own malware, causing a whole slew of new security threats. The good thing is that the good guys can quickly create security patches to prevent the exploits from doing their nefarious deeds. Automatic updates keep your system current with *security patches* that fix the flaws that malware programs attempt to exploit.

Enabling Automatic Updates

Administrators now can have more control over updates by altering the update deferral increment from weeks to days. Changes can be made to the following updates:

- Quality updates can be deferred up to 30 days and paused for 35 days.
- Feature updates can be deferred up to 180 days and paused for 60 days.
- Update deferrals can also be applied to both Current Branch (CB) and Current Branch for Business (CBB). Further explanation of branch management is beyond the scope of this book.
- Drivers can be excluded from updates.

Automatic updates are the best way to keep up with security patches. In fact, chances are, they're already enabled on your system. To find out, open Windows Update. As you know from previous chapters, you simply click Settings to launch the Settings applet. Then click the "Update & security" image. Figure 7.1 shows the Update & security applet.

FIGURE 7.1

The Settings applet showing the Windows Update & security option.

Managing Updates

When you open the Update & security applet, you see the status of your updates. To see if updates are available for download, click the Check for updates button as shown in Figure 7.2. The system searches for updates as shown in Figure 7.3.

FIGURE 7.2

The Windows Update & security applet showing update status.

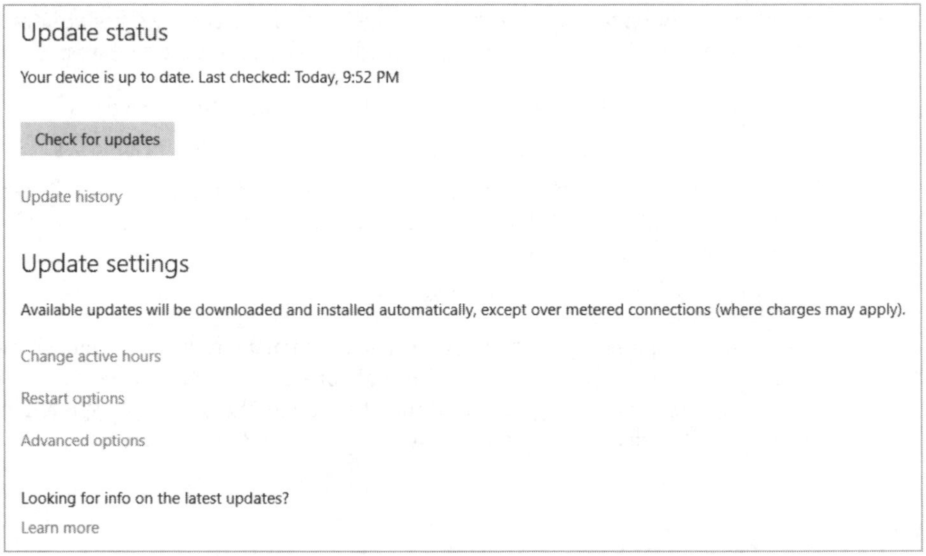

> Update status
>
> Your device is up to date. Last checked: Today, 9:52 PM
>
> Check for updates
>
> Update history
>
> Update settings
>
> Available updates will be downloaded and installed automatically, except over metered connections (where charges may apply).
>
> Change active hours
>
> Restart options
>
> Advanced options
>
> Looking for info on the latest updates?
> Learn more

FIGURE 7.3

The Windows Update & security applet check-ing for updates.

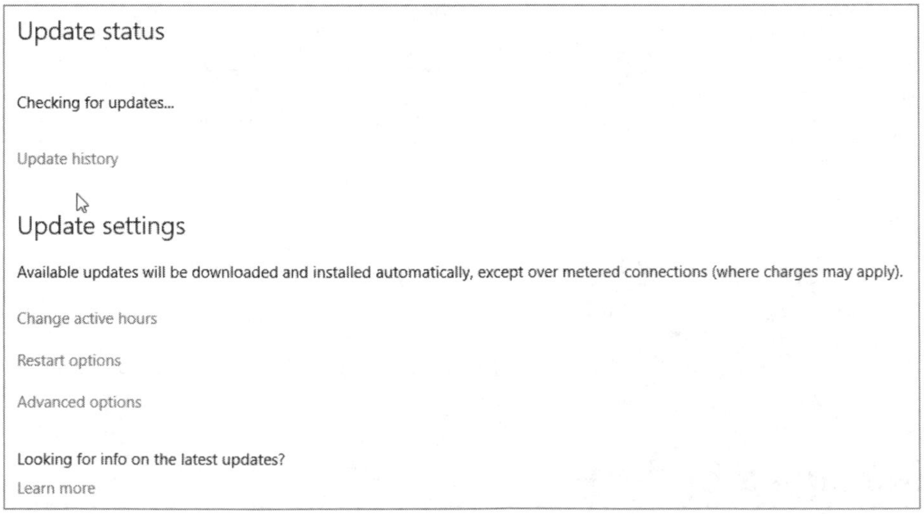

> Update status
>
> Checking for updates...
>
> Update history
>
> Update settings
>
> Available updates will be downloaded and installed automatically, except over metered connections (where charges may apply).
>
> Change active hours
>
> Restart options
>
> Advanced options
>
> Looking for info on the latest updates?
> Learn more

But sometimes you may be faced with optional updates. These updates aren't security related. Instead, they're new versions of drivers, fixes for minor bugs, or some other type of update. They're optional because your computer is secure whether you install the update or not. To see how windows will update other Microsoft products, click Advanced options. This is shown in Figure 7.4.

FIGURE 7.4

The Windows Update & security applet showing how it will update other Microsoft products.

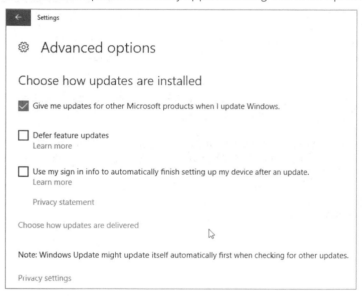

From the Windows Update & Security applet Advanced options, you can choose from these values for the option Choose How Updates Are Installed:

- **Give me updates for other Microsoft products when I update Windows.** By enabling this option through the check box, you are essentially letting Microsoft decide which of its other products, such as Microsoft Office, it will update.

- **Defer feature updates.** If you defer updates, you will not have the newest Windows features when they are available. It could be a few months before they are downloaded.

- **Use my sign in info to automatically finish setting up my device after an update.** This option allows you to not have to sign in to finish the setup process for an update to your device. If you enable this option, Windows 10 finishes the process without the need for you to enter your password.

Note that when checking for other updates, Windows Update might update itself first.

Updates won't download over a metered connection. On a metered connection, charges may apply, as shown in Figure 7.5.

You now can decide when you want to have your computer restart after an update. With the ability to set your active hours; this prevents Windows update from restarting your computer and installs the updates while you are using your machine.

If you want to able to schedule a time when you want a restart to finish installing updates, click Restart options, shown in Figure 7.5. This option temporarily overrides the active hours setting. The computer must be turned on for this feature to run at the scheduled time. This is shown in Figure 7.6.

Also on the applet is a link that allows you to view your update history. When you click this link, the applet opens the pane shown in Figure 7.7 and provides a list of your recent updates, successes, and failures.

You can also select the option "Choose how your download updates." The applet pane for choosing these options appears, as shown in Figure 7.8.

Here you can toggle the option on to get the updates faster by getting them from other machines on your network, or from either other machines on your network or the Internet.

The applet displays the following message: "Getting builds faster means you'll see new things sooner. Getting builds slower could mean more solutions are available for issues."

FIGURE 7.5

The Windows Update & security applet setting for automated updates.

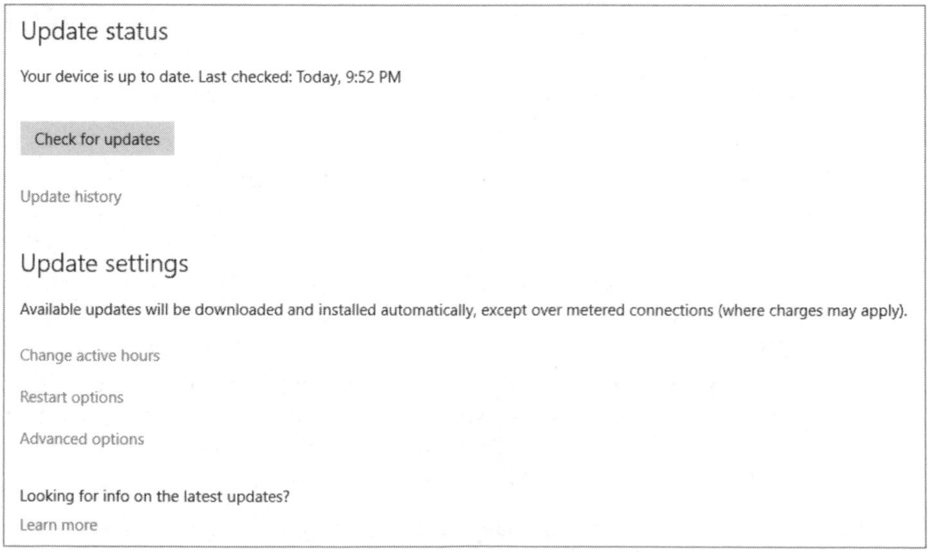

Update status

Your device is up to date. Last checked: Today, 9:52 PM

Check for updates

Update history

Update settings

Available updates will be downloaded and installed automatically, except over metered connections (where charges may apply).

Change active hours

Restart options

Advanced options

Looking for info on the latest updates?

Learn more

FIGURE 7.6

The Windows Update & security applet in prompt to restart mode.

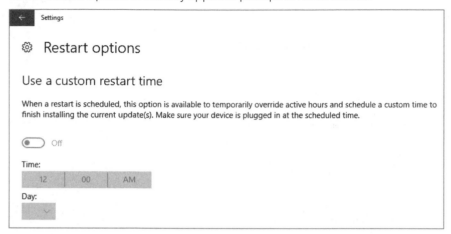

FIGURE 7.7

Windows Update & security applet showing update history.

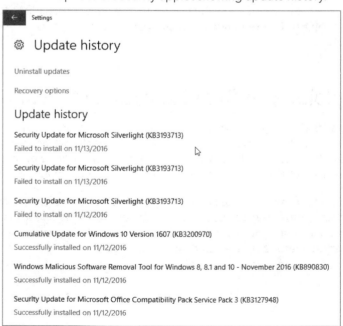

FIGURE 7.8

The Windows Update & security applet provides choices for downloading updates.

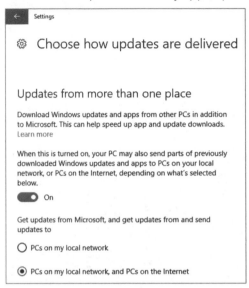

Additionally, you can select the option to get Insider builds. Insider is like a beta tester group at Microsoft that you can join to preview new software that has not yet been released to manufacturing (RTM).

Thwarting Exploits with Data Execution Prevention

Thwarting malware attacks that exploit software vulnerabilities is the most important element of automatic updates. But Windows 10 offers a second way of thwarting such attacks. It's called *Data Execution Prevention (DEP)*. Don't use DEP as an alternative to other techniques described in this part of the book. Instead, use it *in addition* to other techniques.

Many malware attacks use a technique called *buffer overflow* (or *buffer overrun*) to sneak code (program instructions) into areas of memory that only the Windows operating system should be using. Those areas of memory have direct access to everything on your computer. So, any bad code that sneaks into that area can do great damage.

More Security Tricks up Its Sleeve

Some malware techniques rely on well-known memory locations to exploit system vulnerabilities. Windows 10 has a surprise for those programs. It doesn't load essential programs to well-known, predictable locations. Instead, it uses address space layout randomization (ASLR) to load programs in a random location each time you start your computer. So, malware writers can't know in advance where a particular exploit resides in memory, making it much more difficult to exploit those memory addresses.

DEP is a security antidote to such attacks. It monitors programs to make sure they use only safe and appropriate memory locations. If DEP notices a program trying to do something sneaky, it closes that program before it can do any harm.

By default, DEP is enabled for essential Windows programs and services only. When coupled with antivirus protection, that setting is usually adequate. You can crank it up to monitor all programs and services. But if you do, you may also have to individually choose programs that are allowed to bypass DEP. Knowing when that's okay requires technical expertise that goes beyond the scope of this book.

To get to options for DEP, follow these steps:

1. Open Control Panel then System and Security. The System window opens.

2. In the left column, click Advanced System Settings. The System Properties dialog box opens.

3. Select the Advanced tab, click the Settings button on the Performance heading, and then select the Data Execution Prevention tab. You see the options shown in Figure 7.9.

4. By default, the option to apply DEP only to essential Windows programs and services is selected. For stronger protection, you can turn on DEP for all programs and services. If you choose that option, DEP sometimes may shut down a program to prevent it from running.

NOTE

Many modern processors offer *NX technologies*, which prevent buffer overflows at the hardware level. For processors that don't have hardware DEP, Windows uses DEP software to achieve the same result.

FIGURE 7.9

Data Execution Prevention options.

If DEP shuts down a program you need, you have two choices:

- Contact the program manufacturer to find out whether a different version of the program runs under DEP.

- If you trust the program, you can add it to the list of programs that are allowed to bypass DEP. To accomplish that, click the Add button and then navigate to and double-click the executable file that DEP is shutting down. Typically, such a file has the extension .exe.

Wrapping Up

In general computer security, the "big three" items are a firewall, malware protection, and automatic updates. Chapters 7 and this chapter cover those topics. Comprehensive malware strategy is beyond the scope of this book. But don't forget that running under a Standard user account (see Chapter 4) counts, too. Furthermore, you have fewer technical "social" threats to consider, such as phishing scams and pop-up ads.

The main points in this chapter are the following:

- Automatic updates provide a quick and simple way to protect your computer against current software exploitation malware.

- Unless you have a compelling reason to do otherwise, you should allow Windows 10 to automatically download and install updates daily.

- Data Execution Prevention (DEP) offers another layer of protection against threats that work by sneaking errant code into sensitive parts of system memory.

7

Personalizing the Windows 10 Interface

IN THIS CHAPTER

The Windows 10 interface

Working with tiles

Working with tile groups

Customizing the contents of the Start screen

Clearing tile data

The Windows 10 interface presents a clean, streamlined way to interact with your apps, data, and documents, but like the traditional Windows desktop interface, the new interface is just a starting point. You can customize the organization of tiles and tile groups on the Start menu, change the picture on the Lock screen, and much more.

This chapter explores how you can change all these elements of the Windows 10 interface and customize it to suit the way you work and play.

Customizing the Start Screen

Although the Logon screen may be the first thing you see when you start Windows 10, you'll certainly spend a lot more time working with the Start menu, so that's where we start our tour of the tools and settings you can use to customize the interface.

Rearranging tiles

Figure 8.1 shows a typical Windows 10 Start menu. As the figure shows, the tiles on the Start screen are grouped. You can rearrange the tiles on the Start screen, moving them within a group, moving them to other groups, or even creating new groups.

FIGURE 8.1

Tiles on the Windows 10 Start menu.

Moving tiles within a group is easy. If you're using a touch device, tap and hold the tile until a pushpin icon appears near the upper-right corner of the tile; then simply drag it into its new position. If you're using a mouse, just left-click and drag the tile to its new position.

> **TIP**
>
> If the group where you want to place the tile is not shown on the display, drag the tile in the direction of the target group. The screen scrolls automatically.

Adding and removing tiles

You can customize the tiles that appear on the Start menu, adding and removing tiles as desired. For example, you might add the documents or websites you use most often, and remove the apps you seldom or never use. The following sections explain how to add and remove tiles from the Start screen, as well as the Windows taskbar.

Adding tiles

Apps that you add from the Windows Store are not automatically pinned to the Start menu, nor are apps you install manually. So, after you add an app, you may want to add it to the Start menu. Or, if you've removed a tile and you want to add it back, you can easily do so.

TIP

The Recently Added group on the Start menu shows apps that were recently installed. You can also open Search and click or tap Apps in the results list to show all apps.

To add an app, first click or tap the Start menu. Scroll through the list of apps to locate the app that you want to add to the Start menu, and then either right-click or tap and hold the icon. In the resulting pop-up menu (see Figure 8.2), click or tap Pin to Start. If you also want to add the app to the Windows taskbar, open the menu again for the app and click or tap More ➪ Pin to Taskbar.

Removing tiles

Over time, the Start menu may get cluttered with apps you use seldom, if at all. You can uninstall apps you don't need, but in some cases you may prefer to simply remove the app's tile(s) from the Start menu. For example, if you have a utility app that runs in the background and you never need to open it, remove the tile.

Removing a tile is easy. If using a mouse, right-click the tile and then, in the context menu, click Unpin from Start. If using a touch device, tap and hold the tile to open the context menu, and then tap Unpin from Start.

Resizing tiles

Although some tiles have a fixed size, you can change others from small to large, or vice versa. This is particularly handy for live tiles for which you want to provide more space to display their live data. To change the size of a tile, right-click the tile to open the context menu. Click Resize, then click Small, Medium, Large, or Wide, as appropriate.

NOTE

For some apps, Windows 10 does not offer the Wide or Large options for the tile size.

Working with live tiles

In the Windows 10 interface, live tiles are ones that display data dynamically. Examples include the Weather, Mail, and Money tiles. For example, Money shows stock price information for stocks that you've added to your watch list.

FIGURE 8.2

Pin items to the Start screen using the context menu.

You can control whether a live tile–capable app shows data on the Start menu. For example, if you don't use the Weather app much, you may not want it showing data. To turn live tiles on or off, right-click on the tile to open the context menu. Then click or tap More, then either Turn Live Tile Off or Turn Live Tile On (see Figure 8.3), depending on the current state of the tile. On a touch device, tap and hold the tile and click the ellipsis button at the bottom-right corner of the tile, and then choose Turn Live Tile On or Turn Live Tile Off.

Working with groups

You've already seen that the Start menu groups tiles and that you can move tiles from one group to another. Groups enable you to group together tiles on the Start menu in whatever way makes sense to you. For example, you might group your Office apps together in one group, and other items that you use less often into another group.

The "Rearranging tiles" section, earlier in this chapter, explained how to move tiles from one group to another, or within the same group. But there are other actions you can take in regard to groups, including creating new groups and naming them.

FIGURE 8.3

Use the context menu to turn live tiles on or off.

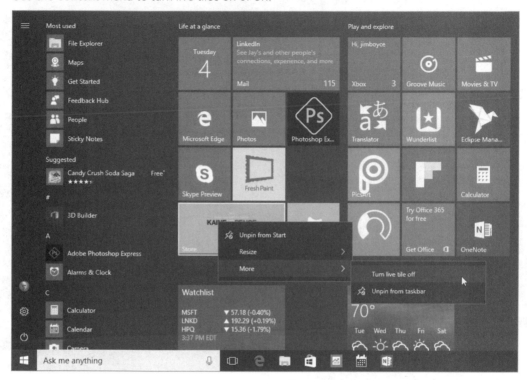

Creating groups

To create a new group, simply drag a tile to an empty space above or below a group. Windows displays a translucent horizontal bar to indicate that it's going to create a new group when you release the tile. Release the tile, and then drag other tiles as desired into the group.

Rearranging groups

You can also change the order of groups on the Start menu. Each group has a title bar, even if the title is blank. To move a group, just click and drag its title bar to a different location (see Figure 8.4). On a touch device, tap and hold the title, and when the double line icon appears at the right edge of the title bar, tap and drag the icon to relocate the group.

Adding administrative tools to the Start screen

One final change you might want to make to the Start menu is to add the Windows 10 administrative tools to it. These tools include Performance Monitor, Computer Management,

FIGURE 8.4

Use a group's title bar to drag and relocate it.

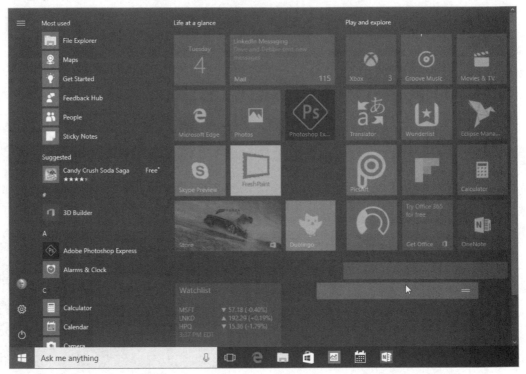

Task Scheduler, and other tools for managing your device. If you use these tools often, or simply want quick access to them, you can add them to the Start menu. To do so, first open the Control Panel. Then, choose Large Icons (or Small Icons) from the View By list. Right-click Administrative Tools and choose Pin to Start. You should then see the Windows Administrative Tools tile on the Start menu.

Changing the Start Menu Color and Transparency

Another change you can make to the Start menu is to change the background color and/or set transparency for the Start screen. To change either of these properties, open the Start menu, click or tap Settings, and then click or tap Personalization.

In the Personalization page, click or tap Colors (see Figure 8.5). The option Automatically Pick a Color from My Background allows Windows to automatically pick a color for some of the items on the Start menu (such as icon color for apps) based on your current color scheme. To assign a specific color, turn off this option and then choose a color from the provided palette.

FIGURE 8.5

Use the Personalization menu to choose a color and background image.

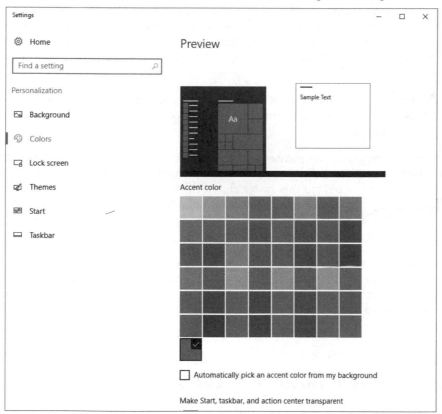

You can also turn color on or off for the Start menu and taskbar. Use the option Show Color on Taskbar and Start Menu to enable or disable color. When this option is on, the Start menu and taskbar appear in the same color as the menu items. Finally, you can apply some transparency to the Start menu and taskbar using the option Make Start, Taskbar, and Action Center Transparent.

Customizing the Lock Screen

Although you probably don't spend much time on the Lock screen, you may still want to customize the way the Lock screen looks and functions. For example, maybe you want to change the picture displayed on the Lock screen. Or maybe you want to choose the apps that run in the background and display information on the Lock screen (such as the Mail app, showing how many unread e-mails you have). Only apps written to do so can display status on the Lock screen. Depending on their design, some apps can display basic information, while others can display detailed status. The Calendar app is an example of an app that can display detailed status.

To customize the Lock screen, open the Start menu, click or tap Settings, and then click or tap Personalization. In the Settings app, click or tap Lock Screen to display the options shown in Figure 8.6.

Windows 10 provides a small number of stock images from which you can choose for the Lock screen. Just click an image to set it as the background for the Lock screen, or click Browse to choose a photo or other image stored on your device. You can also choose Windows Spotlight to have Windows automatically download and use images from Bing as your lock screen image. Windows Spotlight also occasionally highlights Windows 10 features that you may have missed.

The options in the lower half of the Lock Screen page let you choose which apps display status updates on the Lock screen. To add an app, click or tap one of the available boxes (with the plus sign in the middle) and choose an app from the resulting pop-up menu. To change which app displays detailed status, click or tap the detailed status icon and choose the desired app.

Changing Your Account Picture

One final change you'll probably want to make that affects both the Lock screen and the Start menu is your account picture. For example, maybe you want to use your Xbox avatar as your account picture.

FIGURE 8.6

Use the Personalization item to set Lock screen options.

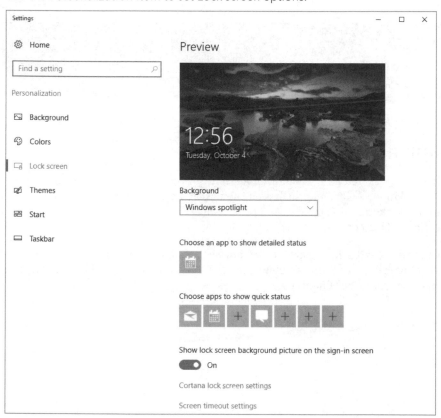

After you have the image you want to use as your account picture, open Settings and click or tap Accounts. The Your Info page shows your currently assigned picture, if you have a picture assigned. To choose a different picture, click or tap Browse for One, choose an image, and click or tap Choose Picture to apply the new image.

> **TIP**
>
> If you want to use your Xbox avatar for your Microsoft or Windows account image, open the Store and install the Xbox Avatars app. Use the app to modify your avatar to your heart's content, then use the Take a Photo feature to capture and save an image of your avatar to disk. Then you can assign the image as your account photo.

Wrapping Up

Windows 10 gives you a fair amount of flexibility over the look and feel of the Start screen and other Windows elements, including the position and grouping of tiles on the Start screen, its background and color, and other properties. You learned how to change those properties in this chapter.

The Windows desktop hasn't gone away, however, and you no doubt want to do at least a little customization of the desktop interface. To learn more about the available customization options, check out Chapter 9.

Personalizing the Desktop

IN THIS CHAPTER

Personalizing your screen, mouse, and keyboard

Personalizing your taskbar

We all like to set up our own desktops and work environments in unique ways. What works best for one person isn't necessarily great for someone else. Fortunately, the way things look and work on your Windows 10 desktop isn't set in stone. You can personalize your desktop and features in a variety of ways to make them look and work the way you like. That's what this chapter is about — setting up your Windows environment your own way.

Most of the options described in this chapter apply only to the user account you're currently logged in to, so the changes you make to your own desktop apply only to you (assuming that you're logged in to your own user account). This means that all users of a computer can have their settings just the way they want them without stepping on each others' toes.

Using the Personalization Page

Many options for personalizing the look and feel of Windows 10 are on the Personalization page, shown in Figure 9.1. As with most aspects of Windows 10, you can get to the Personalization page in several ways. Use the way that is most convenient for you at the moment:

- Right-click the desktop and choose Personalize.
- Open the Start menu and choose Settings, then click or tap Personalization.

The following sections show you how to use the personalization options to fine-tune the look and feel of Windows 10 on your screen.

FIGURE 9.1

The Personalization page.

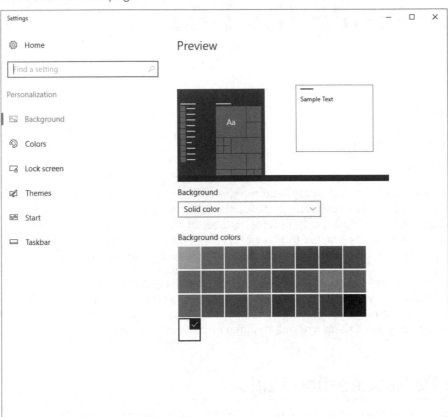

Choosing a theme

A theme is a collection of appearance settings that determine colors, sounds, photos, and other elements of the Windows 10 interface. For example, Figure 9.2 shows how Windows 10 looks with one of the default themes selected. Figure 9.3 shows the result of selecting the Australian Landscapes theme, by Ian Johnson, downloaded from the Microsoft website.

To choose a theme, open the Personalization window, click or tap Themes, and then click or tap Theme Settings. You see a selection of themes from which to choose. A good way to personalize your screen is to choose a theme that looks the most like how you'd like your screen to look. You can modify it to your preferences later, or even create your own custom themes, but a good way to get started is to use a predefined theme that has many of the characteristics you like.

To try a theme, click the theme in the Personalization page. The theme is applied to your desktop. If you don't like the results, click another theme or your previous theme.

Feel free to try as many themes as you like. If you plan to customize your environment further, click Save Theme, a link located on the Themes page. Then enter a name for the theme and click Save.

FIGURE 9.2

One of the Windows 10 themes.

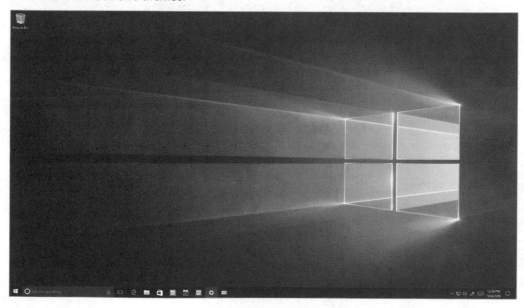

9

FIGURE 9.3

The Australian Landscapes theme.

Personalizing your desktop background

You can *wallpaper* your desktop with any picture or color you like. In the Personalization window, click Background to open the page shown in Figure 9.4.

Click the drop-down button and choose Solid Color to choose a solid-color background for the desktop, or choose Picture to view pictures from your own Pictures folder (see Figure 9.5) and from the shared Public Pictures folder. Of course, if these folders are empty or don't contain any compatible picture types, you don't see any pictures after making your selection. After you choose a category, point to or click any picture to see it applied as your desktop background.

FIGURE 9.4

The Desktop Background page.

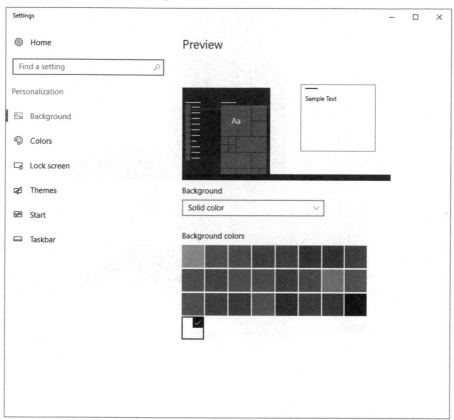

The Slideshow option lets you choose a folder containing photos, and Windows periodically chooses a different photo from the specified folder. You can specify the time interval at which the photo changes.

If you have pictures in some folder other than the Pictures folder for your user account or the Public Pictures folder, click Browse. Navigate to the folder that contains those pictures. Then click (or double-click) the picture you want to use as your desktop background. All pictures from that folder appear in the Desktop Background window. Click the picture you want to use.

9

FIGURE 9.5

Choose a picture for the background.

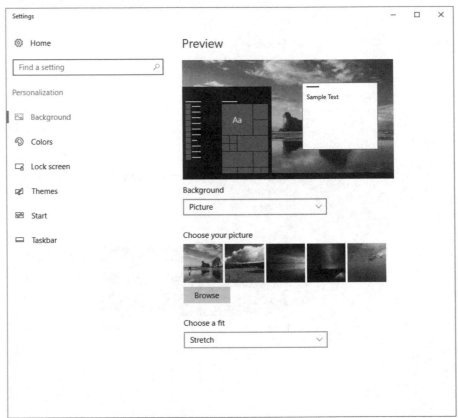

If the desktop is covered, click or tap the Show Desktop button at the lower-right corner of the screen to make all windows invisible and show the desktop. Try different pictures until you find one you like.

Try the options under Choose a Fit to view the image in different ways. The options have little or no effect on large pictures. But if you choose a small picture of your own, the Tile option shows it repeatedly, like tiles. The Center option shows it centered on the screen. If you choose the Center option, you can click Change Background Color to color the desktop surrounding the picture.

If you don't want a picture on your desktop, choose Solid Color from the drop-down list. Then click a color you like.

Making text sharper with ClearType

ClearType is a technology that makes fonts look clearer and smoother on a display. ClearType is particularly effective for LCD and LED displays but can have some effect on CRT displays as well. Windows 10 supports ClearType.

To adjust ClearType on your Windows 10 computer, first open the Display applet from the Control Panel. Then click Adjust ClearType Text. The ClearType Text Tuner appears (see Figure 9.6).

FIGURE 9.6

The ClearType Text Tuner.

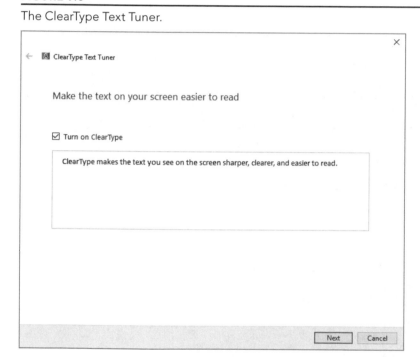

The ClearType Text Tuner is a wizard that steps you through a couple of settings to fine-tune the font display on your computer. Select the Turn On ClearType check box and then click Next. Windows 10 checks your computer's display resolution and offers to change resolution to the display's native resolution or keep the current resolution. Choose the desired option and click Next. Windows 10 then displays four pages with different text samples, prompting you to choose the ones that look the best to you. Click Finish when you're satisfied with your selections.

Personalizing sound effects

You may have noticed some little beeps and whistles as you work in Windows 10. Those are called *sound effects,* and you can customize them from the Personalization window. Just click Themes in the Personalization window and click Advanced Sound Settings to open the Sound dialog box, shown in Figure 9.7.

TIP

You can also open the Sound dialog box from the Control Panel.

FIGURE 9.7

The Sound dialog box.

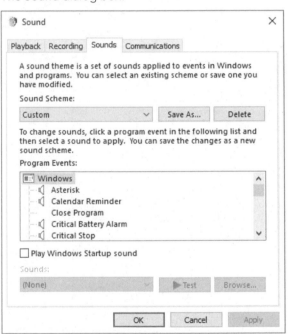

If you don't want to assign sound effects one at a time, you can choose a predefined sound effects scheme from the Sound Scheme drop-down list. Choose No Sounds if you don't want any sound effects.

The Program Events list shows the events to which you can assign sounds. Items that have a speaker icon to the left already have a sound effect associated with them. To hear one, click any program event that shows a speaker icon. The Sounds drop-down menu below the list shows the filename in which the sound effect is stored. Click the Play button to the right of the sound effect name to hear that sound effect.

Sound effects play only when your computer has a sound card with speakers plugged into the correct jack. If the speakers have their own power switch, it must be turned on. Likewise, if the speakers have their own volume control, the volume must be turned up high enough. And if the speakers have a Mute button, it must be turned off. Likewise, the volume control in the notification area must have its volume set to a level you can hear and must not be muted, as in Figure 9.8.

In the Sound dialog box, you can assign any sound effect you like to any program event. First, click the program event to which you would like to assign or change a sound effect. Then click the drop-down button under Sounds to see a list of built-in sound effects. Click the sound effect you'd like to assign. Then click the Play button to hear that sound effect.

FIGURE 9.8

The Windows 10 Volume control.

If you have your own sound effect to assign to a program event, click the Browse button and navigate to the folder that contains your sound effects. Then double-click the sound effect you want to assign to the program event.

If you change the sound effects associated with program events, you can save that work as your own sound scheme. Click the Save As button and give the scheme a name.

Personalizing your screen saver

A screen saver is a moving picture or pattern that fills the screen after a period of inactivity. The name "screen saver" harkens back to the earlier days of computing when leaving a fixed image on the screen for too long a time could cause permanent damage to the screen. This type of burn-in still can be a problem with CRT displays but isn't generally a problem with LCD and LED displays, so a screen saver is typically optional nowadays. Still, it's a nice way to have your screen do something entertaining when the computer is on but nobody is using it. Plus, it can be a way to protect your computer from prying eyes when you walk away from it. Better still, lock your workstation before you leave.

In the Control Panel, open the Personalization page. In the Personalization window, click Screen Saver. The Screen Saver Settings dialog box shown in Figure 9.9 opens. Click the

9

drop-down button to see a list of screen savers from which you can choose. Click any name in that list to get a sneak peek at how it will look if you apply it.

FIGURE 9.9

The Screen Saver Settings dialog box.

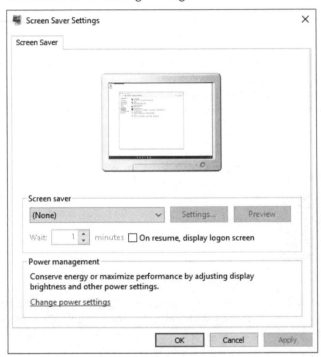

Some screen savers are customizable. Click the Settings button to see whether the screen saver you selected has optional settings you can change. If it does, you see those options in a dialog box. Choose any options that look interesting.

If you have pictures in the Photos app, choose Photos from the drop-down button. Windows 10 creates a slideshow of those pictures and uses it as a screen saver. If you choose Photos from the drop-down list, you can also click the Settings button to see the options shown in Figure 9.10.

FIGURE 9.10

Photo slideshow options.

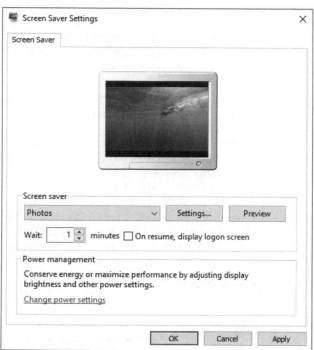

As shown in Figure 9.10, the default setting is for the screen saver to show all pictures and videos from your Pictures library, which includes your own Pictures folder and the Public Pictures folder. You can click Browse to choose a different location, if you prefer.

Click the Slide Show Speed drop-down button to choose the slideshow speed, and choose the Shuffle Pictures option to have Windows randomize the photo selection. Click Save after making your choices.

Regardless of which screen saver and settings you choose, the small preview window in the dialog box shows you how it will look. For a larger view, click the Preview button. Your selected screen saver plays full screen. To make it stop, just move your mouse.

After you've chosen your screen saver, specify how many minutes of inactivity are required before the screen saver starts playing. A period of inactivity means that nobody has touched the touchscreen, mouse, or keyboard. So, if you set the Wait option to five minutes, the screen saver kicks in after the computer has been unused for five minutes. The screen saver plays until someone moves the mouse or presses a key on the keyboard.

Choosing On Resume, Display Logon Screen causes the screen saver to show the login page rather than your desktop when someone moves the mouse. If you're using a password-protected user account, showing the login page prevents that other person from accessing your desktop. It also means that when *you* want to start using the computer again, you have to enter your password to get back to your desktop. Your programs will still be running, so this isn't the same as logging out and logging back in again.

The screen saver doesn't kick in at all if your power options are set to turn off the monitor before the screen saver kicks in. The Change Power Settings link in the dialog box lets you check, and optionally change, when the monitor goes off.

For example, the Power Save plan turns off the monitor after 20 minutes. If you set the screen saver to kick in after 21 or more minutes, you'll never see the screen saver because the monitor will be off. If you prefer the screen saver to an empty screen, make sure to set the screen saver timeout to a shorter period than your screen power-off setting.

 See Chapter 31 for more information on using power options.

When you're happy with your screen saver selections, click OK. Remember that the screen saver doesn't play until you've left the computer alone and untouched for the number of minutes you specified in the Wait box on the Screen Saver Settings dialog box.

Personalizing desktop icons

In the Themes page of the Personalization window in the Settings app, you see a link titled Desktop Icon Settings. Click that link to see the dialog box shown in Figure 9.11. Select the check boxes for any icons you want to see on your desktop. Clear the check box for any icon you don't want to see. As always, choosing icons is purely a matter of personal taste. Also, you can change the icons you see on your desktop at any time. Click OK after choosing the icons you want to see.

Creating your own desktop icons

The Desktop Icons Settings dialog box shows only the few desktop icons built into Windows 10. Many programs you install create other desktop icons. You're also free to create your own desktop icons. Most desktop icons are just *shortcuts* to other places or programs.

Shortcut icons are unique in a couple of ways. For one, they show a little curved arrow like the example in Figure 9.12. For another, deleting a shortcut icon has no effect on the item that the shortcut opens. Instead, deleting a shortcut icon deletes only the icon.

The program or folder to which the icon referred still exists. You can still open that item through a non-shortcut method.

If you often go through a series of clicks or steps to open some item, creating a desktop shortcut makes opening that item quicker and easier. Go to the icon you normally click (or double-click) to open a program, folder, or document. Then right-click that icon and choose Send To ⇨ Desktop (Create Shortcut).

FIGURE 9.11

The Desktop Icon Settings dialog box.

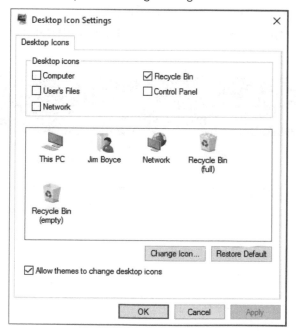

FIGURE 9.12

A sample shortcut icon.

Sizing, arranging, showing, and hiding desktop icons

You can size and arrange desktop icons as you see fit. First, minimize or close all open program windows so that you can see the entire desktop. Then right-click any empty area on the desktop and hover the mouse over the View menu.

The View submenu, shown in Figure 9.13, contains several options for arranging icons. An item on that menu that has a check mark is currently selected and active. An item without a check mark is deselected and inactive. Clicking an item selects it if it isn't already selected, or deselects it if it's selected. Here's what each option does:

- **Large Icons:** Shows desktop icons at a large size.
- **Medium Icons:** Shows desktop icons at a medium size.
- **Small Icons:** Shows desktop icons at a smaller size, similar to earlier Windows versions.

> **TIP**
>
> If your mouse has a wheel, you can make desktop icons almost any size by holding down the Ctrl key as you spin the mouse wheel.

FIGURE 9.13

The View submenu.

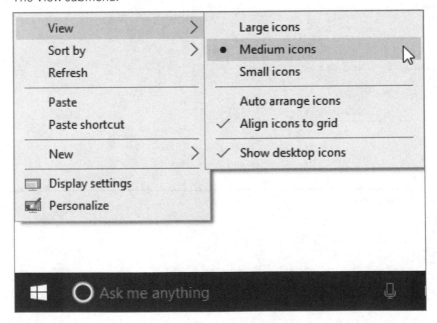

- **Auto Arrange Icons:** Choosing this option keeps icons neatly arranged near the left side of the desktop. If you clear this option, you can put desktop icons wherever you like. Just drag any icon to wherever you want to put it on the desktop.
- **Align Icons to Grid:** Choosing this option keeps icons aligned to an invisible grid. This option makes the spacing between the icons equal.
- **Show Desktop Icons:** If this option is selected (checked), desktop icons are visible. Clearing this option makes the desktop icons invisible. It doesn't delete them, however. They come back into view if you choose this option again.

The Sort By option on the desktop shortcut menu lets you quickly sort icons by name, size, file extension, or date modified. Regardless of which option you choose, built-in icons are always listed first, followed by your own custom icons in whatever order you specified.

The remaining options are similar to their counterparts in folders. The Refresh option ensures that icons on the desktop are up to date with changes you may have made elsewhere in the system. If you accidentally delete a shortcut icon, you can choose Undo Delete (or press Ctrl+Z) to bring it back. The New option lets you create a new folder or document on the desktop. Personalize opens the Personalization page (refer to Figure 9.1).

Customizing icons

To change a built-in icon, open the Desktop Icon Settings dialog box (refer to Figure 9.11). Then click the icon you want to customize, and click Change Icon. To change the appearance of a shortcut icon, right-click it and choose Properties ⇨ Change Icon. The Change Icon dialog box opens, displaying possible alternative icons. Figure 9.14 shows a general example.

FIGURE 9.14

The Change Icon dialog box.

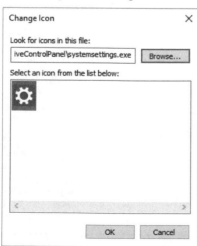

9

> **NOTE**
>
> Not all programs offer optional icons. If the Change Icon button is disabled, that means you can't change that particular icon.

If you have your own .ico files and would prefer to use one of those, click the Browse button in the Change Icon dialog box. Navigate to the folder that contains the .ico file and choose the icon you want to use. Note that some .dll and .exe files also contain icons you can use.

> **TIP**
>
> To explore programs that let you create your own icon pictures, search the web for "icon maker." To find pre-made icons that you can download, search the web using the keywords "download Windows icons."

Choosing a screen resolution

One of the changes you may want to make in Windows is to adjust your screen resolution. This setting determines how much of the desktop can fit on your screen. Resolution is measured in *pixels,* with each pixel representing a tiny, lighted dot on the screen. The higher the resolution, the smaller everything looks, and the more material you can get on the screen. To choose a resolution, right-click the desktop and choose Display Settings, then click Advanced Display Settings on the Display page. Doing so opens the Advanced Display Settings page shown in Figure 9.15.

Choosing a screen resolution setting is a trade-off. A high resolution is good because you can see more of the desktop on your screen. But a high resolution isn't good if things are so small on your screen that you can't see them. On the Advanced Display Settings page, click the Resolution drop-down list and then choose the resolution you want to use. You may need a little trial and error to find a setting that you like.

Other Ways to Size Onscreen Elements

The resolution you choose sets only a basic default size for items on the screen. You have countless other ways to adjust the size of text, icons, and pictures on your screen, and they work no matter what resolution you choose. For example, holding down the Ctrl button while spinning your mouse wheel affects icon size. In Edge, you can hold the Ctrl button and press the – or + keys to change the size of pictures and text on your screen.

Many programs have a View option in their menus that lets you zoom in and out to make things larger or smaller. DPI scaling and the Accessibility Settings described later in this chapter offer many options for making items larger and easier to see onscreen.

FIGURE 9.15

The Customize Your Display page.

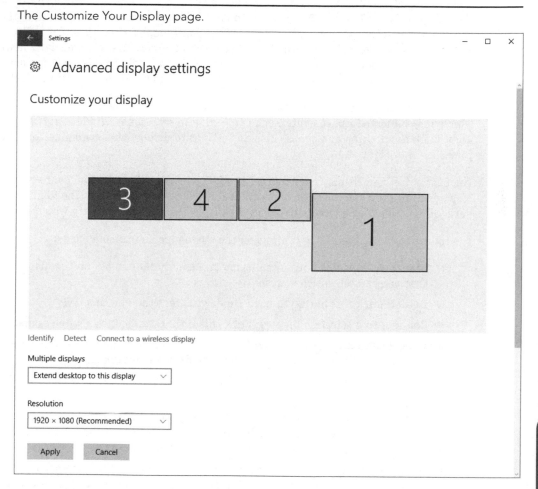

Choose a resolution (for example, 1920 ⇨ 1080) and then click or tap the Apply button. The new resolution is applied to your screen. If the screen goes blank, don't panic: You chose a setting that doesn't work. The setting will be undone automatically in about 15 seconds and everything will be okay again. To try a different resolution, choose another setting and click Apply again. When you find a setting you like, click OK.

Using multiple monitors

Windows 10 supports the use of multiple monitors in a variety of configurations. In many cases, adding a second monitor is a simple matter of connecting to the external monitor and turning it on. If the display supports Extended Display Identification Data (EDID), Windows detects it and adjusts the resolution automatically.

If the external monitor is a television set, you may need to connect, turn on the TV, and then use the Input Select or TV/Video button on the TV or remote control to select the external input (often shown as HDMI, AV1, PC, or Component on the TV screen). You can also add multiple video cards to the PC and connect a monitor to each one. Many newer display adapters support multiple monitors, so you can use a single adapter to drive more than one monitor. Another option is to use a docking station that supports multiple displays.

After you connect to an external monitor and configure it to show input from the plug to which you connected the computer, you can configure settings in Windows for the displays. Right-click the desktop and choose Display Settings to display the Customize Your Display page shown in Figure 9.16.

The Customize Your Display page shows the additional displays after you connect the other displays to the computer. The displays are identified by numbers. Click the Identify link to have Windows display a large number on the display to help you identify which is which.

The following list explains the controls on the Customize Your Display page:

- **Identify:** Click this button to display an identifying number on the displays so that you can tell which is which.
- **Detect:** Click this button to have Windows detect the new display.
- **Connect to a Wireless Display:** Click this link to connect to a wireless display.
- **Lock Rotation of This Display:** Set this option to On to prevent the selected display from automatically rotating when the device is rotated.
- **Adjust Brightness Level:** Use this slider to change the brightness of the selected display.
- **Change Brightness Automatically When Lighting Changes:** Set this option to On to allow Windows to automatically adjust the brightness of the selected display (if the device supports this feature).
- **Multiple Displays:** Choose Duplicate These Displays to display the same information on both displays. Choose Extend These Displays to extend the desktop across both displays. The other two options show the desktop only on display 1 or 2, depending on which you select.
- **Make This My Main Display:** Select this option to make the display number selected in the Display button the main display where the Start menu will appear.

> **TIP**
> Extending Microsoft Excel across two monitors enables you to see twice as many columns!

FIGURE 9.16

Display settings with two monitors working.

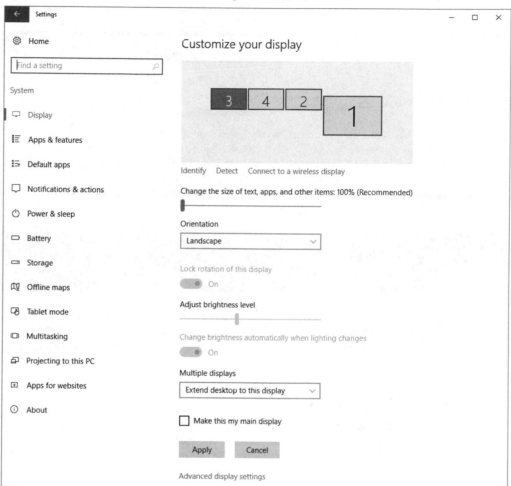

You can also display content on the second monitor only, leaving the first monitor black. If you're using a mobile computer on batteries, this option conserves battery power.

You can use the Customize Your Display page to configure the second monitor. Open the page as described at the beginning of this section. Then click the second monitor's box (with the number 2 in it). If that second monitor is grayed out, choose Extend My Desktop onto This Monitor. Then, click Apply.

More Stuff You Can Do with Monitors

Your monitor attaches to a graphics card or graphics chip inside your computer. That card or chip defines the full range of your visual display. Windows 10 might not give you access to the full range of settings available to you, even after you click the Advanced Display Settings link.

To take full advantage of your graphics card's (or chip's) capabilities, you may want to use the configuration program that came with that device. Many such devices are on the market, and there is no rule that applies to them all. To fully understand the capabilities of your graphics card and the programs for using it, refer to the manual that came with the card or your computer.

NOTE
If you can't get the second monitor to work, make sure it's properly connected and turned on. If the second monitor is a TV, make sure you choose the right input setting using Input Select or TV/Video on the TV or its remote control.

You can arrange the squares in the dialog box to match the arrangement of the monitors. For example, if monitor 2 is to the left of monitor 1, drag the 2 square to the left of the 1 square. If the monitors are stacked with 1 on top of 2, drag the 1 square so that it's above the 2 square.

Adjusting the font size (dpi)

Windows 10 lets you change the size of text and other items on the display, which can be particularly useful for high-resolution displays, making the screen more readable (which becomes more important as we get older!). To change text size, open the Customize Your Display page, and then use the slider control labeled Change the Size of Text, Apps, and Other Items to adjust the size.

NOTE
Be careful to increase the current percentage value only slightly. Otherwise, you might make things so huge that hardly anything fits on the screen.

The new setting will be applied after you log out and log back in again. If the items on your screen are too large, repeat the preceding steps, choosing a smaller size.

Adjusting the font size dpi isn't the only way to enlarge text on the screen. Many programs offer a Zoom option on their View menus that enables you to resize text. The Accessibility options described later in this chapter also offer some alternatives.

Personalizing your mouse

If you grow tired of the same old mouse pointer, or you need to make your mouse pointer easier to see, open the Start menu and choose Settings, then click or tap Devices, and then click or tap Mouse & Touchpad. You see the Mouse & Touchpad page shown in Figure 9.17.

FIGURE 9.17

The Mouse & Touchpad page.

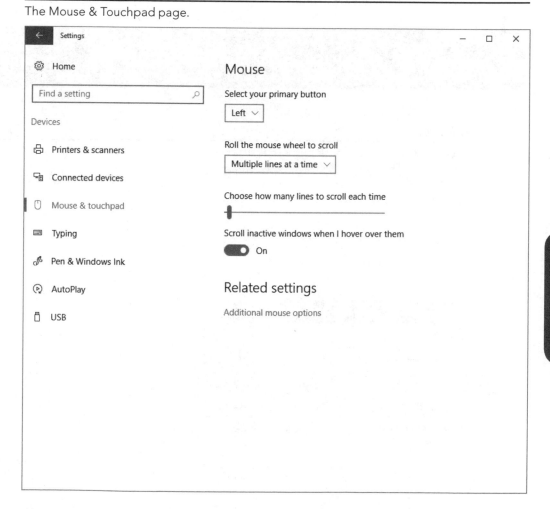

You can specify which button is primary (the button used to select items), whether to scroll by pages or lines using the mouse wheel, and how many lines to scroll at one time. In addition, you can turn on the ability to scroll a window without first activating that window (just hover the pointer over the window and use the mouse wheel to scroll).

You can also change advanced mouse settings. To do so, click the Additional Mouse Options link, which opens the Mouse Properties dialog box. To change your mouse pointers, click the Pointers tab (see Figure 9.18) and choose a scheme from the drop-down menu. The list under the Customize heading shows you how the pointers in that scheme look. You can keep all the mouse pointers in the scheme by clicking OK, or you can assign a mouse pointer of your own. Double-click the pointer you want to change, or click it and click the Browse button. Clicking Browse takes you to a folder named Cursors, which contains all the built-in Windows 10 mouse pointers.

TIP

After you click Browse, you can enlarge the mouse pointer icons in the Browse dialog box for a better look. Hold down the Ctrl key and spin your mouse wheel, or click the Views button and choose Medium icons or a larger size.

FIGURE 9.18

The Pointers tab in the Mouse Properties dialog box.

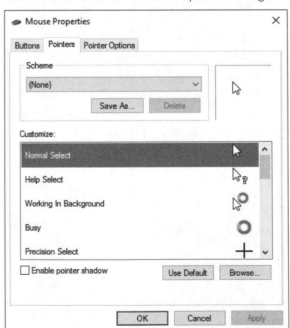

If you assign mouse pointers on a case-by-case basis, click the Save As button to save your selections as a theme with any name you like.

Mice for lefties

If you're left-handed and you want the main mouse button to be below your left index finger, you need to reverse the normal functioning of the buttons. Generally, the left mouse button is the primary button, and the right mouse button is the secondary button. To reverse that setup, open the Mouse page shown in Figure 9.17 and choose Right from the Select Your Primary Button drop-down button.

If you reverse your mouse buttons, you have to adjust all the standard mouse terminology accordingly. Table 10.1 shows how the various mouse terms apply to right-handed and left-handed settings.

TABLE 10.1   Mouse Terminology for Righties and Lefties

Standard Terminology	Righties	Lefties
Primary button	Left button	Right button
Secondary button	Right button	Left button
Click	Left button	Right button
Double-click	Left button	Right button
Drag	Left button	Right button
Right-click	Right button	Left button
Right-drag	Right button	Left button

Adjusting the double-click speed

To double-click an icon, you have to tap the primary mouse button twice very quickly. Otherwise, it counts as two single clicks. If you have trouble tapping the button quickly enough, or if you're so fast that two single clicks are being interpreted as a double-click, adjust the Double-Click speed slider on the Buttons tab of the Mouse Properties dialog box.

To test your current setting, double-click the folder icon. If the closed folder doesn't change to an open one (or vice versa), you didn't double-click fast enough. Move the slider box toward the slow end of the scale and try again. When the slider is at a place where you can easily open and close the little folder next to the slider, that's a good setting for you.

Using ClickLock

If you have difficulty selecting multiple items by dragging the mouse pointer through them, try activating the ClickLock feature. This feature lets you select multiple items without holding down the mouse button. First, choose Turn On ClickLock on the Buttons tab of the Mouse Properties dialog box. Then use the Settings button to specify how long you want to hold down the primary mouse button before the key is "locked."

For example, turn on ClickLock and set the required delay to about one second. To drag the mouse pointer through some items, position the mouse pointer where you plan to start selecting and hold down the mouse pointer for one second. Then release the mouse button and move the mouse pointer through the items you want to select. Those items will be selected as though you were actually holding down the left mouse button.

When you've finished selecting, click some area outside the selection. The mouse pointer returns to its normal function, and the items you selected remain selected.

Speed up or slow down the mouse pointer

Selecting the Pointer Options tab in the Mouse Properties dialog box reveals the options shown in Figure 9.19. The first option, Select a Pointer Speed, controls how far the mouse pointer on the screen moves relative to how far you move the mouse with your hand. If you have difficulty zeroing in on small things on your screen, drag the slider to the slow end of the scale. If you feel you have to move the mouse too much to get from one place to another on the screen, move the slider toward the fast end of the scale.

Selecting Enhance Pointer Precision makes it easier to move the mouse pointer short distances. This feature is especially useful if you move the pointer speed slider to the Fast side of the scale.

Making the mouse pointer more visible

If you keep losing sight of the mouse pointer on your screen, the following pointer options can make finding it easier:

- **Snap To:** If selected, this option causes the mouse pointer to jump to the default button (typically the OK button) automatically as soon as the dialog box opens.
- **Display Pointer Trails:** If selected, this causes the mouse pointer to leave a brief trail when you move it, making it easier to see the pointer.
- **Hide Pointer While Typing:** Clear this check box if you don't want Windows to hide the mouse pointer while you are typing.

- **Show Location of Pointer When I Press the CTRL Key:** If you select this option, you can easily locate the mouse pointer on your screen by holding down the Ctrl key.

FIGURE 9.19

The Pointer Options tab in the Mouse Properties dialog box.

Another way to make your mouse pointer more visible is to use a large or animated mouse pointer.

Changing mouse wheel behavior

The Wheel tab in the Mouse Properties dialog box lets you control how far you scroll when spinning the mouse wheel (if your mouse has one). The default is usually three lines per notch. But you can change that to any value from 1 to 100 lines. Optionally, you can configure the wheel to move an entire page with each notch.

NOTE

The Hardware tab in the Mouse Properties dialog box shows information about your mouse and provides a means for manually updating the mouse driver should the need ever arise.

Don't forget to click OK after making your selection in the Mouse Properties dialog box.

Personalizing the Keyboard

Windows 10 offers several ways to change how the keyboard works. Some are in the Keyboard Properties dialog box, which we cover here. Others are accessibility features and are set using the Ease of Access Center in the Control Panel (not covered in detail in this book). To get to the Keyboard Properties dialog box, open the Keyboard item from the Control Panel (see Figure 9.20).

No setting is right or wrong; you should choose settings that suit your typing style: The options in the Keyboard Properties dialog box are as follows:

- **Repeat Delay:** Determines how long you have to hold down a key before it starts autotyping (repeating itself automatically).
- **Repeat Rate:** Determines how fast the key types automatically while you're holding it down.
- **Cursor Blink Rate:** Determines how rapidly the cursor blinks in a document.

If your keyboard offers programmable buttons, you may not see any options in the Keyboard Properties dialog box for defining those keys. More likely, you need to install and use the program that came with the keyboard. Procedures for defining keys vary widely; consult the instructions that came with the keyboard or the keyboard manufacturer's website.

You can also change settings for the touch keyboard. To do so, open the Start menu and click or tap Settings, then click or tap Devices. Click or tap Typing to open the Typing page shown in Figure 9.21. The options on this page determine how Windows handles misspelled words.

FIGURE 9.20

The Keyboard Properties dialog box.

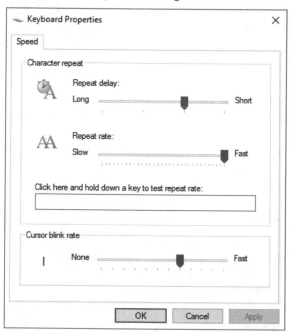

Customizing the Taskbar

The taskbar, which by default is at the bottom of your screen, is one of the most useful tools in Windows. It contains a button for each open desktop program window, icons for any programs that you've pinned to the taskbar, and the notification area. It can also contain some toolbars, such as the Address toolbar, which provides an easy way to open websites, drives, folders, or other items by their path or URL. You can customize the taskbar in many ways, so don't worry if your taskbar doesn't match what you see in this book.

FIGURE 9.21

The Typing page.

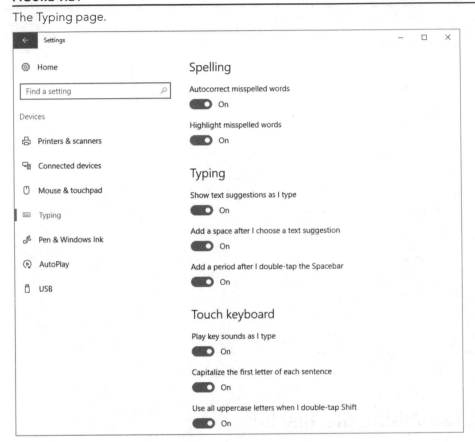

Some options for customizing the taskbar are in the Taskbar Properties dialog box. To open that dialog box, use one of the following techniques:

- Right-click any empty spot on the taskbar and choose Properties.
- Tap the Windows key, type **taskb**, and click Settings ➪ Taskbar Settings.
- In the Control Panel, choose Appearance and Personalization ➪ Taskbar and Navigation.

In the dialog box, select the Taskbar tab to see the options shown in Figure 9.22. The options on that tab are as follows:

- **Lock the Taskbar:** If you select this option, you lock the taskbar, which prevents you from accidentally moving or resizing it. If you want to move or resize the taskbar, deselect this option to unlock the taskbar.

- **Automatically Hide the Taskbar in Desktop Mode:** If you select this option, the taskbar automatically slides out of view in desktop mode when you're not using it, thereby freeing the little bit of screen space it takes up. After the taskbar hides itself, you can rest the tip of the mouse button on the thin line at the bottom of the screen to bring the taskbar out of hiding.

- **Automatically Hide the Taskbar in Tablet Mode:** This option is similar to the previous one, except that is applies to the taskbar when Windows 10 is running in tablet mode.

- **Use Small Taskbar Buttons:** Shows small icons rather than the larger, default-size icons for taskbar items.

- **Taskbar Location on Screen:** Choose on which edge of the display the taskbar will appear.

- **Combine Taskbar Buttons:** Choose whether Windows combines similar items on the taskbar (such as documents for the same program), and whether it combines icons all the time or only when the taskbar is full.

- **Notification Area:** Click the Customize button to specify which items appear in the taskbar's notification area (also called the *system tray*).

- **Replace Command Prompt with Windows PowerShell:** When this option is turned on, when you right-click the Start button, the Command Prompt item is replaced by PowerShell. Use this option if you frequently use PowerShell rather than the Command Prompt.

- **Show Badges on Taskbar Buttons:** Enable this option to show notification badges on the taskbar icons of modern and universal Windows apps. For example, the Mail app taskbar icon shows the number of unread messages in the Inbox when this option is enabled. You cannot control individual app badges.

- **Use Peek to Preview the Desktop:** Choose this option to hide all applications and show the desktop when you hover the mouse over the Show Desktop button at the far bottom-right of the display.

Click OK after making your selections from the dialog box. You can do some other things outside that dialog box to customize the taskbar, as described next.

9

FIGURE 9.22

The Taskbar tab in the Taskbar and Start Menu Properties dialog box.

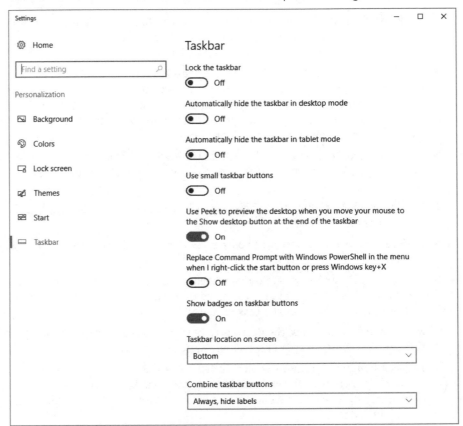

Locking and unlocking the taskbar

The taskbar doesn't have to be at the bottom of the screen, and it doesn't have to be a particular height. When the taskbar is unlocked, you can move and size it at will. If the taskbar is unlocked, putting the tip of the mouse pointer at the inside edge (toward the center of the display) of the taskbar changes the pointer to a two-headed arrow. Additionally, if you have any toolbars on the taskbar, you see a *dragging handle* (columns of dots) next to each toolbar. When you right-click an empty area of the taskbar or the current time, the Lock the Taskbar option on the menu is deselected (see Figure 9.23).

If the taskbar is locked, just right-click an empty area of the taskbar or the current time and click Lock the Taskbar to unlock. You can use the same procedure to lock the taskbar when it's unlocked.

FIGURE 9.23

An unlocked and expanded taskbar.

Moving and sizing the taskbar

When the taskbar is unlocked, you can dock it to any edge of the screen as follows:

1. Place the tip of the mouse pointer on an empty part of the taskbar (not in a toolbar or on a button).
2. Hold down the left mouse button, drag the taskbar to any screen edge, and release the mouse button.

To change the height of the taskbar, put the tip of the mouse pointer on the top of the taskbar so that it changes to a two-headed arrow. Then hold down the primary mouse button and drag up or down until the bar is at a height you like. The minimum height is one row tall. The maximum is about half of the screen.

> **TIP**
>
> If you have any problem getting the taskbar back to the original one-row tall size, close all open toolbars. Then size the taskbar to the height you want and choose the toolbars you want to view.

If you want to hide the taskbar altogether, select the Auto-Hide the Taskbar option in the Taskbar and Start Menu Properties dialog box, described earlier in this chapter. The taskbar stays hidden until you move the mouse pointer to the edge of the screen where you placed the taskbar.

Showing toolbars on the taskbar

Windows 10 comes with some optional toolbars you can add to the taskbar or allow to float freely on the desktop. To show or hide a toolbar, right-click the clock in the lower-right

9

corner of your screen or an empty part of the taskbar and choose Toolbars. You see the names of toolbars shown in Figure 9.24 and summarized here.

FIGURE 9.24

Show or hide optional toolbars.

- **Address:** Displays an Address bar like the one in your web browser. Typing a URL into the bar opens your web browser and the page at the URL.

- **Links:** Displays the contents of Internet Explorer's Links folder as a toolbar.

- **Desktop:** Shows all the icons from your desktop in a condensed toolbar format, along with OneDrive, Libraries, This PC, Network, Control Panel, and your user profile folder.

- **New Toolbar:** Create a custom toolbar containing icons from any folder you wish. For example, after choosing this option, click Documents under Libraries in the New Toolbar dialog box and click OK. The new toolbar that appears provides quick access to all your folders and documents in your Documents folder.

On the Toolbars menu, any toolbar that has a check mark next to its name is "on" and visible in the taskbar. Any toolbar whose name isn't selected is hidden. Click a name to hide, or show, the toolbar.

When you first choose a custom toolbar, you may not have room for it on the taskbar, especially if the taskbar already has many buttons or other toolbars. The next section explains ways to deal with that issue.

Sizing and positioning taskbar toolbars

You don't have much room on the taskbar, so it gets crowded if you add too many items to it. If you use lots of optional toolbars on your taskbar, consider making it taller so that it can show more items. Try moving it to the side of the screen to see whether that helps.

When you have more items on a toolbar than it can show, you see the >> symbol at the right side of the toolbar. Clicking that symbol shows the items that don't fit onscreen. If you have more open program windows than space for taskbar buttons, use the up and down arrows to the right of the visible taskbar buttons to see additional buttons.

> **TIP**
>
> You can switch from one open program window to the next by pressing Alt+Tab.

When the taskbar is unlocked, you see a dragging handle at the left side of each toolbar. You can drag those handles left and right to move and size toolbars. You can also show or hide the toolbar titles. Figure 9.25 shows an example of the titles, a handle, a resize cursor, and taskbar scrolling arrows.

FIGURE 9.25

Taskbar and toolbar handles, titles, resize cursor, and scrolling arrow button.

To show or hide the title or text, right-click the toolbar's title or dragging handle. Then choose Show Title to show or hide the toolbar's title. Click Show Text to show or hide text for icons on the toolbar.

> **NOTE**
>
> Text always appears next to icons when you click >> on a toolbar. The Show Text option has no effect on that behavior. To change the text that appears next to an icon, right-click that text, choose Rename, type the new name (or edit the existing name), and press Enter.

Customizing the Notification Area

The *notification area* (also called the *system tray*) appears at the right side of the taskbar. It contains icons for programs and services that are running in the *background,* which means they typically don't have program windows or taskbar buttons associated with them. Icons in the notification area represent features such as your antivirus software, volume control, and network connection. Pointing to an item displays its name or other information.

To conserve space on the taskbar, you can hide nonessential or inactive icons. When you have hidden items, you see a small up-facing arrow at the left side of the notification area, as shown in Figure 9.26. Click the arrow button (labeled Show Hidden Icons) to see the hidden items.

To customize the notification area icons, open the Taskbar page of the Settings app, and then click or tap the Turn System Icons On or Off link to see the options shown in Figure 9.27.

Use the buttons to show or hide the icon for the selected item. Any items that are disabled (dimmed) aren't relevant to your system, so don't worry about those.

FIGURE 9.26

The notification area.

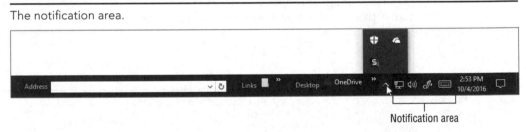

Notification area

Getting rid of notification area icons

You cannot delete a notification area icon by right-clicking and choosing Delete. Unlike toolbar icons, icons in the notification area are not shortcuts for opening programs. Icons in the notification area represent programs that are already running — even though they may be running in the background with nothing showing on the screen.

Getting rid of a notification area icon isn't easy. Hundreds of programs on the market can run in the background and thus can show up in your notification area. To remove such an icon, you may need to prevent that program from auto-starting with your computer, or you may need to remove the program from your system altogether. In some cases, you can simply go to the program's Options dialog box and deselect the check box that makes the program show a notification area icon.

FIGURE 9.27

The Turn System Icons On or Off page.

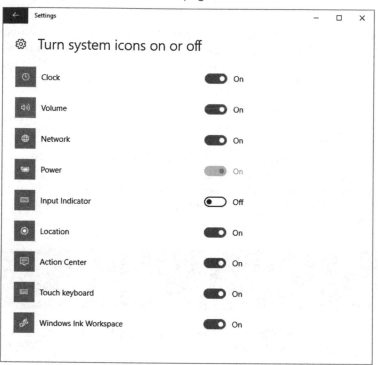

One thing's for sure: You shouldn't delete anything from the notification area unless you know exactly what you're deleting and why. For example, an icon may represent your virus or spyware protection. You shouldn't delete such programs, or prevent them from auto-starting, because you need them running in the background to keep your computer secure.

To see what options are available for a notification area icon, right-click the icon. Some programs that run as icons in the notification area can show up on the screen in a program window. Double-clicking a notification area icon usually opens the program that the icon represents. If the program has a menu bar, choosing Tools ⇨ Options may take you to a dialog box where you can prevent the program from auto-starting or prevent it from showing up in the notification area.

If the notification area icon represents a program you don't want on your system at all, you can remove the program through Control Panel. Just make sure you don't remove a program you need.

 See Chapter 27 for tips on removing programs.

If you want to keep a program but also want to prevent it from auto-starting — and you can't find a way to do that from within the program — other solutions are available. If the program has an icon in your Startup folder, you can remove that icon from that folder. Or you can use the System Configuration tool in the Administrative Tools folder to disable auto-starting of the program.

Tweaking the clock

The clock in the lower-right corner of the screen may look basic, but it's quite useful. If you point to the clock, you see the current date. If you click the clock, you see the current date marked on a calendar and the time on a clock face. If you right-click the time in the taskbar and choose Adjust Date/Time, you come to the page shown in Figure 9.28. There, you have several options.

> **NOTE**
> You need administrative privileges to change some aspects of the date and time. That may sound silly, but in a home environment, it keeps the kids from getting around parental controls that limit when they can use the computer.

You can allow Windows to automatically set the date and time by synchronizing with the time servers on the Internet. The default value for Set Time Automatically is On. Set this to Off if you do not want Windows to automatically synchronize the time and date. If this setting is turned off, you can click the Change button to set the date and time manually.

Use the Time Zone drop-down list to choose your time zone, and use the option Adjust for Daylight Saving Time Automatically if you want Windows to adjust the clock when daylight saving time is in effect.

The Formats settings show the format used by Windows for dates and times, and also specifies the day that Windows will use as the first day of the week. If you want to change these, click the Change Date and Time Formats link to open a page where you can set these values.

Finally, if you want to configure other settings, such as changing your location or adding additional time zones to be displayed in the clock, use the links in the Related Settings group (not shown in Figure 9.28) to do so.

FIGURE 9.28

Date and time properties.

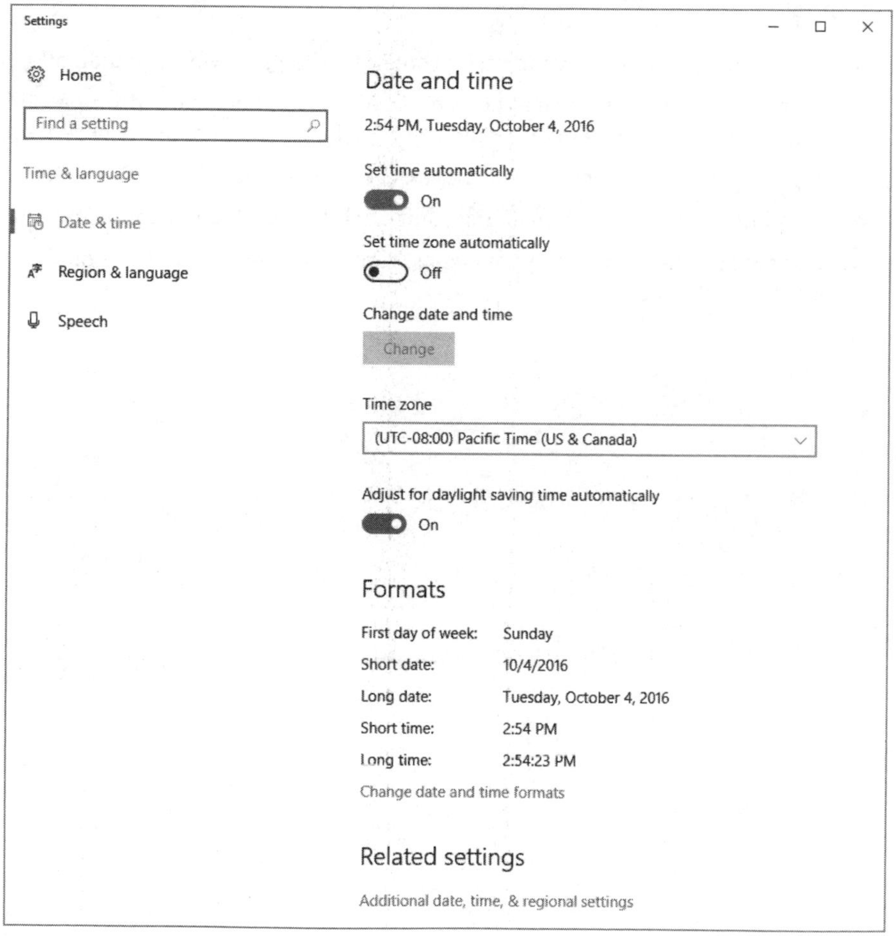

Settings		— □ ×
⚙ Home		
Find a setting 🔍	**Date and time**	
Time & language	2:54 PM, Tuesday, October 4, 2016	
🔂 Date & time	Set time automatically	
⚐ Region & language	⬤ On	
🎤 Speech	Set time zone automatically	
	⬤ Off	
	Change date and time	
	Change	
	Time zone	
	(UTC-08:00) Pacific Time (US & Canada) ⌄	
	Adjust for daylight saving time automatically	
	⬤ On	

Formats

First day of week: Sunday

Short date: 10/4/2016

Long date: Tuesday, October 4, 2016

Short time: 2:54 PM

Long time: 2:54:23 PM

Change date and time formats

Related settings

Additional date, time, & regional settings

Wrapping Up

This chapter has been all about the many ways you can customize the Windows desktop, Start menu, and taskbar to set up your screen in a way that works for you. You have many options. The important thing to keep in mind is that they are *options,* and no setting is right or wrong. You should make the choices that work best for you. Here's a quick recap of the essentials:

- The Windows desktop is your entire screen — the place where you do all your work.
- Many tools for personalizing your system are in the Personalization page of the Control Panel. To get there quickly, right-click the desktop and choose Personalize.
- To personalize your taskbar, right-click the taskbar and choose Properties.
- To add or remove taskbar toolbars, right-click the clock and choose Toolbars.
- To show or hide notification area icons, right-click the clock and choose Customize Notification Icons.

Customizing Startup Options

IN THIS CHAPTER

Understanding applications and services

Starting programs automatically

Preventing programs from auto starting

Managing services

Bypassing the login page

Your computer already has many programs and apps installed on it, and many thousands more that you can add to it. Many are programs that you can start at will from icons on the Start menu or desktop. Some programs start automatically when you log in. Often, these programs run in a window, as an icon on the taskbar, or both.

Another type of program starts automatically as soon as you start your computer. These are referred to as *services*, and services are most often part of the Windows operating system itself or programs that control hardware or other underlying functions. Services generally don't have program windows or have taskbar buttons on your desktop. In fact, you would likely never know that services existed unless you went looking for them.

This chapter is about controlling exactly which programs and services do, and don't, start automatically when you first start your computer and Windows. By controlling these programs, you can streamline the Windows startup and fix problems with performance or function. This chapter focuses primarily on legacy Windows programs rather than new Windows modern apps.

First Things First

First, we need to make a distinction between application programs and services. For the purposes of this chapter, an application program (or *application*) is a program that, when open, usually has a program window on your desktop and a rectangular button in the taskbar. Typically, you open and use such a program to perform some specific task, such as browse the web or perform spreadsheet tasks. Then you close the program when you've finished that task. To close such a program, you can typically click the Close (X) button in the program's upper-right corner or right-click the program's taskbar button and choose Close. You can reopen the program at any time by clicking its icon on the Start menu.

> **TIP**
>
> When in Tablet mode, modern Windows apps can be closed by grabbing the top edge of their window and dragging the app to the bottom of the display. Release the mouse button and the app closes. Or, move the pointer to the top of the window and wait until the close button appears, and then click the close button.

Services are also application programs, but services generally don't provide any means for the user to interact with them. Many services are included as part of the operating system. For example, the Windows Time service provides time synchronization functions for Windows, enabling it to set the computer's time from a remote time server. The DHCP Client service is another example of a service. It is responsible for, among other things, obtaining an IP address for your computer when the computer starts up (or when the address lease expires), enabling your computer to participate on the network.

Neither the Windows Time service nor the DHCP Client service provides any means for you to interact with them; they do their thing in the background with no input from you. In contrast, the Windows Firewall service provides a means for you to interact with it. Even so, Windows Firewall is still a service, and most of the time, you don't interact with it. Services such as this that provide a means for user interaction are by far the exception rather than the rule.

Why are we telling you about services and how they differ from other programs? In most cases, you don't need to manage services or control their startup, but in some situations, doing so is necessary. Most of the time, you're more concerned with which application programs start automatically. But it's important for you to understand the difference so that you can make an educated decision as to how to handle services. One of the main focuses of this chapter is to help you understand how to make programs start automatically that normally don't do so, how to stop certain programs from starting automatically, and why you would want to do either. Let's start with how you make programs start automatically.

Starting Programs Automatically

If you always use a certain program when you start your computer, you can configure Windows to start that program automatically. For example, maybe you use Microsoft Outlook all the time for your e-mail and want it to open as soon as you log in to the computer so that you don't have to start it yourself.

> **CAUTION**
>
> Be aware that some programs provide an option during the program setup wizard to turn on or off auto start features. For many programs that rely on constant network and/or Internet connectivity, you can almost bet that the program needs to auto start each time Windows starts. You may not need other programs, such as graphics tools, to start every time Windows launches, so consider deselecting the option to have the program start when Windows starts.

Using the Startup folder

You have a couple of ways to make programs start automatically when you log in. In previous versions of Windows (for example in Windows 7), you could access the Start menu from the Start button and All Programs menu. Neither Windows 8.1 nor Windows 10 provides this type of access to it. Similarly, you cannot use Search to directly find the Startup folder.

Fortunately, you can pin the Startup folder to the Start screen so you can quickly add or remove programs from it. To do that, use these steps:

1. Press Windows+X and then click Run.

2. Type **shell:startup** and click OK. File Explorer opens so you can see the contents of the Startup folder. Click the Programs folder in the Address bar to go back one subfolder so you can see the Startup subfolder listed in the main Explorer window. Figure 10.1 shows an example Startup folder. You also can enter the following path, using your user profile name in place of <username>:

   `C:\Users\<username>\AppData\Roaming\Microsoft\Windows\Start Menu\Programs`

FIGURE 10.1

The Startup folder.

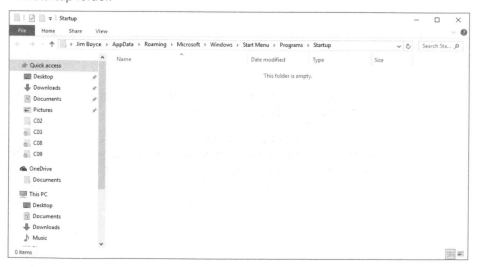

3. Right-click the Startup folder and choose Pin to Start on the context menu, as shown in Figure 10.2. A shortcut of the folder appears in the current folder view.

FIGURE 10.2

Pin the Startup folder to the Start screen.

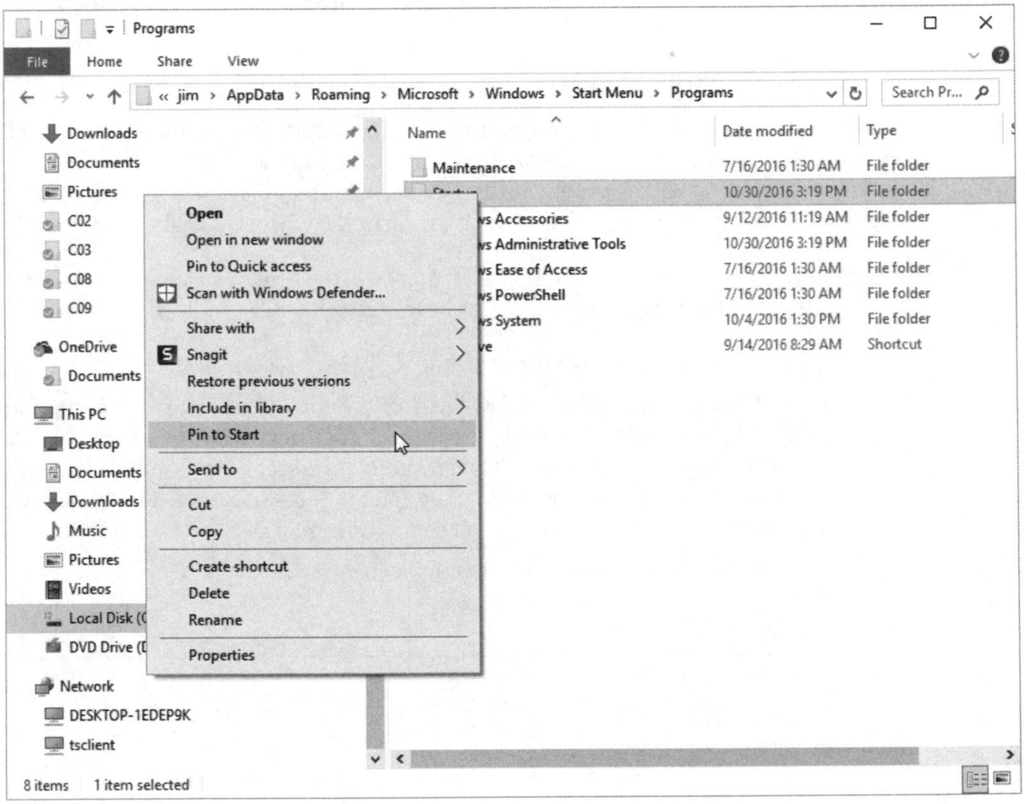

4. Open the Start menu and scroll through it to see the Startup folder pinned to the Start menu, as shown in Figure 10.3.

You can now open the Startup folder to view and manage programs that start when you boot up Windows. If you want a program to start automatically for you, put a shortcut for the program in your Startup folder. If you want a program to start automatically for everyone, you can instead put it in the Startup folder for all users.

FIGURE 10.3

The Startup folder pinned to the Start menu.

If you're already logged in to your user account and pinned the Startup folder to your Start menu, the steps to open your own Startup folder are easy:

1. Open the Start menu.

2. Scroll over until you see the Startup folder tile on the menu.

3. Click or tap that Startup folder tile. The folder opens as a folder on the desktop.

To make an application program auto start, right-drag (drag with the right mouse button) an icon for that program into the Startup folder and drop it there; then choose Create Shortcuts Here.

CAUTION

Keep in mind that the more programs you add to the folder, the longer your computer takes to start. So don't get carried away and put all your favorite programs in there. One or two shouldn't slow down the system.

10

If you're struggling to create a shortcut, open the file location where the application executable is stored, right-click the file, and choose Create Shortcut. Then move the resulting shortcut to the Startup folder.

Using the Task Manager Startup tab

You can use the Windows 10 Task Manager to help you manage and monitor running programs and services. Chapter 27 discusses Task Manager in detail, but it's worthwhile to mention now that you can view and disable properties of programs in your Startup folder with the Startup tab. To open Task Manager, right-click the Start button and choose Task Manager. Or, click or tap in the search box on the Start menu and type **Taskmgr**, and then click or tap on the Task Manager app, which appears at the top of the search results.

Figure 10.4 shows an example of a Startup tab (click More Details to view this tab). Notice the Status column. It tells you if a program is enabled or disabled. To disable a program, right-click the row on which it appears and click Disable. You also can click a program and click the Disable button at the bottom of the Task Manager window.

An interesting part of the Startup tab is the Startup Impact column. That column shows you the relative impact on your system when Windows starts a program automatically.

Stopping auto start applications

Should you ever change your mind about auto start applications, you just need to reopen that Startup folder for your user account. Then delete the shortcut icon for any program you don't want to auto start. Or, if you moved it from another location, move it back (out of the Startup folder). However, not all programs that auto start will be in the Startup folder for your user account. Some may be in the Startup folder for all users. (Still others will be in other locations.)

To view, and optionally remove, programs that start automatically in all user accounts, you need to get to the all users Startup folder, found at the following hidden location:

```
C:\ProgramData\Microsoft\Windows\Start Menu\Programs\Startup
```

You may need administrative privileges to make changes to that folder, so be prepared to enter an administrative password if you're working from a standard account.

FIGURE 10.4

The Startup tab of Task Manager.

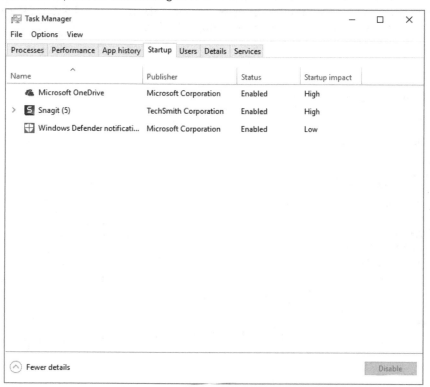

The Startup folder for all users works just like the Startup folder for a single user account. If you want a program to auto start in all user accounts, drag that program's icon into the folder. If you want to stop a program from auto starting in all user accounts, delete its icon from that Startup folder. But again, stick with programs you know. Removing programs from the Startup folder for all users at random could have unpleasant consequences that you weren't expecting.

Using the System Configuration Tool to Control Startup

One tool that has existed in multiple versions of Windows that lets you control program startup is the System Configuration program. That program is also available in Windows 10.

10

To open System Configuration, open the Control Panel, click Large Icons or Small Icons from the View By drop-down list, and click Administrative Tools. Double-click the System Configuration shortcut. Or, press Windows+R and enter **MSCONFIG** in the Run dialog box. Figure 10.5 shows the System Configuration program window.

FIGURE 10.5

The System Configuration program window.

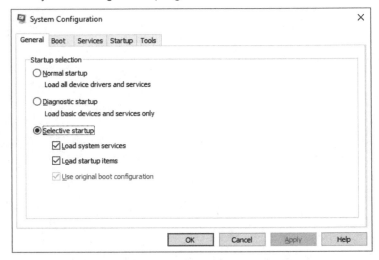

The General tab, shown in Figure 10.5, offers three options for controlling startup:

- **Normal Startup:** Start Windows normally. All items that normally start automatically are started.

- **Diagnostic Startup:** Load only basic device drivers and operating system services but not other services or programs. Use this option to troubleshoot problems with Windows startup that might be caused by a third-party service, device driver, or program.

- **Selective Startup:** Choose which types of items to start automatically. Start Windows with basic devices and services, and optionally other system services and startup programs.

The Boot tab, shown in Figure 10.6, lets you control how Windows boots. The large list box lists all the operating system boot selections. If Windows 10 is the only operating system on the computer, it is the only one listed in the text box. If you have a dual-boot system (for example, with Windows 8.x and Windows 10 on the same computer in different partitions), those additional operating system instances also are listed. Click an instance and then click Set as Default to make that operating system boot by default when the computer starts.

FIGURE 10.6

The Boot tab.

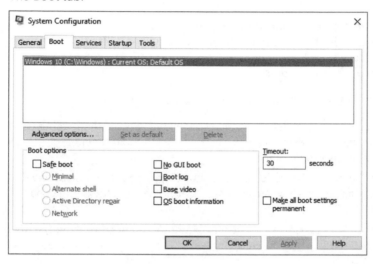

The other options under the Boot Options group enable you to configure options for a safe boot so that the next time you start Windows, it boots with the specified safe boot option. You can also set the following boot options:

- **Safe boot: Minimal:** Windows boots with a graphical user interface (File Explorer) in safe mode running only critical system services, with networking disabled.

- **Safe boot: Alternate shell:** Windows boots to a command prompt in safe mode running only critical system services, with networking and File Explorer disabled.

- **Safe boot: Active Directory repair:** Windows boots to File Explorer in safe mode running critical system services and Active Directory.

- **Safe boot: Network:** Windows boots to File Explorer in safe mode running only critical system services, with networking enabled.

- **No GUI boot:** Windows does not display the Windows Welcome screen when starting.

- **Boot log:** Windows stores logging information from the startup process in the file `%SystemRoot%Ntbtlog.txt`.

10

- **Base video:** Windows boots to File Explorer in minimal VGA mode, which loads standard VGA drivers instead of the video drivers that are specific to the video hardware installed in the device.

- **OS boot information:** Windows shows the names of drivers as the drivers are being loaded during the startup process.

- **Timeout:** This option specifies how long the boot menu is displayed before the default boot entry is automatically selected. The default is 30 seconds.

- **Make all boot settings permanent:** Use this option to have the settings apply for all subsequent boots. You can open System Configuration and change the settings later, as needed. This option is useful when you want to use the same troubleshooting options for several boots.

Click Advanced Options to access the following additional boot options:

- **Number of processors:** Select this check box and specify the number of processors to use on a multiprocessor system. The system will boot using only the number of processors in the drop-down list.

- **Maximum memory:** Use this option to limit the amount of memory available to Windows (simulating a low memory situation). The value in the text box is megabytes (MB).

- **PCI Lock:** Select this option to prevent Windows from reallocating I/O and IRQ resources on the PCI bus. Windows preserves the I/O and memory resources set by the BIOS or UEFI.

- **Debug:** Select this option to enable kernel-mode debugging for device driver development.

- **Global debug settings:** Specify the debugger connection settings on this PC for a kernel debugger to communicate with a debugger host. The debugger connection between the host and target PCs can be Serial, IEEE 1394, or USB.

- **Debug port:** Specify using Serial as the connection type and the serial port. The default port is COM 1.

- **Baud rate:** Specify the baud rate to use when Debug port is selected and the debug connection type is Serial. Valid values for baud are 9600, 19,200, 38,400, 57,600, and 115,200, with 115,200 being the default baud rate.

- **Channel:** Specify using 1394 as the debug connection type and specify the channel number to use. The value for the channel must be a decimal integer between 0 and 62, inclusive, and must match the channel number used by the host PC. The channel specified doesn't depend on the physical 1394 port chosen on the adapter. The default value for the channel is 0.

- **USB target name:** Specify a string value to use when the debug connection type is USB. This string can be any value.

The Services tab (shown in Figure 10.7) gives you a means to disable services so that they don't start when Windows boots. This tab also shows the current state of the services on the computer. Selecting the check box beside a service indicates that the service is enabled. You can disable a service by clearing its check box. If you want to view only third-party services, select the Hide All Microsoft Services check box. This helps you identify services that are not part of the Windows 10 operating system.

FIGURE 10.7

The Services tab.

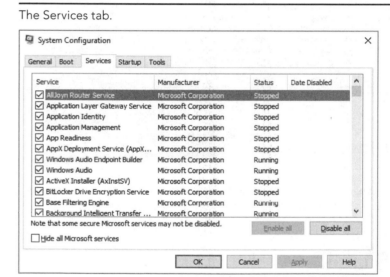

In general, you should avoid disabling services unless you know exactly what the service does and what the consequences of disabling it are. Usually, you want to disable a service only if a tech support engineer or some troubleshooting documentation has directed you to do so.

The Startup tab is pretty useless in Windows 10. It simply has a link to the new and improved Task Manager's Startup tab, which was discussed earlier in the chapter (refer to Figure 10.5).

10

The Tools tab (see Figure 10.8) gathers a selection of useful tools for troubleshooting problems with your computer and compiling more information about programs. Just click a tool and click Launch to open the tool.

FIGURE 10.8

The Tools tab.

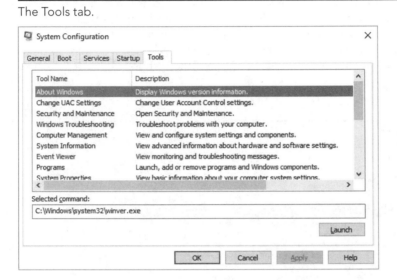

After you make changes to configuration settings in the System Configuration tool, you need to click OK and then restart the computer to make the changes take effect.

Services Snap-In

Windows 10 includes a system management framework tool called the Microsoft Management Console (MMC). The MMC provides access to various *snap-ins,* with each snap-in providing options for different configurations or an interface to manage items such as policies, accounts, and so on. One of these snap-ins is named Services.msc. It isn't a user-friendly program; instead, it's designed for professionals. Beginners and casual users are better off sticking with the Startup folders to work with auto start programs. Even so, beginners can start to understand how some of the underlying pieces of Windows work by looking through the Services console and checking out what some of the services do.

> **NOTE**
> If you want to make any changes in the Services snap-in, log out of any standard accounts and in to an account that has administrative privileges. Or right-click Services and choose Run as Administrator.

To start the Services snap-in, press Windows+R, and enter **SERVICES.MSC**. When the Services snap-in is open, use the View menu options to choose how you want to view icons. Figure 10.9 shows how things are displayed in the Detail view. The toolbar contains a couple of buttons for showing and hiding optional Console Tree and Action panes. (Both are shown in Figure 10.9.) Extended and Standard tabs are near the bottom of the window. Both tabs show the same information, but the Extended tab shows additional information about the selected service, with links for starting and stopping the service. The figure shows the Extended tab.

> **TIP**
>
> You can also start the Services console by opening it in the Administrative Tools folder of the Control Panel. Another way is to type **SERVICES.MSC** in the search box on the Windows Start menu, and click Services.msc in the search results.

FIGURE 10.9

The Services snap-in.

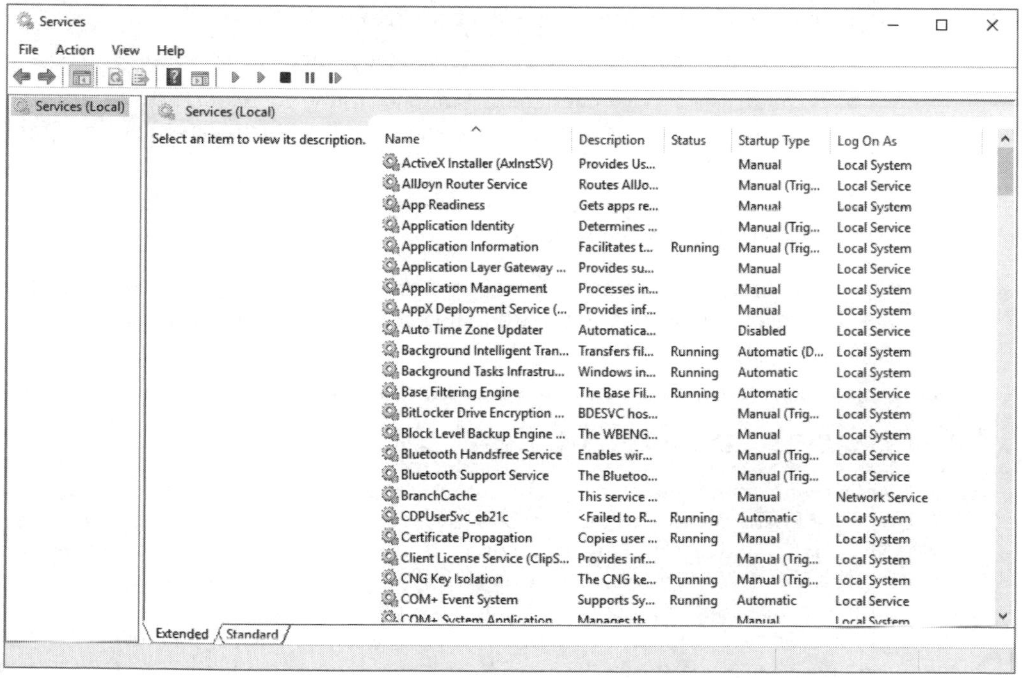

Selecting the Extended tab opens a new pane at the left side of the program window that shows detailed information about any service name you click. It also provides options to start a service that isn't running, or to stop or restart the service if it isn't running correctly.

> **NOTE**
>
> Because of enhanced security in Windows 10, you don't have as much leeway in starting and stopping services as you did in some earlier Windows versions. Some services can't be stopped at all if you don't have administrative privileges.

If you scroll through the list of services, you'll probably see quite a few. Exactly which services are listed varies from one computer to the next. Few, if any, of the services have any meaning to the average computer user. These things are of use only to professional programmers, network administrators, support technicians, or other experienced professionals. What follows is mainly for those folks. We don't summarize what each service does because doing so would eat up several pages and only repeat the information that's already in the Description column.

The Status column shows Running for those services that are currently running. It shows nothing for services that aren't running. The Startup Type column shows whether the service is configured to run automatically, if at all. Common settings are as follows:

- **Automatic (Delayed Start):** The service starts automatically, but only after a delay in time to enable other dependent services to start.
- **Automatic:** The service starts automatically when the computer starts.
- **Manual:** The service doesn't start automatically. You can start the service, however, by right-clicking the service name and choosing Start or by choosing Start from the Action menu.
- **Disabled:** The service is disabled and must be enabled from the Properties dialog box before it can be started.

To get more information about a service or change its Startup type, right-click the service name and choose Properties. You see a dialog box like the one in Figure 10.10.

What Does the DNS Client DO?

IP addresses are what *routers* (networking hardware that move data around) use to locate devices such as servers on the Internet and send traffic back and forth between devices. The DNS client service is called a *DNS resolver* and is critical for networking because it resolves hostnames such as www.wiley.com to IP addresses such as 208.211.179.146. When you type a URL into your web browser and press Enter, the DNS service contacts a Domain Name Server and gives it the hostname (in this example, www.wiley.com), and the name server responds with the IP address (or addresses) that corresponds to the hostname. Then the traffic (in this case, the request for the specified website) gets routed on the Internet to the server based on its IP address. Of course, you can browse the web for the rest of your life without knowing anything about DNS or IP addresses.

FIGURE 10.10

Properties for the DNS client service.

The options you see in Figure 10.10 are typical of the items listed in the Services snap-in. The Description text box provides a description of the services and tells what will happen if you disable or stop the service. The Path to Executable text box shows the location and name of the program that provides the service. The Startup Type option provides the Automatic (Delayed Start), Automatic, Manual, and Disabled options.

The buttons let you stop, pause, resume, or start the service. Some programs accept parameters, which you can add to the Start Parameters text box.

The Log On tab provides options for granting rights to services that need permissions to run. The Recovery tab provides options for dealing with problems when a service fails to start.

The Dependencies tab (see Figure 10.11) is one of the most important of the bunch because it specifies which services the current service depends on (if any) and which services depend on the current service. For example, DNS is a TCP/IP thing (which is the protocol used by the Internet and most modern local networks). If a service isn't starting and you can't figure out why, seeing what services the current one depends on might provide a clue. If the dependent service isn't running, the original one you're looking at can't start, so you need to go to its dependent service and make sure it's starting.

10

FIGURE 10.11

The DNS Client service Dependencies tab.

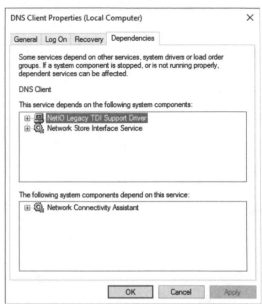

If you're interested in learning more about TCP/IP and how the Internet works, any book on TCP/IP or networking, or any book or course that prepares you for Microsoft Certified Systems Administrator (MCSA) or Microsoft Certified Systems Engineer (MCSE) certification, explains all that in depth. For broader technical coverage of services, consult a technical reference such as Microsoft TechNet at http://technet.microsoft.com.

For more information on Microsoft certifications, see www.microsoft.com/learning/en-us/default.aspx.

Bypassing the Login Page

This is one of those little Windows secrets everyone likes to know about but should be cautious about using. It lets you bypass the login screen and start up Windows 10 in a specific user account automatically. Although it does save you one click at startup, it means anyone who sits at your computer can just turn on the power switch and have full access to everything in the specified user account. Don't do this if you want to keep other people out of the specified user account.

This trick requires administrative privileges. So, you need to know the password or you need to log in to an administrative account first. Here are the steps:

1. Press Windows+R, and enter **netplwiz**. Or you can click in the Search box on the Start menu and enter **netplwiz**. Click netplwiz in the search results. The User Accounts dialog box appears, as shown in Figure 10.12.

FIGURE 10.12

The User Accounts dialog box.

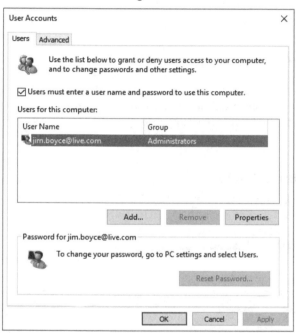

2. Grant permission or enter an administrative password if prompted.
3. Clear the Users Must Enter a User Name and Password to Use This Computer check box.
4. Click Apply.
5. In the dialog box that opens, type the name of the non-administrative user account to which you want to log in automatically.
6. If that user account requires a password, type the password once in the Password box and then again in the second box for confirmation. If the user account isn't password protected, leave both boxes empty.
7. Click OK in each open dialog box.

That's it. The next time you restart your computer, no login page appears. You're taken directly to your user account. If other user accounts exist on the computer, and you want

10

to let another user log in, log out of your account (click the Start button, the arrow next to the lock symbol, and choose Log Off). You're taken to the login page, which works normally. For example, if you want to get into a password-protected administrative account, click that account's icon and enter the correct password.

If you ever change your mind about booting without a logon, just repeat Steps 1 and 2 in the preceding list. This time, however, select the Users Must Enter a Username and Password to Use This Computer check box and click OK.

Troubleshooting Startup

Many things can prevent Windows from starting properly. No simple solution to the problem exists because too many things might be wrong. Typically, you need a professional to fix such problems. But we can tell you a few things that even the average user can try to get things going again.

Get rid of disabled devices

If your computer contains a hardware device that Windows 10 can't use, you should still be able to get to the desktop. But each time you do, you see a notification message about a device being disabled. That can get tiresome. If you manually disable the device through Device Manager, you don't see that message anymore. Also, Windows 10 should take a little less time to start.

> **CAUTION**
>
> Don't take wild guesses when you manually disable devices. If you disable a hardware device you really need, you may not be able to start Windows 10 at all! If in doubt, take the computer to a repair shop and let the pros figure it out.

To disable a device, you need to first log in to a user account that has administrative privileges. Then press Windows+X and click Device Manager on the Power menu. Expand the category to which the device belongs. If you're not sure which category to look in, try the Other Devices category. Look for a device whose icon shows an exclamation point in a tiny yellow triangle. After you find the device, right-click its name and choose Disable.

When you've disabled the device, the yellow icon changes to a white downward-pointing arrow. That means the device is disabled and Windows 10 won't try to reinstall it on future boot-ups, which should mean a slightly quicker boot-up time and no irritating message about the disabled device.

When Windows doesn't start at all

If Windows doesn't start at all, try to start Windows 10 in Safe Mode. This is a special mode in which Windows 10 loads only the minimum services, drivers, and programs it needs to get going. Getting to Safe Mode isn't always easy. Read Chapter 5 on how to enable Safe Mode in Windows 10 and how to boot into it after it's enabled.

Wrapping Up

This chapter has covered all the different ways you can control which programs do, and don't, automatically start when Windows first starts up or when you first log in to your Windows user account.

- Some programs have their own built-in options for choosing whether the program starts automatically and appears in the notification area.

- You can start any application program automatically, or even open a folder automatically, by adding a shortcut for the program to the Startup folder.

- The full set of services that can be started and stopped automatically is listed in the Services.msc snap-in.

- The Services.msc snap-in is an advanced tool designed for professional Information Technology workers and network engineers. As such, it contains very little information that would be useful to the average computer user.

- You can use netplwiz to bypass the login page and go straight to any user account you wish.

- Safe Mode provides a means of starting Windows 10 with the fewest drivers and services. It helps you get the system started so that you can diagnose and repair the problem that is preventing normal startup.

- Use the Navigation tab of the Taskbar and Navigation Properties dialog box to control how and when Windows 10 displays the Start screen and desktop.

10

Part III

Windows 10 for the Enterprise

IN THIS PART

Setting Up Windows 10 Hyper-V

Windows 10 includes native features for virtualizing the user's desktop using the Windows 10 Hyper-V features. Hyper-V lets you run other versions of Windows as well as other systems in a virtual environment on one physical computer. This lets you minimize the expense of purchasing multiple computers for running more than one operating system or network operating system.

To run Hyper-V on Windows, you must turn it on. By default it is disabled. Once you've turned it on, you can install a guest operating system, manage that operating system, and manage the guest from within the host environment. This chapter shows how to enable Hyper-V on Windows 10.

Understanding Windows 10 Hyper-V

Microsoft introduced virtualization to its desktop operating system with Windows 7. With virtualization, a user can set up a virtual copy of an operating system or network operating system within the virtual environment to run multiple instances of operating systems on one physical device. This physical device is called the *host;* the virtual system is called the *guest*. On the guest operating system, you can run applications, services, and other system tasks just as you do on a "normal" physical computer.

The software you set up on the host to run a virtual environment is called the *hypervisor,* or Hyper-V in Windows 10. Hyper-V is a Windows feature that you can enable using the Windows Feature tool of the Programs and Feature applet. Hyper-V runs on the host operating system, on which you can install an additional operating system. The host environment manages the guest Hyper-V environment, and in turn the guest environment manages the virtual system. These guest systems are called *virtual machines,* or VMs for short.

Understanding Hyper-V System Requirements

Before you can enable Hyper-V on your computer, your computer must meet minimum requirements. The following sections show the requirements and how to test your computer to check to see if its compatible with Hyper-V.

For each operating systems and network operating systems you run under a guest VM, you must have a separate license for each system. In addition, for each application you install, you must have the proper license or software agreement for each VM as well.

The following versions of Windows can be installed on a Windows 10 Hyper-V set up:

- Windows 10
- Windows 8.1
- Windows 8
- Windows 7, including Ultimate, Enterprise, and Professional editions (32-bit and 64-bit)
- Windows 7 with Service Pack 1 (SP 1), including Ultimate, Enterprise, and Professional editions (32-bit and 64-bit)
- Windows Vista with Service Pack 2 (SP2), including Business, Enterprise, and Ultimate, including N and KN editions
- Windows Server 2012 R2
- Windows Server 2012
- Windows Server 2008 R2 with Service Pack 1 (SP 1), including Datacenter, Enterprise, Standard and Web editions
- Windows Server 2008 with Service Pack 2 (SP 2), including Datacenter, Enterprise, Standard and Web editions (32-bit and 64-bit)
- Windows Home Server 2011
- Windows Small Business Server 2011

> **TIP**
>
> Several versions of Linux and Free-BSD are supported as VM guests under Windows 10. To get a full description of each and to read about modifications that some versions may require to operate best under Windows 10 Hyper-V, see the following site: https://technet.microsoft.com/windows-server-docs/compute/hyper-v/supported-linux-and-freebsd-virtual-machines-for-hyper-v-on-windows.

Windows 10 Operating System Requirements

The Windows10 operating system requirements that your computer must meet to run Hyper-V are as follows:

- Windows 10 Professional
- Windows 10 Enterprise
- Windows 10 Education

The following Windows 10 versions are *not* compatible with Hyper-V:

- Windows 10 Home
- Windows 10 Mobile
- Windows 10 Mobile Enterprise

If you have Windows 10 Home and need to run Hyper-V, you have the option of upgrading to the Windows 10 Professional version through the Update and Security feature in Windows Settings.

Computer Hardware Requirements

The following are the basic hardware requirements for running Hyper-V on your Windows 10 computer:

- CPU support for VM Monitor Mode Extension (VT-c on Intel CPUs)
- 64-bit Processor with Second Level Address Translation (SLAT)
- Minimum of 4 GB memory

Preparing Windows 10 Computers for Hyper-V

The following items must be enabled in the system BIOS:

- Virtualization Technology — may have a different label depending on motherboard manufacturer
- Hardware Enforced Data Execution Prevention

Before you plan to use a computer for hosting Hyper-V, you might want to run the Windows compatibility tool to ensure your system meets the basic requirements. To run this tool, perform the following steps:

1. Open a command prompt (cmd.exe).
2. Type syseminfo.exe and press enter.

Review the Hyper-V Requirements section (usually at the bottom of the list), as shown in Figure 11.1. Each should read Yes to ensure Hyper-V can run on your system.

FIGURE 11.1

Running systeminfo.exe to find out if your computer can be a Hyper-V host.

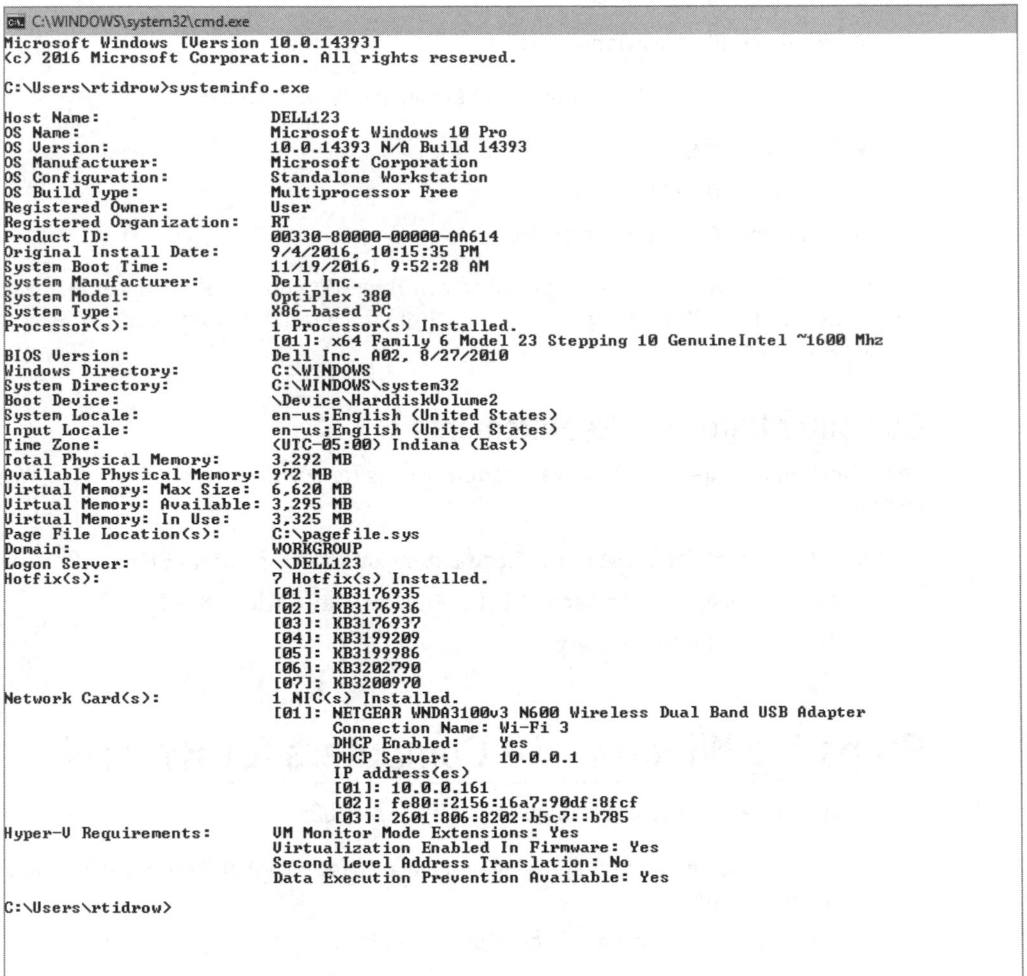

```
C:\WINDOWS\system32\cmd.exe
Microsoft Windows [Version 10.0.14393]
(c) 2016 Microsoft Corporation. All rights reserved.

C:\Users\rtidrow>systeminfo.exe

Host Name:                 DELL123
OS Name:                   Microsoft Windows 10 Pro
OS Version:                10.0.14393 N/A Build 14393
OS Manufacturer:           Microsoft Corporation
OS Configuration:          Standalone Workstation
OS Build Type:             Multiprocessor Free
Registered Owner:          User
Registered Organization:   RT
Product ID:                00330-80000-00000-AA614
Original Install Date:     9/4/2016, 10:15:35 PM
System Boot Time:          11/19/2016, 9:52:28 AM
System Manufacturer:       Dell Inc.
System Model:              OptiPlex 380
System Type:               X86-based PC
Processor(s):              1 Processor(s) Installed.
                           [01]: x64 Family 6 Model 23 Stepping 10 GenuineIntel ~1600 Mhz
BIOS Version:              Dell Inc. A02, 8/27/2010
Windows Directory:         C:\WINDOWS
System Directory:          C:\WINDOWS\system32
Boot Device:               \Device\HarddiskVolume2
System Locale:             en-us;English (United States)
Input Locale:              en-us;English (United States)
Time Zone:                 (UTC-05:00) Indiana (East)
Total Physical Memory:     3,292 MB
Available Physical Memory: 972 MB
Virtual Memory: Max Size:  6,620 MB
Virtual Memory: Available: 3,295 MB
Virtual Memory: In Use:    3,325 MB
Page File Location(s):     C:\pagefile.sys
Domain:                    WORKGROUP
Logon Server:              \\DELL123
Hotfix(s):                 7 Hotfix(s) Installed.
                           [01]: KB3176935
                           [02]: KB3176936
                           [03]: KB3176937
                           [04]: KB3199209
                           [05]: KB3199986
                           [06]: KB3202790
                           [07]: KB3200970
Network Card(s):           1 NIC(s) Installed.
                           [01]: NETGEAR WNDA3100v3 N600 Wireless Dual Band USB Adapter
                                 Connection Name: Wi-Fi 3
                                 DHCP Enabled:    Yes
                                 DHCP Server:     10.0.0.1
                                 IP address(es)
                                 [01]: 10.0.0.161
                                 [02]: fe80::2156:16a7:90df:8fcf
                                 [03]: 2601:806:8202:b5c7::b785
Hyper-V Requirements:      VM Monitor Mode Extensions: Yes
                           Virtualization Enabled In Firmware: Yes
                           Second Level Address Translation: No
                           Data Execution Prevention Available: Yes

C:\Users\rtidrow>
```

If any of the Hyper-V Requirements listed shows a No next to it, you must correct those issues before enabling Hyper-V. In some cases, you must use a different computer entirely.

Keep in mind that each VM requires its own hard drive space. You should have ample hard drive space to enable installing the guest operating system and all the programs and services you plan to run under the guest operating system.

As for memory, Windows10 with 4GB of RAM can run a few (such as three or four) basic virtual machines, but do not expect great performance. As you add VMs, you should add more RAM. Windows 10 can support VMs up to 32 processes and 512GB of RAM. Your host hardware, of course, must support this configuration.

Enabling Hyper-V on Windows 10

Before you start using Hyper-V, you must enable it on your host computer. Once you've enabled it, you can set up a hosted VM on your computer.

Follow these steps to enable Hyper-V on your Windows 10 computer:

1. Right-click the Start and click Programs and Features. The Programs and Features window displays (see Figure 11.2).

FIGURE 11.2

Click Turn Windows Features On or Off to enable the Hyper-V feature.

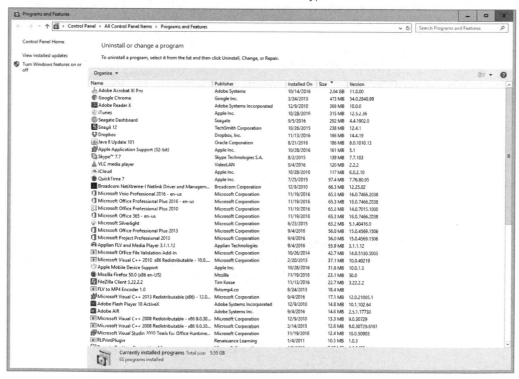

2. Click Turn Windows Features On or Off. The Windows Features dialog box appears (see Figure 11.3).

FIGURE 11.3

Select the Hyper-V option.

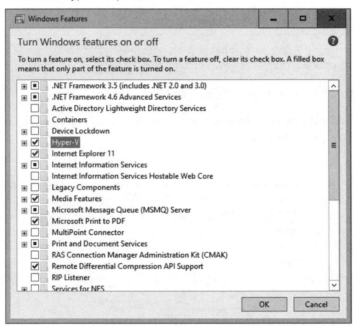

3. Select the Hyper-V option.
4. Click OK. You are prompted to restart your computer to finish enabling Windows 10 for Hyper-V (see Figure 11-4).
5. Click Restart Now to restart Windows 10.

Upon restart, log in to Windows as normal. You are now ready to configure Hyper-V and to set up a virtual machine (VM) on the host. See Chapter 12, "Configuring Windows 10 Hyper-V," for instructions on configuring and setting up the Hyper-V environment.

FIGURE 11.4

After enabling Hyper-V, Windows 10 must be restarted.

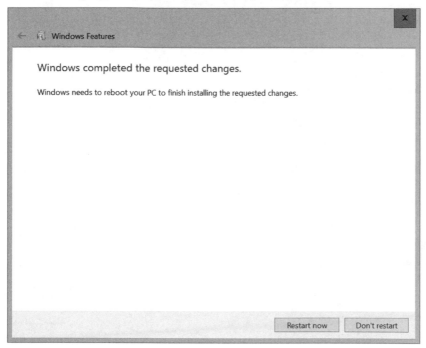

Wrapping Up

Windows 10's Hyper-V feature enables you to use one computer, called the *host*, to install other operating and network systems, called *guests*, in a virtualized environment. This chapter introduced the following points:

- Understanding Windows 10 Hyper-V
- Understanding Hyper-V system requirements
- Preparing Windows 10 computers for Hyper-V
- Enabling Hyper-V on Windows 10

Configuring Windows 10 Hyper-V

IN THIS CHAPTER

Running Hyper-V

Specify a virtual machine server

Creating virtual switches

Creating a virtual machine

In the previous chapter, you enabled Hyper-V as a feature on Windows 10. In this chapter, you learn how to configure the Hyper-V environment and install an operating system as a guest on a Windows 10 Hyper-V host.

To follow along in this chapter, you must first perform the tasks in Chapter 11 to ensure your environment is ready to be configured.

Running Hyper-V

Once Hyper-V is enabled on your host computer, you must start the Hyper-V manager to connect to the host *server,* which is the computer on which you want to run the guest virtual machines (VMs). You can choose to set up the VMs on your local computer (which this chapter shows how to do), or connect to a networked shared computer to set up a VM.

To start Hyper-V Manager, follow these steps:

1. Type **Hyper-V** in the Cortana search field and press Enter.
2. Select Hyper-V Manager from the Best Match list (see Figure 12.1). The Hyper-V Manager window appears.

FIGURE 12.1

Starting the Hyper-V Manager.

FIGURE 12.2

Displaying the Hyper-V Manager.

The Hyper-V Manager has three main panes. The left pane is the Console Pane, which displays all the servers that have VMs set up. Figure 12.2 shows a Console Pane that includes only the label "Hyper-V Manager," with no VMs set up yet. The middle pane includes information about Hyper-V Manager, and will also show information about items you selects in the Console Pane after you have VMs established.

The right pane is called the Action pane. The Action pane provides selectable actions you can perform based on selections you make in the Console pane.

Specify a Virtual Machine Server

To create a virtual machine (VM) server, you use the Hyper-V Manager. Among some of the settings you must select during this procedure is to establish the virtual hard disk location and folder in which you want to create the VM. Keep in mind the amount of space you will need for this task, because the VM folder must accommodate the guest operating system, its services, and any installed programs and apps you want to run on that guest. The following steps lead you through setting up a VM server:

1. Launch Hyper-V Manger.
2. In the Action pane, select Connect to Server. The Select Computer dialog box appears, as shown in Figure 12.3.

FIGURE 12.3

The Select Computer dialog box.

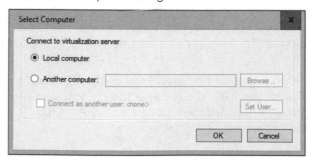

3. Click Local Computer to use your local computer as the VM host.
4. Click OK. Your computer name should appear under the Hyper-V Manager label in the Console pane. This is your VM host.
5. If your host is not selected in the Console pane, click your host. New actions appear in the Actions pane (see Figure 12.4).

FIGURE 12.4

Hyper-V Manager with actions in the Action pane.

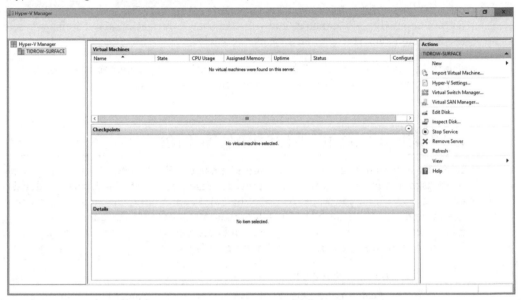

6. Select Hyper-V Settings in the Action pane. The Hyper-V Settings for your host dialog box appears (see Figure 12.5).

7. Select Virtual Hard Disks under the Server label on the left.

8. In the Virtual Hard Disks area on the right, confirm that the default folder is the one you want to use as your virtual hard disk. Or, click the Browse button and navigate to the hard disk you want to use. Click Apply if you select a different hard disk area.

9. Select Virtual Machines under the Server label on the left (see Figure 12.6). Confirm that the location for your virtual machine is the one you want to use for your VM. Or, click the Browse button and navigate to a different location you want to use. Click Apply if you select a different VM location.

FIGURE 12.5

Hyper-V Settings for your host dialog box.

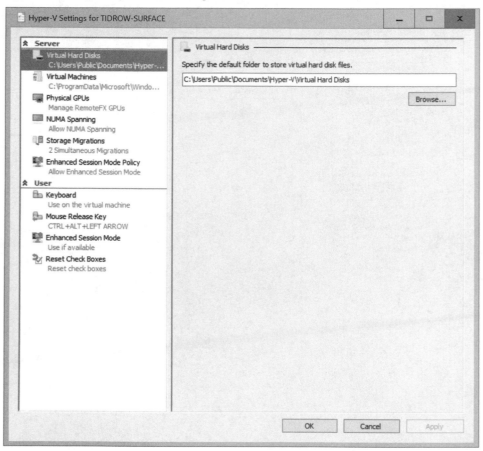

10. Click OK. This returns you to the Hyper-V Manager.

As you become more aware of the settings you may need for each VM, you can set those up as you create future VMs. For now, we are keeping the process simple so that you can get your first VM up and running.

FIGURE 12.6

Use the Hyper-V Settings dialog box to select the location of your virtual hard disk and virtual machine.

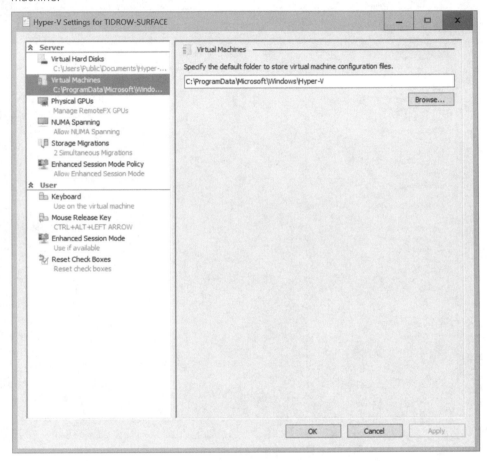

See the next section to continue setting up your first virtual machine.

Creating Virtual Switches

For your virtual machine to use network resources, you must set up a virtual switch. This enables the virtual network interface card (virtual NIC) to communicate with the physical NIC on your host computer.

You can set up three types of virtual switches:

- **External:** If your physical switch is connected to the Internet and you want your VM to connect to the Internet as well, use the external type of virtual switch.

- **Internal:** If you do not want your VM to have Internet access but you want your VM to communicate with other VMs on the same host, use the internal type of virtual switch.

- **Private:** If you want your VM to communicate only with other VMs that run on the host, use the private type of virtual switch. The private type does not allow communication between the host and the VM.

Use the following steps to set up a virtual switch that uses an external virtual switch type:

1. In the Hyper-V Manager window, select your VM in the Console pane.

2. Click Virtual Switch Manager in the Action pane. The Virtual Switch Manager window appears (see Figure 12.7).

FIGURE 12.7

Use Hyper-V Manager to set up a virtual switch for your VM.

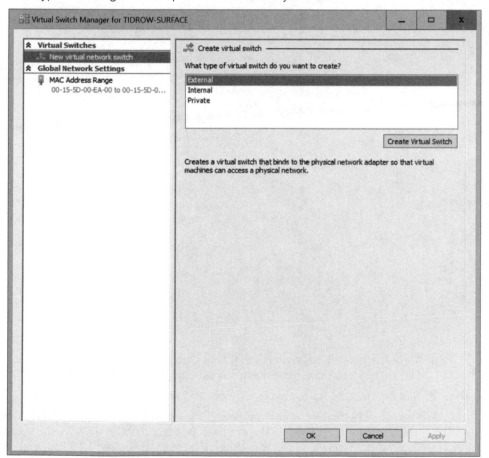

3. Click New Virtual Network Switch in the left pane.

4. Select External.

5. Click Create Virtual Switch. The Virtual Switch Manager appears (see Figure 12.8).

FIGURE 12.8

Use Virtual Switch Manager to set up the virtual switch type for your VM.

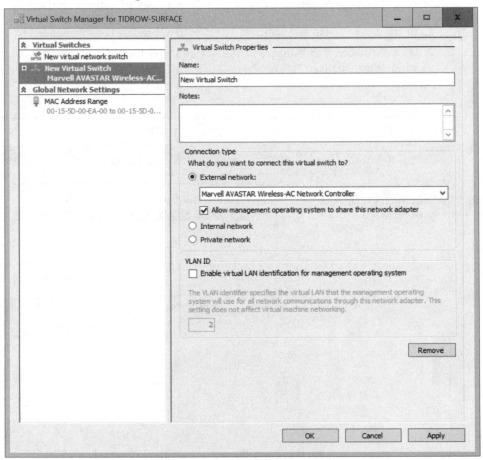

6. Name the new virtual switch something that makes sense to you, such as Acme External Switch (or use the name of your business or organization).

7. Add notes to the Notes area if you need to further identify this switch.

8. From the External Network drop-down list, select the network adapter you want to use for this virtual switch. The example uses Marvell AVASTAR Wireless-AC Network Controller. If your host includes other NICs, such as a wired LAN NIC, you can use it instead.

9. Click Apply.

10. You may see a warning that the new changes may disrupt network connectivity (see Figure 12.9). This disruption is temporary while changes are being applied. Click Yes to continue.

FIGURE 12.9

Your host network connectivity may be disrupted while the new virtual switch settings are being applied.

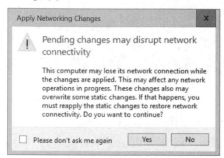

When the changes have been applied, the new virtual switch settings show on the left pane of the Virtual Switch dialog box.

11. Click OK.

When you set up an external virtual switch, your host computer starts using that new switch instead of its previous switch. A new Network Bridge is set up, which allows the host to use the new external virtual switch.

TIP

When setting up an external virtual switch, make sure to select the Allow Management Operating System to Share This Network Adapter. This ensures that both your VM and your physical host computer can use the physical NIC.

Creating a Virtual Machine

After you create a virtual switch, you can set up your virtual machine. To make your VM useable, you must install an operating system or network operating system to it. In this chapter, we use a copy of Windows 7 to illustrate how to set up a VM running an earlier version of Windows. You might want to do this if you need to run specific legacy software or devices on a system, deploy an older version of a web browser for a particular task (such as running older hardware controllers for a heating and air conditioning system), or similar reasons.

To install the operating system, you must have a copy of the operating system you want to deploy. You might, for example, have the original media or .ISO file for the operating system. Use the following steps to set up an operating system on your new virtual machine. These steps show how to set up Windows 8.1 on the VM, but you can use any operating system supported by Hyper-V and that you have on hand.

> **TIP**
>
> Microsoft provides users access to free evaluation copies of its operating systems (such as Windows) and its other software (such as Microsoft Office). You can download these evaluation versions at the Technet Evaluation Center located at http://www.microsoft.com/en-us/evalcenter. You're required to sign up for a Microsoft account, but the account is free as well. The evaluations can be used for a specified amount of time before they expire, such as 90 days. At or before the expiration time you must uninstall the product or purchase license(s) to continue using the product.

1. Launch Hyper-V Manager and select the virtual machine you just created.
2. Select the virtual server you want to use in the Console pane.
3. Choose Action ⇨ New ⇨ Virtual Machine. The New Virtual Machine Wizard appears (see Figure 10).

FIGURE 12.10

Use the New Virtual Machine Wizard to set up a new VM and install an operating system on it.

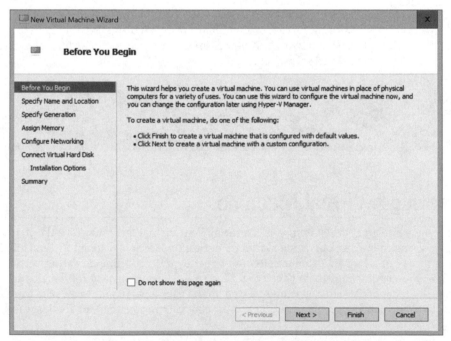

4. Click Next.

5. Enter a name for the virtual machine. For example, this example uses the name VM-WIN8-1. See Figure 12.11.

FIGURE 12.11

Enter the name of the new VM.

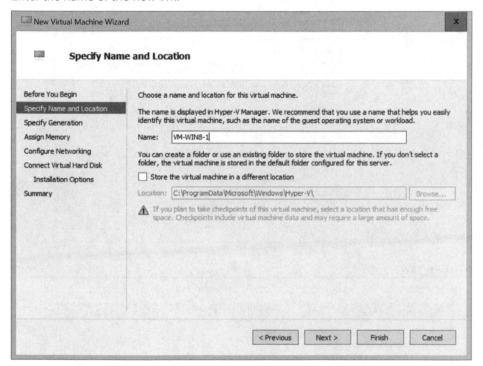

6. Click Next.

7. Select the type of generation for this virtual machine (see Figure 12-12). General 1 provides support for older systems, including 32-bit and 64-bit guest operating systems. General 2 supports newer features available in virtualization software and supports only 64-bit operating systems. This example uses Generation 1.

FIGURE 12.12

Select the type of VM generation to use. You can choose Generation 1 or Generation 2.

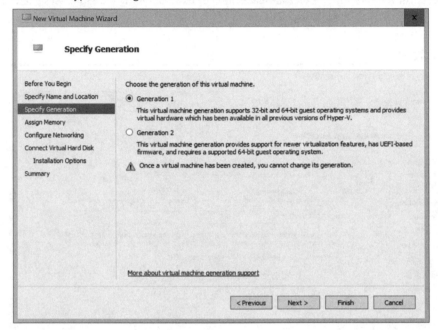

FIGURE 12.13

Specify the amount of memory to allocate for your VM.

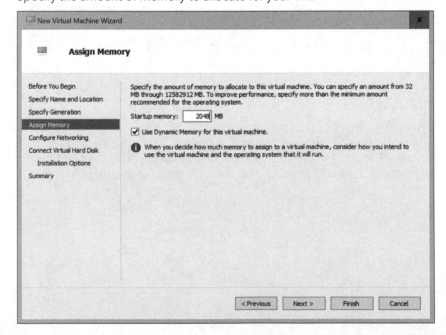

8. Click Next.

9. Enter 2048MB as the starting RAM for your new virtual machine (see Figure 12.13). You can increase this amount after your VM is configured if necessary.

10. Click Next.

11. On the Configure Networking wizard screen, click the Connection drop-down list and select the name of the virtual switch you created earlier in this chapter. The example (see Figure 12.14) uses a switch named Acme External Switch.

FIGURE 12.14

Select the virtual switch to use for your VM.

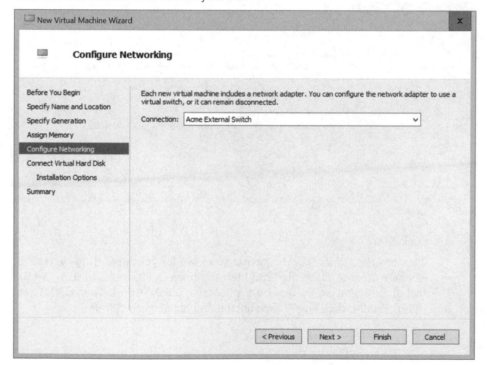

12. Click Next.

13. Create or select a virtual hard disk. In the example, we create a new one (see Figure 12.15).

FIGURE 12.15

Select the virtual hard disk for your VM.

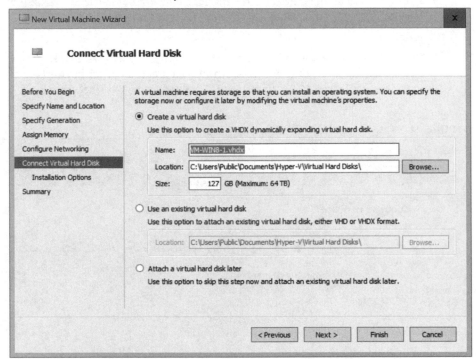

14. Click Next.

15. Click the type of installation media you have for your operating system. The example uses an image file (.ISO file), as shown in Figure 12.16. For .ISO files, click Install an Operating System from a Bootable CD/DVD-ROM. Then click Image File (.ISO). Finally, click the Browse button and locate your .ISO file.

FIGURE 12.16

Specify the installation media and location of the operating system you want to install on the new VM.

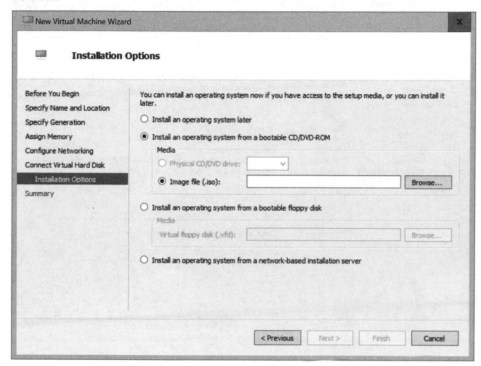

16. Click Next to see the summary of the new VM set up, such as the one shown in Figure 12.17.

FIGURE 12.17

This wizard screen shows the summary of the new VM.

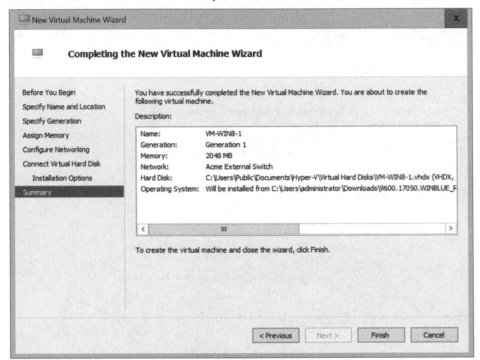

17. Click Finish. The Hyper-V Manager displays the new virtual machines and displays new options in the bottom part of the Actions pane listed under the name of the additional VM (VM-WIN8-1 in the example).

Now that the VM is set up and you have specified the operating system to install, you are still not quite finished. To finish, you must start the VM and then complete the installation of the new operating system on that VM. Use the following steps:

1. In the Hyper-V Manager, select the VM name.

2. Choose Action and then Start. The VM starts. Notice in the Hyper-V Manager that the word "Running" appears in the State column (see Figure 12.18).

3. Double-click the VM. A Virtual Machine Connection window appears, as shown in Figure 12.19. This window may now look familiar if you've ever installed a version of Windows 8 or similar operating system.

FIGURE 12.18

You must start the VM prior to completing the operating system installation on that VM.

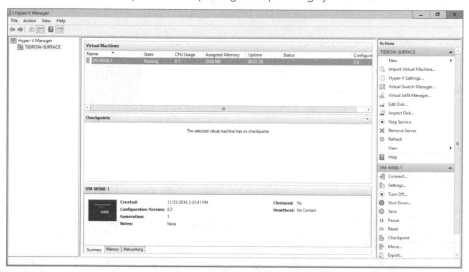

FIGURE 12.19

The Windows Setup screen appears in the Virtual Machine Connection window.

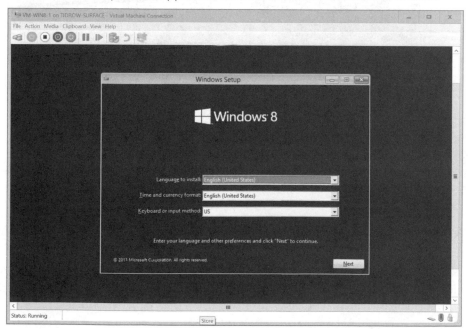

4. Work through the installation process for the virtual machine's operating system. This process can take some time depending on the operating system and the options you choose during the installation.

Figure 12.20 shows an example of how the virtual machine running Windows 8.1 displays inside the Virtual Machine Connection window. This copy of Windows behaves like any other Windows even though it is running inside the virtualized Hyper-V environment. You can install programs, use apps, configure settings, and other Windows tasks within that copy of Windows.

FIGURE 12.20

The finished virtual machine running Windows 8.1 evaluation.

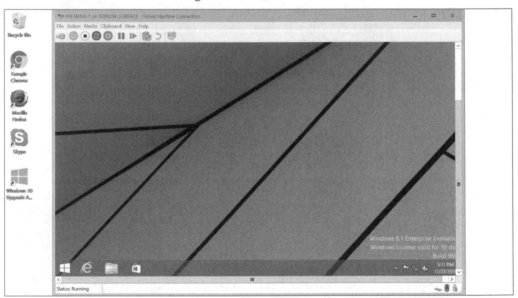

Wrapping Up

Setting up a virtual machine (VM) requires you to set up a virtual switch, specify the hard disks you plan to use, and set up the server (host computer) on which to run the virtualized environment.

After you set up a VM, you can install an operating system or even a network operating system (such as Microsoft Windows 2012 Server) on the virtual machine.

This chapter introduced the following points:

- Running Hyper-V
- Specifying a virtual machine server
- Creating virtual switches
- Creating a virtual machine

Using Computers Remotely

IN THIS CHAPTER

Getting Remote Assistance

Using Remote Desktop App

Using Classic Remote Desktop Connection

R emote Assistance lets you turn control of your computer over to a trusted expert for advice, troubleshooting, or general support. Remote Desktop allows you to control a remote computer from whatever computer you happen to be using. This chapter covers both of these topics.

Using Remote Assistance

Remote Assistance is a way to give control of your computer to a trusted expert. A trusted expert is any computer expert you trust not to damage your computer or steal any personal information. It may be someone from Desktop Support at your place of business. It may be a friend or relative who happens to be a computer expert. Whoever it is, you have to find that person yourself. Remote Assistance provides you with only the *ability* to let a trusted expert operate your computer from afar—it doesn't provide the trusted expert.

Remote Assistance and Firewalls

If you have any trouble using Remote Assistance, make sure that it's listed as an exception in Windows Firewall. To do so, open Windows Firewall from the Control Panel. Click the Allow an App or Feature through Windows Firewall link. Select Remote Assistance and click OK. Note that to send e-mail requests for Remote Assistance, you must enable Windows Remote Assistance for Public connections. In addition, if your computer sits behind a perimeter firewall (DSL router, wireless access point, or other hardware firewall), both your local firewall and the remote firewall must support Universal Plug and Play (UPnP) to support Remote Assistance without any special configuration. Or, if the firewall in front of the system requesting Remote Assistance doesn't support UPnP, you need to use port forwarding to get the incoming Remote Assistance traffic to the computer. How you set up port forwarding depends entirely on the type of firewall you have. Essentially, you need to create a rule in the firewall to forward incoming traffic for port 3389 to the computer that needs Remote Assistance. For additional information, contact your local ISP or contact your network administrator.

Setting up Remote Assistance

Before you try to use Remote Assistance, make sure that it's enabled in your user account. Doing so requires administrative privileges. You find options for enabling and disabling Remote Assistance in the System Properties dialog box. Here's a quick and easy way to get to those options:

1. At the Windows taskbar, start typing the word **assistance.** The Allow Remote Assistance Invitations to Be Sent from This Computer link appears in the results area. Clicking this option opens the System Properties dialog box direct to the Remote tab. (To open Remote Assistance open Control Panel and click the System option.) Choose the Allow Remote Access to Your Computer option in this dialog box.

2. If prompted, enter an administrative password. The Remote tab of the System Properties dialog box, shown in Figure 13.1, opens.

FIGURE 13.1

The Remote tab of the System Properties dialog box.

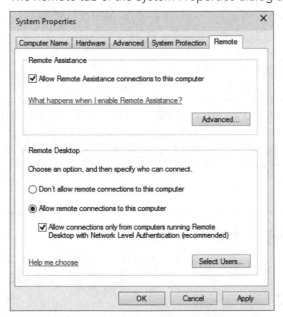

3. If you want to allow the computer to be used in Remote Assistance sessions, select the Allow Remote Assistance connections to this computer check box. Otherwise, the computer cannot be used for Remote Assistance.

4. Optionally, click the Advanced button. Then, to allow trusted experts to control the computer remotely, select the Allow this computer to be controlled remotely option.

5. Optionally, set a time limit on how long Remote Assistance invitations remain open, as shown in Figure 13.2. Also, you can limit Remote Assistance to other computers running Windows Vista or later versions of Windows.

6. Click OK.

7. Click OK again.

FIGURE 13.2

The Windows Remote Assistance Settings screen.

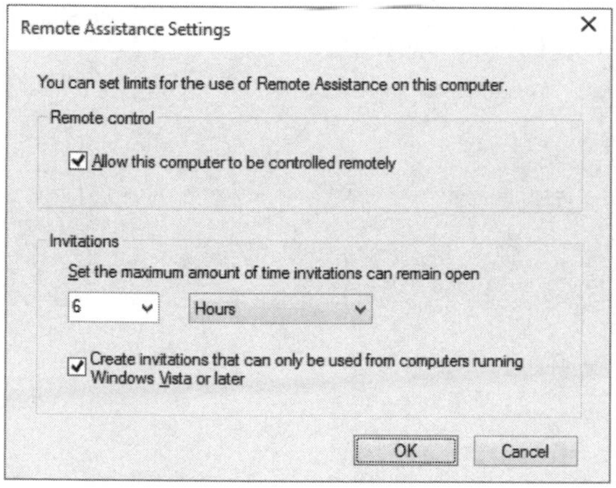

13

The next section assumes that you've allowed Remote Assistance in the preceding steps.

Requesting Remote Assistance

Before you allow a trusted expert to take over your computer online, you need to agree on a time. For security, you should agree over the phone or in person.

If you know the e-mail address of an expert you can trust to help with your computer, follow these steps and then send a Remote Assistance request:

1. Open Control Panel, choose System and Security, select Troubleshoot common computer problems, and then select Get help from a friend from the left side panel.

2. The Remote Assistance dialog loads with information on how to request Remote Assistance, as shown in Figure 13.3.

3. Click the Invite someone to help you option. A window like the one shown in Figure 13.4 appears.

How you proceed from there depends on how you use e-mail. If you use Windows Mail or another e-mail client that's compatible with Windows 10, follow these steps:

1. Click Use e-mail to send an invitation. You e-mail client loads with an invitation e-mail ready to send.

2. Type the expert's e-mail address in the To box and click Send.

3. If your e-mail client isn't configured to send mail immediately, open that program and perform a Send/Receive.

FIGURE 13.3

Creating an invitation for someone to help you solve a problem on your computer.

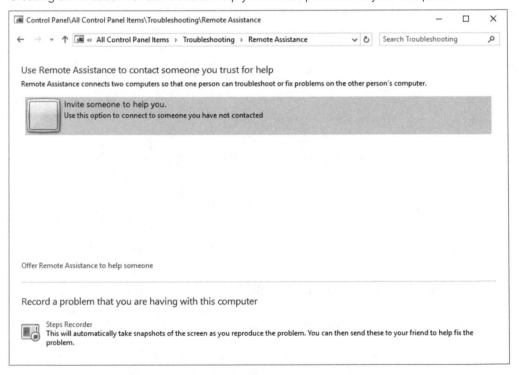

If you use a browser-based e-mail client, follow these steps instead:

1. Click Save this invitation as a file.

2. Choose a location in which to save the file and click Save.

3. Compose an e-mail message to the expert and attach the Invitation (or `Invitation.msrcincident`) file to that message using the standard method for your e-mail service. Then send the message normally.

FIGURE 13.4

The Windows Remote Assistance window.

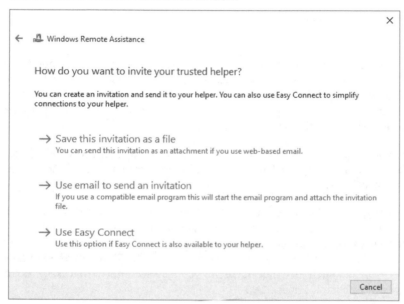

4. Compose a second message to the expert and enter the Remote Assistance password that shows on your screen. Send the message.

TIP

If you don't know how to attach files to messages, search your e-mail service's support using "Attach" as the keyword, or ask your trusted expert.

The e-mail message is sent to the trusted expert. In the meantime you will receive a Windows Remote Assistance message providing you with the helper's connection password. This is shown in Figure 13.5.

NOTE

If you close the Windows Remote Assistance window, your invitation expires and the expert won't be able to connect. If that happens, repeat the previous steps to create a new invitation.

FIGURE 13.5

The Windows Remote Assistance password window.

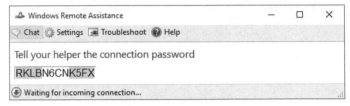

The trusted expert needs to receive your e-mail and open the attached file. Remember to also provide the password in the Remote Assistance window to your trusted expert. Remote Assistance doesn't send that password in the e-mail so you must send it to the other person in a separate e-mail or by phone. Then the trusted expert can enter the password in the Remote Assistance window on his or her end.

After your expert has done that, you see a new message on the screen (like the one shown in Figure 13.6), asking whether you're willing to allow that person to connect to your computer. Choose Yes.

When connected, the trusted expert sees your screen and options for chatting, requesting control of the computer, sending a file, and starting a voice conversation. To operate your computer from afar, the expert takes control of your computer, which he or she can do by clicking Request Control at her end. Depending on the Windows version that the trusted expert is using (such as Windows Vista), you may see another message asking if you're willing to share control. Choose Yes.

FIGURE 13.6

Allowing someone to connect to your computer.

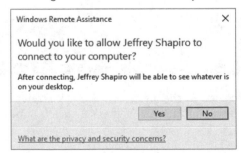

You can see everything the expert is doing while they have control of your computer. On your computer and the expert's computer, the following icons represent the main actions that can be performed in the Remote Assistance window for actions:

- **Request Control:** Seen from the helper's windows, this option allows the expert to take control of your computer from a remote location.

- **Stop Sharing:** On your side, this keeps the expert connected visually, but the expert can't operate your computer.

- **Pause:** On your side, this temporarily breaks the expert's connection to your computer. Click Continue to reestablish the connection.

- **Settings:** This takes you to a Settings dialog box, where you can opt to exchange contact information or save a log of the session. On your side, there is also an option to use the Esc button to stop sharing. This option is provided in case you lose control of your mouse and need to end the sharing immediately.

- **Chat:** This opens a chat window so that you and the expert can communicate during the session.

- **Help:** This opens Windows Help and Support.

At any time, you can click the Stop Sharing button on your screen to take back control of your computer. Similarly, the expert on the other end can click Stop Sharing to stop the sharing session and give you back control of your computer.

While the expert has control of your computer, he or she can use your computer just as you can. As the expert moves around your computer, opening applications, setting options, or displaying the Windows 10 interface, you can sit back and watch. This is one way in which you can learn new troubleshooting steps or application procedures if you're stumped on how to make something work or improve Windows performance.

When the expert has finished working or if you want to stop sharing your desktop, click the Stop Sharing button and close the Remote Assistance window. The expert can click the Disconnect button to end the session.

Using the Remote Desktop App

The Remote Desktop app allows you to control a computer from a remote location. It's often used to access computers on a corporate network from a home PC or vice versa. It's also very commonly used by system administrators to remotely manage Windows servers. The Remote Desktop app is different from Remote Assistance in that, with Remote Desktop app, you're remotely logging on to a computer and controlling it remotely as a single user. With Remote Assistance, the session includes the local user and the remote expert.

Before you can connect to a remote computer on your office network, a network administrator on the corporate side needs to set up that capability, enabling Remote Desktop Connection inbound to the network (or providing a VPN connection to the remote network for the user). Likewise, if you want to connect to your home computer from the office, you need to configure your home firewall to forward port 3389 to the home computer you want to manage. How you configure the firewall depends on the firewall, so we can't give you specific steps. At this point, we assume that whichever direction you're going, the necessary network and firewall changes are in place to make it possible.

> **TIP**
>
> If you're connecting to another computer on the same network segment as the one your computer is on, no local firewall configuration is needed other than having Remote Assistance in Windows Firewall enabled.

To connect to the remote computer, you need to know either the hostname of the computer or its IP address. If the computer is on your local network segment, you can use the computer name. To connect to a computer on a remote network segment, you need to use either the fully qualified domain name (FQDN) of the remote computer, a private IP address on a private network or its externally (public) facing IP address. This IP address is the public address that is mapped in the firewall to the private address assigned to the computer. The computers you connect to must be set up to allow Remote Desktop connectivity.

> **NOTE**
>
> An FQDN is a name in the common `host.domain.tld` format.

When you have the information you need, making the connection should be easy. You have to be online, of course. If the company requires connecting through a virtual private network (VPN), make that connection as specified by your company's network administrator. With Windows 10, you also have the option of using a Remote Desktop Gateway server, if your company allows it. With the Remote Desktop Gateway server, a VPN is not required to be set up.

Next, open Remote Desktop by clicking the Windows 10 Remote Desktop on your computer section of the All apps list. The Remote Desktop app opens, as shown, expanded, in Figure 13.7. If you can't find the Remote Desktop app for some reason, connect to Windows Store and search for Remote Desktop App and install it (don't confuse this app with the classic Remote Desktop Connection application, which is built in to Windows 10). The screen in Figure 13.7 appears.

When you first open the app, you can connect directly to a PC by entering the name in the search bar at the bottom of the screen. You can also connect to apps and desktops that an administrator has granted you access to, as well as connect to a corporate network by way of a Desktop Gateway server.

FIGURE 13.7

The Remote Desktop app.

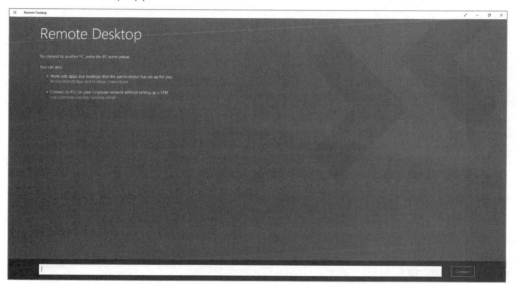

To add a connection, click the top left of the screen and select Settings. This brings up a window on the right side of the screen. Select Manage RemoteApp and desktops. Choose Add a new connection. Enter either the email address or the URL of the computer you wish to connect to.

If the remote computer is password protected, the Log In window appears, as shown in Figure 13.8. Enter credentials that will allow you access to the remote computer. If you don't have an account on the remote computer, or you don't know the username and password of a user on that remote computer, you aren't allowed to connect to it.

After you enter the credentials, you can click the Remember My Credentials check box to store those credentials for the remote computer. This enables you to connect to the remote computer next time without entering credentials. Click Connect.

If the identity of the remote computer cannot be verified or reached, the following message appears: "RemoteApp and desktop resources aren't available. Talk to your network administrator to find out how to access these resources" (see Figure 13.9).

FIGURE 13.8

Enter credentials to connect to the remote computer.

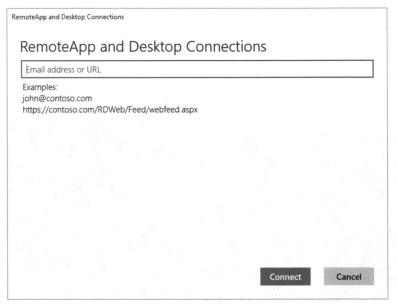

FIGURE 13.9

The Remote Desktop app cannot connect to a remote PC.

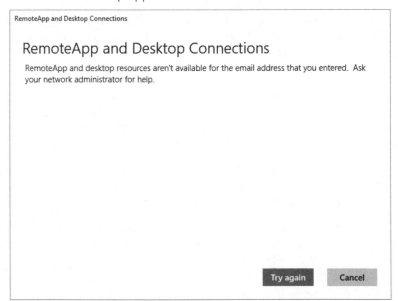

To connect to Remote App and desktops, you need to supply the email address or URL from your organization to gain access to the apps and desktops that you have authorization for.

Allowing remote connections on a home network

You can also use Remote Desktop to control your Windows 10 PC from any other PC within your home network. For example, say you have a notebook computer that you use for work, and a home computer for personal use. You no longer need to hook up a monitor, keyboard, or mouse to the home computer; instead, you can simply open a Remote Desktop connection to the home computer any time you need to use it. Likewise, you can connect to the other computers in the house when you need to fix something on them.

> **NOTE**
>
> Remote Desktop is not required for normal home networking tasks such as sharing folders, files, and printers. Nor is it required to access those shared resources. You use Remote Desktop only if you want to operate the remote computer from the screen, keyboard, and mouse on another computer in the network.

Because the notebook computer has a wireless connection to your home network, you can use your personal PCs from anywhere in the house, even outside on the deck when the weather is nice.

To set up this type of remote connection, you first need a home network. The computer you want to control remotely needs a version of Windows that offers Remote Desktop, including all versions of Windows 10, 8/8.1, Windows 7, Windows Vista, and Windows XP. Finally, you can log in only to password protected accounts on the Windows computer. The account can be a standard account, but it must be password protected.

The remote computer also must have an edition of Windows that supports Remote Desktop. Home editions of Windows, such as Windows 10 Home, do not include Remote Desktop capability, which would allow you to connect to them remotely. However, they include a client that enables them to connect to other computers that do support Remote Desktop.

Assuming that you have all the hardware and software to meet the requirements, the first step is to set up the Windows 10 computer to allow remote connections. Doing so requires administrative privileges and the following steps:

1. On the Windows 10 computer, log in to an account that has administrative privileges.
2. Display the Desktop.
3. Press Windows+X.
4. Launch Control Panel.
5. Choose Large Icons or Small Icons from the View By drop-down list.

13

6. Choose System and then click on the Advanced system shield icons in the left side of the dialog box. The System Properties dialog box now loads.

7. On the Remote tab, under the Remote Desktop heading, choose the Allow remote connections to this computer option.

> **NOTE**
>
> The last option in the list of Remote Desktop choices, NLA (Network Level Authentication), provides more-secure Remote Desktop connections but isn't available in older Windows versions. For more information, click the Help Me Choose link.

8. Click the Select Users button.

9. Use the Add button to add usernames of people who are allowed to connect remotely. The administrator is added to the list automatically. In Figure 13.10, we've added the username Kevin as the third person who can connect remotely.

10. Click OK in each open dialog box.

FIGURE 13.10

After adding a user (Kevin) as a Remote Desktop user.

Make sure you know the computer name or IP address of the Windows 10 computer. You can see the name to the right of the Computer Name label on the main page of System Properties. To find the IP address of the computer, log in to the computer you want to control remotely. On the desktop, press Windows+X and choose the Command prompt. Then type **ipconfig** in the command console window and press Enter. The IP address appears on the IPv4 Address line and is in a form similar to the following: 192.168.2.12.

Connecting from a remote home network PC

To connect remotely to the Windows 10 PC from another network in your local area network (LAN) or home network, you can also open the Remote Desktop app we discussed earlier on your local computer. However, for this task we will use the classic Remote Desktop

Connection application, which you can launch from the Windows Accessories in the All Apps list. See also the next section in this chapter.

In the window that opens, enter the remote computer's IP address or computer name and click Connect. If the user account name of the computer at which you're sitting is different from the user account on the Windows 10 computer, click Use Another User. Type in the username and password for the user account on the Windows 10 computer and click OK or press Enter.

Depending on the display settings you used for the connection, the remote computer's screen either appears in a window or fills your local display. If you're running the connection in full-screen mode, move the mouse to the top of the screen to access the connection bar, which you can use to minimize, restore, or close the connection. From the local computer, you use the remote computer exactly as you would if you were sitting at that computer. When you've finished with your remote session, log out of the remote user account. That is, click the connection bar and click the close button. If you're connecting remotely to an earlier version of Windows, such as Windows 8.1, 8, 7, or Windows Vista, click the Start button on the remote computer and choose the Log Off option.

For more information, check the Remote Desktop Help on both computers that you intend to use in your own local network.

Using Classic Remote Desktop

Although the new Windows 10 Remote Desktop app provides a Windows 10 interface and is easy to use, you may be more comfortable using the previous version of Remote Desktop Connection. If so, you can still run it, but you must launch it from its executable filename: MSTSC.EXE. Use either of these methods to launch it:

- Click the Start button, click on All apps, and from the Windows Accessories folder, click the Remote Desktop Connection icon.
- Open the command prompt. Type **MSTSC** and press Enter.

The Remote Desktop Connection window appears (see Figure 13.11).

Before you connect to a remote computer, you may want to click the Show Options button and look at the options on the various tabs. The only required option is the name or IP address of the computer to which you're connecting. The following sections describe the tabs and options.

Display

Use the Display Configuration settings on the Display tab (shown in Figure 13.12) to specify the screen resolution for the Remote Desktop Connection. If you have multiple monitors connected to the local computer, you can select the option Use All My Monitors for the Remote Session to span the Remote Desktop session across your multiple monitors.

FIGURE 13.11

The classic Remote Desktop Connection window.

FIGURE 13.12

The classic Remote Desktop Connection Display tab.

Use the Colors drop-down list to specify the color depth for the remote session. A lower color depth provides faster response for the remote session.

The Display the Connection Bar When I Use the Full Screen option, if enabled, causes Remote Desktop to display a connection bar at the top of the display when the remote session is using full-screen mode. Moving the mouse to the top of the display shows the connection bar, which then enables you to minimize, restore, or close the remote session window.

Local Resources

The settings on the Local Resources tab (shown in Figure 13.13) enable you to configure how Remote Desktop uses local and remote resources. For example, click the Settings button in the Remote Audio group to open a dialog box that enables you to specify whether Remote Desktop plays audio from the remote computer at the remote computer, brings it to your local computer, or does not play the sounds. You can also specify similar settings for remote recording.

FIGURE 13.13

The classic Remote Desktop Connection Local Resources tab.

Use the drop-down list in the Keyboard group to specify how Remote Desktop treats Windows key combinations such as Alt+Tab—sending them to the local computer or remote computer, or sending them to the remote computer only when using full-screen mode.

The Local Devices and Resources group lets you specify how local resources such as your printers, Windows Clipboard, ports, disk drives, and other resources are made available during the remote session. This capability can be extremely useful. For example, by enabling the drives on your local computer for the connection, you make them accessible in the File Manager on the remote computer. This means that you can easily drag and drop files between the two systems. By enabling the Clipboard, you can cut and paste between the systems.

Experience

The options on the Experience tab (see Figure 13.14) help you control the performance for the remote session. You can choose an option from the drop-down list, which determines which options in the list below the drop-down are enabled. You can also simply select the options you want to use.

FIGURE 13.14

The classic Remote Desktop Connection Experience tab.

Advanced

The Advanced tab (shown in Figure 13.15) offers options that control authentication alerts and Remote Desktop Gateway. The drop-down list on the Advanced tab lets you specify what action Remote Desktop Connection takes when you connect to a remote computer that doesn't satisfy the security requirements as defined by your local system security policy. You can choose to have Remote Desktop Connection drop the connection, warn you so that you can choose the action to take, or connect without warning you.

FIGURE 13.15

The classic Remote Desktop Connection Advanced tab.

The Settings button opens the RD Gateway Server Settings dialog box (see Figure 13.16), which lets you specify how Remote Desktop Connection works with a Terminal Services Gateway Server, now called Remote Desktop Gateway Server. RD Gateway acts essentially as an intermediary between your computer on the Internet and remote computers behind a firewall, such as at your office. RD Gateway uses SSL (port 443) rather than the usual port 3389 used by Remote Desktop Connection. RD Gateway, therefore, makes connecting to remote computers possible without having a VPN or opening port 3389 in the firewall. What's more, it enables connection to multiple back-end computers, rather than just the one that would otherwise be possible with a hole in the firewall for port 3389.

FIGURE 13.16

The RD Gateway Server Settings dialog box.

Remote Desktop Connection can detect the RD Gateway server settings automatically, or you can specify them manually. The first two options on the RD Gateway Server Settings dialog box let you specify which method to use. If you choose to specify the settings yourself, you can enter the server name, login method, and whether to bypass the gateway for computers on your local network. If you enter the settings manually, you also have the option of specifying that Remote Desktop Connection will use your RD Gateway credentials to authenticate on the remote computer to which you are connecting.

> **TIP**
>
> In most cases, you can open a remote session in Remote Desktop Connection without changing any options.

Wrapping Up

Remote Assistance and Remote Desktop Connection provide a means to both view and remotely control other computers. Key points of this chapter are as follows:

- If you know a trusted computer expert who can help with your computer, use Remote Assistance to get live help online.

- Some corporations allow employees to connect to a corporate network from home using Remote Desktop Connection.

- If you have a home network and suitable versions of Windows, you can use Remote Desktop to control one PC on the network from another PC in the same network, or from the Internet.

13

Managing Windows 10 Hyper-V in an Enterprise

A s the Windows 10 operating system grows more pervasive in the corporate world, managing Windows 10 clients becomes more important to the system administrator and other enterprise-level users. System administrators are tasked with becoming more familiar with Windows 10 to manage it in larger organizations.

Virtual machines are one way administrators have found to become more adept at Windows 10 features, application enrichments, device driver issues, and other elements of the operating system.

Understanding Hyper-V in Enterprises

Here are a few ways how running Hyper-V in an enterprise can be beneficial:

- Hyper-V provides a way to "try out" new operating systems without fully committing to them on production clients. If you are interested in a new operating system (say, the latest version of Windows 10), but you are not sure you are ready to take the plunge, fire up a Hyper-V virtual machine of the latest and greatest version and give it a spin. If you are not sure about jumping feet first into the latest version, simply remove the virtual machine and you are finished with it.

- Installing Hyper-V on a workstation, even an old workstation or laptop, enables you to install older versions of software to test how that software operates under Windows 10.

- Hyper-V provides a "closed" environment if you need it. With this environment, you can run tests on applications, device driver settings, network infrastructure modifications, and other tasks that you don't want on your production environment.

- Hyper-V enables administrators to set up multiple occurrences of operating systems, such as Windows 8, Windows 10, Linux, and so on, on a single computer. This makes it easy to test applications, device drivers, networking features, and more, without dedicating multiple computers for each operating system.

- Hyper-V provides a way to set up and customize organizational infrastructures on a single host. Once ready, that Hyper-V infrastructure can be exported and set up on another host or more powerful server hardware.

Migrating Virtual Machines

You can migrate a virtual machine from one host to another. This makes it convenient for testing operating systems, applications, and other issues. To migrate a virtual machine from one host to another, you use the Export Virtual Machine command and Import Virtual Machine wizard.

During the export process, files associated with that VM are bundled in the export. The bundle includes virtual hard drive files, checkpoints, and configuration files.

> **TIP**
>
> Keep in mind that when you place a virtual machine on a different host that the new host must have the same virtual switch settings as the original host. The host should use the exact same name as the old host (the host from which you are migrating the virtual machine). If the names do not match, when you migrate that VM to the new host, you will not have network connectivity. If this is the case, you need to go into the VM and manually set it to the new host's virtual switch setting.

Upgrading Virtual Machine Configurations

Sometimes you need to upgrade the Hyper-V virtual machine configurations to the latest version. This way, your virtual machines can take advantage of new features released during the upgrade.

To upgrade, follow these steps:

1. Upgrade your local Windows 10 host to the latest version.
2. In Hyper-V Manager, stop the virtual machine you want to upgrade.
3. Select the Action menu. Look for the Upgrade Configuration Version. If this option is not available, your virtual machine has the highest configuration version that is supported by the Hyper-V host.
4. Select Upgrade Configuration Version and work through the upgrade steps.

Once your VM is upgraded, you can restart the VM using the controls in Hyper-V Manager.

Understanding Hyper-V Checkpoints

Hyper-V provides a way to create checkpoints of your virtual machines. *Checkpoints* can be used to specify a specific point in time to which you would like to roll back a virtual machine. Checkpoints must be established prior to rolling back to them, but you can automate the creation of checkpoints. You also can manually create a checkpoint.

> **NOTE**
>
> In previous versions of some operating systems and network operating systems, including Windows Server 2008, Windows 2008 R2, and Windows Server 2012, the term *snapshots* was used instead of *checkpoints*. Other systems, such as Windows Server 2012 R2 and Microsoft System Center Virtual Machine Manager (SCVM), referred to *checkpoints*. To eliminate confusion, Microsoft has started referring to these system points as *checkpoints*.

Checkpoints are handy if you experience issues within the virtual machine operating environment. For example, say you install an application on a virtual machine and the application changes configuration settings on the VM operating system, creating an unstable environment. In some cases, simply uninstalling the application may undo the damage. However, in other cases, the system may still operate unpredictably.

In that scenario, it would be nice to stop, reverse the system back to the time before the errant application was installed, and resume as if nothing happened. To make sure you can do this, create a checkpoint before you start installing applications and making changes to your system. Then, if you experience an issue after the installation, you can restore the system to the checkpoint and your system will run just as it did before the installation. The key is to stop and make the checkpoints *prior* to the installation process.

Creating a Checkpoint

To create a Hyper-V checkpoint, perform the following steps:

1. Start Hyper-V Manager.
2. In the Virtual Machines column, right-click the VM for which you want to create a checkpoint.
3. Click Checkpoint (see Figure 14.1). Hyper-V starts the process of creating the checkpoint. You can see that Hyper-V is creating the checkpoint by looking in the Actions column for the "Cancel creating checkpoint" action, as shown in Figure 14.2.

FIGURE 14.1

Click Checkpoint to create a checkpoint for a selected VM.

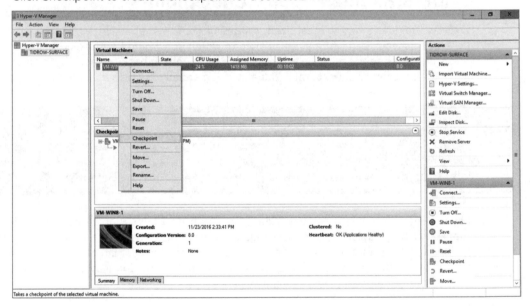

4. After the checkpoint is created, the Virtual Machine Checkpoint dialog box appears (see Figure 14.3). Click OK.

FIGURE 14.2

While a checkpoint is being created, you can watch its progress.

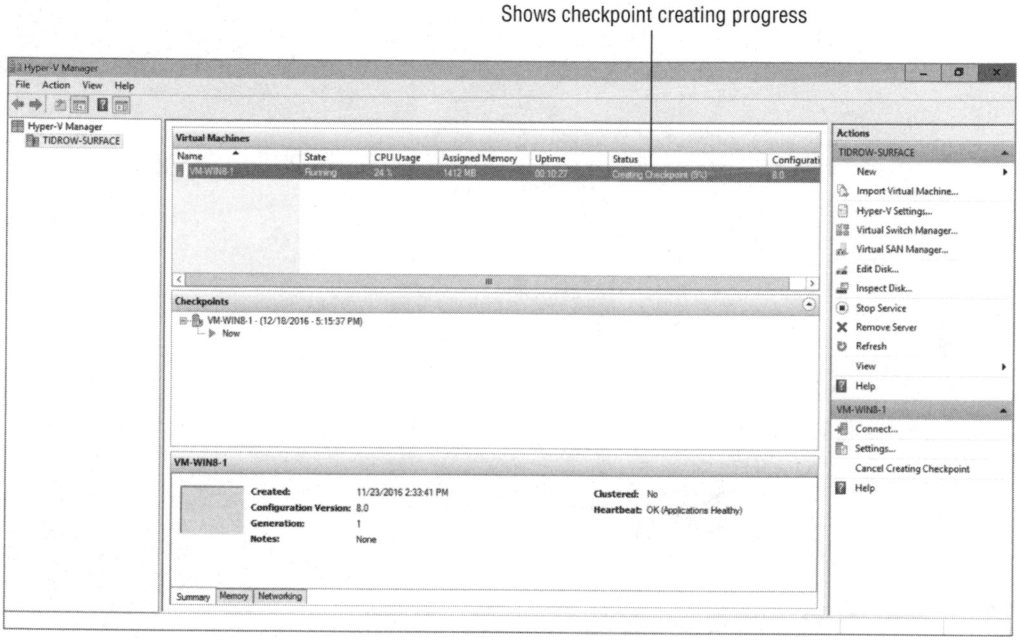

Shows checkpoint creating progress

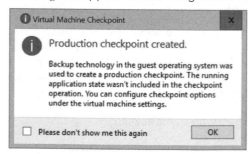

FIGURE 14.3

A dialog box appears announcing when the checkpoint process is finished.

5. The new checkpoint appears in the Checkpoints area in the Hyper-V Manager (see Figure 14.4).

FIGURE 14.4

The new checkpoint appears in the Checkpoint area of the Hyper-V Manager.

New checkpoint

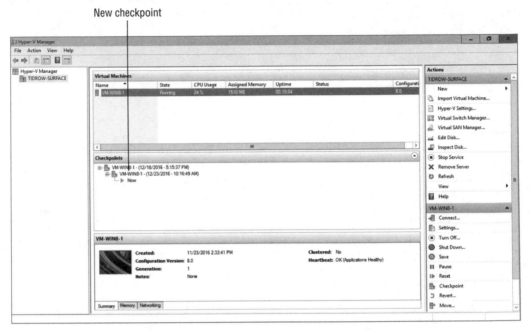

You can create as many checkpoints as you want.

Applying a Checkpoint

To revert to a system state using a checkpoint is called *applying a checkpoint*. This simply returns the VM to its state at the time the checkpoint was created. In many cases, you should create a checkpoint of the current state of the VM just in case you want to return to it if the previous checkpoint does not meet your needs. You can do this manually before you begin the apply process, or do it during the applying a checkpoint process.

To create a checkpoint and apply a checkpoint, do the following:

1. Start Hyper-V Manager.

2. Click the VM on which want to apply a checkpoint.

3. In the Checkpoint area, right-click the checkpoint you want to apply (see Figure 14.5).

FIGURE 14.5

You can apply a checkpoint to return the VM to that state.

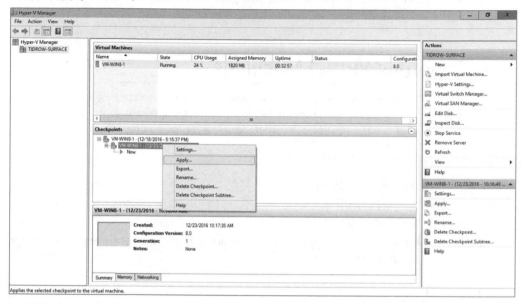

4. Click Apply. The Apply Checkpoint dialog box appears (see Figure 14.6).

FIGURE 14.6

The Apply Checkpoint dialog box warns you that VM's current state will be lost.

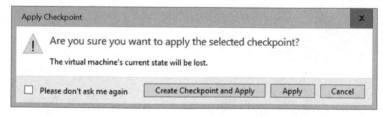

5. Click Create Checkpoint and Apply. Click Apply if you want to apply a check-point without creating a current checkpoint. Also, if the VM is running, Hyper-V Manager shuts down the VM, creates the checkpoint, and then applies the selected checkpoint.

6. Restart the VM to view the system state.

If you have an issue with the older checkpoint, apply the checkpoint you created in Step 5 to return to the latest system state. This procedure should allow you to start your VM in a known working state.

Exporting Virtual Machines

Virtual Machines can be exported from one device and imported on another. This provides a way to share system environments between devices to make it easy to set up VMs on different hosts for testing purposes, evaluating software, and so on.

To export a VM, do the following:

1. Start Hyper-V Manager.
2. Turn off the VM you want to export. (Right-click the VM, click Turn Off, and then click Turn Off).
3. Right-click the VM you want to export in the Virtual Machines column (see Figure 14.7).

FIGURE 14.7

You can export a VM from the Hyper-V Manager.

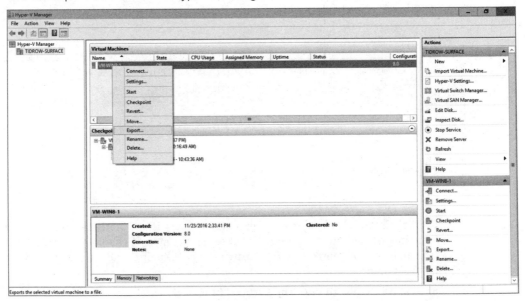

4. Click Export.

5. The Export Virtual Machine dialog box appears (see Figure 14.8).

FIGURE 14.8

Specify the location of the exported VM.

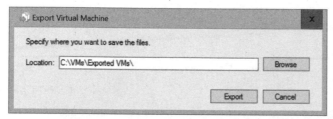

6. Specify the location where you want to save the exported VM. Make sure the location has enough space for the exported VM. Many Windows 10 VMs are of considerable size, such as over 6–10GB.

7. Click Export.

The VM exports.

Importing Virtual Machines

An exported VM can be imported into Hyper-V Manager to allow you to share VMs from one host to another. This feature is handy when you have a working VM on one computer and want to bring up the VM on another computer to share its capabilities or to see how that VM runs on a different host.

When you're importing, Hyper-V offers the following three types of imports:

- **Register in-place:** Export files are in the location in which you will store and run the virtual machine. The VM you import will have the same ID as it did when you exported it.

- **Restore the virtual machine:** This option restores the VM to a different location of your choosing. You also can use the default Hyper-V location. The VM you import creates a copy of the exported files (with the same ID) and moves them to the selected location.

- **Copy the virtual machine:** This option restores the VM to a different location and creates a new unique ID for the VM. This allows you to import the VM to the same host multiple times.

14

To import a virtual machine, do the following:

1. Export the VM you want to import using the steps provided in the preceding section.
2. Start Hyper-V Manager on the host on which you want to import the VM.
3. In the Actions pane, click Import Virtual Machine (see Figure 14.9). The Import Virtual Machine wizard appears (see Figure 14.10).

FIGURE 14.9

Click Import Virtual Machine to begin the VM import process.

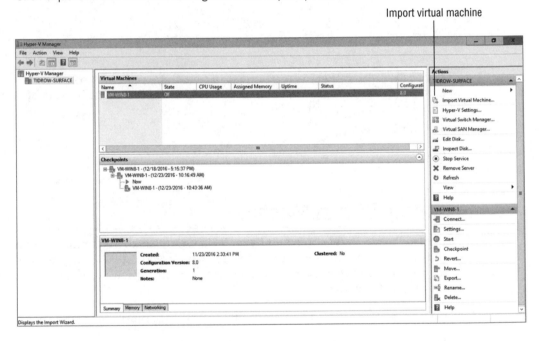

4. Click Next. The Locate Folder wizard screen appears (see Figure 14.11).

FIGURE 14.10

The Import Virtual Machine wizard.

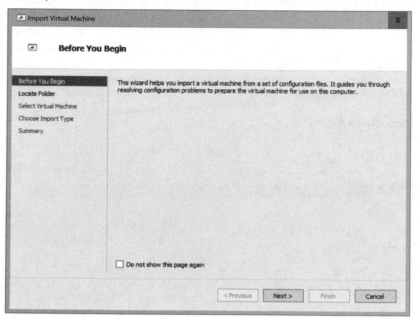

FIGURE 14.11

Specify the location of the VM you want to import.

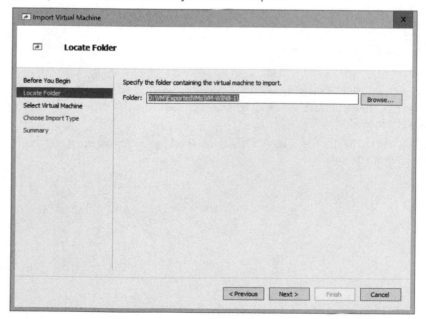

5. Specify the location of the imported VM file.

6. Click Next. The Select Virtual Machine wizard screen appears (see Figure 14.12).

FIGURE 14.12

Specify the virtual machine you want to import.

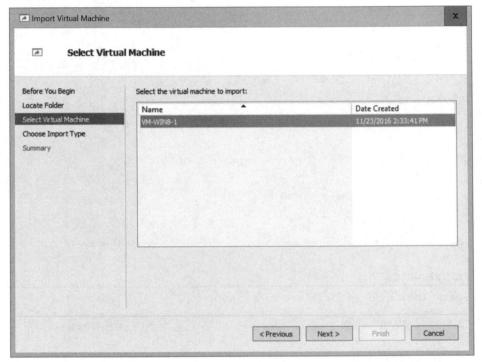

7. Click Next. The Choose Import Type wizard screen appears (see Figure 14.13). In this example we will create a new ID by selecting Copy the Virtual Machine (Create a New Unique ID).

8. Click Next. The Choose Folders for Virtual Machine Files wizard screen appears (see Figure 14.14).

FIGURE 14.13

Specify the type of VM import.

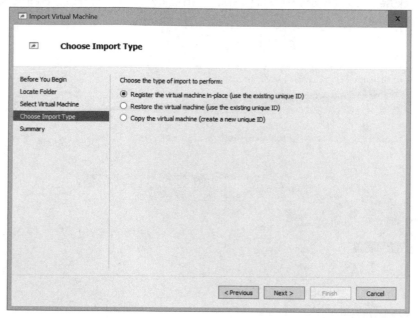

FIGURE 14.14

Specify the location of the imported VM.

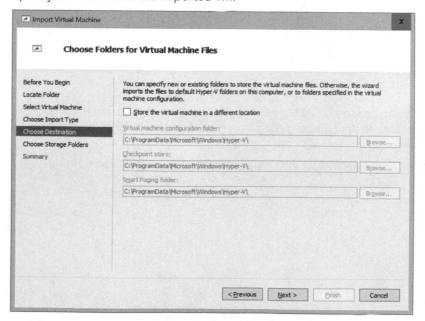

9. Specify the location of the imported VM, such as a new or existing folder.

10. Click Next. The Choose Folders to Store Virtual Hard Disks wizard screen appear (see Figure 14.15).

FIGURE 14.15

Specify the location of the import VM hard disks.

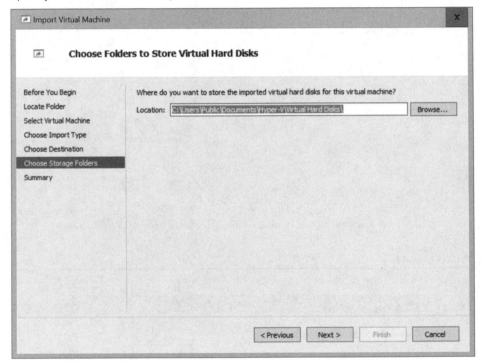

11. Specify the location of the import VM hard disks. By default, Hyper-V attempts to store the hard disks in the same location as the one you have on that host. To avoid an error, specify a new location.

12. Click Next. The Completing Import Wizard screen appears (see Figure 14.16).

FIGURE 14.16

The Completing Import Wizard screen shows a summary of the import settings.

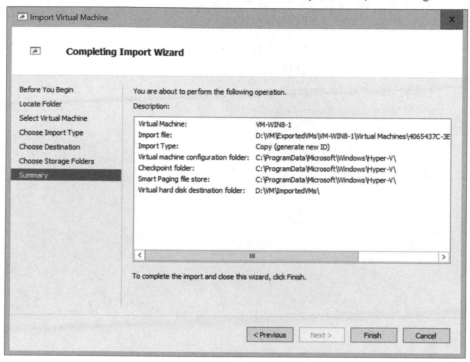

13. Read the summary description to ensure your import settings are correct. You can click the Previous button to return to a screen to correct any mistakes in the import settings.

14. Click Finish.

After the import process, you can start the VM from Hyper-V Manager.

Wrapping Up

Virtual machines are one way administrators have found to become more adept at Windows 10 features, application enrichments, device driver issues, and other elements of the operating system. You can manage them using the Hyper-V Manager in Windows 10 to perform several tasks, such as migrating VMs, creating VM checkpoints, exporting VMs, and importing VMs.

This chapter introduced the following points:

- Understanding Hyper-V in enterprises
- Migrating virtual machines
- Upgrading virtual machines
- Understanding Hyper-V checkpoints
- Exporting virtual machines
- Importing virtual machines

Working in the Cloud and with Azure

IN THIS CHAPTER

Understanding the cloud

Accessing OneDrive and Azure files

Using OneDrive and Azure

In 2005, Microsoft introduced an online web portal where users could store files, get their e-mail, communicate with other users, and share files. This web portal was known originally as Windows Live, but has been rebranded as Office 365. Chapter 12 discusses it in more detail. In this chapter, however, you learn about working in the cloud with Microsoft OneDrive, an online file sharing and file storage tool. To go to OneDrive using a web browser simply open `https://OneDrive.com` or `https://OneDrive.live.com` in your browser.

Microsoft OneDrive provides an area online where you can store and share photos, presentations, and other files. With Windows 10, an app is available to help you manage and add files to OneDrive. This chapter shows you how to use the OneDrive Windows syncing application.

In previous versions of Windows, OneDrive was an app you downloaded and installed. In Windows 10, OneDrive functionality is fully integrated with the operating system and the service appears as a separate drive or device to all applications.

Even if you aren't connected to the Internet, you can use OneDrive locally, use its features to sync your files with the online portal, and share files with other applications that are OneDrive-aware.

Synchronizing files among all your devices is as simple as setting up your devices to support and sign in to OneDrive with your Microsoft account. You can copy files to each local drive or simply access and work with a single instance of your file.

In 2010, Microsoft introduced Azure, a cloud computing platform and infrastructure that was designed for building, executing, and managing applications and services through a global network of Microsoft-managed data centers. Azure supports many different programming languages, tools, and frameworks, as well as both Microsoft-specific and third-party software and systems.

By entering `https://azure.microsoft.com/en-us` in your web browser, you can access the Azure site.

Understanding the Cloud

Computer users have been limited in the ways in which they can access files on disparate systems. Traditionally, users store their files on a local hard drive (such as the `C:` drive) or on a network drive at work. To use those files on a different computer, that computer must have a network connection to the user's network drive, or the user must transfer files using a removable drive such as a flash drive.

With cloud technology, the user only needs access to the Internet in order to work on files. Microsoft OneDrive is Microsoft's cloud-based technology that provides access to users' files from any location at any time. The advantage of cloud technologies is that you aren't limited to a company network location or a removable drive strategy. Storing files in the cloud also provides a more flexible way for users to share files with other users. You no longer have to rely on the network administrator in your organization to establish shares for your teams, colleagues, or other people with whom you want to share files.

> **NOTE**
>
> As with most systems, cloud-based systems have some disadvantages. First, you must have an Internet connection to access files. Second, your company may have rules against storing files in a cloud-based system because of confidentiality and/or file security regulations. Finally, your files may be subject to terms and conditions imposed by the cloud company that gives it rights to read and access your files. Currently, Microsoft OneDrive does not indicate that it has those rights, but you should be aware of that possibility as you decide to store your photos, documents, videos, and other items in the cloud.

Microsoft has a vision that every user should have access to his or her files any time and anywhere he or she wants them (with Internet connectivity, of course). In addition, the device you use to access your files should be irrelevant. For example, users should be able to access files using a personal computer, a tablet device with Wi-Fi connectivity, a smartphone, or a laptop. In fact, with Microsoft OneDrive, any user who has a Microsoft Phone, Xbox, an Apple iPhone, iPad, or iPod Touch, or a Google Android-based tablet or smartphone can access OneDrive files as well.

In addition to Microsoft OneDrive, other cloud-based file-storage services exist. This chapter focuses on Microsoft OneDrive, but you're welcome to learn about other services to see which is best for you and your organization. The following are a few of the most popular online storage services:

- **Google Drive:** https://drive.google.com
- **Sugar Sync:** www.sugarsync.com
- **Dropbox:** www.dropbox.com
- **Box:** www.box.com
- **Cubby:** www.cubby.com

Setting Up a OneDrive Account

OneDrive has been available for users in the Microsoft Live family of products for several years. With OneDrive, you can store many types of files online, including word processing documents, spreadsheets, text files, photos, presentations, and videos.

To begin using OneDrive, you need a Windows OneDrive account. This chapter assumes you have a Microsoft or Live ID account. To ensure you can start using OneDrive, read Chapter 12 to see how to set up an account and to confirm that you can log in to Windows OneDrive. Also refer to Chapter 4, which shows you how to create a Microsoft account that syncs you into both your PC account and the Microsoft Cloud resources like OneDrive.

Signing in to your computer with a local account only lets you use the OneDrive app to browse your PC. You can't access your files unless you also log in to OneDrive.com.

Accessing OneDrive Files

With Windows 10, you have three primary ways to access files stored in your OneDrive environment:

- **OneDrive Device:** OneDrive appears as a drive to File Explorer and all applications. Simply click it as you would your C: drive or any other storage device. This option is shown in Figure 15.1.

FIGURE 15.1

You can access OneDrive using File Explorer.

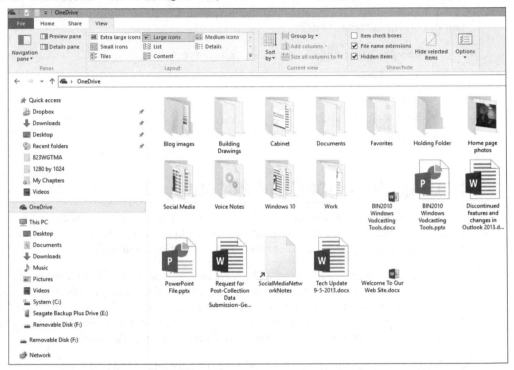

- **Web-based:** You can navigate to Windows OneDrive from a web browser and access files from the OneDrive menu. Figure 15.2 shows an example of this approach. You can also navigate to `https://OneDrive.live.com`, which automatically reroutes you to the Windows OneDrive website.

- **OneDrive Windows 10 notification application:** The built-in taskbar notification applications lets you manage and configure your OneDrive account. The taskbar application is shown in Figure 15.3.

FIGURE 15.2

You can access OneDrive using a web browser, such as Microsoft Internet Explorer.

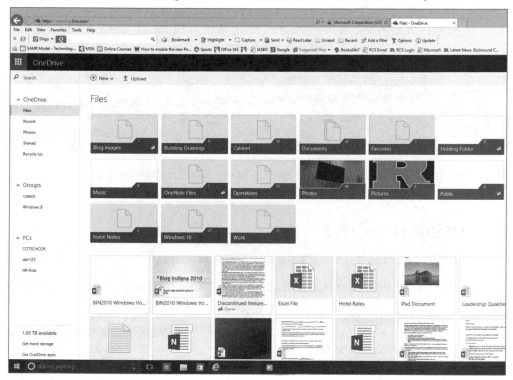

FIGURE 15.3

Accessing OneDrive's taskbar notification application.

Using OneDrive

As you've read, OneDrive is now a folder on your computer. Files and folders you put into your OneDrive folder get synced with the OneDrive (Windows OneDrive) web portal and will sync with other devices that run OneDrive apps.

> **TIP**
>
> If you have an Apple iPad or iPod Touch, consider downloading the free OneDrive app from the Apple iTunes Store. The OneDrive app enables you to view your OneDrive files, delete them, move them to different folders, add folders, send photos or videos to OneDrive, and open files (if you have a support app for that file type).

The following section describes the use of OneDrive in Windows 10.

Using OneDrive

OneDrive is available on the Windows Start menu. Click it now to start using it.

When the application first appears, if you don't have a Microsoft account on your local PC, you're prompted to enter your Microsoft OneDrive login credentials. Do so to continue with the initial setup process. You can view OneDrive items in one of two ways: in a browser window or from File Explorer. To access your OneDrive folders from File Explorer, simply open OneDrive from the Start menu. The screen in Figure 15.2 opens. You can use the regular File Explorer tools to change the view. Figure 15.4, for example, shows the OneDrive in thumbnail view.

Adding files to OneDrive

One of the tasks that you can perform with OneDrive in File Explorer is to add files to your OneDrive folders. You can add files from your computer to OneDrive by using the following steps:

1. In File Explorer, navigate to your folders and select a file or a collection of files. Right-click the files and choose Copy.
2. Click the OneDrive folder icon in the left pane of the File Explorer window.
3. Right-click and choose Paste to paste the files into your OneDrive. Pasting files is shown in Figure 15.5.

FIGURE 15.4

OneDrive app in Extra Large Icons view.

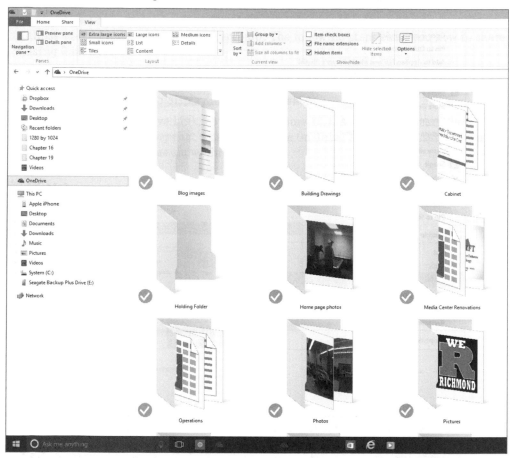

OneDrive uploads the files to your OneDrive account online and displays those files in your OneDrive folder on the Internet. Figure 15.6 shows an example of what this looks like if you view your copy and pasted files in Internet Explorer.

The beauty of working with OneDrive is that you can use the full functionality of Windows drag and drop with OneDrive.

15

FIGURE 15.8

A shared OneDrive file link is created so you can send the link to other people.

4. Open your e-mail application. You will use e-mail to share the new link to other people who you want to access your shared OneDrive file.

5. Enter the e-mail address of the recipient of the file.

6. Right-click and choose Paste in the body of the e-mail message to paste the shared OneDrive link in the e-mail message. Figure 15.9 shows an example of how this looks.

7. Click the Send button. Upon receipt of the message, the recipient simply clicks the link and has access to your shared file.

FIGURE 15.9

We're sending a file from OneDrive to someone using e-mail.

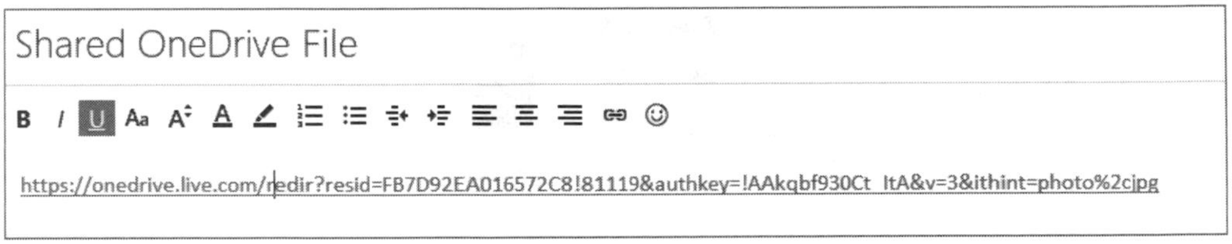

Shared OneDrive File

B *I* U Aa A² A ∠ ☰ ☰ ⇥ ⇤ ☰ ☰ ☰ ⊝ ☺

https://onedrive.live.com/redir?resid=FB7D92EA016572C8!81119&authkey=!AAkqbf930Ct_ItA&v=3&ithint=photo%2cjpg

Configuring OneDrive

To configure your OneDrive, right-click the OneDrive taskbar notification application and select Settings. Select the Settings tab as shown in Figure 15.10. You can set the following items on this tab:

- **Start OneDrive automatically when I sign in to Windows:** Use this option to start OneDrive when you start Windows.

- **Let me use OneDrive to fetch any of my files on this PC:** Use this option to set OneDrive to use the Fetch Files features to access your files from a different computer using the OneDrive website. Click the More Info link under this option to learn more about this feature and its limitations.

- **Use Office to sync files faster and work on files with other people at the same time:** Use this option to share files from OneDrive with other Microsoft Office users. This option is available only when your system has Microsoft Office installed.

Then click OK when your settings are configured as needed.

FIGURE 15.10

The Microsoft OneDrive options screen.

Wrapping Up

Windows 10 provides a good platform for using the Microsoft OneDrive cloud service. You can use a web browser or File Explorer to access and manage your OneDrive files.

In summary:

- OneDrive is a cloud-based file storage and sharing tool.
- OneDrive is integrated into File Explorer, which includes a OneDrive folder icon in the left pane.
- OneDrive Windows app provides a way to view and share your OneDrive files.

15

Part IV

Managing Your Content

IN THIS PART

Searching for Files and Messages on Your Computer

H ard disk storage in the 21st century is reliable, fast, and cheap. Just about every computer sold in the past few years has lots of it. The result is that people now store many thousands of files on their computers. To organize their folders, people use lots of folders and subfolders. Although having lots of well-organized files on your hard disk is certainly good, it has a couple of downsides. For one, drilling down through a ton of folders to get to a file gets tedious. For another, you can easily forget where you put a file and what you named it.

In earlier versions of Windows, you could use shortcuts and searches to help with these problems, but too many shortcuts just added clutter to the screen. The old style of searching is slow and tedious. Searching in Windows 10 is more like searching on the Internet. You don't have to search for filenames; you can search by content and meaning. And in most cases, the search results are instantaneous. You don't have to wait for the system to slog through the whole file system looking at every file.

Basics of Searching

Like filing cabinets, computers store information. The information in your filing cabinet has no "meaning" to your filing cabinet. Likewise, the information in your computer has no meaning to the computer. Searching a computer is much like searching through a filing cabinet or the index at the back of a book: a list of multiple items sorted according to some criteria.

In the next sections, we try to clear up some common misconceptions about searching. Along the way, we offer some tips and techniques that should help you find what you need more easily.

You aren't asking questions

The most basic thing you need to understand about searching is that you aren't asking the computer a question. Computers don't understand human languages the way people do. As mentioned, searching a computer (or the Internet) is much like searching the index at the back of a book. You need to zero in on a specific word or phrase. The more specific that word or phrase, the more specific the search results.

Let's use the Internet as an example. You certainly can search for something like the following:

What is the capital of Kansas?

You'll likely get the correct answer from any Internet search engine. However, you'd probably get the same or similar results if you searched for:

capital Kansas

The keywords in the search are **capital** and **Kansas**. The other words don't help to narrow the search much because you're searching for words, not meaning. Virtually every page on the Internet contains the words **what**, **is**, **the**, and **of**, even if the page has nothing to do with Kansas or capital.

We aren't saying you *can't* conduct a search for **What is the capital of Kansas?** You can do that if you want to, and you will get results. However, the results won't be much different than if you left out the *noise words* (words that appear in virtually all written documents and don't help describe what the page is about). Examples of noise words include the following:

a	it	the	want	who
about	me	then	was	will
an	my	there	we	with
are	of	these	were	would
but	should	they	what	you
did	so	this	when	your
how	than	to	where	
is	that	too	which	

Some search programs remove the noise words before conducting the search. Others include them. But sometimes that works against you because you find things in your search results that have nothing to do with what you were really searching for.

The bottom line is this: When you search for something, don't try to word it as a question. Instead, search for an exact word or phrase that has a specific meaning.

Be specific

The key to successful searches, whether on the Internet or on your computer, is to be specific. The more specific you are about what you're searching for, the better the results.

Here's an Internet search as an example. Suppose you're looking for quotes by Benjamin Franklin on health. If you search Google for **health**, you get links to billions of pages. That doesn't help much because a lifetime isn't enough time to look through all those pages. If you search Google for **Benjamin Franklin**, you get links to more than 30 million web pages. That's still too many.

If you search Google for **Benjamin Franklin health**, you get links to 16 million pages. If you search for **Benjamin Franklin quotation health**, you get links to 5 thousand pages. Now, if you add the word **wise** to the search (because the quote contains that word), you get about 500,000 hits. Notice how the more specific words there are in the search, the smaller (and also better targeted) the search results. In fact, one of the first pages listed probably contains exactly what you're looking for. The moral of the story is: The more specific the search, the more specific the search results.

> **TIP**
>
> After you've clicked a link to a page, you can search that page for a word. In Microsoft Internet Explorer or Microsoft Edge, which is the default browser for Windows 10, click the ellipsis at the far right of the menu bar and then click Find on page (or press Ctrl+F). If you use a different web browser, check its Edit menu or Help for a similar feature. You can switch to IE if you prefer.

Of course, searching the Internet and searching your own computer are two entirely different things, for the simple reason that the Internet exists *outside* your computer, and its searches don't include things that are inside your computer. But the general rule of specificity applies to all searches.

Spelling counts

When you write text for a human to read, you can get away with lots of spelling errors. For example, the following sentence is loaded with spelling errors, but you can probably figure out what the sentence says:

Th kwik brwn dogg jmpt ovr teh lzy mune.

You can figure it out because you have a brain, and brains have many strategies for figuring things out based on context, the sounds the letters make when read aloud, and so on. Computers don't have brains and can't figure things out.

Plenty of computer programs (including tools built directly into Windows 10) are available that can correct your spelling and suggest alternate spellings but those programs aren't as good as a human brain. Some people are good at spelling, and other people aren't.

If you aren't sure how to spell something, try typing it into a word processor that has spell checking. Or, if that isn't an option for you, try an online service such as www .spellcheck.net or www.dictionary.reference.com. If you're looking for a tech term, try www.webopedia.com.

Where you start the search matters

You can search in many different places and for many different kinds of things. Where you start your search and what you search for matter a lot. For example, searching the Internet makes no sense when you're looking for something that's in your own computer.

Inside your own computer are basically two types of searches to consider. One is a search for *help*. There, you're typically looking for instructions on how to perform some task. Chapter 6 provides strategies for getting help with Windows 10. You also can rely on app- or application-specific help for assistance while using an app or program.

This chapter is mostly about searching for programs, folders, files, and messages that are inside, or directly connected to, your computer — the kinds of things you can use even when you're *offline* (not connected to the Internet).

How Searching Works

Understanding how searches work in Windows 10 is critical to performing quick, successful searches. Most searches are performed on an *index*. The index is like the index at the back of this or any other book. It's basically a list of keywords. Of course, Windows 10's index doesn't contain page numbers. In place of page numbers, it contains filenames and locations. You never see the index with your own eyes. The index is built, maintained, and searched behind the scenes without any intervention on your part.

Some searches search the entire index. Others search only for programs, files, e-mail messages, or contacts. Still others ignore the index and search through every single folder on one or more drives. It all depends on where you start the search and how you perform the search. Let's start with common, everyday searches that are fast and easy to do.

Quick Searches

The quick and easy way to find a program, Windows 10 app, favorite website, file, contact, or e-mail message is to search right from the taskbar search field (see Figure 16.1). Put your cursor in the Search box, to the immediate right of the Start button where it says Ask me anything.

FIGURE 16.1

The Search box at the bottom right of the Start button.

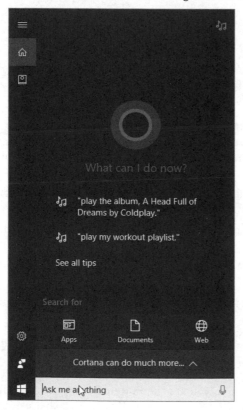

Windows 10 breaks down the type of searches into the following categories. The default is "Everywhere," but here's a list of some of the popular locations into which Search reaches:

- **Apps:** Searches apps and programs that are currently installed on your computer and ready to use.

- **Settings:** Searches Windows configuration settings, such as those that can change the display resolution on your computer.

- **Files:** Searches documents and other files on your hard drive. Search also drills into OneDrive, which is integrated into Windows 10.

- **People:** Searches contacts stored on your computer.

- **Finance:** Searches current financial information about a company.

- **Microsoft Edge:** Displays the Bing search engine and searches on the word or term you enter.

- **Mail:** Searches your local e-mail account for messages containing the search criteria.

- **Maps:** Displays the Maps app and searches for the location you specify.

- **Music:** Searches the Music app for music stored on your computer and available through the Music Marketplace. Through the Marketplace, you can preview and purchase songs.

- **Photos:** Searches the Photos app for photos matching your search criteria.

- **Store:** Displays the Windows Store and returns apps that meet your search criteria. You can click an app to learn more about it. If you like it, you can download it to your computer.

- **Video:** Displays the Video app and returns videos based on the search criteria you enter.

- **Weather:** Displays the Weather app and returns weather information and forecasts about the location you specify.

- **Xbox Companion:** Displays the Microsoft Xbox Companion app to search using an Xbox console.

- **Xbox Live Games:** Displays the Microsoft Xbox Live Games marketplace to enable you to search Xbox Live content.

As soon as you type one character, the search results appear. Each character you type reduces the search results to include only items that contain those letters. You get instant feedback as you type, so you can keep typing as many characters as necessary until you see the item you want. If the results are slim, you are then offered an option to Search my stuff or Search the web. To search within a category, such as Music, click that category after you type in a few letters. An example of a search result for something matching the word *product* or *productivity* is shown in Figure 16.2. The search results begin to appear with anything that matches your search criteria.

FIGURE 16.2

Results of searching on the word *productivity*.

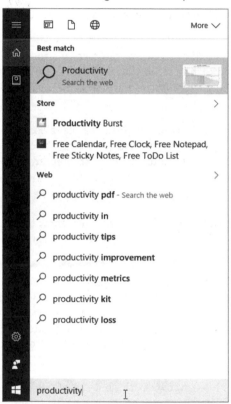

When conducting searches in Windows 10, the searches do not look exclusively at file and folder names — they look at the contents of files, tags, and properties as well. (And with Windows 10, Search can even scan inside images for hidden text.) We talk about what those things are in Chapter 18. We mention it here in case you're wondering why some of your recent search results include search criteria not necessarily found in the names of files or folders. For example, if you search on the term **money**, some of the files and folders that display as a result may not have the word *money* in them. That's because the word *money* appears within the message or contact's information.

You can do many things with the search results:

- To open an item, click it.
- To see other things you can do with an item, right-click it.
- If an item you were expecting to find doesn't show up, or if you want to improve the search, redo the search with other criteria.
- To discard the search results, press Esc or choose something else from the Charms Bar.

You can do wildcard searches from the Quick access menu, where * stands for any characters and **?** stands for a single character. But keep in mind that when you search from the Search box, you're only searching the index, not the entire hard disk. So, don't be surprised if some files don't show up.

You can also do **AND** and **OR** searches from the Start menu. For example, a search for ***.jpg OR *.jpeg** finds files that have either a .jpg or .jpeg extension. We talk about these kinds of searches in more detail later in this chapter and in the next chapter.

Customizing Windows Search

You can customize Windows Search to store a history of your searches, show the most popular searched apps at the top of the search list, and include or exclude certain apps to search.

To set these options, open the Settings window by choosing the Settings item from the Start menu. Enter Search in the Find a setting search field in the top of the Settings page. Once on the Settings window, search settings that have "search" in the name. Then click Cortana & Search settings. This is also directly accessible from the Search interface, which loads when you place the cursor into the Search the web and Windows field to the right of the Start button.

You have many settings to choose from in this window. At the bottom of the list, you have the following options for History, Bing SafeSearch, and Other privacy settings as shown in Figure 16.3.

- **History view:** Shows app, settings, web, search and other history in Cortana home.
- **My device history:** From signed-in devices, you can improve searches using app, settings, and other history.
- **Bing SafeSearch:** Specifies safe search options to filter out adult results from your searches.
- **Other privacy settings:** Manage personal information settings and see the privacy statement.

FIGURE 16.3

Search settings options.

Extending a Start menu search

If the thing you're looking for doesn't show up in your search, check your spelling. Make sure the word you're searching for matches something on your computer. For example, if you're looking for photos of your dog named Spot, a search for **Spot** doesn't find them unless the photos have Spot in the filename, tags, or properties.

Search box searches are ideal for finding the kinds of things most people use most often — apps, music, programs, folders, Control Panel dialog boxes, favorite websites, messages, and documents (text, worksheets, pictures, music, and videos). If you're a quick typist, using the Search box can save you lots of time you'd otherwise spend clicking and opening things through the traditional methods. But Search box searches aren't the end of the story — not by a long shot. There's much more, as you'll see.

> **TIP**
>
> The Search box in File Explorer's upper-right corner provides a quick-and-easy way to search the current folder and its subfolders.

Searching Folders and Views

By now you may have noticed File Explorer has a Search box in its upper-right corner. The Search box, by default, includes text that describes the search context, such as Local Disk, as in Figure 16.4.

FIGURE 16.4

The Search box in Explorer (all folders).

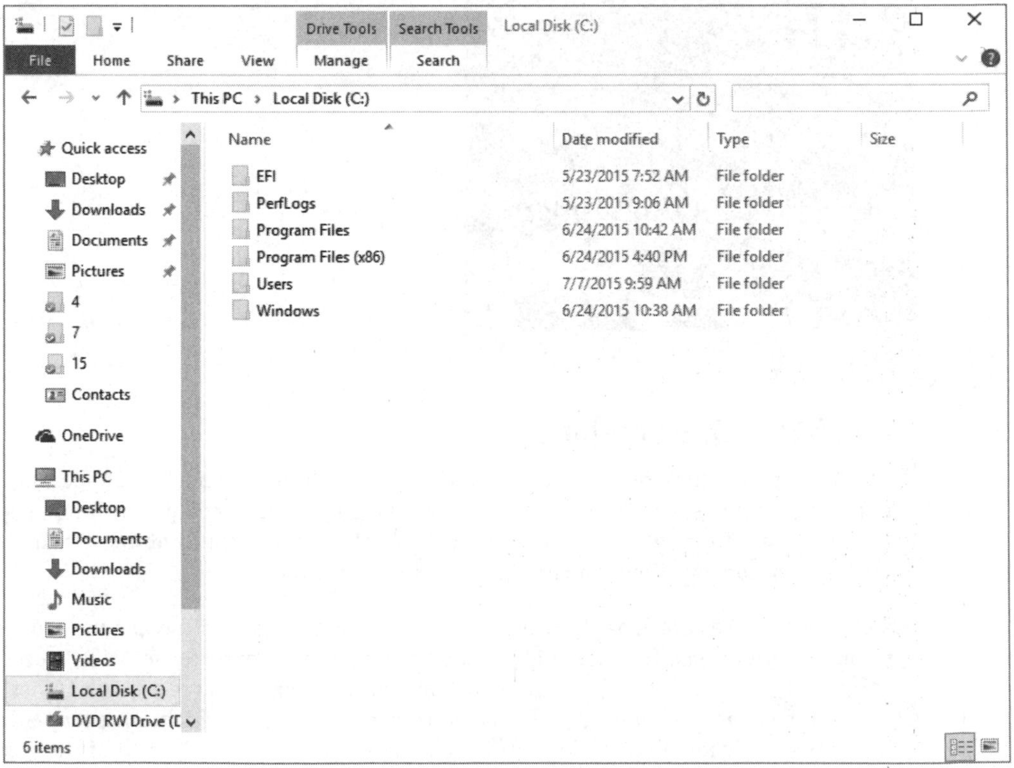

Like the Search box on the taskbar, the one in File Explorer gives you instant, keystroke-by-keystroke search results. With Windows 10, you can search for different kinds of items from the Explorer window. You aren't limited to files and folders. You can, for example, search for music playlists, programs, recorded TV programs, tasks, and other kinds of items. The view consists of all files and subfolders you see in the main content pane, but it can be expanded to search for all subfolders. The Search box in Explorer doesn't look strictly at file and folder names either. It looks at the contents of files that contain text, tags, and other metadata. So, once again, you use it in much the same way you use an Internet search engine: not just to search for a specific filename, but to search for keywords or phrases.

The Search box in Explorer works best when you have some idea where the item you're looking for is located. For example, say you have thousands of songs in your Music folder and its subfolders. You want to see all songs in the Jazz genre. Step 1 is to open your Music folder. Step 2 is to type **Jazz** into the Search box. Instantly, you see all songs in the jazz genre. To ensure that you're searching all the subfolders, click the All Subfolders option on the Search Tool tab of File Explorer.

You certainly aren't limited to searching a genre. You can type an artist's name to see all songs by that artist. You can type a few characters from a song title. You can type anything you want to find. Just keep in mind that you're searching only the current folder or its subfolders.

When you're learning to use the Search box in Explorer, sometimes you don't find a file you may have been expecting to find. This can happen for several reasons:

- The file isn't in the folder you're searching (or one of its subfolders).
- The way you spelled the search term in the Search box doesn't match the way it's spelled in the file(s).
- The file you were expecting to find isn't one of the file types selected from the Kind drop-down list (shown in Figure 16.5).

If you get more results than you were expecting, keep in mind that the search isn't looking only at the filenames, or only at the columns you see in the results. It's searching properties that may not even be visible in the Details view and the contents of files that contain text.

Specifying search criteria

Anything you type into a Search box is a *search criterion*. As soon as you click in the search box, the Search ribbon appears at the top of File Explorer under Search Tools. The ribbon gives you access to the most advanced search options yet to be included in Windows. Basically, the search criterion is telling Windows 10, "Show me all items that have these characteristics." The "items" are things such as files, folders, music, contacts, messages, and Microsoft Edge favorites.

The search criterion can be as simple as a few characters of text. For example, you can click in the Search box, type a person's name, and find the files and messages on your computer that contain that person's name. You can also use multiple search criteria to locate items. First, let's look at how to perform a search using different types of search criteria.

FIGURE 16.5

You can specify the kind of file you're searching for.

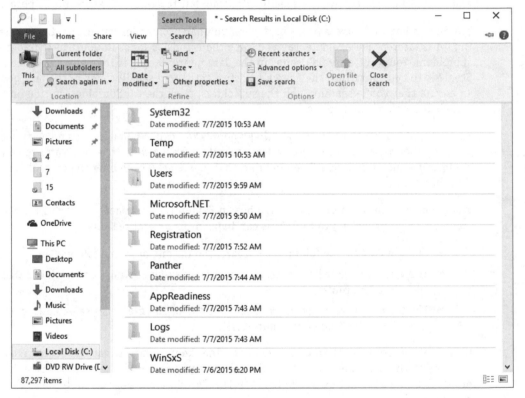

Search by date

You can narrow your search to specific kinds of dates by adding a date filter to your search. For example, you can search by using the following Date Modified options (the last time you opened, changed, and saved the file):

- Today
- Yesterday

- This Week
- Last Week
- This Month
- Last Month
- This Year
- Last Year

To select a date option, click the Date Modified button on the Search tab. Figure 16.6 shows these options.

FIGURE 16.6

You can specify the modify date of files you're searching.

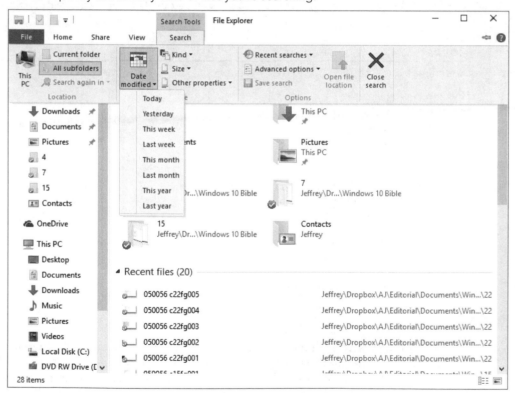

If you're working in the Pictures folder, you can choose Date Taken from the File Explorer search box to find pictures taken (created) on a particular day or in a particular date range.

Here's an example: In File Explorer, click in the Search box and then click Date Modified from the drop-down menu that appears. You can then click a date from the date picker or click an option like Yesterday or This Month. Windows 10 searches in your libraries for the files that meet those criteria.

Although Date Modified is the only date option available when you search at the Libraries level, it isn't the only date criteria you can use to search. For example, you can search by date created, date modified, and last accessed.

Let's say today is October 9, 2016, and you've just created or downloaded a file. The problem is, you clicked the Save button without choosing where to put the file, and you didn't notice the name of the file. So, now you don't know where it is. Open the parent folder where you downloaded the file, click in the Search box, and type **datecreated:today** to see all files created today. That may help you find the file. When you do this, Windows 10 displays a helpful calendar tool and the set of Date Modified options in case you want to select a different date or date range. Figure 16.7 shows an example of how this feature works.

FIGURE 16.7

Searching a date range.

To search for files within a range of dates, choose one of the date criteria (like Date Modified). In the calendar that drops down, click the start or end date. Then hold down the Shift key and click the other date. Or simply click and drag across the date range with the mouse. Both dates, and all the dates in between, are highlighted. Windows 10 displays the files that fill the criteria within that date range.

Search by size

The Size option lets you search for files that are an exact size, or files that are larger or smaller than some size. For example, say you bought a second hard drive and want to move some large video files to it. You can search for Size and choose the Gigantic option, which finds files larger than 128MB. Or, you can specify a particular size, such as 500MB or 1GB. To search by a specific size, click the Size option in the Search box and then type a size after the colon. Use the modifiers K for kilobyte, M for megabyte, and G for gigabyte.

> **NOTE**
>
> A megabyte (MB) is about 1,000KB (exactly 1,024KB). A gigabyte (GB) is about 1,000,000KB (exactly 1,048,576KB).

Search by filename or subject

In the Search box, you can type a specific filename or part of a filename. For example, a search for **sunset** finds all files that have the word *sunset* in the filename. You can use wild-card characters as in earlier versions of Windows (and DOS). Use **?** to stand for a single character, and ***** to stand for any group of characters. For example, say you have files named Sunset (1), Sunset (2), Sunset (3), and so on. A search for **sunset*** finds them all.

You can include filename extensions to narrow the search. For example, a search for **.jpg** finds all files that have a .jpg extension. A search for **sunset*.jpg** finds all files that start with *sunset* and end with a .jpg filename extension.

You can use the word **OR** (in uppercase letters, with a space before and after the word) to extend the search to multiple criteria. For example, consider the following typed into the Filename box:

*.jpg OR *.jpeg

When you click the Search button, you get all files that have either a .jpg extension or a .jpeg extension. Similarly, to find all files that start with *sunset* and end with either .jpg or .jpeg, you can search for the following:

sunset*.jpg OR sunset*.jpeg

You aren't limited to one **OR**. For example, to find all files that end with .avi, .wmv, .mpg, or .mpeg, place the following in the Filename box:

*.avi OR *.wmv OR *.mpg OR *.mpeg

16

CAUTION

Make sure you use OR, not AND. This is a common misunderstanding that we discuss in Chapter 23.

If you're searching a folder that contains e-mail messages, you can search using e-mail–specific criteria. For example, you can search for e-mail messages that have a certain word or phrase in the Subject line. You don't need to use wildcards or filename extensions because the Subject line is text, not a filename. To search by subject, click in the Search box and type **subject:(subject text)**. In this example, *subject text* is the text for which you're searching. You can also simply type the text in the Search box without the **subject:** modifier, but you'll return results from matches other than in the subject of the e-mail messages. You can use other criteria such as From and To when searching for e-mail messages, as well as enter text that appears in the body of the message.

Search by kind

Windows 10 enables you to search by the type of object you want to find. For example, you can search for contacts, documents, e-mail, feeds, folders, games, and more. On the Search tab, Windows 10 displays the Kind tool (refer to Figure 16.5). This tool enables you to choose the kind(s) of objects to search for.

TIP

To search for multiple kinds of objects, use the OR logical operator with multiple kind: specifications.

Search by tags, authors, title, and others

Depending on what type of folder you're searching in, you see other boxes such as Tags, Authors, or Title for specifying search criteria. These correspond to metadata stored in file properties. You can type any word or phrase to search for files that have that word or phrase in the corresponding property.

 We talk more about those properties in Chapter 18.

Saving a search

You can use searches in two ways. In some cases, you may be looking for a file you've lost track of. In that case, after you've found the file, you probably won't need to repeat the search in the future. Just double-click the found file to open it. Then close the Search by clicking the Close Search button on the Search tab in File Explorer.

Sometimes you've constructed a search to pull together files from multiple folders. For example, a search for ***.avi OR *.wmv OR *.mpg OR *.mpeg** shows all video files with those extensions. If you want to check up on your current video files often, you don't need to re-create the search from scratch each time. You can save the search. Any time you want to check up on your current video files, open the saved search. It shows you all *current* files that meet those criteria.

Saving a search is easy. After you've performed the search, you see a Save Search button on the Search tab. Just click that button and a Save As dialog box opens. The name of the search reflects the search criteria you specified. But you don't need to keep that name. Type any name that will be easy to recognize in the future. For example, Figure 16.8 shows a named search about to be saved as Video Files. Windows 10 suggests putting it in the Searches folder for your user account. That's as good a place as any to keep it, so don't change that unless you have a good reason.

TIP

Windows stores these saved searches using the Saved Search format, which is `.search-ms`. This is good to know if you ever need to look for saved searches on your system.

FIGURE 16.8

Saving a search for video files.

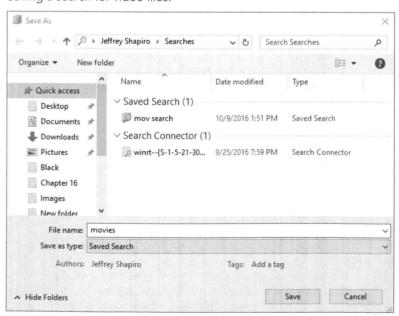

At the bottom of the Save As dialog box, your username is saved as the default author, but you can click that name and change it to another name or add author names. To add a tag to the saved search file, click the Add a Tag item if you like. Then click the Save button.

Using saved searches

Unless you specify otherwise, your saved searches are stored in the Searches folder for your user account. Your searches are also added to the Favorites folder. You can open the Searches folder using the following methods:

- Choose Search from the taskbar and type **searches** in the Search box. In the Results area, click the Searches folder.
- Open File Explorer from the Windows 10 interface, click your user account name, and open the Searches folder.
- If you're in a folder and the Navigation pane is open, click the saved search under Favorites.
- Choose Windows+X from the desktop, click Search, and type **searches** in the Search box. Click the Searches folder to open it.

Unless you opened a specific search, the Searches folder opens. You see searches you've saved.

To perform a saved search, open it by double-clicking its icon. The opened search looks like any real folder, and you can treat it just as you would any folder. The only difference between a saved search and another folder is that the saved search doesn't contain files. The saved search is a *virtual folder* that looks and acts like a real folder, but the files you see in the saved search are still in the folders where you originally saved them. The virtual folder lets you see all the files that match the search criteria *as though* they were all in one folder. This feature allows you to work with the files as a unit, regardless of their actual physical location in folders.

A search in Windows 10 is similar to an Internet search. When you search in Windows 10, or open a saved search, you're looking at links to files that match the search criteria. But be aware that when you do something to a file in the search results, you perform that action on the actual file. For example, when you delete a file from a saved search, you delete it from its actual location. Likewise, if you restore that file from the Recycle Bin, you restore it to its original location.

Wrapping Up

You have many ways to find things in Windows 10. The primary method includes typing a word in the Search box on the Search page to find items that contain that word, or searching in File Explorer using a wide range of criteria.

Each box is similar to a mini search engine for finding documents and messages based on content, properties, tags, or name. By default, only items in your user account are searched.

 If you want to include more items in those searches, see Chapter 18.

Here's a quick review of the main points covered in this chapter:

- Windows 10 has a built-in index of programs, files, folders, and messages in your user account. When you search the index, you get keystroke-by-keystroke results.

- To search from the Windows 10 interface or the Windows desktop, choose Search from the taskbar. Then start typing your search text.

- To search for a file when you know its general location, open the folder or a parent folder of the item. Then use the Search box in Explorer's upper-right corner to search.

- You can specify multiple criteria in both the Search box and in File Explorer by entering search keywords such as date modified, subject, size, and others, followed by a colon and the search parameter. You can combine multiple criteria in a single search.

- To save a search for future use, click Save Search on the Search tab of File Explorer.

- To reuse saved searches, click Search from the taskbar, type **searches** in the Search box, and click the Searches folder. Or click Searches under Favorites (if available) in the Navigation pane of any folder.

 If you frequently use files that are outside your user account folders, see Chapter 18 for information on adding those folders to your search index.

Using Cortana for Searching

C ortana is a digital personal assistant tool built into Windows 10. It provides you a way to access information by typing search criteria or by speaking commands. Information searches, files, calendar events, news, weather, sports updates, and other information is available through Cortana.

Cortana is available on Windows desktops, Windows tablets (such as Microsoft Surface tablets), and handheld mobile devices. Microsoft provides iOS (Apple iPhone) and Android apps as well, to provide you with Cortana access even when you are not using Windows-based devices.

Understanding Cortana

Cortana, named for the fictional artificial intelligence character in the Halo game series, was introduced on the Windows Phone 8.1 platform. It is an intelligent personal assistant that can help you set reminders, perform searches, answer questions, recognize music, and launch apps using voice or text commands. If you speak a question, Cortana typically speaks the answer. If you type a question, Cortana answers with a text response.

Cortana (if you let it) can learn about you, your interests and habits, locations you often visit, and other information to simplify your work or personal life. For example, Cortana can search for and detect flight schedules in your e-mails and add the information to your calendar for you, or identify tracking information in e-mails to keep you up to date on whether your online orders are in transit or still sitting in the seller's warehouse.

Setting Up Cortana

By default, Cortana is installed and set up ready to use when you install Windows 10 Anniversary Edition. Cortana appears in the Search field on the Windows Taskbar next to the Start button and is labeled Ask Me Anything. Figure 17.1 shows the taskbar field where Cortana is located.

FIGURE 17.1

Find Cortana on the taskbar next to the Start button.

To use Cortana, you must have an Internet connection, microphone, and speakers set up on your computer. You can prompt it to action in a few different ways under Windows 10:

- Say "Hey Cortana" out loud. The Cortana window appears, as shown in Figure 17.2. When the Cortana window appears, it awaits your search criteria, but also provides hints and suggestions to help you learn how it works. For example, in Figure 17.2, Cortana displays a tip that reads "Try, 'my groceries.'"

FIGURE 17.2

Say "Hey Cortana" to open the Cortana window.

- Click the microphone icon in the taskbar next to the Start button.
- Press the Windows+S to open Cortana (see Figure 17.3).
- Type a command or search term in the Ask Me Anything field. Figure 17.4 shows an example of Cortana after typing the search "Today's weather."

FIGURE 17.3

Press Windows+S to view the larger Cortana window.

FIGURE 17.4

Cortana shows today's weather.

TIP

To get a verbal response from Cortana, you must issue a voice command to it. If you type a command, you do not get a verbal response.

Using Cortana

The best way to become familiar with Cortana and its features is to use it. The following are some basic tasks you may want to perform with Cortana to get know it better. Once you know its features, you may want to modify them to suit your needs.

Perform a Search for News

To perform a search for the latest headline news using verbal commands, do the following:

1. Say "Hey Cortana." The Cortana window appears.
2. Say "What is today's news?" Figure 17.5 shows the initial Cortana window as you speak your command. Once you deliver your command and Cortana locates the search criteria, the window in Figure 17.6 appears, and Cortana reads you the first item found. In this example, Cortana reads the initial headline.

FIGURE 17.5

Asking Cortana to find today's headline news.

After you see the list of news stories that Cortana finds, you can click one to display it in more detail, as shown Figure 17.7. In this example, Cortana opens the Microsoft Edge browser to display the headline news report. You can exit the browser when you are finished.

FIGURE 17.6

Cortana displaying and reading today's news.

FIGURE 17.7

Click a news item or other search result that Cortana finds to open it in a web browser.

Display Your Calendar

One useful feature of Cortana is to use it to find out your daily calendar of events. Follow these steps to locate your calendar via Cortana:

1. Say "Hey Cortana." The Cortana window appears.

2. Say "What is on my calendar for tomorrow?" Cortana displays a list of meetings for tomorrow, as shown in Figure 17.8, and reads them to you.

FIGURE 17.8

View upcoming calendar events using Cortana.

3. To show more details about an event or meeting, click a calendar item. The Calendar app displays (see Figure 17.9).

FIGURE 17.9

You can see more information about your calendar by clicking a Cortana item.

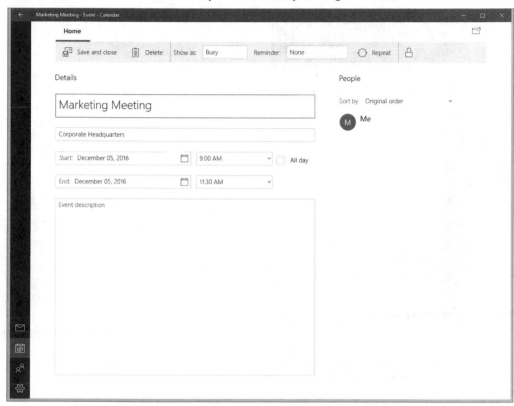

Getting the Time

Cortana can display the time for your current location or for a location anywhere in the world. Follow these steps:

1. Say "Hey Cortana." The Cortana window appears.
2. Say "What time is it?" Figure 17.10 shows the current time for my location.

FIGURE 17.10

You can ask Cortana your local time.

3. Say "What time is it in Venice, Italy?" Figure 17.11 shows the time in a remote location (Venice in this example).

Getting Weather Updates

To get weather reports from Cortana, use the following steps:

1. Say "Hey Cortana." The Cortana window appears.

2. Say "What's the weather here?" Figure 17.12 shows the results of a weather search for the local weather (which is for Richmond, IN, for this example). When you first use Cortana for a location-based query, such as the weather, Cortana may ask you for permission to collect information about your location. Respond that it's OK to collect this information.

FIGURE 17.11

You also can ask Cortana the time for any location, such as Venice, Italy.

17

FIGURE 17.12

Use Cortana to find out your weather.

3. Say "What's the weather like in Salt Lake City, Utah?" to find the weather for a remote location. Figure 17.13 shows the results.

FIGURE 17.13

Use Cortana to see the weather in a remote location.

Opening a Program or App

Cortana has commands for opening programs or apps installed on your computer. To open a program or app, do the following:

1. Say "Hey Cortana." The Cortana window appears.

2. Say "Open" and then the name of the program or app. For example, say "Microsoft Excel." Cortana locates and opens the application, in this case Excel. See Figure 17.14.

FIGURE 17.14

Use Cortana to open a program or app, such as Microsoft Excel.

Searching a File

To use Cortana to search for a file, follow these steps:

1. Say "Hey Cortana." The Cortana window appears.

2. Say "Find" and then the name of the document. For example, to find a document named Corporate Directors Meeting, say "Find document Corporate Directors Meeting," as shown in Figure 17.15.

FIGURE 17.15

Use Cortana to search for a file or document.

Locating a Photo of Cortana

You can also use Cortana for fun. You may, for example, want to know what Cortana looks like, or at least what her character in the Halo game looks like. To find out, do the following:

1. Say "Hey Cortana." The Cortana window appears.

2. Say "Show picture of Cortana." Cortana returns images named as Cortana, as shown in Figure 17.16.

FIGURE 17.16

Use Cortana to locate an image of the Cortana character.

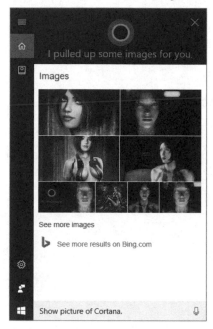

Modifying Cortana

You can customize Cortana using the Cortana Settings tool and the Cortana Notebook. The Settings tool provides access to common Cortana options, such as how it responds to you, allowing taskbar tidbits to display, and more. The Cortana Notebook includes items and settings you want Cortana to remember, such as your name and your favorite places.

To display the Settings tool, perform the following steps:

1. Click the Cortana search field. The Cortana menu opens (see Figure 17.17).

FIGURE 17.17

Displaying the Cortana menu.

Notebook ———

Settings ———

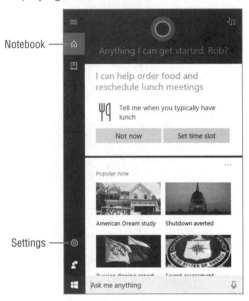

FIGURE 17.18

Use Cortana's Setting features to adjust Cortana's actions.

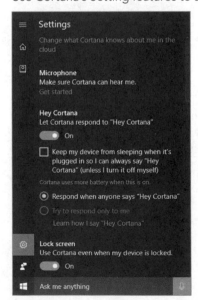

2. Click the Settings button, which is located toward the bottom left side of the Cortana menu. Figure 17.17 shows the location of the Settings button. Figure 17.18 shows the Settings menu.

Within Settings, you can adjust the following:

- **Tailor Cortana to your voice:** You can train Cortana to respond only to your voice when you or someone else uses the "Hey Cortana" phrase. Click "Learn How I Say Cortana" and walk through the prompts to train Cortana. This process takes several minutes, so do it when you have time to devote to training Cortana to recognize your voice.

- **Use Cortana even when the system is locked:** You can have Cortana respond to your request while your computer is locked. When the system is locked, Cortana can access your calendar, e-mail, messages, and Power BI (Microsoft's Power Business Intelligence data tool).

- **Taskbar tidbits:** Cortana can display on your taskbar helpful hints on what commands to use with Cortana.

- **Send notifications between devices:** With this feature, you can enable Cortana to display your phone notifications on your computer or device. You must also allow notifications to be sent from your phone by clicking the Edit Sync Settings options on the Settings menu. On the My Devices menu, set these two options to On:

  - Get Notifications From This PC On My Phone
  - Upload Notifications From This PC To the Cloud

  Both options must be set to On for this feature to work. Click each of them to set the status to On or Off, depending on your preference.

- **Set your local language:** Choose the language for your region, such as English (United States) if you speak English in the U.S.

- **Set history view:** Set History View to On to allow Cortana to display apps, settings, web activity, searches, and other history when you display the Cortana Home screen.

- **View device history:** You can use history from signed-in devices to help improve Cortana's performance when searching from apps, settings, and other history. To remove all device history, click Clear My Device History.

- **My search history:** You can use search history from Microsoft Edge to help improve Cortana searching performance. To modify history settings, click the Search History Settings link.

- **Bing SafeSearch settings:** Click this link to display Bing's SafeSearch feature. Adjust settings for your preferences for how Cortana interacts with SafeSearch, including restricting access to websites that are deemed adult or not safe for children.

- **Other privacy settings:** Click this link to open the Windows 10 Change Privacy Options. From here you can modify several Windows 10 privacy features, such as turning on the SmartScreen filter to check URLs that the Windows Store uses.

To review and adjust your Cortana Notebook settings, click the Notebook icon on the left side of the Cortana menu. The Notebook menu appears, as shown in Figure 17.19.

FIGURE 17.19

Cortana's Notebook feature stores personalized information and settings on how Cortana should respond to your commands.

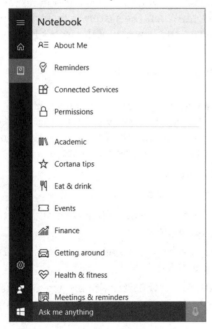

Cortana has a number of Notebook settings, shown in Figure 17.19. The following list details a few of these settings:

- **About Me:** Use this Notebook setting to change your name in Cortana and edit the Favorite places that Cortana uses for you. Favorite places include your home, work, and other locations you want to save, such as your favorite restaurant, workout facility, and day-care. You can also view the account name under which you are currently logged in.

- **Reminders:** Set reminders in Cortana. For example, Cortana can prompt you to perform an action (such as make a phone call at a particular time of day). You can set a Remember To action for that task. Figure 17.20 shows an example of Cortana displaying a reminder to call "Mike Smith" today.

FIGURE 17.20

Use the Reminder Notebook to add items for Cortana to remind you of.

- **Events:** Cortana can provide you with local events based on event categories you set. Click the Events Notebook and then click Add an Event Category. You can choose from Music, Performing Arts, and Sports & Outdoors.

- **Weather:** Use the Weather Notebook to set Cortana actions that relate to weather conditions in your area. For example, you can set Notify Me When There Are Weather Incidents to prompt Cortana to let you know about severe weather.

TIP

If you no longer want to use Cortana on your device or computer, you can turn it off. To do so, use the following steps:

1. Click the Cortana field in the Taskbar.

2. Choose Notebook.

3. Choose About me.

4. Select your user account. A window appears with your account name.

5. Click your user account name.

6. Select Sign Out.

Using Cortana on Mobile Devices

Microsoft has released a Cortana mobile app to use on your smartphone, such as the Apple iPhone and Android phones. To download the app, visit the app store for your phone and search for Cortana. Download the app to your phone and open the app. Within the app, you can perform many of the same functions you can with Cortana on a PC, such as searching with Cortana, setting an alarm using a voice command, viewing reminders, and other items.

To use Cortana on your smartphone, open the app by clicking its icon on your smartphone. Figure 17.21 shows an example of the main Cortana screen on the iPhone app.

FIGURE 17.21

You can use Cortana on your smartphone by downloading the Microsoft Cortana app from your phone's app store.

Click the microphone button on the app to ask Cortana a question or instruct it to perform a task. Figure 17.22 shows the Cortana app waiting for a response from the user. Figure 17.23 shows the iPhone Cortana app with the results of the question, "How Big is Earth?"

FIGURE 17.22

Speak to the Cortana smartphone app to use Cortana in a mobile situation.

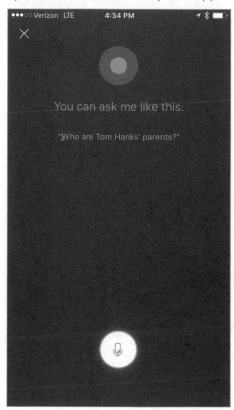

To see Notebook and Cortana Settings, click the Settings button at the top left of the app. This shows Home, Notebook, Settings, Help, and Feedback & Support options. Click the option you want to use to navigate to that item. For example, click Notebook see similar Notebook items that you have on your computer via Cortana. Click the Home button to return to the main window of Cortana.

> **TIP**
>
> To perform other Cortana tasks in the Cortana app, click the options button. This button is located on the lower right of the iPhone app. From here, you can set reminders, see weather items, show scheduled meetings, make a phone call, create a text message, set alarms, see news stories and movie listings, hear a joke, or listen to a song sung by Cortana.

FIGURE 17.23

Cortana shows results of your search.

Wrapping Up

Cortana is a digital personal assistant tool built into Windows 10. It provides you a way to access information by typing in search criteria or by speaking in commands. Information searches, files, calendar events, news, weather, sports updates, and other information is available through Cortana.

This chapter introduced the following points:

- Understanding Cortana
- Setting up Cortana
- Using Cortana
- Modifying Cortana
- Using Cortana on mobile devices

Metadata and Power Searches

C hapter 16 covers different ways you can search your computer. When you search for files, you actually search an index of filenames and properties. You don't see the index on the screen, nor do you have to do anything to create or update the index. Windows 10 takes care of all the details automatically. The beauty of the index is that it allows Windows 10 to find files much more quickly than it could without the index.

The information about files that's in the index comes from each file's properties. Those properties are sometimes referred to as *metadata* because they're different from the file's content. The file's content is what you see on the screen when you open the file. The file's properties are stored in the file and are visible from the file's properties sheet.

Properties provide a way of organizing files that goes beyond their physical location in folders. This is a great help to people who have many files to manage — sometimes a simple folder name and filename just aren't enough. Sometimes you want to see all files based on authorship, date created, tags, subject, or even comments you've jotted down about the file. In other words, you want to pull together and work with files in a way that transcends their physical locations in folders. Metadata in Windows 10's indexed searches allows you to do that quickly and easily.

Working with File Properties

Taking a wild guess, we'd say you can put several thousand different types of files on a PC. No one person needs them all or uses them all. Some file types are so esoteric that you might never come across one.

In File Explorer, you can view and edit a file's properties in many ways. One way is to open the folder in which the file is contained and then select the file's icon. The Details pane, if open, displays the file's properties. If the Details pane isn't open, select the View tab and click the Details Pane button.

Initially, the Details pane may be too short to show all the file's properties, but you can drag its top border upward to see more properties. Figure 18.1 shows an example displaying the properties for a Microsoft Word 2016 document. Other file types have other properties.

FIGURE 18.1

A file's properties in the Details pane.

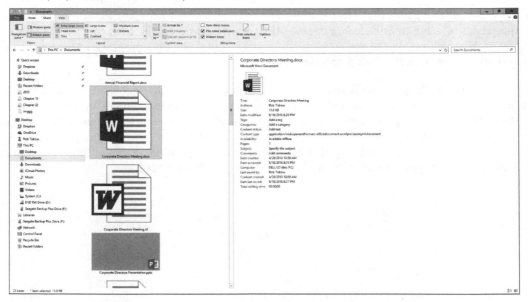

Viewing properties sheets

Here's another way to view a file's properties: Right-click the file's icon and choose Properties. A dialog box opens. If that dialog box has a Details tab, that's where you're most likely to find properties you can create and edit. You often hear the term *properties sheet* used to describe that set of properties because it's like a sheet of paper on which properties are written.

Figure 18.2 shows a couple of sample properties sheets. On the left is the properties sheet for the Word document shown in Figure 18.1. On the right is the properties sheet for a .doc document file. When you have more properties than fit in the box, use the scroll bar at the right side of the box to see others.

FIGURE 18.2

Examples of properties sheets for two files.

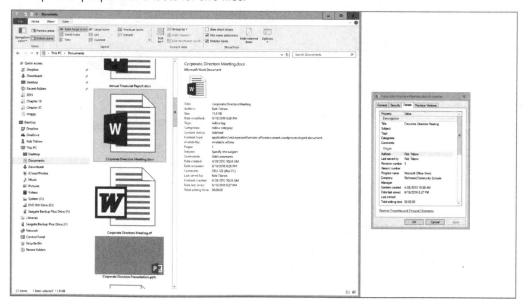

Every property has a name and a *value* (some text, date, or number that's assigned to the property). In the properties sheets, the property names are listed down the left column. The value assigned to each property (if any) appears to the right of the property name.

Viewing properties in columns

A third way to view properties is through the Details view in File Explorer. In any folder (including the results of a search), select the View tab and choose Details. You see a few columns across the top of the contents pane. But what you see isn't necessarily all the available information. The horizontal scroll bar across the bottom of the pane lets you scroll to other columns. You can add columns to the view (or remove columns) by right-clicking any column heading, as in Figure 18.3. The menu that appears shows a few other columns from which you can choose. Click More at the bottom of that menu to see others.

FIGURE 18.3

Choosing columns in Details view.

Editing properties

To change a file's properties (some properties are not editable), select its icon and make your changes in the Details pane. Or right-click the file's icon, choose Properties, select the Details tab, and make your changes there.

You can change properties for multiple files using the same basic method. You just have to select the icons for the files first. But there is a catch: You're limited to changing properties that all the selected files have in common. This limitation can be a pain when you're working with multiple file types. For example, many different types of files for storing pictures exist — JPEG, TIFF, PNG, BMP, and GIF, to name a few. The newer file types — JPEG, TIFF, and PNG — offer many properties. The older file types — BMP and GIF — offer relatively few.

Figure 18.4 shows an example of what can happen when you select multiple file types. We selected all the icons in the folder, each of which is a picture. Then we right-clicked one of them, chose Properties, and selected the Details tab. Hardly any properties are showing because those file types have few properties in common.

FIGURE 18.4

Properties for multiple files.

With old file types that support few properties, about the only thing you can do is convert them to newer file types. For example, you may have lots of GIF images on your system. That file type doesn't offer any usable properties. To resolve this problem, you can use the batch conversion feature of your graphics program (PaintShop Pro) to convert the files to PNG files. We suggest PNG because it supports transparency, as GIF does.

NOTE

PNG does not support animation, so you may not want to convert animated GIFs to PNG.

If you have many files that you want to assign new properties to, consider creating a search that brings similar files together all under one roof, so to speak. Open the Documents folder (or other folder that is a parent of the one you want to search) and click in the Search box to specify the types of files you want to work with. In Figure 18.5, we typed the following into the Filename box:

```
*.jpg OR *.jpeg OR *.tif OR *.tiff OR *.png
```

FIGURE 18.5

Specify the types of files in the Search box.

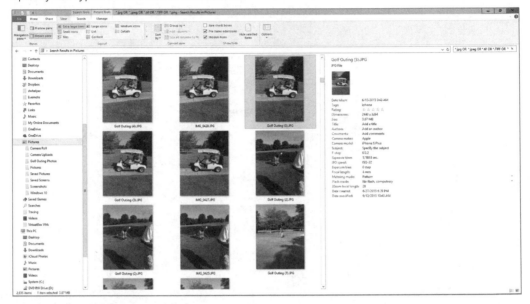

That brings together all the TIFF, JPEG, and PNG files in the search scope. Perform the search and then use column headings to sort items based on their current folder location. You can add columns that allow you to see the properties you intend to work with. Of course, that's just an example. You can set up searches to find and organize files as you see fit.

Save the search when you're finished so you can open and use it whenever you have time to work with properties. To change properties for any single file, click its name. To assign the same property value to multiple files, select their icons. Then use the Details pane or properties sheet to make your changes. The procedure takes some time if you have a number of files to work with. But having all the files together in one place, and the properties of interest in plain view, can make the job less daunting.

> **TIP**
>
> Windows 10's Save As dialog box offers tools for entering metadata (such as tags) when you save a file.

Setting Properties When You Save

Search indexes are nothing new. Database administrators have been using them for decades. Every time you do an Internet search, you're searching an index of websites somewhere. Windows XP and other operating systems allowed some limited, indexed searching through add-on programs. But Windows Vista was the first Windows version to have indexed searching — its own built-in search engine — built in from the ground up. Windows 7 and 8.1 expanded upon and improved the search capabilities introduced in Vista, with capabilities to search Windows apps, the Windows Marketplace, Xbox LIVE, and Xbox Companion areas from within Windows. Other software developers understand the value of that feature. As the years roll by, new versions of old programs will include the capability to tag files and set properties at the moment you first save the program. In addition, the relationship of the desktop environment to the online environment is much tighter and more seamless in Windows 10.

When you save a new file, be sure to look for options in the Save As dialog box that allow you to add tags or properties. Figure 18.6 shows an example of the Save As dialog box for a Microsoft PowerPoint 2016 presentation. The dialog box allows you to add tags and authors right on the spot.

When you're faced with such options, think about words you can type into a Search box to find the file in the future. Ask yourself, "If I need this thing six months from now and forget its filename, what word can I use to search for it?" or "How should I categorize this file in relation to other similar kinds of documents?" As your collection of files grows, and your searching skills grow, the few moments you spend thinking up keywords for tags and properties will pay off in spades.

FIGURE 18.6

Save As dialog box for PowerPoint 2016.

Personalizing Searches

Getting the most from Windows 10's searches includes knowing how to tweak its settings to work in ways that support the kinds of things you do. You can tweak some aspects of indexed searches through the Folder and Search Options dialog box. To get to the search options, do either of the following:

- If you're in a folder, select the View tab and click the Options button.
- Type **file option** in the Cortana search box and then click File Explorer Options in the Search Results area.

The File Explorer Options dialog box opens. Select the Search tab to see the options shown in Figure 18.7.

The Don't Use the Index When Searching in File Folders for System Files (Searches Might Take Longer) option applies when you search non-indexed locations. When you select that option, searches outside the index work like non-indexed searches from older Windows versions. The search looks at every file in every folder and doesn't even look at the search option. When you leave that option unselected, the search still uses the index for files in indexed locations. So, that part of the search goes quickly. Then it falls back to the old non-indexed method, but only for files that aren't indexed.

The last three options apply only when you're searching non-indexed locations. Choose Include System Directories if you want non-indexed searches to include Windows and other program files that are essential to proper functioning of your PC. These are not files you normally open or modify yourself. So, choose this option only if you're a power user or administrator who needs frequent access to files in those locations. Otherwise, you're slowing down your searches for no good reason.

FIGURE 18.7

Search options.

Choosing the Include Compressed Files (ZIP, CAB...) option extends the search into compressed Zip folders and the like. (CAB files are "cabinet" files, and they're compressed as well.) Typically, people use compressed files for archived files that they don't use often because the compression and decompression add time to opening and closing the files. Including their contents in searches can also slow searches. But if you want to include those files' contents in your non-indexed searches, select the check box.

The option Always Search File Names and Contents (This Might Take Several Minutes) — forces searches to look at the contents of non-indexed files, which can really slow you down. Better to index the non-indexed document files to get the speedier index searches.

As always, clicking Restore Defaults sets all options back to their original defaults. Those are the options that provide the best performance for indexed searches and cover the things most people typically want included in their searches.

Managing the Search Index

To get the best performance and value from the search index, make sure it includes all the files you regularly use in your work. But don't go overboard and include files you never, or rarely, use. If you do, you force Windows to search through thousands of filenames and properties for no good reason. By default, Windows 10 maximizes the search index by including messages and documents from a limited number of folders.

> **TIP**
>
> Some indexing settings can be changed by standard users. Advanced settings can only be changed by a user with administrative rights. Of course, many people use multiple hard disks to store their files. If you want to include files from other drives and folders, you need to add them to your search index. But exercise some discretion. The larger the index, the more overhead involved in maintaining the index and the slower things go. Don't add a folder to the index if it contains a bunch of non-document files or files you don't use regularly.

What's with the Offline Files?

Offline files are files that primarily exist on some other computer. You use Sync Center to copy them to and from a portable notebook in a way that prevents the copies on your computer from becoming out of sync with copies on the main computer. The files are included in the search index, by default, because they're usually documents. The search index is all about finding and opening documents quickly.

You can exclude offline files from the search index just by clearing the check box in the Indexed Locations dialog box. Any user can do that; administrative privileges aren't required. If you don't use offline files, leaving that option selected doesn't cause any overhead. After all, if you don't use offline files, the offline folder does not exist in the first place. Indexing a non-existent folder takes no time at all.

Adding indexed locations

Windows 10 indexes certain folders by default. You can add or remove locations through the Indexing Options dialog box (see Figure 18.8) with the following steps:

1. Open the Indexing Options item from the Control Panel to open the Indexing Options dialog box.

2. Click Modify.

3. Click to expand drives and folders, as necessary, to get to the folder(s) you want to add.

> **CAUTION**
>
> Items with check marks are already indexed. Don't clear any check marks unless you specifically want to remove that folder from your index. If you goof and lose track, click Cancel to leave the dialog box without saving any changes.

4. Select (check) the folder(s) you want to add. Choosing a folder automatically chooses all subfolders, so there's no need to select those individually. But you could clear the check mark on one if you wanted to exclude it from the index. Those excluded folders will show up in the Excluded column in Indexing Options.

5. Click OK.

FIGURE 18.8

Indexing options.

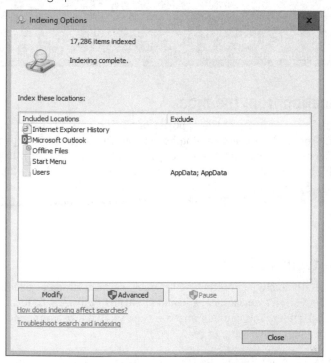

The folder is added to the index without any fanfare. About the only change you see is that the folder name appears in the Index These Locations list in Indexing Options. Use the scroll bar to the right of that list if the folder name isn't immediately visible. Also, if you look at the text near the top of Indexing Options, you'll see the number of items indexed.

If you're actively using the computer, you see a message indicating that indexing speed is reduced due to user activity. Not to worry — it just means that the index-building process is giving priority to things you want to do. This message is replaced by others when the index is being built at full speed, and when indexing is complete.

You can add as many folders as you wish, from as many drives as you wish, using those same methods. But again, prudence is a virtue. *Remember:* Don't add folders just for the heck of it or because you don't know what's in a particular folder. The more you keep your index focused on files you want to find in searches and access through virtual folders, the better performance you get from the index.

> **TIP**
>
> With administrative rights, you can click Show All Locations in the Indexed Locations dialog box to show additional folders that are not shown by default. These include Offline Files folders for all users, rather than just the current user. You can also view user folders for users other than yourself when you click Show All Locations.

Remove a location from the index

Removing a folder from the index is the opposite of adding one. Repeat the preceding steps to get to the Indexed Locations dialog box shown in Figure 18.9. Expand drives and folders, as necessary, so you can see the items you've selected (checked). If you want to exclude some subfolders from one of your indexed folders, expand that folder first. Then clear the check marks from the subfolders you don't want in the index. Those subfolders show up in the Exclude column in the lower pane of the dialog box. Click OK after making your changes.

Choosing file types to index

The index intentionally excludes unknown file types, certain kinds of executable files, and libraries because they aren't normally the kinds of things you want to locate in a quick file search or virtual folder. You can add any file type you like to your index, and you can remove any file type you don't want to see.

Filenames and properties of selected file types are always indexed. For files that contain text, such as word-processing documents and spreadsheets, you can choose whether to index file contents. The advantage of indexing file contents is that when you search for files, the file shows up even if the search term isn't in the filename or properties. The slight disadvantage is that it adds some size to the index. But in this case, the advantage of including file contents probably outweighs the cost, unless you're using older, slower hardware and your searches are very slow.

FIGURE 18.9

The Indexed Locations dialog box.

To change options for file types, open the Indexing Options dialog box and follow these steps:

1. Click the Advanced button (enter an administrative password if prompted).

2. In the dialog box that opens, select the File Types tab. You see a list of all file extensions, as in Figure 18.10. Do any of the following:

   - To include a file type, select its check box.

   - To exclude a file type, clear its check box.

   - If you opted to include a file type, choose whether you want to index properties only or properties and file contents.

3. To add a file extension that isn't in the list, type the extension next to the Add button and click the Add button.

4. Click OK after making your changes.

FIGURE 18.10

Choosing file types to index.

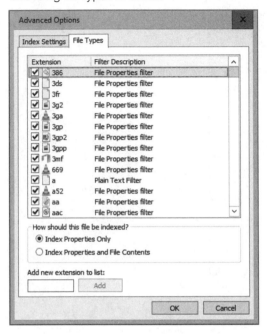

More advanced options

You can make some more advanced tweaks to the index to change how it operates. You see them when you first click the Advanced button in Indexing Options. Figure 18.11 shows those advanced options on the Index Settings tab.

Choosing Index Encrypted Files ensures that encrypted files are included in searches and virtual indexes. People encrypt files to keep out prying eyes. Keeping those files out of the index adds a layer of security by making them invisible to basic file searches. But if that isn't a problem for you, and you want your encrypted files to show up in searches, choose the option to index encrypted files.

A *diacritic* (or diacritical mark) is an accent mark added to a letter to change a word's pronunciation. Some examples include the acute accent (á), circumflex (â), and umlaut (ä). When used in filenames and properties, Windows 10 usually treats characters with diacritics as being identical to the character without the mark. Choosing Treat Similar Words with Diacritics as Different Words changes the search behavior so that the diacritics are no longer lumped together as though they were a single character.

FIGURE 18.11

The Index Settings tab.

The Index Location option lets you specify where you want to store the search index. The default is the C:\ProgramData\Microsoft folder. If you have a separate hard drive that runs faster than your C: drive, you can relocate the index to that drive for better performance. Just make sure you choose a drive that's always attached to the computer, not a removable drive. Click the Select New button and use the Browse for Folder dialog box that appears to navigate the drive and folder in which you want to store the index.

If you see error messages about a corrupt index, or the system crashes when you try to perform a search, the problem may be a corrupted index. You can rebuild the index to see if that helps, but the process can take several hours. So, if at all possible, consider doing this job as an overnighter. The process is simple: Click the Rebuild button on the Index Settings tab of the Advanced Options dialog box (refer to Figure 18.11).

You can continue to use the computer while the index is being rebuilt. Any searches you perform while the index is being rebuilt will likely be incomplete.

Power Searches

The ability to display the Search box, type a few characters, and see all items that contain those characters is a great thing. For most people, it saves lots of time otherwise spent opening programs or navigating through folders to open a program, document, contact, or message. It's so useful that you may not even need to bother with more complex searches.

When you need a more complex search, you can use the Search box in File Explorer to search for particular types of files and limit the search by date, filename, size, or other criteria. You can create complex searches and save them. When you want to do the same search again in the future, that's handy, as well. Folks who want still more can use the query language.

You may have noticed that after you fill in the blanks in an Advanced Search and click the Search button, you see some text in the Search box. Take a look at Figure 18.12 for an example. There the date criterion is set to Date Modified 10/9/2016. This puts the following into the Search box:

```
6datemodified:10/09/2016
```

That little line of text in the Search box, called a *query,* is what returns the search results. When you perform the search, Windows 10 looks through the whole index. But the query acts as a filter. Only items that meet the conditions set forth by the query show in the search results. In this example, only files whose Date Modified date is 6/28/2015 appear in the search results. Items that don't match the criterion don't appear in the search results. Those items aren't deleted or changed in any way. They're simply "filtered out" so as not to show up in the search results.

You can type your own queries into the Search box to perform complex searches. But, it isn't as simple as "asking a question" or typing a bunch of words at random. You have to follow some rules and write the query in such a way that it can be interpreted properly. Otherwise, the search returns the wrong items, or no items at all. The following sections look at some ways you can type your own complex queries.

Searching specific properties

When you type a word into the search box, the results show files that contain that word in their filename, contents, and properties. For example, a search for jazz finds songs in the jazz music genre, any folder or file that has the word *jazz* in its filename or contents, and any file that has the word *jazz* in any property. In other words, you can end up with lots of files in the search results.

You can narrow a search by specifying a property name followed by a colon and the text for which you're searching. For example, a search for genre:jazz finds only music files in the jazz genre.

FIGURE 18.12

Sample search.

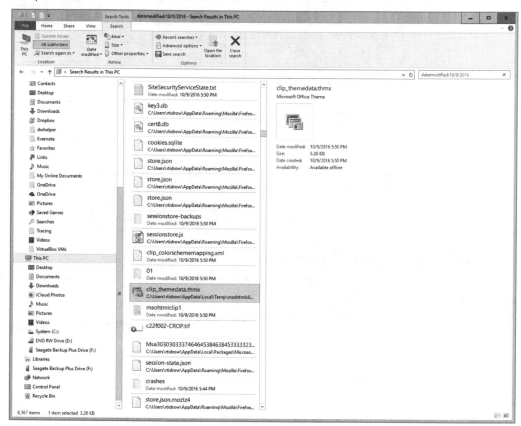

Similarly, a search for `susan` finds all files that have *susan* somewhere in the file, name, or a property, whereas a search for `from:susan` finds only e-mail messages that have the name *susan* in the From address (for a local e-mail client, not a web e-mail client).

You can assign ratings to pictures and music files, and use ratings as a search word. For example, `rating:5 stars` finds files with 5-star ratings.

Greater than and less than

When you're searching for a property that contains a date or a number, you can use the comparison operators shown in Table 23-1.

TABLE 23.1 **Comparison Operators Available with Search**

Operator	Meaning
=	Equal to (this is assumed if you don't specify an operator)
>	Greater than
>=	Greater than or equal to
<	Less than
<=	Less than or equal to
<>	Does not equal

A search for `rating:>=4 stars` finds pictures and music with 4- or 5-star ratings. A search for `width:<600` finds pictures with widths less than 600 pixels. The query `modified:<2015` finds files last modified in 2015 or earlier. A search for `kind:video size:<300KB` finds video files less than 300KB in size.

AND, OR, and NOT searches

You can use the keywords AND, OR, and NOT in searches. You must type the word in upper-case letters. Be sure to include a space before and after the word.

Not using any word is the same as using AND. For example, consider the following search:

```
Datemodified:5/9/2012 name:koala
```

That means the same thing as this:

```
Datemodified:5/9/2012 AND name:koala
```

Any time you create an AND query, you *narrow* the search results. Intuitively, you may expect it to have the opposite effect. But that isn't the way it works. The query is a filter. To show up in the search results, a file must meet *all* criteria posed by the filter. For example, files that don't have *koala* in the Filename property don't show up at all, no matter what's in their Date Modified property. And files that were modified on dates other than 5/9/2012 don't show up either, even if they have *koala* in the Filename field.

Here's a common mistake that illustrates this principle:

```
filename:(*.jpg AND *.jpeg)
```

Intuitively, you might expect this search to identify files with .jpg and .jpeg extensions. But it doesn't. The result of this search is nothing! Why? Because the criterion is a filter, not a question. To get through the filter, a file must have a .jpg extension *and* a .jpeg extension. But a file can't have two extensions. Every file has only one filename extension. Therefore, no single file can get past this filter.

When you want to *broaden,* not narrow, a search, you use OR. For example, take a look at this search:

```
filename:(*.jpg OR *.jpeg)
```

To get past this filter, a file must have either a .jpg or a .jpeg extension. So, the result of the search displays all files that have either a .jpg or .jpeg filename extension.

> **TIP**
>
> If you don't see filename extensions in search results, select the View tab and click the Options button. Then select the View tab, clear the check mark next to Hide Extensions for Known File Types, and click OK.

By the way, you don't have to use the asterisk (*) and dot if you use extension:, ext:, or type: as the property name. For example, this search criterion also shows all files that have .jpg or .jpeg extensions:

```
ext:(jpg OR jpeg)
```

You aren't limited to a single OR. Here's a search that shows all files that have .avi, .wmv, .mpg, and .mpeg extensions:

```
ext:(avi OR wmv OR mpg OR mpeg)
```

When you use type: you can use whatever appears in the Type column (in Details view) rather than the extension. For example, this search finds Microsoft Word documents:

```
type:word
```

This one finds Word documents that have *john* in the filename or inside the document text:

```
john AND type:word
```

Because the keyword AND is assumed if omitted, the following search works the same as the preceding one:

```
john type:word
```

If you want to look only at the filename and not the contents, use the name: property. For example, here's a query that looks for Excel spreadsheets that have the word *festival* in the filename:

```
name:festival type:excel
```

In addition to searching for extensions, you can use kind: to find certain kinds of files. For example, kind:music finds music files; kind:picture finds pictures; kind:contact finds contacts; kind:e-mail finds e-mail messages; and kind:communication finds messages and contacts.

18

The NOT keyword narrows a search by excluding items that match the criterion that follows. For example, when you use the kind: keyword, you get both the file type, as well as shortcuts that open the file type. To hide the shortcut files, use NOT shortcut. For example, here's a search criterion that shows all files that are communication files excluding any shortcuts to those files:

```
kind:(communication NOT shortcut)
```

A search for kind:video shows all video files. This search shows all video files except the ones that have a .mov filename extension:

```
kind:video NOT extension:mov
```

It isn't always necessary to specify the kind or type of file. For example, consider this query:

```
homecity:Cucamonga
```

That one finds all contacts whose Home City is Cucamonga. Because Contacts are the only type of file that have a Home City property, you'd probably get only contacts in the search results even without specifying kind:contact.

You can use tag: as a search property, too. For example, the query tag:(alec OR ashley) finds files that have either *alec* or *ashley* in the Tags property. The query tag:(alec AND ashley) finds files that have both *alec* and *ashley* in the Tags property.

If you use the Comments and Categories properties in files, use comment: and category: to search just those properties. Similarly, you can use title: to search the Title property and subject: to search the Subject property.

Date and number searches

When searching for files based on a date, you can use the following property names for specific dates:

- modified: Date the file was last modified.
- accessed: Date the file was last opened.
- created: Date the file was created.
- sent: Date a message was sent.
- received: Date a message was received.
- taken: Date a picture was taken.

To search a range of dates, use the keywords followed by a start date, two dots (..), and an end date. For example, to find all pictures taken between June 1, 2016, and September 1, 2016, use this criterion:

```
taken:6/1/2016..9/1/2016
```

You can also use comparison operators with date searches. For example, to see all files modified on or after January 1, 2016, use this criterion:

```
modified:>=1/1/2016
```

You can also use the following keywords with dates:

- today
- tomorrow
- yesterday
- this week
- last week
- this month
- last month
- next month
- this year
- last year
- next year

For example, this search finds all files modified today:

```
modified: today
```

This search shows all files that were created this week:

```
created:this week
```

Here's a query that lists all picture files that were taken this month:

```
taken:this month
```

To see all files modified between some date (say 1/1/2016) and today, use this query:

```
modified:>=1/1/2016 AND modified:<=today
```

If you're interested in a certain month and year, use the month name and year like this:

```
modified:july 2016
```

For a day of the week, use the weekday name like this:

```
modified:monday
```

The comparison operators work with numbers, too. When searching sizes, you can use KB, MB, and GB abbreviations. For example, here's a search criterion that finds all files that are 1MB or greater in size:

```
size:>=1MB
```

Here is one that finds files larger than 2GB in size:

```
size:>2GB
```

Here's one that finds files between 500KB and 1,000KB in size:

```
size:>=500KB AND size:<=1000KB
```

If you save music in various bit rates, here's a query that finds all files with bit rates greater than or equal to 300 Kbps:

```
bitrate:>=300kbps
```

If you want only MP3 files with those large bit rates, use this criterion:

```
bitrate:>=300kbps AND type:mp3
```

Here's a query that finds all pictures whose height is 800 pixels or less:

```
kind:picture height:<=800
```

Searching for phrases

When searching for two or more words, you'll likely end up with documents that contain the words you specified, but not necessarily in the order you typed them. To prevent that problem, you can enclose the phrase in quotation marks. For example, typing the following into a Search box displays all files that contain the words *dear* and *wanda* regardless of their relative positions to one another:

```
dear wanda
```

But typing the following into a Search box displays files where the words *dear* and *wanda* appear right next to each other in the document:

```
"dear wanda"
```

Message searching

For Windows Mail messages, key properties include `to:`, `from:`, `about:`, `subject:`, `sent:`, and `received:`. Both `to:` and `from:` can contain any word that appears in the To: and From: columns in the message. The `about:` keyword looks at the contents of the messages, not just the subject line. For example, the following is a query that you could enter in the Search box on the Start menu, which finds all messages from someone named Kay that contain the word *lunch:*

```
from:kay about:lunch
```

Here's a query that shows all messages addressed to Alan that arrived today:

```
to:alan received:today
```

Here's a search that shows all messages addressed to Susan, sent by Alan, that have *contract* in the Subject line:

```
to:susan from:alan subject:contract
```

Here's a query for e-mail messages sent this week from Alan to Wanda that contain the words *chow mein:*

```
to:wanda about:"chow mein" from:alan sent:this week
```

Natural language queries

Earlier in this chapter, you saw the option Use Natural Language Search in the Folder and Search Options dialog box. If you choose that, you can omit the colons after property names and use uppercase or lowercase letters in search queries. This makes typing most queries easier. For example, with natural language, the following query finds all messages from Susan that contain the word *dinner:*

```
from susan about dinner
```

This search finds all video files excluding ones with an .avi filename extension:

```
kind video not avi
```

Here's the natural language version of the query about "chow mein" e-mail messages:

```
to wanda about chow mein from alan sent this week
```

Here's a query that finds all files whose size is greater than 5MB:

```
size > 5MB
```

Here's a natural language query that finds all songs by Led Zeppelin:

```
music by zeppelin
```

This natural language query finds all pictures that have the word *flower* in the filename:

```
flower pictures
```

18

Here's a natural language query that finds all files that contain the word *peas,* the word *carrots,* or both words:

```
peas or carrots
```

Here's a natural language search that finds files that contain the words *peas* and *carrots* (although not necessarily together):

```
peas and carrots
```

Here's one that finds files that contain all three words, *peas and carrots,* together:

```
"peas and carrots"
```

Looking for a file you just downloaded or saved today? Try this natural language search in the Search box on the Start menu:

```
created today
```

Here's a natural language search that lists all files modified yesterday:

```
modified yesterday
```

Here are some other natural language searches you can probably figure out without our telling you what they mean:

- `e-mail received today`
- `e-mail from alec received yesterday`
- `contact message`
- `pictures alec`
- `genre rock`
- `artists Santana`
- `rating 5 stars`

Using natural language syntax doesn't mean you can ignore all the other things described in this chapter. The folder from which you start the search still matters. And all the other options in the Folder and Search Options and Indexing Options dialog boxes still apply. But in most cases you can type a useful search query with minimal fuss. If you can't get a search to work, try turning off natural language searches and use the stricter syntax with colons after property names.

Wrapping Up

Windows 10's searching and indexing features pick up where Windows 7 and Windows 8.1 left off. Search is now a vast improvement over earlier versions of Windows and the add-on

Search Companion used in Windows XP. Windows 10 searching isn't about finding lost files, although you can use it for that. If you use it only for that, you're missing out on the big picture and some key features of Windows 10.

Windows 10 searches use an index of filenames, properties, and file contents to make searches quick and nimble. They also look only at files in the search index because that's much faster than slogging through the entire file system to look at every file in every folder. But searches work correctly only if your index includes all the locations where you keep your frequently used document files.

One thing is for sure. If you've been managing thousands of files in hundreds of folders, and you're sick of opening programs and folders, you're sure to love the new search index. You may not love it at first, because you have to understand how it works. And you may have to spend some time tweaking settings in a couple of dialog boxes. But after you're past that small bump in the road, you'll spend less time *getting to* files, and lots more time *doing* things!

This chapter introduced the following points:

- The search index includes information about files stored in the file's properties sheets.
- When you select a file in a folder, the Details pane shows the properties currently assigned to the file.
- You can also view a file's properties by right-clicking its icon and choosing Properties. Most editable properties are on the Details tab.
- File properties are also visible in any folder's Details view. That includes virtual folders (saved searches).
- The search index generally covers all files in your user account, people in your Contacts folder, and Windows Mail messages.
- The Folder and Search Options dialog box provides some options for personalizing searches.
- The Indexing Options dialog box provides a means of customizing the index to better suit the way you organize your files.

18

Protecting Your Files

S ome things on your hard drive are valuable. Pictures and videos from digital cameras are irreplaceable. Documents you spent hours creating required an investment of your time. You don't want to lose those things because of a technical problem or mistake, so keeping backups is a good idea. That way, if you lose the originals on your hard drive, you can easily restore them from your backup copy.

In addition to the files you create and use yourself, many *system files* reside on your hard drive. These are files that Windows 10 needs to function properly. If those files get messed up, your computer may not work correctly. So, you need some means of backing up those system files as well.

This chapter explains how to back up both your personal files and your system files. (We also cover the ability to save your system settings and configuration to your OneDrive.) Of course, the backups don't do you any good if you can't use them when you need them. So, we discuss how to use those backups if you ever need to get your system back in shape. We also discuss System Protection, which creates restore points to keep copies of some files around temporarily. This feature helps you fix minor mishaps on the spot without fumbling around with external disks.

Simple File Backups

A simple way to back up items from your user account is to copy files to an external disk. Just make sure that the disk to which you're copying has enough space to store what you're copying.

> This chapter focuses on using hard drives, flash drives, and similar local disks to make backups. For ways to back up to the "cloud," read Chapter 15, which covers Microsoft OneDrive and Azure. That chapter shows you how to store files online to give you the ability to back up files to an offsite location, and use those files from any place where you have Internet access.

To see how much material is in a folder in your user account, open File Explorer and then point to the folder you're considering backing up, or right-click that folder and choose Properties. When you point, the size of the folder shows in a tooltip. When you right-click and choose Properties, the size of the folder shows up next to Size on Disk in the Properties dialog box (see Figure 19.1).

FIGURE 19.1

A folder's size shown in the Properties dialog box.

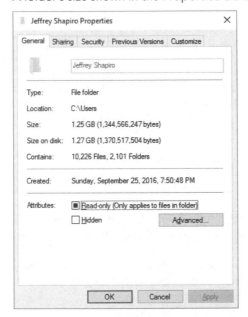

To see how much space is available on a removable disk, such as a flash drive, connect it to a USB port and then open the root folder on your computer. With some kinds of drives, you see the amount of available space right on the icon. For example, drive C: in Figure 19.2 has 35.8GB free.

FIGURE 19.2

A disk's available space.

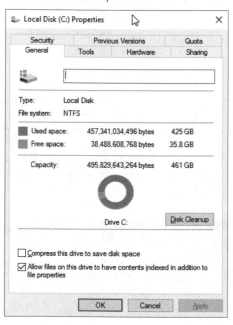

The layout for Windows 10 is very different from previous versions of File Explorer or Windows Explorer. In particular, Windows no longer puts libraries under Favorites.

TIP

1KB is 1024 bytes, 1MB is a little more than a million (1024²) bytes, and 1GB is about a billion (1024³) bytes.

If the disk has enough space for the item you want to copy, copy it to the disk. If you ever lose or damage a file on your hard drive, you can get it back from the copy on the external disk.

> **NOTE**
>
> Dozens, if not hundreds, of e-mail services and multiple e-mail clients exist, and they don't all work the same. In fact, e-mail has nothing to do with Windows 10. E-mail is a service provided by your ISP or mail service provider. Your only resource for information is the tech support provided by your ISP or mail service (or someone who happens to use and know the same service).

That's the quick and easy way to make backups of important files. More elaborate methods exist. The next two sections discuss ways of backing up all your files, and even your entire hard drive.

Using File History

Windows 10's File History feature is an alternative to the simple method for backing up files described earlier and is an upgrade to the Windows Backup feature released with Windows 7. File History can back up individual folders, all files for all user accounts, or even your entire hard drive. It works with an external hard drive, USB drive, or a shared network drive. File History makes recovering files very easy because it allows you to access backed-up files from File Explorer.

> **NOTE**
>
> File History does not use OneDrive as an external drive. You must supply one of the following: a physical hard disk that is attached to your local computer, a drive on a server somewhere in your office, or a drive on a server in the cloud. Drives on servers can be found by configuring network connections to these resources.

Starting File History

File History is a tool for backing up files in all user accounts so you need administrative privileges to run it. If you're logged in to a standard account, log off, or run as administrator. Then log back in to an administrative account.

To launch File History, open Settings, launch the Update and Security application, and then click Backup in menu on the left. Or open Control Panel and click the File History option. File History can be accessed from Settings as shown in Figure 19.3.

By default, File History is turned off under Windows 10. A message on the main File History page indicates such. Also, File History recommends that you use an external drive for your backup storage device, or use a network location for backups. In fact, notice that the Turn On button is grayed out. You cannot even turn on File History until it recognizes a supported drive. In the example shown, File History has accepted an external USB hard drive.

FIGURE 19.3

The File History page from Settings.

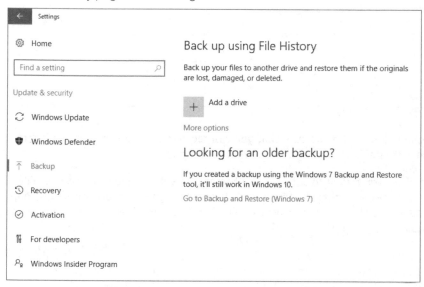

To turn on File History, connect an external drive to your computer. Press F5 on your keyboard or click the Refresh button on the Address bar to refresh the page. If you would rather use a network drive than an external drive, click the Use Network Location link and follow the instructions in the next section, "Backing Up to a Network Location."

The next example here uses an external USB drive to back up files. Figure 19.4 shows what the File History page looks like after plugging in the USB drive and refreshing the page.

Before turning on File History, note that File History backs up files from the following locations by default:

- Libraries
- Desktop
- Contacts
- Favorites

FIGURE 19.4

The File History page after connecting a USB drive.

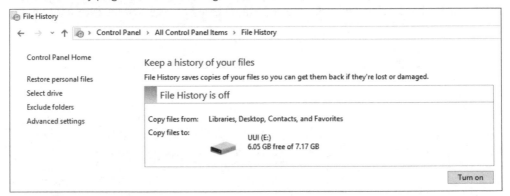

Its main purpose is to make sure that you can recover documents such as pictures, music, and videos if you lose the originals on your hard drive.

Click the Turn On button to activate File History. The Recommend a Drive for File History dialog box appears, asking if you want to allow others in your network homegroup to use this drive as their backup drive as well. (You learn about Windows 10 homegroups in Chapter 39.) If you want to allow this, click Yes; otherwise, click No.

After you activate File History, the File History page changes to show that it's turned on and that File History is making a copy of your files for the first time (see Figure 19.5). This initial backup may take several minutes or even hours, depending on the number of files you have in the folders being backed up.

FIGURE 19.5

File History is now activated.

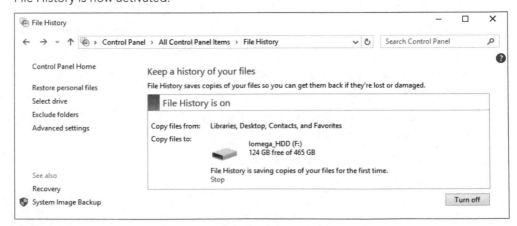

As we mentioned, the first backup may take a while. But subsequent backups copy only files that have changed since the most recent backup, so the backups complete more quickly.

Backing Up to a Network Location

You can use a network location to back up files. This is handy if you have multiple computers in a location and want to use it as a shared backup location. Another benefit to using a network location is access to hard drives that may have large amounts of unused space. Typically, networked computers have larger hard drives than dedicated external drives. In many cases, you can use these larger hard drives to back up files.

To use a network location, click the Use Network Location link when you initially access the File History page. Or click the Select Drive link on the left side of the File History window. This opens the Select Drive window, as shown in Figure 19.6.

FIGURE 19.6

The Select Drive window for choosing drives where you want to back up files.

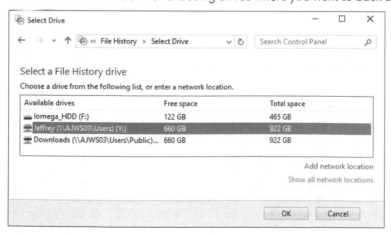

Click the Add Network Location link to display the Select Folder window (shown in Figure 19.7). Find the computer and folder to back up your files to. You must have network access privileges to access a computer and folder on your network. (Chapter 39 discusses sharing resources on a network.) Click Select Folder after you find the location on the network to back up your files.

FIGURE 19.7

Selecting a network location for backups.

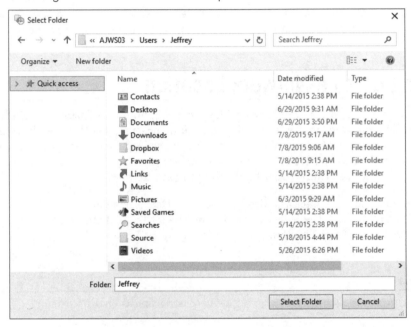

The Select Drive window reappears, listing the network drive you just selected (see Figure 19.8). If it isn't selected, select it and then click OK to save your selection.

For systems on which you've already backed up files to a drive (such as to a USB drive), File History prompts you with a message asking if you want to move your currently backed-up files to the network location. Click Yes to ensure all your backed-up files are available on the new network location. This move may take several minutes or even hours depending on the number of files on your backup drive.

If you use the Select Drive feature again and select a drive that you've previously used for backups (in the example, if you reselect the USB drive), you're presented with a list that shows at least one backup exists (see Figure 19.9). To ensure all your backed-up files are on the most recent drive selection, select an existing backup, choose OK, and then click Yes when prompted to reselect a drive you've previously used.

FIGURE 19.8

The Select Drive window showing the network drive we just selected.

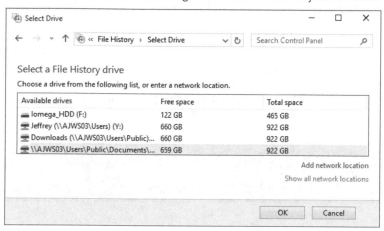

FIGURE 19.9

Reselecting a previously used drive shows existing backups on that drive.

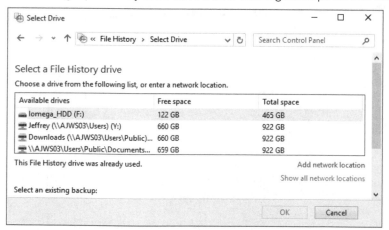

Excluding Folders during Backups

There may be some folders on your computer that you do not need to back up. For example, you may find that all your music is backed up using a different backup utility or music program. In this case, you don't need to use File History resources (backup time and drive space, for example) to back up your music.

To specify folders that you don't want to back up, click the Exclude Folders link on the left side of the File History window. The Exclude Folders window appears, as shown in Figure 19.10. By default, folders are not excluded so your Excluded Folders and Libraries list will simply say No Excluded Items.

Click the Add button to display the Select Folder window. Select a folder to exclude and then click Select Folder. File History adds that selected folder to the list of excluded folders. Continue this process until all the folders you want to exclude from backups are selected. In Figure 19.10, for example, we've added the Music, Videos, and Camera Roll folders to exclude in our backups. Click Save Changes to save your changes.

> **TIP**
>
> If you want to remove folders or libraries from the Exclude Folders list, select the item and then click Remove. This enables File History to back up files in that folder once again.

FIGURE 19.10

The Exclude Folders window.

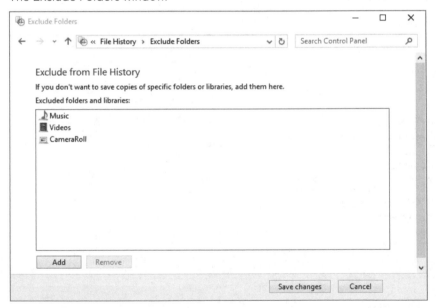

Setting the File History Advanced Option

To change File History advanced settings, click the Advanced Settings link on the File History window. Figure 19.11 shows what the Advanced Settings window looks like. The following paragraphs describe the settings you can modify on this window.

By default, File History looks to see if you've made changes to already backed-up files every hour. If changes have been made, File History saves the most current file to your backup location. If hourly is not an appropriate length of time — too short a time or too long a time — change it by choosing a new time from the Save Copies of Files drop-down list. You have the following options:

- Every 10 Minutes
- Every 15 Minutes
- Every 20 Minutes
- Every 30 Minutes
- Every Hour (Default)
- Every 3 Hours
- Every 6 Hours
- Every 12 Hours
- Daily

FIGURE 19.11

The Advanced Settings window.

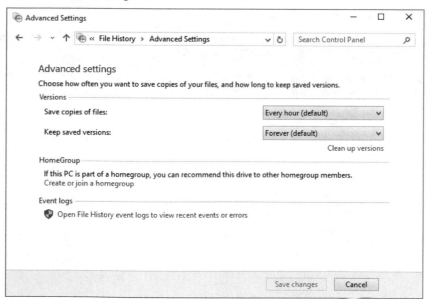

One setting you may want to change is the Keep Saved Versions option. This instructs File History on how long to keep backup copies of your files. File History keeps multiple copies of your files so that you can restore a file to a previous date and time. This feature is great when you accidentally delete a file and want to return to a previous version of that file. The downside comes in the amount of space needed to store all so many multiple copies.

By default, File History saves all copies forever, as long as you have sufficient storage space. You may want to change this to a shorter period of time, such as one month or three months if you know that you won't need to return to all those multiple versions of the same file. File History keeps the last copies within the time frame you choose, so you have the option of returning to more recent copies. But you may not ever return to a version that is two years old, for example.

Your options for saved versions include the following:

- Until Space Is Needed
- 1 Month
- 3 Months
- 6 Months
- 9 Months
- 1 Year
- 2 Years
- Forever (Default)

> **TIP**
>
> Use the Clean Up Versions link when you want to get back some space on your backup drive. Click that link, and File History removes old versions of the same file so that only the most recent copy is on the backup drive.

You can choose the Recommend This Drive option. Use this option only if your computer belongs to a homegroup and you want others on the network to be able to use your drive to back up their files.

Finally, you view File History event logs by clicking the Open File History Event Logs to View Recent Events or Errors option. Event Viewer, which is shown in Figure 19.12, provides helpful information in case you encounter problems with File History.

When you finish modifying the advanced settings for File History, click Save Changes.

FIGURE 19.12

View File History event logs using the Windows 10 Event Viewer.

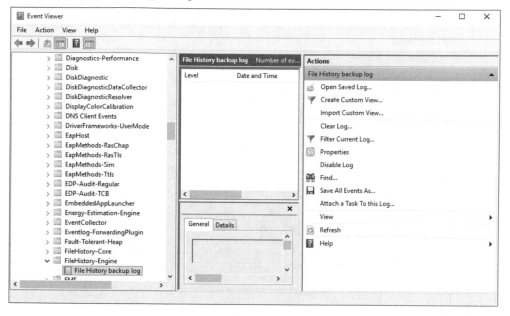

Restoring Files from a Backup

If you ever find that you've lost or destroyed important files, you can restore them from your File History backup. But understand that you need this method only if the files or folders are not in the Windows 10 Recycle Bin. Before you bother with the method described here, open the Recycle Bin and look for the missing file or folder. If you find what you need, right-click it and choose Restore. The deleted item goes right back where it was, and you don't need to proceed with the procedure described here.

If this method does not help you recover the lost items, you can restore from your backup. First, log in to the user account from which you lost the files. Open the File History application (type **File History** in the Search field, for example or open it from Control Panel), click the link Restore Personal Files, and then click the Restore to original location button in the center of the File History window.

The File History window appears, as shown in Figure 19.13. This window shows all your saved folders.

FIGURE 19.13

Restore a file using the File History window.

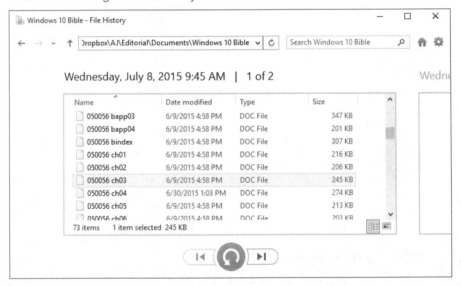

Find the file you want to restore by opening an appropriate folder. If you know the file is in a previous version, for example, you want to return to a version of a file that is several days old, and if you know it isn't the most recent version backed up, click the Restore button at the bottom of the window to navigate back in time to see previous versions.

The next dialog box, shown in Figure 19.14, gives you the following options:

- **Copy and replace:** This option replaces the current file on your hard disk with the backed-up version you just selected.

- **Don't copy:** This option instructs File History to ignore this file during the restore phase. The option makes sense only if you're choosing multiple files to restore or you suddenly want to cancel the current restore.

- **Copy, but keep both files:** Use this option when you want to see file details about the file you selected to restore and the file currently on your hard drive. From the dialog box that appears, you can select the file you want to keep or keep both copies. (A sequential number will be added to the filename of the restored file. Click Continue to complete the restoration process.)

FIGURE 19.14

Click one of the restore options that appear in the Copy File dialog box.

When restoring a file, you can click Preview to preview the file first. If you want to restore the file but restore it to a different location — which makes a copy of that file somewhere other than its original location — click Restore To and specify a location for it to be restored to. Click Select Folder after you select a folder and to complete the restoration of the file.

Not only can you restore individual or multiple files, but you can use the preceding instructions for restoring complete folders as well.

19

The following sections do not use File History, so you can close its window by clicking the red Close button (X).

Using System Protection

System Protection enables you to create a restore point, which is a way to back up important Windows system files. Unlike File History, System Protection doesn't require or use any external disks. Also, it does not back up any installed programs or all of Windows 10. Instead, System Protection creates System restore points that maintain copies of the most important system files needed for Windows 10 to operate properly, as well as hidden *shadow copies* of some of your own personal files.

The idea behind System Protection isn't to protect you from rare catastrophic hard drive disasters; it's to protect you from smaller and much more common mishaps. For example, you install some program or device that wasn't designed for Windows 10 on the grounds that "It worked fine in another version of Windows, so it should work fine here," only to discover that it doesn't work as well as you assumed. Even after uninstalling the program, you find that some Windows 10 features don't work as they did before you got the notion to give the old program or device a try.

Another common mishap occurs when you make some changes to an important file, but they aren't particularly good changes. But you save the changes anyway out of habit, thereby losing the original good copy of the file you started with. Sometimes System Protection can even help you recover a file that you deleted and removed from the Recycle Bin.

Turning System Protection On or Off

System Protection is turned on by default for the drive on which Windows 10 is installed. That means it's protecting your Windows 10 operating system and also documents you keep in your user account folders such as Documents, Pictures, Music, and so on.

If you have documents on other hard drives, you can extend System Protection to protect documents on those drives, too. However, don't try to use System Protection to protect a hard drive that has another operating system installed on it.

System Protection is an optional feature. You can turn it on and off at will (providing you have administrative privileges, because it affects all user accounts). And you can choose for yourself which *volumes* it monitors. (A volume is any hard drive or hard drive partition that looks like a hard drive in your computer's root folder.) To get to the options for controlling System Protection, first open your System folder using any of the following techniques:

- Type **System Protection** in Search and then click the Create a Restore Point option in the results area of the Search page.
- Open the System dialog box from Control Panel.

The System Properties dialog box appears, with the System Protection tab selected (see Figure 19.15).

FIGURE 19.15

The System Protection tab in System Properties.

To ensure that system protection for Windows 10 and user account files is turned on; first look in the Protection Settings box to verify that the Protection column shows "On" for your system disk (typically drive C:). If the Protection column indicates that protection is off, click the Configure button to open the System Protection dialog box. Then choose one of the first two settings in the Restore Settings group. You can also specify how much disk space to allocate to system protection with the Max Usage slider.

CAUTION

If you turn off System Protection, all existing restore points are deleted.

If your computer contains other volumes, whether you apply System Protection to them depends on what's on the volumes and whether you find it worthwhile to enable System Protection on them.

After you've made your selections, click OK. You're finished. Nothing happens immediately, but Windows 10 creates restore points every seven days after the last restore point was created. Each restore point contains copies of your important system files and shadow copies of files on the volumes you specified.

System Protection needs a minimum of 300MB of space on each protected volume for restore points. If necessary, it uses from 3 percent to 5 percent of the total drive capacity. It doesn't grow indefinitely or consume a significant amount of disk space. Instead, it deletes old restore points before creating new ones. (Old restore points are of dubious value anyway.)

Creating a restore point

System Restore is the component of System Protection that protects your important system files — the ones Windows 10 needs to work correctly. System Restore automatically creates a restore point daily. It also creates a restore point when it detects that you're about to do something that changes system files. But you can also create your own restore points. This may be a good idea when you're about to install some older hardware or software that wasn't designed for Windows 10. This technique isn't required, but it's a smart and safe thing to do.

To create a restore point, get to the System Protection tab shown back in Figure 19.15 and click the Create button. When prompted, you can type a brief explanation as to why you manually created the restore point: perhaps "Before Acme widget install" if you're about to install an Acme widget. Then click Create. Windows creates a restore point, after which you can click Close. Click OK to close the System Properties dialog box.

Next, you install your Acme widget. Take it for a spin, and make sure it works. If it works fine and you don't notice any adverse effects, great. You can forget about the restore point and go on your merry way.

If you find that the change you made wasn't such a great idea after all, first you have to uninstall whatever you installed. That's true whether it's hardware or software.

After you've uninstalled the bad device or program, you can make sure no remnants of it lag behind by returning to the restore point you specifically set up for that program or device.

If you install other programs or devices after the bad one, don't skip over other restore points to the one you created for the new item. If you do, you also undo the good changes made by the good programs and devices, which will likely make them stop working! Be methodical: Set the restore point, install the program or device, and test the program or device. If (and only if) you encounter problems, uninstall the device or program and return to the last restore point you set.

Returning to a previous restore point

Say you installed something that didn't work out, you uninstalled it, and now you want to make sure your system files are exactly as they were before. Open the System Properties dialog box and select the System Protection tab. Click System Restore (see Figure 19.16).

The System Restore starts. Click the Recommended Restore option and click Next. This launches the System Restore Wizard. Click Finish to undo the most recent update, driver installation, or software install (for example, our Acme Widget installation). Windows 10 makes those changes and then restarts your computer. Upon restart, you see a confirmation about restoring your system files.

FIGURE 19.16

Using a restore point can fix issues with the way Windows runs.

 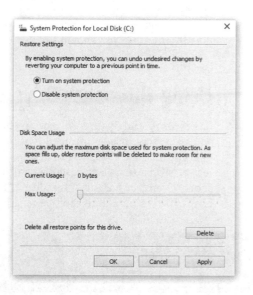

> **NOTE**
>
> For technical readers, we should mention that you can run System Restore from a command prompt. This is good to know if you can only start the computer in Safe Mode with the command prompt. Type `rstrui.exe` at the command prompt, and press Enter.

Undoing a System Restore

If you use System Restore and restore points exactly as described in the preceding sections, the process should go smoothly. If you try to use it in other ways, you may not have good results. In fact, returning your system to an earlier restore point sometimes causes more problems than it solves. When that happens, you can undo the most recent restore. Here's how:

1. Open System Restore.
2. Click System Restore and then click Next.
3. Choose the restore point labeled Undo and click Next.
4. Click Finish and follow the onscreen instructions.

Your computer restarts, and you see a confirmation message about undoing the restore point.

System Restore and the restore points you've just learned about have nothing to do with your document files. System Restore does not change, delete, undelete, or affect document files in any way. You should use System Restore and restore points exactly as described.

Using BitLocker Drive Encryption

File History and System Protection ensure the *availability* of your files, in that they allow you to restore lost or damaged files by restoring from a backup copy. BitLocker drive encryption isn't about availability — it's about *confidentiality*. If your notebook computer is lost or stolen, that's certainly a bad thing. But if your computer contains confidential personal, client, or patient information, that's even worse. BitLocker drive encryption ensures that lost or stolen data can't be read by prying eyes.

> **TIP**
> BitLocker differs from the Encrypting File System (EFS) in that EFS encrypts individual folders and files, whereas BitLocker encrypts the whole disk.

BitLocker drive encryption works by encrypting all the data on a hard drive. With BitLocker drive encryption active, you can use the computer normally. All the necessary encryption and decryption takes place automatically behind the scenes. But a thief can't access data, passwords, or confidential information on the drive.

> **TIP**
> BitLocker drive encryption ensures the confidentiality of data stored in portable computers.

BitLocker hardware requirements

BitLocker drive encryption uses an encryption key to encrypt and decrypt data. That key must be stored in a Trusted Platform Module (TPM) Version 1.2 microchip and compatible BIOS. Only newer computers come with the appropriate hardware preinstalled. You also need a USB flash drive to store a copy of the password.

Caution, Caution, and More Caution

BitLocker drive encryption is primarily designed for organizations that have sensitive data stored on notebooks and PCs. Theft of that data could have a negative impact on the organization, its customers, or its shareholders. While transparent to the user, the act of setting up BitLocker is normally entrusted to IT professionals within the organization.

If you aren't an IT professional, you need to be aware of the risks involved, especially if you plan to set up BitLocker on a hard drive that already contains files. First, always back up your data before repartitioning a drive. Although many programs on the market allow you to repartition a disk without losing data, there's always a risk. A backup is your only real insurance. More important, you should understand that BitLocker is not for the technologically faint-of-heart. You have no way to undo any bad guesses or mistakes. If not handled with the utmost care, BitLocker can render your computer useless and your data unrecoverable. If you aren't technologically inclined, but you have a serious need for drive encryption, consider getting professional support in setting up BitLocker for your system.

NOTE

The first time you open the BitLocker task page, you see a message indicating whether you have a TPM Version 1.2 chip installed. If you're certain that you have such a chip, but Windows 10 fails to recognize it, check with your computer manufacturer for instructions on making it available to Windows 10.

In addition to a TPM chip, your hard drive must contain at least two volumes (also called *partitions*). One volume, called the *system volume,* must be at least 1.5GB in size. That volume contains some startup files and cannot be encrypted. The other volume, called the *operating system volume,* contains Windows 10, your installed programs, and user account folders. Both volumes must be formatted with NTFS.

Encrypting the volume

When all the necessary hardware is in place, setting up BitLocker drive encryption is a relatively easy task:

1. Select **BitLocker** Drive Encryption from Control Panel.

   If your hardware setup doesn't support BitLocker, you see messages to that effect. You cannot continue without appropriate hardware and disk partitions.

19

2. If all systems are go, the BitLocker Drive Encryption window appears (see Figure 19.17).

3. Click Turn On BitLocker. If your TPM isn't initialized, a wizard takes you through the steps to initialize it. Follow the onscreen instructions to complete the initialization.

4. When prompted, choose your preferred password storage method, store the password, and click Next.

FIGURE 19.17

The BitLocker Drive Encryption window.

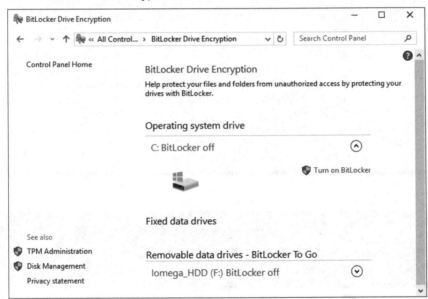

5. On the encryption page, select Run BitLocker System Check and click Continue.

6. Insert the password recovery USB flash drive (or whatever medium you used for password recovery) and click Restart Now.

7. Follow the onscreen instructions.

The wizard ensures that all systems are working and it's safe to encrypt the drive. Just follow the instructions to the end to complete the procedure.

Make sure you password-protect all user accounts to prevent unauthorized access to the system. Otherwise, a thief can get at the encrypted data just by logging in to a user account that requires no password!

When the computer won't start

After BitLocker is enabled, you should be able to start the computer and log in to it normally. BitLocker only prevents normal startup if it detects changes that could indicate tampering. For example, putting the drive in a different computer, or even making BIOS changes that look like tampering, causes BitLocker to prevent bootup. To get past the block, you need to supply the appropriate password.

Turning off BitLocker

If you ever change your mind about using BitLocker, repeat the steps in the section "Encrypting the volume" and choose the option to turn off BitLocker drive encryption.

More info on BitLocker

The setup wizard for BitLocker drive encryption is designed to simplify the process as much as possible for people using computers with TPM 1.2. Other scenarios are possible, but they go beyond the scope of this book. For more information, search Windows Help for "BitLocker." Or better yet, browse to www.technet.com or technet.microsoft.com and search for "BitLocker."

Performing a System Image Backup

Performing a system image backup lets you capture your system's image and save it to a remote device. The system image is a copy of the drive on which Windows is installed. If some of the files get destroyed or the drive gets damaged, you may have to restore your system image as a last resort to getting back up and running. (The system image can be saved to any remote media, such as a DVD, or the same external drive used by File History.)

A system image backup combined with File History is an excellent and reliable (and free) alternative to a costly local or online backup service or software.

To capture your system image, click the Create a system image link on the bottom-left corner of the Backup and Restore screen (refer to Figure 19.4). A dialog box opens to allow you to select a remote device or location for the system backup. This is shown in Figure 19.18.

The next screen prompts you to confirm your choices and start the backup. (Notice that the System Backup is still the old System Backup from Windows 7 days. Looks like a good thing lasts forever.)

FIGURE 19.18

The backup in progress showing the backup location for the system image.

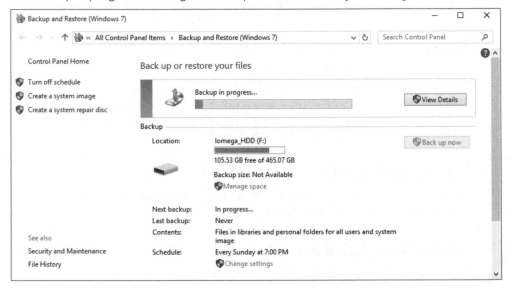

Wrapping Up

Any way you slice it, having two or more copies of important files is better than having only one copy. The reason is simple and obvious: If you have two or more copies, you can afford to lose one. This chapter is about different ways to make backup copies of important files. Here's a summary:

- To make simple backups of files on the fly, copy them to external disks as convenient.

- To restore an accidentally deleted file, first try to restore it from the Recycle Bin.

- To back up files in the Libraries, Desktop, Contacts, and Favorites folders, use File History.

- To recover deleted files, use the Restore Personal Files link on the File History window.

- Use System Protection to make automatic daily backups of important system files and documents. These don't protect you from a hard drive disaster because they're on the same disk as the system files and documents. But they provide a relatively easy means of recovering from minor mishaps without messing with external disks.

- To use System Restore properly, create a restore point just before installing new hardware or software. If the new product creates a problem, uninstall it. Then return to your restore point to ensure all traces of the installation are wiped away.

- For data confidentiality on portable computers, Windows 10 offers BitLocker drive encryption.

- Windows 10 includes features to let you take a system image of your computer. This image can be used to restore a "broken" system. Combining this feature with File History, you can get a computer that refuses to reboot or restore back up and running within an hour.

19

Part V

Printing and Managing Printers

IN THIS PART

Installing and Managing Printers

Installing a printer is usually an easy job. One rule applies to installing any hardware, and it certainly applies to printers: *Read the instructions that came with the printer first.* Trying to save time by ignoring the instructions and "winging it" is likely to cost you more time in getting the thing to work.

In many cases, you have the option to connect the printer to a USB port or a printer port. If your computer is a member of a network, you may want to install a shared printer that's physically connected to some other computer or a printer that is directly connected to the network. This chapter looks at different ways of installing printers, including using the Windows 10 Devices tool, which you can run from Settings, as well as techniques for managing installed printers using the legacy Devices and Printers tool in Control Panel.

Windows 10 also includes support for wireless printing and far easier and more efficient support for ad-hoc connection to printers. Windows 10 also supports NFC (Near Field Communications) tap-to-pair technology.

You don't have to do anything special to connect to printers using these technologies. Both WI-FI Direct and NFC tap-to-pair implementation depends on the printers. Newer printers support WI-FI Direct, while older printers can use NFC tap-to-pair if you attach NFC tags to them. On the client side, you don't have to do anything extra to connect to printers using this technology with Windows 10. NFC tap-to-pair is a boon for users on tablets, phones, and other handheld devices. (Tap-to-pair is not practical from your desktop computer.)

Printer Properties versus Printing Properties

Two types of properties are covered in this chapter: *printer properties* and *printing prefer-ences*. The distinction isn't obvious from the terminology, so here's a general description:

- **Printer properties:** These properties apply to the printer itself, such as the way it's connected to the computer, whether and how it's shared on the network, the way the computer sends information to the printer, when the printer is available, and more.

- **Printing preferences:** These properties apply to how the printer creates a printed document, including such features as paper source, paper size, duplex printing, paper quality settings, print scaling, watermarks, and other document output properties.

In a way, you can think of printer properties as related to how the printer prints *all* docu-ments, and printing preferences as related to how the printer prints *specific* documents. That isn't 100 percent accurate, but it should begin to help you understand the distinction between the two.

If you're a typical Windows user, you're more likely to spend time configuring printing pref-erences than printer properties. If you're a power user or administrator, however, you'll no doubt spend some time configuring printer properties to control how the printer operates.

Before diving into printer properties and printing preferences, you need to get your printer installed. That's covered in the following section.

> **TIP**
>
> Windows 10 has two ways to view and manage your printers. First, the Windows 10 Printers and Scanners tool lets you view, add, and remove hardware devices, such printers and scanners. The Devices and Printers folder, which was introduced in Windows 7, is still around. It is the place to go to manage hardware devices such as displays, keyboards, input devices, wireless network adapters, and printers.

Adding a Printer with the Devices Tool

Windows 10 introduces the Devices tool in the Settings area. The tool provides a way to add, remove, and view your hardware devices, such as a printer, Bluetooth devices (see Chapter 30), scanners, and so on. We've found that when Windows 10 has recognized a new printer connected to your computer, regardless of whether you're actively using the tool, Windows 10 automatically installs device drivers for it (as long as those device drivers are part of the Windows 10 installation).

To get to the tool, do the following:

1. Click Start.
2. Click Settings.

3. Click the Devices panel.

The Printers and scanners settings are shown in Figure 20.1.

In this example, a printer has been added to the printers list. If your printer is not showing up in this list, make sure the printer is connected to an active USB port (or other printer port) and ensure the printer is turned on. If, after you've done these checks, the printer does not start installing, click the Add a Device button on the Devices and Printers page. Windows 10 looks for the new device (your printer in this case), and upon locating it, installs the necessary drivers or prompts you for a location to find the drivers. Sometimes you can find those drivers on the printer manufacturer's website. In other cases, the drivers are provided on a distribution disk that was bundled with your printer.

FIGURE 20.1

The Windows 10 Devices.

You can learn more about installing printers in the "Installing a New Printer" section later in this chapter.

After you have a printer installed, you can do two other things in the Devices tool. You can view the name of the printer, such as NPIA236A, and you can remove a device from your computer. To remove a device, select it and click the Remove device button that appears in the menu ribbon when the printer is selected (see Figure 20.2). A message pops up asking if you're sure you want to uninstall the device. Click Yes. (If you aren't sure and you want to keep the device installed as is, press Esc on the keyboard.)

FIGURE 20.2

Removing a printer using the Devices tool.

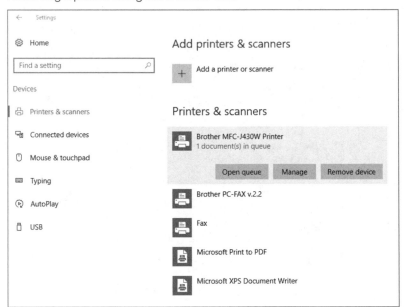

Opening the Devices and Printers Folder

Another tool to use for setting up and managing printers is the legacy Devices and Printers folder that is still part of Control Panel. This folder includes the same features as the new Windows 10 Devices tool (see the preceding section), but it also adds management of printer properties and printer options and a number of tasks that are available to you.

Aside from actually printing documents, just about everything you do with printers takes place in the Devices and Printers folder.

As with everything else in Windows 10, you can get to the Devices and Printers folder in several ways. Use whichever of these two ways works for you and is most convenient at the moment:

- In Search, type **dev** and click the Settings link. On the Settings page, click the Devices and Printers link in the panel.

- On the Windows desktop, press Windows+X, choose Control Panel ⇨ View Devices and Printers under Hardware and Sound.

When you're in the Devices and Printers folder, you see an icon for each printer (or similar device) that you can print to. Figure 20.3 shows an example; your folder will look different.

FIGURE 20.3

A sample Devices and Printers folder.

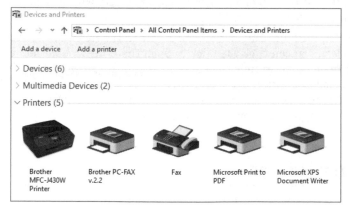

Setting the default printer

If your Devices and Printers folder contains more than one printer icon, only one of them is the *default* device for printing. By "default," we mean the printer that's used automatically if you don't specify something else. For example, many programs allow you to print a document to the default printer by pressing Ctrl+P. The program may not ask what printer you want to use. Instead, it simply sends the document to the default printer.

In the Devices and Printers folder, a check mark indicates the default printer. If you want to change the default printer, right-click the printer's icon and choose Set As Default

Printer. The printer or device you specified now sports the green check mark, and will be used for printing when you don't specify another printer or device.

Testing a printer

If you've installed a printer and you want to test it, follow these steps (we assume that you're already in the Devices and Printers folder):

1. Right-click the printer's icon and choose Printer Properties. (Be careful not to click Printing Preferences or the Printer Properties items.)

2. Select the General tab.

3. At the bottom of the Properties dialog box that opens, click the Print Test Page button.

4. Wait a few seconds (few printers start immediately). The printer should print a sample page.

   - If the page prints and doesn't look garbled, click OK in each open box.

   - If nothing prints within 15 or 30 seconds, click Get Help with Printing for tips on solving the problem.

If you had to click Get Help with Printing, follow the advice in the Help documentation first to resolve the problem. You can click the Click to Open the Print Troubleshooter link to launch the printing troubleshooter from the Control Panel. Also, keep in mind that hundreds of makes and models of printers are on the market, and no single rule applies to all. So, don't overlook the documentation that came with your printer or the printer manufacturer's website, which may provide troubleshooting advice.

Installing a New Printer

- Before you can use a new printer, you need to connect it to the computer and install it. This section looks at adding a printer using the Devices and Printers folder. Many printers give you the choice of using the USB port to connect the printer or a parallel printer port. In most cases, USB works just fine for printing. Most of today's standard computer configurations don't even have a parallel printer port, so USB may be your only option. Likewise, most new printers don't have parallel or serial port connections.

> **TIP**
> If your printer offers only a parallel port and your computer doesn't have one, you can either buy an add-on adapter card to add the parallel port or buy a new printer that supports USB.

As mentioned at the beginning of this chapter, the main rule for installing a printer is to follow the instructions that came with it. Sometimes you need to install drivers first;

sometimes you don't. No "one rule fits all" when you're installing printers or any other hardware device. But in a pinch, when you have no instructions, the techniques in the following sections are your best bet.

Installing printers with USB and infrared connections

If you have the option of connecting the printer through a USB port or by infrared, the installation procedure should go this way:

1. Close all open programs on your Windows desktop so that you're at the Windows desktop with nothing else showing.

2. Check the documentation that came with the printer, and if directed to install the drivers before connecting the printer to the computer, do so.

3. Plug the printer into the power outlet; connect the printer to the computer with its USB connection, or configure the infrared connection as instructed by the printer manufacturer.

4. Turn on the printer, and wait a few seconds.

You should see a message in the notification area that tells you the device is connected and ready to use. You're finished. The printer is installed and ready to go.

Regardless of which of these methods you use, you should test the printer, and perhaps make it the default printer, as discussed later in this chapter.

> **TIP**
>
> If the printer documentation tells you to install the software before you attach the printer to the computer for the first time, don't skip that step. If you connect the printer before installing the drivers, Windows may have problems detecting the printer.

Installing printers with parallel and serial port connections

If your printer is an older model that is not a typical plug-and-play USB printer (for example, an older HP LaserJet that you refuse to get rid of), it probably connects to the computer via an LPT port or COM port. The following is the best approach to installing it on Windows 10:

1. Save any unsaved work, close all open programs, shut down Windows, and shut down your computer.

2. Plug the printer into the power outlet, connect the printer to the computer's LPT or serial port, turn on the printer, and turn on the computer.

3. When Windows restarts, look for the Found New Hardware notification message to appear.

20

Several things may happen next. You may be prompted for a disk if Windows can't find the driver for the printer. If you see a notification message indicating that the printer is installed and ready to use, you're probably finished.

If Windows doesn't locate your printer automatically, consider using Google or Bing to locate instructions on the web for setting up your printer in Windows 10. Because so many different printers are available, this book cannot show how to install your particular printer. Often, the manufacturer's website includes updated device drivers and/or updated instructions on how to get older printers working with the latest operating systems such as Windows 10.

You can also try installing the printer using the Program Compatibility feature of Windows 10.

Installing a network, wireless, or Bluetooth printer

If your computer is a member of a home or small business network, and you know of a shared printer on another computer in that network, you can use the technique described next to install that printer on your own computer. The same is true of many wireless and Bluetooth printers. But again, this procedure may not be necessary because Windows 10 often detects network printers and makes them available automatically. Be sure to check the manual that came with a wireless or Bluetooth printer for an alternative procedure before trying the method described here. Also, be sure to turn on the printer before you try to install it.

If you're trying to install a printer that's attached to another computer in your private network, make sure that both the printer and the computer to which the printer is physically connected are turned on. Make sure your network is set up and you've enabled discovery and sharing as discussed in Part VIII of this book. Then go to the computer that you're trying to use to access the network printer and perform the steps for that computer. You install a network, wireless, or Bluetooth printer in much the same way as you install a local printer.

First, open the Devices and Printers folder using any technique described at the beginning of this chapter.

If the printer's name appears in the Devices and Printers tool of the Settings area or in the Devices and Printers folder, you don't need to install it. If you want to make it the default printer, right-click its icon and choose Set As Default Printer (only available while in the Devices and Printers folder). Then close the Devices and Printers folder. You can then use the printer as described in Chapter 21.

If you see no sign of the printer in the Devices and Printers tool or in your Devices and Printers folder, open the Devices and Printers folder and follow these instructions to install it:

1. Click Add a Printer in the toolbar. The Add Printer Wizard opens.

2. If the printer is located automatically, select it and click Next to work through the wizard to install it. If the printer is not located, click The Printer That I Want Isn't Listed. The Find a Printer by Other Options window opens, as shown Figure 20.4.

FIGURE 20.4

Setting up a network shared printer.

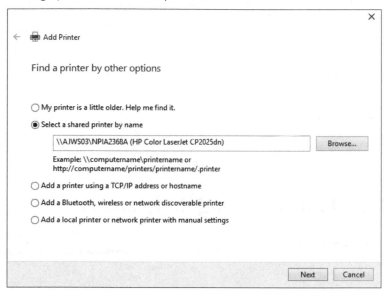

3. If you know the UNC name or IP address of the printer to which you want to connect, fill in the appropriate information. Otherwise, click Browse, and navigate to the computer and printer to which you want to connect. Click the printer's name and click Select. Then click Next.

4. After the printer is successfully installed, click Next. On the next wizard page, you can opt to print a test page and make the shared printer your default printer. Make your choices and click Finish.

An icon for the shared printer will appear in your Devices and Printers folder. If you made it the default printer, it will also show a check mark.

Managing Printer Drivers

Virtually all hardware devices, including printers, come with a special program called a *device driver,* or just *driver* for short. The driver provides the interface between the device and a specific operating system, such as Windows 10, Windows 8, Windows 8.1, Windows 7, Windows

20

Vista, or Windows XP. You must have the correct and current printer driver installed on your computer in order for your printer to work correctly.

> **TIP**
>
> In most cases, the Windows 8/8.1 or earlier version of a printer driver works just fine for Windows 10. However, you should use the Windows 10 version of a printer driver if one is available to ensure you have access to all your printer's features. Additionally, keep in mind that if you have Windows 10 64-bit installed, you need 64-bit printer drivers.

Many printers come with drivers on a CD. How you install a driver from the disk depends on the printer you're using, but an older printer may not have a Windows 10 driver to offer. In that case, you need to look for a current driver online. Try Windows Update first.

If Windows Update doesn't find an updated driver, that may mean your printer manufacturer hasn't posted the driver online yet. Browse to the printer manufacturer's website and look for a Drivers link or Support page with downloads. Or go to the Support page and send an e-mail asking if an updated driver is available for your printer model.

Setting Default Printing Preferences

Remember the discussion early in this chapter about printing preferences versus printer properties? This section explains how to configure the default printing properties that a printer will use to print documents.

As with objects on your screen, many devices have properties that you can customize. Most printers have such properties. You can make selections from those properties to define defaults for the printer. Those default settings for properties aren't set in stone; you can override the defaults any time you print a document.

A printer's properties are accessible from its icons. To view the properties for an installed printer, first open the Devices and Printers folder if you haven't already done so. Then right-click the printer's icon and choose Printing Preferences. The options available to you depend on your printer. The options shown in Figure 20.5 are for the NPIA236A printer.

The Printing Preferences dialog box varies from one printer to the next and often offers multiple tabs, each with several options. The following sections cover some of the common settings that you may want to set for your printer.

Portrait versus landscape printing

Unless your printing needs are very unusual, you'll probably print most of your documents in a portrait orientation. That's the orientation that letters and most other documents use, so you should almost always choose Portrait as your default orientation, as shown in Figure 20.6.

FIGURE 20.5

FIGURE 20.5

Printer properties.

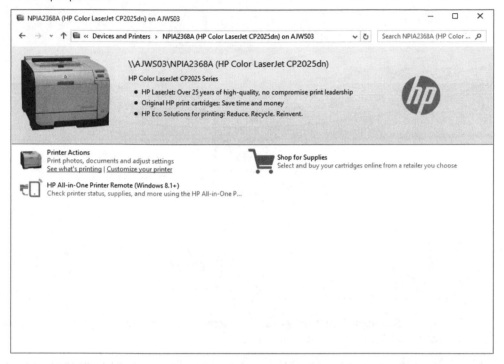

You can always override that default and print the occasional document in Landscape orientation (sideways, so the page is wider than it is tall).

Printing on both sides

On some printers, you have the option of printing a multi-page document on both sides of a sheet of paper. For our example, this option is located in the Print on Both Sides drop-down list. You can choose None, which prints on a single side of a piece of paper. The Flip on Long Edge option results in a multi-page document being printed front to back, also called duplex printing or *duplexing*. The Flip on Short Edge option prints on both sides, but is usually used for documents printed in landscape mode.

Making pages print in the correct order

When you print a multi-page document, you don't want to have to shuffle the pages around to put them in the correct order. You want the pages to come out of the printer in order.

20

FIGURE 20.6

Sample printing preferences.

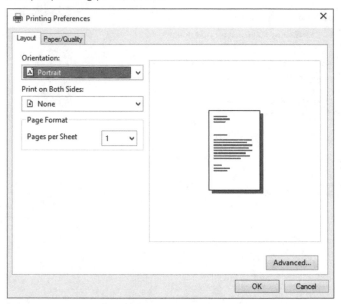

The Page Order property is the option that determines whether the pages are printed in the correct order. The rules are as follows:

- If the pages come out of the printer face down, use Front to Back order.
- If the pages come out of the printer face up, use Back to Front order.

> **TIP**
>
> If you have to reshuffle printed pages, choose the Page Order option that currently *isn't* selected.

Saving time and money

Most printers are just plain slow. That's because they're clunky mechanical devices, and they take time to move a page through and apply ink or toner. Fast printers are typically more expensive than slow ones. But no matter what the cost or general speed of your printer, one general rule applies: The higher the print quality of the document you're printing at the moment, the longer it takes to print.

> **TIP**
>
> Many printers are cheap, but ink cartridges typically are not. In some cases, buying a new printer is cheaper than buying replacement cartridges for your old printer. Additionally, some manufacturers ship new printers with starter cartridges, which typically contain less than a full-size replacement cartridge.

The printer property that most determines how quickly your documents print and how much ink or laser toner you use per document is called *print quality*. The higher the print quality, the longer the document takes to print, and the more ink or laser toner you use in the process. You can save time and money by doing your day-to-day printing in draft quality, perhaps even without color if you want to conserve color ink or laser toner.

On the printer shown in Figure 20.7, quality settings are on the Paper/Quality tab.

As with other printer properties, setting the printer defaults to low-quality and black-and-white settings doesn't prevent you from printing the occasional color document. You can override those defaults any time you print a document. When you want to print a professional-looking report or a fine photo, increase the print quality and activate color for that one print job.

Beyond these features, the properties vary greatly from one printer to the next. The only resource for learning all the details of your particular make and model of printer is the documentation that came with that printer, or the printer manufacturer's website.

FIGURE 20.7

Paper/Quality settings.

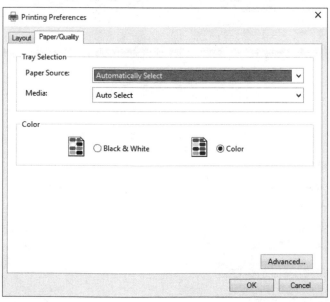

397

Setting Printer Properties

If you're an average Windows user, you may never need to configure printer properties for a printer. In most cases, you're more concerned with printing preferences that control how the printed documents look. If you're an advanced user or administrator, however, you likely need to understand how to configure printer properties.

To configure properties for a printer, start by opening the Devices and Printers folder, as described earlier in this chapter (you should find it on the Control Panel). Then right-click the printer and choose Printing Properties to open a Properties dialog box similar to the one shown in Figure 20.8.

The tabs shown in the Properties dialog box for a printer can vary from one type of printer to another, but some settings are common to most of them. The following sections use the NPIA236A as an example to illustrate common concepts such as port configuration, printer pooling, spooling options, and more.

FIGURE 20.8

A sample Properties dialog box.

TIP
Use the Print Test Page button on the General tab of a printer's Properties dialog box to test the printer.

Configuring shared printers

The Sharing tab (see Figure 20.9) enables you to set up your printer so that you can share it with others on your home or work network. Clicking Settings ➪ Devices, and select the printer that you want to share. Click the image and select Manage. Choose Printer properties and then the Share This Printer option. You will then enable sharing, and must provide a share name for the printer. You can use the default, which is the name of the printer, or name it something more descriptive. For example, you can name it "Rob's Printer" or "Laser Printer in Room 100" so others in your network know which printer it is by looking at the name.

FIGURE 20.9

The Sharing tab.

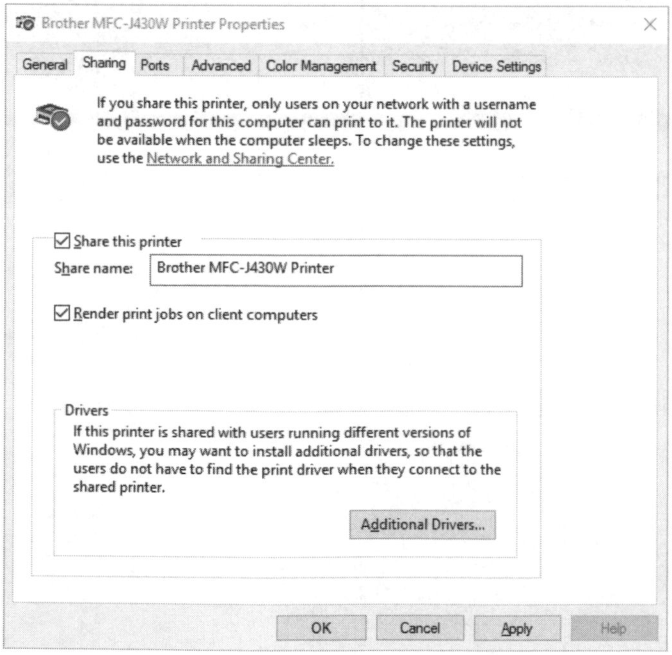

20

The Additional Drivers button contains a way for you to install additional drivers to support multiple versions of Windows. For example, you may be running Windows 10 on your computer, but the person down the hallway or in another part of the house may be on Windows 8.1 or Windows Vista. By installing those drivers now, you can be assured that users of those other versions of Windows will have an easier time setting up to use your shared printer.

After you set up these options, click Apply. You may be prompted to shut down and restart Windows before your sharing takes effect.

Configuring printer ports

The Ports tab (see Figure 20.10) lets you view and configure the printer's ports, which define the way the printer is connected to the computer. Typically, a printer has only one port, but multiple ports are possible.

FIGURE 20.10

The Ports tab.

Users visit the Ports tab for two primary reasons: to configure a printer for a different network port, or to switch from one LPT port to another. You can also configure the printer to print by default to a file by selecting the File port.

Some port types offer settings that you can configure. LPT ports, for example, enable you to specify the Transmission Retry setting, which determines how long the computer will wait for a response from the printer before timing out. For serial printers on a COM port, you can specify several settings that control the speed of the port and how data flows from the computer to the printer. To configure a port, select the port from the list and click Configure Port. Use the settings in the resulting dialog box to specify settings for the port.

If you need to add a new port for a printer, click the Add Port button. Windows displays the Printer Ports dialog box shown in Figure 20.11. Select the type of port you want to create and click New Port. If the selected port type supports creating new ports, Windows displays a dialog box or a wizard (depending on the port type) that you use to specify the settings for the new port.

FIGURE 20.11

Printer Ports dialog box.

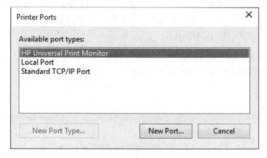

Setting up printer pooling

A *printer pool* is a group of identical printers that Windows treats as a single printer instance. You can then print to the printer pool as if it were a single printer, and Windows handles sending the document to an appropriate printer in the pool. Before we explain pooling in more detail, take a look at how a *printer driver instance* differs from a *printer*.

The printer that you see listed in the Devices and Printers folder is really not a printer as such. Instead, it's an *instance* of a printer driver representing the particular printer. The printer driver is the middleware between Windows and the printer hardware (the real *printer* in this discussion) that enables Windows to communicate with the printer. The phrase *instance of a printer driver* refers to a named copy of the printer driver that has its own set of properties. You can have two instances of the same printer driver with different settings, both of which control the same printer. Or you can have one instance of a printer driver that controls more than one printer.

20

For example, assume your office has three identical network printers. You can create a printer pool using those three printers, assigning three ports to the single instance of the printer driver in your Devices and Printers folder. So, you may have one HP LaserJet 1250N network printer in your Devices and Printers folder, for example, but that instance of the driver may actually print to any of the three printers.

Why would you want to set up your printers that way? First, you need to manage only one instance of the printer driver in your computer, which can simplify printer and document management, particularly if you typically use the same settings for each one. Second, you don't have to worry about selecting a printer when you print. Instead, assuming you've assigned the printer driver instance for the pool as your default printer, you just click Print and send the document on its way. Windows decides which printer to send the document to.

To set up a printer pool, follow these steps:

1. Install the printer driver for the printers in the pool.
2. Open the properties for the printer from the Devices and Printers folder and select the Enable Printer Pooling option on the Ports tab. When that option is selected, you can select multiple ports from the ports list.
3. Add ports as needed (such as additional TCP/IP ports for network printers), and select the ports for all the printers in the pool.
4. Click OK.

Configuring printer availability

You can specify when a printer is available. For example, you can restrict access to a printer to business hours to keep people from using it when no one else is in the office. Whatever the reason, you configure printer availability from the Advanced tab of the Printer Properties dialog box (see Figure 20.12).

By default, a printer is configured to be always available. To limit its availability, click the Available From option; then use the spin controls to set the start and end times for the time range when the printer will be available. If you or a network user of a shared printer sends a document to a printer when it isn't available, the document is held in the printer queue on the sending computer until the printer becomes available.

Setting other advanced options

As Figure 20.12 illustrates, Windows offers several other advanced options for configuring a printer. For example, the spooling options determine how the printer driver sends data to the printer. The option Spool Print Documents So Program Finishes Printing Faster causes documents to be spooled to an on-disk queue, where it waits until the printer driver can send it to the printer. To the printing application, printing is complete as soon as the last page of the document is sent to the queue. You can then continue using the program.

FIGURE 20.12

The Advanced tab.

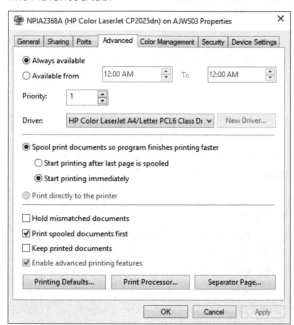

Alternatively, you can configure the printer driver to print directly to the printer, bypassing the on-disk document queue. The downside to this option is that you can't use the program until it finishes printing, which can potentially take much longer than sending the document to a queue if the document is complex or very large.

In most cases, today's computers are fast enough and have enough disk capacity that you never need to print directly to the printer. If you're trying to print a huge document and you have very little free space on your disk, however, sending the document directly to the printer may enable the document to print when it might not otherwise.

Following are some additional settings on the Advanced tab:

- **Hold Mismatched Documents:** The spooler checks the configuration of the printer against the document setup before sending the document to the printer. If the document setup doesn't match the printer, the document is held in the queue and not sent to the printer. You can then address the configuration mismatch, and restart the document from the queue to send it to the printer.

- **Print Spooled Documents First:** Documents that have completed spooling to the queue are printed before documents that are still spooling, even if they have a lower priority.

20

■ **Keep Printed Documents:** Documents remain in the queue even after they're printed, enabling you to restart the document from the queue if you need to reprint them.

 These aren't the only properties available for a printer. We cover other properties, such as the sharing properties, in other chapters. For more information about managing print jobs, turn to Chapter 21.

Wrapping Up

That about wraps up installing and managing printers. In the next chapter, you learn how to print documents, choose color and quality settings on the fly, and manage your print jobs. The main points from this chapter are as follows:

■ Many makes and models of printers exist. The best resource for your printer is the documentation that came with that printer.

■ Installed printers, and options for installing printers, are in the Windows 10 Devices and Printers folder, which is found in Control Panel.

■ If you have access to multiple printers, right-click the icon for the printer you want to use on a day-to-day basis and choose Set As Default Printer.

■ To test a printer, right-click its icon and choose Printer Properties. Then click the Print Test Page button.

■ To connect a printer by USB, don't shut down the computer. Instead, leave the computer on, connect the printer to the computer, and then turn on the printer. Check the printer documentation to see whether you need to install the drivers before connecting the printer.

■ The typical scenario for installing a printer that connects to a printer port (LPT port) is to shut down the computer, connect the printer and turn it on, and then restart the computer.

■ To ensure that your printer driver is appropriate for your operating system, check the Windows Update service and the printer manufacturer's website.

■ To set default preferences for day-to-day printing, right-click the printer's icon and choose Printing Preferences.

Managing Print Jobs

IN THIS CHAPTER

How printing works

Making a shortcut to a printer

Stopping the printer

Printing XPS documents

Learning how to print from Windows 10 apps

When you print a document, more happens than you might expect. The printer doesn't immediately start printing. Instead, the computer converts your document to a set of instructions that tell the printer what to do. Then those printer instructions are sent to the printer in small chunks because the printer is a slow mechanical device compared to a computer.

Each document you print becomes a *print job* that waits its turn in line if other documents are already printing, or waiting to be printed. Most of this activity takes place in the background; you don't have to do anything to make it happen. In fact, you can continue using your computer normally while the document is printing.

How Printing Works

When you print a document, quite a bit of work takes place invisibly in the background before the printer even "knows" it has a document to print. First, a program called a *print spooler* (or *spooler* for short) makes a special copy of the document containing instructions for the printer. Those instructions don't look anything like the document you're printing. They're codes that tell the printer what to do so that the document it spits out looks like the document you printed.

After the spooler creates the special printer file, it can't hand the whole thing off to the printer as one giant set of instructions. Most printers are slow mechanical devices that can hold only a small amount of information at a time in a *buffer*. The buffer is a storage area within the printer that holds the data until it's printed. The amount of data that can reside in the buffer depends on the size of the buffer. In some cases, the buffer holds a large number of pages. In others, it may hold only a single page. If you're printing a complex document such as a photo, and the buffer is relatively small, only part of the page may fit in the buffer at one time.

When the spooler has finished creating the special printer file, another document may already be printing. You may even have several documents waiting to be printed. So, the spooler puts all the print jobs into a *queue* (line). All this activity takes the computer time. And because each document is fed to the printer in small chunks, you often have time to cancel a document you've told Windows to print but that hasn't been fully printed.

To manage print jobs, you use the *print queue*. If a document is already printing, or waiting to print, you see a tiny printer icon in the notification area. When you point to that icon, the number of documents waiting to be printed appears in a tooltip. Double-click that small icon to open the print queue as shown in Figure 21.1. (We set the printer offline to catch the item in queue.)

FIGURE 21.1

The printer queue.

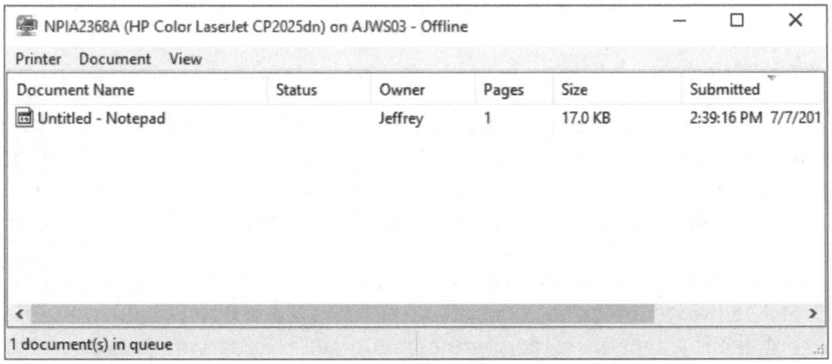

As an alternative to using the notification area, you can get to the print queue from the Devices and Printers folder. To open your Devices and Printers folder, press Windows+X, click Control Panel, and click View Devices and Printers.

After you're in the Devices and Printers folder, double-click the printer's icon to open its print queue. Some printers, such as HP, bring up their own printing control panel when you double-click the printer.

> **TIP**
>
> To make a desktop shortcut to a specific printer, right-click the printer's icon in the Devices and Printers folder and choose Create Shortcut. Any time you need to open the printer's queue, double-click (or click) that shortcut icon on the desktop.

Managing Print Jobs

The print queue for a printer contains all the documents that are currently printing or waiting to print. In the example in Figure 21.1, one document has been sent to the printer and is being spooled for printing.

Managing a single document

To pause or cancel a specific print job, right-click its line in the print queue and choose one of the following options from the shortcut menu that appears:

- **Pause:** Stops printing the document until you restart it.
- **Resume:** Resume restarts the paused print job.
- **Restart:** Restarts the paused print job.
- **Cancel:** Cancels the print job so that it doesn't print and removes the job from the print queue.
- **Properties:** Provides detailed information about the print job. You can also set the document's priority. The higher the priority, the more likely the print job is to cut in line ahead of other documents waiting to be printed.

Managing several documents

To pause, restart, or cancel several documents in the queue, select their icons. For example, click the first job you want to change. Then hold down the Shift key and select the last one. Optionally, you can select (or deselect) icons by holding down the Ctrl key as you click. Then right-click any selected item, or choose Document from the menu bar, and choose an action. The action is applied to all selected icons.

Managing all documents

You can use commands on the print queue's Printer menu, shown in Figure 21.2, to manage all the documents in the queue without selecting any items first. The following options apply to all documents:

- **Pause Printing:** Pause the current print job and all those waiting in line. See the section "Printing Offline," later in this chapter, for an example of when this would be useful.
- **Cancel All Documents:** You guessed it — this cancels the current print job and all those waiting to be printed.

FIGURE 21.2

The Printer menu in the print queue.

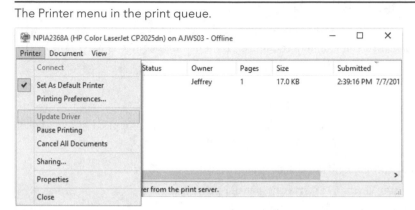

How Do I Stop This Thing?

Don't expect a paused or canceled print job to stop right away. Several more pages may print. That's because the print queue sends chunks of a document to the printer's buffer. The buffer, in turn, holds information waiting to be printed. Canceling a print job prevents any more data from being sent to the buffer, but the printer doesn't stop printing until its buffer is empty (unless, of course, you turn off the printer, which you should not do while paper is being fed through the printer).

Changing the print queue order

In the print queue, you can change the order in which documents in the queue print. For example, if you need a particular printout right now, and a long line of documents is waiting ahead of it, you can give your document a higher priority so it prints sooner. Your print job gets to cut in line ahead of others.

To change an item in the print queue's priority, right-click the item in the queue and choose Properties. On the General tab of the dialog box that opens, drag the Priority slider, shown in Figure 21.3, to the right. The farther you drag, the higher your document's priority. Click OK. Your document doesn't stop the document that's currently printing, but it may be the next one to print.

You can close the print queue as you would any other window — by clicking the Close button in the upper-right corner or by choosing Printer ⇨ Close from the menu bar.

FIGURE 21.3

The Priority slider in a print queue item's Properties dialog box.

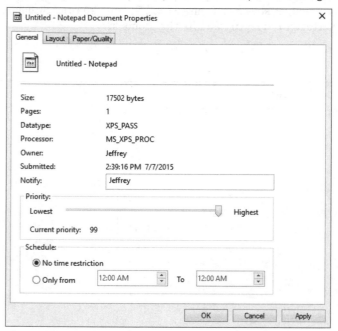

Solving Common Printer Problems

If you experience a problem printing a document, the problem may be something to do with the printer. Before you assume the worst and delve into any major troubleshooting, check for some of the more common problems that cause such errors:

- Is the printer turned on and set online?
- Are both ends of the printer cable plugged in securely?
- Is there paper in the printer, and is it inserted properly?
- Is there a paper jam in the printer?
- Does the printer still have ink or toner?

More often than not, the printer problem is something as simple as the printer being out of paper or ink.

If you don't find any issues with the printer itself, do some troubleshooting in Windows. Open the Devices and Printers folder, right-click the printer, click Manage and choose Troubleshoot in the left column, as shown in Figure 21.4. Windows 10 runs through several troubleshooting steps to attempt to identify and fix the problem.

FIGURE 21.4

Troubleshoot a printer from Devices and Printers.

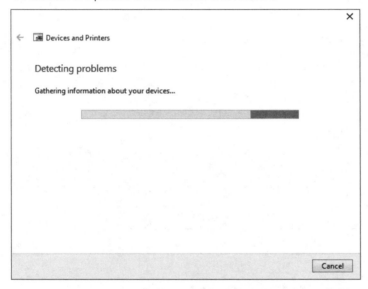

In some situations, Windows 10 identifies the problem and fixes it for you. In others, Windows 10 suggests a fix.

Printing Offline

Printing offline is a means of creating a spool file for the printer without printing the document. Sometimes this technique is useful, such as when you're working on a notebook computer with no printer attached but you intend to print later.

To make this method work, open the printer's queue and choose Use Printer Offline from the Printer menu, as shown in Figure 21.5. The printer's icon dims and shows the word *offline.* You can disconnect the printer from the computer.

FIGURE 21.5

Use Printer Offline.

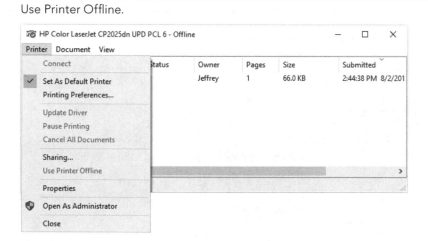

You can print any document while the printer is offline. The document doesn't actually print because the printer isn't connected. When you get back to the printer, connect the printer to the computer again. Open the Printers folder, right-click the printer's icon, and uncheck the Use Printer Offline option to set the printer online again. Any documents you "printed" while disconnected from the printer start printing.

Creating XPS Documents

As an alternative to printing on paper, you can print to an XPS document. The XPS document looks exactly like the printed document will look, but it is a file rather than a sheet of paper. You can e-mail that XPS document to other people. Or, if you have a website, let people download it from your site.

> **TIP**
> You can use XPS documents to print other people's web pages to files on your own hard disk. You can view that file at any time — you needn't be online.

To print to an XPS document, start printing as you normally would. For example, choose File ⇨ Print from the program's menu bar. Or if you're in Internet Explorer or any other web browser, click Print from the menu. When the Print dialog box opens, choose Microsoft XPS Document Writer instead of your usual printer, as shown in Figure 21.6. Then click OK or Print.

FIGURE 21.6

Print to an XPS document.

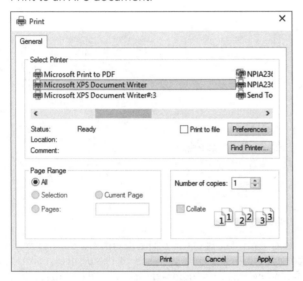

Because you're printing to a file, a Save As dialog box opens. There you can choose the folder in which you want to place the file and give the file a name. Figure 21.7 shows a file named crimemap.xps located in the Documents folder about to be printed. Click Save.

The Save As dialog box closes. To verify that the document was printed to a file, open the folder you printed to. The file is closed so it looks like an icon (see Figure 21.8), but you can treat it as any other document. For example, double-click the icon to open it into the Windows 10 Windows Reader app. Or, if you want to e-mail it to someone using an installed e-mail program, such as Microsoft Outlook, right-click the icon and choose Send To ⇨ Mail Recipient.

FIGURE 21.7

Printing crimemap.xps.

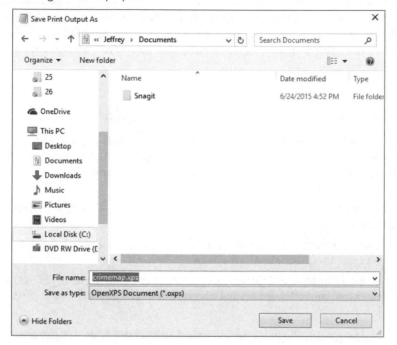

FIGURE 21.8

The icon for an XPS document.

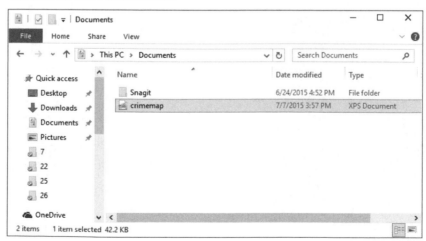

Wrapping Up

The typical printing scenario is that you choose File ⇨ Print from a program's menu bar, or press Ctrl+P, to print the document you're viewing at the moment. But as you've seen in this chapter, more is going on behind the scenes, and you have ways to manage your print jobs.

This chapter covered the following points:

- Every document you print is a print job, temporarily stored in a print queue.
- To open the print queue, double-click the printer icon in the notification area, or the printer's icon in the Printers folder. As mentioned earlier in this chapter, some printers such as HP bring up their own printing control panel when you double-click the printer.
- To manage print jobs in the queue, right-click any job and choose an option from the shortcut menu.
- To cancel all documents that are waiting to be printed, choose Printer ⇨ Cancel All Documents from the print queue's menu bar.
- To print to an XPS document rather than paper, start printing and get to the Print dialog box as you normally would, but choose Microsoft XPS Document Writer as the printer.
- To read an XPS document, open it in the Windows Reader app.

Part VI

Installing and Removing Programs

Adding and Managing Windows 10 Applications

T he Windows Store is an online location where you can find and install Windows 10 apps. When you find an app you like, you must install it on your computer before you can start using it. This chapter explores how to access the Windows Store, how to navigate it, how to install apps, how to look for and install app updates, and how to remove apps.

Using the Windows Store

The Windows Store (shown in Figure 22.1) is a new feature of Windows 8 and Windows 10. It provides an online area where you can download Windows 10 apps for your computer, tablet, or Windows phone. Windows 10 apps are typically single-functioning applications (for example, reading and responding to Twitter feeds) designed for the Windows 10 interface and must adhere to strict application development guidelines before they're approved for the Windows Store. Users can browse the Windows Store for apps.

FIGURE 22.1

The Windows Store available with Windows 10.

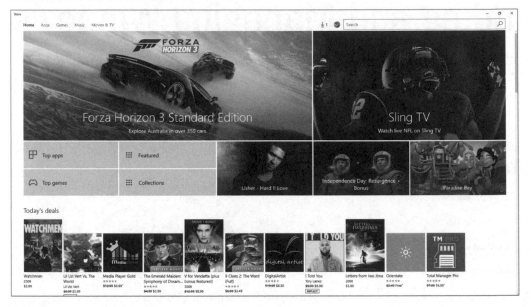

The Windows 10 interface leverages the touch-based interaction features from Windows 8 and Windows 8.1. But Windows 10 is not only about touch; it's also about simplification and putting applications within easy reach. The Windows Store makes acquiring apps easy and quick. The Windows Store is available online and requires that your computer meet the following requirements:

- A high-speed Internet connection.

- Screen resolution of at least 1024 × 768.

- For the Snap feature to work (see Chapter 2), your screen resolution must be set to a minimum of 1280 × 800.

To use the Windows Store, show the Start menu and click the Store app. You also can click the Store app on the Windows taskbar (shown in Figure 22.2). The Windows Store page appears (refer to Figure 22.1).

Reviewing Windows 10 apps

Using the Windows Store is pretty straightforward. When you enter the site, the Spotlight area highlights some of the most popular apps. To see the apps and your account, click the account button on the top right of the screen (next to the Search box). The Store menu drops down giving you access to your apps, app categories, and your account. The Store menu is shown in Figure 22.3.

FIGURE 22.2

The Windows Store app located on the Windows taskbar.

FIGURE 22.3

The Windows Store account menu.

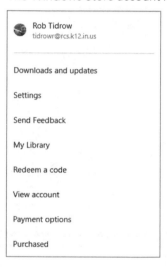

Rob Tidrow
tidrowr@rcs.k12.in.us

Downloads and updates

Settings

Send Feedback

My Library

Redeem a code

View account

Payment options

Purchased

> **NOTE**
>
> Microsoft releases guidelines for programmers who want to create Windows 10 apps. Besides programming require-ments, the guidelines also list general requirements for all apps: For example, apps cannot contain adult material; cannot include defamatory or obscene material; and cannot include content that encourages irresponsible use of alcohol, tobacco, drugs, or weapons.

To learn more about an app, click its tile. A page appears that includes information about the app, such as cost (many apps are free), ratings, description, and features.

Figure 22.4 shows an example of the app page for a free calculator.

To learn what other users have to say about the app, scroll to the Ratings and Reviews area (see Figure 22.5). This shows any reviews that have been added for the app. After you download an app, you can add a review as well by clicking a star under the Rate and Review This App heading and then filling out the Write a Review section of the resulting form.

FIGURE 22.4

The details page of a free calculator app.

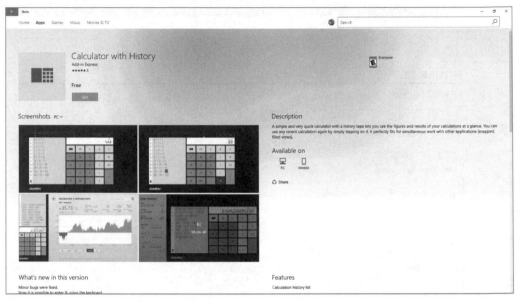

FIGURE 22.5

The review page of a free calculator app.

Navigating the Windows Store

Navigating the Windows Store is like navigating a full-screen web page. All the information for a page is displayed on a single page so you don't have to scroll down very much. Instead, additional Windows Store pages are accessed by scrolling to the right using one of the following methods:

- If you have a scroll wheel on your mouse, scroll toward you to scroll to pages to the right. Scroll away from you to return to previous pages on the left.

- Drag the scrollbar at the bottom of the page to the right to see additional pages to the right. Scroll to the left to return to previous pages on the left.

- On touch devices, swipe from right to left to see pages on the right. Swipe from left to right to return to previous pages on the left.

You can navigate back to the main Windows Store page by using the following methods:

- **Clicking the Back button on the top left of the window:** You may have to do this several times if you've viewed several pages already.

- **Using any of the three methods in the preceding bullet list to return to previous pages to the left until you arrive at the main Windows Store page.**

- **Right-clicking the top of a page or swiping down from the top edge of the page to show the app menu:** From this menu, click Home to return immediately to the Windows Store home page.

Windows Store categories

The Windows Store displays apps in categories to help you locate them. Apps are available within the following main categories:

- **Books & Reference:** Shows apps relating to books, e-books, references, the Bible, and online magazines.

- **Business:** Shows apps that help you in the business world, such as myStarjob, Captain Dash, and Presenter.

- **Developer Tools:** Shows apps that are used by software developers.

- **Education:** Provides educational apps, such as SATmax, My Baby Piano, Star Chart, and ICT Break.

- **Entertainment:** Shows apps that provide entertainment value, such as the Naturespace holographic audio app, Kids Song Machine apps, and the CW TV network app.

- **Food & Dining:** Provides recipe and food- and drink-related apps, such as Fine Cooking, Cocktail Flow, Matias Winery, and Allrecipes.

- **Government & Politics:** Lists government-related and politics-related apps.

22

- **Health & Fitness:** Lists apps for helping you stay healthy, get in shape, and lose weight, including Fitball and MedicineCabinet.

- **Kids & Family:** Lists apps that are family-friendly.

- **Lifestyle:** Lists apps that fall into general lifestyle areas, such as AutoTrader and PRINZ Cityguide.

- **Medical:** Lists medical-related apps.

- **Multimedia Design:** Lists apps used for creating and modifying multimedia documents and files.

- **Music:** Shows apps for accessing podcasts, listening to Internet radio, and working with music. Apps you can find in this category include Givit, SlapDash Podcasts, and Slacker Radio.

- **Navigation & Maps:** Provides apps related to maps and navigation.

- **News & Weather:** Provides apps for news and weather resources, such as the Los Angeles Times, USA Today, and AccuWeather.com.

- **Personal Finance:** Provides apps for helping you manage finances, including the Finance app and the Ameriprise Financial app.

- **Personalization:** Provides apps for customizing and personalizing your Windows 10 environment, including free wallpapers, pins, and other items.

- **Photo & Video:** Lists digital photography and video apps, such as Camera, Composite, and Fhotoroom.

- **Productivity:** Includes apps for computer and tablet productivity, including EverNote, Skitch, and Quick Note.

- **Security:** Lists computer security-related apps.

- **Shopping:** Shows apps for shopping, such as Yellow Pages, Amazon Windows 10 for Windows, and CBAZAAR.

- **Social:** Provides apps for accessing social media sites, such as Rowi and Tweetro for Twitter, WordPress.com for WordPress sites, FlipToast for Facebook and Twitter, and more.

- **Sports:** Provides sports-related apps, such as Major League Soccer, Basketball Coach's Clipboard, and New Zealand Cricket.

- **Travel:** Lists travel-related apps, such as Kayak Hotels, INRIX Traffic, and NAVITIME.

- **Utilities & Tools:** Shows computer tools, such as WinZip 16.5, Maps, and Dr.eye.

Within each category, individual apps are showcased. Some categories also show an All Stars category for apps that have been rated the highest for a category, a New Releases category for just released apps, and a Top Free category that lists top-rated free apps.

In addition to standard apps, the Windows Store provides access to games, music and movies & TV shows.

- **Games:** Provides game apps, such as Fruit Ninja, Cut the Rope, Mahjong Deluxe, and more.
- **Music:** Download and listen to music provided on the Microsoft Groove Music site. Additional costs apply to join Groove.
- **Movies and TV:** Buy and rent motion pictures and television shows. Additional costs apply to buy or rent movies and television shows.

Costs of apps

The costs of apps vary. Typically, the costs fall into one of three payment structures:

- **Free:** Many free apps are free because they include built-in advertisements to offset the cost of development, support, and upgrades. In some cases, you have the option of upgrading from a free version to a full-featured version that includes additional features and no ads.
- **Trial:** Gives you many of the features available in a full paid version, but for a limited time period.
- **Paid:** Gives you access to a full version of the app. Costs vary from 99 cents to several hundred dollars.

Searching for apps

Because the Windows Store is itself a Windows 10 app, you can use the Cortana search tool to locate apps in the Windows Store. To do this, access Cortana. In the Search field, type an app name or a keyword for an app and press Enter. The Windows Store returns a list of apps that meet your search criteria. Figure 22.6, for example, shows a screen with the Search field visible and the Windows Store showing the **Calculator Free** app selected.

Installing Windows 10 apps

When you find an app you like, you must first install it before you can use it on your computer or tablet. Installing apps is easy. Click an app tile to show the app's description page. Next, click the Install button on the left side of the page. The Windows Store shows a message at the top of the page indicating that your app is installing. Windows then displays a message notifying you that the installation is complete.

22

FIGURE 22.6

Use Cortana to locate Windows Store apps.

After the app has been installed on your computer, the install button is no longer available when you go to the app's page in the Windows Store. Instead, the page shows that the selected app is already installed on your computer, as shown in Figure 22.7.

If you already own an app, but have not installed it on a particular device, Windows Store shows a label that says "You own this product" and provides an Install button.

To start using the app, display the Start screen and click the app's tile.

FIGURE 22.7

The Windows Store showing that you own the app and that it is installed.

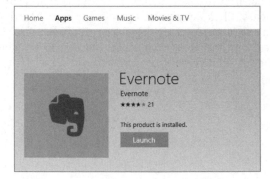

Updating Apps

Periodically, app developers provide an update that enhances an app by adding features or improving performance. If updates are available, the Store tile on the Windows Start screen shows a number corresponding to the number of updates available.

Click that tile to open the Windows Store. At the top right of the Windows Store, click the download arrow. You may also see a number next to the arrow showing you the in-progress or pending downloads and updates. On the Download and Installs page, click Check for Updates. Windows searches for updates and begins downloading the available updates for your installed apps. These updates run in the background. When they're complete, a message indicates that the updates have been installed on your computer.

Removing Apps

If you no longer want an app installed on your computer, you can remove it by uninstalling it. To do this, follow these steps:

1. Display the Start menu.
2. Right-click the app that you want to remove (see Figure 22.8).

FIGURE 22.8

Use the Uninstall feature to remove an app from your computer.

3. Click Uninstall in the menu. A message appears telling you that the app will be removed and any information related to that app will also be removed.

4. Click the Uninstall button to remove the selected app.

Wrapping Up

The Windows Store provides access to many different types of apps, including productivity apps, games, news apps, and more.

Here's a quick summary of the main points presented in this chapter:

- You use the Windows Store to install apps to your computer.
- Apps are divided into categories in the Windows Store, such as Social, Entertainment, Business, and Productivity.
- Many apps are free.
- You use the Windows Store to install updates to your installed apps.
- To remove an app from Windows, right-click it and click Uninstall. Click Uninstall to confirm that you want to remove that app.

Installing and Upgrading Legacy Programs

IN THIS CHAPTER

Playing it safe with program installations

Updating versus upgrading

Installing programs from disks

U nlike documents, which you can freely copy to your hard disk and use on the spot, most new programs you acquire must be installed before you can use them. The installation process configures the software to work with your particular hardware and software. The process also creates an icon or program group on the Windows 10 Start menu so that you can start the new program as you would any other.

> **NOTE**
>
> If you're upgrading from Windows 7 or earlier, don't take for granted that upgrading to Windows 10 preserves all your legacy applications. Even Microsoft Office 2016 applications are at risk. Before you upgrade, make sure that you have your legacy software installation media and registration or license keys handy, and be prepared to reinstall.

You need to install a program only once, not each time you intend to use it. After you've installed a program from a disk, you can put the disk away for safekeeping. You need the original installation disk to reinstall the program only if you accidentally delete the program from your hard disk or if some sort of hard disk crash damages the program.

This chapter explores the common methods and issues you may experience when installing programs for Windows 10. Keep in mind that the installation process, although similar across different programs, can vary from one program to the next. So, the examples in this chapter are general, rather than specific.

> **NOTE**
>
> One type of program does not require installation. Self-contained program files (such as .MSI programs) simply copy to your computer and require you to double-click them to run.

Playing It Safe with Program Installations

Programs you buy in a store aren't likely to contain any malicious code such as viruses, worms, or spyware. Those things tend to be spread by e-mail attachments and free downloads from the web. However, you face an outside chance that the new program is incompatible with Windows 10 or a hardware device on your computer. So, sometimes you need to uninstall a program and then get all your system files back into shape to undo any changes made to your system by the new program.

> **NOTE**
>
> This chapter covers installing legacy applications on Windows 10.

Windows 10 System Protection greatly simplifies the task of getting your system back in shape if a program installation or upgrade causes problems. But it helps only if it's turned on and you know how to use it. For details, see Windows 10 online help.

Updates Versus Upgrades

Non-technical people often assume that updates and upgrades are the same thing. They aren't. An *update* is usually something you do online. You have nothing to buy at a store, no disk to insert in a disk drive. Updates are generally free, and often automatic (many programs scan for updates and offer them to you automatically). You don't have to make an effort to seek those out and install them.

Updates for some programs may not be quite so automatic. But you can often find out if any updates are available right from the program's Help menu or similar area.

> **TIP**
>
> You can use Windows Update to check for Microsoft product updates. See Chapter 8 to learn about Windows Update.

Unlike updates, upgrades are usually not free. You have to purchase them and install them. For example, say you have Microsoft Office 2013 installed on a computer. You want to get

Office 2016 on that computer. In that case, seek out Office 2016 or Office 365. Then install that upgrade over your existing version. For software that is delivered as software-as-a-service (SaaS), you may be required to upgrade or pay an additional subscription fee when upgrading to Windows 10. Contact your subscription service for details on upgrading to Windows 10. For example, Adobe Photoshop is subscription-based software.

Installing and Upgrading from a Disk

Before you begin installing and upgrading from a disk, you must have administrative privileges to install a program. You need to know the password for an administrative account on your computer. If you have a limited user account and don't know the administrative password, you need an administrator to install the program for you.

Most programs that you purchase are delivered on a CD, DVD, or via an Internet download. Always follow the installation instructions that come with such a program. But just so that you know what to expect, here's how the process usually works, after you have the installation files or CD/DVD in hand:

1. Although this step is not required, you should run the installation with no other programs running to make sure you have plenty of system resources available. This step ensures that no files that the installation will upgrade are in use. Close all open program windows on your desktop by clicking their Close buttons or by right-clicking their taskbar buttons and choosing Close.

23

NOTE
You don't need to close programs whose icons are in the notification area, unless specifically instructed to by the installation instructions for the program you're installing.

2. For programs released on a disk, insert the CD or DVD into your computer's CD or DVD drive and wait a few seconds. Wait for the installation program to appear on your screen. If it doesn't appear within 30 seconds, see the section "Using the installed program" later in this chapter. Skip to Step 4.

3. For programs released on a download from the Internet, find the installation or setup file, which usually has an .exe file extension. Double-click that file to launch it.

4. Follow the onscreen instructions to perform the installation.

That's installation in a nutshell. You're presented with some questions and options along the way. Exactly what you see varies from one program to the next, but some common items include the end-user license agreement (EULA) and the option to choose a folder in which to store the program, which we discuss in a moment.

For programs on a CD/DVD, sometimes your Windows setup may not launch the installation program automatically. If nothing happens within half a minute or so after you have inserted a program's installation CD/DVD into your computer's CD/DVD drive, you may need to start the installation program manually. Here's how:

1. Open your Computer folder by clicking the File Explorer icon on the desktop taskbar and choosing This PC.

2. Open the icon that represents the drive into which you placed the disk.

3. If the installation program doesn't start automatically in a few seconds, click (or double-click) the icon named Setup or Setup.exe.

That should be enough to get the installation program started. From there you can follow the onscreen instructions to complete the installation.

The onscreen instructions and prompts you see during the installation vary from one program to the next. The next section discusses some common things you're likely to come across when installing just about any program.

Common Installation Prompts

Even though every program is unique, you're likely to encounter some common elements during a program installation. When you install a program, you likely won't see all the prompts described in the sections that follow, so don't be alarmed if your installation procedure is much simpler. (Be thankful instead.)

The initial CD or DVD prompt

Shortly after you insert the installation disk for a program, you may see a prompt like the one in Figure 23.1. This is a new setup feature. Click this message to display the actions you can take with the installation disk. Figure 23.2 shows examples of setup options Windows 10 provides. The most common option is Run SETUP.EXE, which is what you would click.

FIGURE 23.1

The first prompt after inserting an installation disk.

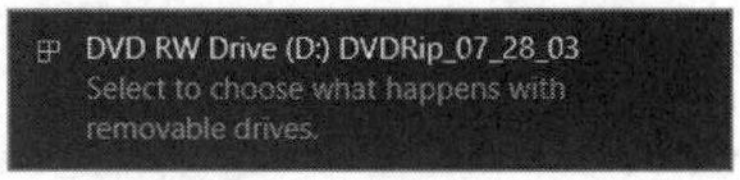

DVD RW Drive (D:) DVDRip_07_28_03
Select to choose what happens with
removable drives.

FIGURE 23.2

Windows 10 displays a message when it recognizes a disk with a setup program on it.

Entering an administrator password

Only people with administrative privileges can install programs in Windows 10. If you're signed into a limited account, you see a dialog box asking you to enter an administrative password. If you're already logged on with an administrative account, Windows 10 asks you if you want to allow the program to make changes to the computer. Click Yes to continue with Setup.

The product key or serial number

Many programs (including ones published by Microsoft, Adobe, and Apple) require that you enter a product key or serial number to install the program. That number is usually on a sticker on the case or sleeve in which the program was delivered.

> **TIP**
>
> You may want to keep track of all your product keys in a word processing or spreadsheet document in case you ever need to reinstall something. Print a copy of the document and keep it safe in case your hard disk crashes. Magical Jelly Bean Finder (www.magicaljellybean.com/keyfinder) is a free program that lists the product keys for all your installed programs, as well as a good deal more useful information about your systems.

If you need to enter a product key or serial number, you see a prompt asking you for the product key, license number, or similar title. Type the product key exactly as it is provided by the software manufacturer, and click Continue (or whatever button the installation program offers to continue the installation process).

Compliance check

If you're installing an upgrade of a new program and you already have the older version installed on your computer, the installation program likely will detect the existing product and move through the upgrade. In other situations, particularly where you don't already have a previous edition of the program installed, you may be prompted to insert the CD/ DVD for the old version and/or enter the product key for the old version. This process depends entirely on the requirements of the application's upgrade program. Follow the prompts displayed by the upgrade program to provide the requested information.

> **NOTE**
>
> You may see a message asking what you want to do with the CD/DVD you just inserted. You do *not* want to install the program on the CD/DVD. The goal is to simply prove you have the older version, not to install the older version. So, if you see a dialog box asking what you want to do with the CD/DVD, click the Close (X) button in the upper-right corner of that dialog box.

User information prompt

Some programs offer prompts that ask for your username or initials. These are optional but useful. The username is automatically entered as the author name in any documents you create with the program. The initials are used in settings where multiple people edit documents to identify changes you made to the document.

The End User License Agreement

Just about every commercial program and most freeware and open-source programs require that you accept the end-user license agreement (EULA) as part of the installation process. Figure 23.3 shows an example. The agreement is a legal document that defines your rights to the program, as well as the developer's retained rights.

The EULA differs from one program to the next. In most cases, the EULA gives you the right to install a program on one computer. However, that is not always the case. The EULA for Microsoft Office 2013 applications, for example, allows you to install the software on a licensed device (such as your desktop computer) and one portable device (such as your notebook PC). The intent of this clause is that you'll use the software on only one computer at a time. In addition, you can access and use the software on the device remotely from any other device. For example, this means you can connect to your office PC from home and run the Office application remotely on your office PC (or vice versa).

FIGURE 23.3

A sample end-user license agreement.

Although many people never read the EULA when installing a program, you should take the time to do so. You'll discover interesting bits of information (such as the fact that you can install Office on more than one computer) and also potential problems. For example, we've seen EULAs for shareware and commercial programs that explain that the Setup program installs other, third-party applications along with the program, and that by accepting the EULA you're indicating your acceptance of those other programs. These programs may have nothing to do with the program you're installing, such as weather monitors, web browser add-ons, toolbars, and so on. Often, the installation program gives you the option of not installing these additional programs, but that isn't always the case. So, our best advice is to always read the EULA.

You can't install the program if you don't accept the terms of the agreement, so assuming you're happy with (or at least resigned to) the terms of the EULA, check the I Accept option and click Next, Continue, or whatever button continues the installation process.

Type of installation

Sometimes you're given some choices as to how and where you want to install the program. Figure 23.4 shows an example from Microsoft Office Professional 2013. Unless your computer is low on disk space, generally you should install the program with all features. Otherwise, months later you may try to use some advanced feature of the program and get an error message saying it isn't installed.

FIGURE 23.4

Type of installation.

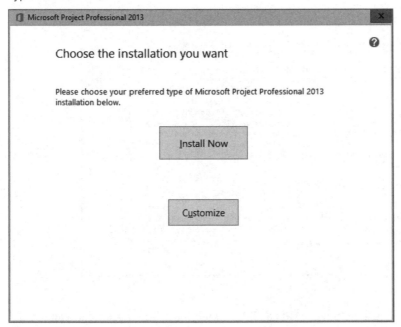

As to the *where* to install the program, you rarely have any reason to change the suggested location, which is typically some folder in C:\Program Files. Don't change that location without a good reason. Whatever you do, don't make the common newbie mistake of installing a program in your Documents folder. You aren't installing a document. You're installing a program. The Documents folder is intended to store documents for easy retrieval later. And we recommend keeping all your programs in subfolders under C:\Program Files.

Installation summary

The installation procedure may give you a summary of the options you chose along the way. Typically, you have a Back button or some other means to return to previous screens and make changes if needed.

Setup completed

The last page of the installation options may offer a couple of final options, as in the example shown in Figure 23.5. Whether you choose these options is relatively unimportant. You can check the web for updates and additional downloads at any time, whether through the program itself or by visiting the software company's website (or the Microsoft Update site).

FIGURE 23.5

Setup complete.

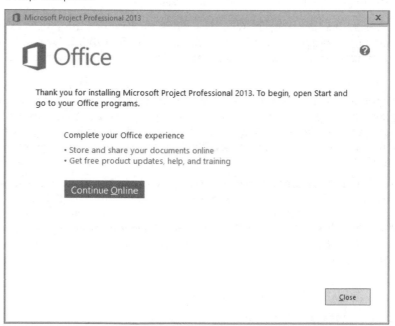

Some applications give you the option of keeping installation files on the computer rather than deleting them. Keeping the installation files can simplify the process of changing program settings or installing missing components in the future. Installation files usually don't take up any significant amount of disk space. Click Finish, remove the CD/DVD from the drive, and put it someplace safe in case you ever need to reinstall.

You may also be prompted to shut down and restart Windows after the program is installed. If prompted, you can click Yes to restart now or click No to restart later. In any event, you must restart at least once before running the program for the first time.

> **NOTE**
> Most insurance policies don't cover computer software. So, if at all possible, consider keeping your original program DVD or CDs in a fireproof safe.

Using the installed program

After the program is installed, you can run it from the Windows 10 Start menu. The preceding steps installed Microsoft Office Professional 2013. To run the program, show the Windows 10 Start menu, click All Apps, scroll over to the application you want to start, and click its tile.

Wrapping Up

Installing programs from files, CDs, or DVDs is easy. It's a matter of running the executable file, or putting the program installation disk into your CD or DVD drive and following the onscreen instructions. Here's a quick summary of the main points presented in this chapter:

- Consider creating a system restore point (see Chapter 24) before installing any program. That way, if the new program creates problems, use that restore point and return to the protection point to undo every change made during the program installation. In most situations, Windows 10 creates a restore point for you automatically.

- You need to install a program only once, not each time you want to use it. After you've installed the program, you run it from the new Windows 10 Start screen, without the program CD or DVD in the drive. In a few cases, the program requires the CD or DVD in the drive to validate that you have a licensed copy of the program (because possession of the CD or DVD implies that you haven't installed it by using someone else's media).

- If you're upgrading a program that's already installed, do not remove the existing version unless the installation instructions tell you to do so.

- The typical procedure for installing a new program is to insert the program's installation CD or DVD and follow the onscreen instructions. For a program that you download from the Internet, you simply need to double-click its setup filename.

- If nothing happens within a minute of inserting the installation disk, open your This PC folder, open the icon for the CD drive, and double-click the Setup or Setup. exe icon on the CD.

- When the installation is complete, store the installation disk in a safe place. In most cases you don't need it to run the program. But you may need it to reinstall the program should some mishap cause you to lose the program.

Getting Older Programs to Run

IN THIS CHAPTER

Recognizing old programs to avoid

Installing incompatible programs

Checking for compatibility

Using DOS commands in Windows 10

Y ou can run almost any program that's installed on your computer just by clicking its tile on the Windows 10 Start menu. But every rule has exceptions. Chief among the list of exceptions are old programs that were written to work with earlier versions of Windows. Or, even worse, programs that were written to run on DOS.

That isn't to say Windows *can't* run old programs. Most of the time, it can run an older program as is, without any changes at all on your part. This is especially true if the program was written for Windows XP or later versions of Windows. So, before you assume that you have to do something to try to get an older program to run, try running the program normally. If it runs, you're set. If it doesn't run, this is the chapter you need.

Understanding Program Types

A couple of types of programs can be considered "old" in the context of this chapter:

- **DOS programs:** These programs were developed to run under various versions of the Disk Operating System (DOS), the precursor to Windows.
- **16-bit Windows programs:** These Windows applications were written for Windows ME and earlier versions of Windows.

What does "16-bit" mean? Three classes of Windows applications exist: 16-bit, 32-bit, and 64-bit. The number of bits indicates the maximum amount of addressable memory supported by the program. Table 24.1 indicates the differences.

TABLE 24.1   **Processor Technology and Directly Addressable Memory**

Technology	Meaning	Memory Addresses
16-bit	16	65,536
32-bit	32	4,294,967,296
64-bit	64	18,446,744,073,709,600,000

Windows NT, Windows 2000, and Windows XP were all originally 32-bit operating systems. Windows XP was also offered in a 64-bit edition. Windows 98 and earlier were 16-bit operating systems. Windows Vista and Windows 7 were offered in two versions, 32-bit and 64-bit. Likewise, Windows 8/8.1 and Windows 10 are available in 32-bit and 64-bit versions. Suffice it to say, the higher the bits, the more capable the operating system. For the purposes of this chapter, the key point is that you can run a program on the OS it was designed for or (possibly) on a later version, but you can't go backward. For example, you can run a 32-bit application on a 64-bit OS, but you can't run a 64-bit program on a 32-bit OS.

DOS programs

Let's make a distinction between DOS programs and DOS commands that you can run in Windows 10. *DOS programs* were written specifically to run on a DOS without (and before) Windows. It's so unlikely that you would want to run an old DOS program on Windows 10 that we don't even cover the topic in this chapter (although we do have a copy of Zork — an interactive adventure game from the late 1970s — lying around somewhere that would be fun to play again...). That doesn't mean you *can't* run that DOS program under Windows 10. Many of them run without any major problems.

DOS commands are developed by Microsoft and included as part of the Windows package, instead of being developed and marketed by third parties. We cover DOS commands to some degree later in this chapter.

Old programs to avoid altogether

Windows 10 is a revision of the Windows 8.1 operating system, so almost all Windows 8.1 programs should have no problems running on Windows 10. Likewise, many of your basic Windows 7, Vista, and Windows XP application programs work. But you should validate compatibility for other kinds of programs before attempting to run them under Windows 10. These include:

- **Old disk utility programs:** Older disk utility programs such as Norton Utilities (later it went by Symantec Norton Utilities) and various disk compression and partitioning tools should never be run on Windows 10. Many older DVD- or

CD-burning programs are likely to cause problems, too. If you have such a program, you should upgrade to the Windows 10 version of that program or find a similar product that's designed to work with Windows 10.

- **Old backup programs:** If you have an older backup program, using it in compatibility mode could prove disastrous. Even if you can perform the backup, there's an outside chance you won't be able to restore from the backup if and when you need to. Consider using Windows File History, which comes with your copy of Windows 10.

- **Old cleanup programs:** Older programs that purport to keep your computer running in tip-top shape, clean up your registry, and so on should not be used at all in Windows 10. If you like the program, look into getting a version that's specifically written for or certified by the developer as compatible with Windows 10.

- **Old optimizing programs:** Programs designed to make your computer run at maximum performance don't necessarily make Windows 10 run that way. In fact, they may do more harm than good. If you use such programs, check to see if a Windows 10 version is available before you install the old version.

- **Old antivirus programs:** Virus detection and removal is dicey business and must be handled with great care. Antivirus programs written for pre–Windows 10 versions of Windows should *never* be installed or run on a Windows 10 computer unless certified by the developer as compatible. The same goes for anti-spyware and other anti-malware programs. Better to seek out a Windows 10 version of the program than to presume the older version will work. Better yet, use Windows Defender, which comes preinstalled on your computer.

 Read Chapter 5 on how to deal with malicious software that attacks your computer.

Installing Incompatible Programs

To install an older program, first try installing it normally. For example, if it's on a CD, insert the CD and wait for the installation program to appear automatically. If nothing starts automatically, open your root folder (open File Explorer and choose the root folder or This PC). Then click the icon to open the drive that contains the installation disc and double-click the setup launcher program (typically setup.exe, setup, install.exe, or install). If Windows 10 determines that the program is older, you see the Program Compatibility Assistant.

If you believe that the program installed normally, click the option that indicates that the program installed properly. Otherwise, click the option that specifies compatibility mode. Windows 10 assigns some compatibility mode attributes to the program and tries the installation again. With any luck, the second try does the trick.

If you still have problems, here are some things to consider:

- If you're installing from a standard user account, log out and log in to an administrative account; then try to install from that account.

- If you have to create any file or folder names, use names that conform to the DOS 8.3 conventions (keep filenames to eight characters maximum with no blank spaces and provide a three-character extension).

- If you get stuck in an installation program, use the Applications tab in Task Manager to end the stuck program.

 See Chapter 27 for details on Task Manager.

If all else fails, contact the program publisher (if it's still in business) or look for information about that program online. Only the program publisher really knows if the program runs in Windows 10 and what's required to get it to run.

Using the Program Compatibility Troubleshooter

Installing a program is one thing; getting it to run after it's installed is another. If an installed program doesn't start or isn't working right, try using the Program Compatibility Troubleshooter on it.

The Program Compatibility Troubleshooter provides a step-by-step means of configuring and testing an older program so that it runs in Windows 10. Before you bother to use the troubleshooter, try running the installed program without it. You may discover that the program runs just fine without any compatibility settings and save yourself quite a bit of trouble.

If you're sure an installed program isn't running, or is not running correctly, follow these steps to start the Program Compatibility Troubleshooter:

> **TIP**
> You can right-click a program's icon on the Start menu, choose More, choose Open File Location, right-click the file, and then choose Troubleshoot Compatibility to launch the Program Compatibility Wizard.

1. Open Control Panel and click the Troubleshooting icon.
2. When the Troubleshooting applet opens, click the Programs option and then click the Program Compatibility Troubleshooter.

3. On the first page of the troubleshooter, click Next. The troubleshooter now gathers a list of applications for troubleshooting (see Figure 24.1).

4. Select a program and click Next.

5. If you want Windows 10 to try to determine the right settings on its own, click Try Recommended Settings. To specify your own settings, click Troubleshoot Program. The following steps assume you've selected the second option.

FIGURE 24.1

Program Compatibility Troubleshooter.

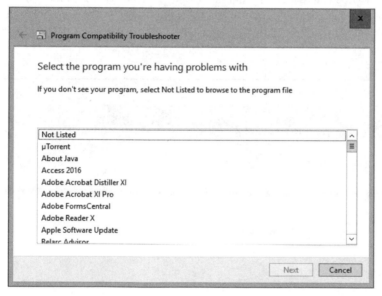

6. Next, the wizard prompts you to answer questions about the program (see Figure 24.2). Selecting any of the first three options causes the wizard to prompt you with related questions. For example, if you choose the option The Program Worked in Earlier Versions of Windows But Won't Install or Run Now, the wizard asks you to specify on which version of the OS it worked previously (see Figure 24.3). Likewise, choosing the option The Program Opens But Doesn't Display Correctly results in a screen that prompts you to the test the program for display setting issues.

Complete the wizard by selecting options that relate to the problems you're having with the program.

24

The process is mostly trial and error. If the program runs when you finish the wizard, great. Otherwise you can run it again to try different settings until you get the program to work correctly.

Here are some general guidelines to help you get your program running:

- If the program doesn't install or doesn't run, run the wizard, choose the option The Program Worked in Earlier Versions of Windows But Won't Install or Run Now and specify the operating system for which the program was written. For example, if it is a Windows XP game, choose Windows XP from the OS list provided by the wizard.

- If you have problems with the program's display, choose the option The Program Opens But Doesn't Display Correctly and click Next. Choose the symptoms the program is exhibiting and click Next to let the wizard set display options as needed.

FIGURE 24.2

Program Compatibility questions.

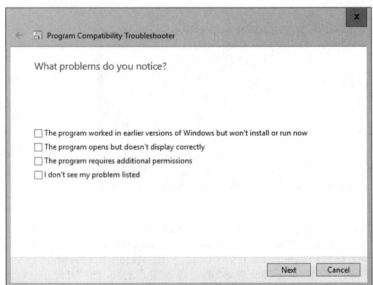

FIGURE 24.3

Select a Windows version under which your program previously worked.

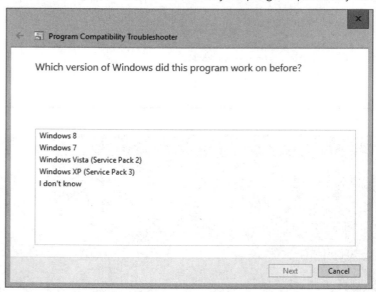

- If you think the program is having permissions issues (for example, the program says it can't write a file), choose the option The Program Requires Additional Permissions. The wizard configures the program to run as an administrator, which should resolve the issue.

You have no guarantee that the Program Compatibility Troubleshooter will make the program run. Some programs are so old and so far removed from modern computing capabilities that you have no way to force them to run. In those cases, the only hope is to contact the program publisher or search online for solutions or a compatible version of the program.

24

Quick-and-Dirty Program Compatibility

The Program Compatibility Wizard provides an easy way to choose and test settings for program compatibility. Those settings are stored on the Compatibility tab of the program file's properties sheet. You can use the wizard to change compatibility settings, or you change settings manually right in the properties sheet by following these steps:

1. On the Start menu, right-click the program shortcut you want to examine. Choose More.

2. Choose Open File Location (see Figure 24.4).

FIGURE 24.4

Display program options.

3. Right-click the program's icon and choose Properties.

4. In the Properties dialog box that opens, select the Compatibility tab. You'll see the options shown in Figure 24.5.

5. Select the Run This Program in Compatibility Mode For check box, and then choose the operating system for which the program was written. If the program installs and runs, but exhibits other symptoms (such as display problems), leave this option unselected.

6. If you're having problems with the program's display, choose appropriate display settings in the Settings group.

7. If the program seems to have permission problems, select Run This Program as an Administrator.

FIGURE 24.5

Compatibility settings.

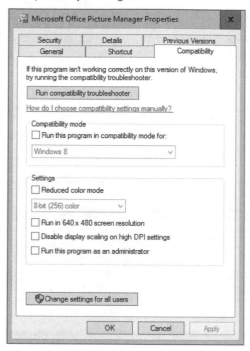

8. If you want to apply the settings for everyone who uses the program, click the Change Settings for All Users button to open a similar Properties dialog box and set properties there as needed.

9. Click OK.

The compatibility settings stick to the program so you can start the program normally, from the All Programs menu, at any time. Keep in mind that you can't force all programs to run in Windows 10.

Using DOS Commands in Windows 10

If you've used personal computers since the DOS days, you may want to enter the occasional DOS command. DOS commands let you do things you can't do in Windows. For example, in those rare instances where you can't delete a file in Windows, using a DOS erase or del command with the /F switch often does the trick. You can use the DOS `dir` command to print filenames from a folder to print out or a text file.

Using commands in Windows 10 has one big catch. User Account Control (UAC) may prevent you from doing things you'd otherwise take for granted. You can get around many of those by using the Run as Administrator option to open the command prompt. Here are two different ways to open the Command Prompt window, but not as an Administrator:

- From the desktop, press Windows+X and click Command Prompt.
- In the Cortana search box, type **cmd** and press Enter. The Command Prompt window appears (see Figure 24.6).

FIGURE 24.6

Open Command Prompt.

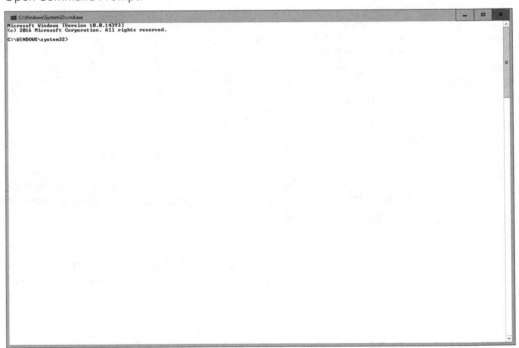

The Command Prompt window that opens is much like DOS. By default, when logging in under an account that is not the Administrator account you're taken to the home directory for your user account. But you can navigate around using the DOS `cd` command.

For example, enter **cd..** to go to the parent directory, or **cd "program files"** to go to the Program Files folders.

To see a list of all supported commands, enter **help** at the command prompt. For the syntax of a command, type the command followed by **/?**. For example, entering **dir /?** displays the Help for the dir command.

> **NOTE**
>
> You can change the height and width of the Command Prompt window. To do so, click its control menu in the upper-left corner and choose Properties.

You can copy and paste a lengthy pathname to a cd command to simplify opening that folder in a DOS window. In Windows, open the folder in File Explorer, click the folder to the left of the breadcrumb list, and highlight the path in the address bar as in Figure 24.7, and press Ctrl+C to copy it.

> **TIP**
>
> While using File Explorer, you can see the name you need to type to launch any program, right-click the program's icon on the All Programs menu and choose Properties. The filename at the end of the Target path is the name you type in the Search or Run box.

In the Command Prompt window, type **cd** and a space. Then right-click the Command Prompt window, right-click, and click Paste. Press Enter, and you'll be in that folder.

Use the dir command with various switches to view, or optionally print, all the filenames in a folder and also its subfolders if you like. For example, say you navigate to the Music folder for your account (C:\Users\yourUserName\Music). From that folder, entering **dir /s** lists all file and folder names for all artists, albums, and songs in your Music folder.

You can use the /b, /n, and /w switches to choose how you want the information displayed. For example, entering **dir /s /w.** shows filenames in the wide format.

You can send the output to a text file so you can open and edit the file before you import it into Excel or Access to make it more like tabular data. To send output to a file, end the command with a filename (or path and filename). For example, entering the following from the Music folder puts the output listing in a file named MyMusic.txt in the Music folder.

```
dir /s /w >MyMusic.txt
```

You can then open that MyMusic.txt file with any text editor or word processor to clean it up. If you have database management skills, you can import the data to Access or a similar program and treat it like any other tabular data.

FIGURE 24.7

Select a directory path.

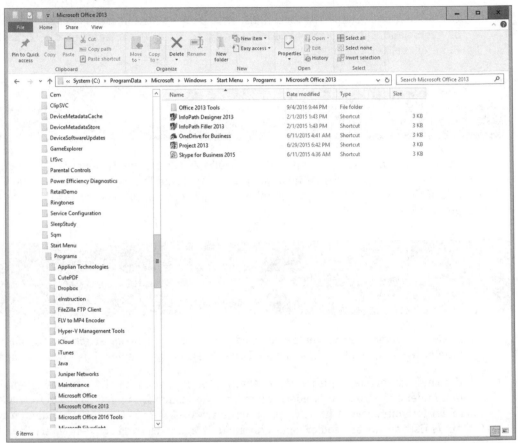

> **CAUTION**
> This section is just a side topic for people who are already familiar with DOS. Don't experiment with DOS commands carelessly. You could lose a lot of files and have no means of getting them back!

To exit the Command Prompt window, enter the exit command or just close the window.

Wrapping Up

This chapter has focused on techniques for getting older programs to work in Windows 10. Windows 10 offers several tools to help with compatibility issues. Whether you have any luck with them depends on how old and how incompatible the program is. Most of your programs will run fine under Windows 10. A few won't, until you upgrade to the Windows 10 version, but those should be few and far between. The main points are as follows:

- Most programs written for Windows Vista, Windows 7, and Windows 8.1 are already compatible with Windows 10 and require no special handling.
- When you attempt to install an older program, the Program Compatibility Assistant kicks in automatically to help out.
- The Program Compatibility Wizard helps you with installed programs that don't start or run correctly.
- Compatibility settings are stored in the program file's properties sheet on the Compatibility tab.
- To use DOS commands in Windows 10 with minimal flack from UAC, choose Run as Administrator to open the Command Prompt window.

24

Repairing and Removing Programs

Most of the time, your applications operate smoothly and without incident. Occasionally, however, you need to repair a program that is having problems. Or, you may want to remove a program or a Windows feature that you aren't using.

In this chapter, you learn techniques for managing installed programs. You learn how to change or repair programs as well as how to remove programs you no longer need or want. You do most of these tasks in the Control Panel's Programs and Features applet or from the Windows Start menu.

Changing and Repairing Programs

Some large programs let you choose how you want to install the program. For example, you may be given options to do a Minimum Install, Typical Install, or Complete Install. You might do a Minimum or Typical installation to conserve disk space but later discover you need a feature that only the Complete Install would have provided.

Sometimes a program becomes corrupted and stops working properly. That can happen if you inadvertently delete a file that the program needs. Or it may be caused by a minor glitch that compromises an important file.

The first step to changing or repairing a program is to get to the Programs and Features applet in the Control Panel. Here's how:

1. Press Windows+X on the desktop and click Control Panel.
2. In the category view, click Programs.
3. Click Programs and Features.

You can also get to Programs and Features from Cortana. Simply start typing **pro** and click Programs and Features.

The page that opens lists all your installed application programs. (It doesn't include programs that come with Windows 10.)

Not all programs offer change or repair options. To see what options an installed program offers, right-click the program name. Or, click the program name and take a look at the buttons above the list of program names. Things you can do with that program are listed in a toolbar above the list. For example, in Figure 25.1, we clicked Bonjour, which offers options to Uninstall and Repair.

In most cases, you need the CD or DVD that you originally used to install the program to change or repair the program. If you have the CD handy, put it into the CD drive. If Windows asks what you want to do with the disk, choose Take No Action. If the installation program opens automatically, cancel or close that program.

> **NOTE**
> Changes you make to a program affect all users. Therefore, you must know the password for an Administrator account on your computer to change or repair programs.

Exactly how the process plays out from here varies from one program to the next, so we can only provide some general guidelines and examples. But all you have to do is make your selections and follow the instructions on the screen. For example, to repair a corrupted program, click the Repair button and do whatever the resulting instructions tell you to do.

The Change option for a program is generally for adding components you didn't install the first time around, although you can also remove any components you don't need. The exact process varies from one program to the next, but a typical approach is to provide different install options, like the example in Figure 25.2.

FIGURE 25.1

A list of installed programs.

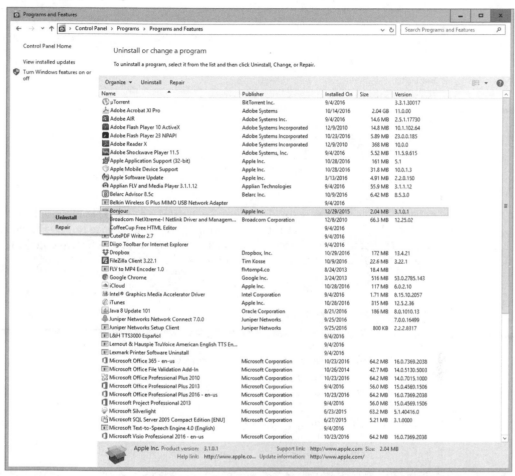

> **NOTE**
>
> Don't use Programs and Features to change settings within a program. Instead, use the program's Options or Preferences dialog box. Open the program as you normally would and look through its menus for a Tools or Preferences option. Or search that program's help for the word *preferences* or *options*.

25

FIGURE 25.2

Click an installation or update option.

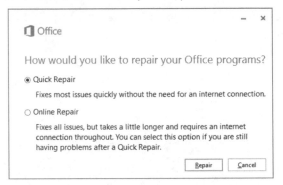

In the tree, click a program feature to choose an action. For example, choose Run from My Computer to install a feature. To remove an optional feature, choose Not Available. That feature is then removed and its icon displays a red X. When you've finished making your selections, click OK or Next and follow the onscreen instructions.

Uninstalling Programs

Unlike documents and other files, copying a program to your hard disk isn't enough to make it usable. You have to *install* programs before you can use them. Likewise, simply deleting the startup icon for a program isn't enough to remove the program from your system. You have to *uninstall* the program. These steps are necessary because a program often consists of many files. For example, Microsoft Office comprises hundreds of files! Furthermore, installing a program makes other changes to the system. Uninstalling is necessary to undo those changes.

> **NOTE**
> You must be logged in to an administrative account, or know the administrator password for your PC, to remove a program.

Before you remove (uninstall) any program, make sure you know what you're removing and why. Just because you don't know what a program is or what purpose it serves doesn't mean you should remove it. Removing programs isn't likely to solve any computer problems.

> **CAUTION**
> You can't use an Undo or Recycle Bin to reinstate removed programs. The only way to get a removed program back is to reinstall it from its original installation CD or DVD, or to download it again from the original website.

With all those cautions out of the way, removing a program is quite simple. Windows 10 provides two methods for uninstalling programs. From the Start menu, right-click a program icon and choose Uninstall. Or you can use the Programs and Features Control Panel applet. Assuming you're already in the applet, right-click the name of the program you want to remove and choose Uninstall. Or select that program's icon or name and click the Uninstall button in the toolbar. If prompted, enter an administrative password. Follow any additional instructions that appear on the screen.

Unpinning from Start

If the program that you want to remove doesn't appear in Programs and Features, you may be able to remove its icon from Start, the area on the right side of the Start menu when you display the Start menu. When a program is on Start, it's pinned to the menu. To unpin it, right-click the icon you want to remove and click Unpin from Start, like the example in Figure 25.3. If you find such an option, you can click it to remove the program from your system.

FIGURE 25.3

Unpinning from the Start screen.

Dealing with stuck programs

Occasionally, you find a situation where removing a program generates an error message before the program is completely removed. The first thing to do, of course, is to read the error message and see what options it offers. You may be able to finish the removal just by choosing options that the error message provides.

If you can't get rid of a program through the normal means or error message, your next best bet is to install the program again. That may seem counterproductive, but the problem may be that the program only partially installed. A partially installed program may not have enough application files installed to do a thorough removal. After you've completed the initial installation, you should be able to remove the program without any problems.

Turning Windows Features On and Off

Windows 10 comes with many programs and features built right in. How many depends on which edition of Windows 10 you purchased. Your edition may include some features you want to use and some you don't.

> **TIP**
>
> Unlike Add/Remove Programs in Windows XP, program features in Windows Vista, Windows 7, Windows 8/8.1, and Windows 10 allow you to turn features on and off without the hassle of installing and uninstalling.

To turn Windows Features on or off, open the Programs and Features Control Panel applet discussed earlier in this chapter. Then click Turn Windows Features On or Off in the left pane. A list of available Windows Features opens, as shown in Figure 25.4. Items that are selected are currently installed and working. Unselected features are not active. A filled check box represents a feature that's active but that also has additional subfeatures. Click the plus sign next to a feature to see what subfeatures it offers.

> **CAUTION**
>
> Turn off only those program features that you're certain you don't need. If you don't know what a feature is or does, better to err in favor of keeping it active than to find out, the hard way, that you shouldn't have disabled it!

The rest is easy. To disable a feature or subfeature, clear its check box. To enable a disabled feature, click its empty check box to select it. Click OK after making your changes.

FIGURE 25.4

Windows features.

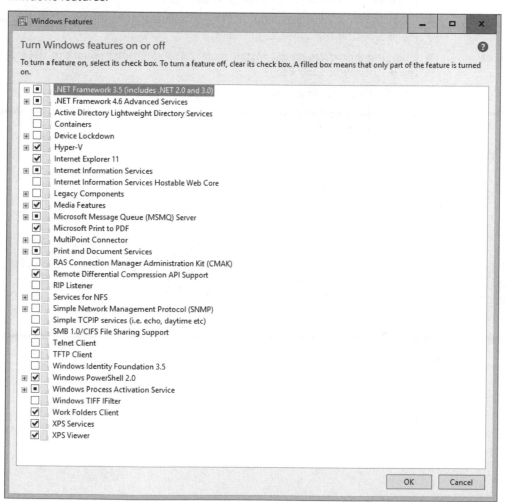

Wrapping Up

Managing installed programs in Windows 10 is easy enough. It all takes place through the Programs and Features page. Here's a quick review of what's involved:

- You need administrative privileges to change, repair, or remove programs.
- Use Programs and Features to change, repair, or remove installed programs (open Control Panel and click Programs).

25

- To see what options an installed program offers, click its name in Programs and Features and look at the buttons in the toolbar.

- Repairing a program generally involves reinstalling it from the original CD or redownloading the application from the web.

- Changing a program means installing features you didn't choose initially or removing features you don't use.

- Uninstalling a program removes it from your computer and from all user accounts.

- The Programs and Features window also provides an option to turn Windows features on and off.

Setting Default Programs

A s everyone knows, you can buy many different brands of toothpaste, shampoo, cars, and just about every other kind of product. The same is true of software. Everyone uses a web browser to browse the Internet, and you have many different web browsers to choose from. One is Microsoft Edge, which comes with Windows 10. Others are Internet Explorer, Opera, Firefox, and Google Chrome, to name a few.

If you're looking for a media player, Windows 10 comes with Media Player. In addition, you can choose QuickTime, Musicbee, and many others. When you have two or more programs capable of handling the same type of file, consider making one the *default program* that opens automatically when you open that type of file. Setting such defaults is what this chapter is all about.

Setting Default Programs for Files

Typed text, pictures, music files, and video clips are all examples of documents and other types of files that you can create or download to your computer. Thousands of file types exist. Each type is indicated by its filename extension. For example, a picture may be a JPEG (`.jpeg` or `.jpg`), BMP (`.bmp`), GIF (`.gif`), TIFF (`.tif` or `.tiff`), PNG (`.png`), or any of a couple of dozen other formats.

When you click (or double-click) a file icon while in File Explorer, the file opens in whatever is the default program for its type. If you have more than one program that can open the file type, you can override the default and open the file with some other program. Right-click the file's icon and choose Open With, as shown in Figure 26.1. The Open With option is available only if you have two or more programs installed that can open that type of file.

If you want to keep the current default program for this type of file, and override that just this time, click the name of the program you want to use to open the file.

FIGURE 26.1

Using the Open With option.

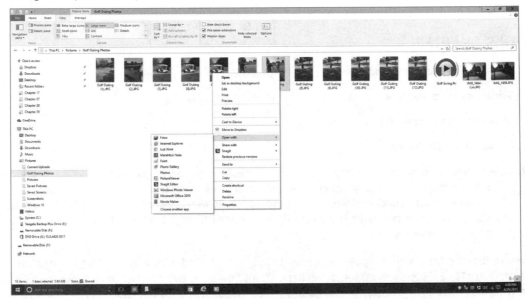

If you want to change the default program that Windows always uses to open that type of file, click Choose Another App at the bottom of the Open With menu. The Open With dialog box opens. An example of this box when a .jpg file is selected is shown in Figure 26.2.

I Don't See Any Filename Extensions

If Windows is configured to hide known filename extensions, you don't see them in your Pictures folder or other folders. But you can point to a file icon and see the filename extension in the tooltip that appears at the mouse pointer. Optionally, you can make filename extensions visible by clicking the File Name Extensions item on the View tab in Windows File Explorer.

Click whatever program you want to use for opening that type of document. Also, make sure the Always Use This App To Open *<filetype>* Files option is selected (checked). Otherwise your new choice isn't saved.

FIGURE 26.2

The Open With dialog box.

If you can't find the program you want to use as the default, you can click the More Apps link to look for it (you may need to scroll down the list to see this link). Just make sure that the program you want to use is capable of opening that type of document.

Setting default programs using the Open With dialog box is just one way to do it. Many programs have options within them that enable you to choose which file types you want to associate with the program. The settings within the program might even override the settings you specify in Windows. So sometimes you have to go into the program that's acting as the default for a file type and make a change there.

Unfortunately, no single rule applies to the hundreds of programs that allow you to change associations within a program. Typically you start by opening the program and choosing Tools ⇨ Options or Edit ⇨ Preferences, or something similar, to get to the program's main options. To illustrate, we'll use QuickTime as an example because many people have that program.

In QuickTime, you first open the QuickTime Player from the Windows 10 Start menu. Then choose Edit ⇨ Preferences ⇨ QuickTime Preferences from its menu bar. Select the Browser tab, click File Types, and you're taken to a dialog box where you can specify file types that should open automatically in QuickTime. Select the file types you want to open in QuickTime automatically. Clear the check marks for those file types for which QuickTime should not act as the default program. Figure 26.3 shows an example.

When you associate a program with a file type, make sure to specify a program that *can* open files of that type. For example, don't associate video or audio files with Word or Excel because those programs don't play multimedia files.

FIGURE 26.3

Select QuickTime as the default program for audio and video file types.

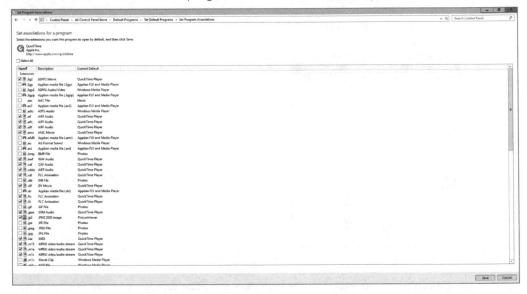

If the program you're setting up does not have a preferences option, open Control Panel, select All Control Panel Options, Default Programs, Set Your Default Programs, and then choose Set This Program As Default from the dialog box that loads.

Using the Default Programs Page

Right-clicking a document's icon and choosing Choose Another App is the quick and easy way to set a default program on the fly, but it isn't the only method, and you aren't limited to setting defaults based on file types. You can also set defaults for protocols. A *protocol* is a standardized way of doing something. Different Internet services use different protocols. For example, web browsing uses HTTP, which stands for Hypertext Transfer Protocol.

You can also set default actions for CDs, DVDs, and devices you connect to your computer. Use the Default Programs page in the Control Panel to set all these different kinds of defaults. To get there, use whichever method is easiest for you:

- Press Windows+X and choose Control Panel ⇨ Programs ⇨ Default Programs.
- From Cortana, type **default** and choose Default Programs.

You see the options shown in Figure 26.4 and summarized here.

- **Set Your Default Programs:** Use this option to choose default programs for your user account only.
- **Associate a File Type or Protocol with a Program:** This option works like the preceding item, except that you start by choosing a file type or protocol rather than a program.
- **Change AutoPlay Settings:** Use this option to change what happens when you insert a CD or DVD, or when your connect a camera to your computer.
- **Set Program Access and Computer Defaults:** This option is strictly for administrators. It sets defaults for Internet access and media players for all user accounts.

The following sections describe each option.

FIGURE 26.4

Setting programs in the Default Programs tool.

Setting default programs

The first item in Default Programs lets you choose which file types and protocols you want to associate with programs. When you click Set Your Default Programs, you're taken to a page like the one in Figure 26.5.

Click a program name in the left column to see a description of that program in the right column. Then you can choose one of the following options:

- **Set This Program as Default:** Choose this option to make the selected program the default for all file types and protocols it can handle.

- **Choose Defaults for This Program:** Limit the program to act as the default for only certain file types and protocols.

FIGURE 26.5

Setting programs as defaults for file types and protocols.

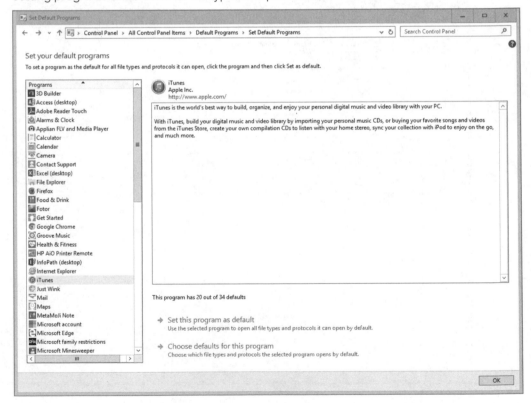

Choosing the second option takes you to a list of all the file types and protocols that the program supports, as shown in Figure 26.6. You can scroll through the list and select the file types and protocols for which the program should act as default. Clear the check box of any file type or protocol for which you want some other program to act as the default. Then click Save to return to the previous page.

When you've finished choosing defaults for programs, click OK to return to the main Default Programs page.

You also can choose a default app for Windows 10 apps from the Windows 10 Settings page. Open the Start menu and select Settings. When the Windows 10 Settings page opens, click System and then select Default Apps. The screen shown in Figure 26.7 loads.

FIGURE 26.6

Setting file type associations for a program.

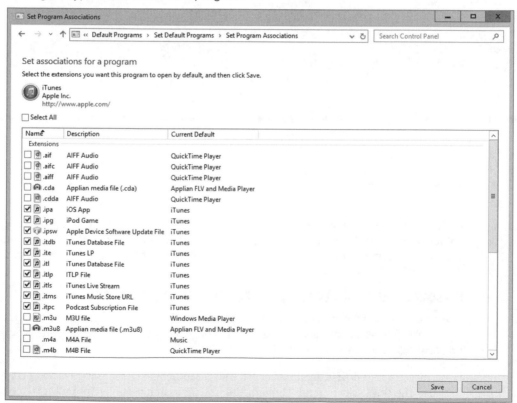

FIGURE 26.7

The Defaults screen for setting defaults for apps.

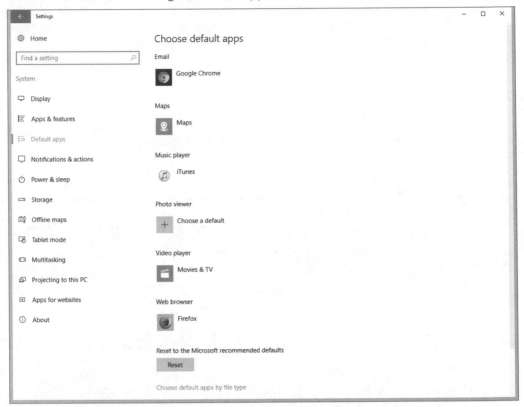

In Figure 26.7, we haven't chosen a default program for the Photo Editor app. To select a default program click the Choose a Default link next to the program that has no default. The menu shown in Figure 26.8 loads. Continue to select the program you want to use.

Associating a file type or protocol with a program

The second option in Default Programs is similar to the first. But instead of starting with a program, you start with a file type or protocol. When you click Choose Default Apps by Protocol, you see options similar to those in Figure 26.9.

File types are listed first, in alphabetical order. Protocols are separate at the bottom of the list. Use the scroll bar to scroll through the list. To assign a default program to a file type or protocol, click the item you want to change and click the Change Program button. Then use the Open With dialog box that opens to choose a program.

Choosing default apps by file type and/or protocol is also possible from Settings. Click the respective link at the bottom of the Associate a File Type or Protocol With Specific Apps page.

> **NOTE**
> Don't worry about items marked as Unknown Application. Most of those aren't files you interact with with directly anyway and don't need a default program. You don't have to assign a default program to every item in the list.

FIGURE 26.8

The options presented for setting defaults for apps.

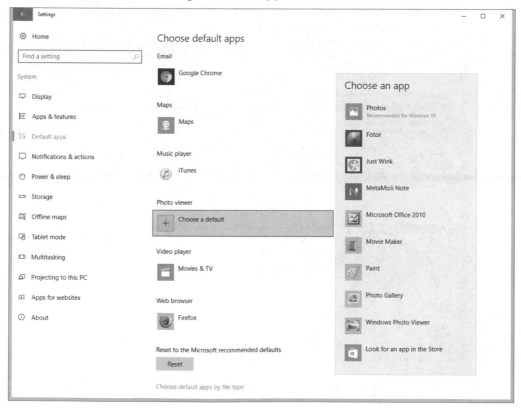

Changing AutoPlay settings

AutoPlay is a Windows feature that lets you choose which program you want to use to play content on CDs, DVDs, and devices (such as MP3 devices). Chances are you've already seen the AutoPlay screen at least once, after you inserted a CD or DVD, or connected a camera, mobile phone, or disk drive. Figure 26.10 shows an example.

Click the AutoPlay screen to see a list of actions to take. The AutoPlay dialog box lets you choose the action you want to take with the selected media. For a removable device that always has pictures on it, you might choose one of the Import Pictures and Videos options. Or, as the example in Figure 26.11 shows, the actions for the iPad that we connected to our computer include open in Microsoft Word, Import Pictures and Videos, and Open Device To View Files. Until you set a default AutoPlay option, however, Windows continues to ask you what you want to do when you attach the device.

FIGURE 26.9

Setting protocols with programs.

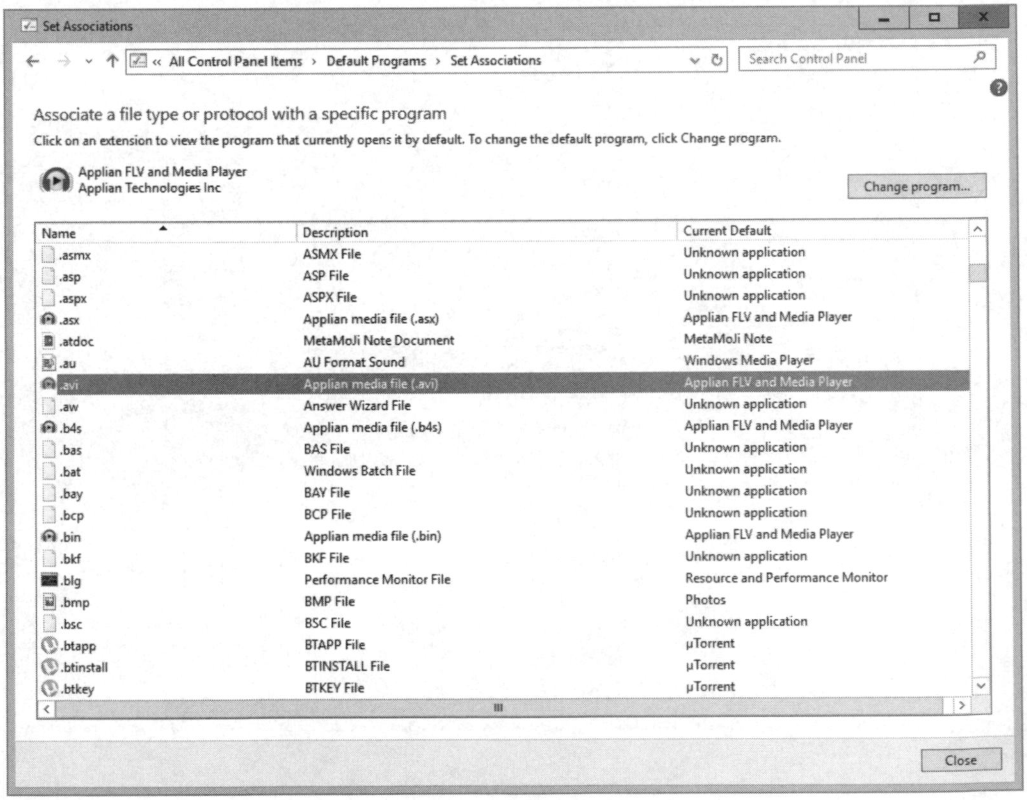

When you click Change AutoPlay Options in the Control Panel, you get to see all your current AutoPlay default settings, as in Figure 26.12. You can also get there by clicking Change AutoPlay Settings in the Default Programs item in the Control Panel. Scroll to the bottom of the list to find icons for devices you connect to your computer, such as digital cameras.

FIGURE 26.10

The Windows 10 AutoPlay screen appears at the bottom of the window.

FIGURE 26.11

Selecting an action to take when connecting a device.

The Shift Key Doesn't Work the Way It Used To

In previous versions of Windows, you could hold down the Shift key while inserting a disc or connecting a device to override the default action for the device. You can do that in Windows 10, but the AutoPlay dialog box opens. (The default program doesn't open.) To prevent the AutoPlay dialog box from opening when using the Shift key, you need to deselect the Use AutoPlay for All Media and Devices check box at the top of the AutoPlay page shown in Figure 26.12.

FIGURE 26.12

Setting AutoPlay options for each type of media or device you attach to your PC.

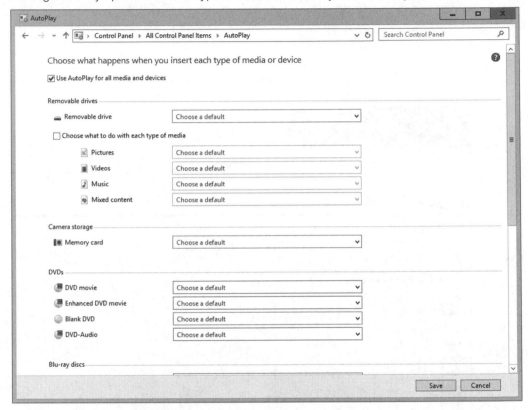

To change the default action for any item, click the current action and choose the action you want from the menu that drops down. Click Save after making your changes to return to Program Defaults.

Setting program access and computer defaults

Anybody who has a user account can choose defaults using any of the methods described in this chapter. The Set Program Access and Computer Defaults option (see Figure 26.13) is strictly for computer administrators. It sets defaults that apply to all user accounts, and can even be used to limit programs that they can use. This is most often used in corporate settings when administrators want tight control over how staff members use their computers. But anyone with an administrative user account on a home computer can use it to control family members' program use as well.

Because the Set Program Access and Computer Defaults option can so severely limit what all users can do, you need administrative privileges just to start it. If you're in a standard user account, you need to log out. Then log in to an administrative account to open that option. When you first open it, you see these three options:

- **Microsoft Windows:** Choose this option if you want to set the programs that came with Windows 10 as the default programs.

- **Non-Microsoft:** Choose this option if you don't want to use any Microsoft programs.

- **Custom:** Choose this option if you want to use a combination of Microsoft and non-Microsoft programs.

After you choose one of these options, more options appear under that category. The exact options vary depending on what you choose. But they work in a similar manner. We'll use the Custom category, shown in Figure 26.13, as an example, because it offers the most options.

FIGURE 26.13

Setting program access and computer defaults.

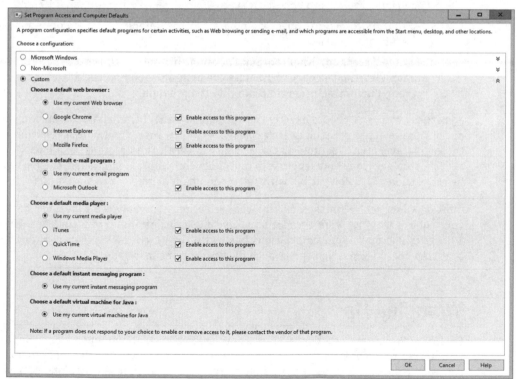

What's a Java Virtual Machine?

Java is a programming language often used with Internet programs and *applets* (small programs embedded in web pages). The virtual machine (also called a runtime environment) allows those programs to run on your computer. It isn't a mandatory item unless you use programs that require it or visit websites that require it.

Typically, if you need the Java Virtual Machine, you're prompted to download it automatically when it's required. You can also download and install it at any time from www.java.com/download.

As shown in Figure 26.13, the first options let you choose the default web browser, e-mail client, and media player for online music and video. Scrolling down enables you to choose a default instant messaging program and Java virtual machine. The options available to you depend on what programs you have installed on your computer at the moment. For each program, you have the following options:

- **Use My Current:** Choose this option to keep whatever program you're currently using as the default program. This will be the only option when you don't have multiple programs to choose from.

- *<Program Name>:* To specify a program as the default, click the option button to the left of its name.

- **Enable Access to This Program:** Choosing this option allows users to run the program. Clearing the check box hides the program's icon on the Start menu and elsewhere, preventing users from running the program.

Sometimes you can't choose exactly the option you want. Other times, when you choose an option, the selected program doesn't comply. That's because the programmers who create these programs aren't required to make them work with the Program Defaults selections. If that's a problem, your only recourse is to contact the program publisher. They may have a newer version that's compatible with setting program defaults in Windows 10.

Click OK when you've finished making your selections. You may see a message stating that your choices may not work because of current file associations. If you click Yes, Windows 10 tries to change the file associations to go with the new default program automatically. If that step doesn't work, you can change file associations manually.

Wrapping Up

Default programs are programs that start automatically when you open a document or use an Internet protocol such as e-mail or the web. When you have two or more programs that can open a document or use an Internet protocol, you can choose which one acts as the default. Choosing a default doesn't preclude using other programs. The default only determines which program is used when you don't specify otherwise. Windows 10 offers several methods of choosing default programs:

■ To set the default for a file type on the fly, right-click a file's icon and choose Open With ⇨ Choose Another App.

■ To use some program other than the default for a document, right-click the icon, and choose Open With and the name of the program you want to use.

■ The Program Defaults page in the Control Panel provides ways of setting multiple default programs from a single page.

■ The Set Your Default Programs option enables you to choose a program and specify the documents and protocols for which it should act as the default.

■ The Associate a File Type or Protocol with a Program option enables you to first choose a filename extension or protocol, and then choose the program that will be the default.

■ The Change AutoPlay Settings option enables you to choose what happens when you insert a disc or connect a device.

■ The Set Program Access and Computer Defaults option allows an administrator to control defaults and programs for all user accounts.

Managing Programs and Processes

Y ou are no doubt familiar with the terms *application* and *program*. These two terms describe
program code that, whether one component or several components, serves a specific function.
For example, a word processor is an application. Some applications, however, comprise multiple
processes running at the same time. In addition, a process can comprise multiple threads of execution, each performing a specific task. Although you typically concern yourself with programs, you
sometimes need to think about the processes that make up a program, particularly if one of those
processes fails. That's where Task Manager comes into play.

Task Manager is a program included with Windows 10 for viewing and managing running programs
and processes. You can use it to seek out performance bottlenecks, close stalled programs and processes without restarting the system, and more.

Getting to Know Task Manager

Task Manager is a program that lets you view and manage running programs and processes, as
well as view performance data for your computer and network. Starting with Windows 8 and con-
tinuing with Windows 10, Task Manager has changed from releases prior to Windows 8. If you're
familiar with Task Manager in Windows 7, for example, you're in for quite a change with the new
(and, in our opinion, improved) Task Manager.

You can start Task Manager in several ways:

- Press Ctrl+Alt+Del and click Task Manager.
- Right-click the clock or an empty spot on the taskbar and choose Task Manager.
- Display Cortana, and type **task**. Click Task Manager on the Apps screen.

TIP

If a program is hung (frozen), right-clicking the taskbar may not work. But pressing Ctrl+Alt+Del may still work. If Ctrl+Alt+Del doesn't work to bring up Task Manager and the computer is unresponsive, turning the computer off and back on is generally the only way to get it going again.

Figure 27.1 shows the Task Manager and a number of apps and programs running. Task Manager behaves much like any program window. It has a button on the Windows taskbar when open. You can drag the program window around by its title bar and size it by dragging any corner or edge. You can also configure it so it stays on the top of the stack of open windows so you can always see it. You can change that by selecting Options from the top ribbon and selecting Always On Top.

FIGURE 27.1

Task Manager in its normal view.

Viewing more and less detail

With Windows 10 Task Manager, you have the choice of showing a list of just the running applications, as shown in Figure 27.1, or a display with multiple tabs filled with system and application data (as shown in Figure 27.2). The former view shows fewer details while the latter shows more details. When showing less detail, you have fewer options for controlling and viewing application information, but you can still stop an app or application.

FIGURE 27.2

Task Manager in its detailed view.

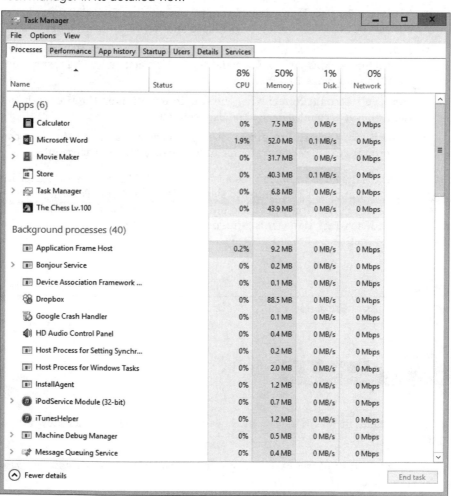

To switch between detail views, click the More Details button on the bottom of Task Manager. When viewing the More Details view, you can click the Fewer Details button to display the less detailed view.

Choosing Task Manager views

While viewing Task Manager in the More Details view, you can view and use Task Manager in several ways. On the Options menu in the menu bar, you have the following options:

- **Always On Top:** Choosing this option ensures that Task Manager is always on the top of the stack when it's open, so no other program windows can cover it.

- **Minimize On Use:** If selected, this option minimizes Task Manager whenever you choose the Switch To option to switch to another running program.

- **Hide When Minimized:** Normally when you minimize Task Manager, only its task-bar button remains visible. Choosing this option also hides the taskbar button when you minimize Task Manager.

- **Show Full Account Name:** When viewing information on the Users tab, you show the full user account name in the User column.

- **Show History for All Processes:** This option activates when you select the App History tab. It shows your resource usage history for the past month.

Whenever Task Manager is open, you see a small greenish-blue square in the notification area unless Task Manager is configured to show notifications only. Pointing to that icon displays the current CPU (central processing unit), Memory, Disk and Network usage, as shown in Figure 27.3. When Task Manager is minimized, you can double-click that little square to bring Task Manager back onto the desktop.

FIGURE 27.3

The Task Manager notification icon.

On the View menu in Task Manager, you have the following choices, as shown in Figure 27.4:

- **Refresh Now:** Causes Task Manager to refresh all its data immediately, regardless of the Update Speed setting.

- **Update Speed:** Task Manager needs to use some computer resources to keep itself up to date with what's happening in the system at the moment. The Update Speed option lets you choose how often Task Manager updates itself, as follows:

- **High:** Updates Task Manager twice per second.
- **Normal:** Updates Task Manager every two seconds.
- **Low:** Updates Task Manager every four seconds.
- **Paused:** Updates Task Manager only when you choose View ➪ Refresh Now.

- **Group by Type:** Shows apps, Windows process, and background processes in groups.
- **Expand All:** Expands the lists of apps and processes to show any open documents, open websites (if you're running Internet Explorer or another browser), and subprocesses.
- **Collapse All:** Collapses the list of running apps and processes.
- **Status Values:** Displays on the Processes tab only and shows the status of suspended processes.

27

FIGURE 27.4

Task Manager's View menu.

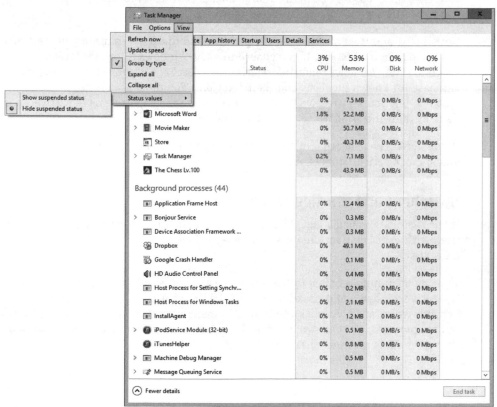

479

Not Responding? Task Manager to the Rescue

One of Task Manager's most useful roles is that of dealing with problems that cause programs, or your whole computer, to *hang* (freeze up, so that the mouse and keyboard don't work normally). Even when you can't get the mouse or keyboard to work, pressing Ctrl+Alt+Del and choosing Start Task Manager may get Task Manager open for you.

Closing frozen programs

Once Task Manager is open, select the Details tab, as shown in Figure 27.5. If a particular program is hung, its Status column usually reads Not Responding rather than Running. To close the hung program, click its name in the Name column, and then click the End Task button, which appears at the bottom right of the window. Task Manager tries to close the program normally, so that if you were working on a document at the time, you may be able to save any changes. (So, don't expect the program to close immediately.)

If the program doesn't close, you see a warning that moving ahead will close the program and leave unsaved work behind. To forge ahead, click End Process. The program may try to restart itself, depending on how it's designed.

Most likely, a process of reporting the problem and finding a solution will start after you end a program in this way. If you choose to allow Windows to send information about the program error, Windows sends information to a database of problems and searches that database for known problems and their solutions. You don't always get a solution to the problem, but you may receive information about an incompatible device driver or other issue by allowing Windows to report the problem.

If you don't have time to wait through that reporting process, you can cancel out of each dialog box by clicking its Cancel button.

Switching and starting tasks

If the system is so badly hung that you can't use the taskbar normally, and you want to work with open program windows individually, Task Manager provides some ways to accomplish that.

To bring a running program to the top of the stack of windows on the screen and make it the active window, right-click its name in the list of running tasks on Task Manager's Fewer Details screen, and then click the Switch To menu item. If you were working on a document in that program, you can save your work, and then exit the program normally (assuming that program is running normally).

FIGURE 27.5

Task Manager's Details tab.

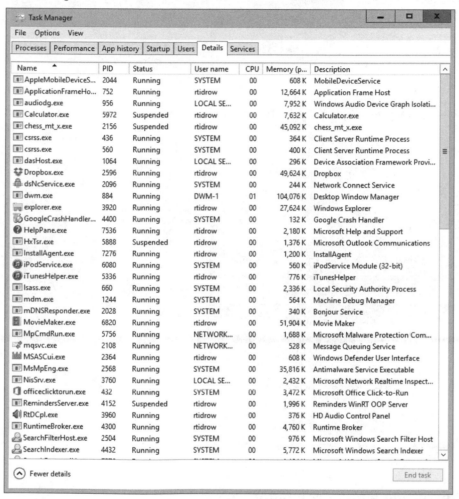

If you need to bring up a diagnostic program or debugger, or simply need to start some other program, and you know the startup command for that program, right-click an application in the Task Manager window and choose Run New Task. The Create New Task dialog box, shown in Figure 27.6, opens. Type the startup command for the program (or the complete path to the program, if necessary), and click OK. You can also access this dialog box when in the More Details view. Choose File ➪ Run New Task.

FIGURE 27.6

The Create New Task dialog box.

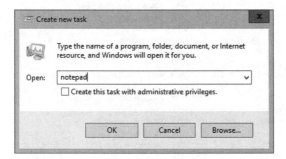

Restarting a hung computer

If your computer is so locked up that you can't get to Task Manager, or stop the offending program, you can try other things. If pressing Ctrl+Alt+Del works, you are taken to a Windows 10 screen with four options: Lock, Switch User, Sign Out, and Task Manager. You also have the Shut Down option and Ease of Access option at the lower right of the screen. Logging off or restarting is likely your best bet. If at all possible, Windows attempts to give you a chance to save your unsaved work.

If the program that's hung is also the one that contains the unsaved work, you may have no way to save that work. You may have to restart without saving. For this reason, you should save your work often.

Monitoring Performance with Task Manager

In addition to helping you deal with hung programs, Task Manager lets you see which processes in your system are using computer resources. On the Performance tab, as shown in Figure 27.7, you can see these key resources. The Performance tab in Task Manager provides both graphical and numeric summaries of CPU, memory, disk, and network hardware resource usage. To watch resource usage, leave Task Manager open and always on top as you run programs and use your computer in the usual ways. If you have multiple processors or a multi-core processor, each may be represented in a separate pane in the CPU history.

27

The Performance charts are useful for identifying major *performance bottlenecks*. For example, if the CPU charts run high, your CPU is working very hard. An errant application can consume inordinate amounts of CPU capacity. Also, reducing the number of running programs reduces CPU load.

A common performance bottleneck is limited physical memory. Running lots of programs when memory is limited forces the system to use lots of virtual memory, which in turn slows down performance because of the added overhead of swapping pages in and out of the hard disk. Increasing the amount of virtual memory (as discussed in Chapter 36) can help, but the best solution is to add more RAM (physical memory) to the system.

FIGURE 27.7

The Performance tab shows performance data.

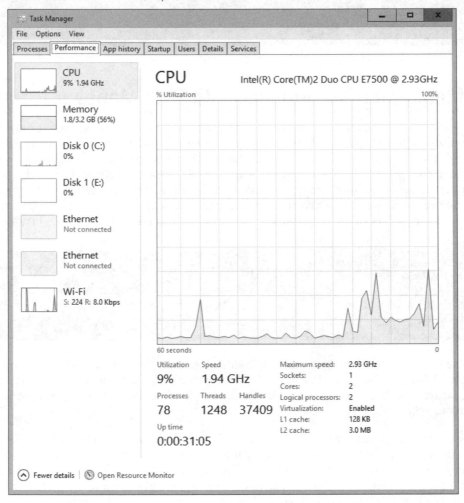

Some of the resources you may see include the following:

- **CPU:** Shows information about your computer's central processing unit. Data includes utilization, speed, processes, threads, handles, and up time. The bar graph shows a 60-second view of the CPU usage. Refer back to Figure 27.7 for an example of the CPU data.

- **Memory:** Provides data about the RAM in your computer, including the amount of RAM in use, how much is available in your computer, the committed memory (RAM plus virtual memory), cached memory, the Windows paged pool, and the non-paged pool (shown in Figure 27.8).

FIGURE 27.8

The Performance tab shows memory data.

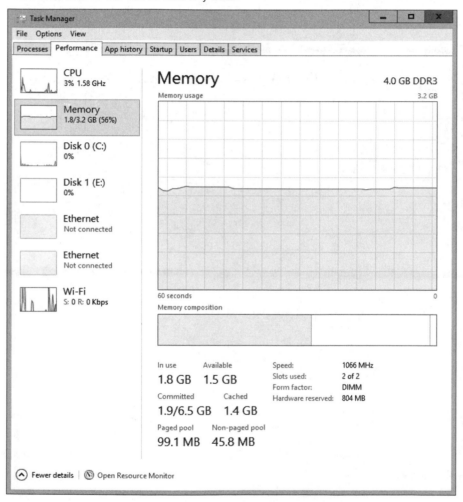

- **Disk:** Provides data about your installed hard disks, including disk transfer rate, active time in percentage, average response time, disk read speed, and disk write speed (shown in Figure 27.9).
- **Bluetooth:** Provides performance data about your Bluetooth devices.

- **Wi-Fi:** Displays data about wireless network devices installed on your computer. You can see send and receive data (see Figure 27.10).

FIGURE 27.9

The Performance tab shows disk data.

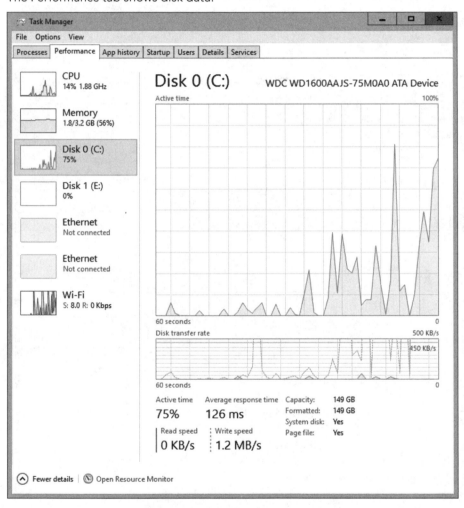

Exactly how fast your computer runs at any given moment depends on the resources available to it at that moment. For example, if you have half a dozen programs running, all doing intensive tasks, they're eating up CPU resources. If you start another program, that program may run slower than usual, because the other running programs are consuming CPU resources.

Likewise, everything you open stores something in RAM. If RAM is nearly full, and you start another program that needs more memory than what's currently left in RAM, Windows has to start sloughing some of what's currently in RAM off to the hard disk (called *virtual memory*) to make room. That takes time, so everything slows down.

FIGURE 27.10

The Performance tab shows Wi-Fi data.

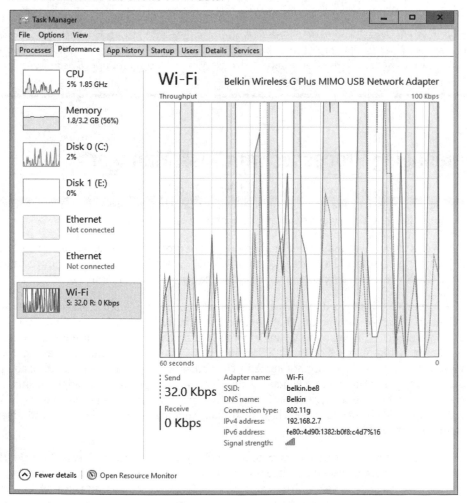

Physical Memory versus Virtual Memory

The term *physical memory* refers to the actual amount of RAM, on computer chips, installed in your computer. When you press Windows+X and choose System, the number to the right of the words *Installed Memory (RAM)* indicates the amount of physical memory installed on the motherboard inside your computer.

When applications and processes are busy in RAM, Windows moves some lesser-used items out to a special section of the hard disk called a *paging file*. The paging file looks and acts like RAM (to the CPU), even though it's actually space on your hard disk. Although Windows can be configured to not use a paging file, Windows, by default, sets aside some hard disk space for this paging file and uses it even if all available RAM is not used. (More on that topic in Chapter 31.)

A *page fault* is when the CPU "expects" to find something in RAM but has to fetch it from virtual memory instead. The term *fault* is a bit harsh here, because a certain amount of memory paging is normal and to be expected. Other terms used in this context include *nonpaged memory* for physical memory and *paged memory* for virtual memory.

Managing Processes with Task Manager

Whereas applications usually run in windows and are listed on the Processes tab in Task Manager, processes have no program window. We say that processes run in the background because they don't show anything in particular on the screen.

Your running applications are actually one or more processes. To see all currently running processes, select the Processes tab in Task Manager. Each process is shown under the Windows Process category heading, as in the example shown in Figure 27.11.

The Processes tab shows its information in columns. To help you differentiate between data values (that is, for data points that are low, medium, or high), Windows 10 uses a "heat map" paradigm. This type of display lets you look across columns and rows and data that represent different types of data (CPU, memory, disk, and network usages) and get a quick view of the data and see any hot spots in the values. For example, if memory usage for a process or application is high compared to other running processes or applications, the heat map shows a brighter orange color. Lower values are in lighter shades, such as light tan or light yellow. Microsoft designed these heat maps to allow users to visualize and digest the information quickly.

You can sort items by clicking any column heading. For example, you can click the Memory column to sort processes by the amount of memory each one takes up, in ascending order (smallest to largest) or descending order (largest to smallest). Seeing those in largest-to-smallest order lets you know which processes are using up the most memory.

Here's what each column shows:

- **CPU:** The percent of CPU resources that the process is currently using.
- **Memory:** The amount of memory the process is currently using.
- **Disks:** The current throughput the process is currently consuming.
- **Network:** The current throughput being consumed by the process.

FIGURE 27.11

The Processes tab in Task Manager.

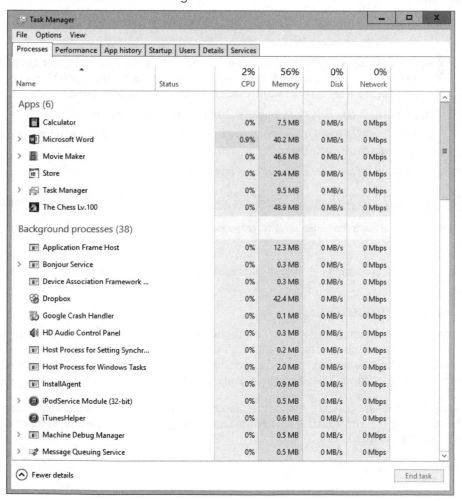

Memory usage is probably the main cause of slow-running computers. The more stuff you cram into RAM, the more Windows has to use the paging file, and hence the slower everything goes. You can see which processes are hogging up the most RAM just by clicking the Memory column heading until the largest numbers are at the top of the list.

Showing other columns

Windows 10 Task Manager provides additional columns of data that you can view on the Process tab. To see these columns, right-click on the column area. A menu appears with the names of the available columns, including the following ones that are not shown by default:

- **Type:** Displays the same information at the group type, such as App, Background Process, or Windows Process.
- **Status:** Displays information about Windows Store apps and whether they are suspended or not. To see what apps are suspended, select View, open the Status values, and choose whether you want to show or hide suspended status.
- **Publisher:** Name of the company that produces the application.
- **PID:** Process ID number, which is a unique number created by Windows for each process that is running.
- **Process Name:** Shows the executable name of the process.

Figure 27.12 shows what Task Manager looks like when you turn on all the columns. The information shown in the default columns (CPU, Memory, Disks, and Network) appears on the far right of Task Manager, and in this example the window is too wide to fit in this screenshot.

You can resize columns by dragging the separator line between the columns.

Common processes

You can end any running process by right-clicking its name and choosing End Task (or by clicking its name and clicking the End Task button). But doing so isn't a good idea unless you know exactly what service you're terminating. If a process represents a running program with unsaved work, ending the process closes the program without saving the work.

Some processes are required for normal operation of the computer. For example, Desktop Window Manager and Runtime Broker are important parts of Windows 10 so you definitely shouldn't mess with those.

FIGURE 27.12

The Processes tab with additional columns showing.

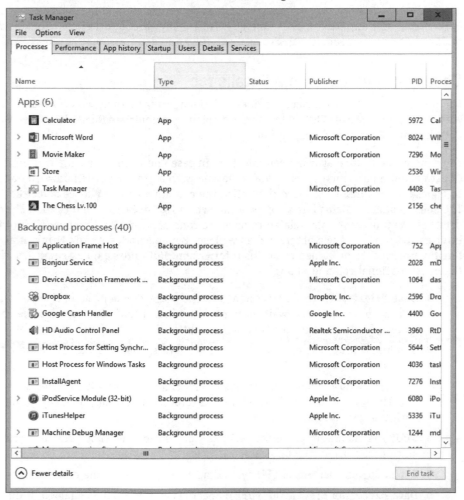

27

If you're unsure about a process, you can search for it by name on Google, Bing, or any other search engine. Just be sure to check out multiple sources and read carefully. Virtually every resource you find will tell you that perfectly legitimate and necessary processes such as dwm.exe and explorer.exe could be a Trojan, spyware, or other malicious item. But *could* is not synonymous with *is*. So, read carefully and don't assume the worst.

Choosing columns on the Details tab

The Details tab on Task Manager provides additional ways to analyze performance issues with running processes. The columns that display by default are Name, PID, User Name, CPU, Memory, Status, and Description.

You can choose to display other columns here in case you need to capture different types of data about a particular problem you're having with a program or Windows in general. To choose other columns to view, right-click the column area and choose Select Columns. The Select Columns dialog box appears (as shown in Figure 27.13). Each column shows some detail of the process, mostly related to resource consumption. A programmer might use this information to fine-tune a program she's writing. Beyond that, we can't think of anything terribly practical to be gained from this information. But here's a quick summary of what the other, optional columns show:

- **Base Priority:** The priority assigned to the process. When the CPU is busy, low-priority processes must wait for normal and high-priority processes to be completed. To change a process's priority, right-click its name and choose Set Priority.

- **Command Line:** The command, with parameters, that was used to initiate the process.

- **CPU Time:** Total number of seconds of CPU time this process has used since starting. The number will be doubled for dual-processor systems, quadrupled for systems with four processors.

- **CPU:** The amount of processor time, as a percent of the whole, this process has used since first started (the CPU column).

- **Cycle:** Current percent of CPU cycle time consumption by the process.

- **Data Execution Prevention (DEP):** Specifies whether DEP is enabled or disabled for the specified process. DEP is a set of hardware and software technologies that help prevent malicious code from running by marking some areas of memory as non-executable.

- **Description:** A description of the process.

- **Elevated:** Specifies whether the process is being elevated or not.

- **GDI Objects:** The number of Graphics Device Interface (GDI) objects used by this process, since starting, to display content on the screen.

- **Handles:** The number of objects to which the process currently has handles.

FIGURE 27.13

Picking additional columns for the Details tab.

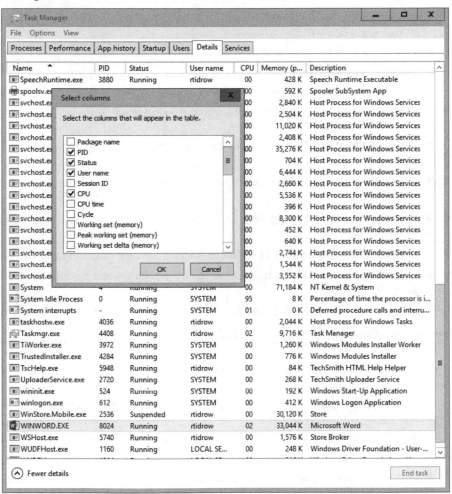

- **I/O Other:** Non-disk input/output calls made by the object since it started. Excludes file, network, and device operations.
- **I/O Other Bytes:** The number of bytes transferred to devices since the process started. Excludes file, network, and device operations.
- **I/O Reads:** The number of file, network, and device Read input/output operations since the process started.
- **I/O Read Bytes:** The number of bytes transferred by Read file, network, and device input/output operations.

- **I/O Writes:** The number of file, network, and device Write input/output operations since the process started.
- **I/O Write Bytes:** The number of bytes transferred by Write file, network, and device input/output operations.
- **Image Path Name:** The path to the executable specified in the Image Name column.
- **Working Set Memory:** The amount of memory used by the process (also called the process's *working set*) since starting.
- **Peak Working Set (Memory):** The largest amount of physical memory used by the process since it started.
- **Working Set Delta (Memory):** The change in memory usage since the last Task Manager update.
- **Memory (Private Working Set):** The amount of memory allocated to the process's private data.
- **Memory (Shared Working Set):** The amount of memory allocated to the process's shared data.
- **Commit Size:** The amount of virtual memory currently committed to the process.
- **Operating System Context:** Specifies the operating system context in which the process is operating.
- **Paged Pool:** The amount of system-allocated virtual memory that's been committed to the process by the operating system.
- **NP Pool:** The amount of physical RAM used by the process since starting.
- **Page Faults:** The number of times the process has read data from virtual memory since starting.
- **PF Delta:** The change in the number of page faults since the last Task Manager update.
- **PID:** A number assigned to the process at startup. The operating system accesses all processes by their numbers, not their names.
- **Platform:** Specifies whether the process is running on a 32-bit or 64-bit platform.
- **Session ID:** The Terminal Session ID that owns the process. Always zero unless Terminal Services are in use on the network.
- **Status:** Shows if the process is running or suspended.
- **Threads:** The number of threads running in a process.

> **TIP**
> A *thread* is a tiny sequence of instructions that the CPU must carry out to perform some tasks. Some programs divide tasks into separate threads that can be executed in parallel (simultaneously), to speed execution. This is called *multi-threaded execution.*

- **UAC Virtualization:** Specifies whether User Account Control (UAC) is virtualized for the specified process. When enabled, data is written to a user area rather than to a system area.
- **User Name:** The user, user account, or service that started the process.
- **User Objects:** The number of objects from Window Manager used by the object, including program windows, cursors, icons, and other objects.

App History tab

The Windows 10 Task Manager includes the App History tab shown in Figure 27.14. This tab lists all the apps that you've used on this computer since a given time. By default, you can see history since the time you installed Windows 10. In actuality, you may want to click the Delete Usage History link periodically to remove all old app history. This limits the amount of data Windows keeps stored in a log file somewhere on your hard drive.

The columns available on the App History tab include the following:

- **Name:** The name of the app that has been used.
- **CPU Time:** The amount of CPU time consumed by an app.
- **Network:** The amount of network data utilized by an app.
- **Metered Network:** The amount of metered network resources consumed by an app.
- **Tile Updates:** The amount of resources used for updating Windows 10 app tile information.
- **Non-Metered Network:** The amount of network data consumed by an app that is not considered metered data.
- **Downloads:** The amount of data an app downloads from the Internet or other network resource.
- **Uploads:** The amount of data an app uploads to a network resource.

To launch an app or see related apps under a category of apps (look for an arrow to the left of a name), double-click the app name.

Startup tab

The Startup tab shows a list of the apps that start when you start Windows 10. Figure 27.15 shows an example of the Startup tab and the application that will start at boot up time. In this example, several applications will start when Windows starts.

FIGURE 27.14

The App History tab in Task Manager.

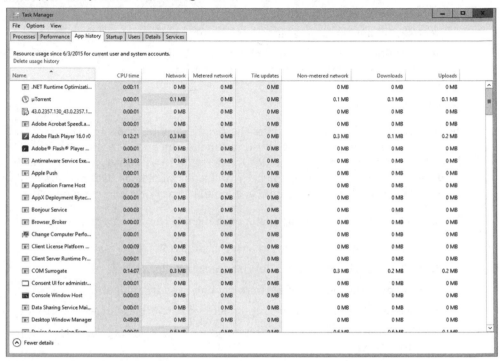

The columns on this tab include the following:

- **Name:** The name of the app that will start at boot time.
- **Publisher:** The company that distributes the app.
- **Status:** Lists either Enabled or Disabled depending on whether the app will (Enabled) or will not (Disabled) start at boot time.
- **Startup Impact:** Shows a relative rating of the impact the app will have during boot time.
- **Startup Type:** Shows the type of app that starts, such as one that is hidden (such as running from a Registry key), or one that launches from the interface.
- **Disk I/O at Startup:** Displays the amount of memory used at startup by the app.
- **CPU at Startup:** Displays the amount of CPU resources used at startup by the app.

- **Running Now:** Lists only those apps currently running under Windows.
- **Disabled Time:** Lists the amount of time the app is disabled.
- **Command Line:** Shows the hard drive path of the listed app.

If you don't want the app to start at boot time, select it and then click the Disable button.

FIGURE 27.15

The Startup tab of Task Manager.

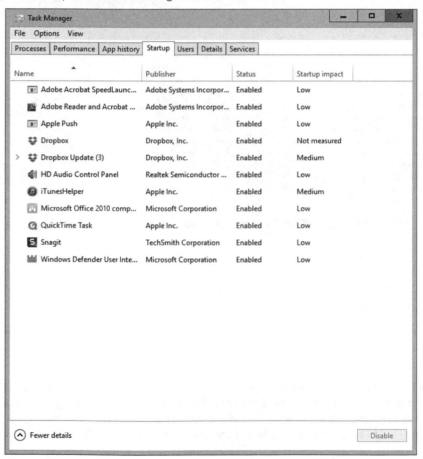

Users tab

The Users tab in Task Manager displays information about your user accounts. The Users tab (shown in Figure 27.16) shows the names of people currently logged in to the computer. Standard users see only themselves, even if other users are logged in.

FIGURE 27.16

The Users tab of Task Manager.

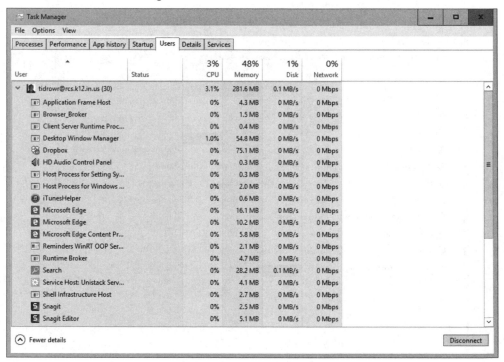

If your system is running slowly because users are not logging out of their accounts, you can send a message to those users asking them to log off when done using the computer. Click a username and click Disconnect to disconnect that user. Any unsaved data is lost. In general, this is a bad idea, so try to get the user to log off normally before taking this action.

To see the apps and processes that a user uses, double-click the username. Figure 27.16, for example, shows the apps listed under the tidrow user.

Figure 27.16 shows the default columns on the User tab, but the tab can show the following columns:

- **ID:** A unique integer for each user signed on to the computer.
- **Session:** The type of session, including console or remote.
- **Client name:** The name of a computer ("client") connected to your computer.
- **User:** The name of the user logged into the computer.
- **Status:** Whether an app is suspended or disabled.
- **CPU:** The amount of CPU a user is using.
- **Memory:** The amount of RAM a user is using.
- **Disk:** The amount of disk resources a user is using.
- **Network:** The amount of network resources a user is using.

Services tab

The Services tab provides a view of the services running under Windows. This tab is discussed in more detail in Chapter 10.

Wrapping Up

The Windows 10 Task Manager is a handy tool for terminating hung programs (programs that are not responding) and for monitoring computer resource usage. Task Manager also provides detailed information that's of interest only to programmers and network administrators. The following are the main things to remember about Task Manager:

- To open Task Manager, press Ctrl+Alt+Del and click Start Task Manager, or right-click the time and choose Start Task Manager.
- The Processes tab shows the names of all running applications. To end a program that's not responding, right-click its name and choose End Task.
- To see which process an application relates to, right-click the application name and choose Go to Details.
- The Processes tab shows all running processes, including application programs, background programs such as antivirus software, and operating system processes.
- The Performance tab presents a bird's-eye view of overall CPU and memory usage.
- The Users tab shows which users are currently logged in.

Troubleshooting Software Problems

IN THIS CHAPTER

Troubleshooting installations

Troubleshooting programs

Researching application errors

Editing the Windows Registry

Most programs designed for Windows 7 and 8.1 (and possibly Windows Vista) work with Windows 10. However, not all programs that were designed for Windows XP (or earlier versions of Windows) work with Windows 10. This chapter helps you troubleshoot problems with programs running on Windows 10.

> **NOTE**
> Microsoft support for the Windows XP operating system ended on April 8, 2014. For more information on Windows lifecycles, visit http://windows.microsoft.com/en-us/windows/lifecycle.

Troubleshooting Installations

Avoid installing utility and security programs unless they're specifically written for Windows 10. (Most basic application programs run fine.) If you can't get an older program to install, or it doesn't work after you install it, check the program manufacturer's website to see if a Windows 10 version is available. Or, use the methods discussed in Chapter 24 to configure settings that might enable the older program to run on Windows 10. Or, consider installing and using Windows XP Mode using Hyper-V to run the application. If these steps fail, you can take some general troubleshooting steps to get the program working properly.

Troubleshooting Programs

Because so many programs are available for Windows, no troubleshooting magic bullets exist that solve all problems. Every program and every problem is unique, but pinpointing what's causing the problem is often easy.

One of the most common mistakes users make is that they don't invest time in learning how to use a program. They guess and hack their way through it, and when the results aren't what they expected, they think something is wrong with the program. In fact, the problem is that the person using the program has no clue how to use it correctly. Troubleshooting can't fix ignorance; only learning can fix that.

Most programs have their own built-in Help feature for a reason — because every program is unique. The only ways to get information about a specific program are from the Help that came with that program or from the support website for that program. The Help feature, which is usually the last item on a menu bar or tab, provides all the Help options available to you.

The whole concept of troubleshooting applies only when you *do* know how to do something, but the program isn't working the way the documentation says it should.

The trick is to explore a number of different avenues for help. No book, web page, person, place, or thing has all the answers to all questions, nor the solutions to all problems. Sometimes you have to dig for a solution. Start with the narrowest, simplest solution and work your way out from there, as follows:

- Try the Help that's available from the program's menu bar or tab.

- Try the program manufacturer's website. You may want to try searching www .bing.com, http://support.microsoft.com, or http://office.micro-soft.com for Microsoft Office products. At the program manufacturer's website, look around for other support options such as Frequently Asked Questions (FAQs), troubleshooting information, and discussion groups or newsgroups.

- For Microsoft products, go to http://support.microsoft.com and click a product link for links to support for particular products. A great resource for Microsoft products is the Microsoft Community "Answers" website (as shown in Figure 28.1) at http://answers.microsoft.com. This page takes you to areas for specific products where you can post questions and get answers.

Don't forget, too, that you can search the entire planet using a search engine like Google or Bing. However, when you're searching the entire planet, use as many exact, descriptive words as possible in your search. Otherwise, you'll get links to more pages than you can visit in a lifetime. Include the product name, version number, and specific words that describe what you're looking for.

FIGURE 28.1

The Microsoft Community website.

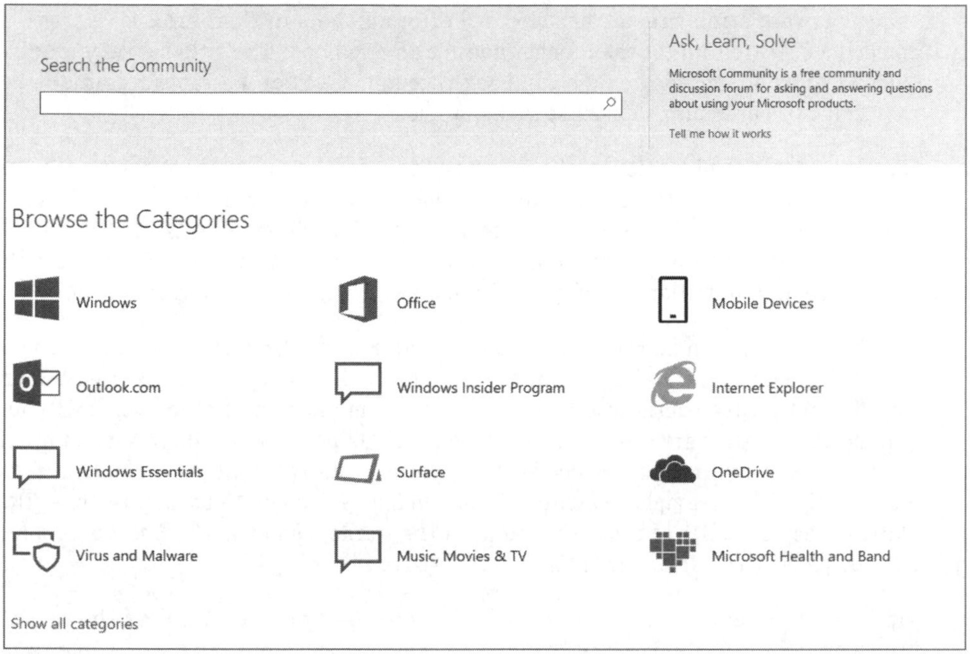

Search the Community

Ask, Learn, Solve

Microsoft Community is a free community and discussion forum for asking and answering questions about using your Microsoft products.

Tell me how it works

Browse the Categories

Windows	Office	Mobile Devices
Outlook.com	Windows Insider Program	Internet Explorer
Windows Essentials	Surface	OneDrive
Virus and Malware	Music, Movies & TV	Microsoft Health and Band

Show all categories

TIP

To find out what version of a program you're using, choose the program's Help ⇨ About command. On newer programs, the About information sometimes can be located by selecting the File tab and then clicking Help. Or you can also check the version in the Control Panel: Open the Control Panel, click Programs, and click Programs and Features. The Version column shows the program version.

When searching the web, use specific keywords and skip the noise words like *how*. For example, if you're looking for help with Mail backups, get all the appropriate words into your search, as in "Backup Mail." To find specific phrases, enclose the phrase in quotes. Be as specific as you can be. The more specific you are when typing your search words, the better your results will be.

NOTE

We would be lost without Google. When our team experiences a problem with a server for which we don't have a ready fix, invariably the first place we turn is Google. We aren't alone in that. Even some auto repair shops search Google to find the probable cause for engine lights that come on.

Researching Application Errors

Many software errors provide hexadecimal error numbers in their error messages. Sometimes, searching for the number doesn't do any good. The title bar may provide some clues as to what caused the problem. Look through the error messages for unique keywords that you can enter into support search engines.

Searching for a combination of the program name and keywords from the error message text can sometimes provide clues. You may want to start with a narrow search, such as http://support.microsoft.com, to avoid getting too many hits. If that doesn't work, you can broaden the search to all of Microsoft.com (www.bing.com). If all else fails, you can search all five billion (or so) pages in Google's index at www.google.com.

But the key thing, in all searches, is to get unique words from the message into your search string. For example, if searching for the hexadecimal memory addresses from the error message doesn't return useful results, you can try a combination of other words. If you keep getting results that are clearly not germane, such as pages about UNIX system problems when you're searching for a Windows issue, preface the keyword you want to exclude with a minus sign. For example, searching Google using "Windows 10 backup restore –UNIX –Linux" returns a list of pages that contain the words *Windows, 101, backup,* and *restore,* but not pages that also include the words *UNIX* or *Linux.*

Ideally, try to dig up as much information about the error as you can via the web. Search the company's website; because they created the application, they may be able to provide additional information.

Editing the Registry

After researching a software problem, you may find that the solution involves a "Registry hack," also known as "editing the Windows Registry." This is serious business with little margin for error. Never attempt to fix a problem by guessing at a Registry hack. When you get specific instructions on making a Registry change, make sure you make *exactly* the change indicated in the message. Even the slightest typographical error can cause a world of problems. If you're not a technical person and don't want to risk creating a big mess you can't rectify, consider hiring a professional to resolve the problem. In any event, if you're going to make a Registry change, back up your Registry by doing a System Image backup as described in Chapter 19. File History also keeps a copy of your Registry (see also "Backing up the Registry," later in this chapter).

Before you launch into Registry hacking, you need to understand what the Registry is and how to work with it. First, be aware that the Registry is a database where Windows and other programs store data that they need to operate properly on your computer. The average computer user typically doesn't need to know that the Registry exists. Absolutely nothing about the Registry is user friendly. Microsoft provides the Registry Editor described in this chapter because programmers and other IT professionals occasionally need to view or modify Registry entries.

> **CAUTION**
> The Windows Registry is not a safe place to mess around. Pay attention to all cautions in this chapter!

How Registry data is organized

The Windows Registry comprises several *hives,* each of which holds specific types of data. Within each hive, the registry uses *keys* and *subkeys* to organize data. Just as a folder can contain subfolders, a key can contain subkeys.

The Registry doesn't store files or documents, however. Instead, it stores *values.* Some of these values make sense to the average user, but some do not. For example, if you have Microsoft Office 2013 installed, a value in the Registry stores the path to the Office installation folder, and the value is typically `C:\Program Files\Microsoft Office\Office15\`. That's easy to understand. However, you also find values in the Registry that look something like `{89820200-ECBD-11cf-8B85-00AA005B4383}!8,0,7100,0`, and it's highly unlikely that this value means anything to you. But whether the value of a Registry entry makes sense to you, it makes sense to the application that is using the value, and that value must be entered exactly as required.

Hives, keys, and subkeys

We get into the specifics of editing the Registry in a moment. But first, Figure 28.2 shows an example of the Registry Editor as it might look when you first open it. The names listed down the left column are hives. As defined by Microsoft, a *hive* is a logical group of keys, subkeys, and values in the Registry that has a set of supporting files containing backups of its data. So, each hive contains keys, subkeys, and data. Each hive stores a particular type of information, as summarized in Table 28.1. Note that most keys have a standard abbreviation, such as HKCU for HKEY_CURRENT_USER.

TABLE 28.1   Standard Root Keys

Name	Abbreviation	Description
HKEY_CLASSES_ROOT	HKCR	Stores information about document types and extensions, registered programs that can open each file type, the default program for each file type, and options that appear when you right-click an icon.
HKEY_CURRENT_USER	HKCU	Stores information about the person who is currently using the computer, based on which user account that person is logged in to, and settings that particular user chose within his or her account.

Continues

505

TABLE 28.1 *(continued)*

Name	Abbreviation	Description
HKEY_LOCAL_MACHINE	HKLM	Stores information about all the hardware that's available to the computer, including devices that might not be plugged in at the moment.
HKEY_USERS	HKU	Stores information about all users, based on user accounts you've defined via the Control Panel.
HKEY_CURRENT_CONFIG	N/A	Similar to HKEY_LOCAL_MACHINE, this key stores information about hardware available to the computer. However, this key limits its storage to hardware that's connected and functioning currently.

FIGURE 28.2

Standard hives at left in the Registry Editor.

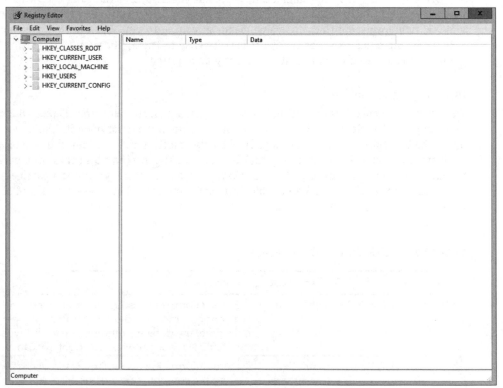

28

> **TIP**
>
> To open Registry Editor, press Windows+X, click Run, type *regedit*, and press Enter. You also can display Cortana and type *regedit*. Click `Regedit.exe` on the Apps screen.

When you click the gray triangle next to a hive, the hive expands to display its keys. Most of the keys have subkeys, and those subkeys may also have subkeys of their own. In that case, the subkey itself has a gray triangle, as well, which you can click to see another level of subkeys. For example, in Figure 28.3, the HKEY_CLASSES_ROOT key is expanded to reveal its subkeys. Each subkey represents a particular file type in that case. A few subkeys are also expanded in this example.

FIGURE 28.3

The HKEY_CLASSES_ROOT and some subkeys expanded.

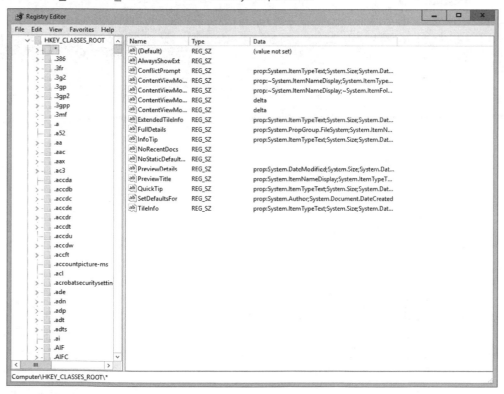

Often, a reference to a specific subkey is expressed as a path, in much the same way that a file's location and name are expressed as a path. For example, the path to a file might be expressed as `C:\Users\rtidrow\Pictures\Summit01.jpg`. The path tells Windows exactly where to find the file `Summit01.jpg` in my Pictures folder.

A registry path is the same idea, and even uses backslashes to separate the key and subkey names. For example, the highlighted subkey in Figure 28.3 is at `Computer \HKEY_CLASSES_ROOT\*`.

Sometimes you see instructions telling you the path to a key or subkey, as in `HKEY_ CURRENT_USER\Control Panel\Appearance\Schemes`. You have to manually expand each folder down the path to get to the subkey. Figure 28.4 shows the result of following that sample path. The values in the Data column for that key are mostly binary numbers — a good example of just how user *un*friendly the Registry can be!

FIGURE 28.4

The `HKEY_CURRENT_USER\Control Panel\Appearance\Schemes` subkey selected.

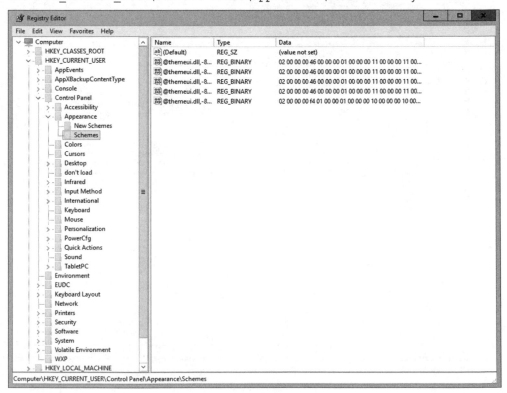

Key values

The data stored in a subkey is called a *value*. The value is a specific piece of information that can be stored as a string (text) or a number. However, the terms *string* and *number* don't tell the whole story because those types can be further broken down into the specific *data types* listed in Table 28.2.

TABLE 28.2   Registry Value Data Types

Name	Data Type	Description
Binary value	REG_BINARY	Raw binary data used mostly by hardware components. Often displayed in hexadecimal format.
DWORD value	REG_DWORD	An integer often used to store parameters for device drivers and services. Subtypes include related types such as DWORD_LITTLE_ENDIAN and REG_DWORD_BIG_ENDIAN with the least significant bit at the lowest/highest address, respectively.
Expandable string value	REG_EXPAND_SZ	A variable-length string often used to store data for application programs and services.
Multistring value	REG_MULTI_SZ	A string that actually consists of multiple substrings separated by spaces, commas, or other special characters.
String value	REG_SZ	A simple fixed-length text string.
Binary value	REG_RESOURCE_LIST	A series of nested arrays (lists) often used by hardware and device drivers. Usually displayed in hexadecimal.
Binary value	REG_RESOURCE_REQUIREMENTS_LIST	A series of nested arrays (lists) containing a device driver's hardware resources, displayed in hexadecimal.
Binary value	REG_FULL_RESOURCE_DESCRIPTOR	A series of nested lists of actual hardware device capabilities, usually displayed in hexadecimal.
None	REG_NONE	Data with no particular type that's displayed as a binary value in hexadecimal.
Link	REG_LINK	A string naming a symbolic link.
QWORD value	REG_QWORD	A 64-bit number displayed as a binary value.

28

In the vast majority of situations, you work with strings, DWORDs, or QWORDs when you create or modify Registry entries. Entering a string in the Registry is just like entering characters in a text box. When you enter DWORD and QWORD values, however, you enter those either as a decimal or a hexadecimal value. We don't go into detail about the differences here, and if you want a clearer understanding of hexadecimal numbering, a quick search on the web will turn up lots of explanations and examples. Keep in mind that when you edit a DWORD or QWORD value, you need to choose the option that matches the value you're entering. Figure 28.5 shows an example of a value entered as a hexadecimal number.

FIGURE 28.5

The Edit DWORD (32-bit) Value dialog box.

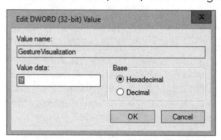

If the troubleshooting steps that you're using direct you to enter a decimal value, click the Decimal option and then type the value specified. If you need to enter a hexadecimal value, click the Hexadecimal option before you type the value.

Backing up the Registry

Every time you start your computer, Windows automatically updates the Registry based on the hardware and software available to it. Then it makes a backup copy of that Registry. When you plan to manually change the Registry, you should also make a backup copy of the Registry just before you make your change. When you're editing the Registry, you have no margin for error. Even a tiny typographical error can have far-reaching, unpleasant consequences.

> **TIP**
> The System Restore feature described in Chapter 31 also makes periodic backup copies of the Registry.

You need administrative privileges to edit the Registry. The program you use is named regedit. You can start it using either of these methods:

- Type **regedit** in the Cortana search field and click `regedit.exe` on the search screen.
- Press Windows+X, choose Run, type **regedit**, and press Enter.

The Registry Editor opens. You should *always* make a backup of the Registry before you change anything. It's easy to do:

1. Choose ➪ Export from the menu bar in the Registry Editor.
2. Choose a folder and enter a filename of your own choosing.
3. To export the entire Registry, choose All under the Export Range heading.
4. Click the Save button.

That's it. In the event of a disaster, you can choose File ➪ Import from the Registry Editor's menu bar to restore the entries you copied in the preceding steps.

Making the Registry change

You can change any value in the Registry. First, you need to find the appropriate subkey. For example, say that you've found the solution to a problem via Microsoft's website. Part of that solution involves changing a value in the following subkey:

```
HKEY_LOCAL_MACHINE\SOFTWARE\Microsoft\Windows\CurrentVersion\Run
```

The first step is to get to the subkey by expanding the HKEY_LOCAL_MACHINE\ SOFTWARE\Microsoft\Windows\CurrentVersion node. Then click Run. The pane to the right shows values in the subkey. The status bar shows the complete path name, as in Figure 28.6.

To change a subkey's value, double-click that value. A dialog box opens, allowing you to make a change. The appearance of the dialog box depends on the type of value you're editing. Figure 28.7 shows a general example.

28

> **CAUTION**
>
> Make sure you get to the correct key, and make *exactly* the change your instructions tell you to. Even the slightest mistake here can cause big problems down the road.

The Value Data box contains the value you can edit. Make your change there and click OK. Then close the Registry Editor. You've finished making your Registry change.

Whether you see any change on the screen depends on the value you changed. Many Registry hacks have no effect until you restart the application or the computer.

If it turns out that you created more problems than you solved, you can restore your Registry from the backup you made. Open the Registry Editor and choose File ➪ Import to import the backed-up Registry file. Otherwise, if all seems well, you can delete the backed-up Registry file.

FIGURE 28.6

HKEY_LOCAL_MACHINE\SOFTWARE\Microsoft\Windows\CurrentVersion\Run selected.

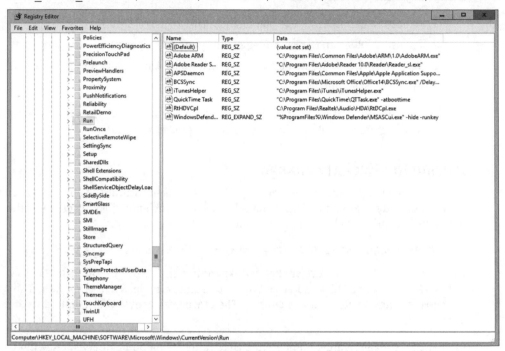

FIGURE 28.7

The dialog box to edit a string value.

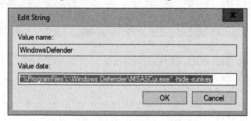

Troubleshooting Tips

One important approach helps ensure your troubleshooting success: You *must* be methodical.

Don't change program settings, Windows settings, or Registry settings; delete files; or take other actions without an understanding of what the Registry is and how to use it. Just as important, don't make lots of changes at once. Instead, make a single change, see if it fixes the problem, and then try the next change if needed.

Here are some key pieces of advice:

- When searching the web for answers, be as precise as possible. Include as many keywords as possible that are related to the issue. If you receive an error message, enclose the exact error message in quotes in your search.

- Ask yourself what has changed. Did you add something new? Did you change a setting? Knowing when the problem started occurring and what changes happened right before it began can give you a great head start on finding the solution.

- Make one change at a time, testing the problem after each change to see if it's been resolved.

- Keep notes. As you make a change or test something, make a note of it so you'll know what you changed and when.

- Don't be surprised to find that what appears to be a single problem is actually multiple problems.

- Use restore points to restore your system to the state it was in just before the problem started occurring.

- Make backups of your critical data before you make any drastic changes.

- Make backup copies of the Registry key in which you're about to make changes before you make those changes.

TIP

For more help with troubleshooting programs, search Windows Help and Support or post a question in the appropriate area online at Microsoft Communities.

Wrapping Up

As you work in Windows 10, you'll notice that some older programs run better than others. Generally speaking, programs designed for Windows Vista, Windows 7, or Windows 8.1 work with Windows 10. You may find, however, that not all programs that were designed for Windows XP or earlier versions of Windows work with Windows 10.

This chapter discussed how to troubleshoot software problems in Windows 10. Specifically, this chapter discussed the following:

- How to troubleshoot problems that may occur during software installation.
- How to troubleshoot problems with programs running under Windows 10.
- How to research application errors that occur under Windows 10.
- How to edit the Windows Registry.

Part VII

Hardware and Performance Tuning

IN THIS PART

Installing and Removing Hardware

A typical computer consists of hardware, firmware, and software. These three components work together to make the computer both usable and useful. This chapter helps you understand each of these with a focus on installing and removing hardware in Windows 10.

Before jumping into hardware-related tasks, take a quick look at just what hardware, firmware, and software really are.

Hardware, Firmware, and Software Demystified

Hardware is any physical device used by the computer, whether internal to the computer (such as the CPU on the computer's motherboard) or attached externally to the computer. A discrete hardware component that performs a given function is generally referred to as a *hardware device* or just *device* for short. You can use numerous types of hardware devices with a computer. Printers, scanners, mice, keyboards, monitors, disk drives, digital cameras, iPods, MP3 players, modems, and routers are all examples of hardware devices.

Before we describe firmware, you need a better understanding of *software*. Software is program code that is written to perform a given function. For example, all the program code that makes up WordPad is software. Likewise, all the program code that constitutes Windows 10 is software.

Device drivers are also software. A device driver is a program that serves as an intermediary between a piece of hardware and an application or the operating system. For example, a display driver enables Windows 10 to communicate with and control your computer's display. Likewise, a printer driver enables Windows 10 to communicate with and control a printer.

Firmware is also software, in the context that it is program code. The difference is in how the program code is stored. *Firmware* is program code stored in a hardware device, typically in non-volatile memory such as read-only memory or flash memory. For example, the program code that makes your Apple iPad or your digital camera work is firmware.

Generally, as a typical Windows 10 user, you deal with firmware only when updating firmware on your removable devices, such as MP3 players. You add device drivers and work with Windows updates much more than you do with firmware.

A Few Words about Device Drivers

As indicated in the previous section, device drivers enable the Windows operating system to communicate with and control devices. Although Windows 10 comes with a very large number of device drivers for a wide range of devices, most device drivers are written and distributed by the manufacturers of a given device. For example, your video adapter's device driver was written by the company that designed and manufactured the adapter.

Device drivers are very much device-specific. That is, a device driver written for one device doesn't work for a different type of device. For that reason, make sure you have the necessary device driver(s) for a device before you install it. If you've just purchased a new device that requires a device driver not included with Windows, that driver is included with the new device, typically on a CD or available for download on the manufacturer's website. Because the version of the device driver was developed specifically for the device, you don't have to obtain an updated driver before installing the new device. However, you can visit the manufacturer's website to see if an updated driver is available that adds features or fixes issues with the version you have. We recommend installing the device with the driver you have, and then checking later for an updated driver as needed.

Support for 3D Printers?

Windows 10 supports 3D printers, which are devices that use laser and lathe-like technology to "print" three-dimensional objects from solids, such as certain prototyping plastics and metals. Because Microsoft provides 3D printer manufacturers with a 3D printing API, Windows 10 users will find installing and supporting these new devices as simple as connecting standard printers.

Using Hot-Pluggable Devices

Many modern hardware devices are *hot-pluggable,* which means you simply connect them to your computer and start using them. You don't have to shut down the computer before connecting the device. Nor do you need to go through a formal installation process after you connect the device. However, you should read the instructions that came with a device before you connect it for the first time because sometimes you need to install software before you connect the device. When that's the case, as mentioned earlier, the software is usually on a CD that comes with the device.

> **TIP**
>
> Because Windows 10 includes a large library of device drivers, you can just connect a device and begin using it without installing a device driver yourself. For example, you can connect a USB flash drive or one of many USB external hard drives and begin using them right away. Because most digital cameras look and act to Windows 10 as flash drives, you can do the same with cameras.

Hot-pluggable devices generally connect to the computer through USB, IEEE 1392 (FireWire), or PC Card (different versions called PCMCIA, Cardbus, and ExpressCard). The latter two types of connections are not as popular now as they were several years ago because of advances in other types of connections. USB has become the predominant hot-pluggable connection on most desktop computers, laptops, and some tablets.

We look at USB in the sections that follow.

Connecting USB devices

Universal Serial Bus (USB) is the most common type of hot-pluggable device. USB is used by flash drives, smartphones, digital cameras, some types of microphones and headphones, external disk drives, and many other types of devices. Like most technologies, USB has evolved over the years, and several versions of USB are currently on the market.

The main differences among USB standard versions have to do with speed. USB 1.0 and 1.1 have two speeds: Low Speed (1.5 Mbps) used by mice and keyboards, and Full Speed (12 Mbps), more often used by digital cameras and disk drives. USB 2.0 added a third, High Speed, data rate, which can transfer data at the much faster rate of 480 Mbps. USB 3.0 and USB 3.1 now transfer data 5 Gbps and higher.

USB 2.0 is downwardly compatible with USB 1.1 and 1.0, which means that you can use a USB 2.0 device in a computer with USB 1.x ports. However, the device transfers at the 12 Mbps speed rather than the 480 Mbps speed available only in USB 2.0. (Although 480

29

Mbps is the highest speed possible, most devices do not meet that limit.) So, you don't need to know exactly which type of USB your computer has. If you plug a USB 2.0 device into a USB 1.0 or 1.1 port, Windows displays a message telling you that you'd get better performance from a USB 2.0 port. The device works; it's just slower than if you'd plugged it into a USB 2.0 port.

Released in 2008, USB 3.0 is the latest specification for USB. It has a speed that is ten times faster than USB 2.0, with a transfer speed of 5 gigabits per second (625MB per second). USB 3.0 is backward compatible with USB 2.0. In 2013, USB 3.1 was released. USB 3.1, named SuperSpeed+ USB, transfers at 10 gigabits per second.

Five USB plug shapes are available: Type A, Type B, Type C, Mini-USB or On-the-Go (OTG), and Micro-USB. The computer has female Type A ports, into which you plug the male Type A plug on the cable. The device may have Type A, B, C, or a mini-port. Figure 29.1 shows the symbol for USB and the general shape of USB ports on the computer. An example of the Type A plug is third from the left in that figure. USB plugs are all keyed so that they fit only one way. Try pushing the plug gently into the port, and if it doesn't fit, flip the plug over and try again.

FIGURE 29.1

USB symbol, ports, and plug types.

Type-C

Connecting a USB device should be easy, provided you've done any preliminary installations required by your specific device. The steps are as follows:

1. If the device has an on/off switch, turn it off.
2. Connect the device to the computer using the appropriate USB cable.
3. If the device has an on/off switch, turn it on.

The very first time you connect a device, you may get some feedback on the screen indicating that Windows is loading drivers for the device. That message is followed by one indicating that the device is ready for use.

In many cases, you get a Windows 10 message instructing you to tap it to see options after you've connected a device. After you tap (or click) that message, a list appears with options so you can choose what you want to do with the device. In the case of a hard drive, that would most likely be the Open Folder to View Files option, unless you were using that hard drive to store one specific type of file.

What's "Speed Up My System" and ReadyBoost?

Some USB devices can be used to speed up your system with ReadyBoost. When you plug a flash drive into a USB port, AutoPlay options may include an option to speed up your system using ReadyBoost, which is a Windows 10 feature designed to speed up some operations by using flash memory as intermediary storage between the processor and the hard drive. It works only with USB devices that can play that role. Flash memory has fast random I/O capabilities, and therefore isn't supported by all USB devices. See Chapter 31 for more information on ReadyBoost.

Connecting IEEE 1394 devices

IEEE 1394 (often called 1394 for short) is a high-speed (800 Mbps) standard typically used to connect digital video cameras and high-speed disk drives to computers. The symbol and plug shape for an IEEE 1394 port are shown in Figure 29.2. IEEE 1394 also goes by the names FireWire and iLink. FireWire was once a popular standard, but it has been losing ground the last few years to USB 3.1. New hardware devices typically do not use the FireWire specification.

FIGURE 29.2

The FireWire symbol and plug shape.

TIP

1394a supports speeds up to 400 Mbps, and 1394b supports speeds up to 800 Mbps.

Connecting a 1394 device is much the same as connecting a USB device:

1. Leave the computer running, and turn the device off (if it has an on/off switch).
2. Connect one end of the 1394 cable to the computer and the other end to the device.
3. Turn on the device and wait.

What happens next depends on the device. For example, some devices transfer drivers and software to Windows to complete specific tasks (such as copying video files).

PC cards

PC Cards, PCMCIA, Cardbus, and ExpressCard cards were once commonly used on laptop computers. Newer laptops rarely have PC card capabilities because of the availability and pervasiveness of USB devices. However, you may still have a computer that includes a PC card slot and those devices can operate with Windows 10. You may need to hunt around for a device driver that supports Windows 10 (or even Windows Vista, Windows 7, or Windows 8/8.1) for that device to work.

A PC card device is usually a little larger and thicker than a credit card. Figure 29.3 shows an example of a PC ExpressCard wireless network adapter.

FIGURE 29.3

A PC card.

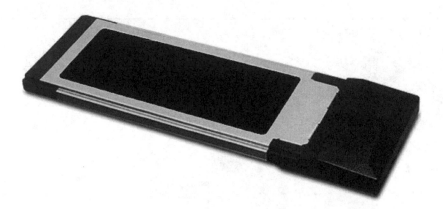

Connecting a PC card to a notebook computer is simple: Just slide the card into the slot, right side up, and push until it's firmly seated. As with USB and FireWire devices, you should get some feedback on the screen indicating when the device is connected and ready for use. How you use the device depends on the type of device you inserted.

Using memory cards

Memory cards are hot-pluggable storage devices. Figure 29.4 shows examples of some memory cards. Most memory cards are used in digital cameras, tablet computers, and jump drives. You just connect the camera or jump drive to a USB port to access the content on the memory card. However, if your computer has slots for memory cards, you can also insert the card directly into the appropriate slot.

FIGURE 29.4

Examples of memory cards.

After you insert a memory card into a slot, you should get some feedback on the screen indicating that the card is ready for use. That may be in the form of the Windows 10 auto play dialog box, or an Explorer window may open to show you the contents of the card. Either way, the card is treated as a USB mass storage device, as discussed next.

Memory cards and USB mass storage

Memory cards and USB devices that store data act like disk drives when you connect them to a computer. As such, each will have an icon in your Computer folder when it's connected. Figure 29.5 shows an example where we have connected a flash drive named ATTACHE (drive F:), and an external Hard Disk (made by Seagate) through USB ports.

Using such a device is no different from using any other disk drive. To see the contents of the device, open its icon. Use the standard techniques to navigate through folders, to delete files and folders, and to move and copy files and folders. See Chapters 20 and 21 for the necessary buzzwords and basic skills.

29

FIGURE 29.5

External devices in the Computer folder.

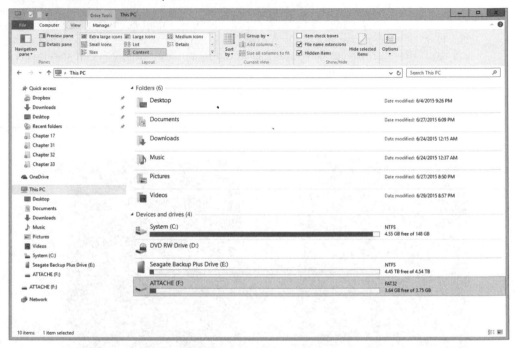

Disconnecting hot-pluggable devices

Before you disconnect a hot-pluggable device from a computer, you may want to make sure it isn't in the middle of a file transfer or holding a file that you have open in a program. To do that, look in the notification area for an icon that looks like the one shown in Figure 29.6. (That icon shows only when you have a storage device attached.) The icon's tooltip reads "Safely Remove Hardware and Eject Media."

FIGURE 29.6

The Safely Remove Hardware and Eject Media icon.

To safely remove a device, click the Safely Remove Hardware and Eject Media icon. The menu shown in Figure 29.7 opens, listing each connected mass storage device. Click the action you want to take.

FIGURE 29.7

Safely Remove Hardware menu.

Simply click the Eject command for the drive you want to disconnect. The media does not physically eject from the computer, but Windows closes it and displays a message that the device can safely be disconnected from the computer. You can then safely remove it from the computer.

Not all devices are hot-pluggable. Some require a more elaborate connection and installation procedures. Those devices are discussed in the next section.

Not-So-Hot-Pluggable Devices

Hardware devices that aren't hot-pluggable require a bit more effort than hot-pluggable devices. Most require that you turn off the computer, connect the device, turn the device on, and then turn the computer back on. You may also need to install some software to get the device to work. It all depends on the device you're connecting. As always, you have to read the instructions that came with the device for specifics. We can provide only general guidelines and examples.

Most computers have the ports shown in Figure 29.8. Your computer may have more or fewer such ports, and your ports probably aren't arranged exactly like those in the figure. On a notebook computer, some of the ports are likely to be on the side of the computer, perhaps hidden under a sliding or hinged door. But the basic shape of each port is as shown in the figure.

You can install some devices inside the computer case. These connect to sockets inside the computer case on the *motherboard* (also called the *mainboard*). The motherboard is a circuit board that provides the wiring among all the hardware devices that make up the system, including the CPU, memory (RAM), internal disk drives, and everything else. The sockets that accept these devices are called *expansion slots,* and the devices that go in them are typically called *adapter cards.*

FIGURE 29.8

Ports on the back of a computer.

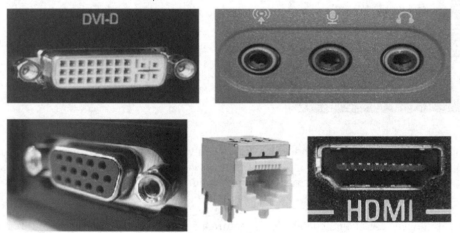

Figure 29.9 provides a general idea of what different types of internal slots and ports look like.

Installing expansion cards

Many internal hardware devices are PCI cards, which slide into a PCI slot. The slots are positioned so that one end of the card lines up with the back of the computer, exposing one or more external connectors. Figure 29.10 shows a general example of what such a card looks like.

FIGURE 29.9

Slots on a computer motherboard.

Many motherboards may have PCI Express (PCIe) and PCI Express 16. These provide faster communication between the motherboard, which in turn allows for more powerful expansion cards. The PCI Express 16 slot is ideal for high-powered graphics cards designed to work with advanced graphics and large high-definition TV screens. The Accelerated Graphics Port (AGP) is designed specifically for a graphics card.

Before you buy an expansion card, you need to know what slots are available on your motherboard. Either open the computer case and make note of the available slots or contact your computer manufacturer for that information. Before you install a card, read the instructions that came with it. No one-size-fits-all rule applies to the thousands of hardware devices you can add to a PC. You should install the device exactly as instructed in the instructions provided by the manufacturer of the device.

Be sure to turn off the computer before opening the case to install a card. Remove the power cord as well. Ideally, you should wear an antistatic wrist strap so that you don't generate static electricity that could damage the components in the computer.

29

FIGURE 29.10

A sample expansion card.

Many AGP and PCIe 16 slots have a locking mechanism to hold the card steady in the slot. You have to make sure that it's in the unlocked position before you try to insert the card into the slot. When installing the card, push firmly on the card to insert it. Don't force it and break it, but push it in well enough to ensure that it's firmly and evenly seated in its slot. If the slot has a locking mechanism, push it into the locked position. Put the case cover back together again, plug in the power cord, and then turn on the PC.

If the device is plug-and-play (as many modern devices are), the rest of the procedure should be easy. The computer should boot up normally, but you don't necessarily get to the desktop right away. Instead, Windows should detect the new device and go through an installation procedure to get the device working. You get some feedback on the screen in the form of notification area messages. When the notification messages stop and the desktop looks normal, the device should be ready to use.

Installing more memory (RAM)

Installing more RAM isn't exactly like installing other devices because you aren't likely to get any feedback at all on the Windows desktop when you're done. RAM is such an integral part of the computer that it doesn't really get "installed." The processor detects it as soon as you turn on the power. One of the few places you'd even see that you have more RAM is on the System screen of the Control Panel applets.

The key consideration to adding more RAM is finding the right type of memory. You need to match the type and speed of your existing RAM chip, and you need an available DIMM slot on the motherboard. In addition, every motherboard has a limit as to the maximum speed and type of memory it can handle. When you build a PC, you know these specifications. But when you buy a prebuilt PC, finding this information isn't always easy.

Upgrading the CPU

Every motherboard has a certain maximum CPU speed it can handle. You don't know what that is unless you can get the specs for your exact motherboard. Rather than try to upgrade just the CPU, you're probably better off upgrading the motherboard, CPU, and RAM. That way you can speed up everything but still use your existing hard drive, DVD drive, mouse, keyboard, and monitor. Or, for a little extra, you can probably purchase a new PC almost as inexpensively as upgrading your old one.

A barebones kit may be the best way to go. With a barebones kit you can get a motherboard, CPU, RAM, and power supply already assembled in a new case. You then transfer your existing hard drive, CD drive, mouse, keyboard, and monitor to that new case. You get the benefits of a newer, faster computer without the expense of buying an entirely new PC. A word of caution: Windows may require you to reenter the product key after a hardware upgrade.

29

Your best bet is to go to the computer manufacturer's website and find the main web page for your exact model of computer. You can often find out exactly what type and speed of RAM chip is currently installed using that method. PNY (a company that sells RAM chips) has memory information on its website (www.pny.com) to help you understand terms and product offerings.

TIP

The PNY site also has installation guides, which may help you when you purchase more RAM. Remember to look inside the computer and see if you have an available slot for adding more RAM first.

Even so, installing more RAM isn't something for the technologically timid to undertake. Even the slightest mistake can prevent the computer from starting at all. If the speed of the new chip doesn't exactly match the speed of the existing chip, the computer may start but you're likely to end up with error messages when you try to work with the computer. When purchasing and installing RAM, consider installing them in pairs because this allows your computer to run faster. Finally, sites that offer RAM are numerous, but a few you might consider include Crucial.com and Kahlon.com.

Installing a second hard drive

If you need more hard disk space, installing a second hard drive is a good option. Hard disk space is cheap, and adding another drive is much easier than pinching a few more megabytes out of a single drive by compressing files and moving them to removable disks.

Most internal drives are relatively easy to install, and today's computers automatically detect the drive type when they boot. If you don't feel up to the task of installing a new internal drive, however, consider an external drive.

> **TIP**
> If the computer doesn't recognize the new drive, enter the computer's BIOS Setup program and make sure the BIOS is configured to auto-detect drives on the new drive's interface. If you are not sure how to enter the BIOS, refer to your computer's help documentation.

Installing an external hard drive is relatively simple; just connect the drive to a USB or FireWire port. If you already bought an internal hard drive but you haven't connected it, you can convert it to an external drive by putting it in an external drive enclosure. Just make sure you get an enclosure that has the right internal connectors (IDE or SATA) for your drive.

> **TIP**
> To see examples of hard drive enclosures, search an online retailer such as www.newegg.com, www.tigerdirect.com, or even www.google.com/shopping for "external drive enclosure." Drives that connect via USB 2.0 can move data at 480 Mbps, which is plenty fast for a hard drive and isn't a performance bottleneck. USB 3.0/3.1-compatible drives can move data at 5 to 10 Gbps.

Hard drives for most non-server PCs fall into two main categories: Serial ATA (SATA) and Parallel ATA (PATA), more commonly referred to as Integrated Drive Electronics (IDE) drives. (The ATA stands for Advanced Technology Attachment.) SATA III is the newer, faster, and easier technology.

The original SATA drives moved data at a good 150 Mbps (150 million bits per second). The newer SATA 3.2 drives move data at speeds up to 2GB/s. Before adding a second SATA drive, refer to your computer's documentation to ensure your motherboard has SATA connectors, and whether they're the appropriate connectors for the type of SATA device you want to install.

IDE drives come in multiple speeds, too, ranging from 33 Mbps to 133 Mbps. The maximum speed your PC can use depends on the speed of the IDE connectors on the motherboard.

IDE drives have an unusual configuration where you can connect two drives to a single IDE port. One drive is called the *master drive;* the other, the *slave drive.* You physically set a jumper on the drive to make the drive either master or slave. Then you connect the drive to the right place on the cable. The master goes at the end of the cable. The slave goes on the plug in the center of the cable.

Again, your best bet before installing any hardware device is to follow the instructions that came with the device — to the letter — before you even turn the computer back on and use Windows to configure the device. If in doubt, have a pro install the hardware for you. But, assuming you've installed the drive, either internally or externally, you can then use Windows 10 to partition and format the drive.

Primary and extended partitions

You can divide a basic disk into multiple *partitions.* Each partition looks like a separate item in your This PC folder. The drive can be divided into a maximum of four *primary* partitions, or three primary partitions and one *extended* partition. The difference is that a primary partition can be used as a *system partition,* meaning you can install an operating system on it and boot the computer from it. An extended partition can't be a boot disk and can't contain an operating system. However, you can divide an extended partition into multiple logical drives, where each logical drive has its own drive letter and icon in the This PC folder, and looks like a separate drive.

In Windows XP and previous versions of Windows, you could explicitly create extended partitions using the Disk Management console. Microsoft changed that in Windows Vista, and that change carries over to Windows 10. Now, instead of giving you the option to create either a primary partition or an extended partition, Disk Management gives you the option of creating a new simple volume. The type of volume created when you use this command

29

depends on the number of partitions already on the disk. The first three partitions you create are created as primary partitions. The fourth is created as an extended partition.

> **TIP**
>
> If you need an extended partition, you can use the DiskPart command in a command console to create it. To learn more about DiskPart, open a command console and enter diskpart. At the DiskPart command prompt, enter Help to see a list of commands.

You can use two types of disks in Windows 10:

- **Basic:** This is the type of disk supported by DOS and all previous versions of Windows.
- **Dynamic:** This type of disk was introduced in Windows 2000. Dynamic disks support the following types of volumes:
  - **Simple:** These volumes make up space for a single dynamic disk and can use a single region on the disk or multiple regions on the disk.
  - **Spanned:** These volumes make up space on more than one physical disk (they span multiple physical drives — hence, the name).
  - **Striped:** These volumes stripe the data for a single logical volume across multiple physical disks, providing improved performance by distributing the read/write load across multiple disks.
  - **GPT:** This stands for Globally Unique Identifier Partition Table. GPT supports theoretical volume sizes up to 16 EB. The primary advantages to using GPT are the very large volume size and the large number of partitions you can create on a GPT disk. Disk structure is also optimized for performance and reliability.

> **TIP**
>
> EB stands for exabyte, which is equal to about a million terabytes. A terabyte (TB) is about a trillion bytes or 1,024GB.

Which disk type you choose depends on the type of disk and your needs. If you're reinstalling a very high-capacity disk in a Windows 10 computer, we recommend using GPT. If you need to create a spanned or striped volume, use a dynamic disk. For general-purpose disks, a basic disk is fine.

Partitioning and formatting the disk

After you have a new hard drive installed, you can start Windows 10 and use the Disk Management tool to partition and format the drive. Log in to an account with administrative privileges for this task. If the Computer Management tool doesn't start automatically after you've logged in, you can get to it by following these steps:

1. On the desktop, press Windows+X.
2. Click Disk Management from the Quick Link menu.

> **CAUTION**
>
> Repartitioning and/or reformatting a disk that already contains files will result in the permanent loss of all files on that disk. You should not attempt to repartition or reformat an existing disk unless you fully understand the consequences and are fully prepared to recover any lost files. Again, if you don't have formal training and experience in technical matters, leave this sort of thing to the pros. An in-depth treatment of these more technical hardware matters is beyond the scope of this book.

The new drive appears at the bottom of the display, most likely as Disk 1 (assuming the system has one other disk drive, which will show as Disk 0), as shown in Figure 29.11. The drive's space is indicated by a dark bar showing Unallocated in the lower-left corner.

To partition the drive as a basic disk with a simple volume:

1. Right-click within the unallocated space of the new drive and choose New Simple Volume.
2. On the first page of the New Simple Volume Wizard that opens, click Next.
3. The next wizard page asks what size you want to make the partition and suggests the full capacity of the disk. You can choose a smaller size if you intend to divide the disk into multiple partitions. After you make your selection, click Next.
4. The next wizard page asks you to assign a drive letter to the drive. It suggests the next available drive letter, which is a good choice. Click Next.
5. The next wizard page asks how you want to format and label the disk. Your options are as follows:

   - **Do Not Format This Volume:** If you choose this option, you'll have to format the partition later. We don't suggest choosing this option.
   - **File System:** Your choices here depend on the disk type. For volumes on basic and dynamic disks, you can choose between exFAT and NTFS. On a GPT disk, you can choose only NTFS.
   - **Allocation Unit Size:** This defines the cluster size. The Default option automatically chooses the best allocation unit size given the type and capacity of the disk, so that would be your best choice.
   - **Volume Label:** This is the name that appears with the drive's icon in This PC. You can also change that name at any time in the future.

29

- **Perform a Quick Format:** If you choose this option, formatting goes quickly, but the drive isn't checked for errors. Better to leave this option unselected.

- **Enable File and Folder Compression:** Only available if you chose NTFS as the file system, this option automatically compresses all files and folders on the drive. This conserves disk space, but there is a minimal performance overhead for the compression/decompression as the drive is used. You can still compress individual files and folders if you leave this option unselected.

FIGURE 29.11

The Disk Management tool.

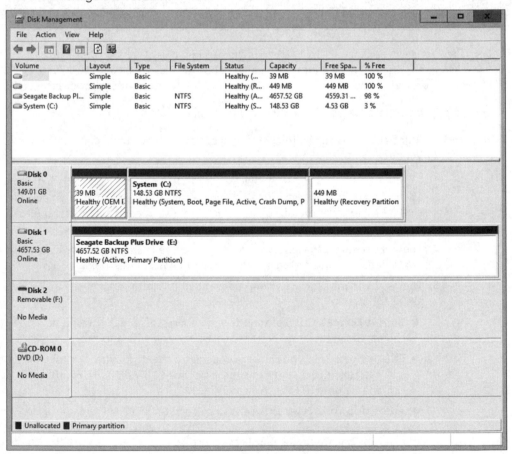

6. Click Next after making your selections.

7. The last wizard page summarizes your selections. Click Finish.

Now you get to wait for the disk to be formatted. This can take some time, depending on the size of the volume and if you chose the quick format option. You can continue to use your computer while the drive is being formatted or you can wait until it finishes.

If you set up the drive as one large partition, you're finished when the Formatting indicator reaches 100 percent. You can close the Disk Management tool.

If you're partitioning the disk into smaller units, you can repeat the steps outlined previously for each partition. Just make sure that you right-click an unpartitioned portion of the disk in Step 1. If you create an extended partition with the DiskPart command, you need to add one or more physical volumes to the disk through the Disk Management console. Just right-click the extended partition and choose New Simple Volume; then follow the steps described previously to create the new volume. Repeat the process for any other volumes you want to create in the extended partition.

When the partitioning and formatting are complete, exit the Disk Management tool. Access the drive as you would any other — through the This PC folder. Figure 29.11 shows an example. Notice how each Hard Disk Drive icon represents a drive (or partition) defined in the Disk Management tool.

Other hard drive operations

This section covers some general issues concerning hard disks. All these operations pose some risk of data loss and should be attempted only by people who understand the risks and are confident they have backups of all important data.

Converting a disk to NTFS

Windows 10 offers two different file systems for formatting a hard drive. FAT32 was introduced with Windows 95. New Technology File System (NTFS) was introduced in Windows NT 4.0, largely to support user access control required in domain networking. Extended FAT (exFAT) is a new file system that removes several limitations of the older FAT file systems while providing compatibility with other operating systems and devices.

When you divide a hard drive into multiple volumes, you can format each independently of the other. (A *volume* is any partition or logical drive that has its own drive letter and icon in File Explorer's This PC view.) NTFS is the preferred file system for Windows 10 because of its better performance and stronger security. You don't need exFAT file systems unless you have multiple operating systems installed and can choose one or the other at startup. For example, if you can boot to Windows 10 and Linux, the Linux operating system will not be able to access files on a local NTFS volume (without adding third-party Linux tools).

Each file system imposes minimum and maximum volume sizes, and a maximum file size. Keep in mind that these file systems apply only to the hard drives, not to media such as USB flash drives, CDs, or DVDs. Table 29.1 summarizes the differences among the file systems.

TABLE 29.1 Differences among NTFS, exFAT, and FAT32 File Systems for Hard Drives

Description	NTFS	exFAT	FAT32
Locally accessible to	Windows 10, Windows 8/8.1, Windows 7, 2008 Server, Windows Vista, 2003, XP, and 2000	Windows XP, Vista, and 7; Linux	Windows 95 and later
Minimum volume size	10MB		512MB
Maximum volume size	More than 2TB	64ZB*	32GB
Maximum file size	Entire volume	16EB	4GB
Access Control Lists (ACLs)	Yes	No	No

* Zettabyte, a sextillion bytes or 1 billion terabytes

TIP

See the section, "The exFAT file system," later in this chapter to learn more about the exFAT file system.

CAUTION

Changing the file system on a drive poses some risk of data loss and should be attempted only by people who understand the risks and are prepared to recover from possible loss of data.

You can convert a FAT32 file system to NTFS, but you can't go in the other direction. That is, you can always upgrade to NTFS, but you can't downgrade. Be sure to close all open documents and program windows before starting the conversion. To convert a FAT32 volume to NTFS, use the following syntax with the command console `convert` command:

```
convert volume: /fs:ntfs
```

In this syntax, *volume* is the letter of the hard drive you want to convert. Advanced users can enter **convert /?** at the command prompt or search Windows Help and Support for more advanced options. To enter the command, follow these steps:

1. Close all open documents and program windows.
2. Press Windows+X and choose Command Prompt (Admin).

3. Type the command using the syntax shown. For example, to convert hard disk drive D: from FAT32 to NTFS, type **convert d: /fs:ntfs**.

4. Press Enter and follow the instructions on the screen.

If you're converting your system drive (C:), you need to restart the computer to start the conversion. Don't use the computer during the conversion process.

Shrinking and extending partitions

> **TIP**
>
> You can shrink and extend partitions without reformatting, either from the Disk Management tool or by using the DISKPART command.

You can shrink existing partitions to free up unallocated space. And if you have any unallocated space, you can extend existing partitions into that space. This procedure presents some risks. Therefore, you should back up everything before attempting to shrink or extend a partition.

> **CAUTION**
>
> The techniques described in this section do not increase the amount of hard disk space you have. These techniques are best left to professionals and highly knowledgeable computer users. The slightest error can cost you everything on your hard drive! These procedures are not recommended for casual computer users.

You can shrink a basic volume that's either raw (unformatted) or formatted with NTFS quite easily right in the Disk Management tool. You can shrink to the current used space size or to the first unmovable files (such as a paging file) on the volume. To shrink a volume, right-click it at the bottom of the Disk Management screen and choose Shrink Volume. A dialog box opens to show how far you can shrink the selected volume. Make your selection and click OK.

Likewise, if you have some unallocated space on the drive, you can extend an existing partition into that space. Within the Disk Management tool, you can choose to extend an existing partition. When you choose to do this, a wizard opens to take you step-by-step through the process.

For more information on extending and shrinking volumes, including spanned volumes, search the Help in the Disk Management tool.

Changing a volume label

A *volume label* is the name of a volume as it appears in your This PC folder. By default, each volume is labeled Local Disk. To change a drive's volume label, right-click its icon in your

29

This PC folder and choose Properties. On the General tab of the properties sheet, type the new name into the first text box, where you see New Volume in Figure 29.12.

FIGURE 29.12

Changing a volume label.

Changing a drive letter

Drive letters A, B, and C are reserved for floppy disk drives and your hard drive. They cannot be changed. Beyond those first three letters, you can assign drive letters as you see fit. Be aware that when you do, Windows does *not* update your settings and programs to reflect those changes. All settings you've made concerning locations of files in all programs become invalid. Virtual folders and items in Media Player and Live Photo Gallery must be updated to reflect the new drive locations. If you aren't sure how to deal with these issues, don't try to change any drive letters.

> **CAUTION**
> Changing drive letters is best left to experienced users who understand the consequences and can solve, on their own, the problems that are likely to follow.

No two drives can have the same drive letter. If you need to swap two drive letters (for example, change drive E: to drive F: and change drive F: to drive E:), temporarily leave one of the drives without a letter or assign it an unused drive letter. The Disk Management tool, which you need to make this change, allows you to do that. Here's how the procedure works:

1. Navigate to the Disk Management tool described at the beginning of this section.
2. Right-click the graphical representation of the drive whose letter you want to change. Or, to change a removable drive, right-click its drive letter as shown in Figure 29.13. Choose Change Drive Letter and Paths.

   The new drive letter shows up the next time you open your This PC folder.

FIGURE 29.13

Changing a drive letter.

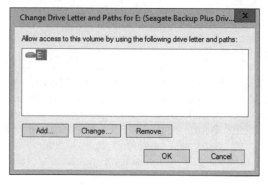

3. If the new letter to which you want to assign the drive is available, click Change, choose the new drive letter, and click OK. Otherwise, if you want to assign the current drive's letter to a different drive, click Remove and click Yes.
4. Repeat steps 2 and 3 until all drives have the letters you want them to have. Then close the Disk Management tool.

The exFAT file system

Microsoft developed a file system called exFAT, for Extended FAT. exFAT is also sometimes referred to as FAT 64 (for 64-bit).

exFAT is not intended as a replacement for NTFS. Instead, exFAT is geared primarily toward mobile personal storage, as used in MP3 players and other mobile devices. exFAT offers several advantages:

29

- Theoretical volume size of 64ZB (recommended size 512TB)
- Theoretical maximum file size of 16EiB-1 Byte (recommended size 512TB)
- Supports more than 1,000 files per directory
- Provides cluster bitmap for fast storage allocation
- Better contiguous on-disk layout, useful for recording movies
- Is extensible

exFAT is supported natively by Windows 10, Windows 8/8/1, Windows 7, and Windows Vista. Windows Vista does not support the use of exFAT with ReadyBoost, but Windows 7, Windows 8/8.1, and Windows 10 do support it. exFAT is also supported under Linux through kernel update.

If you want to optimize performance for removable media such as flash drives, consider formatting the drive with exFAT. However, keep in mind that the device will be usable only in a computer that supports exFAT.

Removing Hardware

Hot-pluggable devices don't employ the type of removal discussed in this section. To remove a USB or FireWire device, or a PC card or memory card, see the section "Disconnecting hot-pluggable devices" earlier in this chapter. This section is about removing more complex devices such as internal components. Before you follow the procedures described in this section, make sure you understand what you're removing and why you're removing it. Do not attempt to fix a problem by removing devices based on guesswork.

You need administrative privileges to perform the tasks described here. We suggest signing into a user account before you begin so you don't have to rely on Windows to prompt you to sign on as administrator later.

Before you physically remove a device from the system, first uninstall its driver through Device Manager by following these steps:

1. Open File Explorer and right-click This PC.
2. Choose Manage and then click Device Manager in the left pane to open Device Manager.
3. Expand the category in which the device is listed. Then, right-click the name of the device you intend to remove and choose Uninstall, as shown in Figure 29.14.
4. Click OK.

Now you need to shut down the computer, unplug the power cord, and physically remove the device from the system. Then plug the machine in, start it, and everything should be back to the way it was before you installed the device. If you set a restore point (see Chapter 19 for steps to creating a restore point) just before installing the hardware, you can return to that protection point just to make sure.

FIGURE 29.14

Uninstall a hardware device.

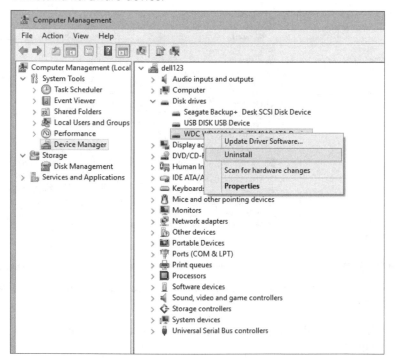

Updating Drivers

At the start of this chapter, we discussed the importance of using Windows 10 drivers with your hardware. The quickest and easiest way to get an updated driver for a device is usually to search for it online by following these steps:

1. Open Device Manager (press Windows+X and choose Device Manager).

2. Right-click the device that needs an updated driver and choose Update Driver Software, as shown in Figure 29.15.

FIGURE 29.15

Update a device driver.

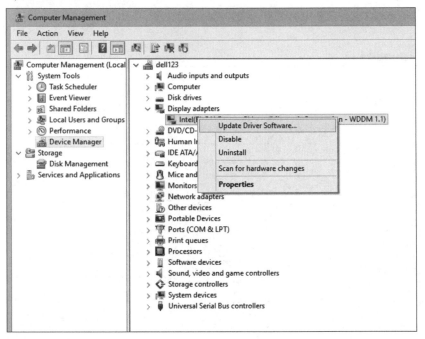

3. Click Search Automatically for Updated Driver Software and follow the onscreen instructions.

Often, that's all you need to do. You may need to restart the computer after the driver installation is complete.

If that method doesn't work, you may have to go to the product manufacturer's website and search for a Windows 10 driver there. If you find the driver, be sure to follow the manufacturer's instructions carefully to download and install the updated driver. If you can't find a driver specifically for Windows 10 and Windows 8/8.1 but you find one for Windows 7 or Vista, that driver should work.

Dealing with Devices That Prevent Windows 10 from Starting

Sometimes a newly installed hardware device prevents Windows 10 from starting properly. In most cases, such devices are disabled automatically so that Windows 10 can start. If your device works that way, you can typically follow the steps described in the preceding section to try to get the updated driver online.

If Windows 10 can't disable or work with the new device, you may be able to start in Safe Mode with Networking and either get updated drivers there or disable the device manually. You also need to log in with the Administrator account.

 To learn how to boot your Windows 10 computer in Safe Mode, see Chapter 6.

When you're at the desktop, follow the procedure described in the preceding section to search for updated drivers. If you can't find updated drivers, your best bet may be to disable the device by right-clicking its name and choosing Disable from the shortcut menu. Close Device Manager and restart the computer again normally.

If you had to disable the device, it won't work when you restart the computer normally. But at least you can get Windows 10 started and try to find an updated driver through the product manufacturer's website.

Wrapping Up

This chapter has been about connecting, installing, and removing hardware. Some of this material is intended for more advanced users who are familiar with computer hardware. If some of the content is beyond your technical capabilities or comfort level and you need to install or remove hardware, consider having the job done professionally. The following are the main points to take away from this chapter:

- Most modern devices are hot-pluggable, which means you simply connect them to the computer as needed.
- Always read and follow the instructions that come with a device before connecting it to your computer. "Winging it" will likely result in frustration.
- Hot-pluggable devices that act as storage devices have icons in your This PC folder while connected. You can transfer files to and from such a device using basic techniques described in Chapter 20.
- More-advanced hardware devices generally require shutting down the computer, connecting the device, turning on the device, and then starting the computer again.
- Use the Disk Management tool to partition and format a new drive.
- To remove a hot-pluggable storage device, click the Safely Remove Hardware icon in the notification area and stop the device before physically removing it.
- To remove other devices, first uninstall them in Device Manager. Then shut down the computer and physically remove the device from the system.

29

Using Wireless Bluetooth Devices

IN THIS CHAPTER

What Bluetooth is all about

Connecting and configuring a Bluetooth adapter

Associating with Bluetooth devices

Connecting to a Bluetooth-enabled personal area network

Transferring files between two systems using the personal area network

In a nutshell, Bluetooth is a wireless technology that provides wireless communications among computers, printers, mobile phones, tablets, digital cameras, and other electronic devices. You can connect as many as eight devices together with Bluetooth, with one device acting as the master device and up to seven slave devices. (This labyrinth of connected devices is called a *piconet;* you can have up to two piconets.) For example, you can have a desktop PC, a laptop, a smartphone, digital camera, MP3 player, digital video camera, and headphones all linked wirelessly. They can share a high-speed Internet connection, share data, and use a single printer.

The World of Bluetooth

Bluetooth is a wireless specification intended to replace the need to use physical cables between devices. For example, Bluetooth enables you to wirelessly connect keyboards, mice, and printers to your laptop or computer. You also can use Bluetooth to wirelessly connect a mobile phone to your computer or laptop to sync settings, transfer photos or videos, or share contacts. Many other types of Bluetooth devices are available as well, including some that don't even connect to computers or laptops, such as devices used inside automobiles, exercise equipment, and games.

Bluetooth uses radio waves to transmit signals, much like many other types of technologies such as FM radio, television, and Wi-Fi. One primary difference between Bluetooth and other radio wave technologies is the distance between devices. Bluetooth is designed for very small distances; Bluetooth is personal. You set up connections among your devices in a personal area network (called a PAN). Bluetooth is good within about 164 feet (50 meters), whereas other radio wave technologies can reach miles or hundreds of miles.

At the time of this writing, the current Bluetooth version is 5. Bluetooth 5 has low-energy wireless transfers to allow small, low-powered devices to use Bluetooth. Transfer rates for Bluetooth 5 are up to 2 Mbit/s instead of the usual 1 Mbit/s. If you're thinking of setting up a permanent wireless network between computers, however, you may want to stick with the 802.11 standards described in Chapter 33. But when you're connecting non-computer Bluetooth devices, wirelessly connecting a printer, or occasionally transferring files between computers, Bluetooth can't be beat.

The following are some Bluetooth buzzwords and concepts that you'll encounter in this section, as well as in the instructions that come with Bluetooth devices:

- **Discovery:** A Bluetooth device finds other Bluetooth devices to which it can connect through a process called *discovery*. To prevent Bluetooth devices from connecting at random, discovery is usually turned off by default on a Bluetooth device. You manually turn on discovery when you're ready for that device to be discovered. After a device has been discovered, you can turn discovery off.

- **Discoverable:** A *discoverable* (or visible) Bluetooth device is one that has discovery turned on, so other Bluetooth devices within range can see and connect to the device.

- **Pairing:** After two or more Bluetooth devices have discovered one another and have been *paired* (connected), you can turn off their discovery features. The devices will forever be able to connect to one another, and unauthorized foreign devices will not be able to discover and hack into the paired devices.

- **Encryption:** A process by which transferred data is encoded to make it unreadable to any unauthorized device that picks up a signal from the device. Bluetooth offers powerful 128-bit data encryption to secure the content of all transferred data.

- **Passkey:** Similar to a password; only devices that share a passkey can communicate with one another. This is another means of preventing unauthorized access to data transmitted across Bluetooth radio waves.

- **Bluejacking:** A process by which one user sends a picture or message to an unsuspecting person's Bluetooth device.

A non-computer gadget such as a smartphone, MP3 player, or electronic pedometer that supports Bluetooth is called a *Bluetooth device*. A standard desktop PC or laptop computer usually isn't a Bluetooth device, although many laptops include built-in Bluetooth capabilities. As a rule, turning your PC or laptop into a Bluetooth device is easy. You simply plug a Bluetooth USB adapter — a tiny device about the size of your thumbnail — into any available USB port, and presto, your computer is a Bluetooth device. Making your computer into a Bluetooth device doesn't limit it in any way. Bluetooth extends the capabilities of your computer so that you can do things such as the following:

- Connect a Bluetooth mouse, keyboard, or other pointing device.
- Use the Devices applet in the Settings area to add a Bluetooth device.
- Use the Add Printer Wizard to use a Bluetooth printer wirelessly.
- Use a Bluetooth-enabled phone or dial-up device as a modem.
- Transfer files between Bluetooth-ready computers or devices by using Bluetooth.
- Join an ad hoc PAN of Bluetooth-connected devices (an ad hoc network is an informal network, where devices connect and disconnect on an as-needed basis, without the need for a central hub or base station).

When you install a Bluetooth adapter on your PC or laptop, you also install *radio drivers*. Windows 10 comes with many radio drivers preinstalled.

> **NOTE**
> If a built-in radio driver doesn't work with your device, install the drivers that came with the device per the device manufacturer's instructions.

Configuring Your Bluetooth Adapter

If you plan to share a single Internet account among several computers or Bluetooth devices, you should install your first Bluetooth USB adapter in the computer that connects directly to the router. That will give other Bluetooth devices that you add later easy access to the Internet through that computer's Internet connection.

After you've installed a Bluetooth adapter, or if your device is itself a Bluetooth device, you'll find a new icon named Bluetooth in the Settings applet. You also can view Bluetooth information in the Device Manager.

To view the Devices list, choose Settings, click Devices. Figure 30.1 shows the Bluetooth menu option that appears in Settings when a Bluetooth device is attached or built into the computer.

To see how the same device looks in Device Manager, show the desktop and press Windows+X. Choose Device Manager and expand the Bluetooth list, as shown in Figure 30.2. Your list may be different from the one shown here, but the important point is that you can view and manage the Bluetooth device in this list as well as in the Devices app.

30

You will have a Bluetooth icon (which looks very similar to the letter *B*) in the notification area of the Windows desktop taskbar. The Bluetooth Settings screen is your central point for installing Bluetooth. To open that screen, click Settings from the Start menu, or double-click the Bluetooth Devices notification area icon (see Figure 30.3). Initially, the Devices list is empty. If you don't see a Bluetooth Devices icon in the notification area, make sure to select the Show the Bluetooth Icon in the Notification Area check box.

FIGURE 30.1

The Bluetooth option on the Settings page.

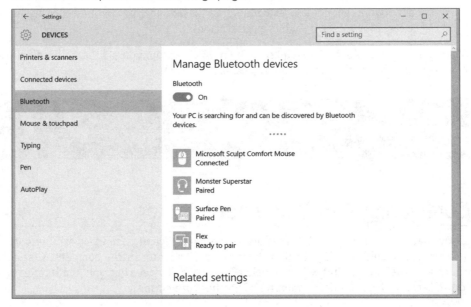

As you install devices and join devices to a Bluetooth PAN, you see the names of those devices listed on that screen.

The shortcut icon that appears when you right-click the notification area provides options for adding a Bluetooth device, sending and receiving files, and joining a PAN.

FIGURE 30.2

Bluetooth USB device showing on the Devices list.

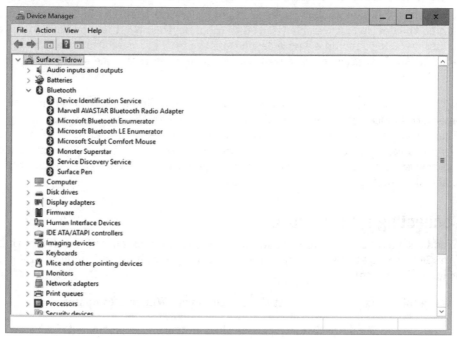

FIGURE 30.3

Bluetooth icon shown in the notification area.

30

Adding Bluetooth-Enabled Devices

Many types of Bluetooth devices are available on the market. Most have some means of making the device discoverable (visible) to other devices. Whether you have to make your PC discoverable to install a device depends on the type of installation you're about to perform. As always, you need to read the documentation that came with your device for specifics.

On the shortcut menu for the Bluetooth Devices notification icon, clicking the Add a Bluetooth Device option opens the Settings window with the Devices option showing. Windows attempts to locate any devices available. The sections that follow show you how easily you can connect Bluetooth devices to your laptop or computer. This example shows you how to connect a smartphone to your computer. We then walk you through the process of transferring files to and from that device.

Connecting a smartphone

To add a smartphone to your computer using Bluetooth, you must have a device that supports Bluetooth. Also, your computer or laptop must have built-in Bluetooth or a Bluetooth adapter plugged into it.

Use the following steps to connect the device to your Windows computer:

1. On the Windows 10 desktop, click the Bluetooth icon on the notification bar.
2. Click Add a Bluetooth Device, as shown in Figure 30.4. The Devices screen appears.

FIGURE 30.4

Choose to add a Bluetooth device.

3. Turn on the Bluetooth feature on the device. In the example shown, we're going to add an iPhone. How you do that depends on the version of your device and the model of phone. The device listed uses the Settings menu in the iPhone. From there, you can turn on the Bluetooth feature and then use the Bluetooth settings item to make the phone discoverable. Windows searches for all Bluetooth devices that are nearby, including the phone.

4. When the computer and phone find each other, a window similar to the one shown in Figure 30.5 appears. Click the item you want to connect with in Windows.

FIGURE 30.5

Windows finds the phone device.

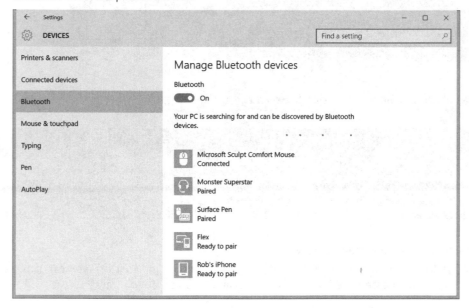

5. Click the Pair button.

6. A message appears on both your phone and in Windows. A passcode should appear that is identical on both devices. If they are, click Pair on your phone (at least in the case of an Apple iPhone 6 or above; your message may vary depending on the smartphone you use) and Yes in Windows to set up the Bluetooth connection. Figure 30.6 shows an example of a passcode that appears during this transaction.

30

FIGURE 30.6

Windows and your phone display a passcode.

Compare the passcodes

Compare the passcodes

Does the passcode on Rob's iPhone match this one?

515258

Yes   No   Cancel

Windows sets up a connection between the two devices.

> **NOTE**
>
> On some devices, you may need to type in the passcode that appears on the Windows screen. If so, be aware that you have a short amount of time to enter the code (approximately 60 seconds) before Windows and your device decide that you don't want a connection at this time. If the passcode screen disappears, restart the connection process to get the two devices to "see" each other again.

Joining a personal area network

After your two devices are connected, you can join them as a PAN so you can transfer files between them using the Bluetooth connection. To do so, follow these steps:

1. Click the Bluetooth icon on the desktop notification bar.
2. Click the Join a Personal Area Network option, as shown in Figure 30.7. The Devices and Printers window appears (see Figure 30.8).
3. Click the device you want to join to the PAN, which in our case is a printer.
4. Click Connect Using ⇨ Access Point. Once connected to the PAN, the command choices change to Disconnect from Device Network. Your device will say something like Connected to PAN or similar.

Now that your devices are joined to a PAN, you can transfer files between them, print to a Bluetooth printer, and so on. Read the following two sections to find out how to do this.

FIGURE 30.7

Setting up a PAN.

FIGURE 30.8

Selecting a device to connect to the PAN.

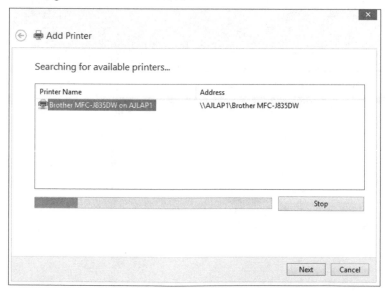

Receiving files from a Bluetooth device

You can't do much when you connect a smartphone to a computer via Bluetooth. One feature that is handy, however, is the feature to send files from your phone to Windows.

You can, for example, send picture or video files from your phone to your computer. To do this, follow these steps:

1. Click the Bluetooth icon on the desktop notification bar.
2. Click Receive a File, as shown in Figure 30.9. The Bluetooth File Transfer window appears (see Figure 30.10). Windows 10 now waits until files from your phone begin transmitting to your computer.

FIGURE 30.9

Receive a file from a smartphone.

FIGURE 30.10

The Bluetooth File Transfer window.

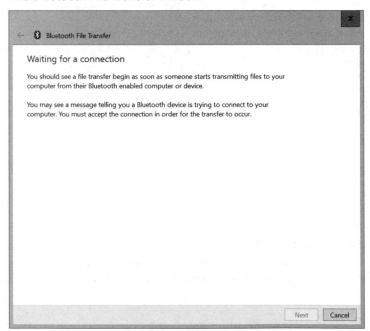

3. On your phone, locate the feature that enables you to send files to a remote location or a media-sharing app. Some Android-based phones include an app called Media Share. With this app, you can share media files (pictures, videos, and audio) with devices on a Bluetooth connection.

4. On your phone, select the file you want to transfer to Windows and transfer it.

5. In Windows, the Bluetooth File Transfer window shows device information, file information, and progress of the file transfer. Figure 30.11 shows an example. In Figure 30.12, the transfer is finished and you can see the filename and size of file, and browse to the location to which it was saved.

FIGURE 30.11

Receiving a file from a smartphone.

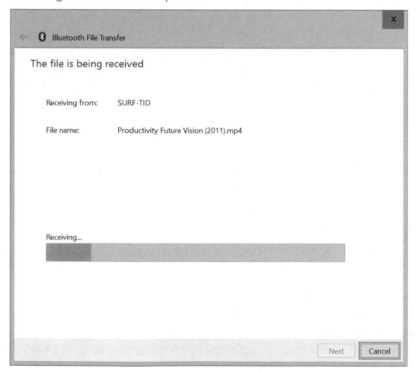

6. Click Finish when you're finished sharing files from the phone.

30

FIGURE 30.12

After Windows receives the transferred file.

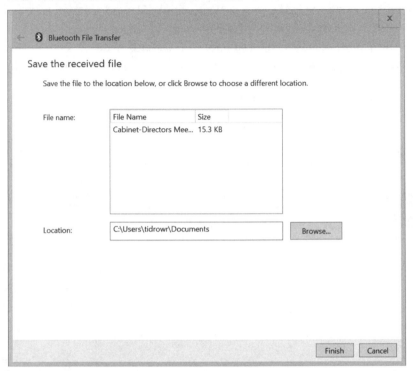

Sending files to a Bluetooth device

Not only does Windows 10 make receiving files from a Bluetooth device, such as an Android-based smartphone, easy; it also simplifies sending them to the device. Follow these steps:

1. Click the Bluetooth icon on the desktop notification bar.

2. Click Send a File. You can see this option in Figure 30.9 earlier in this chapter.

3. Select the Bluetooth device to which you want to send the file. In the example shown in Figure 30.13, our choice is the SURF-TID device. In some cases, you may have multiple devices showing, so be sure to choose the correct one.

FIGURE 30.13

Select a device to send a file to.

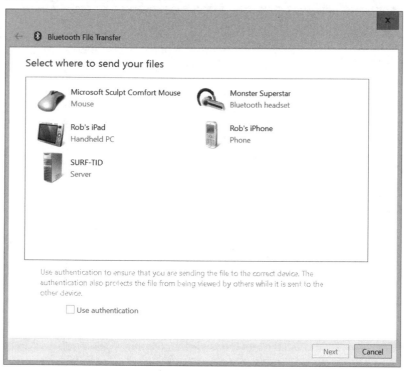

4. Click Next.

5. Specify the path and name of the file you want to share, as shown in Figure 30.14. Use the Browse button to locate the file(s) to send. If you choose multiple files, they're separated by a semicolon.

6. Click Next. The Bluetooth File Transfer window appears showing the progress of the file being sent. Make sure your other device is turned on. You may need to confirm the file transfer on your other device.

Windows sends the file(s) from your computer to your other device. Depending on the size of the files, the transfer process may take several minutes.

30

FIGURE 30.14

Select files to send.

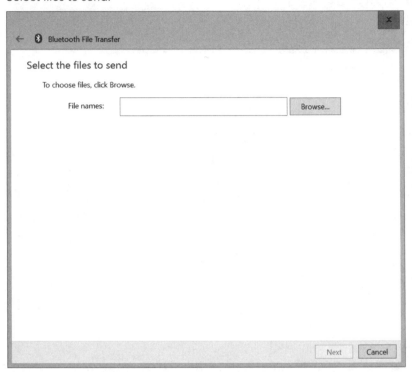

Creating a Bluetooth personal area network

You've seen how to create a PAN to allow a smartphone to connect to your computer. You also can create a Bluetooth PAN as a short-range wireless network to connect other types of devices together wirelessly. A PAN is commonly used to connect a laptop to a desktop PC, although it can be used to connect other types of Bluetooth devices. As a rule, joining Bluetooth devices to a Bluetooth network is a simple matter. Most of the action takes place automatically, behind the scenes.

To understand the basic procedure, assume you already have a desktop computer with a functional Internet connection. You've already installed a Bluetooth USB adapter on that computer, so it's now a Bluetooth device. On that desktop computer, click the Bluetooth adapter icon in the notification area of the Windows desktop. Click Open Settings and make sure Allow Bluetooth Devices to Find This PC is selected, as shown in Figure 30.15. Click OK.

FIGURE 30.15

Make sure Bluetooth is set up on both computers.

On a laptop computer (or a second computer), activate Bluetooth or, if necessary, plug in a second Bluetooth USB adapter. The objective is to connect the laptop to the desktop in a PAN. To do so, starting from the laptop computer, follow these steps:

1. Right-click the Bluetooth Devices notification area icon and choose Join a Personal Area Network. A list of Bluetooth devices should appear. If at least one device does *not* appear, click the Add a Bluetooth Device button and follow the steps to locate a Bluetooth-enabled computer. When the search completes, you should see a list of all of the available devices.

2. Click the name of the computer to which you want to connect. If the Properties page for that device appears, click OK to close that page.

3. Click Connect Using. A drop-down menu appears, as shown in Figure 30.16.

After the connection is established, you should have Internet access on both computers. You can share printers and folders, and move and copy files between computers using the techniques described in Chapter 16 and Chapter 20.

30

Note, however, that if you made the Bluetooth connection to only one computer in an existing local area network (LAN), you have access only to the shared resources on the Bluetooth-enabled computer, not all the computers in the LAN.

FIGURE 30.16

Select Direct Connection when setting up a PAN.

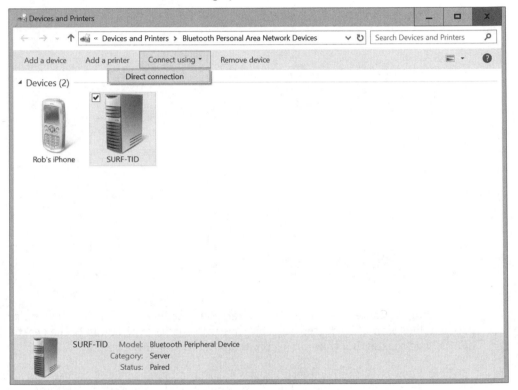

Troubleshooting a Bluetooth network connection

If you can't get any connectivity at all using Bluetooth, try the following remedy:

1. Go to the computer that's having trouble connecting to the PAN.
2. Open the Network and Sharing Center by pressing Windows+X and choosing Control Panel ➪ Network and Internet ➪ Network and Internet ➪ Network and Sharing Center.
3. Scroll down to the Bluetooth Network Connection group. If you can't find the Bluetooth Network Connection group, follow the steps outlined earlier.

The Network and Sharing Center folders on each PC should have similar Bluetooth network entries.

Sharing an Internet connection

If you can't get Internet connectivity from the computer you're connecting to the PAN (assuming the PAN already has Internet connectivity), go to a computer that's connected to the cable modem or router. Open the Network and Sharing Center and click the network item next to the Connections label. In the Activity area, click Properties and select the Sharing tab. Choose Allow Other Network Users to Connect through This Computer's Internet Connection and click OK twice to save your settings.

If you still have problems connecting to the Internet, check the settings for the Windows Firewall. In the Cortana search box, type **fire**, and then click Windows Firewall in the results area. Double-click a rule from the inbound or outbound rules list to adjust the settings.

With these settings, you should be able to connect to the Internet from the other computers in the PAN.

Remember that many different Bluetooth devices are available on the market. If none of the techniques described here help you make the connection between two computers in a PAN, refer to the instructions that came with your Bluetooth device.

Wrapping Up

This chapter has been about installing and configuring Bluetooth devices and Bluetooth networks. Bluetooth devices provide an excellent alternative to many commonly wired devices. They're usually fast and easy to set up and can provide a great way for users to communicate between computers without relying on more complex networking. Here's a recap of the technologies covered in this chapter:

- Bluetooth is currently at version 5 and allows you to connect smartphones, mice, keyboards, exercise equipment, and other Bluetooth devices.

- To turn a computer into a Bluetooth device, simply connect a Bluetooth USB adapter to a USB port on the computer.

- To connect a Bluetooth device to a computer, activate discovery on the device, bring it within range of the computer, click the Bluetooth Devices icon in the notification area, and choose Add a Device.

- To create a PAN between two or more computers, add a Bluetooth USB adapter to each computer, or use the built-in Bluetooth if applicable. Then click the Bluetooth Devices notification area icon and choose Join a Personal Area Network.

- Regardless of what type of device you intend to connect to your computer, always read the instructions that came with the device first.

30

Performance-Tuning Your System

C ompared to most machines, a computer requires virtually no maintenance. That's because it has fewer moving parts compared to other machines. And the new mobile and handheld devices that Windows 10 runs on have practically no moving parts. However, you can take some steps to keep your computer running at its optimum.

For example, the more the hard drive is used to store data, the more fragmented the data on the drive becomes. That doesn't pose any problems for reading the data, but it slows down the process. To speed it up again, you can defragment the drive. This topic, and others that will help you optimize your computer's performance, are covered in this chapter.

Getting to Know Your System

A computer system is made up of many components. The two main components that make up the actual "computer" are the CPU and RAM. The overall speed of your system is largely determined by the speed of your CPU and the amount of RAM in your system. The speed of a CPU is measured in gigahertz (GHz), billions of instructions per second.

The amount of RAM determines how much data the CPU can work with at any one time without accessing the much slower hard drive. RAM chips come in various speeds. But the amount of RAM you have, more so than its speed, determines the overall speed of your system. RAM is measured in megabytes (MB) or gigabytes (GB). A megabyte is roughly a million bytes. (A byte is the amount of memory required to store approximately a single character, such as the letter *A*.) A gigabyte (GB) is 1,024 megabytes. In short, the faster your CPU and the more RAM the computer has, the better its performance.

Knowing your CPU and RAM

To see the brand name and speed of your processor and the amount of RAM you have, right-click your This PC icon from File Explorer and choose Properties. The System Control Panel applet that opens shows the basic computer information, as well as information about the version of Windows you're using, as shown in Figure 31.1.

FIGURE 31.1

The System Control Panel applet.

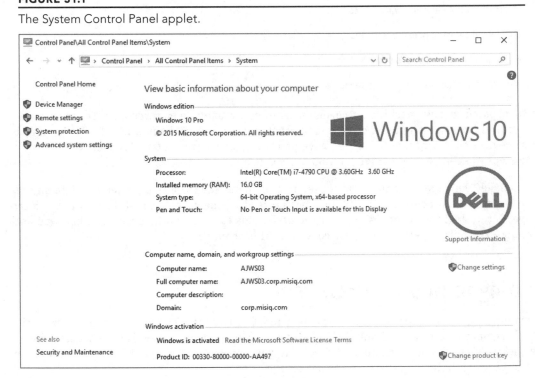

NOTE

The Windows Experience Index (WEI) that provided a quick snapshot of the major components that determined how you experience Windows 8 on your computer is no longer available. Microsoft pulled the WEI out of Windows 8.1. The Performance Information and Tools applet has also been removed.

For advanced performance analysis, Microsoft includes the Windows Performance Analyzer (WPA) and the Windows Performance Recorder (WPR) in Windows 10. Use WPR to collect performance data of your computer. This data is then saved to an XML file or kept in memory and then loaded into WPA for analysis.

To access WPA and WPR, click in Search, search on **perf**, and select Performance Monitor. These tools are extremely powerful and discussing them is beyond the scope of this book. Full documentation is, however, available from the Windows Performance Toolkit, which can be downloaded directly from Microsoft.

Getting more detailed information about your PC

You can get more detailed information about all the components that make up your computer system from the System Information program. To open System Information, display the desktop and press Windows+X. Click Run, type **msinfo32**, and press Enter. The System Information window shown in Figure.31.2 opens.

FIGURE 31.2

The System Information program window.

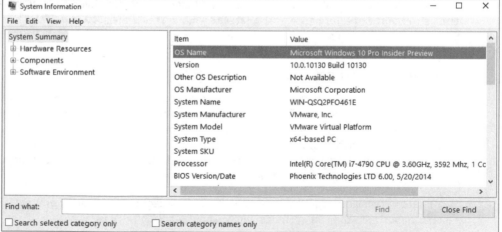

The left column of the System Information window organizes your system information into expandable and collapsible categories. For example, clicking the plus sign next to the Components category expands that category to display subcategories and the names of specific device types. When you click a specific type, such as Drives under the Storage category, the pane on the right shows information about the components installed in your computer system.

You don't actually do any work in the System Information program. Its job is to present the facts about your computer's installed hardware and software. However, you can export a copy of the System Information data to a text file, which in turn you can open, format, or print using any word processing program or text editor. To export a copy of your system information to a file, just choose File ➪ Export from System Information's menu bar.

You can also print your system information, either in whole or in part. To print all your system information, first click System Summary at the top of the left column. To print just a category, first click a category name, such as Components. Then choose File ➪ Print from System Information's menu bar. In the Print dialog box that opens, choose All if you want to print everything, choose Selection to print just the text you may have selected, or choose Current Page to print the page you're viewing. To close System Information, click its Close (X) button or choose File ➪ Exit.

Maximizing CPU and Memory Resources

Windows 10 takes care of managing the CPU and memory for you. Even so, you can do some things to improve performance as it relates to your system's memory and CPU. The following sections offer some tips.

Conserving memory

One of the best things you can do to improve your computer's performance is to ensure that it has plenty of memory. Initially, that means making sure the computer has a sufficient amount of physical memory installed. You should consider 2GB a minimum, although Windows can run with 1GB. If you use lots of programs at once, or use applications that require a lot of memory, consider using the 64-bit version of Windows and having at least 4GB of RAM in the computer, if not more.

Having lots of memory is part of the solution, but managing the memory you have is equally important. You can optimize your computer's RAM in these ways:

- **Reduce the number of programs you run concurrently:** If you aren't using a program, close it to reclaim the memory it's using. You can open it again later if you need it.

- **Minimize the number of programs you install on your computer:** Do you really need a program on the tray that tells you what the weather is like outside? All the little add-on programs you install and run on your computer, even if they're running in the background, consume resources. The fewer programs, the better.

Reducing the number of programs running at one time not only improves performance by freeing up memory, but also reduces the load on the CPU, making processing cycles available to those programs that do need to be running.

Managing virtual memory

31

In the very early days of DOS, a computer could run only one program at a time. Programs had to be written to fit in the available (and minimal) memory in the computer. In Windows 10, you can run almost as many programs as you want at one time as a result of the design of today's CPUs and of the OS itself. The capability to manage memory effectively for all those programs is due, in part, to the use of *virtual memory.*

Modern computers can use two types of memory. The first type is *physical memory* (RAM), which consists of physical memory chips on memory modules (small circuit boards) that plug into the computer's motherboard.

> **TIP**
>
> The amount of RAM shown in the System section of the System Control Panel applet (refer to Figure 31.1) is the amount of physical RAM in your system.

The second type of memory is *virtual memory,* and Windows 10 uses the computer's hard drive for that, using a file on the drive as a place to store data as an alternative to physical memory. The area on the hard drive that's used as virtual memory is called a *paging file* because data is swapped back and forth between physical and virtual memory in small chunks called *pages*. When you fill up both your physical memory and virtual memory, the computer doesn't just stop and display an error. Instead, it displays a message in advance, warning that the computer is running low on virtual memory and suggesting that you make room for more.

Because the virtual memory is just a paging file on the hard drive, you can easily add more just by increasing the size of the paging file. You don't have to buy or install anything. This is unlike physical memory in that the only way to increase physical memory is to buy and install more RAM. One downside to virtual memory is that it's much slower than physical memory because hard drives are slower than RAM chips.

To manage virtual memory in Windows 10, open the System applet from the Control Panel and click the Advanced System Settings link on the System applet. The link appears on the left of this page, as shown in the left side of Figure 31.3. In the resulting System Properties dialog box, click the Advanced tab, and then click the Settings button in the Performance group. Then select the Advanced tab in the resulting Performance Options dialog box (see the left side of Figure 31.4). The Virtual Memory area on this dialog box shows the total paging file size for all drives. To adjust the settings, click the Change button to open the Virtual Memory dialog box shown in the right side of Figure 31.4.

FIGURE 31.3

The Advanced System Settings link (left); the Advanced tab of the System Properties dialog box (right).

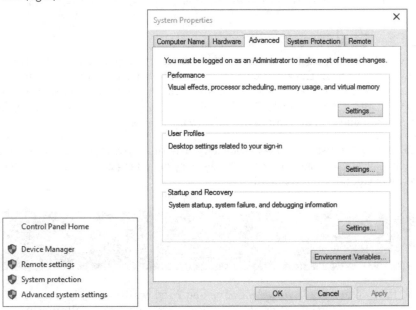

In most cases, you can simply select the top check box, Automatically Manage Paging File Size for All Drives, to allow Windows to adjust the page file.

If you don't want Windows to manage the page file for you, your main options in the Paging File Size for Each Drive area of the Virtual Memory dialog box are as follows:

- **Custom Size:** You choose where you want to put your paging file(s), their initial size, and maximum size.

- **System Managed Size:** Tells Windows to create and size the paging file automatically for you.

- **No Paging File:** Eliminates the paging file from a drive. Not recommended unless you're moving the paging file from one drive to another.

If you have multiple hard drives, you can get the best performance by using the least busy drive for virtual memory. For example, if you have a D: drive on which you store documents, it may be better to use that, rather than the C: drive, because the C: drive is pretty busy with Windows and your installed programs.

If you have multiple *physical drives,* you can get a little performance boost by splitting the paging file across the two drives. A single drive that's partitioned into two or more partitions, to look like multiple drives, doesn't count. Don't divide the paging file across multiple partitions on a single drive because that has the reverse effect and slows operations down.

FIGURE 31.4

The Advanced tab of the Performance Options dialog box (left); the Virtual Memory dialog box (right).

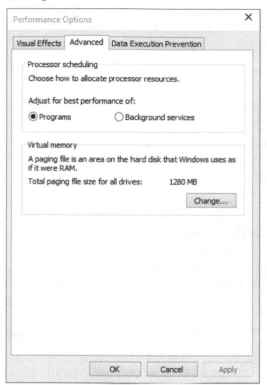

If you opt for a custom size, you can work with any one hard drive at a time. The drives are listed by letter and labeled at the top of the dialog box. In the example shown, all the partitions reside on a single drive.

> **TIP**
>
> The Disk Management tool discussed in Chapter 29 lists hard drives by number. If you have a single physical hard drive, it is Disk 0. If you have two physical hard drives, they're listed as Drive 0, Drive 1, and so on.

If you don't select the check box at the top of the Virtual Memory dialog box, you need to set the paging file sizes individually. For example, to move the paging from drive C: to D:, first click drive C: at the top of the dialog box, choose No Paging File, and then click the Set button. Then click drive D:, choose Custom Size, set the sizes, and click Set.

The Total Paging File Size for All Drives section at the bottom of the dialog box shows the minimum allowable size, a recommended size, and the currently allocated size (the last measurement being the sum of all the Initial Size settings). The recommended size is usually about 1.5 times the amount of physical memory. The objective is to prevent you from loading up way more stuff than you have physical RAM to handle, which would definitely make your computer run more slowly.

If your computer keeps showing messages about running out of virtual memory, you definitely should increase the initial and maximum size of the paging file. A gigabyte (1,024MB) is a nice round number. But if the computer runs slowly after you increase the amount of virtual memory, the best solution is to add more physical RAM.

If you change the Virtual Memory settings and click OK, you're asked if you want to restart your computer. If you have programs or documents open, choose No and close everything first. But because the paging file is created when you only start your computer, you eventually need to restart the computer to take advantage of your new settings.

Priorities, foreground, and background

Your computer's CPU and RAM are very busy places, with potentially thousands of tasks occurring at one time. To try to optimize performance, Windows prioritizes those tasks. Your application programs typically run in the *foreground,* which means that when you click an item with your mouse or do something at the keyboard, fulfilling that request gets top priority in terms of being sent to the CPU for execution.

Most processes, by comparison, run in the *background.* This means that they get a lower priority and have to momentarily step aside when you tell Windows or an application to do something. For example, printing a document is treated as a low-priority background process, and for good reason. Printers are slow mechanical devices. So, by making printing a low-priority process, you can continue to use your computer at near normal speeds while the printer is slowly churning out its printed pages.

Controlling CPU priorities

By default, programs that you're using are given a higher priority than background processes. You can reverse that order by giving processes a higher priority than applications. If you have an intensive background task running, you can give it a higher priority. Or if you want to make sure that your applications are getting top priority, as they should be, follow these steps:

1. Open the System window for your system.

TIP

The System icon in the Control Panel also opens the System window. If the Control Panel opens in Category view, click System and Security and click the System link.

2. Click the Advanced System Settings link on the left side of the screen to bring up the System Properties dialog box. Select the Advanced tab in the System Properties dialog box.

3. Under the Performance heading, click the Settings button. The Performance Options dialog box opens.

4. In the Performance Options dialog box, select the Advanced tab (refer to Figure 31.3).

The Processor Scheduling options determine whether your actions, or processes, get top priority when vying for CPU resources to do their jobs. If you choose Background Services, your computer may not be as responsive as you'd like, but background tasks get higher priority. So, for example, if you're running a scan of your system in the background and you want it to finish faster, select Background Services in the Performance Options dialog box and click OK.

> **NOTE**
> Choosing Background Services doesn't make your printer print any faster. You can't do anything to speed printing, other than use the printer's Draft mode (if it has one). But even so, printers are simply slow, mechanical devices.

Monitoring and Adjusting Performance

Windows 10 includes a great selection of tools to help you monitor and tune your system's performance. You've already seen a couple of them, notably the Performance Monitor. The following sections explore this tool in more detail, along with several others that will help you keep your system running at its best.

Performance Monitor

Performance Monitor, included in Windows 10, has also been available in previous versions of Windows. It provides an interface for viewing performance counters on your system. To open Performance Monitor, press Windows+X. Click Run, type **perfmon**, and press Enter, or type **perf** in the Cortana search. The Performance Monitor window shown in Figure 31.5 opens.

> **NOTE**
> Performance Monitor is a very complex application, and we could easily devote several chapters to it. For this reason, we cover only some of the basic functions of the application. To get more information, search for Performance Monitor under Windows Help.

FIGURE 31.5

Performance Monitor.

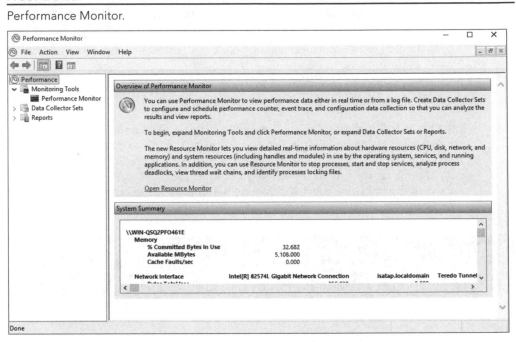

When Performance Monitor opens, the Performance branch in the left pane is selected and the Performance Monitor window displays general information about the program, a system summary, and some links to learn more about using Performance Monitor. Although the System Summary area shows current performance data, you'll probably prefer to see a visual representation. To do so, click Performance Monitor under the Monitoring Tools branch in the left pane. Figure 31.6 shows an example.

The line crossing the screen as you watch the Performance Monitor plots your system's CPU activity. The graph has a timeline along the bottom and a percentage on the side. Tracking only the CPU doesn't provide much more information than what Task Manager provides. By adding counters to the grid, you can track your system's performance. To add more counters to the graph, follow these steps:

1. Start by clicking the plus sign in the toolbar located just above the graph.
2. The Add Counters dialog box, shown in Figure 31.7, shows all the available performance objects for your system. In the left column, click the arrow to the right of the performance objects to expand and display the available counters for that object. We've selected Network Interface in Figure 31.7.

FIGURE 31.6

Performance graphs in Performance Monitor.

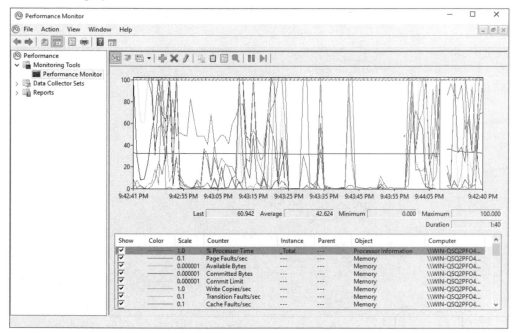

3. Depending on the counter you select, you may also have the option of selecting an instance of that counter. In the case of the Network Interface object, depending on your computer system, you may have multiple network interfaces, as shown in the Instances of Selected Object list box. This figure shows the Bytes Total/Sec selected as the counter and the wireless adapter for the instance.

4. Optionally, you can select the Show Description check box so you can view additional information about the counter.

5. Click the Add button to move the selection over to the Added Counters section of the window.

6. When you've selected all the counters you want to monitor, click OK to return to the graph.

7. As shown in Figure 31.8, the counter is added to the bottom of the window. If you select the counter in the list and click the highlighter icon in the toolbar, it highlights that specific counter. In this case, it has changed the color to a bold black. This is very helpful when you have several counters on the screen at the same time. When the highlighter is turned on, clicking any counter in the list causes that counter to be highlighted.

FIGURE 31.7

The Add Counters dialog box.

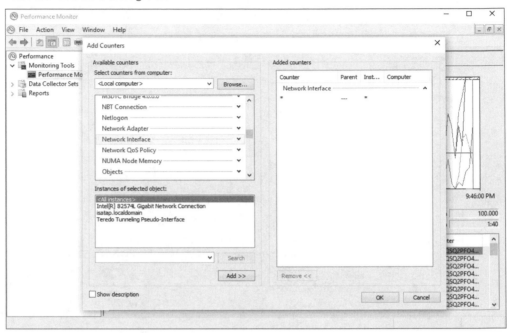

The scale of the graph is set automatically. In the case of the previous example, if the network utilization went off the screen, you'd be able to adjust the scale for that specific counter so you'd have more meaningful information instead of a line running off the top of the graph.

Data collector sets and reports

The Performance Monitor interface provides a mechanism to log the information and events that occur on your system. Besides just logging the information, it also provides a way for you to use reports to look at the information.

In the previous section, you learned about performance counters in Performance Monitor through the use of one example, Bytes Total/Sec. A data collector set, as its name implies, is a set of objects that collect data about your computer. So, you might create a data collector set that gathers data about specific items. For example, you could create a data collector set to gather information about network performance through the use of a variety of network counters. Or you might create one to analyze drive performance by using multiple drive counters.

FIGURE 31.8

Network Interface object added to Performance Monitor.

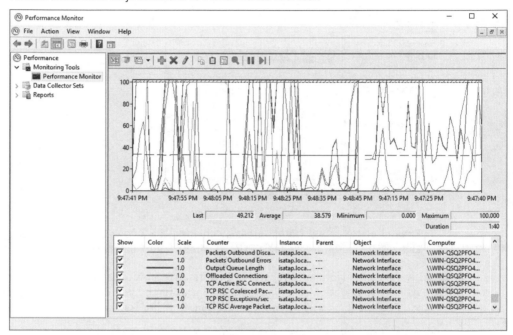

Within the Performance Monitor interface, you can create user-defined data collector sets, but let's start with the predefined data collector sets. To get started, follow these steps:

1. Click the arrow to the left of Data Collector Sets to expand the tree beneath it. Then expand the System icon beneath Data Collector Sets and click System Performance.

2. Right-click System Performance and choose Start, or click the Start button in the toolbar. The system starts collecting data for the different components of the collector.

3. Let the system run for a while, and when you're ready, right-click System Performance again and choose Stop this time, or click the Stop button in the toolbar. Stopping the collector may take a few seconds.

4. Navigate to the Reports section within Performance Monitor and expand the System branch, as shown in Figure 31.9. In this figure, two performance reports are listed.

FIGURE 31.9

System Performance reports.

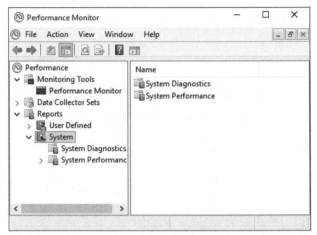

5. Expand or collapse different areas by clicking the arrows next to each group. Use the vertical scroll bar to see all the different report categories.

Generating system performance reports in Performance Monitor can help you understand where bottlenecks might exist in your system. For example, you can quickly identify an overtaxed CPU, problems with network saturation, or other issues.

In addition to creating performance reports with Performance Monitor, you can also create diagnostic reports. In the left pane, under Data Collector Sets, expand System and click System Diagnostics. Then click Start in the toolbar. Wait as Performance Monitor creates the report. While the report data is being gathered, the icon next to the System Diagnostics branch shows a small green arrow. This is replaced by an hourglass while Performance Monitor generates the report. When the icon returns to normal, the report is finished. You'll find a new report under the Reports ⇨ System ⇨ System Diagnostics branch in the left pane. Click the report to view its contents. Figure 31.10 shows an example of a diagnostics report.

As with a performance report, expand and collapse any categories in the report to view the information in the report. The information in the report can help you pinpoint hardware errors and other problems.

FIGURE 31.10

A diagnostics report.

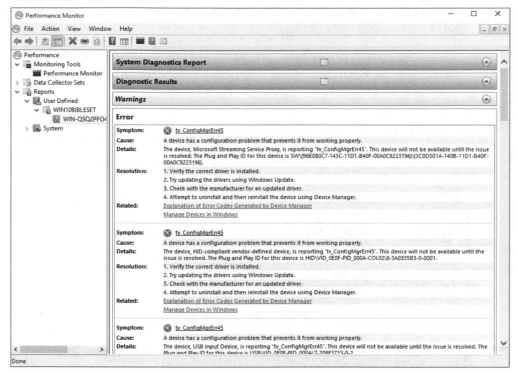

Creating data collector sets

You can create your own user-defined data collector sets, which involves adding data from one of the four categories. From the properties window of the collector, you can set a variety of properties for each type, such as the sample interval maximum number of samples, Registry keys to monitor, and many more.

You can add the following four types of data collectors to your custom data collector sets:

- **Performance Counter Data:** This information is the same information that you can gather from Performance Monitor, discussed earlier in the chapter.

- **Event Trace data:** This data is gathered when system events occur on your system.

- **Configuration data:** This data is gathered from changes to your system's Registry.

- **Performance Counter Alert:** This data is gathered when a performance counter you specify reaches a point either above or below a value that you define.

As explained previously, creating data collector sets assumes a certain level of technical capability and knowledge about how the computer and its components function. Those topics are far outside the scope of this book. So, instead, we focus on the mechanics of creating the data collector set:

1. Open Performance Monitor and expand the Data Collector Sets branch.
2. Right-click User Defined and choose New ⇨ Data Collector Set to start the Create New Data Collector Set Wizard (see Figure 31.11).

FIGURE 31.11

Create New Data Collector Set Wizard.

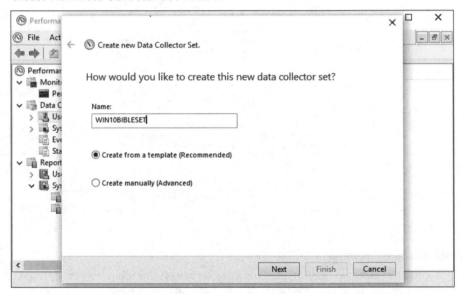

3. Enter a descriptive name in the Name text box.
4. Decide whether to create the data collector set from a template or from scratch (manually). If you choose the Create from a Template option, you can add data collectors to the ones already in the template. Click Next.
5. If you opted to start from a template, the wizard next prompts you to choose a template. Select one and click Next. Otherwise, the wizard prompts you to choose a type of data collector to add. In this example, let's assume you choose to start from a template, so choose Basic from the offered templates and then click Next.
6. Specify the directory where you want the data to be saved and click Next.
7. In the final page of the wizard, click Finish.

The new data collector set should now appear under the User Defined branch in the left pane. Let's assume that you now want to add some additional data collectors to the set. Right-click in the right pane (or on the new data collector set's name in the left pane) and choose New ⇨ Data Collector.

Performance Monitor opens the Create New Data Collector Wizard (see Figure 31.12). Specify a name for the collector and choose one of the four collector types, as described previously in this section. For example, to add a performance counter, choose Performance Counter Data Collector. Then click Next.

FIGURE 31.12

The Create New Data Collector Wizard.

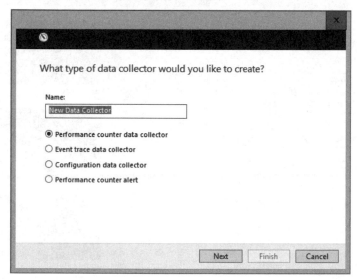

Depending on the type of collector you choose, the wizard prompts you for information about the collector. Specify the information needed to configure the collector to obtain the data you're looking for, and then click Finish.

After you create the data collector set, you can use it just as you can the predefined ones in the System branch.

Resource Monitor

Another handy tool for monitoring system performance is Resource Monitor, which collects and displays real-time information about the CPU, disk, network, and memory.

To open Resource Monitor, select the root node in Performance Monitor and then click the Open Resource Monitor link. You can also open Resource Monitor by running **resmon** from the Cortana search as described for running **perfmon** (see "Performance Monitor," earlier in this chapter). Figure 31.13 shows Resource Monitor.

FIGURE 31.13

Resource Monitor.

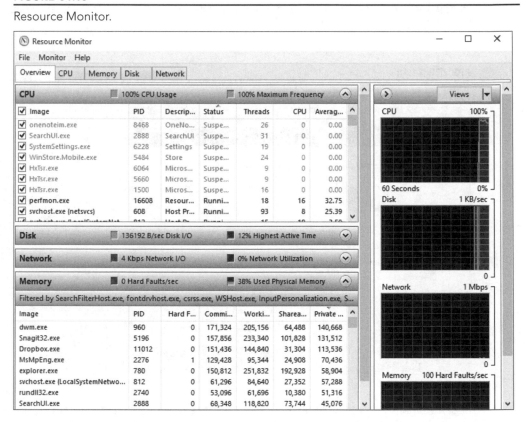

The Overview tab, shown in Figure.31.14, offers summary information about each of the four categories. To view activity for a particular process, select the check box next to the process's image name in the CPU list. Then click the category header for a category to view the data filtered by the selected process. For example, Figure 31.14 shows network activity filtered for Dropbox.

FIGURE 31.14

Network activity filtered for Dropbox.

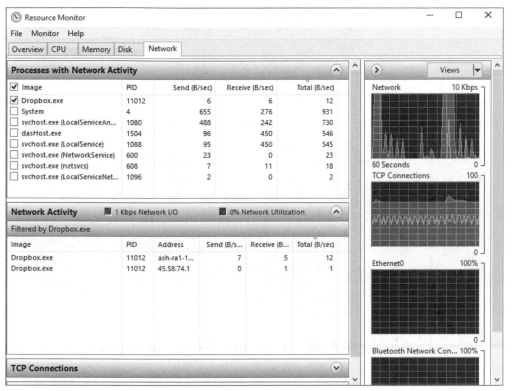

Each of the other tabs in Resource Monitor provides data specific to the specified category. For example, to see detailed information about memory utilization, select the Memory tab. The top area of each tab shows the running processes. You can filter by one or more processes by selecting them from the list. Deselect the Image check box to clear the filter.

Reliability Monitor

Reliability Monitor provides information regarding your system's overall stability. It tracks data and generates a report similar to the one shown in Figure 31.15, which indicates a relative reliability index from 1 to 10. Reliability Monitor uses five groups of information to determine the index, including application failures, Windows failures, miscellaneous failures, warnings, and informational events. To open Reliability Monitor, open Control Panel and search for Reliability. Then click the Reliability Monitor Report.

FIGURE 31.15

Reliability Monitor report of overall system stability.

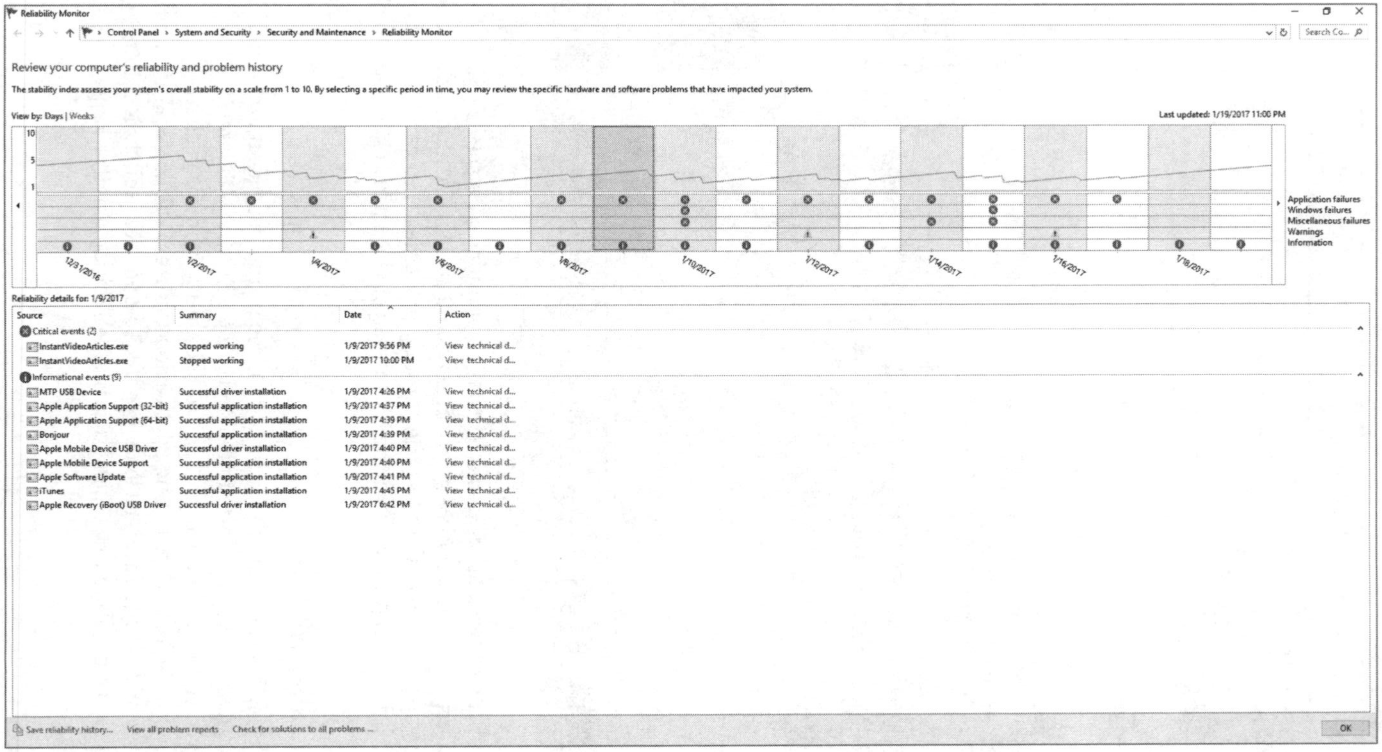

TIP

Reliability Monitor starts monitoring your system right after the operating system is installed and keeps one year's worth of data for analysis. Reliability Monitor requires 28 days of information before it accurately determines a stability index. The line in the graph is dashed until Reliability Monitor has 28 days of information.

The icons on the chart in Reliability Monitor indicate the type of event that occurred on the specified date. The letter *i* inside a blue circle is an informational event, such as an update being applied successfully to the system. A yellow triangle with an exclamation point inside indicates a warning — for example, a warning that a driver did not install successfully. Failures are indicated by a white X inside a red circle. Examples include an application hanging or Windows shutting down unexpectedly.

You can view the events for a particular day by clicking that day in the chart. Details for that day appear in the bottom Details pane. When viewing the graph in Weeks view, clicking a week in the graph shows all items for that week in the Details pane. Whichever view you use, double-clicking an item in the Details pane displays full information about the event. For example, Figure 31.16 shows the results of double-clicking an event related to an application hang event.

Reliability Monitor is a great tool for keeping track of the events that have occurred with your computer over a long period of time. It can be particularly useful in identifying repetitive problems or problems with specific items.

TIP

Windows ReadyBoost uses flash memory, rather than your hard drive, for the paging file. This allows programs to get drive data more quickly, providing a faster, more fluid computing experience.

Using Windows ReadyBoost

Historically, PCs had two ways to store data: memory and the hard drive. Memory (RAM) is very fast. But it's volatile, meaning everything in it gets erased the moment you shut down the computer. The hard drive isn't nearly as fast. But it has *persistence,* meaning that it retains information even when the computer is turned off.

RAM is also more expensive than hard drive storage. For example, a typical desktop computer might have 2GB of RAM. The hard drive, on the other hand, most likely holds hundreds or even thousands of gigabytes (called *terabytes*) of data.

Windows 10 automatically uses the paging file (discussed earlier in this chapter) to store the data and conserve RAM.

FIGURE 31.16

Details for an event in Reliability Monitor.

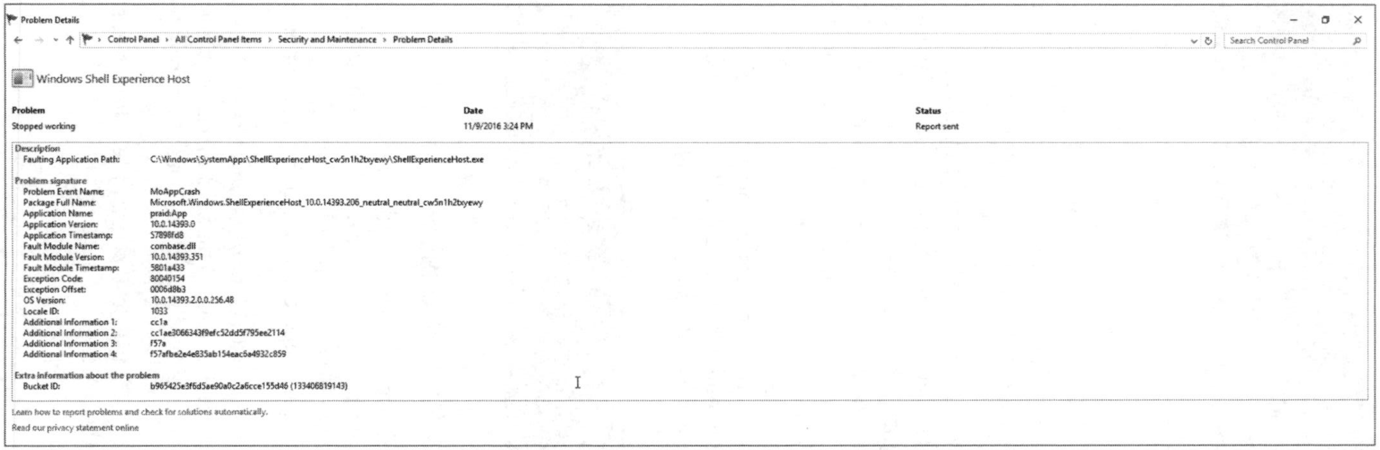

Problem Details

Control Panel › All Control Panel Items › Security and Maintenance › Problem Details

Search Control Panel

Windows Shell Experience Host

Problem	Date
Stopped working	11/9/2016 3:24 PM

Status
Report sent

Description
Faulting Application Path: C:\Windows\SystemApps\ShellExperienceHost_cw5n1h2txyewy\ShellExperienceHost.exe

Problem signature
Problem Event Name: MoAppCrash
Package Full Name: Microsoft.Windows.ShellExperienceHost_10.0.14393.206_neutral_neutral_cw5n1h2txyewy
Application Name: praid:App
Application Version: 10.0.14393.0
Application Timestamp: 57899fe8
Fault Module Name: combase.dll
Fault Module Version: 10.0.14393.351
Fault Module Timestamp: 58014d33
Exception Code: 80040154
Exception Offset: 000dd8b3
OS Version: 10.0.14393.2.0.0.256.48
Locale ID: 1033
Additional Information 1: cc1a
Additional Information 2: cc1ea0b6342f9fef.c32dd9f793eec2114
Additional Information 3: f57a
Additional Information 4: f57afba2e4e833ab1154aec3a4832cd59

Extra information about the problem
Bucket ID: b96542a3f6d5ae9a0c2a6cce155d46 (133408619143)

Learn how to report problems and check for solutions automatically.

Read our privacy statement online

The downside to using the paging file is that the processor can't move data to and from it as quickly as it can with RAM. The paging file becomes a little performance bottleneck. Prior to Windows Vista, no solution to this problem existed. Windows Vista introduced a solution called ReadyBoost that lets Windows 10 use flash memory for the paging file. For paging file operations, flash memory is about ten times faster than a hard drive, which means ReadyBoost can get rid of many little, short delays and offer a faster, smoother overall computing experience. Windows 7 through Windows 10 support ReadyBoost.

> **NOTE**
>
> Contrary to popular belief, ReadyBoost doesn't add more RAM to your computer. It improves performance by using flash memory, rather than the hard drive, to store and access frequently used disk data.
>
> Windows 10 takes care of all the potential problems that using flash memory for disk data can impose. For example, Windows 10 keeps the actual paging file on the drive in sync with the copy on the flash drive. So, if the flash memory suddenly disappears (as when you pull a flash drive out of its USB slot), you don't lose any data. Windows 10 even compresses and encrypts the data on the flash drive using high-strength AES encryption. If someone steals a ReadyBoost flash drive from your computer, he or she can't read data from it to steal sensitive information.

You have three ways to get ReadyBoost capabilities in your system:

- Use a *hybrid* hard drive, which puts NAND flash memory right on the drive.
- Have ReadyBoost capability on the computer's motherboard.
- Use a USB flash drive (a small device, usually small enough to fit on a keychain, which you just plug into a USB 2.0 or 3.0 port on your computer) for ReadyBoost.

Not all flash drives are ReadyBoost-capable. They vary greatly in their capacity and speed. Windows 10 uses a flash drive for ReadyBoost only. An 8GB flash drive with fast random I/O capability is a good choice for ReadyBoost.

If you already have a USB flash drive and want to see if it's ReadyBoost-capable, plug the drive into a USB slot. After Windows 10 recognizes and analyzes the drive, you get some feedback on the screen letting you know that you can speed up your system by utilizing the available space on your device.

Some systems, such as newer laptops that use solid-state hard drives, are fast enough that ReadyBoost doesn't provide any serious performance gains. Figure 31.17 shows an example of the ReadyBoost properties tab for a USB 2.0 flash drive. Notice that using ReadyBoost would not provide additional performance benefit to laptops or handheld devices. Right-click the USB device in File Explorer and select properties. The ReadyBoost tab as shown in Figure 31.17 lets you know if the USB drive selected can be used for ReadyBoost.

FIGURE 31.17

Windows lets you know if the USB flash drive would not benefit from ReadyBoost.

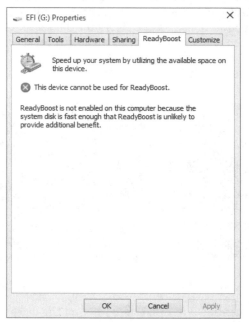

If you want to use the device as virtual memory, select the Speed Up My System option. After you've selected that option, the properties for the removable disk pop up. You can also bring up that dialog box by opening your Computer folder, right-clicking the drive's icon, and choosing Properties.

Select the Use This Device option, and then you can set the amount of space for ReadyBoost. By default, Windows sets the value to the recommended amount and lets you know that the space you allocate won't be available for general use. When you've set the value, click OK.

ReadyBoost copies as much of the information as possible from virtual memory to the USB thumb drive. A copy of all the information remains within virtual memory, but the system now knows to look at the ReadyBoost device first. If the system can't find the information there, it looks to the real virtual memory located on your hard drive. By keeping the original copy on your hard drive, you can remove your USB thumb drive without disrupting the computer.

Don't expect to see your computer suddenly run faster with ReadyBoost. Its benefits may not be immediate. *Remember:* The main purpose of ReadyBoost is to eliminate the short delays you may experience when loading certain programs, switching among open programs, and performing other activities that usually involve a paging file. With time, you should experience quicker response times in those areas. You may even find your computer starts more quickly because programs load more quickly at startup.

Trading pretty for performance

All the visual effects you see on your screen while using Windows come with a price. It takes CPU resources to show drop-shadows beneath 3D objects, make objects fade into and out of view, and so forth. On an old system that has minimal CPU capabilities and memory, those little visual extras can bog down the system.

To change settings that control visual effects, open Control Panel, select the System link, and then select Advanced system settings. The System Properties dialog box loads. Select the Advanced tab and then click the Performance Options Settings button. The Performance Options dialog box shown in Figure 31.18 loads.

FIGURE 31.18

The Visual Effects tab of the Performance Options dialog box.

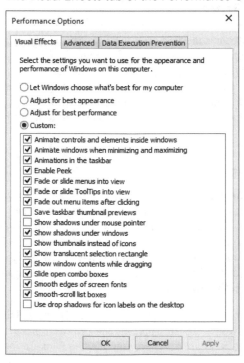

The Visual Effects tab of the Performance Options dialog box lets you choose how much performance you're willing to part with for a "pretty" interface. As shown in Figure 31.18, the Visual Effects tab gives you four main options:

- **Let Windows Choose What's Best for My Computer:** Use this option to enable Windows to automatically choose visual effects based on the capabilities of your computer.

- **Adjust for Best Appearance:** If selected, all visual effects are used, even at the cost of slowing down performance.

- **Adjust for Best Performance:** This option minimizes visual effects to preserve overall speed and responsiveness.

- **Custom:** With this option, you can pick and choose any or all of the visual effects listed beneath the Custom option.

How you choose options is entirely up to you. If you have a powerful system, the visual effects don't affect performance very much, if at all. So, you don't need to turn off the visual effects. But if your computer isn't immediately responsive to operations that involve opening and closing menus, dragging, and other things you do on the screen, eliminating some visual effects should help make your computer more responsive.

Maintaining Your Hard Drive

The CPU and RAM are the most important factors for system performance, but your hard drive plays an important role in determining the overall speed of your computer. That's because the hard drive comes into play when you open programs or documents, when you save documents, or when you move and copy files. By moving less-used applications to your hard drive from RAM, the hard drive also comes into play when you're running low on RAM. So, keeping the hard drive running as near to peak performance as possible has a positive impact on system performance.

Recovering wasted hard drive space

At any time, some of the space on your hard drive is being eaten up by *temporary files.* As the name implies, temporary files are not like the programs you install or documents you save. Programs, apps, and documents are "forever," in the sense that Windows never deletes them at random. The only time a program is deleted, for example, is when you use Programs in the Control Panel to remove the program. Likewise, documents aren't deleted unless you intentionally delete them and also empty the Recycle Bin. And Windows 10 apps aren't deleted unless you remove them from the Windows 10 interface.

In contrast, the files in your *Internet cache,* also called your Temporary Internet Files folder, are temporary files. Every time you visit a web page, all the text and pictures that make up that page are stored in your Internet cache. When you use the Back or Forward button to revisit a page you've viewed recently, your browser pulls a copy of the page out of the Internet cache. That saves lots of time when compared to how long it would take to redownload a page each time you click the Back or Forward button to revisit a recently viewed page.

> **CAUTION**
> Before you click the Disk Cleanup tool, be forewarned that the process can take several minutes and maybe longer. You never need to use Disk Cleanup to get rid of temporary files.

To recover some wasted disk space, click the Disk Cleanup button on the properties sheet for the hard drive. Open the This PC folder, right-click a drive, and choose Properties. In the Properties dialog box, click the Disk Cleanup button on the General tab. Disk Cleanup then analyzes the drive for expendable files. When the analysis is complete, you see the Disk Cleanup dialog box shown in Figure 31.19. The Files to Delete list shows categories of temporary files. When you click a category name, the Description below the names explains the types of files in that category. All the categories represent temporary files that you definitely can safely delete. Important programs or documents you saved on your own never appear in the list of temporary files.

FIGURE 31.19

The Disk Cleanup dialog box.

The number to the right of each category name indicates how much drive space the files in that category are using and how much space you'll gain if you delete them. Choose which categories of files you want to delete by selecting (checking) their check boxes. If you don't want to delete a category of files, clear the check mark for that category. The amount of drive space you'll recover by deleting all the selected categories appears under the list. After you've selected the categories of files you want to delete, click OK. The files are deleted and the dialog box closes.

Deleting system restore files and unwanted features

If you click the Clean Up System Files button in Disk Cleanup, a More Options tab appears on the Disk Cleanup dialog box. Clicking that tab provides two more options for freeing up drive space:

- **Programs and Features:** Takes you to the Programs and Features window, where you can uninstall programs and Windows Features you don't use.

- **System Restore and Shadow Copies:** Deletes all restore points except the most recent one. This can be significant because system protection files are allowed to consume up to 15 percent of your available drive space.

 For more information on removing programs, see Chapter 27. For more information on restore points, see Chapter 19.

Defragmenting and optimizing your hard drive

When a drive is newly formatted, most of the free space on the drive is available in a contiguous chunk. This means the disk *clusters* (the smallest amount of storage space that can be allocated) are side-by-side in contiguous fashion. As Windows writes a file, it can do so in contiguous clusters, writing the entire file in one pass. When it reads the file back, it can also do so in one pass, making drive performance as good as possible.

However, the more a drive is used, the more fragmented the data becomes. Instead of writing data contiguously, Windows writes it here and there on the drive, splitting up the file into fragments (thus, the term *fragmentation*).

> **TIP**
>
> Data on solid-state hard drives isn't stored the same way it's stored on traditional hard drives. Because of this difference, fragmentation of data does not exist on solid-state drives, so defragmenting them is not necessary.

When that happens, the drive heads move around quite a bit to read and write files. You may even be able to hear the drive chattering when files get seriously fragmented across the drive. This movement puts extra stress on the mechanics of the drive and also slows it down a bit.

To get your drive running more smoothly, you can *defragment* (or *defrag* for short) the drive. When you do, Windows takes most of the files that are split up into little chunks and brings the pieces together to make each file contiguous again. It also moves most files to the beginning of the drive, where they're easiest to get to. The result is a drive that's no longer fragmented, doesn't chatter as much, and runs faster.

You don't need to defragment your drive too frequently; four or five times a year is probably sufficient. The process can take a few minutes or up to several hours, so consider running it overnight. However, note that Windows 10 automatically defragments the drive. You can view the current schedule, if any, in the Disk Defragmenter program.

> **TIP**
> You don't have to stop using the computer while Windows defragments the drive. You can continue to use it as you normally would. Doing so, however, continues to generate read/write operations on the drive, which ultimately slows the defragmentation process. For that reason, you should run the defragmentation operation while you are not using the computer. See Step 5 in the following list to choose the best time to run optimization.

To defragment a hard drive, follow these steps, starting at the desktop:

1. Open the This PC folder in File Explorer.
2. Right-click the icon for your hard drive (C:), and choose Properties.
3. In the Properties dialog box that opens, select the Tools tab.
4. Click the Optimize button. The Optimize Drives program opens, as shown in Figure 31.20.

> **TIP**
> When you see a message that says you don't need to defragment, that doesn't mean that you can't or shouldn't. It just means the drive isn't badly fragmented. But you can still defragment it.

5. In the Optimize Drives dialog box, you can set up a schedule to run the optimizer. Click Change Settings to establish that schedule. You also can click the Analyze button to get the current status of the drive and to see if an optimization process (defragmentation) would be beneficial. The program starts analyzing your drive and may take as little as a few minutes or as much as a few hours.
6. When the defragmentation is complete, the Current Status column shows an OK (0% Fragmented) message for the drive you optimized.

When you optimize the drive, the Disk Defragmenter tool defragments all the fragmented files and moves some frequently used files to the beginning of the drive, where they can be accessed in the least time with the least effort. Some files aren't moved. That's normal. If Windows decides to leave them where they are, it has a good reason.

FIGURE 31.20

The Optimize Drives applet.

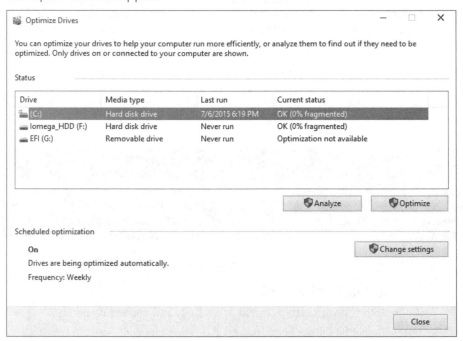

You may hear lots of drive chatter as Disk Defragmenter is working. That's because the drive heads are moving files around to get them into a better position for defragmentation.

When Disk Defragmenter is finished, close any open dialog boxes and the Disk Defragmenter program window.

The Power Settings

The power settings under Power Options in the Control Panel provide features that enable you to adjust the performance of your system while conserving energy. To get to the power options for your system, open the Control Panel. If the Control Panel opens in Category view, click the System and Security link. Then click the Power Options icon. The Power Options applet opens, as shown in Figure 31.21. Click the down arrow beside Show Additional Plans to show the High performance plan.

The Power Options applet provides the basic configuration for the power options on your system. The three plans listed — Balanced, Power Saver, and High Performance — are the default power plans for the system. You can alter the settings for the three default plans by either clicking the Change Plan Settings link beside the plan or, for the selected plan, clicking either Choose When to Turn Off the Display or Change When the Computer Sleeps from the left column. Clicking any of these links brings up the Edit Plan Settings dialog box shown in Figure 31.22.

FIGURE 31.21

The options for power settings for a powerful computer.

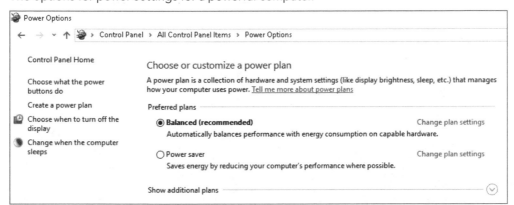

FIGURE 31.22

The basic options for setting the power conservation features of Windows 10 running on a powerful computer.

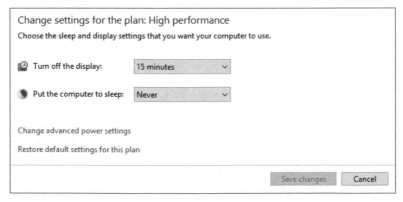

Adjusting either of these options alters the default plan you've selected. Clicking the Change Advanced Power Settings link brings up the Power Options dialog box, which includes the Advanced Settings tab shown in Figure 31.23.

With these options, you can drill down on individual options at a more advanced level. If you change something that you think you shouldn't have, you can click the Restore Default Settings for This Plan link to get back to where you were. Note that notebook computers have additional power options not typically available on desktops.

FIGURE 31.23

The Advanced Settings tab.

Create a power plan

If none of the default options meets your needs and you'd like to build your own power plan, click the third link on the left side of the Power Options applet, Create a power plan. Clicking this link brings up the window shown in Figure 31.24.

To make it easier, Windows lets you create your power plan from one of the three defaults. You also can name the plan on this page. After you've set the name of your plan, click Next. The next window allows you to set when you want to turn off the display and when you want to put the computer to sleep.

After you've configured these last two options, click the Create button. When you're back at the Power Options applet, your plan should be first on the list and selected. If you want to change some of the advanced options in your plans, click the Change Plan Settings link and then click Change Advanced Power Settings, as mentioned earlier in the chapter.

FIGURE 31.24

The first step to creating your own power plan.

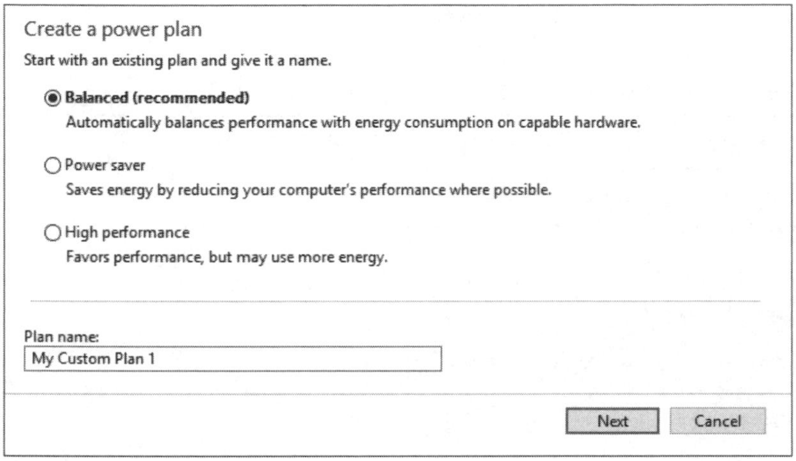

Create a power plan
Start with an existing plan and give it a name.

● **Balanced (recommended)**
  Automatically balances performance with energy consumption on capable hardware.

○ Power saver
  Saves energy by reducing your computer's performance where possible.

○ High performance
  Favors performance, but may use more energy.

Plan name:
My Custom Plan 1

[Next] [Cancel]

System settings

Choosing What the Power Button Does located at the left of the Power plan applet takes you to the System Settings page shown in Figure 31.25.

With older computers, when you pressed the power button, the system would power off. With current computers, the power buttons take on a different role. Under the first heading in this window, Power Button Settings, you determine what happens when the power button is pushed. You're given two options:

- **Do Nothing:** Nothing happens when you press the power button.
- **Sleep:** If you select this option, the data you're working on is stored in memory and to the hard drive. The system runs using very little power until you press a key on the keyboard or move the mouse. On a notebook computer, when Windows notices that the system is running low on battery power, Windows starts writing the information to the hard drive. Upon restarting, the system moves all the information from the hard drive to memory, just as the system was left originally. Usually, bringing the computer back from Sleep takes two to three seconds. Sleep mode is not limited to notebooks. Most newer desktop computers also support it.

- **Hibernate:** The computer shuts down but saves data to a disk in order to resume where it left off when you power back up.

- **Shut Down:** This selection shuts down the computer without saving any of the data you have in memory. Windows prompts you to save your work before you shut down. This method does a gradual shutdown of Windows.

- **Turn off the display:** This selection is mainly for laptops and handhelds. The display is turned off to conserve power.

FIGURE 31.25

Options for power buttons and password protection on a powerful computer.

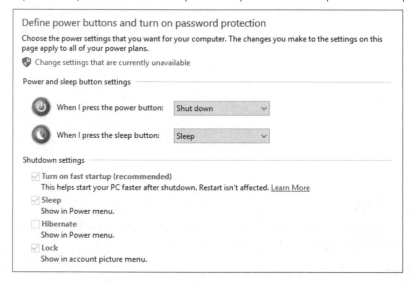

After you've decided which option you want, click the Save Changes button.

On the System Settings window, you also can set the password option for what happens when the computer wakes up. As indicated by the text next to each of the options, when your system wakes from Sleep, the user may be prompted for a password. Obviously, the more secure option is to use a password. However, if this is your home system and you're the only one with physical access to the system, the second option is good enough.

> **NOTE**
>
> The settings described in this section are the most common settings based on the hardware. For example, if you're using a laptop, you may have two additional or different options on the left side of the Power Options window: Choose What Closing the Lid Does and Choose What Power Buttons Do. These options are specific to the system and offer additional options for power management.

With all the power options available in Windows 10, you should be able to conserve resources on your system while still making your system very responsive. The power options probably benefit portable users more than desktop users.

Wrapping Up

The components of your computer system that most affect performance are its CPU and memory, but hard drive performance also affects overall system performance. (Internet access speed is determined primarily by the bandwidth of your Internet connection but can also be affected by slow system performance.) As an alternative to buying a faster computer, you can do some things to make your current computer run faster and keep it running at top speed. The main points in this chapter are as follows:

- The System Information program provides detailed information about all the components that make up your computer system.

- To ensure that your computer is responsive to your every mouse click and keyboard tap, Windows automatically prioritizes programs as foreground (high-priority) and background (low-priority) tasks.

- Windows automatically uses a portion of the hard drive as virtual memory to handle the overflow.

- ReadyBoost uses flash memory to store frequently accessed disk files to provide a faster, more fluid computing experience.

- If your computer is usually sluggish and unresponsive, consider turning off some of Windows 10's visual effects.

- The speed of your hard drive determines how long it takes to open and save files.

- To keep your hard drive running at top speed, consider deleting temporary files, scanning for and fixing bad sectors, and defragmenting the drive four or five times a year depending on how much time you spend at the computer.

- Power settings play a role in your system's overall performance and can also be adjusted to conserve power, especially when using a laptop.

Troubleshooting Hardware and Performance

IN THIS CHAPTER

Troubleshooting common hardware and device driver issues

Troubleshooting startup issues using System Recovery Options

Troubleshooting slow or unresponsive system performance

This chapter discusses the components of your computer and addresses some common problems and their solutions. Additionally, you'll find information for troubleshooting Bluetooth connectivity. Finally, we provide information for troubleshooting general performance issues.

First Aid for Troubleshooting Hardware

Whenever you have a hardware problem that's causing a device to misbehave or not work at all, finding an updated driver is usually your best bet. But before you do that, you may want to try Windows' built-in troubleshooting tools to see if they can resolve the problem.

To get help on programs, hardware, and drivers, you should open the Troubleshooting applet from the Control Panel (see Figure 32.1). After you have the applet open, you can click on a number of categories. Each of the items in this Control Panel applet provides a troubleshooting wizard that can automatically search for, detect, and potentially fix problems. The applet offers the following groups:

- **Programs:** Launch the Program Compatibility Troubleshooter, which enables you to apply settings to programs to make them run as if they were running in an earlier version of Windows. For example, you can potentially run a Windows XP program under Windows 10 by configuring its compatibility settings for Windows XP. This troubleshooting group also provides help for Internet Explorer issues, printer issues, and Media Player problems.

- **Hardware and Sound:** Use the Hardware and Sound item to scan for hardware changes and troubleshoot problems with general devices, printers, network adapters, and audio devices.

- **Network and Internet:** Troubleshoot problems connecting to the Internet or accessing shared files and folders on a local area network. Also troubleshoot HomeGroup and incoming network connections.

- **System and Security:** Troubleshoot problems with Windows Update, modify power settings, check for computer performance issues, and run maintenance tasks, including cleaning up unused files and shortcuts. Also, check search and indexing problems, and adjust performance settings.

FIGURE 32.1

The Troubleshooting applet provides options for troubleshooting hardware and driver issues.

The Troubleshooting applet lists only some of the items for each category. Click the group name (such as Hardware and Sound or Network and Internet) to see all the troubleshooting tools for that category. Figure 32.2, for example, shows the System and Security category.

FIGURE 32.2

The System and Security category.

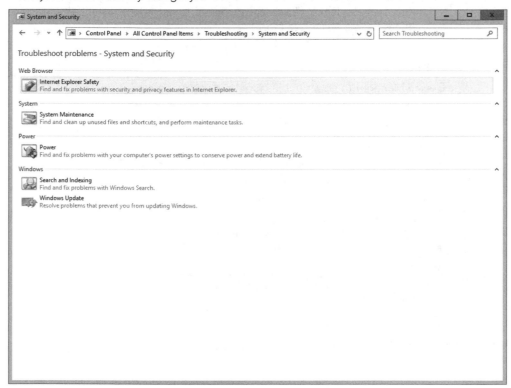

An alternative is to troubleshoot from the hardware device's Properties dialog box in Device Manager. To open Device Manager, press Windows+X and click Device Manager. You also can use Cortana to open it by typing **dev** and then clicking Device Manager. In Device Manager, follow these steps:

1. Right-click the name of the device that's causing problems and choose Properties.

2. If the device shows an error in the Device Manager (see Figure 32.3), use that information to begin troubleshooting. For example, if Device Manager indicates that no driver is installed, try installing or reinstalling the device's driver.

3. If necessary, use the options on the Driver tab to reinstall the drivers for the device. You can also disable the device from this tab and eliminate potential conflicts with other devices.

4. On the Resources tab (see Figure 32.4), check for a conflict message under Conflicting Device List and resolve problems by reassigning resources to the conflicting devices, or by disabling one of them. Note that not all hardware devices have a Resources tab.

FIGURE 32.3

Use Device Manager to help troubleshoot hardware problems.

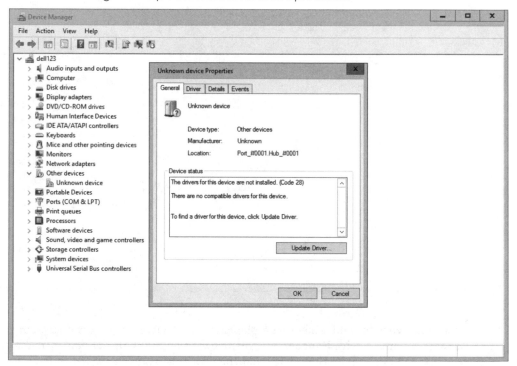

> **TIP**
> If you've made a hardware change but Windows hasn't noticed the change, open Device Manager and choose Action ⇨ Scan for Hardware Changes to have Windows rescan the system.

FIGURE 32.4

The Resources tab.

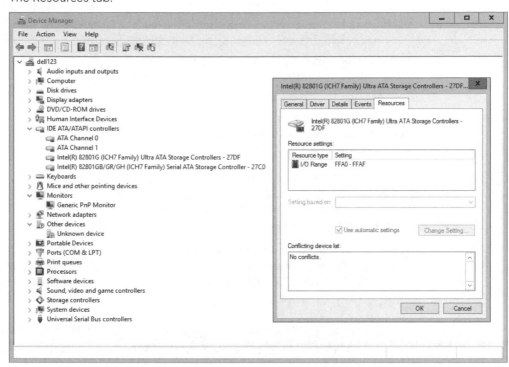

Dealing with Error Messages

Error messages come in all forms, from simple warnings to the *stop errors* and the blue
screen of death, which causes the computer to stop dead in its tracks. If you were a user
of Windows 8.1, you more than likely saw a decrease in the number of blue screen events.
In Windows 10, that same pattern will more than likely follow — Windows 10 seems to be a
stable operating system.

The more serious errors are often accompanied by one or more of the following pieces of information:

- **An error number:** An error number is often a hexadecimal number in the format 0x00000*xxx*, where the *xxx* can be any numbers in the message.
- **Symbolic error name:** Symbolic error names are usually shown in all uppercase with underlines between words, such as PAGE_FAULT_IN_NONPAGED_AREA.
- **Driver details:** If a device driver caused the problem, you may see a filename with a .sys extension in the error message.
- **Troubleshooting info:** Some errors have their own built-in troubleshooting advice or a Help button. Use that information to learn more about what went wrong.

Whenever you get an error message about a problem that you can't solve by reading the advice presented on the screen, go to http://support.microsoft.com. Search there for the error number, the symbolic error name, the driver name, or some combination of words in the text of the error message.

If searching Microsoft's support site doesn't do the trick, consider searching the Internet using Google or Bing. You never know — someone else may have had the same problem and posted the solution. When using a search engine, provide as much detail as possible to get the best results.

TIP

Oddly, a Google search often turns up pages on Microsoft's support site that can be difficult to find when searching at the Microsoft site. You can include "site:support.microsoft.com" in the search criteria in Google to help narrow your search results to the Microsoft Support site.

Performing a Clean Boot

The biggest problem with hardware errors is that even a tiny error can have seemingly catastrophic results, such as suddenly shutting down the system and making a restart difficult. Clean booting can help with software problems that prevent the computer from starting normally or cause frequent errors.

Not for the technologically challenged, this procedure is best left to more experienced users who can use it to diagnose the source of a problem that prevents the computer from starting normally. The procedure for performing a clean boot is as follows:

> **NOTE**
>
> A clean boot is not the same as a clean install. During a clean boot, you may temporarily lose some normal function-ality. But after you perform a normal startup, you should regain access to all your programs and documents, and full functionality.

1. Close all open programs and save any work in progress.
2. At the Windows desktop, press Windows+X, click Run, and enter **msconfig**.
3. The System Configuration tool opens, as shown in Figure 32.5.

FIGURE 32.5

System Configuration.

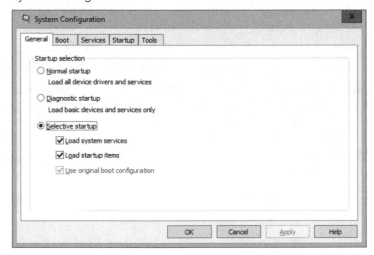

4. On the General tab, choose Selective Startup and make sure the Load Startup Items check box is cleared.
5. Click the Services tab.
6. Select Hide All Microsoft Services and click the Disable All button.
7. Click OK.
8. Click the Restart button.

To return to normal startup after diagnosis, open the System Configuration tool. On the Services tab, click Enable All. On the General tab, choose Normal Startup and click OK.

Using the System Recovery Options

For more severe problems that require repairing an existing Windows 10 installation, troubleshooting startup issues, performing system and complete PC restoration, using the Windows Memory Diagnostic Tool, or getting to a command prompt, you need to use the System Recovery Options. This method should be used only by experienced users who can perform such tasks from a command prompt.

To boot from the Windows disk, first make sure that the drive is enabled as a boot device in the BIOS with a higher priority than any hard drives. Insert the Windows disk into the drive. Restart the computer and follow these steps:

1. During the POST, watch for the Press Any Key to Boot From CD or DVD prompt, and press a key.

2. After all files load from the disk, click the Next button on the page that is prompting for language, currency, and keyboard type.

3. On the next page, click the Repair Your Computer link near the bottom of the page.

4. On the resulting page, choose Troubleshoot, reset your PC, or see advanced options.

5. Windows opens the System Recovery Options dialog box, which looks for an existing installation of Windows 10. If your system requires special hard drive controller drivers, you can click the Load Drivers button so your installation of Windows 10 can be located. If you see your version of Windows 10 in the list box, select it and click the Next button.

6. The next window shows all your options for recovery.

The Troubleshooting/Advanced window provides troubleshooting tools based on your set of circumstances:

- **Startup Repair:** Use this option if your system won't start. This may happen for any number of reasons, including a bad or misconfigured driver, an application that attempts to start at startup but causes the system to hang, or a faulty piece of hardware.

- **System Restore:** System Restore restores to a designated restore point. By default, Windows makes restore points of your computer (see Chapter 19 for more information on Windows restore points) that store the state of your system. You can choose a restore point for your system from a previous day when you know your system was performing correctly. The System Restore option doesn't alter any of your personal data or documents.

- **System Image Recovery:** For this feature to work, you need to have done a backup in the past. Windows searches hard drives and DVDs for valid backups from which to restore. See Chapter 19 for information on backing up your system.

- **Windows Memory Diagnostic:** Some of the issues you are experiencing may be the result of memory problems. Windows Memory Diagnostic Tool performs tests against the RAM in your system to check for problems. To run this tool, click the link, which prompts you to restart your computer now and check for problems or to check for problems the next time you restart.

- **Command Prompt:** The Command Prompt option is for experienced users who need to access the file system and run commands specific to Windows 10. Choose this option only if you're sure you need it.

When you're finished using the System Recovery Options, you can click either Restart or Exit to exit. For additional information on System Recovery Options, use Help and Support and search on "System Recovery Options."

Troubleshooting Performance Problems

This section covers basic troubleshooting in terms of using Task Manager and Control Panel tools to monitor and troubleshoot performance. Keep in mind that hardware and software go hand in hand, so performance problems can be caused by either one. For example, a device that is malfunctioning or improperly configured can lead to performance problems. Likewise, having too many programs running at one time can eat up valuable memory and processor time, also foiling performance. So, don't assume that performance problems are always caused by hardware or software — the problem may well be one, the other, or both.

If your CPU Usage chart consistently runs at a high percentage in Task Manager, it may point to the running of two or more firewalls. Most likely, you need to disable and remove any third-party firewalls, or disable the built-in Windows Firewall.

Also, scan your system for viruses, adware, and other malware, and remove all that you can find to eliminate their resource consumption.

If neither of the previous suggestions fixes your problem, you may need to see if an individual process is keeping your system overly busy. To do this, use one of these methods to start Task Manager:

- With Windows running and while logged on to the computer, press Ctrl+Alt+Del and click Start Task Manager.
- Press Windows+X, click Run, and type **taskmgr** to locate and start Task Manager.
- Right-click the taskbar and click Start Task Manager.

Once you're in Task Manager, click More Details, and select the Processes tab. Next, sort the CPU column, as shown in Figure 32.6. Just click the CPU column to sort by CPU utilization.

> **TIP**
>
> If a task is spiking CPU utilization but not staying at a consistently high rate, first identify the processes by sorting by CPU. Then, when you've determined which processes are using the most CPU time, sort by process name to watch how those processes are using the CPU.

You should be able to identify the process that is using the majority of your CPU. You have a couple of options at this point:

- Use the name of the process under the Name column to search the Internet to see if the process is a valid file or a potential virus. If it is a virus of some form, you need to update your virus definitions and rerun your virus scan. If it does not appear to be a virus, contact the software vendor for help troubleshooting the problem.

- In the short term, you can right-click the process and choose End Task. Sometimes applications run into situations the developer never imagined and the process gets stuck in a loop, which taxes the CPU. Restarting the application resets the process, and with any luck, you'll avoid the circumstances that put the application in a loop.

FIGURE 32.6

Task Manager sorting the processes based on CPU percentage.

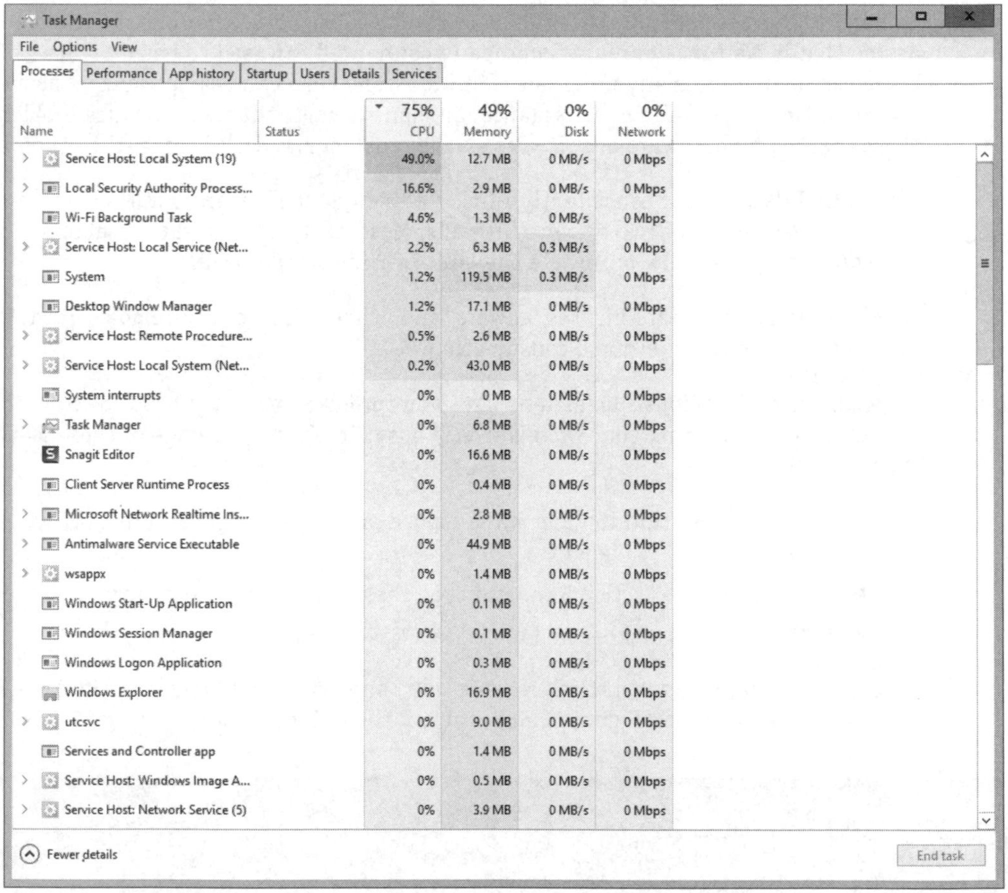

Wrapping Up

Many thousands of hardware devices are available to use with Windows, and no single rule applies to troubleshooting all of them. So, you'll likely have to consider all your resources. Be sure to check the manual that came with the hardware device first. If that doesn't work, the device manufacturer's website is your next best bet.

32

Part VIII

Networking and Sharing

Creating a Small Office or Home Network

I f you have two or more computers, you may already be using what's known as a *sneaker network*. For example, to get files from one computer to another, you copy files to a flash drive or CD. Then, you walk over to the other computer and copy the files from the disk to that computer. Wouldn't it be nice if you could drag icons from one computer to the other without using a flash drive or CD?

What if you have several computers, but only one printer, one Internet connection, or one DVD burner? Wouldn't it be nice if all the computers could use that one printer, that one Internet connection, and that one DVD burner? All these things are possible if you connect the computers to one another in a *local area network* (LAN) or a private wireless network (Wi-Fi).

After you've purchased and installed networking hardware, you're ready to set up your network. Windows 10 includes features that remove the complexities commonly associated with network configurations.

This chapter describes how to configure Windows for different types of hardware setups. Remember that you should always follow the instructions that came with your networking hardware first. After all, those instructions are written for the exact products you've purchased.

What Is a LAN?

A *local area network* (sometimes referred to as a LAN, a *workgroup*, a *private network*, or just a *network*) is a small group of computers within a relatively small geographic area such as a campus, single building, or household that can communicate with one another and share *resources*. A resource is anything useful to the computer. For example:

- All computers in the LAN can use a single printer.
- All computers in the LAN can connect to the Internet through a single Internet connection and Internet account.
- All computers in the LAN can access shared files and folders on any other computer in the LAN.

In addition, you can move and copy files and folders among computers using exactly the same techniques you use to move and copy files among folders on a single computer. However, you don't need to move or copy a document that you want to work on, because if a document is in a shared folder, you can open and edit it from any computer in the network. This is good because you have only one copy of the document, and you don't have to worry about having multiple, slightly different copies of the same document.

Planning a LAN

To create a LAN, you need a plan and special hardware to make that plan work. For one thing, each computer needs a device known as a *network interface card* (NIC) or *Ethernet card*. You can purchase and install those yourself. Many PCs, however, come with an Ethernet card already installed for connecting to a wired network. In that case, you have an RJ-45 port on the back of the computer. It looks like the plug for a telephone, but is a little bigger. Plug one end of an Ethernet cable into that port, and plug the other end of the cable into a network hub or wall jack. You can also connect computers without any cables at all by using wireless networking hardware. Exactly what you need, in terms of hardware, depends on what you want to do. This chapter describes your options.

Creating a Wired LAN

If you have two or more computers to connect, and they're in the same room and close to one another, you can use a traditional Ethernet switch and Ethernet cables to connect the computers with cables. You need exactly one NIC and one Ethernet cable for each computer in the LAN. Figure 33.1 shows an example of four computers connected in a traditional LAN. Notice how each computer connects to the hub only — no cables run directly from one computer to another computer.

By the way, in Figure 33.1, a printer can be connected to any computer on the LAN. In fact, you can have several printers connected to several computers. All computers can use all printers, no matter which computer that printer is (or those printers are) connected to. In addition, a printer with a network interface need not be connected to a computer at all, but rather can be connected directly to the network.

FIGURE 33.1

Four computers connected in a traditional Ethernet LAN.

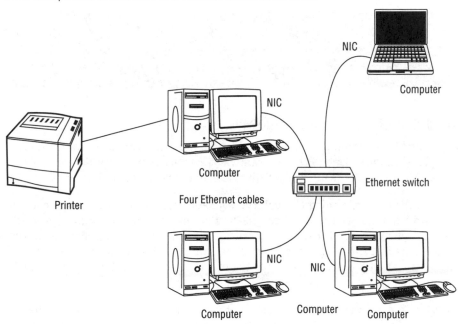

Traditional Ethernet speeds

When the time comes to purchase network interface cards, cables, and a switch, you need to decide on the speed you want. As with most things in the computer industry, network speed costs money. However, in the case of networks, the cost differences are minor, whereas the speed differences are huge. The three possible speeds for Ethernet LANs are listed in Table 33.1.

TABLE 33.1   Common Ethernet Network Component Speeds

Name	Transfer Rate (speed)	Bits per Second	Cable
10Base-T	10 Mbps	10 million	Category 3 or better
100Base-T	100 Mbps	100 million	Category 5 or better
Gigabit Ethernet	1 Gbps	1,000 million (billion)	Category 6 or better

To relate the numbers to actual transfer rates, consider a dial-up modem, which tops out at about 50 Kbps. That's 51,000 bits per second. A 100Base-T network moves 100,000,000 bits per second. That's 2,000 times faster; you only have to wait 1/2,000 as long for the same file to transfer across a 100Base-T connection. So, a file that takes 33 minutes (2,000 seconds) to transfer over a dial-up modem takes 1 second to transfer over a 100Base-T network.

> **TIP**
>
> You can set up a 10 Gbps network that operates at ten times the speed of a 1 Gbps network. However, 10 Gbps network hardware is still generally much more expensive than 1 Gbps hardware, making it a less likely candidate for a home or small office network. For that reason, we don't cover 10 Gbps networks in this chapter.

The slowest component rules

When purchasing hardware, understand that the slowest component always rules. For example, if you get gigabit Ethernet cards, but connect them to a 100Base-T hub, the LAN runs at 100 Mbps. The faster gigabit NICs can't force the slower hub to move any faster.

Envision the electrons going through the wire as cars on a freeway. Lots of cars are zooming down a ten-lane freeway, but the freeway narrows to one lane because of road construction. Cars pile up behind that point because the one-lane portion is slowing traffic. Where the one lane reopens back to ten lanes, cars trickle out of the *bottleneck* — the single lane — one at a time. The ten lanes at the other side of the bottleneck can't "suck the cars through" the bottleneck any faster than one car at a time.

Likewise, if your computers are connected together with a gigabit LAN, but they all share a single 512 Kbps broadband connection to the Internet, your Internet connection is still 512 Kbps. Your fast LAN can't force the data from your ISP to get to your computer any faster than 512 Kbps. Furthermore, if two people are using the 512 Kbps broadband connection at the same time, they have to share the available bandwidth, meaning that each user may get only a portion of the available bandwidth. But if only one person is online, she gets the full 512 Kbps because she isn't sharing bandwidth with anyone else.

> **NOTE**
>
> If you have only two computers to connect, and each has an Ethernet card, you don't need a switch. Instead, you can connect the two computers directly using an Ethernet *crossover cable*. However, this technique doesn't enable the computers to connect to anything other than one another.

Creating a Wireless Network

Wireless networking reigns supreme when it comes to convenience and ease of use. As the name implies, with wireless networks you don't have to run any cables. Additionally, no computer is tied down to any one cable. For example, you can use your notebook computer in any room in the house, or even out on the patio, and still have Internet access without being tied to a cable.

To set up a wireless network, you need a wireless NIC for each computer that you want to connect using wireless. To set up an ad-hoc wireless network, that's all you need. The computers can communicate with each other, so long as they're within range of one another. If you want Internet connectivity for all the computers in a wireless LAN, you need some kind of access point that acts as a central location for all the computers and also provides an Internet connection. Typically, that device is a wireless broadband router, as illustrated in Figure 33.2.

FIGURE 33.2

Four computers connected in a wireless network.

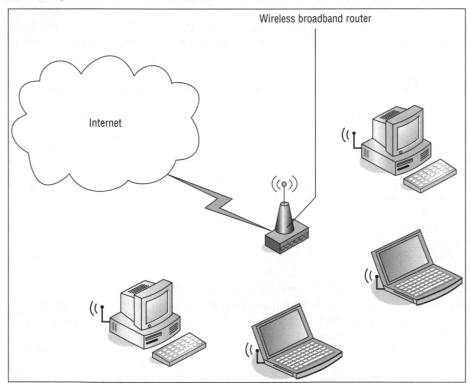

33

Wireless broadband router

The big advantage of wireless networking is, of course, the lack of cables. This is especially handy on a notebook computer or handheld device because the device isn't tethered to one location by a cable. Granted, you can't stray too far from the wireless access point (100 to 150 feet or so), but that is sufficient in most cases.

Also, many universities and retail businesses offer public Internet access from any computer that has an 802 class (802.11b, 802.11g, 802.11n, 802.11ac and so on) wireless network interface. So, if you create your home wireless network using one of those standards, you-can use public Wi-Fi Internet access where it's available.

> **TIP**
>
> The only disadvantages to wireless networking, as compared to wired networks, are speed and reliability. 802.11 ac wireless networks run at a theoretical max of 54 Mbps. It isn't as fast as the 100 Mbps or 1 Gbps speeds of traditional Ethernet cables, but it's more than fast enough for typical networking tasks. Reliability isn't a problem with the technology. Instead, the problem has to do with the rare "blind spot" here and there where the computer can't connect to the network because the signal is blocked or out of range.

Wireless networks are built around four different standards. Table 33.2 summarizes the main differences between the four most common standards in use today. The Public Access column refers to Internet Wi-Fi hotspots such as those found at some airports, hotels, and other places.

TABLE 33.2 Wireless Networking Standards and Speeds

Standard	Speed	Range	Public Access
802.11b	11 Mbps	100–150 feet	Yes
802.11a	54 Mbps	25–75 feet	No
802.11g	54 Mbps	100–150 feet	Yes
802.11n	600 Mbps	150–300 feet	Yes
802.11ac	1733 Mbps	150–300 feet	Yes

In most cases, when setting up your network you're really setting up *two* networks. The first network involves the computer-to-computer communication. This includes the wireless setup or a wired setup discussed earlier in the chapter. The second network is the Internet. Connecting to the Internet involves some form of an ISP. Today, two of the most popular methods are digital subscriber line (DSL) modem connections and (more likely) broadband connections, which your cable TV company may be able to supply. If you're sharing an Internet connection, one device in your network has physical access to the Internet, and the other computers share the connection. The one device that sees the Internet can be a computer, or you can purchase an inexpensive device called a *broadband router*.

Other useful wireless goodies

If you already have a wired network with Internet connectivity and you simply want to add some wireless computers to that network, you don't need a wireless broadband router. Instead, you need a *wireless access point* (WAP). First, configure the WAP, as per the manufacturer's instructions, by connecting it directly to one of the computers in your wired network. Then you can disconnect the WAP from the computer and connect it directly to the switch for your wireless network. The wireless computer can use the same shared Internet connection that the wired network uses.

Getting a wireless network to cover a whole house can be a challenge, especially if you have two or more floors. If you want to extend Wi-Fi to the entire house, you may need to use one or more *wireless range expanders* to extend the reach of the network. Putting one near a staircase is a good idea when you need to reach upstairs or downstairs. You can also use multiple access points to achieve the same results.

A Wi-Fi finder can also be helpful. It's a small device (small enough to fit on a keychain) that measures the strength of a wireless network signal wherever you're standing. It can help you determine where the edge of a signal is. That's a good place to put a range expander to get more coverage.

Acquiring and Installing Network Hardware

Almost all PCs manufactured in the last several years have networking capability built in. So, most likely you needn't buy NICs for your devices. If you need one for a desktop PC and you aren't comfortable installing it, buy a USB network adapter. If you aren't sure, check with your local PC dealer.

If you're new to networking and you want to see what some of this hardware looks like, here are some websites you can visit. They're all network hardware manufacturers, not retailers:

- **D-Link:** www.d-link.com
- **GigaFast:** www.gigafast.com
- **Linksys:** http://www.linksys.com/en-us/home
- **Netgear:** www.netgear.com
- **SMC Networks:** www.smc.com
- **TRENDnet:** www.trendnet.com

In terms of actually purchasing the products, you can find these products at any store that sells computer supplies, including many of the large office supply chains such as Staples and OfficeMax. In addition, you can buy the devices at any website that sells computer products. Shopping jaunts include websites such as www.amazon.com, www.cdw.com, www.cyberguys.com, www.officemax.com, www.staples.com, www.tigerdirect.com, and www.walmart.com, just to name a few.

After you've acquired the hardware, you need to install it. Follow the manufacturer's instructions because each piece of hardware has its own installation requirements. In general, you'll probably follow these steps:

- Get the hub or router (if any) set up first.
- Install the network interface cards second.
- Connect all the cables last.

Once all the hardware is connected and installed, you're ready to set up the network. That part isn't very complicated because Windows does a great job of searching out networks. The next section gets you started.

After the Hardware Setup

A couple of steps are involved in setting up the networking hardware. First, make sure that the hardware you purchased is installed according to the manufacturer's instructions. This procedure may include plugging in the device, then connecting the device to the Internet, and finally plugging in the other computers to the device. When these steps are complete, you can run the Set Up a New Connection or Network Wizard to let Windows finish the process.

> **CAUTION**
>
> Read and follow the network hardware manufacturer's instructions carefully before you configure your network. If you find any conflict between what they say and what's stated in this chapter, do as the manufacturer's instructions say. Failure to do so can lead to many hours of hair-pulling frustration!

Close any open programs and documents before you start configuring your network. The type of network hardware you have set up determines what configuration you need to use. Here's where to look, depending on your network configuration:

- **If you have an Ethernet network, and you're using a modem inside of, or connected to, one computer in the network,** you can use Internet connection sharing

(ICS) to share a single Internet account. Because this scenario is no longer common, we don't cover it in this book. Search the web for "Internet connection sharing" for details.

- **If you have a router or residential gateway that all computers in your network connect to,** each computer will have its own direct access to the Internet via the router. See the section "Setting Up a Wired Network" later in this chapter.

- **If you have a wireless network,** see the section "Setting Up a Wireless Network" later in this chapter.

- If you want to set up a Bluetooth personal area network, see Chapter 30.

> **NOTE**
> In the past, the term *residential gateway* typically referred to relatively low-cost networking devices that combined most or all of the devices needed to connect a LAN to a wide area network (WAN) such as the Internet. Today, the term is used to describe essentially the same type of device, but today's gateways offer much more capability. An example of a residential gateway is a cable modem that includes a hub and provides everything you need to connect your LAN to a cable-based Internet service. Another example is a wireless access point that includes a hub and integrated DSL modem. This chapter uses the term *gateway* to refer to the device that connects your LAN to your Internet service. If you are not sure what you need to connect your LAN to the Internet, check with your local computer store.

Be sure to turn off all computers before you install the networking hardware (unless you're installing a USB adapter). Then install all the networking hardware and turn on all the computers. Chances are, Windows 10 will detect the hardware and start the setup automatically. If you see any prompts asking what type of network you're installing, specify that it's a *private* network (not a public network). When asked about file sharing, make choices that allow for file and printer sharing among computers in the private network.

With those buzzwords and tips in mind, let's move on to the things to do after you get all the network hardware in place and all the computers turned on.

Setting Up a Wired Network

With a wired network, your first step after setting up the hardware and connecting the PCs to the hub (or gateway device that contains the hub) is usually to get online from one computer. To do that, refer to the instructions that came with your router, as well as your ISP's instructions. In a typical scenario, you configure the router or gateway to automatically assign an IP address, default gateway address, and DNS addresses to your computers. Then you configure your devices for automatic address assignment. The computers then should receive their addresses (you generally don't reboot them) and have access to the network and the Internet.

33

TIP

Although the computers on the network should have access to the Internet at this point, they don't necessarily have access to one another's resources such as files and printers. Instead, you need to configure sharing. See Chapter 39 to learn how to set up your computers to share resources.

After connecting and configuring your PCs, Windows attempts to find the network for you. To check your connection status, follow these steps:

1. Open the Control Panel.

2. If the Control Panel opens in Category view, click the Network and Internet icon.

3. Open the View Network Status and Tasks link below Network and Sharing Center.

   As shown in Figure 33.3, the system is connected to a local network with access to the Internet.

4. If the connection doesn't show Internet as the access type, check the gateway configuration and make sure the settings are correct.

In Figure 33.3, Windows sees the local network and also sees the Internet connection from the local network. If your networking hardware is configured correctly, Windows sees the network and sets it up appropriately.

You can see your connection status on the task bar, although with less detail. The best thing to do for complete access to all your network connections is to open the Network & Internet applet from Settings. Figure 33.4 shows this applet.

FIGURE 33.3

A computer connected to the network and also connected to the Internet.

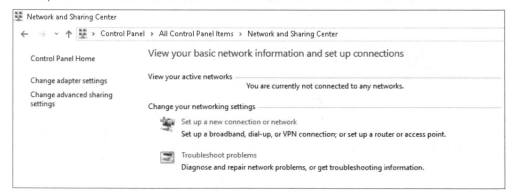

FIGURE 33.4

View the network status.

If your network is configured correctly for the first computer, try configuring your next system on the network using the steps outlined earlier.

If you have wireless devices that you want to connect to the network, follow the instructions in the next section.

Setting Up a Wireless Network

Something about the term *wireless* makes it seem as though it must be easier than *wired*. In truth, wireless networking is quite a bit more complicated, terminology-wise. Wireless involves lots of buzzwords and acronyms that everyone assumes you already know. So, before we get very far into this topic, let's get the terminology out of the way.

The 802.11 standard

The Institute of Electrical and Electronics Engineers, Inc., abbreviated IEEE (pronounced eye-triple-E), is an organization of some 360,000 electrical engineers who develop many of the standards that PC products use to interact with one another. The IEEE isn't big on fancy names. They prefer numbers (which somehow seems fitting). Names often get tacked on later. For example, what is now called *Ethernet* is actually IEEE 802.3. What Apple calls FireWire and Sony calls iLink is actually IEEE 1394.

> **NOTE**
> The home page for IEEE is at `www.ieee.org`.

IEEE created the 802.11 standard for most wireless networking today. Several revisions to the original specification have been proposed, with 802.11a, 802.11b, 802.11g, and 802.11n being the most common (802.22 ac is the latest standard in use). Most likely, you'll use 802.11g or 802.11n or 802.11 ac because they're the standards to which most of the recently released wireless networking products adhere.

Access point, SSID, WEP, and WPA

Wireless networking requires some kind of *wireless access point,* also called a *base station.* The base station is the central unit with which all computers in the network communicate. It's the same idea as a hub in Ethernet networking. The difference is that wireless networking has no wires connecting computers to the access point. Instead, each computer has a wireless network interface card (NIC), as illustrated in Figure 33.5.

The access point in a wireless network plays the same role as the hub in a wired network: All traffic goes to the access point first and is passed on to the appropriate destination from there. The problem is that wireless networks transmit radio waves, which aren't confined to the inside of a wire. Radio waves go all over, the same as when you throw a rock into the water and waves spread out in a circle.

The radio waves can be a problem when multiple wireless networks are close to each other. For example, say that a company has several departments, and each department has its own, separate wireless network.

To avoid that problem, you need a way to discriminate among multiple wireless access points. For example, you need some means of setting rules such as "these six computers in the marketing department communicate only with each other through access point X, and these 12 computers in the accounting department communicate with each other only through access point Z." The way you do that in today's wireless networking is through configuring network resources such as network names, SSID, WEP, and WPA.

About SSIDs

Every wireless network has a unique name called a *service set identifier (SSID),* or just a *wireless network name* for simplicity. The access point in the network holds the SSID. When you start a wireless network computer, it scans the airwaves for SSID. When you set up a wireless network access point (by reading the manufacturer's instructions, of course), you assign an SSID to your access point.

FIGURE 33.5

Wireless communications all go through an access point or base station.

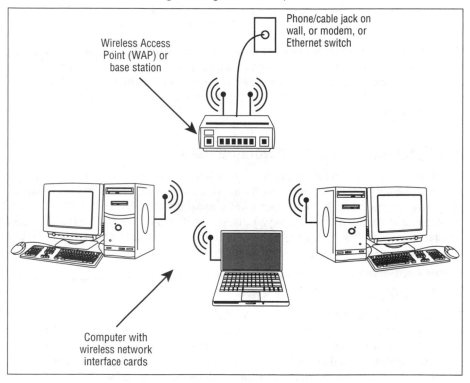

Wireless Access Point (WAP) or base station

Phone/cable jack on wall, or modem, or Ethernet switch

Computer with wireless network interface cards

TIP
You can configure a WAP to not broadcast its SSID, which adds an extra measure of security for your wireless network. Rather than search for available wireless networks, you have to manually specify the network SSID when setting up the wireless connection on your device.

The name you assign doesn't have to be anything fancy, but it should be distinctive enough to avoid conflict with any close neighbors who also have wireless networks. The SSID doesn't provide much network security. After all, the access point broadcasts the SSID out some distance from the access point. So, if some hackers happened to be driving by with a notebook computer, they might be able to pick up the name of your wireless LAN from the car. Then they could join your network and receive data being sent by computers in your network. WEP and WPA are encryption tools designed to avoid such intrusions.

About WEP and WPA

Wired Equivalent Privacy (WEP) is a wireless security protocol that protects wireless network data from falling into the wrong hands. Before any information leaves your computer, it's encrypted using a WEP key. The key is a simple string of characters that you can generate automatically or have Windows generate for you.

Wi-Fi Protected Access (WPA) is a newer and stronger encryption system that supports modern EAP security devices such as smart cards, certificates, token cards, one-time passwords, and biometric devices. WPA2 adds support for the AES encryption algorithm, which provides better security than WPA. If your wireless devices support WPA2, you should use that, rather than WPA.

Installing the wireless networking hardware

The most critical step in setting up a wireless network is installing the hardware devices. You must follow the instructions that came with the device to the letter. In particular, note that even devices that plug into a hot-pluggable port such as USB devices or a PC Card require you to install drives *before* you install the hardware device. That's unusual for hot-pluggable devices. Most people assume that they can plug in the device and go, but wireless networking devices don't work that way.

Connecting to available networks

The main trick to wireless networking is setting up the access point. Typically, you do this by configuring one computer with a static IP address and connecting it to the access point with a wired connection. With both the computer and WAP on the same IP subnet, you can then open a browser and connect to the WAP's web-based configuration pages. Then you configure the access point from that computer. You give the network its name (SSID) and choose your encryption method. The access point then begins transmitting that name at regular intervals.

On any computer that's to join the wireless LAN, you install a wireless network adapter. A notebook computer most likely has an internal card. On a desktop computer, you can install an internal wireless network adapter, or connect one to a USB port.

After you've installed the network adapter, you're ready to connect to the wireless network. If you're working from the Windows 10 interface, open Settings. Then click or tap the

Network & Internet link to view a list of available networks. Click or tap the connection you want to use and then click or tap Connect. If the connection requires you to enter a passphrase, type the passphrase and click or tap Next to connect to the network.

If you need to change network properties, press open Control Panel and go to Network and Sharing Center. Select Change adapter settings. Right-click the connection and select properties as shown in Figure 33.6.

FIGURE 33.6

Wireless Network Properties allow you to configure the connection.

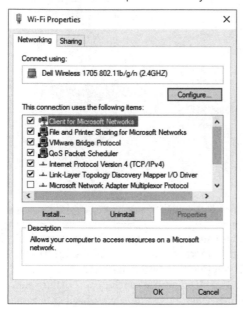

To configure the connection, click the Configure button. The next dialog box to load lets you configure the device as shown in Figure 33.7.

When you've finished, you're ready to move on to Chapter 34, where you learn to share resources and use those shared resources from any computer in the network.

FIGURE 33.7

Configure a wireless network connection.

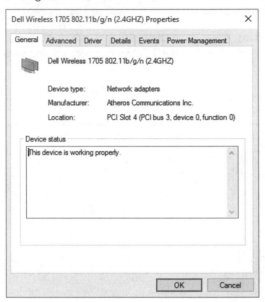

Wrapping Up

A LAN consists of two or more computers that can communicate with one another through networking hardware. Multiple computers in a network can share a single Internet account, printers, and files and folders. Moving and copying files among networked computers is a simple matter of dragging and dropping. No fumbling around with CDs or other removable disks is required. The main points to remember when buying network hardware are as follows:

- The first step in creating a LAN is to purchase the computer networking hardware.
- Each computer in the network must have a NIC installed.
- Ethernet LANs provide the fastest speeds but require running special Ethernet cables.
- Wireless networking provides complete freedom from cables and wires.
- USB networking devices are easy to install and don't require opening the computer case.
- On a notebook computer, you can use a PC Card NIC (not to be confused with a PCI card), USB NIC, or an integrated wireless network card to connect to the network.
- After you acquire your network hardware, you have to set it all up per the manufacturer's instructions. When you've finished that step, you can use the Network and Sharing Center to help configure the hardware.

Sharing Resources on a Network

IN THIS CHAPTER

Understanding your options for sharing

Getting acquainted with homegroups

Turning on sharing and discovery

Sharing media, printers, and folders

A local area network (LAN) consists of two or more computers connected through some sort of networking hardware. In a LAN, you can use *shared resources* from other computers in much the same way as you use local resources on your own computer. In fact, the way you do things in a LAN is almost identical to the way you do things on a single computer.

For example, everything you learned about printing documents on your own computer earlier in this book works just as well for printing on a network printer. Opening a document on some other computer in a network is no different from opening a document on your own computer.

Before you can access shared resources, however, you need to share them. You have more than one method for sharing resources, and this chapter covers those methods. Before getting into the particulars of resource sharing, the following section takes a quick look at some terminology.

Some Networking Buzzwords

Networking has its own set of buzzwords. All the buzzwords you learned in earlier chapters still apply, but you have some new words to learn, as defined here:

- **Resource:** Items you use on the network, including a folder, shared media, a printer, or other device.
- **Shared resource:** A resource accessible to other users within a network. A shared folder is often referred to as a *share* or a *network share*.
- **Local computer:** The computer you're currently using.

- **Local resource:** A folder, printer, or other useful thing on the local computer or directly connected to the local computer. For example, if a printer is connected to your computer by a cable, it's a local resource (or more specifically, a *local printer*).

- **Remote computer:** Any computer in the network other than the one you're currently using.

- **Remote resource:** A folder, printer, or other useful thing on some computer other than the local computer. For example, a printer connected to someone else's computer on the network is a remote resource (or more specifically, a *remote printer*).

Figure 34.1 shows an example of how the terms *local* and *remote* are always used in reference to the computer you're currently using.

FIGURE 34.1

Examples of local and remote resources, from your perspective.

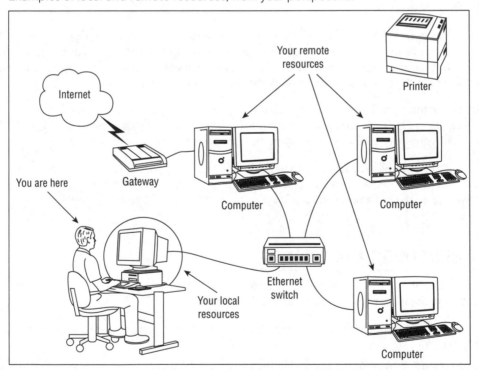

Methods for Sharing in Windows 10

Windows 10 includes three methods for sharing resources, each of which has its own advantages. The following sections explain these different methods.

Homegroups

Homegroups were first introduced as a feature in Windows 7 designed to simplify resource sharing and access for home networks. Homegroups are also available with Windows 10. The first Windows 7, Windows 8/8.1, or Windows 10 computer added to a network creates the homegroup, and then other Windows 7, Windows 8/8.1, or Windows 10 computers on that same network can join the homegroup. After your computer becomes part of the homegroup, you have access to the resources shared by the other computers in the homegroup. (See "Windows 10 Homegroups," later in this chapter, to learn how to create and join a homegroup.)

When you use a homegroup for sharing, you specify which folders you want to share. You can share those folders with either read or read/write permissions with the rest of the homegroup. You can also set permissions on a per-user basis to allow one person to access a folder or file but not others.

Only Windows 7, Windows 8/8.1, Windows Storage Server 2008 R2 Essentials (and even Windows Storage Server 2008) and Windows 10 computers can participate in a homegroup. A computer running any edition of Windows from version 7 through Windows 10 as well as Windows Storage Server 2008 R2 Essentials can join a homegroup, but computers running Windows 7 Home Basic and Windows 7 Starter can only join a homegroup, not create one.

> **NOTE**
> Computers in a homegroup need not belong to the same workgroup.

Workgroup

Although homegroups are a great new way to share resources in a network, only the Windows 7 through Windows 10 computers on the network can participate. Computers running other versions of Windows cannot participate in the homegroup. In these situations, you can use workgroups to share resources on the network.

A Windows PC, regardless of the version of Windows it's running, must be a member of either a workgroup or a domain (covered in the next section). A workgroup isn't a boundary that controls security. Instead, workgroups provide a means for organizing and discovering resources on the network.

The default workgroup name in Windows is, not surprisingly, Workgroup. Computers that share the same workgroup name and reside on the same network segment appear grouped together when you browse the network. Figure 34.2 shows a workgroup.

FIGURE 34.2

Browsing a workgroup for shared resources.

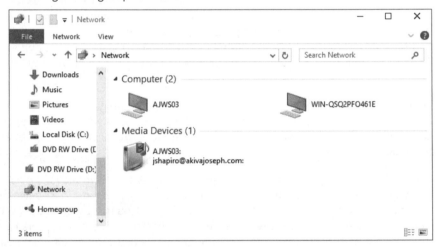

To access shared resources in a workgroup, you must have an account on the computer that is sharing the resource. Assuming a small home network of three computers and the desire to access resources on each one, this means that either you need to have your own account on each computer or you create a common account on each computer that everyone uses for sharing resources.

Domain

In a domain environment, one or more domain controllers running Windows Server host all user accounts in a centralized directory called Active Directory (AD). Typically, instead of belonging to a workgroup, your computer is joined to the domain. When you log on, you log on with a domain account (stored in AD) rather than a local account (stored on your local computer).

In a domain, AD handles authentication services. So, if you share a folder on your computer, you can specify which other domain users or groups can access that shared resource, and what permissions they have in it. The advantage of this type of resource sharing is that every user needs only a single user account in AD, and that account can be used to access resources anywhere on the network.

How to choose

If you're setting up a home network and all your computers are running Windows 7, Windows 8, or Windows 10, a homegroup probably makes the most sense. If your home network includes Windows Vista or Windows XP computers, using a common workgroup to share resources is a good option. Or you can use a hybrid model where your Windows 7, Windows 8, and Windows 10 computers share their resources through a homegroup and other computers use the workgroup.

In a business network, the number of computers generally dictates whether you choose a workgroup or a domain model for sharing. You can set up a Windows workstation as a file server, create an account for each person on the network on that computer, and use it to share resources. Whether you choose that route or use a domain and Windows Server for sharing really depends on how you plan to use the network. In most cases, when you have about five to ten computers, a domain and server make the most sense.

> **TIP**
> Windows client computers running Windows Vista and earlier are limited to a maximum of ten concurrent connections, making them useful for centralized sharing in small networks but not in larger ones. Windows 7, Windows 8, and Windows 10 all support up to 20 concurrent connections.

> **NOTE**
> Using a domain for sharing implies that you have one or more centralized file and print servers on the network, so sharing from your client computer is unlikely (although possible). For that reason, we don't cover domain sharing in detail in this chapter.

Turn On Sharing and Discovery

Before you start sharing resources on your network, you need to make sure you configure Windows 10 to enable it to share and access shared resources. By default, Windows does not make network resources available to everyone. Instead, Windows 10 requires users to explicitly share resources before others can access them.

A first step on each computer is to make sure sharing and discovery are enabled and all computers belong to the same workgroup. When you first connect to a new network, Windows asks if you want to enable sharing (see Figure 34.3). If the connection is a private one, such as your own wireless network at home, choose the option to turn on sharing by opening the Network and Sharing Center applet from the Control Panel and then clicking the Change Advanced Sharing Settings link. If you're connecting to a public network, you should *not* turn on sharing. The sharing options screen is shown in Figure 34.3.

FIGURE 34.3

Choose whether to turn on sharing.

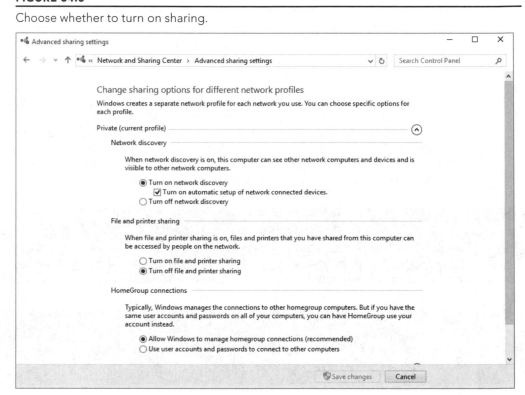

All computers must belong to the same workgroup if you're going to use workgroup sharing rather than a homegroup. So, on each computer you also want to make sure Network Discovery is turned on and all computers have the same workgroup name.

In the Network and Sharing Center section of the Control Panel, click Change Advanced Sharing Settings in the left pane to open the Change Advanced Sharing Settings dialog box (see Figure 34.3). Click the arrow beside Private to access the settings for private networks. Enable the options for network discovery and file and printer sharing if they aren't already on.

If you want to use public folders for sharing, expand the options for All Networks and choose the option to turn on public folder sharing. If you want to enable people to access shared resources without a user account, located at the bottom under Password protected sharing, choose the option Turn Off Password Protected Sharing. Otherwise, turn this option on.

If your network is small and you won't use a domain for sharing, make sure all computers are in the same workgroup. On a Windows 7, Windows 8, or Windows 10 computer, open the Control Panel and then click System. In the resulting System dialog box, click Advanced System Settings to open the Computer Name tab of the System Properties dialog box (see Figure 34.4).

The Computer Name tab shows the current computer name, description, and workgroup name. If the workgroup isn't what you need it to be, click the Change button. In the resulting Computer Name/Domain Changes dialog box, click the Workgroup option and type the required workgroup name in the Workgroup text box. Then click OK. Click OK again to close the System Properties dialog box.

FIGURE 34.4

The Computer Name tab of the System Properties dialog box.

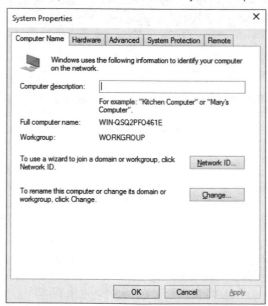

When you've turned on all the Sharing and Discovery options and set the workgroup name, you're ready to move to the next computer in the network and repeat the process. When all the computers have sharing and discovery enabled and belong to the same workgroup, they can find each others' shared resources. But each user can decide what to share. The sections that follow look at techniques for sharing resources.

You can share media files from Windows Media Library, rather than from the folders in which those files are contained. See Chapter 24 for details.

Windows 10 Homegroups

Homegroups are a feature introduced in Windows 7 and carried over to Windows 8 and Windows 10 that simplify setting up a home network and sharing resources on the network. When you set up a Windows 7, Windows 8/8.1, or Windows 10 computer, Windows creates a homegroup automatically if one doesn't already exist and generates a network password for the homegroup. With that network password, other Windows 7, 8/8.1, and Windows 10 computers on the network can join the homegroup, and users on those computers can access resources that are shared by other computers in the homegroup.

> **TIP**
>
> Computers must be running Windows 7, Windows 8, or Windows 10 to participate in a homegroup, and support for homegroups is included in all editions of Windows 7, Windows 8/8.1, and Windows 10. However, Windows 7 Starter and Windows 7 Home Basic and earlier editions of Windows can participate in a homegroup but cannot create one.

Finding or changing the homegroup password

If Windows 10 doesn't find an existing homegroup, it creates one. From that point on, you can add other Windows 7, 8/8.1, or Windows 10 computers to that existing homegroup. All you need is the homegroup password, which Windows creates automatically when it creates the homegroup.

If you don't already know the homegroup password, open the Control Panel and click Network and Sharing; click the HomeGroup link at the bottom left of the dialog box. In the Homegroup applet, click View or print your homegroup password. A dialog box opens (see Figure 34.5) and displays the password. Click Print This Page if you need a printed copy.

As mentioned previously, Windows sets the homegroup password when it sets up the homegroup. If needed, you can change the password. To do so, first make sure all the computers in the homegroup are turned on. Then open the Homegroup applet as explained previously and click Change the Password. In the resulting dialog box, click Change the Password. A new window opens, allowing you to type new password. Click Next when you're satisfied with the new password.

Next, perform the following steps on each of the other computers on the homegroup:

1. Open the Homegroup applet from the Control Panel. Windows detects that the password has changed and gives you the opportunity to change it.

2. Click the Type New Password button, type the new password, and click Next.

3. After you've changed the password, click Finish.

FIGURE 34.5

View or print your homegroup password.

Joining a homegroup

When you add a new Windows 10 computer to your network, you can add it to your homegroup. You don't have to do this unless you want the computer to participate in the homegroup. To add a computer to the homegroup, boot the computer and make sure the computer is on the network. Your computer's network location must also be set to private for security. You don't have to do anything here. If the computer's network location is not set to private you will be prompted to set it. (See Chapter 33 if you need help with that.)

Next, open the Control Panel and then open the Homegroup applet. Click the Join Now button (see Figure 34.6); then, in the resulting Join a Homegroup dialog box, click Next and choose which items you want to share (see Figure 34.7). Then click Next. Type the home-group password, click Next, and click Finish.

FIGURE 34.6

Click Join Now to join the homegroup.

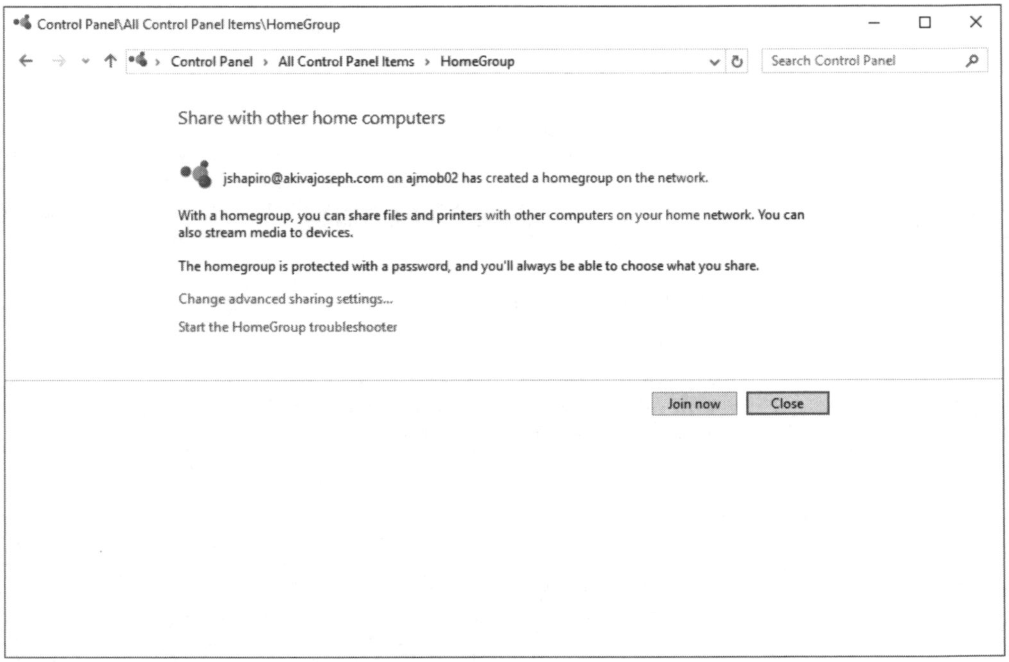

Sharing items with the homegroup

If you change your mind about what you want to share with the homegroup, you can change sharing options accordingly. To do so, open the Homegroup applet from the Control Panel (see Figure 34.7).

You can easily share items with your homegroup. To do so, open the folder containing the item you want to share. For example, if you want to share a folder in the Documents folder, open Documents, click the folder, and select the Share tab on the ribbon ; then choose Homegroup (View) to give others the capability to read items in the folder, Homegroup (View and Edit) to enable them to also write to the folder, or Stop Sharing to remove the folder from sharing. To lock down the homegroup further, you can click the Advanced security button on the Share tab. The Advanced Security Settings for the target folder now load (see Figure 34.7).

Excluding items from sharing

In some situations, you may want to share a folder or library but exclude access to certain folders or even individual files. Excluding a folder or file is simply a matter of selecting the item and clicking Stop Sharing. Open the folder containing the folder you want to exclude, or in the case of an individual file, open the folder containing the file. Click the item you want to exclude, and click Stop Sharing in the ribbon. That library, folder, or file will not show up when others browse the homegroup.

FIGURE 34.7

The Advanced Security Settings dialog box.

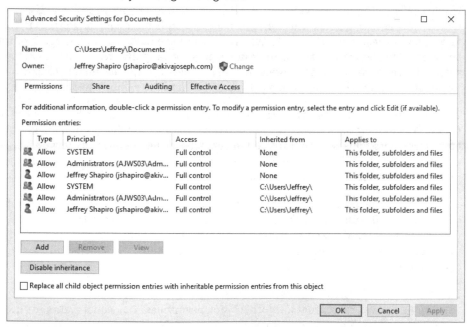

Sharing with individual users

You can also share folders and files with individual users, but those users must have an account on your computer and access the files from that same computer. For example, if you have a single home computer you share with your spouse and children, you may want to share a folder with only your spouse and not the children. To share the folder or file, open the folder containing the item to be shared, click it, and select the Share tab in the ribbon. Choose specific people to open the File Sharing dialog box, choose an account from the drop-down list, and click Add. Then click Share to close the dialog box.

To access a folder or file that has been shared in this way, open the Network folder, and expand the local computer, then the Users folder, and finally the user who is sharing the folder or file.

Using Public Folders

Windows 7, Windows 8, and Windows 10 include a public folder from which files are shared automatically. This feature is similar to the Shared Documents folder in Windows XP and Windows Vista. In previous versions of Windows, even as recently as Windows 8, public folders were accessible from the Libraries node, which is no longer supported. If you wish to view the libraries, you just need to turn them on in the Navigation pane setting; which can be found from the view settings. You can simply move any files that you intend to share across all user accounts or computers in a private network to that folder. To get to that folder, start by opening File Explorer. Figure 34.8 shows the public folders.

The public folders are actually all contained in a single folder named Public in the Users folder. (The default path is `C:\Users\Public`.) The Public folder is organized much like your Documents folders. It contains subfolders for storing documents, downloads, music, pictures, and videos. If you have Media Center installed, it also contains a Recorded TV folder, in which Media Center–recorded TV files are stored.

Perhaps the easiest way to move files into a Public folder is to open one of its subfolders, such as Public Documents or Public Pictures. Then open the folder that contains the files you want to share. Size and position the two windows so you can see both. Then drag files from one folder to the other. See Chapter 21 for more information on moving and copying files.

The Public folder is shared in a way where every user on the computer (and in the network) has free reign over its contents. In other words, every user has equal rights to the Public folder. If you have files you want to share more selectively, such as only with certain people or only with certain permissions, use the method described previously in the section, "Sharing with individual users."

FIGURE 34.8

Public folders.

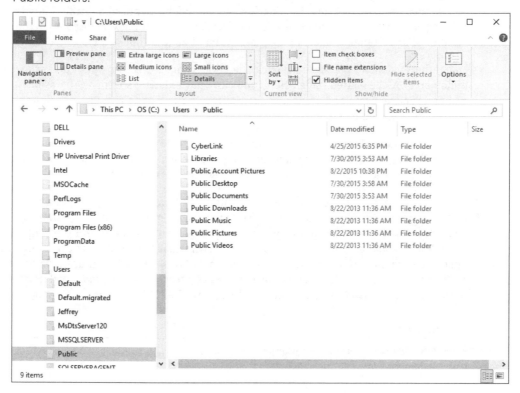

Advanced Sharing

Advanced Sharing allows a user with administrative privileges to set custom permissions for multiple users, control the number of simultaneous connections and caching for offline files, and set other advanced properties. Some of these topics require training in or knowledge of network administration. The Public folder and selective sharing methods described in the preceding sections should be adequate for a home network and much easier to work with.

For people who understand the concepts (and potential problems) involved, we'll quickly run through the process. Locate the folder you want to share, right-click that folder's icon, and choose Properties. Select the Sharing tab and click Advanced Sharing. Elevate your privileges (if prompted) and choose Share This Folder. Then click the Apply button. Set the number of simultaneous users up to a maximum of 20 and (optionally) add a comment.

To configure sharing permissions, click the Permissions button to open the Permissions dialog box for the shared folder. Here, you can view existing sharing permissions and also add and remove users and groups. You're limited to specifying Full Control, Change, or Read permission sharing levels.

If the disk where the shared folder resides is on an NTFS volume, you can set NTFS permissions, which are more flexible than sharing permissions. To set NTFS permissions, open the properties for the folder and select the Security tab (see Figure 34.9).

On the Security tab, you can add or remove users and groups and specify the permission levels for each one. The available permissions are more granular than the sharing permissions described previously, giving you finer control over what each user or group can do in the folder. As you assign permissions, keep in mind that the most restrictive permissions apply. For example, if you share a folder and apply Full Control for all users, but then set NTFS permissions so that all users have only Read access, then the more restrictive NTFS permissions apply and users can only read items in the folder, not modify them.

FIGURE 34.9

The Security tab for NTFS permissions.

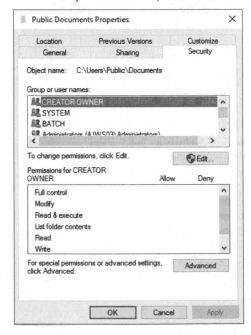

Identifying Shared Folders

In Windows 10, you have a few methods for identifying which folders are shared. First, in File Explorer, open a folder. If the folder is shared, you see the words "State: Shared" in the status bar at the bottom of the window.

You can also use the Shared Folders snap-in with the Computer Management console to see which folders are shared. To open Shared Folders, click Start, right-click the Start button, and choose Computer Management. When the Computer Management console opens, expand the Shared Folders branch and click Shares. The folders that are shared, whether visible or hidden, appear in the right pane.

You can also use the NET command in a command console to see what is shared. Open a command console and type **NET SHARE** to see a listing of shared resources. A full discussion of the NET commands is beyond the scope of this book, but you can get the full command list by searching the web for NET SHARE.

Sharing a Printer

Printers in a LAN are usually connected to one of the computers in that network. To ensure that the printer is shared, so everybody in the network can use it, follow these steps:

> **TIP**
> With the right hardware, you can connect a printer directly to a LAN without going through a computer. With that type of arrangement, you need to make sure that the printer is turned on, connected to the network, and configured with network settings appropriate for your network.

1. Go to the computer to which the printer is connected by cable. If either is turned off, turn on the printer first and the computer second.

2. Open Devices and Printers from the Control Panel.

3. Right-click the printer and choose Printer Properties to open the Properties dialog box for the printer.

4. Select the Sharing tab; then select Share This Printer, type a name in the Share Name text box, and choose to render print jobs on the client, as shown in Figure 34.10.

> **NOTE**
> The Render Print Jobs on Client Computers option lets each user control print jobs from his or her own computer. In earlier versions of Windows, most print jobs had to be managed from the printer to which the computer was physically attached.

5. Click OK.

When you click the printer's icon in Devices and Printers, the status bar indicates that the printer is shared. The printer should show up automatically in all network computers' Print dialog boxes. If it doesn't show up on a particular computer, see Chapter 25 for information on installing a shared network printer.

What about Sharing Programs?

Although you can share folders and documents freely on a LAN, you can't share programs. You can only run programs currently installed on your computer. If you try to open a document on another computer, but you don't have the appropriate program for that document type, you can't open the document.

Don't bother trying to copy an installed program from one computer to another — it doesn't work, except in rare cases. Only programs that you install on your own computer can run on your computer.

The only solution is to install the necessary program on your own computer.

FIGURE 34.10

Sharing a printer.

Wrapping Up

People create computer networks to share resources among computers. Resources include things such as an Internet connection, media files, folders, and printers. Windows 10's sharing and discovery make it relatively easy to share resources and discover them. This chapter has focused on the "sharing" part. The following are some of the key points covered in this chapter:

- To turn on sharing and discovery, open the Network and Sharing Center and choose Advanced Sharing Settings.
- Use a homegroup to easily share resources among Windows 7, Windows 8/8.1, and Windows 10 computers on a small network.
- To share a printer, use the Sharing tab of the printer's Properties dialog box.
- One way to share files is to move them to the Public folder or one of its subfolders.
- Use the Computer Management console or the NET SHARE command to see which folders are shared.

Using Shared Resources

Chapters 33 and 34 covered all the basics of setting up and sharing resources on a private home or small business network. This chapter assumes that you've done that. Nothing in this chapter will work until the network is set up, you've turned on network sharing and discovery on each Windows 7, Window 8/8.1, and Windows 10 computer, and you've shared some files on the network.

This chapter looks at how you find and use shared resources from computers within the network. It looks at opening documents from remote resources, moving and copying files between networked computers, using remote printers, and ways of using shared media.

UNC Paths

Before diving too deeply into methods for accessing network resources, let's take some time to delve into a topic that will help you navigate network resources more easily — UNC paths.

UNC stands for Universal Naming Convention. A UNC path is expressed in this form:

    \\MachineName\PathName

MachineName is the name of the computer and PathName is a folder path on that computer. For example, assume that your network includes a computer named SNOOPY that you use as a file server. On that computer is a folder that you have shared as SharedDocs. Within that SharedDocs folder is a subfolder named Contracts. The UNC path to the Contracts folder is \\<ComputerName>\<Share Name>\Path.

So, for the computer named SNOOPY, it would look like this: \\SNOOPY\SharedDocs\Contracts.

Note that the UNC path is not case-sensitive.

A UNC path makes navigating the network easy, particularly when you know the path name. Using a UNC path is often quicker than navigating to the Network folder, and then to a remote computer, and then drilling down through its shared folders. Instead, you can open the This PC folder, click in the Address bar, and simply type the UNC path to the remote share that you want to use.

Additionally, you can specify the IP address of the remote computer in place of the computer name in the UNC path. So, assuming that our trusty computer named SNOOPY has the IP address 192.168.0.5, the UNC path to the Contracts folder would be \\192.168.0.5\SharedDocs\Contracts.

Now that you're up to speed on UNC paths, let's look at how to access network resources.

Accessing Remote Resources

Every Windows 10 computer on which you've enabled network sharing and discovery should show up in every computer's Network folder. The same is true of any Windows 8/8.1, Windows 7, Vista, and XP computers in the network that have at least one shared resource (such as the built-in Shared Documents folder). To open the Network folder on a Windows 10 computer, open File Explorer and click Network in the folder list.

The first time you open the Network folder on a computer, it may take a few seconds to discover other computers in the network. But within a few seconds you should see an icon for each computer in the network, as in the example shown in Figure 35.1. Each computer is also accessible from the Folders list after you expand the Network category in that list.

Each computer's icon is like a folder; when you open it, you see shared resources from that computer. Shared resources include a folder icon for each shared folder and printer icons for any shared printers connected to that computer.

If you use the Network folder often, make sure you can find its icon easily. To put a Network icon on your desktop, right-click the desktop and choose Personalize. In the Personalization screen, choose Themes in the left column. Then click Desktop icons settings. Select the Network check box (and the check boxes of any other icons you want) and click OK.

To add Network to your Quick Access location in File Explorer, open a folder and make sure you can see the Navigation pane. Open the Folders list and drag the Network icon in the

Folders list of the Quick Access location. This is easier to do with two instances of File Explorer running.

> **TIP**
>
> Any time you're in File Explorer, clicking the leftmost arrow in the Address bar usually displays a quick link to the Network folder.

FIGURE 35.1

A Network folder.

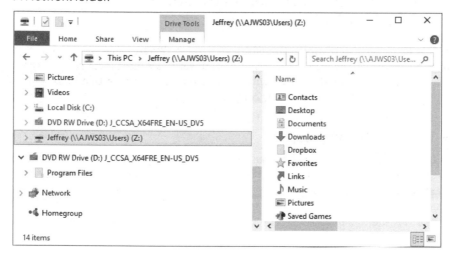

Opening Remote Documents

One of the advantages to having a network is that you can put documents in shared folders and open them from any computer in the network. For example, you can put all your important work documents in a shared folder on your main work computer. If you also have a portable computer that you can use outside on sunny days (or from the sofa on lazy days), you can work directly with those documents from the remote computer.

The process is no different from opening a document on a local computer. You can, for example, navigate to the folder, via the Network folder, in which the document is stored. Or open the Computer folder, type the UNC path to the shared folder in the Address bar, and press Enter. Then double-click (or click) the document you want to edit, and the document

35

opens from the remote computer (providing that the local computer has the appropriate program installed for working with that type of document).

Optionally, you can go through the program's Open dialog box to get to the document. Here's how:

1. Open the program you want to use and choose File ⇨ Open or the command, link, or button to open a file.

2. In the Open dialog box, click Network (if available) at the left side of the dialog box.

3. Select the computer on the network where the document resides. Then navigate to the folder for (or a parent folder to) the document.

4. Click or double-click the document's icon.

After the document is open, you can edit it or print it. When you save the document, your changes are saved at the original location. If you want to save a local copy of the document to work with, choose File ⇨ Save As within the program, navigate to a local folder such as your Documents folder, and save your copy there.

Opening a read-only copy

If you try to open a document that someone already has open on another computer, you may see a message telling you what your options are. Those options vary from one program to the next. For example, you may be offered the option to open a read-only copy of the document or to open an editable copy of the document. If you choose to open a read-only copy, you can then choose File ⇨ Save As in the program and save a local copy that you can modify.

Creating network locations

If you have your own website, or permission to upload to an FTP site, Microsoft SharePoint site, or any other Internet site, you can add an icon for that location to your This PC folder. Doing so allows you to upload files to that location using the same techniques you use to save a file to your own computer.

You need to know the URL (address) to which you can upload. Chances are, you need a username and password as well. The people who own the site to which you're uploading provide that information when you set up your account. They may also provide upload instructions. But as long as you know the URL and your username and password, you should be able to use the technique described here in addition to the method they provide.

To create a link to the Internet location, follow these steps:

1. Open your computer folder, named This PC in Windows 10.

2. Right-click any unused space in the window and choose Add a Network Location.

3. Click Next on the first wizard page.

4. Click Choose a Custom Network Location and click Next.

5. Type the complete URL of the remote site. For example, if you're uploading to a website you own, include the `http://`. In Figure 35.2, we're about to create a shortcut to the site `ftp://ftp.akivajoseph.com`. If the shortcut is to an FTP site for which you have upload permissions, use the `ftp://` prefix on the URL. Click Next. To see a list of examples, click the View Examples link in the middle of the window.

6. If the remote resource requires a username and password, you're prompted to enter your credentials. Enter the credentials and click OK.

7. The next wizard page suggests the URL (without the `http://` or `ftp://` prefix) as the name of the shortcut icon. You can replace that with any name you like because it's used only as the label for the shortcut. Type the desired name and click Next.

FIGURE 35.2

Providing the URL of an Internet resource.

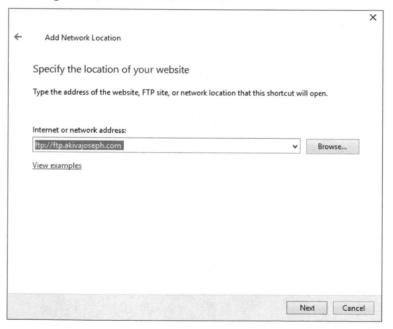

8. On the last wizard page, you can select (check) the check box Open This Network Location When I Click Finish if you want to see the remote folder immediately. Or clear the check box if you don't want to see that right now. Then click Finish.

When you double-click the icon for the remote site, it opens in File Explorer, looking much the same as any local folder on your own hard disk. You may not have quite as many options to choose from in the Explorer bar. In Figure 35.3, we've opened an FTP site.

You can treat the folder as you would any other, provided you have the credentials, permissions, and authority. For example, you can create a new folder, or rename or delete existing files and folders by right-clicking, just as you would in any folder on your C: drive. You can also move and copy files to and from the site. Your computer will be slower because the remote resource may be thousands of miles away, but the techniques should be the same.

> **TIP**
> You can rename any icon under Network Locations, just as you would any other icon. Simply right-click the icon and choose Rename.

FIGURE 35.3

An FTP site as a folder in File Explorer.

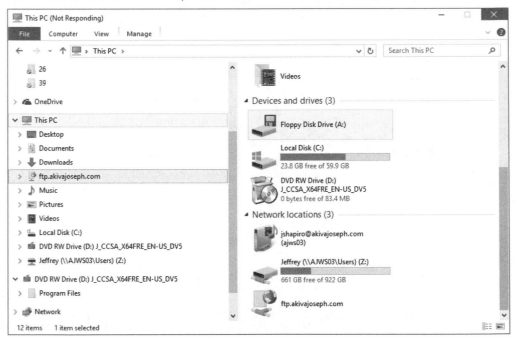

If you have trouble connecting, the people who provided the site are your best resource. They're the only ones who know the details of that site. You may have to provide a user ID and password in order to gain access to the location.

Saving to a Remote Computer

Any time you save a new document — whether it's one you've created yourself or something you're downloading — a Save As dialog box (or something similar) opens, enabling you to save the file. The dialog box has a Folders list so that you can choose where you want to save the document.

As with the Open dialog box, you can choose the Network folder from the Folders list to get to all the locations in your Network folder. Then navigate to wherever you want to save the file. Or click in the text box where you would normally enter the filename and instead enter a UNC path to the folder where you want to store the file. After the folder opens in the dialog box, enter the filename.

Downloading Programs to a Network Share

If you regularly download programs to install on multiple computers, consider using the folder named Public Downloads within your Public folder. After you save a downloaded program file to that folder, you can install it on all the computers in the network. You have to install it on each computer individually, but you don't need to download it on every computer, especially if you're sharing a not-so-speedy Internet connection.

Start by creating the Public Downloads folder in your own Documents folder or on another shared folder on your network. Then initiate the download as you normally would. When the File Download dialog box appears, click Save or Save As. In the Save As dialog box, navigate to the shared Public Downloads folder and save the file there.

TIP

You can download the file from the computer where the Public Downloads folder resides or from another computer on the network. The advantage of performing the download from the computer where the file will be stored is that you minimize network traffic. If you're saving to a shared folder across the network, the file comes through the network to your computer and then goes across the network to the shared folder, effectively doubling the network traffic and slowing the process.

35

After the file has been downloaded, you can access it from any other computer on the network to install the program. Browse the network from the computer where you want to install the program, open the shared Public Downloads folder, and double-click the file to begin the installation.

> **NOTE**
>
> Some programs must be installed from a local copy of the file rather than across the network. If you have problems installing across the network, copy the file across the network to the local computer and install from that local copy.

Transferring Files between Computers

Moving and copying files on a network is virtually identical to doing so on a single computer. You can use any of the techniques described in Chapter 18 to select, move, or copy files from any folder on your own computer to any shared folder or from any shared folder to any folder on your own computer. You can use those same techniques to move and copy files between shared folders on any two remote computers on the network.

For example, say you're sitting at a computer named Hobbes, and you have a bunch of files in a subfolder named Rob-PC\Common Downloads on a computer named Rob-PC. So, the UNC path is \\Rob-PC\SharedDocs\Common Downloads (where SharedDocs is the name of the shared documents folder). You want to copy one or more files to the Downloads folder of your own user account on HP-Rob. Open the Network folder, and then open the Rob-PC\ SharedDocs\Common Downloads folder. Then open the Documents folder for your user account. We suggest you size and position the windows so you can see the contents of both, as in Figure 35.4.

With both folders open, as in the figure, you can select the files you want to copy in the remote folder using any technique you like, as discussed in Chapter 21. To copy (rather than move) the items to the remote folder, right-drag any selected icon to the remote folder and then choose Copy Here after you release the mouse button. (You also can drag using the left mouse button; the files are copied from the remote location to the local one.) That's the entire procedure. As we said, it's no different from moving and copying files between folders and drives on your own computer, except that you use the Network folder or a UNC path to open the remote folder.

FIGURE 35.4

Remote shared folder (front) and local folder (behind).

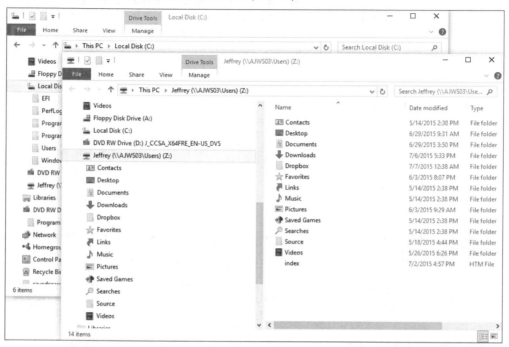

Mapping Drive Letters to Shared Folders

Some programs require that you assign a drive letter to remote resources. You can assign any unused drive letter to a resource. For example, if you already have drives A: through F: in use, you can assign drive letters G: through Z: to any shared resource. Use the following steps to map a drive letter to a shared folder:

1. Go to the computer on which you need to assign a drive letter to a remote shared resource.

2. Open any folder (such as the This PC folder), select the Computer tab, and click Map Network Drive. The Map Network Drive dialog box opens.

35

3. Click the Browse button to open the Browse for Folder dialog box.

4. In the Browse for Folder dialog box, click the name of the shared resource to which you want to map a drive letter, so its name is selected (highlighted). For example, in Figure 35.5, we're about to map the drive letter Y: to the shared Download folder on a computer.

5. Click OK.

6. If you want the drive to be mapped automatically each time you log on, select the Reconnect at Sign-In check box.

7. Click Finish.

The remote resource opens. You can close that folder and also close the Network folder. Because you've mapped a drive letter to the remote resource, it appears in your This PC folder. In Figure 35.6, we've mapped two resources: Y: is mapped to the Users\Jeffrey folder on the computer named AJWS03 and Z: is mapped to Users\Public on drive C:.

Hidden Shares

Windows creates a hidden administrative share for each drive connected to the computer. These shares, which share the root of the drive, take the name of the drive letter followed by a $ sign. For example, the administrative share for drive C: is C$, for drive E: is E$, and so on. If you have an administrative account (or have access to the administrative shares) on the remote computer, you can map to its hidden share using the UNC path. For example, to connect to drive C: on a computer named Spock, you would use the UNC path \\Spock\C$.

These shares are called "hidden shares" because they don't appear when you browse the network for resources. For example, you don't see these shares in the Network folder. In addition, you can create your own hidden shares. When you share the resource, just add a $ sign at the end of the share name. See Chapter 34 to learn more about sharing resources on the network.

From that point on, you can access the folder either by going through the Network folder as usual, or just by opening your This PC folder and opening the resource's icon under Network Location.

NOTE

Even though a mapped network drive shows up as a disk drive in the Computer folder, a shared network resource need not be a disk drive at all. It can be a folder. The term *network drive* just refers to the fact that the shared resource "looks like" a drive because it has a drive letter and icon in your Computer folder.

FIGURE 35.5

The Map Network Drive dialog box.

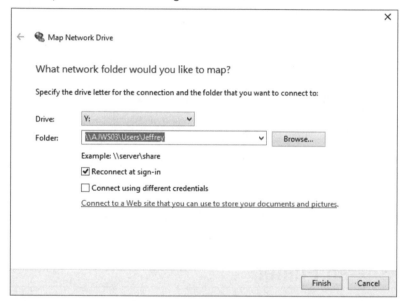

Disconnecting from a Network Drive

In your This PC folder, you can disconnect from any network drive by right-clicking the drive's icon and choosing Disconnect. If you chose the option Reconnect At Sign-In when you previously mapped the drive, the shared resource will no longer be mapped the next time you log on to the computer.

35

FIGURE 35.6

Drives Y: and Z: are actually shared resources on other computers.

Using a Shared Printer

You use a shared printer from a remote computer exactly as you use a local printer. Choose File ⇨ Print from the program's menu bar. When the Print dialog box opens, look for the shared printer, click it, and click the Print button.

If the shared printer doesn't show up in the Print dialog box, you can either add it right from the Print dialog box or install it from the Devices and Printers applet. To install it from the Devices and Printers Control Panel applet, click Add a Printer to open the Add Printer dialog box. Windows 10 automatically searches for all local and shared network printers and displays them in the Add a Device dialog box (see Figure 35.7).

FIGURE 35.7

Windows 10 does a great job finding networked printers.

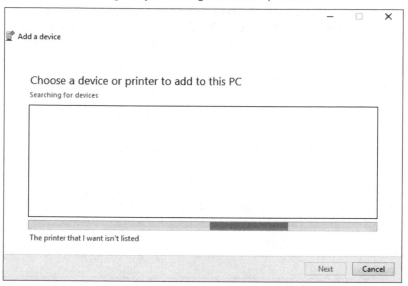

Select the printer you want to add to your list of printers and click Next. Windows 10 attempts to install the necessary printer driver for the networked printer. If it does not find one, you're shown a message that Windows could not find a driver. Click OK to manually specify where the necessary drivers are for the printer you want to set up.

After the drivers are installed, you return to the Devices and Printers folder. If that's the printer you'll use most often, make it the default printer as described in Chapter 20.

Whichever method you use to add the printer, after the printer is installed, choose File ⇨ Print, select the newly installed printer, and click Print.

TIP

You can play shared media from a Windows 10 computer on any other Windows 10 computer in the network and on compatible networked digital media players.

Using Shared Media

Shared media are different from shared files because they're *streamed* to the local computer when played. This allows you to play the media files on non-computer network devices such as the Xbox One or a networked digital media player. Exactly how you work such a device depends on the device. Refer to the instructions that came with the device for specifics. You also can use the Windows 10 Xbox LIVE Games app from the Windows 10 interface to connect your Windows computer or tablet with a Microsoft Xbox device.

You can access the shared media by opening Windows Media Player normally. In the left pane, you should see each of the devices on the network that are sharing their media. Click the arrow next to a device to access its shared music, as shown in Figure 35.8.

You can also browse for media devices (and computers that are sharing their music libraries) from the Network folder. When you open the Network folder, you see a section named Media Devices that shows all the streaming media devices on the network. Double-click a device to open its library in Media Player.

FIGURE 35.8

Accessing a remote shared library.

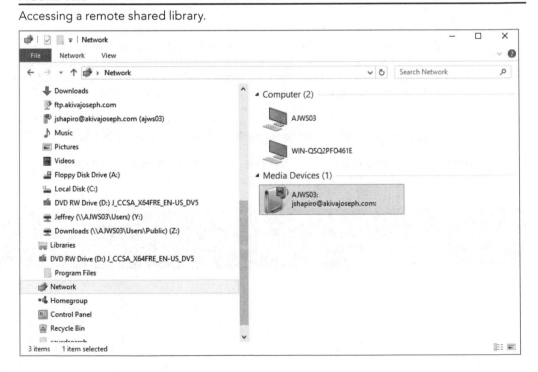

Wrapping Up

This chapter looked at ways to access shared network resources from computers in the same private network. We covered these points:

- To get to shared folders on other computers in the network, first open the Network folder on the computer at which you're sitting.

- To open a remote document from within a program, choose File ⇨ Open from that program, as usual. Then choose the Network folder from the Folders drop-down list in the Open dialog box.

- To save a document to a remote computer, choose File ⇨ Save (or File ⇨ Save As), and choose your Network folder from the Folders drop-down list.

- To create a Network Location link to an Internet site, right-click within your Computer folder and choose Add a Network Location.

- To move or copy files between computers in a network, use your Network folder to open the source and/or destination folders. Then use the standard techniques described in Chapter 16 to select, move, or copy the files.

- To use a shared printer, print normally but select the shared printer's name in the Print dialog box.

- If you don't see a shared printer in the Print dialog box, install the printer on the local computer using techniques described in Chapter 20.

- To play shared media using Windows Media Player, open the Network folder and double-click the shared media's icon.

35

Part IX

Managing Windows 10 in an Enterprise

IN THIS PART

Imaging and Deploying Windows 10

W indows 10 is gaining more presence in larger companies, schools, and corporations as a standard operating system. To meet the high demands that corporations and large businesses have for maintaining and deploying systems, larger organization and corporations need a way to set up and configure individual client desktops quickly and efficiently. In addition, client desktops generally must be standardized in an enterprise so each base system functions identically.

Windows 10's imaging capabilities provides a way to standardize a base installation and then deploy that "image" or copy to other desktops quickly and efficiently. This chapter describes Windows 10 imaging, how to use the system preparation tools, and how to deploy and modify images.

Understanding Windows 10 Imaging

Imaging provides a way to install Windows 10 on devices in a way that lets system administrators duplicate installs on multiple computers in a pseudo-automated way. Once a Windows 10 image is created, including customizations, applications, mappings, device drivers, and so on, administrators can use that image to deploy Windows to other similar types of devices.

Imaging is helpful when an organization purchases a number of computers that it has to place out in the organization. For example, say a company's IT department receives 1,000 new desktop computers to be distributed to its call center. To prepare each computer for call center employees, the IT department would have to install Windows on each computer, and likely would perform the following duties on each one:

1. Customize the Windows environment for each computer manually. For example, simply adding a custom corporate logo to each wallpaper setting would require manually copying the image to the new computer and then specifying it as the computer's wallpaper via the Personalization settings in the Control Panel.

2. Install and customize each application manually. Many applications may be customized when installed on corporate computers, such as turning on or off specific features, specifying installation folders, and similar application settings.

3. Set drive mappings and other network file locations manually.

4. Install proper device drivers for all devices, including network interface card drivers, printer drivers, and video display drivers, and other system settings.

With imaging, the IT department sets up and configures one desktop client, then clones that client to the other 999 computers. This process increases efficiency, reduces mistakes, and provides other system-wide processes (such as a way to inventory the devices quickly, for example).

You can image and deploy Windows in the following ways:

- Use the set of tools provided in the Microsoft System Center Configuration Manager (SCCM).

- Use the Microsoft Deployment Toolkit (MDT).

> **TIP**
>
> SCCM and MDT are a powerful and complex set of tools that, unless you have a dedicated administrator or team of administrators, can be overwhelming for small to medium-sized corporations. If you do not need the power of SCCM or MDT, but still need a convenient and efficient way to deploy a Windows image, consider using the Windows Assessment and Deployment Kit (ADK).

Using Windows Assessment and Deployment Kit (ADK)

You use the Windows Assessment and Deployment Kit (ADK) to access the tools you need to create an image of your system. The Windows ADK includes Windows Imaging and Configuration Designer (ICD). The ICD provides a way to create a *provisioning* package to use to automate configuration of multiple computers.

Understanding Provisioning Packages

A provisioning package (PPKG) is a good choice when you need to apply the image over an existing Windows 10 deployment. For example, say your company or organization receives a shipment of 1,000 computers that have a version of Windows already installed, but include programs, OEM programs, drivers, apps, settings, and other items that you do not want each device to have.

In some cases this could include an OEM (original equipment manufacturer) help desk system that adds files and "bloatware" to your computers. Another type of software many vendors ship standard on new computers is free antivirus software (free, but limited to a time period, such as 90 days). In these cases, you likely will want to remove these tools, install an approved set of device drivers, and include other settings standard for your company. Creating and deploying a provisioning package is a good way to configure your devices efficiently.

Accessing the Windows Assessment and Deployment Kit (ADK)

To download the Windows Assessment and Deployment Kit (ADK), use the following steps:

1. Open a web browser, such as Microsoft Edge.

2. Navigate to `https://developer.microsoft.com/en-us/windows/hardware/windows-assessment-deployment-kit`.

3. Click Get Windows ADK for Windows 10, version 1607 (see Figure 36.1). Make sure you download the ADK for version 1607 or later.

FIGURE 36.1

Visit the Download the Windows ADK web site to download the Windows ADK to enable you to image on Windows 10.

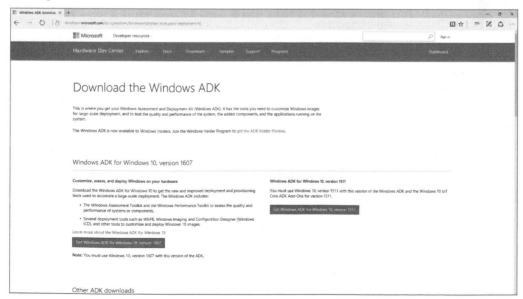

4. Click Save to save the ADKSETUP.EXE file to your computer. By default, it is downloaded to your Downloads folder.

5. After the file downloads, click the View Downloads button and click ADKSETUP .EXE in the Downloads pane to continue the ADK download and installation process. The Specify Location screen of the Windows Assessment and Deployment Kit — Windows 10 program appears. See Figure 36.2.

FIGURE 36.2

Specify the location to install the Windows ADK.

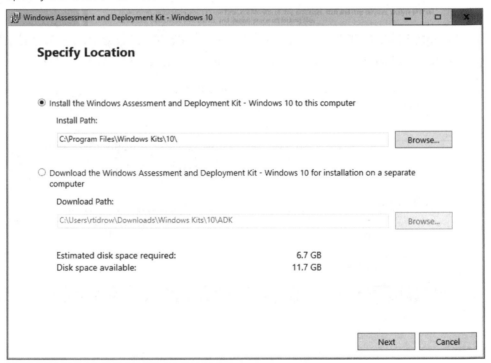

6. Click Next. The Windows Kits Privacy window appears (see Figure 36.3). Click Yes to participate in the Windows Customer Experience Improvement Program, or No if you don't want to participate.

FIGURE 36.3

The Windows Kits Privacy window.

7. Click Next. The License Agreement window appears (see Figure 36.4).

FIGURE 36.4

The Windows ADK License Agreement window.

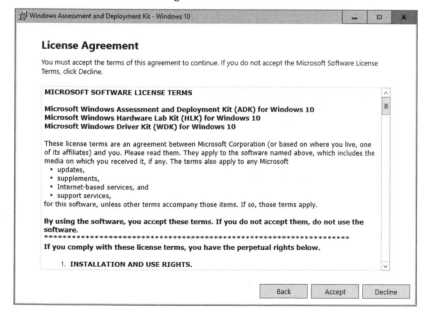

8. Select Accept. The Select the Features You Want To Install window appears (see Figure 36.5). Select those features you want to install. In most cases, you can keep all the default features selected.

FIGURE 36.5

The Select the Features You Want to Install window.

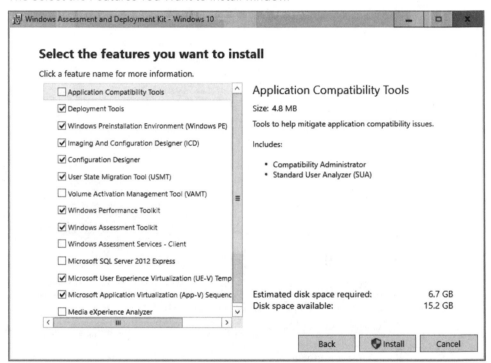

9. Click Install. The Installing Features window appears as the ADK is downloaded and installed on your computer. When finished, the Welcome to the Windows Assessment and Deployment Kit — Windows 10 window appears (see Figure 36.6).

FIGURE 36.6

After the Windows 10 ADK downloads and installs, you can close the installation window.

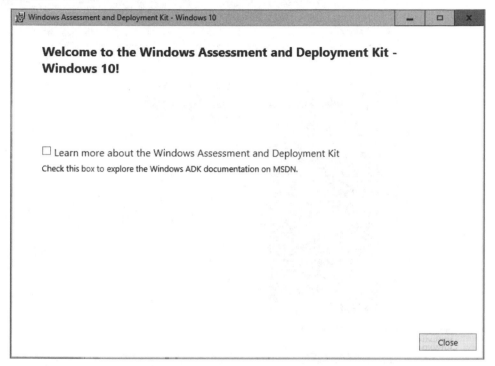

10. Click Close to end the installation process.

Once installed, the Windows ADK's Imaging and Configuration Designer (ICD) can be executed to start the imaging process. The following section describes running the ICD.

Running Windows Imaging and Configuration Designer (ICD)

You use the Windows Imaging and Configuration Designer (ICD) to create an image of your Windows 10 setup. The following steps show how to use ICD to create a provisioning package to install on top of an existing Windows 10 installation.

1. Start ICD by choosing the Start button and navigating to Windows Kit.
2. Click Windows Imaging and Configuration Designer to display the Windows Imaging and Configuration Designer windows (see Figure 36.7).

FIGURE 36.7

Start the ICD from the Windows Kit folder on the Start menu.

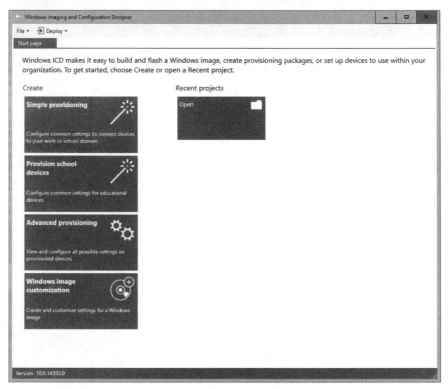

3. Click Simple Provisioning. The New Project window appears (see Figure 36.8).

FIGURE 36.8

Name and specify a location for your new image in the New Project window.

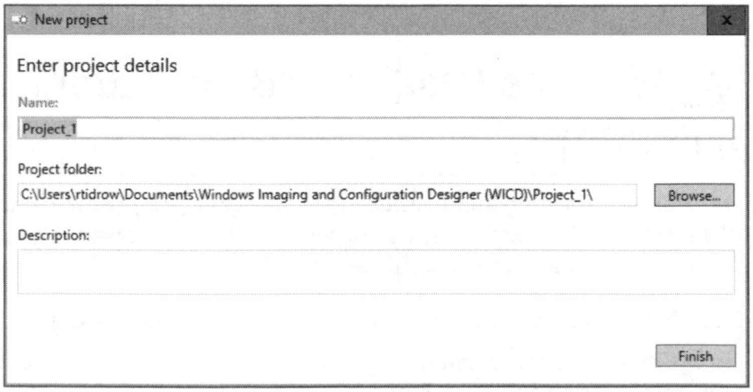

4. Type a name for the new image in the Name box. The default name is Project 1, but you may want to be more descriptive.

5. Specify a location for the image in the Project Folder box.

6. Type a description of the image in the Description box.

7. Click Finish. A new tab in the ICD window is created, using the name of the image you entered in Step 4. Figure 36.9 shows this tab, named "Windows10Image" in this example.

FIGURE 36.9

The ICD shows the tab in which you can specify image details.

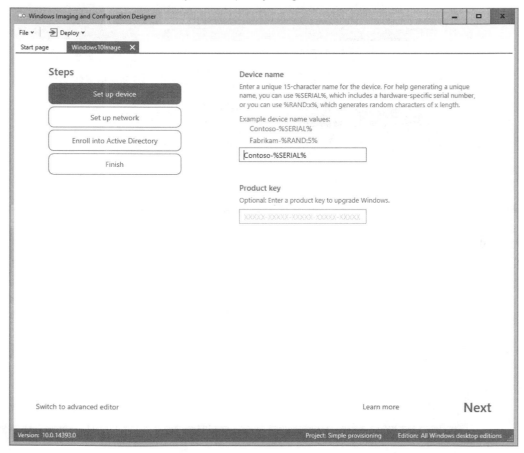

8. Enter a device name that the image can use for naming your computers as they are being imaged. The name can be up to 15 characters long. For names that are to

include random characters, use %RAND%. For names that include serial number for a device, use %SERIAL%.

9. If you are upgrading Windows during the imaging process, enter a Windows product key in the Product Key box.

10. Click Set Up Network to display network configuration settings for the image (see Figure 36.10). You can set the network name, SSID, network type (open or secure), and, if the network is secure, the password for the network.

FIGURE 36.10

Set network configuration settings for your image.

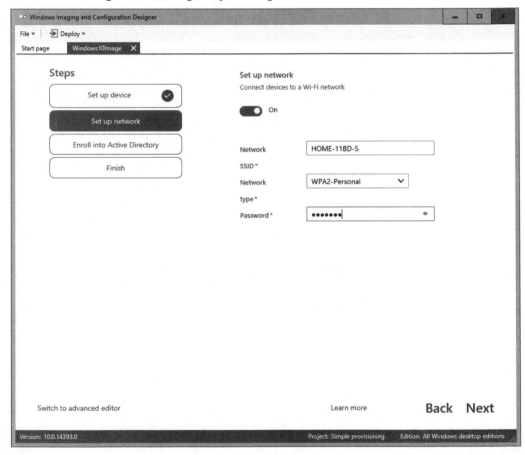

11. Click Enroll into Active Directory to display settings for enrolling devices into the active directory during the deployment process (see Figure 36.11). *Enrolling devices*

means setting them up. Enter the domain name, username, and user password for the domain. Optionally, you can enter a username and password for a local administrator account.

FIGURE 36.11

Set active directory settings for your image.

12. Click Finish to display the Summary window (see Figure 36.12). Read the summary to ensure your settings are correct. Also, to password-protect the image package, select the Yes slider under Protect Your Package and enter a password.

FIGURE 36.12

The ICD Summary screen.

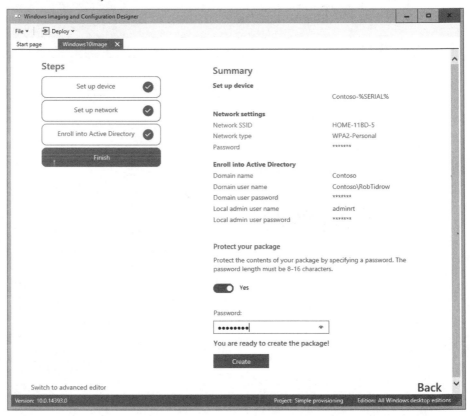

13. Click Create. The Windows ICD begins working, building the new image package.

As the package builds, a note appears above the Create button you clicked in Step 13.

> **TIP**
> Keep in mind that building an image package takes a long time. In some cases, it may take several hours.

Deploying Windows Using an ICD Package

The provisioning package can be distributed to other computers using a USB flash drive, network drive, or external hard drive. To deploy the PPKG package, perform the following steps:

1. Boot the computer on which you want to run the provisioning package.
2. Locate the provisioning package using Windows Explorer.

3. Double-click the provisioning file to launch it.

4. Click Allow to enable the provisioning package to configure the device.

This procedure allows you to completely configure a new device without having to perform the steps manually on each device.

Modifying Windows 10 Images

Many times you want to ensure your system is configured a certain way before you create an image. You can customize settings in Windows using the Windows Imaging and Configuration Designer. Some of the customizations you can perform include adding apps to the installation, choosing device drivers to set up, setting up Windows settings, and more.

To customize settings for a Windows image, use the following steps:

1. Start Windows Imaging and Configuration Designer.

2. In the Windows Imaging and Configuration Designer window (see Figure 36.13), click Windows Image Customization. The New Project window appears (see Figure 36.14).

FIGURE 36.13

Use the Windows Image Customization option to modify settings for Windows images.

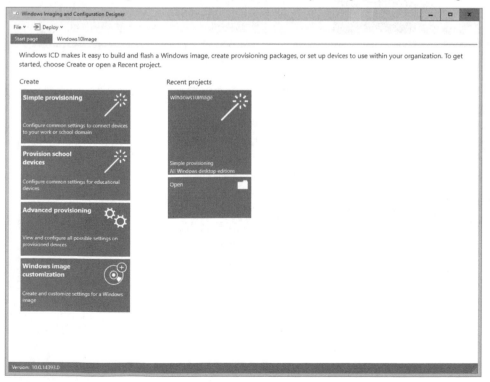

FIGURE 36.14

Name the new image project.

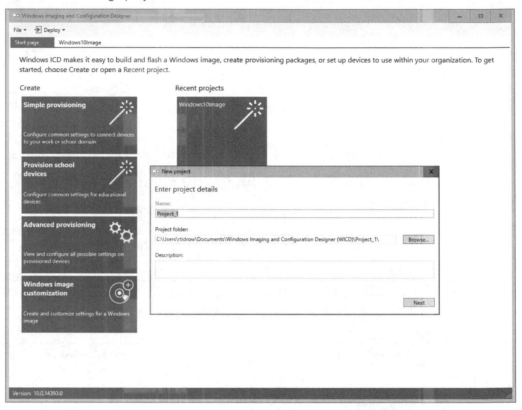

3. Type a name in the Name field, specify a location to store the new image, and type a description.

4. Click Next. The Select Imaging Source Format window appears, as shown in Figure 36.15.

FIGURE 36.15

The Select Imaging Source Format window specifies the image type.

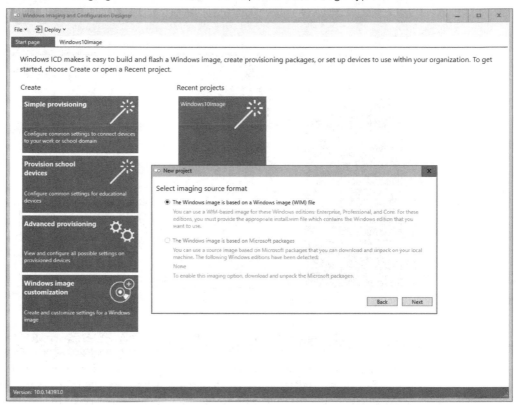

5. Select The Windows Image Is Based on a Windows Image (WIM) File option. Unless you have downloaded and unpacked other Windows packages, only the first option is available.

6. Click Next. The Select Image window appears. You need to specify the .WIM file to use. Click Browse to locate the .WIM file and click Open to select it. Figure 36.16 shows an example of selecting the install.wim file for Windows 10 and the available images in the Available Images list.

FIGURE 36.16

Select a Windows image file.

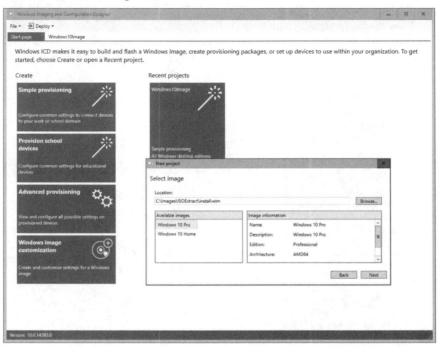

7. Click Next. The Import a Provisioning Package (Optional) window appears (see Figure 36.17). Select the package you want to modify. This step is optional, so if you do not have a provisioning package, skip to the next step without selecting a package.

FIGURE 36.17

As an option, you can specify the provisioning package you want to customize with the image.

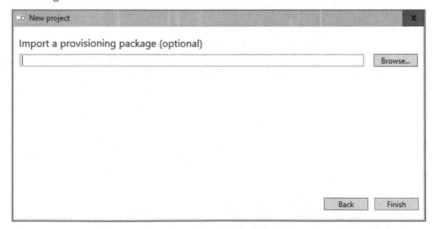

8. Click Finish. The new project is created and the Windows Imaging and Configuration Designer window appears with the new project tab showing (see Figure 36.18).

FIGURE 36.18

Use the Windows Imaging and Configuration Designer to customize individual settings.

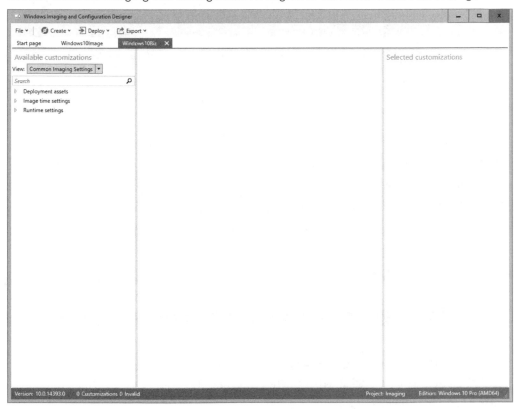

9. In the Available Customizations column (left column), click the View drop-down list to see a list of setting categories (such as Common Imaging Settings, Common OEM Settings, and so on). As you select an item from the View drop-down list, the settings change below the Search field. For example, when you select Common Imaging Settings, the following settings appear: Deployment Assets, Image Time Settings, and Runtime Settings.

Expand a category to see a specific setting. Figure 36.19 shows the Deployment Assets category expanded with the Applications item selected.

FIGURE 36.19

Windows ICD includes hundreds of image settings you can customize.

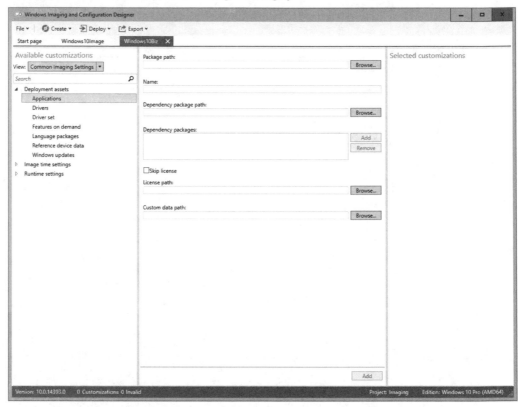

10. Customize the image as needed using the ICD.

11. When finished, click Create and choose Production Media. The Build window appears.

12. Click FFU (Full Flash Update file), as shown in Figure 36.20. FFU provides a more efficient method for deploying the image because it is sector-based and not file-based. This allows the FFU file to capture the full set of drive information (such as partitions) on a single file, as opposed to a WIM file, which stores all in a set of files.

FIGURE 36.20

Use the FFU option for a more streamlined imaging file.

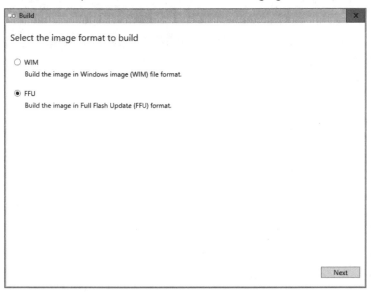

13. Click Next. The Select Imaging Options window appears.

14. Click Yes (see Figure 36.21) to compact the operating system image.

FIGURE 36.21

Select to compact the image file to reduce its size.

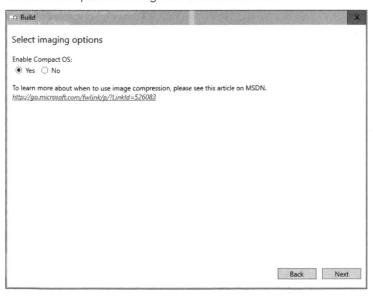

15. Click Next. The Configure Audit Mode Boot window appears (see Figure 36.22).

FIGURE 36.22

You can keep the default audit settings for this image.

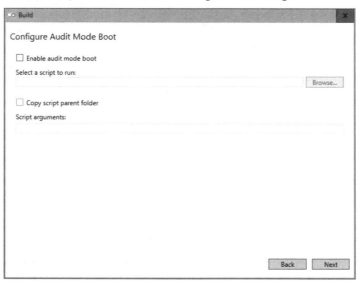

16. Keep the defaults in the Configure Audit Mode Boot window.
17. Click Next. The Choose Where the FFU File Is Saved window appears (see Figure 36.23).

FIGURE 36.23

Specify the file location destination and file name for the image file.

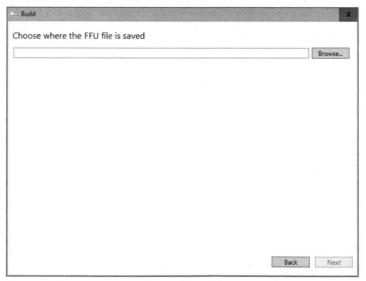

17. Enter the location where the FFU file is to be stored. In addition, you must specify a name for the file.

18. Click Next. The Build the Windows Image window appears (see Figure 36.24).

FIGURE 36.24

The Build the Windows Image window details the image file.

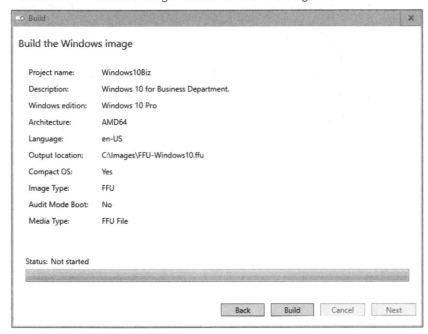

19. Click Build to start the build process.

After the image is built, which can take some time, you can copy the FFU file to a removable storage device. You can use an external USB drive, for example, to make the image file highly portable.

TIP

As you become more comfortable creating and editing images, you can create custom images for departments, regional locations, and other categories important to your organization.

Wrapping Up

You can create images to help speed the process of preparing a large number of computers in your organization. With the Windows Imaging and Configuration Designer (ICD), you can create provisioning images to deploy Windows 10 installations.

The ICD also provides options for customizing images so you can create images that are specific to the needs of your organization. This chapter introduced the following points:

- Understanding Windows 10 imaging
- Using Windows system preparation tools
- Running Windows Imaging and Configuration Designer
- Deploying Windows using ICD
- Modifying Windows 10 images

Using Windows 10 Group Policies on a Network

IN THIS CHAPTER

Understanding Windows 10 group policies

Editing group policies

Deploying group policies

Viewing new Windows 10 group policies on a client

G roup policies provide a way to configure settings for a group of users or computers and have those settings replicated throughout an organization or enterprise. These settings range from basic interface settings (such as how the taskbar behaves) to settings that modify how a client works on the corporate network (such as looking for system updates from a Microsoft Windows Server Update Service server).

As new versions of Windows are released, new group policies are made available to take advantage of new system components, apps, and features. Conversely, some group policies are removed for security or other reasons not explained by Microsoft.

Understanding Windows 10 Group Policies

When you are responsible for multiple computers, whether it's as few as 100 computers or as many as thousands, you need a way to establish baseline installations of your Windows 10 environment. Creating and managing images is one good way to set this baseline of applications, components, networking settings, device drivers, and the like. Chapter 36 discusses imaging.

However, once you get an image set and deployed, sometimes (or most likely *always*) you need to make a change to your clients, but you don't have time or the personnel to re-image all systems for that one, minor change. This is when Microsoft's group policy feature is helpful.

With group policies, you can change settings using the Group Policy Editor and then replicate those changes to all your client computers. The Group Policy Editor modifies policy on a local computer. To edit policies for domains, you use the Group Policy Management Console (GPMC). GPMC can modify computers in a site or computers in an Organizational Unit (OU). The latter is helpful when you have OUs set up for specific departments or types of users and you want group policies to affect only those computers, not the entire site or domain.

Editing Group Policies

With group policies, you can change settings using the Group Policy Editor. The Group Policy Editor modifies policy on a local computer. When you set group policies on a local computer using the Group Policy Editor, users on that computer will not be allowed to modify those settings without using the Group Policy Editor. Essentially it locks in that setting change.

To edit policies for domains, you use the GPMC. GPMC can modify computers in a site or computers in an OU, and then you can replicate those changes to all your client computers. The latter is helpful when you have OUs set up for specific departments or types of users and you want group policies to affect only those computers, not the entire site or domain.

The following steps show how to use the Group Policy Editor to make group policy changes on a local computer:

1. In the Cortana Search field, type **GPEDIT**.
2. Select Edit Group Policy (Control Panel). The Local Group Policy opens (see Figure 37.1).

FIGURE 37.1

The Group Policy Editor enables you to modify group policies on a local computer.

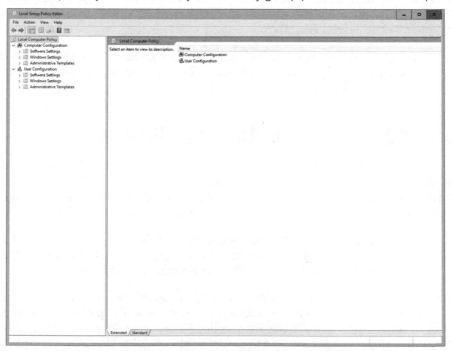

3. Use the left pane to select the general category of the setting you want to make. Computer Configuration policies enable you to modify settings that pertain to the computer or device. User Configuration policies are settings established per logged in user.

4. Expand Administrative Templates.

5. Expand Start Menu and Folders. Your view should look similar to Figure 37.2.

FIGURE 37.2

Editing the Start Menu and Taskbar policies.

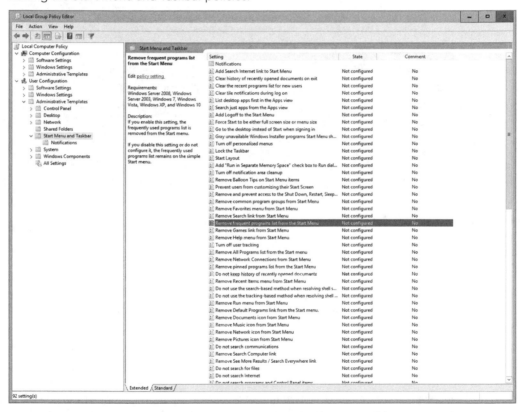

6. In the right pane, double-click the Remove Frequent Programs List from the Start Menu setting. It appears about midway down the list of the settings.

7. In the Remove Frequent Programs List dialog box (see Figure 37.3), click Enabled. This removes the list of frequently used programs that by default displays at the top of the Start menu.

689

FIGURE 37.3

Group policy settings have dialog boxes like this one that describe the setting and provide options.

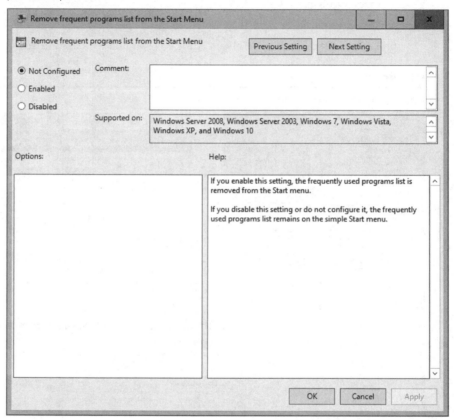

8. Click Apply.

9. Click OK.

If you want to re-enable the setting, you must use the Group Policy Editor to edit the setting and restore to its original setting. In the example, you would change the setting back to Not Configured. Click Apply and OK to finish the editing process.

Deploying Group Policies

For group policies you want to edit through the GPMC on Windows 10, you first need to download the Administrative Templates (.admx) for Windows 10 from Microsoft. You then can run the GPMC and edit group policies with these templates for multiple computers.

To download the Administrative Templates for Windows 10, use the following steps:

1. Open a web browser.
2. Navigate to the following website:

   `https://www.microsoft.com/en-us/download/details.aspx?id=53430`
3. Click the Download button located on the website (see Figure 37.4).

FIGURE 37.4

Visit the Administrative Templates web page to download the Group Policy Management Console.

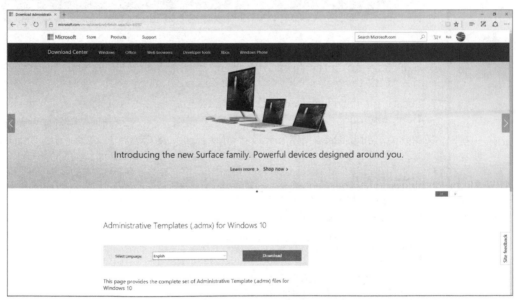

4. Select Windows 10 and Windows Server 2016 ADMX.msi (see Figure 37.5).

FIGURE 37.5

Select the ADMX templates to download.

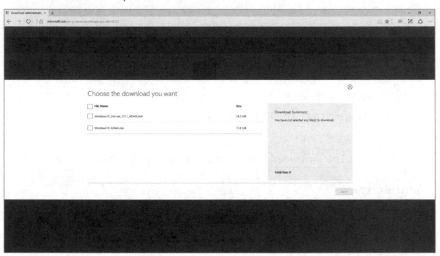

5. Click Next.

6. Click Save As on the download bar and specify a location on your system to save the ADMX templates. This downloads the program to your computer.

7. Locate the download and double-click it. It is an .MSI package, which is an installation program.

8. Work through the ADMX installation wizard (see Figure 37.6). As you proceed through the wizard, you can retain all the default settings.

FIGURE 37.6

Work through the ADMX installation wizard.

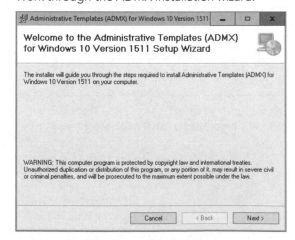

9. After you install the ADMX templates, launch the GPMC.

GPMC has a similar look and capabilities as the Group Policy Editor. Select the Computer Configuration or User Configuration categories to edit the settings of your choosing.

Viewing New Windows 10 Group Policies on a Client

As with previous versions of Windows, Windows 10 includes additional group policies not available on other Windows versions. Table 37.1 lists the new group policies available with Windows 10.

TABLE 37.1   New Windows 10 Group Policies

Group Policy Setting	Category	Location of Policy	Description
Use enhanced anti-spoofing when available	Machine	Windows Components\Biometrics\Facial Features	This policy determines whether enhanced anti-spoofing is configured for devices that support it.
Configure Windows Spotlight on lock screen	User	Windows Components\Cloud Content	This policy lets you configure Windows Spotlight on the lock screen.
Do not show Windows Tips	Machine	Windows Components\Cloud Content	This policy prevents Windows Tips from being shown to users.
Turn off all Windows Spotlight features	User	Windows Components\Cloud Content	This policy lets you turn off all Windows Spotlight features at once.
Turn off Microsoft consumer experiences	Machine	Windows Components\Cloud Content	This policy turns off experiences that help consumers make the most of their devices and Microsoft accounts.
Do not suggest third-party content in Windows Spotlight	User	Windows Components\Cloud Content	If you enable this policy, Windows Spotlight on lock screen, Windows tips, Microsoft consumer features, and other related features will no longer suggest apps and content from third-party software publishers.
Absolute max cache size (in GB)	Machine	Windows Components\Delivery Optimization	Specifies the maximum size in GB of the Delivery Optimization cache.

Continues

TABLE 37.1   *(continued)*

Group Policy Setting	Category	Location of Policy	Description
Download mode	Machine	Windows Components\Delivery Optimization	Set this policy to configure the use of Windows Update Delivery Optimization in downloads of Windows apps and updates.
Group ID	Machine	Windows Components\Delivery Optimization	Group ID must be set as a GUID.
Max cache age (in seconds)	Machine	Windows Components\Delivery Optimization	Set this policy to define the max time that each file is held in the Delivery Optimization cache.
Max cache size (percentage)	Machine	Windows Components\Delivery Optimization	Set this policy to define the max cache size Delivery Optimization can utilize, as a percentage of available disk space.
Max upload bandwidth (in KB/s)	Machine	Windows Components\Delivery Optimization	Set this policy to define a cap for the upload bandwidth a device will utilize across all concurrent upload activity via Delivery Optimization (set in KB/s).
Maximum download bandwidth (in KB/s)	Machine	Windows Components\Delivery Optimization	Specifies the maximum download bandwidth in KB/s that the device can use across all concurrent download activities using Delivery Optimization.
Maximum download bandwidth (percentage)	Machine	Windows Components\Delivery Optimization	Specifies the maximum download bandwidth that Delivery Optimization uses across all concurrent download activities as a percentage of available download bandwidth.
Minimum background QoS (in KB/s)	Machine	Windows Components\Delivery Optimization	Specifies the minimum download QoS (quality of service or speed) for background downloads in KB/s.
Modify cache drive	Machine	Windows Components\Delivery Optimization	Specifies the drive Delivery Optimization will use for its cache.
Monthly upload data cap (in GB)	Machine	Windows Components\Delivery Optimization	Specifies the maximum total bytes in GB that Delivery Optimization is allowed to upload to Internet peers in each calendar month.

TABLE 37.1 *(continued)*

Group Policy Setting	Category	Location of Policy	Description
Disable MDM enrollment	Machine	Windows Components\MDM	This policy setting specifies whether Mobile Device Management (MDM) enrollment is allowed.
Force Start to be either full-screen size or menu size	User	Start Menu and Taskbar	If you enable this policy and set it to Start menu or full screen Start, Start will be that size. Users will be unable to change the size of Start in Settings.
Configure pre-boot recovery message and URL	Machine	Windows Components\BitLocker Drive Encryption\ Operating System Drives	This policy lets you configure the entire recovery message or replace the existing hyperlinks that are displayed on the pre-boot key recovery screen when the OS drive is locked.
Allow suggested apps in Windows Ink Workspace	Machine	Windows Components\Windows Ink Workspace	Allow suggested apps in Windows Ink Workspace.
Allow Windows Ink Workspace	Machine	Windows Components\Windows Ink Workspace	Allow Windows Ink Workspace.
Turn off automatic download and update of map data	Machine	Windows Components\Maps	Enables or disables the automatic download and update of map data.
Turn off unsolicited network traffic on the Offline Maps settings page	Machine	Windows Components\Maps	This policy setting allows you to turn on or turn off unsolicited network traffic on the Offline Maps page.
Don't allow this PC to be projected to	Machine	Windows Components\Connect	This policy setting allows you to turn off projection to a computer.
Require personal identification number (PIN) for pairing	Machine	Windows Components\Connect	This policy setting allows you to require a personal identification number (PIN) for pairing
Allow Windows to automatically connect to suggested open hotspots, to networks shared by contacts, and to hotspots offering paid services	Machine	Network\WLAN Service\WLAN Settings	This policy setting determines whether users can enable the following WLAN settings: "Connect to suggested open hotspots," "Connect to networks shared by my contacts," and "Enable paid services."

37

> **TIP**
>
> To learn more about specific group policy settings and which policies apply to specific Windows version, visit `https://technet.microsoft.com/en-us/itpro/windows/manage/group-policies-for-enterprise-and-education-editions`.

Wrapping Up

Group policies provide a way to configure settings for a group of users or computers and have those settings replicated throughout an organization or enterprise. These settings range from basic interface settings (such as how the taskbar behaves) to settings that modify how a client works on the corporate network (such as looking for system updates from a WSUS server).

This chapter introduced the following points:

- Understanding Windows 10 group policies
- Editing group policies
- Deploying group policies
- Viewing new Windows 10 group policies on a client

Securing Windows 10 for the Enterprise

IN THIS CHAPTER

Understanding why Windows 10 security is important

Securing Windows 10

Protecting against malicious software

T he security of client computer resources on a network should be a matter of utmost importance to any system administrator or information technology manager. A single client computer can make a enterprise vulnerable to outside agencies, including computer hackers, foreign governments, or other entities who are looking for ways into your network. For that matter, always make sure your Windows 10 client computers are secure.

As you learn in this chapter, several forms of malicious software (also called *malware*) exist, including viruses, worms, spyware, and adware. As you also discover in this chapter, you can take actions to prevent your computer from getting malware. And when it's too late for that, you can take steps to get rid of the malware.

Understanding Why Windows 10 Security Is Important

With a penetration rate of upwards of 90 percent of the world's desktops and business applications, Microsoft Windows is a large security target. Windows products have been the subjected to security breaches and attempted security breaches. These breaches come in the form of viruses, worms, Trojan horses, malware, and more.

To help combat these issues, Windows 10 includes a free version of Microsoft Defender anti-virus software. This tool is installed and activated by default when Windows is installed.

> **NOTE**
>
> Your Internet service provider (ISP) might provide perimeter protection for viruses, which means viruses are detected and removed by your ISP before they ever get to your computer. There is no extra charge for that. You pay for it when you pay the monthly bill for your Internet connection. Furthermore, you don't have to do anything to keep your virus protection up to date. Your ISP takes care of that, too. The same is true if your business provides perimeter protection — a device on your network actively scans all incoming and outgoing traffic, looking for and eliminating viruses. However, perimeter protection cannot protect your computer against viruses on a flash drive or other removable media. Also, if a virus gets past the ISP perimeter defense, you still need an antivirus program or similar tool on your local computer to detect and remove the virus.

Malicious software comes in many forms. All forms have certain things in common, though. For one, they're invisible — you don't even know they're there. For another, they all do something bad, something you don't really want happening on your computer. Third, they're all written by human programmers to intentionally do these bad things. The differences have to do with how they spread and what they do after they're on your computer. We tell you about the differences in the sections to follow.

Viruses and Worms

Viruses and *worms* are self-replicating programs that spread from one computer to the next, usually via the Internet. A virus needs a *host file* to spread from one computer to the next. The host file can be anything, although viruses are typically hidden in e-mail attachments and programs you download.

A worm is similar to a virus in that it can replicate itself and spread. However, unlike a virus, a worm doesn't need a host file to travel around. It can go from one computer to the next right through your Internet connection. That's one reason it's important to always have a firewall up when you're online — to keep out worms that travel through Internet connections.

The harm caused by viruses and worms ranges from minor pranks to serious damage. A minor prank might be something like a small message that appears somewhere on your screen where you don't want it. A more serious virus might erase important system files, rendering your computer useless.

Spyware and Adware

Spyware and *adware* is malware that isn't designed to specifically harm your computer. Rather, it's designed to help people sell you stuff. A common spyware tactic is to send information about the websites you visit to computers that send out advertisements on the Internet. That computer analyzes the websites you visit to figure out what types of products you're most likely to buy. That computer then sends ads about such products to your computer.

Adware is the mechanism that allows ads to appear on your computer screen. When you get advertisements on your screen, seemingly out of the clear blue sky, there's usually some form of adware behind it. Spyware and adware often work in conjunction with one another. The adware provides the means to display ads. The spyware helps the ad server (the computer sending the ads) choose ads for products you're most likely to buy.

Trojan Horses and Rootkits

You may have heard the term *Trojan horse* in relation to early mythology. The story goes like this. After 10 years of war with the city of Troy, the Greeks decided to call it quits. As a peace offering, they gave the people of Troy a huge horse statue named the Trojan horse.

While the people of Troy were busy celebrating the end of the war, Greek soldiers hidden inside the horse snuck out and opened the gates to the city from inside. They allowed other Greek soldiers, lying in wait hidden outside the city, to storm into the town and conquer it. (This is a case in which it would have been wise to look a gift horse in the mouth.)

A Trojan horse is a program that works in a similar manner. In contrast to other forms of malware, a Trojan horse is a program you can see on your screen and use. On the surface, it does something useful. However, hidden inside the program is a smaller program that does bad things, usually without your knowledge.

A Trojan horse can also be a program that hides nothing but could be used in bad ways. Take, for example, a program that can recover lost passwords. On the one hand, it can be a good thing if you use it to recover forgotten passwords from files you created yourself. But it can be a bad thing when used to break into other people's password-protected files.

A *rootkit* is a program that can hide itself, and the malicious intent of other programs, from the user and even from the system. As with Trojan horses, not all rootkits are inherently malicious. However, they can be used in malicious ways. Windows 10 protects your system from rootkits on many fronts, including Windows Defender.

Some rootkits can remain hidden on a computer for long periods of time, even for as much as several years. Rootkits provide a stealthy way for a person or organization (such as a rogue government or company) to infect a device. The rootkit stays dormant on the computer until a specific time or event, when it activates and causes malicious behavior to occur. Some of the most commonly known rootkits are Alureon, Sirefef, Rustock, Sinowal, and Cutwail.

Securing Windows 10

There are basically two ways to deal with malicious software. The best is to *prevent* them before they infect your system. The other is to detect and remove them after your computer has already been infected.

38

As you read earlier, viruses can potentially cause a great deal of harm to your computer. Therefore, it's best to always run an anti-virus program, such as Microsoft Windows Defender, which comes standard with Windows 10. Windows Defender is designed to locate and eradicate viruses and spyware.

Spyware (and its close cousin adware) isn't specifically designed to cause your computer harm. But even without the direct intent to do harm, spyware can have serious consequences. Too much spyware can bog your system down, causing everything to run more slowly than it should. Spyware can make unwanted changes to your Internet settings, causing your web browser to act in unexpected ways. Spyware can lead to many annoying pop-up ads. In the worst cases, it can send personally identifiable information about you to identity thieves.

Most spyware comes from software that you can download for free, such as screen savers, custom toolbars, and file-sharing programs. However, it can also be installed automatically from scripts and programs embedded in web pages.

Many programs on the market are designed to prevent and eliminate spyware (and adware). But you don't have to spend money or download a third-party program to protect your system from these threats. You can use Windows Defender, which comes with Windows 10 for free. Despite its focus on spyware, Defender protects your computer from any potentially unwanted programs. That includes many types of adware, Trojan horses, and rootkits.

> **NOTE**
>
> Computer security is always a moving target. The good guys come up with ways to thwart existing malware (including viruses). The bad guys keep inventing new ways to create viruses and other bad programs. To keep up to date with current threats, most antivirus programs need to download current *signatures* on a regular basis. Each signature basically tells the antivirus program what to look for to detect malicious software and what to block to keep your computer free of viruses.

With Windows 10 Anniversary, Microsoft has added several enhancements to Windows Defender. Two new features include Cloud-Based Protection and Automatic Sample Submission. They are turned on by default, but the first time you launch Windows Defender, you can explicitly turn on the features in case they have been shut down for some reason.

Cloud Protection works by referring to the cloud services to determine if a file should be blocked. It analyzes the file using file analysis and heuristics, along with machine learning, to determine if a file poses a potential threat. It does this in real-time to mitigate issues almost immediately, instead of potentially hours, days, or longer.

With Automatic Sample Submission, infected files are automatically uploaded to Microsoft, thereby allowing the company to perform in-depth analysis of the file. Microsoft can then release updates to Defender and more quickly protect other computers as well.

The Microsoft Edge web browser has enhanced security as well. By not supporting ActiveX or Java add-ins, Edge is less vulnerable to some of the attacks that Microsoft Internet Explorer historically was susceptible to.

Protecting against Malicious Software

You don't need to open Windows Defender to protect your computer. Defender runs in the background and starts when you log in to Windows. But you can do other things with Defender that require opening the program.

To launch the Windows Defender interface, perform the following steps:

1. Type **Windows Defender** in the Cortana Search field.
2. Click Windows Defender — Desktop App. You might also see Windows Defender — Trusted Windows Store App. *Do not* click that item. Figure 38.1 shows the Windows Defender window.

FIGURE 38.1

The Windows Defender main window.

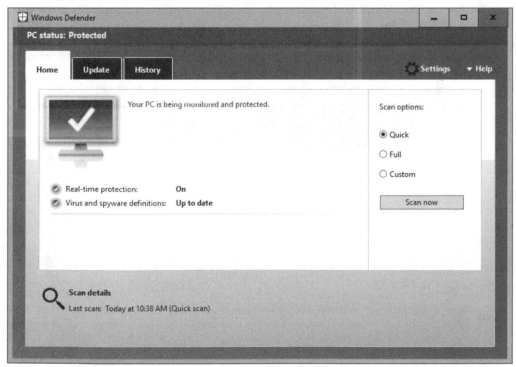

Removing Malicious Software

Windows Defender offers many tools for fighting malicious software. One of them is the ability to scan your system for malicious programs or files that you might have already acquired. On the Home tab of Windows Defender, you see these three scan options:

- **Quick:** As its name implies, the quick scan takes less time because it focuses on areas where malicious software is most likely hiding.
- **Full:** A full scan takes a while but gives you the peace of mind of knowing that your system is free of malicious software.
- **Custom:** A custom scan lets you choose which drives you want to scan.

To perform a scan, select the desired scan option and click the Scan Now button, as shown in Figure 38.2.

FIGURE 38.2

Windows Defender performing a manual scan.

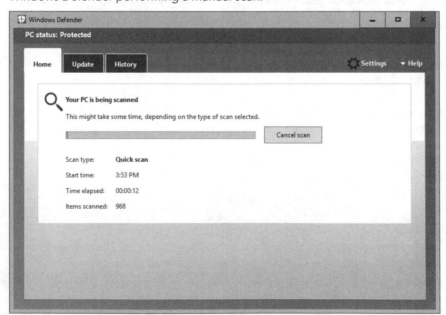

A full scan takes several minutes (or longer depending on the size of the storage drives you are scanning), so you need to be patient. When the scan is complete, you should see a clean bill of health. If not, suspicious items will be *quarantined* (disabled). You should be taken to the quarantined list automatically, though you can get there any time by choosing History⇨Quarantined Items and then clicking View Details. You can see details on quarantined items, allowed items (which are items you let run on your computer), or all detected items.

Each item in the quarantined list has an alert level associated with it. Here's what each alert level means:

- **Severe or High:** This item is known to compromise the security of your computer. Or, this item may be too new to be well known. But all indications point to malicious intent, so the item should be removed immediately.

- **Medium:** This item appears to collect personal information or change Internet settings. Review the item details. If you do not recognize or trust the publisher, block or remove the item.

- **Low:** This is a potentially unwanted item that you should remove if you did not intentionally install it yourself.

To remove an item, click its name and click Remove. You can usually click Remove All, because valid, useful programs are rarely detected as viruses, spyware, or other potentially unwanted items. If in doubt, you can leave the item quarantined for a while. Use your computer normally to see whether some useful program no longer works. After you've determined that everything is okay, you can go back into Quarantined Items and remove anything you left behind.

> **TIP**
>
> Should you ever encounter a false positive (where an innocent program is quarantined), don't remove it. Instead, click its name and then click Restore.

Doing a Quick Scan

A full scan takes some time because it scans every file on your hard disk. You can save some time by doing a quick scan. A quick scan checks only new files and the kinds of files commonly used by viruses, spyware, or other malicious software. After you've done a single full scan, quick scans are sufficient.

Doing a Custom Scan

A custom scan lets you scan a specific drive or folder. For example, if someone sends you a flash drive, you might want to check that disk before copying or opening any files from it.

For downloads, you might consider creating a subfolder within your Downloads folder, perhaps named Unscanned or something similar. Whenever you download a file or save an e-mail attachment that you don't trust 100 percent, save it to that Unscanned folder. Then scan just the folder to make sure all is well. If the files check out okay, you can then move them to any folder you like. Or, in the case of a downloaded program, click the icon to start the program installation.

To do a custom scan, choose the Custom option on the Home tab in Windows Defender and click the Scan Now button. Click to select the drive you want to scan, like the example shown in Figure 38.3. Or, expand any drive icon and select the specific folder you want to scan. Then click OK to start the scan.

FIGURE 38.3

Use Custom scan to scan only specific drives or folders.

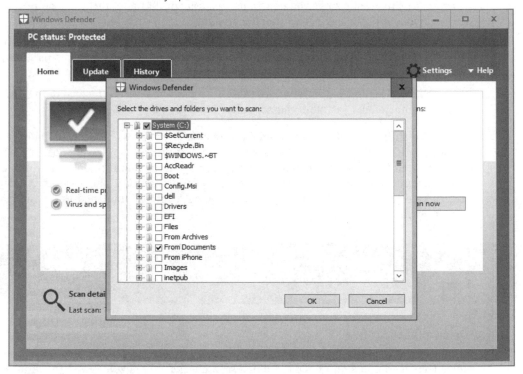

Preventing Malicious Software from Using Real-Time Scanning

You've probably heard the saying "An ounce of prevention is worth a pound of cure." That's certainly true of viruses, spyware, and other malicious software. Getting rid of malicious software that has already infected your computer is a good thing. But preventing it from getting there in the first place is even better. That's where *real-time protection* comes into play. The term "real-time" means "as it's happening."

The Windows Defender real-time protection analyzes files as they approach your computer from the Internet. Any virus, spyware, or suspicious-looking files are blocked to keep your computer from being infected. If Defender detects a potential threat, it alerts you to the issue and quarantines the threat.

To turn on real-time protection (it is turned on by default), perform the following steps:

1. Click the Settings button. The Windows Defender settings window appears (see Figure 38.4).

FIGURE 38.4

Configure Windows Defender options with this screen.

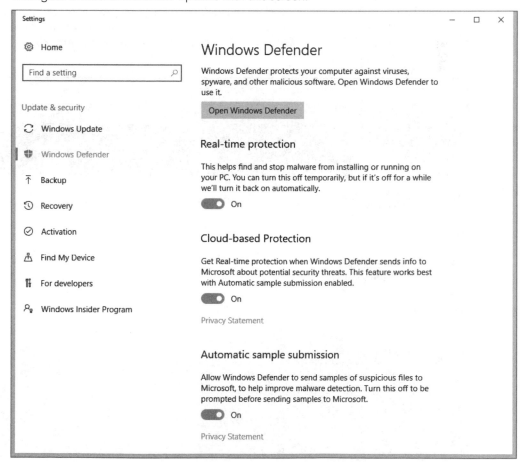

2. Click the Real-Time Protection option to On.
3. Click the close button at the top right of the window to return to the Windows Defender window.

If you turn off real-time scanning, Windows displays a red banner on the top of the Windows Defender window that specifies that your PC is at risk. In addition, a Windows alert appears on the task bar indicating that you need to protect your computer, which you can do by re-enabling the real-time protection option.

Windows Defender Updates

Each virus and malware item that Defender identifies has a *definition* that specifies its intent, severity, and recommended actions. The definitions are created by human experts who have previously found and analyzed the item. To keep up with threats posed on the Internet and other online locations, Windows Defender definitions are added seemingly every day.

To keep your system as safe as possible, definitions are updated automatically to Windows Defender based on your Windows Update schedule. See Chapter 7 for more information about Windows Updates. You can view information about the Windows Defender updates by clicking the Update tab on the Windows Defender window, as seen in Figure 38.5.

FIGURE 38.5

Review the Windows Defender update information.

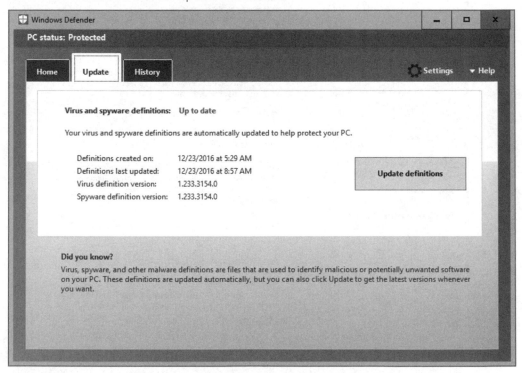

The Update tab includes the date and time when the last definitions were created and the last time you updated your copy of Windows Defender. You also can see the version numbers of the virus and spyware defenders installed on your computer. This information can be helpful for troubleshooting in the future.

If you want to update your definitions manually, click the Update Definitions button. Windows Defender searches for and downloads all new virus and spyware definitions.

Excluding Files and Folders

In some situations, you might want to exclude certain files or folders from being scanned by Windows Defender. For example, if you know certain folders or files are safe, and they may take a long time for Windows Defender to scan, or they may cause problems when scanned, you can exclude them. You can also exclude files based on their file type. Finally, you can exclude processes, including .exe, .com, and .scr files.

To set exclusions, perform the following steps:

1. Click the Settings button on the Windows Defender window. The Windows Defender settings window appears (as shown earlier in Figure 38.4).

2. Click the Add an Exclusion link under the Exclusions area. The Add an Exclusion window appears (see Figure 38.6).

FIGURE 38.6

You can exclude files, folder, file extensions, and processes from being scanned.

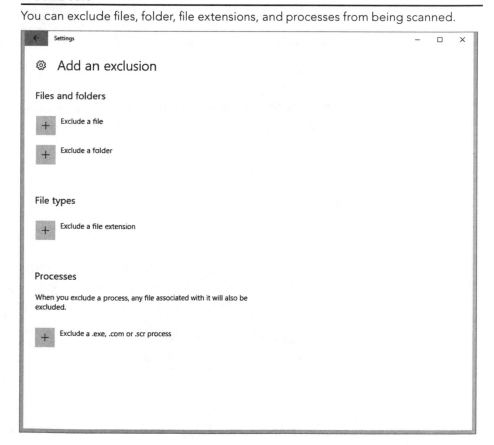

3. Click Exclude a File. The Open dialog box appears, as shown in Figure 38.7.

FIGURE 38.7

Specify the file to exclude during scanning.

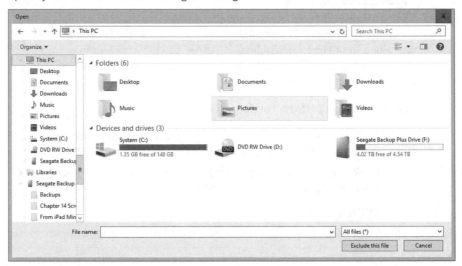

4. Locate and select the file you want to exclude.

5. Click Exclude This File button. The file name is added below the Exclude a Folder option. As you add files and folders to exclude, this list grows.

6. Click Exclude a Folder to specify a folder to exclude. The Open dialog box appears.

7. Locate and select a folder you want to exclude.

8. Click the Exclude This Folder button. The folder name is added below the Exclude a Folder option.

9. Click the Exclude a File Extension. The Add Exclusion window appears (see figure 38.8).

FIGURE 38.8

Specify a file extension to exclude from scanning.

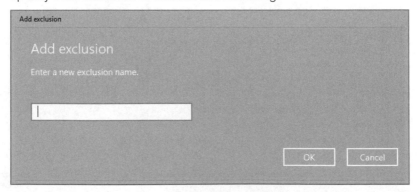

10. Type a file extension, such as .jpg, into the Enter a New Exclusion Name field.

11. Click OK. The file extension is added below the Exclude a File Extension Name option.

12. Click Exclude a .exe, .com, or .scr. The Add Exclusion window appears (see Figure 38.9).

FIGURE 38.9

Specify a process to exclude from scanning.

13. Type a process name, such as the name of a program you want to exclude. You might, for example, choose to exclude Microsoft Word from scanning processes. Type **WORD.EXE** in the field.

14. Click OK. The process you entered is added below the Add a Process option.

15. Repeat the process for any other exclusion.

16. When finished, click the close button on the top right of the window.

Wrapping Up

Malicious software (called *malware* for short) is computer software that's intentionally written to invade your privacy or cause harm. This is not the kind of thing you purchase or download from legitimate software vendors. Nor does it announce its presence to you on the screen. Rather, it sneaks into your computer through tainted programs and e-mail attachments without your knowledge.

This chapter introduced the following points:

- Understanding why Windows 10 security is important
- Securing Windows 10
- Protecting against malicious software

Part X

Appendixes

Upgrading to Windows 10

IN THIS APPENDIX

Windows 10 system requirements

Preinstallation housekeeping

Installing Windows 10

If you purchased your PC with Windows 10 already installed and have no interest in dual-booting, this appendix isn't for you. Go straight to the Introduction, or Chapter 1, at the beginning of this book, and forget all about upgrading.

If you purchased an upgrade version of Windows 10 to replace your current version of Windows and you haven't installed that upgrade, this appendix helps you complete the upgrade. However, you don't have to read the entire appendix to install your upgrade. Just do this:

1. Insert the disk that came with your Windows 10 upgrade into your computer's disk drive and wait a few seconds.

2. Follow the instructions that appear on the screen to install Windows 10 by upgrading your current version of Windows.

When the installation is complete, remove the disk from your disk drive, put it someplace safe, and ignore the rest of this appendix. If these two steps don't quite get the job done, read on.

> **NOTE**
>
> Be aware that Windows 10 can upgrade *only* from Windows 7 or Windows 8.x. If you have a version of Windows *earlier than* Windows 7, you need to back up all your data and then perform a "clean install" of Windows 10 on the computer. Doing so causes all the data on your computer to be erased, so you need to restore your data after installing Windows 10. (If you do not have SP1 installed on Windows 7, first install SP1 and then run the Windows 10 upgrade, unless you want to do a clean install.) If you are updating to Windows 10 using Windows Update from Windows 7, you must have SP1 installed.

> **TIP**
>
> Windows 10 was free for one year after release (through July 29, 2016) for qualified Windows 7 and Windows 8.1 devices. In addition, if you were enrolled in the Windows Insider program as of the July 29, 2015 release date, and you continue in the program, you will continue to receive updated builds of Windows 10 on enrolled devices.

Windows 10 System Requirements

Windows 10 has the same hardware requirements as Windows 7 and Windows 8.x, but it requires a bit more hardware horsepower than versions of Windows prior to 7. The more hardware capability you have, the better Windows 10 runs. The recommended minimum hardware requirements are as follows:

- 1GB of RAM for 32-bit (x86) versions; 2GB of RAM for 64-bit (x64) versions
- A 1.0 GHz 32-bit (x86) or 64-bit (x64) processor
- At least 16GB free space available for 32-bit (x86) versions; 20GB for 64-bit (x64) versions
- DirectX 9–capable GPU with WDDM 1.0 driver or higher
- Screen resolution of at least 1024 × 768 for modern Windows apps, although Windows 10 will also support 800 × 600.
- A Microsoft account and Internet access

When you run the installation program for Windows 10, it automatically runs the Windows 10 Installation Compatibility Advisor tool on your computer. This tool tests to ensure your computer meets minimum requirements for Windows 10. It also checks many of your installed programs for known problems with those programs running with Windows 10.

Preinstallation Housekeeping

If you've been using your PC for a while with an earlier version of Windows, you have a few things to do before you begin your upgrade:

- If your computer has any time-out features, such as the power-down features found on some portable PCs, disable those features now.
- If you have an antivirus program handy, run it now to check for, and delete, dormant viruses that may be lurking on your hard drive.

- Make sure that any external devices (printers, external disk drives, and so on) are connected and turned on so that Windows 10 can detect them during installation.

- If at all possible, back up the entire hard drive. At the very least, jot down all the information you need to connect to the Internet. Back up all your documents, e-mail messages, contacts, and anything else you'll need after you complete the upgrade.

Most enterprise IT environments provide at least some mechanism for backing up your documents and other data. Services such as Backblaze (www.backblaze.com), Carbonite (www.carbonite.com), and Mozy (www.mozy.com) enable you to back up your computer outside the enterprise environment (such as at home). But even in the absence of those backup options, you can back up documents, e-mail messages, names and addresses, and so on.

 See Chapter 19 for general pointers on backing up documents.

Installing Windows 10

To upgrade an existing version of Windows 7 SP1 or Windows 8.x, first start the computer and get to a clean desktop with no open program windows or dialog boxes. You have a few options for starting the upgrade. Perhaps the easiest is to use Windows Update, available from the Settings app. Or, you can update Windows through the Microsoft Store. The third option is to use a Windows 10 disk.

Regardless of the method you use to start the update, after the installation procedure begins, you may notice that the screen goes blank once in a while during the installation. Don't be alarmed — that's normal. If the screen goes blank for a long time, try moving the mouse to bring it back. To complete the installation, just follow the instructions provided by Setup. The following sections will help you understand the choices you will be offered during setup.

Installation options

Next, the setup routine requests several pieces of information. The exact procedure varies a bit, depending on which version of Windows 10 you're installing. Also, the routine may

A

request slightly different information depending on the hardware that's connected to your computer. Here's a summary of the items you're likely to encounter along the way.

- **Product key:** Type the product key. You should be able to find it on the sleeve in which the Windows 10 disk was delivered. If you downloaded Windows 10, you should have received a license key via e-mail.

- **License terms:** If you agree with the terms and conditions of the license, select the I Accept the License Terms check box.

- **Upgrade or custom installation:** If you decide to do a fresh installation, choose the Custom option. This option does not keep your personal files and programs. The Upgrade option keeps them. For tips on choosing a clean (custom) installation over an upgrade, see Appendix B.

Re-enabling old startup programs

You may discover that some of the programs that used to start automatically on your computer don't do so after you've installed Windows 10. You can follow these steps to get those programs to start automatically again in the future:

1. Click the Start button, type **Task Manager**, and click Task Manager in the search results. This runs the Task Manager tool.

2. Click the More Details link and then select the Startup tab.

3. Right-click a program that shows Disabled in the Status column and click Enable. Or click a program that shows Disabled in the Status column and click the Enable button at the bottom of the Task Manager window.

4. Choose File ⇨ Exit to close the Task Manager.

Windows 10 should restart with the programs from your previous version of Windows.

Installing Windows 10 on a New System

IN THIS APPENDIX

Gearing up for a clean installation

Doing the clean installation

Completing the installation

If you've just built a new computer from scratch, or if you've replaced your old hard drive C: with a new hard drive, you have to perform a *clean install* of Windows 10.

You can opt to do a clean install even if you already have a version of Windows installed on the hard drive; however, you must realize that doing so is *very* serious business. When you do a clean install, you wipe out everything on your hard drive. And we do mean *everything* — all programs, documents, settings, and Internet account information. You can't get *any* of that stuff back, either.

> **CAUTION**
> The procedures described in this chapter are for advanced users only. You should know your hardware; your system's BIOS/firmware setup; all your Internet account information; how to export, back up, and restore messages, contacts, favorites, and the like; and how to find technical information about your hardware components on your own before attempting any of the techniques described in this chapter.

Gearing Up for a Clean Install

Most experts prefer to do a clean install when they upgrade to a new version of Windows, largely because this method ensures a pristine installation of Windows with no issues or files lingering from the previous installation. Besides, a clean install is a great excuse for upgrading to a bigger and faster hard drive. You can use your original hard drive as a second hard drive and easily transfer documents from that drive to the new drive after you've installed Windows 10 on the new drive. However, you still need to reinstall all your programs and redo all your settings after you complete the installation.

Back up all your data

If you intend to keep your existing C: as the C: drive after the clean install, understand that you will *permanently* lose everything on that drive during the clean install. Therefore, you should do the following:

- Write down all your Internet connection data so that you can reestablish your connection after the clean install.

- Back up or export all your e-mail messages, contacts, and favorites so that you can recover them. ***Remember:*** Everything you don't save will be lost forever. However, this does not apply for web-based e-mail accounts that don't store messages on your computer.

- Back up all your documents because every one of them will be wiped out along with Windows and all your programs.

> **CAUTION**
>
> A clean install permanently erases everything on your hard drive, which is basically everything that's "in your computer." Users who don't fully understand the ramifications of this should not attempt to do a clean install of Windows 10 or any other operating system. It's extremely difficult to recover data from an erased drive, but if you need that kind of help, you can turn to a data recovery service. Search the web for "hard drive recovery" for resources.

Because hard drives are so inexpensive these days, it almost seems a shame *not* to start the clean install from a new hard drive. You don't have to worry about losing any data from the old drive if you do a clean install of Windows 10 to a new drive. The data from your old drive will stay intact because Windows will be installed on the new drive.

Make sure you can boot from your DVD

By far, the easiest way to do a clean install on a new drive is to boot from the Windows 10 disk. Make sure that you *can* do this before you do anything inside the computer. Most disks aren't bootable, so insert the Windows disk into the drive and restart the computer. Watch for a message that says, "Press any key to boot from CD or DVD countdown," and tap the spacebar before the countdown runs out. (In case you're curious, it's five seconds.)

If you see a message that tells you that Windows is loading files, you know you can boot from a disk. Press Ctrl+Alt+Del to reboot before setup starts, and remove the disk from the drive while the system is rebooting. Then shut down the PC altogether.

If you can't boot the system from the Windows disk, you need to adjust your BIOS settings. We can't tell you specifically how to do this because the procedure depends on your system's BIOS. The usual scenario is to press F2, F12, or Del as the computer is starting up to get to your BIOS setup. After you get into the BIOS settings, make sure that booting from the disk drive is enabled and that the disk drive has a higher priority than the hard drive.

If you'd rather not adjust your BIOS settings, many computers give you the option to select the boot device. Pressing a key during the startup process tells the BIOS that you want to select your boot device this one time. It can be the F10, F11, or F12 key; check your computer's documentation to find out which key it is.

If you opt to change the BIOS settings, put the Windows disk back into the disk drive, save your BIOS settings, and exit so that the computer reboots again. If you got it right, you should see a message telling you Windows is loading files again on restart, indicating that you've successfully booted from the disk. Cancel that startup as well, by pressing Ctrl+Alt+Del, and remove the disk from the drive before the computer gets another chance to boot from the disk.

Performing the Clean Install

When you feel confident that you'll be able to get back everything you want from your hard drive from backups that you have made, you're ready to start the clean install. Put the Windows disk in the disk drive and shut down the computer. Then restart the computer and boot from the disk. Your system's screen goes blank with a progress bar across the bottom of the screen while it copies some setup files. After the copy, the screen changes to a blue and green background, and you're given a mouse pointer. Follow these steps to continue the installation:

1. At the Windows Setup dialog box, select the Language, Time, and Currency format and the type of keyboard; then click the Next button.

2. Click the Install Now link. If prompted to do so, enter the product key, and then click the Next button.

3. If you accept the license terms, select the I Accept the License Terms box and click the Next button.

4. Select the Custom: Install Windows Only (Advanced) option to continue.

5. The next dialog box lists all the drives and partitions that the installation application sees on your system. Select the partition on which you want to install Windows 10 and click Next.

   If you don't see your drive, the controller to which your hard drive is connected may require a special driver that the installation application doesn't know about. You can click the Load Driver link to load the driver provided by the controller's manufacturer. Clicking the Drive Options (Advanced) link enables the option to format the drive before installing Windows 10. Select the partition on which Windows 10 will be installed and click the Format link. The installation application prompts you to confirm that the data on the drive will be erased and permanently deleted. Click OK if you're sure your database has been saved elsewhere.

B

6. After the drive is formatted, the Total Size and Free Space columns should be almost identical. Don't worry about discrepancies. They're a result of how file systems and the formatting process work. Click the Next button to continue, and the installation application starts copying files.

The Rest of the Installation

Copying the files and installing them to your system takes some time. When the installation continues, follow these steps:

1. Click Use Express Settings.

2. When prompted to specify whether the PC belongs to your company or to you, choose the appropriate response. This determines the type of account that Setup will prompt you for.

3. If setting up the PC for yourself, you're prompted to enter either an Office 365 account or your Microsoft account. You need the Microsoft account to enable purchases from the Windows store and optional synchronization of settings across multiple devices. Enter your Microsoft account if you have one and click Sign In, or choose the option to create one.

Windows installation continues for several minutes as it finalizes and prepares your computer to be used. After Windows 10 has been installed, you see a sign-on screen that you can use to log in to Windows 10.

Universal Shortcut Keys

IN THIS APPENDIX

General, dialog box, and Explorer shortcut keys

Ease of Access shortcut keys

Text-editing shortcut keys

This appendix is a quick reference to shortcut keys that are used throughout Windows 10. Many application programs use the same shortcut keys. That's why we titled this appendix "Universal Shortcut Keys." Of course, any program can have additional shortcuts to its own unique features. For example, the Advanced page of the Word 2016 Options window shows underlined characters, denoting them as hotkeys for activating an option. The first option is Typing Replaces Selected Text. The hotkey for this option is T. For programs still using menus, the *key+key* combination to the right of each menu command is the shortcut key for using that command from the keyboard without the menu.

Virtually every program also comes with its own Help. Typically, you get to that by pressing Help (F1) while the program is in the active window. Or you choose the ? or Help from that program's menu bar. Use the Help feature of that program to search for the term "shortcut" or "shortcut keys" to see whether you can find a summary of that program's shortcut keys.

Tables C.1 through C.6 provide lots of detail and make a handy reference.

TABLE C.1   **General Shortcut Keys**

To Do This	Press This Key
Copy selected item(s).	Ctrl+C
Cut selected item(s).	Ctrl+X
Paste cut or copied text or item(s) to current folder.	Ctrl+V
Undo your most recent action.	Ctrl+Z
Delete selected item(s) to Recycle Bin.	Delete or DEL
Delete selected item(s) without moving to Recycle Bin.	Shift+Delete
Rename selected item(s).	F2
Extend selection through additional item.	Shift+any arrow key
Select all items or content in a document or window.	Ctrl+A
Open search.	F3
Display properties for selected item.	Alt+Enter
Close program in the active window.	Alt+F4
Open the shortcut menu for the active window.	Alt+Spacebar
Close the active document in a multiple-document program.	Ctrl+F4
Switch between open programs.	Alt+Tab
Cycle through open programs in the order in which they were opened.	Alt+Esc
Display the shortcut menu for the selected item.	Shift+F10
Open/close the Start screen.	Ctrl+Esc or Windows key
Open menu or perform menu command.	Alt+underlined letter
View menu bar in active program.	F10 or Alt
Move left or right in menu bar.	← and →
Move up or down in menu.	↑ and ↓
Select highlighted menu command.	Enter
Refresh the active window.	F5
View the folder one level up in File Explorer.	Backspace
Cancel the current task.	Esc
Open Task Manager.	Ctrl+Shift+Esc
Copy dragged item to destination.	Ctrl+drag
Move dragged item to destination.	Ctrl+Shift+drag

TABLE C.2   **Dialog Box Keyboard Shortcuts**

To Do This	Press This Key
Choose the option with the underlined letter.	Alt+letter
Select a button if the active option is a group of option buttons.	Arrow keys
Open a folder one level up if a folder is selected in the Save As or Open dialog box.	Backspace
Go to the previous tab.	Ctrl+Shift+Tab
Go to the next tab.	Ctrl+Tab
Execute the selected action (similar to clicking OK).	Enter
Cancel the current action (similar to clicking cancel).	Esc
Get Help.	F1 key
Display the items in the active list.	F4 key
Move to the previous option.	Shift+Tab
Select or clear the check box.	Spacebar
Move to the next option.	Tab

TABLE C.3   **Windows 10 Start Screen Keyboard Shortcuts**

To Do This	Press This Key
Launch File Explorer on the classic desktop.	Windows+E
Launch Narrator.	Windows+Enter
Open the Feedback Hub.	Windows+F
Open the Share pane.	Windows+H
Open the Settings app.	Windows+I
Opens the Connect pane.	Windows+K
Lock Screen.	Windows+L
Launch the desktop.	Windows+M
Lock the device orientation.	Windows+O
Set second screen — projector mode.	Windows+P
Open Run on the desktop.	Windows+R
Open Cortana from the Start menu	Windows+S
Start the Ease of Access Center.	Windows+U
Open Windows Ink Workspace.	Windows+W
Open the Quick Links menu (Advanced Tools menu) on the desktop.	Windows+X

C

TABLE C.4 **Ease of Access Keyboard Shortcuts**

To Do This	Press This Key
Open the Ease of Access center.	Windows+U
Switch the MouseKeys on or off.	Left Alt+Left Shift+Num Lock
Switch High Contrast on or off.	Left Alt+Left Shift+Print Screen
Switch the ToggleKeys on or off.	Num Lock for 5 seconds
Switch FilterKeys on or off.	Right Shift for 8 seconds
Switch the StickyKeys on or off	Shift five times

TABLE C.5 **Keyboard Shortcuts**

To Do This	Press This Key
Display or hide the Start menu.	Windows key
Lock the computer.	Windows+L
Display the System Properties dialog box.	Windows+Break
Show the desktop.	Windows+D
Open File Explorer.	Windows+E
Open the Start menu.	Windows+F
Search for computers.	Ctrl+Windows+F
Display online Windows Help.	Windows+F1
Minimize all the windows.	Windows+M
Restore all minimized windows.	Windows+Shift+M
Open the Run dialog box.	Windows+R
Switch apps.	Windows+Tab
Open the Ease of Access Center.	Windows+U

TABLE C.6 **Text Navigation and Editing Shortcuts**

To Do This	Press This Key
Move the cursor down one line.	↓
Move the cursor left one character.	←
Move the cursor right one character.	→

To Do This	Press This Key
Move the cursor up one line.	↑
Delete the character to the left of the cursor.	Backspace
Move the cursor to the start of the next paragraph.	Ctrl+↓
Move the cursor to the start of the previous paragraph.	Ctrl+↑
Move the cursor to the start of the previous word.	Ctrl+←
Move the cursor to the start of the next word.	Ctrl+→
Select all.	Ctrl+A
Copy to the Clipboard.	Ctrl+C
Copy the selected text to the destination.	Ctrl+drag
Select to the end of the paragraph.	Ctrl+Shift+End
Select to the end of the word.	Ctrl+Shift+→
Select to the beginning of the word.	Ctrl+Shift+←
Select to the beginning of the paragraph.	Ctrl+Shift+↑
Select to the end of the document.	Ctrl+Shift+End
Select to the top of the document.	Ctrl+Shift+Home
Paste the Clipboard contents to the cursor position.	Ctrl+V
Cut to the Clipboard.	Ctrl+X
Undo the last action.	Ctrl+Z
Delete the selected text or character at the cursor.	Del
Cancel the current task.	Esc
Select to the character in the line above.	Shift+↑
Select to the character in the line below.	Shift+↓
Select the character to the left.	Shift+←
Select the character to the right.	Shift+→
Select from the cursor to here.	Shift+click
Select to the end of the line.	Shift+End
Select to the beginning of the line.	Shift+Home
Select the text down one screen.	Shift+PgDown
Select the text up one screen.	Shift+PgUp

C

Windows 10 Touch Gestures

IN THIS APPENDIX

Getting acquainted with the touch interface

Exploring Windows 10 touch gestures

On laptop or desktop computers, you use keyboard and mouse movements for most tasks, but with Windows-based tablets, you can use Windows 10 touch interface gestures. These are hand gestures that you can use instead of keystrokes or mouse clicks.

Table D.1 lists touch gestures and a description of those gestures. Other gestures may be available for a particular Windows app that you're running, and not all these gestures in the table are available with every app. Each app has only the gestures that the app developer programmed into it.

> **TIP**
> Microsoft Windows 10 apps use Semantic Zoom to help you navigate large amounts of data presented in a single view. For example, you can view full-size maps by pinching and zooming into a region on the map or a small location on the map. Conversely, you can zoom out from a point on a map to a larger view.

TABLE D.1 **Windows 10 Touch Interface Gestures**

This Action	Does This
Slide your finger left or right.	Scrolls through the screens.
Tap once.	Starts an app.
Swipe from the right side of the screen toward the middle.	Displays the Action Center, which also includes controls for tablet mode, VPN connections, connecting devices, and opening the Settings app.
Swipe down.	Displays additional menus.
Press and hold down on an item and then move it.	Enables you to move an item onscreen.
Tap and hold.	Shows the name of the element or the type of action you can perform with it.

This Action	Does This
Swipe down on an item.	Selects the item.
Swipe down past an item.	Allows movement of the item so you can move it from its current placement on the screen.
Slide an item from left or right.	Enables you to drag the item across the screen.
Place two or more fingers on an item and rotate your fingers.	Rotates an object.
Pinch inward with two or more fingers.	Zooms in on an item that uses Semantic Zoom, such as an object on an interactive map.
Pinch outward with two or move fingers.	Zooms out from an item that uses Semantic Zoom, such as zooming out on a photo or picture.
Swipe from left to right or right to left in Microsoft Edge.	Enables you to navigate from page to page while web browsing.
Press and hold down on an app, and then drag to the bottom of the screen.	Closes the app.
Swipe from the left and release.	Switches the active app.

Index

X-Y-Z